American Politics

American Politics

POLICIES, POWER, AND CHANGE

Third Edition, Revised

Kenneth M. Dolbeare   *University of Massachusetts, Amherst*

Murray J. Edelman   *University of Wisconsin*

D. C. HEATH AND COMPANY
Lexington, Massachusetts   Toronto

International Standard Book Number: 0–669–01724–8

Library of Congress Catalog Card Number: 78–78191

Preface to the
Third Edition, Revised

The third edition, published in 1977, added two new chapters, expanded others, and generally simplified our approach. We planned then to incorporate the results of the 1978 elections and perhaps one or two other changes in a contemplated "Congressional Printing" in early 1979, when depleted stocks would normally require reprinting. Two considerations intervened, however, to make this a more substantial alteration of the third edition. One was a concern for our own credibility in the eyes of teachers and students: We did not think it fair to present as "new" a printing in which only ten or a dozen pages differed from the basic third edition. The other was the number of compelling developments that it seemed necessary to integrate into our analysis: Several events and actions, not just one or two, required reporting and/or updating or expansion of points covered in the third edition.

As a result, we now offer an "updated third edition", a midterm printing that varies considerably from but remains predominantly the third edition. Specifically, this new third edition includes eleven new or completely updated tables or figures in six different chapters. Substantive changes have been made in eight chapters—including current discussions of the 1978 "tax revolt," the status of women and the ERA, President Carter's anti-inflation gamble, the Carter Presidency, and the 1978 election as it affects both the Congress and national politics into the future.

We want to again thank the reviewers whose insights and challenges helped so much in shaping the third edition. Major reviews were received from Merlyn J. Clarke, East Stroudsburg State College; Paul D. Schumaker, University of Kansas; and Goetz Wolff, University of North Carolina, Asheville. We also wish to thank the following people for their reviews and suggestions: M. O. Boss, Indiana University; Martin L. Brownstein, Ithaca College; Joan B. Davis, Keene State College; Robert Durden, Oxford College of Emory University; George Durrie, Eastern Washington State College; Alfred Evans, Jr., California State University, Fresno; J. Eldon Fields, University of Kansas; Charles C. Fishburne, Edison Community College; E. Friedman, University of Wisconsin; Dale E. Hess, Westminster College; Jeffrey A. James, State University of New York at Genesee; Stephan Johnson, University of Washington; James R. Klonoski, University of Oregon; Fred A. Kramer, University of Massachusetts, Amherst; Gary E. Monell, San Diego Mesa College; Jeffrey R. Orenstein, Kent State University, Stark; Richard C. Rich, Indiana University, Bloomington; John Paul Ryan, Vassar College; Robert V. Watson, University of Houston; Alexander Wilde, University of Wisconsin; Jarrell Willoughby, Clayton Junior College; and Robert M. Wilson, Malibu, California. We also received vital assistance from Joan De-Bardeleben of the University of Wisconsin and Pat Cowles, Bill Hill, Linda Medcalf, and Fred Vanderbeck of the University of Massachusetts.

K.M.D.
M.J.E.

Contents

PART ③ Contrasting Ideologies

PART 4　**Institutions and Processes:
The Role of Elites**　　183

PART 6   **Political Change**

Introduction

Why are we here?
Where are we going?

      Why are we here? Where are we going? These questions may occur to students confronting a new textbook, as well as to Americans facing multiplying social problems. This introduction tells where the book is going and why. *American Politics,* properly used, will help to explain why our political system works as it does, what difference its workings make to people and problems, and where *it* is going. If we are successful, it should also help readers to ask the right questions, and either to get what they want or to reconstruct the system so they can.

      This is not a book for those who think they can avoid or transcend the effects of politics. The moral dilemmas of mankind, and the failures and successes of human efforts to build a decent world, deserve our best understanding and active responses. We think this book can help. We

2

Introduction: Why are we here? Where are we going?

shall describe our goals, themes, and strategy, and then let readers decide for themselves—about the book and about American politics.

Goals

Our primary purposes are to help people see their political system more clearly, to develop their skills of analysis and evaluation, and to enable them to act more effectively to gain their ends in politics—whether through, around, or in spite of the established political system. To do these things honestly forces us to look critically at many of the revered institutions and values of the United States, to challenge some familiar myths, and to depart from some of the standard approaches of academic political science.

Naturally, this book is biased. Every textbook is. There is no such thing as a "neutral" or "objective" textbook. Some books may *appear* neutral or objective because they say things we have heard many times before. That is, they reiterate dominant beliefs and familiar interpretations, whose familiarity causes us to respond favorably. But this is to say only that we have not *recognized* the biases that lie hidden in those orthodox points of view, or that reside unconsciously in our minds and shape our responses. The most scrupulously "neutral" authors must select certain facts, present them within a particular conceptual framework, suggest ways of interpreting them so that they become meaningful, and so on. At every stage, the authors' assumptions and preferences—in short, their biases—determine what will be presented as truth to their readers. The best that authors can do is to declare frankly where they stand and warn their readers to be skeptical—another of the purposes of this introduction.

But if all books are thus biased, why read any except those we agree with? What can a serious reader expect to gain from a biased book? This brings us to a vital point. We believe that it is possible, even necessary, to be both honestly critical and frankly biased without sacrificing intellectual quality, rigor, or utility. The key lies in our conviction that readers must become independent thinkers, and in our determination to provide them the tools to do so. A critical stance that points up the culture-bound, parochial, self-congratulatory, or otherwise limiting elements of standard American beliefs is absolutely essential for this purpose. Only thus can people begin to analyze where power is located, and how and for whose benefit it is used.

Finally, becoming a truly independent person requires that one make repeated value judgments—about particular policies and practices, about the political system itself, and about alternatives to both. Change is constant, and more drastic changes appear to lie ahead. Choices must be made, and conscious action taken, to shape the future. To do these things, people must learn to identify their present values and preferences, and to ask the right questions about both present and future so that they can effectively further the values they conclude are desirable. A substantial portion of this book is devoted to presenting these questions systematically and exploring their implications and possible answers. Therefore, although we readily acknowledge the biases of this book, we argue that such biases are functional—in fact, necessary—for the purpose of forcing questions to the surface and equipping the reader to become a truly independent thinker.

Thus, this is not the usual civics book. But neither is it a mere polemic, another in the long series of attacks on things American. It is a set of tools and questions, applied to the real world of American politics, to enable readers to gain a better understanding of the political system and of themselves—in short, to help them decide what they want and how to get it. To aid in the process of developing critical judgment skills, we occasionally describe the judgments *we* make in response to a particular set of facts, or between alternative values. If we have done our job, and if readers do theirs, the result should be greater independence of mind and enhanced ability to cope with the deepening crises of the American future.

Themes

This book has two major themes or arguments. The first is that the United States is facing a severe social crisis, one that may be unique in our history, because of the many different forces and factors that have converged on us. The term "crisis" is much overworked these days, to the point that it may seem meaningless. And a prevalent kind of popular self-hypnosis causes people to agree complacently that things are very, very bad, and then to go about their daily routines as always. But we invoke the term precisely, deliberately, and in all seriousness. Moreover, we see this crisis as such an overwhelming convergence of economic, racial, international, ecological, intellectual, technological, and moral problems that only substantial change can ensue.

In other words, we believe that the one thing that cannot be predicted is a future that automatically incorporates the basic outlines of the present. Throughout our history, it has always been safest to predict that tomorrow will look very much like today, only slightly more so. We do not believe this is true any longer. We may well come to a crossroads, for example, at which the only choices will be socialism or fascism. But this does not mean that there is nothing people can do, that the results are predetermined, or that such powerful forces are at work that in-

4

Introduction: Why are we here? Where are we going?

dividuals cannot affect the outcome of events. Men and women make history, and this is a time when history is malleable, open, and subject to the determined efforts of knowledgeable individuals.

Our second theme is that a relatively few people possess the bulk of the wealth, status, and power that exist in the United States. Their stature results in part from their class and family origins and in part from their positions in the major economic and social institutions of the society, which enable them to affect nearly all major political decisions made at the national level. Their interests are principally those of maintaining and furthering the American economic system. To fulfill the basic needs of that system, they act in a united way and tolerate no significant opposition. With respect to less important matters, there may well be conflict within the ruling group, and political decisions may favor first one group or interest and then another.

The domination of the ruling group is not grossly or blatantly undertaken, however, and is sometimes not even publicly visible. Social control is accomplished in many subtle ways—through the educational system, the media, legal rules and procedures, the symbolic rituals of leaders, and the like—and only infrequently is it necessary to resort to outright coercion. Drastic repression may create a sense of hopelessness among people. Management of the society is, therefore, usually a peaceful process.

Strategy

What is distinctive about this book? The intent to help others become independent thinkers is often voiced, though rarely implemented. Indeed, we anticipate that only full study of this book will convince those who have heard this goal invoked regularly that we are indeed serious about it. Though neither a critical posture toward the American political system, nor the view that it is dominated by the needs of the economic system, are unique to this book, it is distinctive in its systematic and evidential demonstration of how and why this happens.

The method of presentation we have chosen is unprecedented. We feel that it is a major contribution to clear understanding of American politics. Part One of the book briefly presents some basic tools for analysis and evaluation. In each of the six chapters in Part Two, we examine what the U.S. government has actually done with regard to a particular problem in the last few years. By looking at the actual outcomes of public policies, and by asking who was affected and in what ways by a government action, we shall understand for whom government works. We believe that the performance of government can best be measured by results, and that is why we focus on the consequences of governmental actions. Our questions in Part Two will be: Who wins and who loses as a result of this policy? What effect did this policy have on the problem or goal involved?

Once we can recognize who gets what from government policies, and how people and problems are affected, we shall be in a position to ask why this is so. Our inquiry proceeds in two ways. First, in Part Three we look at contrasting ideological justifications or explanations of these outcomes. What values, assumptions, and goals are apparent in these policies and their effects? The orthodox American ideology, dominant for decades, pervades the practices of government and the words and actions of leaders. A radical-populist challenge to the validity or propriety of this established ideology is also apparent, however, though usually in the complaints of deprived groups and the writings of a minority of intellectuals. The contrasts between these two sets of beliefs are sharp, and they raise some vital questions of fact and interpretation for us as analysts. They also, quite obviously, indicate some of the reasons for continued conflict in American politics today.

Then, in Parts Four and Five, we turn to an analysis of power and decisionmaking. We look not just at the institutions of the national government but also at the structure of power in the society generally. Much of what is done by government institutions reflects needs and preferences flowing from the economic or social structures of the society.

In effect, we will be using our knowledge of the consequences of public policies as a kind of prism through which to look at power and decisionmaking. We can see far more clearly how power is distributed and used in this way than by focusing on elections or politicians' rhetoric, and it is undeniably better than merely describing how government institutions work in isolation. Many benevolent assumptions and democratic myths may be exposed as false, but that is both necessary and proper in an accurate political analysis. Where we know the long-term patterns of benefit and burden from government policies—who consistently wins and loses—and we find that the beneficiaries have the apparent power to shape decisions as they wish, we have a solid basis for inferring that they in fact do so for their own benefit. This is the primary focus of analysis in this book.

A final and important feature of our approach is its concern with the process of political change, a concern that culminates in the three chapters of Part Six. Why do we try to discover who rules and for whose benefit, except to ask whether and, if so, how this situation should be changed? And yet very few analyses of American politics systematically explore the conditions and actions that permit, promote, or impede change in this society. Our analysis, from the first chapter on, is undertaken from the perspective of these findings' implications for change. In Part Six, we first reach some conclusions about the structure of power in the United States. Then we look at the many ways in which the symbols and appearance of change often substitute for the reality. Finally, we propose a general theory of change, and apply it to our

6

Introduction: Why are we here? Where are we going?

present circumstances to forecast possible changes in the United States in the next decade. This is a potentially controversial endeavor, but we think it is a necessary and desirable sequel to the analysis undertaken earlier. Moreover, it should be both rigorous and provocative enough to enable readers to test their skills of independent political judgment.

This book may be difficult in spots. If the writing is at fault, we are to blame. More often, we think, the difficulty is due to the complexity of the subject matter, and to misconceptions and incapacities produced by the dominant American ideology, which not only teaches that all is well and need not be examined closely, but also erects verbal and conceptual barriers against doing so. We must establish factual points thoroughly, on the basis of data and other evidence where possible; thus there are many tables and charts in this book. To meet a high standard of proof, some precise definitions and carefully detailed considerations are essential. Because we must comprehensively synthesize and interpret a vast body of material—the totality of the American econopolitical system and process—repeated conceptual clarification is necessary. For all these reasons, we ask that readers respond to difficult sections by trying a little harder. The end product—understanding of how and why the system works as it does, and for whom, and what can be done about it—is surely worth the trouble.

PART 1

The Study of Politics

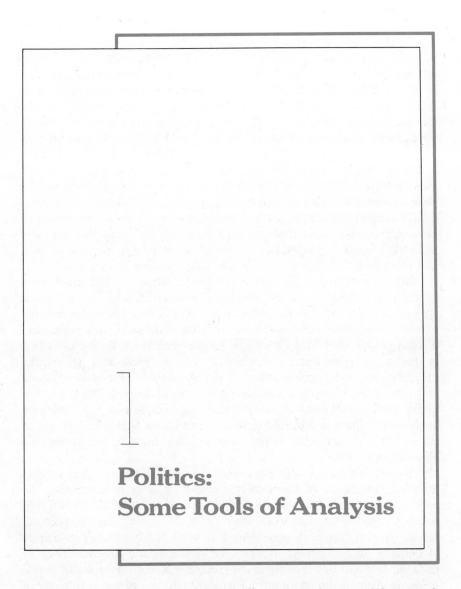

1

Politics:
Some Tools of Analysis

Let us begin by briefly illustrating why a careful approach is essential, using a problem that will remain with us throughout the book. Then we can move on to develop the necessary tools of analysis.

The United States is a capitalist society. This is one of the most meaningful statements that can be made about American politics. It is not a very startling or original observation, but Americans react to it in sharply contrasting ways. Most people never understand its implications. Others are so shocked by the discovery and its implications that they believe there is nothing more to be said. Much recent talk about American politics falls into the latter category, interpreting all political attitudes, behavior, institutions, processes, and prospects exclusively in terms of the (bad) characteristics of capitalism.

Neither of these two responses satisfies the demands of sophisticated political analysis. Both result from a lack of understanding of the interrelationship of economic, social, cultural, and ideological factors in shaping politics. These two types of intellectual failure define our task in this book. We must develop concepts, methods, and other tools of analysis that enable us to transcend these responses to the point of understanding, for example, how much of our politics is traceable to the capitalist nature of the American social order and how much is due to other factors.

What does it mean that the United States is a capitalist society? First, it means that the productive resources of the society—farms, factories, mines, and so on—are all owned by private individuals or corporations and operated so as to produce profits for those owners. Services such as transportation, advertising, communications, and the like are also privately owned and operated for profit. Most people are not owners, and must earn their livelihoods by working for those who are.

Next, it means that the social structure is shaped in important ways by patterns of wealth and income distribution created by that economic system. A relatively few people—mostly owners, but also some salaried managers and other persons—receive a large share of all the wealth and income produced. A larger group of people with specially useful skills—engineers, lawyers, accountants, salesmen—also receives a substantial proportion. A still larger number of people, mostly blue-collar workers and minorities, receives a smaller proportion of income. They are not highly skilled, and hold those jobs that are both low-paying and most likely to be eliminated during economic recessions. Status and power in the society are distributed in the same stratified manner, giving rise to a class system.

A capitalist society also has certain cultural and ideological characteristics. The values of the society support kinds of behavior that are consistent with the economic system and social structure. Individual self-seeking, materialism, the work ethic or profit motive, and respect for private property are both basic American values and necessary principles of behavior in a capitalist society. The characteristic American way of thinking is also (but less obviously) consistent with a capitalist social order. It assumes the continuity of existing patterns of ownership, social structure, and values, and unconsciously tries to fit all it sees or imagines into that mold. It asks only questions that are answerable in these terms, and employs only words that express attitudes appropriate to such a society. For example, it looks at higher education chiefly as a means to prepare young people for jobs and income in a technological society. It either cannot imagine other purposes or considers them uneconomical "frills"—or possibly even subversive.

Finally, although all societies generate self-congratulatory and justifying ideologies, that associated with a capitalist society has certain special features. It holds that economic activity is separate from (and morally superior to) politics. And it teaches that human nature itself is the basis of capitalism: people are naturally competitive and self-seeking, and thus capitalism is the "natural" economic system. American ideology includes many other beliefs as well, as we shall see in a later chapter; but the outlooks just identified are specially linked to the capitalist nature of the American system.

All these economic, social, cultural, and ideological characteristics play significant parts in our politics. They are not the only major factors in politics, of course. But they are often so familiar as to pass unrecognized, or so much a part of our way of thinking as to control our perceptions and judgments. How do we identify precisely the parts played by different factors in our politics? Clearly, we must cast our analytical net wide enough to include all major causal factors—and we must be alert enough to see them after we have caught them. Part of the answer lies in some careful definitions.

Some Preliminary Reflections on Politics

In order to live together on a continuing basis and to achieve their various goals in life, people seek and employ power in ways that affect the lives of their fellows. In other words, they engage in politics. They erect governments to maintain order, further mutual goals, and promote general well-being. Around and within the framework of that government, they continue to seek their individual and group goals. People can no more live without politics in this sense than they can forego food, love, or other basic human needs and desires. Politics is the activity by which they seek their goals, maintain a context that allows them to pursue those goals, or defend what they have already gained. For many people, of course, politics serves all three purposes.

Those individuals who possess the resources of power—such as wealth, prestige, strength, or oratorical talent—are often able to persuade or compel others to alter their intended patterns of behavior. Others, by combining their lesser resources, may influence or even reverse the decisions of the more powerful. In the broadest sense of the term, political activity occurs whenever an individual or group of people brings resources of power to bear, not only on government but also on any other individual or group whose behavior they desire to change. If tenants withhold rent in order to induce a landlord to make needed improvements on a building, they are, in a general sense, engaging in political activity.

But regardless of how seldom individuals employ their own political resources to influence the actions of others, they cannot escape the consequences of political decisions. If only as a consumer of the political products generated by the actions of others, every one of us is involved. Thus we are all in politics, whether we like it or not, inevitably and permanently.

Because war has been a continuing fact of history, politics has always had life-or-death importance for at least some people. With the advent of nuclear weapons, politics has come to have such meaning for practically everybody. But it is not only in relation to other countries that politics has life-or-death significance. The more powerful elements in a society prescribe the behavior that is in their eyes consistent with the established order of things, and fix punishments for those who break the rules. Further, thousands of men are hired and equipped with weapons to enforce such codes of behavior. For those whose situations and/or preferences make them able and willing to accept the rules, the political preferences they reflect and the power exercised to enforce them create no great problems. For those not satisfied with the *status quo,* however, the same rules may serve as apparently unjust obstacles to desired change. But violation of the rules, or even talk of the justice of doing so, often brings swift retribution in the form of imprisonment, physical injury, or death.

Politics is also routine. At every hour of the day, in practically any activity in which an individual engages, he or she is affected by the consequences of politics. Consider so prosaic an act as driving to a drugstore to buy a pack of cigarettes. The driver (licensed by the state) gets into the car (licensed and registered with the state; fitted with safety devices according to federal specifications; sold at prices reflecting the manufacturer's response to federal antitrust laws, labor-management relations practices, and interstate commerce rate controls; and taxed by federal, state, and local governments). He or she drives (according to local and state ordinances, and subject to local traffic officers) to the drugstore (where the state-licensed pharmacist is closely regulated as to the hours he may do business and the prescriptions he may sell to customers), and buys (with federal currency) the cigarettes (which have been the subject of extensive federal testing for danger to health, carry a required warning to users, and are taxed by both federal and state governments). And so forth.

The point is that the relationship of the individual to politics *never* ends. And every instance of contact with politics implies a prior history of conflict and governmental choice made in keeping with the preferences of those with the greatest amount of power at a particular time or over a particular issue. Thus, the individual exists in a world shaped by the decisions of others, and not even the most determined effort to extricate oneself from such effects can be successful.

Politics: A Definition and Its Implications

Politics is a process (1) in which power is employed to gain rewards, and (2) through which the interests of broad segments of the population are affected. We like the shorthand phrasing of a leading political scientist, who characterized politics as "who gets what, when, and how." [1] This is a wide-ranging definition (which we shall have to refine shortly), for it points well beyond "government" or "the state" to focus on other holders of power in the society and the ways they achieve their goals and affect others' lives.

Nothing is more tedious, or more important, than precise definition of what we are talking about. This is particularly true of the emotion-laden subject of politics. We have deliberately adopted a distinctive definition of politics in order to employ the widest possible, and least ideologically shaped, frame of reference for our inquiry. But even at the risk of tedium, we must spell out in detail what is implied by our definition, and how it differs from the more familiar and more limited (and more self-congratulatory) definitions usually employed.

We believe that we must include in our definition extragovernmental activity that bears on who rules, who benefits, and how change comes about, because government is only one of several channels through which vital goals are obtained. The use of government therefore implies change or confirmation of pre-existing patterns of benefits—either of which is of vital concern to political participants. Fundamentally revealing uses of power are more often prompted by the question of *whether* government should act in a given area than by *the way in which* government is to act. For example, the "natural" residential pattern in most areas is one of racial segregation. Neighborhood schools thus tend to be enclaves of whites or minorities. Some like this situation, but others do not. Should there be national governmental involvement in this area? Some will gain and some will lose in either event. The consequences for ordinary people, who inevitably feel the impact of this struggle in one form or another, may be very great—and eminently a product of politics.

Further, a concern for the nature of problems and the character of extragovernmental activity will alert us to the processes by which an issue becomes recognized as a possible subject for political debate or governmental action. Some matters are routinely understood as appropriate for governmental action, some (such as poverty and racial discrimination) are seen as such only at very late stages, and some (such as nationalization of major industries and compensation for victims of crime) not at all. Sometimes a subject initially appears quite outside the range of "practical" political consideration, but after a period of years moves into the field of political debate and finally takes a place among the policies of government. This was the case, for example, with medical care for the aged and, more recently, with the guaranteed annual wage or "negative income tax."

Throughout the period when some political actors are trying to move

---

[1] Harold Lasswell, *Politics: Who Gets What, When, How* (New York: McGraw-Hill, 1936).

a subject from the unthinkable stage to the stage of debate and even action, many forces are at work to shape opinion about whether the issue should be a subject for government and, if so, what should be done about it. These shaping forces reach deep into the underpinnings of our politics. Our understanding of what is proper for government action, for example, is strongly affected by the cultural values and assumptions we have acquired while growing up.

But these values and assumptions are not coincidental: somebody or something has taught them to us. The result is that some participants in politics—usually those who do not need governmental protection or might be hindered by it in some way—are better able than others to gain their ends. Nevertheless, some issues and problems do elicit public attention and are acted upon by government. Which issues do this, and why, and under what conditions? And when they do, who acts how to shape our understanding of the nature of these issues? What is at stake?

The temptation is strong to try to understand too much, to treat almost every event and pattern of social and economic activity as if it had political implications. The fact is, of course, that almost everything does. But we must exclude much of this activity in order to cope concretely with some of it. We shall limit ourselves to matters that have a direct and immediate relation to the present character or future prospect of government action. Our definition of politics then becomes: *the process by which power is employed to affect whether and how government will act on any given matter.* Power is the possession of resources, ranging from money and prestige to official authority, that cause other political actors to modify their behavior and conform to what they perceive the possessor of the resources prefers. Such resources need not be tangible; what counts is others' perceptions of one's resources. They need not actually be mobilized and employed in any particular situation, because others may act in anticipation or expectation. Indeed, much politically significant behavior occurs because of "voluntary" conformity with the perceived expectations of others.

One of the major resources of power, of course, is *legitimacy*. Legitimacy is a status conferred by people generally on the institutions, acts, and officials of their government. When people believe that their government is the right one—that it works properly and for desirable ends —they place their trust in it and grant it their obedience. Elected officials, bureaucrats, and law enforcement personnel all acquire some of this special status by virtue of their institutional positions. This enables higher officials, at least, to exert considerable influence over what people believe, to draw support for their actions, and (under normal circumstances) to shape the agenda of politics so as to gain their ends more easily.

But legitimacy is a fluid and intangible attribute. It can be undermined by frequent requests for uncritical support, actions inconsistent with expectations or traditions, and extreme misconduct. It may be withdrawn by a segment, or even by most, of the people. Under such circumstances, voluntary compliance with the acts of government and normal cooperative routines may cease. If this occurs among a large proportion of the population, people in government may have to fall back on outright coercion to achieve their ends. The shift to this form of power, of course, means that the political system is close to breakdown.

Thus politics is a vast interactive process of power applications which, although sometimes unintentionally, nearly always has consequences for others. From our early acquisition of ideology to the present process of defining a "problem" for government, we are subject to the effects of past and present power. Fortunately, our limited definition of politics as those uses of power that bear directly on whether or how government will be employed makes it unnecessary to trace the entire web of power transactions in society. The delineation of what bears "directly" on the use of government will not always be clear-cut. But we shall try, by holding on to what is tangible and demonstrable, to keep our definition manageable.

Understanding and Action in Politics

The purpose of understanding what is happening in politics, and why, is to be able to judge and then to act. Of course, all understandings, judgments, and actions are not equally sound. Some are clearly better than others, in terms of factual accuracy, human values, or both. Our task is to find the ways of understanding, judging, and acting that can lead to a more just and decent society.

Most of the tools useful in this effort can only be demonstrated in concrete situations. As we proceed in our analysis, we shall employ three central questions, and observe several cautions. We shall also explore the nature and implications of various standards of evaluation frequently employed to reach judgments about political questions. All these questions, cautions, and evaluative considerations are explained and examined in Appendix I, and other applications of them are cross-referenced with the Appendix. (Readers may wish to consult Appendix I now, for purposes of a preliminary overview.)

We can, however, make two general points here about these tools. First, much emphasis, particularly in the first few chapters, will be on problems involving *how we look at or think about the political world*. In a sense, we shall argue, much of "politics" is really *in ourselves*—in the categories and assumptions in our minds that shape our understanding of events or conditions. We must try to identify the presuppositions in our minds—and to replace them with frameworks more of our own choosing. In Chapter 2 we start this process by considering the context of government in a new, or at least unfamiliar, way.

Second, we shall emphasize *what government actually does*. By assembling facts about the distribution of *burdens* (taxes, regulations, and

Source: Cartoon by Fernando Krahn, *The Atlantic,* October 1972. Reprinted by permission of Russell & Volkening as agents for the cartoonist. Copyright © 1972 by Fernando Krahn.

The Last Laugh

the like) and *benefits* (services, money, and so on) we shall see for whom government works. We shall move beyond many assumptions and beliefs about how government should or does work to build a base of facts about what government actually does. Then we can begin to consider the interesting question of why it functions as it does. Each chapter of Part Two will examine such facts in a particular subject area. Once we organize these facts into regular patterns, we shall proceed to analyze the reasons for such patterns.

PART 2

Problems
and Policies

WHO WIN'S
WHO LOSSES

2

The American Political Economy

What you see depends on what you are looking for; how you understand the world depends on the *concepts* (images and expectations) in your mind as you undertake your inquiry. All concepts reflect assumptions and suggest conclusions. For example, many people conceive of "politics" as sharply distinct from "economics." The former is associated with Democrats and Republicans, the President on television, and occasional elections; the latter with a complicated system of production and distribution within which one has to find a job and produce income. The two are treated as separate compartments of social life, with no necessary connection to each other.

An older—and newer—conceptual approach is to see economic and political life as a single integrated whole. Eighteenth-century insight and today's common sense both resist such artificial distinctions. Economy and government are interpenetrating and mutually supportive; no meaningful boundaries can be drawn between them. The term *political economy* is used to refer to this system of institutions and human activity.

What difference does it make how we conceive of economy-and-government? In social analysis, the most useful concepts are usually those that take the most factors into account. And we want to be able to look beyond mere facts in search of *relationships* and *explanations*. The compartmentalized approach to politics and economics obscures many such vital connections, while the integrated political economy approach is deliberately inclusive.

We consider the political economy concept valuable and rewarding, but it will not always be easy to think (or write or read) in that framework, because we all are so used to the idea of separate compartments. It will take deliberate effort for each of us to abandon our familiar habits of thought. In this chapter, for example, we shall characterize our present political economy and describe some of its problems and prospects. But this material should not evoke images of "government" managing "the economy," which would represent a return to the two-compartments concept. Instead, we should be searching for interests, trends, power, and potential actions wherever they exist within the single entity under analysis. Our focus will shift from one sector of the political economy to another, and we shall look at aspects of our problems and prospects separately. But our entire inquiry will proceed within this integrated conceptual framework.

The Structure of the American Political Economy

It is becoming increasingly standard to characterize the American economy as having two parts, or *sectors*. One sector is composed of massive and often multinational corporations and banks, a few of which dominate national and world industries or markets. The other sector is made up of a much larger number of small businesses, mostly retail and service-providing, and is characterized by real competition and the operation of market principles. To this orthodox view, we shall add two factors. First, we shall explore separately the nature of the integration between government and the two sectors—the needs of each, and the supports and services that flow from government in response. Second, we shall treat the government as an additional part or sector, and explore its consumption, investment, and other fiscal and monetary activities. Most of our effort in this chapter will be conceptual, oriented toward painting a broad picture of the American political economy today. Step by step, we shall fill in the details in later chapters.

The (Multinational) Corporate and Banking Sector

The basic character and workings of the American political economy are shaped by wealthy, service-demanding, and often multinational corporations. Perhaps the most obvious characteristic of the individual units in this system is sheer size. The General Motors Corporation is often used as an example. In economic, political, and social terms, it is comparable only to the more important nations of the world. Its annual sales receipts are larger than the *combined* general revenues of the eleven populous northeastern states: New York, New Jersey, Pennsylvania, Ohio, Delaware, Massachusetts, and the other five New England states.[1] It has 1,300,000 stockholders and more than 700,000 employees in 46 countries. Although General Motors is the largest of the great American corporations, it is not distinctively different from several others. Here is a government lawyer's characterization of Standard Oil of New Jersey:

> With more than a hundred thousand employees around the world (it has three times as many people overseas as the U.S. State Department), a six-million-ton tanker fleet (half again bigger than Russia's), and $17 billion in assets (nearly equal to the combined assessed valuation of Chicago and Los Angeles), it can more easily be thought of as a nation-state than a commercial enterprise.[2]

These two companies, and a handful of others like them, dominate the American economy in sales, assets, and profitability. In part, this is because two, three, or four giants so dominate key markets that competition is replaced by tacit cooperation. For example, the aluminum market is shared entirely by Alcoa, Reynolds, and Kaiser; more than 95 percent of automobiles are manufactured by General Motors, Ford, and Chrysler; more than 90 percent of telephone equipment by Western Electric; more than 75 percent of steel by U.S. Steel, Bethlehem, and Republic; and 90 percent of copper by Anaconda, Kennecott, Phelps Dodge, and American Smelting. Nor are these proportions unique. Concentration is particularly high throughout the industrial core of the economy—manufacturing, finance, utilities, transportation, and communications; from two to four firms share upwards of 70–80 percent of the markets in such areas.[3]

In proportion to the total economy, the largest corporations account for the lion's share of assets and profits. For the last twenty years, *Fortune* magazine has been reporting the sales, assets, and profits of the five hundred largest American nonfinancial corporations according to their sales ranking. Table 2.1 lists the top twenty for 1977. In general, these companies have grown faster and absorbed larger proportions of sales and

---

[1] Richard J. Barber, *The American Corporation* (New York: E. P. Dutton, 1970), pp. 19–20. Unless otherwise indicated, all data in this and the next two paragraphs are from this source.

[2] *Ibid.*, p. 20.

[3] William Shepherd, *Market Power and Economic Welfare* (New York: Random House, 1970), pp. 152–153.

net income than have other companies. But the performance of the top 500 as a whole is even more striking: having accounted for about half of all industrial sales in 1954, these corporations are now responsible for two-thirds of all such sales. Their share of all industrial earnings has risen from two-thirds to three-quarters in the same two decades.[4]

Of equal importance is the multinational scope of these giants. All of the biggest—but, of course, not all even of the "Fortune 500"—are global in character (that is, they have plants or other major facilities in more than one country). The top twenty listed in Table 2.1 include thirteen of the top twenty companies in the *world.* Many of these corporations have more economic resources than most of the nations of the world. Over 300 U.S.-based corporations conduct business all over the world; investments abroad in 1975 totalled over $70 billion.[5] In the last decade there have been sharp increases in these corporations' overseas employment, sales, and profits. More than 20 percent of all corporate profits are currently derived from abroad. The international network—exports, imports, and production and sales in foreign countries —is thus crucial not only to the *size* of profit margins but also to the very question of profitability itself, for many large U.S. corporations.

But nonfinancial corporations are only one component of the dominant sector of our political economy. The nation's largest banks are one of its most potent sources of leverage over the entire system. Even the largest corporations must borrow to finance expansion and growth. And banks' profits depend on making such loans at the most advantageous risk-to-earnings-rate ratio. Only 220 banks account for practically all lending in the United States. And a mere *nine* banks, six of them associated with the Rockefeller-Morgan group and *all* in New York City, accounted for more than 26 percent of all commercial and industrial lending by U.S. banks in 1973. About half of this money is lent to global corporations. One authority estimates that 90 percent of the entire indebtedness of the U.S. petroleum and natural gas industry, three-quarters of that of the machinery and metal products industry, and two-thirds of that of the chemical and rubber industry, is held by the same nine New York banks.

In the process of making loans, banks make judgments about the management and activities of prospective debtor-corporations, and also gain influence over them in such other ways as obtaining positions on their boards of directors in exchange for loans. The more loans they make, the more their interests are associated with those of the major corporations. In recent decades banks have loaned larger and larger proportions of their deposits, a phenomenon that contributes both to

[4] *Fortune, 41,* No. 5 (May 1975), p. 241.
[5] Data in this and the next paragraph are drawn from Richard J. Barnet and Ronald Muller, "The Negative Effects of Multinational Corporations" in David Mermelstein, ed. *The Economic Crisis Reader* (New York: Random House, 1975), pp. 153–155.

TABLE 2.1 *The Top Twenty U.S. Industrial Corporations, 1977 (ranked by sales; $ in millions)*

Rank '77	Rank '76	Company	Sales*	Assets*	Rank	Net Income	Rank	Employees Number	Rank
1	2	General Motors (Detroit)	54,961	26,658	2	3,337	1	797,000	1
2	1	Exxon (New York)	54,126	38,453	1	2,422	3	127,000	14
3	3	Ford Motor (Dearborn, Mich.)	37,841	19,241	4	1,672	4	479,300	2
4	5	Mobil (New York)	32,125	20,575	3	1,004	8	200,700	7
5	4	Texaco (White Plains, N.Y.)	27,920	18,926	6	930	9	70,646	37
6	6	Standard Oil of California (San Francisco)	20,917	14,822	7	1,016	6	38,283	105
7	8	International Business Machines (Armonk, N.Y.)	18,133	18,978	5	2,719	2	310,155	5
8	7	Gulf Oil (Pittsburgh)	17,840	14,225	8	752	10	59,400	51
9	9	General Electric (Fairfield, Conn.)	17,518	13,696	9	1,088	5	384,000	3
10	10	Chrysler (Highland Park, Mich.)	16,708	7,668	18	163	66	250,833	6
11	11	International Tel. & Tel. (New York)	13,145	12,285	11	550	15	375,000	4
12	12	Standard Oil (Ind.) (Chicago)	13,019	12,884	10	1,011	7	46,667	79
13	15	Atlantic Richfield (Los Angeles)	10,969	11,119	12	701	12	51,666	66
14	13	Shell Oil (Houston)	10,112	8,876	14	735	11	33,548	124
15	14	U.S. Steel (Pittsburgh)	9,609	9,914	13	137	84	165,845	8
16	16	E. I. du Pont de Nemours (Wilmington, Del.)	9,434	7,430	19	545	16	131,317	13
17	17	Continental Oil (Stamford, Conn.)	8,700	6,625	21	380	26	43,141	90
18	18	Western Electric (New York)	8,134	5,875	23	490	18	162,000	9
19	20	Tenneco (Houston)	7,440	8,278	15	426	21	93,000	25
20	19	Proctor & Gamble (Cincinnati)[1]	7,284	4,487	31	461	19	53,700	58

Source: Fortune, 97, No. 9 (May 1978), pp. 240–241.

* Because dollar totals are in *millions*, these figures represent *billions* of dollars.

greater influence and shared interests *and* to dependence on conditions that facilitate repayment of such loans. In 1950, for example, the large New York banks had loans outstanding of about $10 billion, or less than 40 percent of their deposits; in 1974 their loans totaled $79 billion, or more than 84 percent of all their deposits.[6]

The other major components of this sector—insurance companies, other investment trusts (real estate, mutual or pension funds, and the like), and utilities—have in common domination of their fields or markets, ownership or control over vast sums of money or capital investment, and close ties to the banks and corporations just described. Together, the relatively few—but giant—units in this sector account for the overwhelming preponderance of the total economy's sales, assets, and profits. In a basic and compelling way, their needs for profit, secure investment opportunities, and general economic and social predictability create the context and establish the leading priorities for all actions by major American institutions, both private (corporations, trade associations, unions) and public (Congress, the President, the political parties).

The Competitive Sector [7]

The contrast between the corporate-banking sector and the competitive sector is sharp and growing in every dimension. The number of businesses in this sector has been estimated at around 250,000. Many are started, and more fail, every year. Production is usually on a small scale, and markets are local or regional. Typical examples are repair shops, restaurants, independent drug and grocery stores, cleaners, and other service-providing businesses. Nearly one-third of the U.S. labor force is employed in this sector, approximately the same number as in each of the other two sectors.

While the largest corporations and banks dominate markets and thus achieve relative control over supplies, costs, prices, and profits, the situation of the competitive firms is normally the opposite. The market is real; suppliers and purchasers come and go, prices fluctuate widely, and unpredictability reigns. Profit margins are often narrow and highly unstable. Employment is irregular, and many workers are marginal and/or part-time (minorities, many women, students, and so on). Wages are substantially lower than in the corporate-banking sector, and unions are few and far between. Incomes are inadequate and constantly in need of supplementation, increasingly from some governmental source.

The corporate-banking and competitive sectors also differ markedly in their respective needs for services and supports from the national government. The size, scope, market domination, and profitability of units in the corporate-banking sector make it possible for them to encourage

[6] Harry Magdoff and Paul M. Sweezy, "Banks: Skating on Thin Ice," in Mermelstein, *Economic Crisis Reader*, p. 200.

[7] This section and the following are derived from James O'Connor, *The Fiscal Crisis of the State* (New York: St. Martin's Press, 1973), pp. 13–18.

unions, survive recessions, and wield massive influence over governmental policy. At the same time, their international interests require extensive diplomatic and military support. They need an educated work force, elaborate scientific and technological research and development, and a network of governmental programs to assure stability of demand (unemployment insurance, welfare, Social Security, and the like). And their size enables them to avoid the burdensome aspects of controls and regulations that also help assure stability and predictability.

For the fragmented and relatively powerless competitive sector, on the other hand, governmental policy is much more often oppressive. Taxes are a greater burden, for example, and demand-assuring spending is of lesser benefit. Prices cannot be raised to compensate for increased taxes, nor are as many ways available to defer or conceal income. Unemployment and welfare benefits reduce the number of workers willing to work for the lowest wages, and minimum-wage laws also push pay levels up. Education and other services are of much less value to this sector, in which highly skilled workers are largely unnecessary and employment tends to be short-term. A large military is of little direct benefit, and research and development are irrelevant.

These differences in the character and interests of the two sectors, and the resulting contrast in their costs and benefits from governmental policies, is not readily recognized. A widely promulgated and almost as widely shared set of beliefs holds that (a) all business is essentially the same—competitive and dependent on market forces; (b) government should normally keep "hands off" the activities of the "private economy"; and (c), public services and social insurance benefits are aimed exclusively at people in need. That points (a) and (c) are inaccurate, and that (b) is deliberately and regularly violated—due to the character and needs of the corporate-banking sector—is only the beginning of our reconceptualization of the United States' political economy.

The State as a Sector of the Integrated Political Economy

Part of the reason for the corporate-banking sector's dominance over the competitive sector is the massive size of the units in the former, which enables them to control markets, withstand bad times and other threats, and exert powerful influence over public policy. Thus the state (considering national, state, and local governments as a unit for the moment) might appear to be a potential rival of the corporate-banking sector. This is in some respects true: the sheer magnitude of revenue raised and expenditures made does place the state squarely on a par with the corporate-banking sector. The federal budget for 1976 alone calls for an income larger than the *combined* total sales of the top twenty corporations listed in Table 2.1. And expenditures ($350 billion) equal about one-third of the total gross national product (the sum of all goods and services produced) estimated for the same year.

But for two major reasons, the state is not an economic *rival* but an effective *ally* of the corporate-banking sector. First, "the state" is thoroughly fragmented into independent and sometimes competing units, each responsive to a particular constituency. This is as true of the federal government as of the more obviously independent states, cities, counties, towns, and villages.

Second, the key unit, the federal government, is heavily influenced—if not dominated—by the corporate-banking sector. Full demonstration of this point requires detailed analysis, which is undertaken in later chapters. Basically, however, many of the crucial decisions that shape governmental taxing, spending, fiscal or monetary actions, and other economy-related policies are made in one or more of the following ways:

1. by the corporate-banking sector directly, such as decisions to buy or not buy municipal or state bonds, or decisions on the part of the World Bank to lend or not lend, and on what terms,

2. jointly by the corporate-banking sector and governmental officials, operating through an agency of the government, such as the Federal Reserve System,

3. by corporate-banking sector managers who are temporarily governmental officials in most cases, such as in the U.S. Treasury, the Office of Management and Budget, and other agencies,

4. by governmental officials and decisionmakers who, though not actually part of the corporate-banking sector, recognize that unless its needs are served there will be serious unemployment or such other undesirable consequences, as tax cuts to spur business investment or create new jobs,

5. in response to developments within the economy as a whole that trigger pre-existing commitments on the part of the national government, such as unemployment insurance benefits.

In many respects, in other words, *the national government is the corporate-banking sector by another name.* (Jules Feiffer, a noted political cartoonist, appears to agree; see the accompanying cartoon.) We shall explore how taxing and spending policies benefit business at the cost of others in Chapter 5; how governmental supports, subsidies, and regulations sustain big business, and the nature of various business influences on governmental decisionmaking in Chapters 12 through 16. Here we shall sketch the integration of the federal government in the larger political economy in general conceptual terms. If it is true that money talks, it should be the starting-point.

The amount of money expended by all levels of government in the United States has risen steadily since World War Two, and now amounts to about $500 billion, or nearly 40 percent of the gross national product. During this period, state and local governments' expenditures have more than doubled; the sources of their income is derived not only from local taxes but also from substantial transfers by the federal government ($60

Source: Copyright © Jules Feiffer.

Feiffer

billion in 1976) and, of course, borrowing from banks and other investors. As we have said, the large and loosely connected set of enterprises that constitutes the state employs about one-third of the entire U.S. labor force. Clearly, no treatment of our political economy would be complete without consideration of all this activity.

One way to grasp the nature of the state's impact on, and its close connection to, the rest of the economy is to consider the national budget. Of the nearly $350 billion in estimated expenditures for 1976, about 1 percent is for maintenance of the government itself, such as upkeep of buildings, salaries of civilian employees, and the like. About 27 percent is required for maintenance of the military establishment. Much of this $94 billion is designated for purchases of weapons and other supplies, and a significant proportion of the corporate-banking sector is engaged almost exclusively in such production. The relationship between expenditures and employment here is so direct, according to a study analyzing the 1965–1970 period, that each billion dollars in additional purchases created 75,000 jobs.[8] Presumably, the same ratio applies to reductions; if so, the military cutbacks of 1969–1970 are alone responsible for the subsequent 2 percent rise in the unemployment rate.

Another major component of federal expenditures ($70 billion) is Social Security payments to retired or disabled workers. Of course, these workers and their employers pay taxes over an extended period of time to cover a large proportion of these costs; in 1976 nearly a third of all

[8] Richard P. Oliver, "Increase in Defense-Related Employment During Vietnam Buildup," *Monthly Labor Review* 93 (February 1970), p. 3.

federal income will be derived from such taxes. A similar partially tax-supported expenditure is unemployment compensation, which in 1976 totalled almost $19 billion. Such payments obviously help significantly to maintain the purchasing power of millions of people.

Interest payments to banks and investors who hold U.S. Treasury bonds and other securities represent a different sort of tie to the other sectors of the economy. Roughly 10 percent of the 1976 budget, or more than $34 billion, is devoted to such interest payments. The U.S. government is the single most secure investment banks and other investors can find, because its taxing capability (as well as its capacity to print money) represents complete assurance of its ability to repay except in the direst emergencies. This helps explain why banks and investors have been willing to finance and refinance a federal debt now nearing $600 billion. It also suggests that other borrowers will find it difficult to obtain needed loans when the U.S. Treasury is seeking them, as it must whenever there is a *deficit*—more expenditures than revenues in a given year—in the federal budget. In 1976, for example, the Treasury had to seek more than $50 billion in loans to cover the deficit in the national budget. This sum was in effect diverted from other potential borrowers, such as cities and corporations, which then had trouble paying their debts or increasing their capabilities.

A final category of government expenditure is devoted to building roads, financing railroads, operating the mail service, supporting agriculture, conducting scientific research and development, operating and supporting schools, and the like. Some of these functions are performed by state and local governments using federal funds. These numerous and diverse direct services are often understood as efforts to help people generally, or as the result of pressures from various specific interests. But they may also be understood, in conjunction with the other supporting efforts of government, as providing the *infrastructure*—underlying but necessary building-blocks—on which businesses can build to become profitable. The fact that the costs are public and the profits private leads to the assertion that the general public has made vast social investments in order that a few people can enjoy substantial profits.[9]

How It Works: A Case Study

Continuing to focus on money, let us illustrate how the corporate-banking sector interlocks with the national government to determine the integrated political economy's most basic directions. The Federal Reserve System was created by Congress in 1913 and empowered

[9] For a full version of this argument, see O'Connor, *Fiscal Crisis,* and Michael Best and William Connolly, *The Politicized Economy* (Lexington, Mass.: D. C. Heath, 1976).

to regulate the nation's money supply. This is an immensely significant power. By managing the amount of money in circulation, and thus (indirectly) nationwide interest rates, the Federal Reserve Board (Fed) can affect the whole economy. By rapidly increasing the money supply and thus lowering interest rates, it can give the economy a major push, in effect speeding up all its buying, selling, production, and other transactions—and increasing employment. By slowing the rate of increase in the money supply, it can have the opposite effect—raising interest rates and forcing cutbacks, credit crises, and unemployment.

The Fed's powers do not give it complete control; no single entity could exercise total authority over an economy as complex and international as ours. But they are sufficient, for example, to completely offset the effects of a tax cut intended to spur the economy, such as the anti-recession tax cut of $23 billion in 1975. Refusal to make loans or release reserves to other banks to do so can drive states and cities into default and bankruptcy. Or the extension of massive credit to a failing bank can keep it afloat long enough to preserve the stability of the rest of the banking system. *All of these actions were taken in the period from 1974 to 1976.* More immediately, there is no question but that the most vital aspects of the daily lives of all Americans—jobs, living costs, taxes, credit —are profoundly affected by Fed actions.

In light of the vast scope of their power and its impact on business and personal lives, it might be expected that there would be some form of public accountability and control over those who make such fateful decisions. There is, but it is so indirect that one can accurately say that the nation's money supply is managed by the nation's bankers. *How* and *in whose interests* they do so, and *their priorities with regard to the conflicting goals of full employment and low inflation,* is a matter of continuing controversy.

The Fed is headed by a seven-member Board of Governors, appointed by the President to seven-year terms and subject to confirmation by the Senate. All major banks are members of the Federal Reserve System, and their needs are served by twelve Federal Reserve Banks in various parts of the country. Banks are, of course, profit-oriented enterprises, whose goal is to make as many loans as possible at the highest possible interest rates—and then to see that those loans are repaid in money of the same or higher value (that is, with as little inflation as possible). No matter how decisions are made, or who makes them, a system made up of banks that have such needs and interests will be concerned about preserving the profitability of banks by limiting inflation.

The key decision-making unit of the Fed is the Federal Open Market Committee (FOMC), which consists of the chairman, the other six governors, and five of the twelve presidents of Federal Reserve Banks. This group meets every Friday to decide on Fed policy for the next week with regard to buying and selling government securities (Treasury bonds and notes). If the Fed *buys,* it pays by crediting the selling banks with new reserves in their accounts at the Fed, a transaction that in effect creates new money. The selling banks, which are only the very largest, are now able to make more loans themselves; their borrower banks in turn can make more loans. As this new money circulates, the economy picks up speed. If the Fed *sells* government securities, it reduces the reserves in the biggest banks, makes money more difficult to acquire, pushes interest rates up, and slows the economy down. The meetings at which such decisions are made are completely secret, and the Fed does all it can to mask its strategy in the complex securities market so that it can work its will effectively.

Who are the members of the FOMC? Table 2.2 lists their backgrounds. Not surprisingly, all have considerable banking and/or corporate executive experience. Many also have money-management experience in the executive branch of the federal government, in this case with Republican administrations because Republican Presidents have made all appointments to the FOMC since 1969. An exception of sorts is Arthur Burns, the current chairman, an economist who was an academic for many years. For the last twenty years, however, Burns has been in public life, often as an adviser or officeholder in Republican administrations. He replaced banker William McChesney Martin, who served as chairman for twenty-five years.

What does the corporate-banking background of FOMC members mean? At the very least, it suggests a special concern for the stability of the currency, that is, a determination to prevent inflation at almost any cost. In this respect, Chairman Burns is more like a banker than some bankers: throughout 1975, he continued to fight against increasing the money supply, despite the pleas and arguments of many in business and in Congress that the Fed was thereby threatening the economy with still more recessionary pressure and even more unemployment. *Business Week,* a journal known neither for sensationalism nor for special sympathy to working people, published an analysis of the Fed under the title "Burns: Architect of the Worst Recession?" in 1975.[10] At about the same time, Representative Wright Patman, long-time chairman of the House Banking Committee, described the FOMC as "one of our most secret societies. These twelve men decide what happens in the economy.... In making decisions they check with no one—not the President, not the Congress, not the people." [11]

The FOMC's secrecy and power have persisted, and the Fed has stood firm against the economy-spurring actions of the rest of the federal government. It is *able* to do so because it is an independent agency, subject to none but the most indirect control by elected officials. And it *wants* to do so because its decisionmakers are bankers and others who think as they do. In effect, the Fed is a "public" agency run by leading

[10] *Business Week* 2377 (21 April 1975), p. 106.
[11] Quoted in *Parade,* 26 October 1975.

members of the "private" banking industry in accordance with their own view of what is desirable.

The Role of Political Institutions

We have touched only on the most essential units of the integrated economic-political system. In subsequent chapters, we shall examine the parts played by universities, the communications media, foundations, and other institutions. But this brief sketch should create a frame of reference for the analyses that now follow. *All* major institutions, of which political institutions are only a fraction, give rise to positions of power and influence. Political institutions are units in an extensive web of relationships, animated by forces beyond their control. Because they are staffed by the same kinds of people who are dominant elsewhere in the system, and because they respond principally to its dominant needs and goals, they should be seen as linked *horizontally* to the upper layers of that system. It is a form of tunnel vision to see the Congress, presidency, and Supreme Court as a separate set of institutions linked vertically to "the people." Such democratic mythology, which suggests that popular wants and needs are communicated to political decisionmakers through political parties and elections and are ultimately expressed in policymaking, obscures more than it reveals.

This is not to say that nothing of consequence occurs within political institutions. Much does, but it must not be understood as the whole story of politics, or as the major source of initiative and control over the rest of the system. We shall analyze these institutions both as units of importance in their own right and as aspects of the context that gives them their real meaning.

By way of example, let us quickly summarize the situation of the American political economy and the role of government in it during the 1960s. Though the 1960s are fading from memory now, the seeds of our present crisis were sown in that decade. The corporate-banking sector and its multinational component came into being in its present form in the early 1960s, as a result of a wave of mergers and a surge of overseas investment. Once the effects of the recession of 1957–1961 were overcome, in part due to the strong stimulus of a massive federal income tax cut, economic growth was rapid and sustained. The Vietnam War was a further stimulant; new jobs were created and profits were spurred by still higher federal spending. During most of this period, inflation was only modest, averaging less than 3 percent per year. Unemployment averaged 5–6 percent most of this time, but dropped below 4 percent during the peak war years of 1966–1968.

To most people, the times seemed very good—at least economically. For the poor and minorities, of course, they were not good, and this very disparity led to new militance. Ironically, this militance was used by politicians and the media to confirm the view that the United States was

TABLE 2.2 *Members of the Federal Open Market Committee, 1975*

Name and Age	Position and Date of Appointment	Education, Highest Degree	Principal Occupation
Arthur Burns, 71	Chairman, FRB and FOMC; 1970	Columbia PhD	Economist. Former Chairman, Council of Economic Advisers
Stephen S. Gardner, 54	Vice-Chairman, FRB; 1976	Harvard, MBA	Banker: Girard Trust Company; U.S. Treasury Department
Paul Volcker, 48	Vice-Chairman, FOMC; President, N.Y. Reserve Bank; 1975	Princeton, Harvard, London School of Economics, MBA	Banker: Chase Manhattan Bank; U.S. Treasury Department
Henry Wallich, 60	Governor; 1974	Oxford, Harvard, PhD	Economist. Former Treasury official, member of Council of Economic Advisers
Robert Holland, 50	Governor; 1973	University of Nebraska, University of Pennsylvania, PhD	Banker: Federal Reserve Bank, Chicago

Name, age	Position; year	Education	Background
Philip Coldwell, 52	Governor; 1974	University of Illinois, University of Wisconsin, PhD	Banker: President, Federal Reserve Bank of Dallas
Jeffrey Bucher, 42	Governor; 1972	Occidental College, Stanford, LLB	Banker and lawyer: United California Bank
John Sheehan, 45	Governor; 1972	U.S. Naval Academy, Harvard Business School, MBA	Business executive of a manufacturing corporation
Robert Mayo, 59	President, Federal Reserve Bank of Chicago; 1970	University of Washington, MA	Banker: U.S. Treasury Department, Continental Illinois Bank
Ernest Baughman, 59	President, Federal Reserve Bank of Dallas; 1974	University of Minnesota, BA	Banker: Chicago Federal Reserve Bank
David Eastburn, 54	President, Federal Reserve Bank of Philadelphia; 1970	Amherst College, University of Pennsylvania, PhD	Banker: Philadelphia Federal Reserve Bank
Bruce MacLaury, 43	President, Federal Reserve Bank of Minneapolis; 1971	Princeton, Harvard, PhD	Banker: N.Y. Federal Reserve Bank, U.S. Treasury Department

indeed an "affluent" society that could afford to devote its apparently limitless resources both to pacifying the complainants *and* to fighting a vastly expensive war. In part because economic conditions seemed good, many people ignored or resisted both the civil rights movement and the antiwar effort that succeded it. And these bitter social conflicts in turn helped to divert attention from the growing problems of the economy—the advent of worldwide inflation, overexpansion of debt and credit, and increasingly unstable monetary and trade patterns.

The role of government in this period seemed clear and feasible to the administrations in power. It was to stabilize the economy, maintaining predictability and profitability so that steady growth with minimum inflation could continue. By aggressively promoting and defending American business overseas, and by "fine-tuning" through taxing and spending policies at home, it was assumed, government was able to perform its functions well. And because the resulting prosperity seemed to be in the best interests of all, there was widespread popular tolerance and general optimism. In a national survey undertaken in 1964, for example, confidence in the future reached all-time highs among all portions of the population.[12] But the storm clouds were gathering, and by 1970 it was becoming clear that a new set of problems threatened the fundamental character of the American political economy.

Politics in Capitalist America

We return now to the problem with which we began Chapter 1—that of understanding the significance of capitalism for the character of American politics. We are about to undertake an analysis of the ways in which capitalism—and other social, cultural, and ideological factors—affect politics in the United States.

In Chapters 3–7, we will analyze five problem areas and the effects of government policies in each. In all five areas the nature of the economic system is relevant; it would, in fact, be difficult to find important areas in which it is not. But the potential role of the economic system and associated values and ideology could be quite different in each area.

Taken together, these five problem areas encompass much of the content of American politics. One of our tasks is to see (1) these problems, (2) the characteristics of the capitalist economic and social system, and (3) the actions of government, as a single large and connected whole, an interrelated entity. One way to do so is to focus on the patterns of policy consequences (burdens for some, benefits for others), which may be linked to characteristics of the larger social system. But first we concentrate simply on the effects of governmental policies in each area. Some basic questions that readers should try to answer clearly are:

[12] *The New York Times*, 26 October 1975, p. 1.

What does the United States government *do* in these areas?
Who gets what as a result of a given policy?
What, if any, patterns of (1) governmental actions, and (2) effects of such actions, are evident in the five areas taken together?

It is not too soon to speculate about *why* things happen as they do, but it is essential to keep in mind that the evidence has yet to be assembled. Another set of questions, similarly speculative, may be more directly applicable at this point:

Can identifiable purposes or goals (consistent or conflicting) fairly be inferred from the answers to the first questions?
If so, what are the priorities among such purposes or goals: which are foremost and which are secondary?

After we have explored each of these areas, we shall turn to the task of understanding why things happen as they do. In Part Three, our inquiry will be directed at two standard explanations: a version of capitalist ideology, strongly held by most Americans, and a counter to it perhaps best known as radicalism. Each of these ideologies offers a complete explanation for the pattern of American public policies, one justifying and the other condemning. We shall explore each in detail. Among other purposes, this will help us to generate appropriate questions for the subsequent analyses of power and decisionmaking.

Summary

Taking stock of what we have begun in this chapter, two steps stand out. The first is our effort to build a conceptual framework broad enough in scope to enable us to understand the workings of economy-and-government. In effect, we have set the stage and described some of the background so that the story about to be told will "make sense." Both basic facts and underlying relationships have been sketched, so that we can begin to see how the integrated system operates. We have also been concerned with the part played (at least potentially) by pre-existing beliefs and assumptions—some of which help to conceal important relationships.

Second, we have located the role of government in this context. After all, it *is* government-and-politics that we seek to understand here. But because we can do so adequately only in terms of its connection to the rest of economic and social life, we have had to begin there. Perhaps our belabored definition of politics in Chapter 1 now seems more meaningful. In any event, all further analysis will assume that such connections and relationships exist in some form, and will search for facts that demonstrate *how* they apply in particular areas or cases.

3

The 1970s:
From Confidence
to Crisis

At the beginning of the 1970s, most observers thought they saw a war-induced inflation that required merely standard anti-inflationary policies on the part of the U.S. government. Accordingly, the Nixon administration used reduced war expenditures and increased revenues due to the 1968 tax increase to generate a federal budget surplus in fiscal 1969 (the year ending June 30, 1969). The result in 1970 was curtailment of economic growth (the first negative-growth year in a decade) and the sharpest jump in unemployment in a decade.

According to all the principles of conventional economic wisdom, such rigorous restraint should have halted inflation. But inflation kept rising. Not only was such wisdom confounded by the totally unprecedented combination of inflation and unemployment—heretofore polar opposites, one rising as the other fell—but another blow awaited. For several reasons, the fiscally conservative Nixon administration had the highest peacetime budget deficit in American history (to that point) in 1971, some $24 billion. According to conventional principles, this deficit should have sharply reduced unemployment. Instead, unemployment continued its steady upward climb.

In a desperate about-face, the Nixon administration then imposed the most severe wage-and-price controls in peacetime history. Though wage increases were slowed, prices continued to increase and profits jumped. And both inflation and unemployment continued to rise. Moreover, these conditions were worldwide: all industrial nations except the socialist countries were experiencing both phenomena at the same time. The value of currencies, including the American dollar, began to fluctuate widely. This effect threatened world trade patterns, since traders must know the probable value of the currencies in which they are dealing in order to calculate whether they can make a profit on a transaction.

When, in time, the new controls were eased, there promptly began a new wave of inflation and unemployment. Clearly, the capitalist world economic situation was a many-faceted crisis inexplicable in terms of conventional economics. No known remedies seemed to work. Either the newly interdependent world economy had distinctive new characteristics or it had reached a newly unmanageable stage. The only precedent that seemed at all relevant was the Great Depression of the 1930s. Those who only a few years before had talked confidently of the efficacy of "built-in economic stabilizers" to prevent instability and maintain steady growth now faced the specter of worldwide depression.

In this chapter, we shall initially survey the key dimensions of the crisis: inflation, unemployment, bankruptcy of governments, and credit and capital problems. Then we shall focus on the economic aspects of the energy crisis as a case study. Finally, we shall explore the contrast with the 1930s, the policy options available to the U.S. government, and the implications of each for peoples' lives in the United States.

Inflation

Inflation is a general rise in the prices of goods and services, such that the *real* or purchasing-power value of money is reduced. Three dollars are necessary today to buy what two dollars bought yesterday. Conventional wisdom acknowledges three types of inflation; the differences among them bear importantly on who suffers most and on whether government can control inflation at all.

In *demand-pull inflation,* an excess of money in the hands of consumers bids up the prices of goods. This may happen during periods when consumer goods are scarce, such as wartime, or as a result of governmental spending in excess of its revenues—in which case it is injecting new money (or increased demand) into the economy. A second type of inflation is *cost-push inflation,* in which the rising costs of production (raw materials, interest on loans, wages, and the like) force producers to charge more for their products.

The third form is *profit-push inflation,* in which those producers or investors who have sufficient control over the market for their products or capital to flourish seek to make more profit by raising prices, or by maintaining them at an artificially high level when other prices are declining. In this type of inflation, of course, a noncompetitive market situation is assumed. As we shall see later, this is the case for many American industries, dominated by a few large corporations. Thus the prospect of this form of inflation, while new, is real.

Combinations of these three types of inflation are also possible. For example, producers may use slight rises in the costs of production as grounds for large price increases. Or a period of inflation may be initiated by one form of inflation, such as governmental spending in excess of revenues for a sustained period (such as the Vietnam War), and prolonged by one or both of the other forms.

While nearly everybody suffers from inflation, people do not suffer equally; and some do not suffer at all. In the case of demand-pull inflation, for example, the need for more workers to produce more goods may result in a sudden increase in the availability of jobs and/or higher income for people who are usually unemployed or poorly paid. This is the case during periods of heavy military expenditures; since World War Two, unemployment has dropped below 4 percent only during the Korean and Vietnam Wars. Since periods characterized by this type of inflation are apparently the only times such people experience full employment or decent incomes, they may be said to benefit. Some workers, usually those in the unionized fields (less than 20 percent of the labor force) *may* be able to stay ahead of inflation. But those whose incomes are derived from ownership of corporate stock stand the best chance of staying ahead of inflation, since profits and stock value are quite likely to rise in value faster than the rate of inflation.

Most wage earners and all those on fixed incomes (such as retired persons) stand to lose—often severely—from inflation. In a study of the effects of inflation in 1974–1975, for example, one business magazine identified eight categories of wage earners who had experienced gains in their real wages, and thirty-four who had had losses. Some of the latter had fallen behind by as much as $77.52 per *week* (farmers) and several had had their weekly wages effectively reduced by $15–$30.[1] Moreover, a similar journal saw the middle class in a particular squeeze:

> . . . the middle class is on its way to becoming another "lost generation" like the one that disappeared in the 1929 crash. Battered by inflation

---

[1] *U.S. News and World Report,* 12 May 1975, p. 89.

and the country's worst recession in 40 years, shaken by political scandals unparalleled in American history, and troubled by massive strains in the world economy, the middle class is growing angrier and more frustrated day by expensive day. Within the last two years, it has seen the purchasing power of its dollar shrink nearly 20%, the value of household savings and other wealth or assets decline 11.5%, and the size of household debts rise 18.6%.[2]

There are many ways to characterize what has been happening to ordinary Americans as a result of inflation. Since 1967 the dollar has declined in purchasing power by 48 percent, staggeringly affecting how much money is now required to support a family. As real wages dropped in the years 1974–1975, however, the spending power of corporate profits rose 24 percent.[3]

Businesses may benefit from inflation individually, or for brief periods generally, but it is a threat to them also. Major corporations and banks, for example, most need predictability and stability. They must be able to plan ahead. If profits are to be assured, return on investments must exceed the rate of inflation. If loans and other investments made this year are repaid ten years from now in money of substantially lower value, they will return insufficient real profits to investors—and soon there will be no willing investors. Similarly, businesses must be confident that their investments in plant and equipment today will lead to sales at prices that will mean real profits tomorrow. Thus, it is not so much the prospect of inflation itself (which can be planned for), but the prospect of uncertainty—uneven or unpredictable rates of inflation—that is most troublesome to business and financial interests.

Inflation also has several combined economic and psychological effects. If the expectation of inflation is widely shared, people may act to protect themselves against its effects and thereby generate a *self-fulfilling prophecy*—a prediction that comes true because people act as if it were true. Such attitudes and behavior fuel the upward movement of prices, but at uneven and unpredictable rates. Moreover, inflation in one nation reduces the value of that nation's currency in relation to that of countries not experiencing inflation. Speculators may anticipate the devaluation of the nation's currency, and thus sell their holdings of that currency for a stronger currency—thereby creating further devaluative pressure. The result of such speculation may be instability throughout the international monetary system, interfering with normal world trade and causing unemployment in various countries.

Finally, inflation, if prolonged, is likely to have an unsettling effect on broad segments of the population. Those who have fallen behind economically, and even those who by dint of special efforts have managed to stay even, begin to feel the pressure and to express resentment of the

---

[2] *Business Week*, 10 March 1975, p. 52.
[3] The data in this paragraph are calculated from *Economic Report of the President, 1975* (Washington, D.C.: Government Printing Office, 1975).

economic and political system that has permitted such conditions. Over a prolonged period, their resentment may give rise to rejection of that system and action to fundamentally change it.

The special—and perhaps intractable—character of the inflation of the 1970s becomes apparent from simultaneous examination of the experience of the United States and other major countries. In one five-year stretch from 1974 through 1978, the United States experienced an unprecedented inflation of roughly 40 percent. Britain and Italy underwent inflation nearly double that, while Germany and Japan had a somewhat lower rate than the United States. This widespread inflation has ominous implications: (1) The major countries appear to be so interdependent that what affects one affects them all, and no national economy can be relied on to provide a stabilizing influence. (2) As inflation surges substantially but unpredictably, national currency values also fluctuate widely and in such a manner as to encourage potentially damaging speculation against the world's major currency, the U.S. dollar, *and* to threaten world trading patterns.

In 1978, American inflation appeared headed back toward the 10 percent or higher rates of the mid-1970s, and the value of the U.S. dollar accordingly dropped sharply in the international money exchanges. In addition to causes of inflation built into the modern American economy, the United States was regularly incurring deficits in its trade balances (payments for imports far exceeded receipts for exports). It was also running staggering deficits in the national government budget accounts (spending exceeded revenue by $51 billion in fiscal year 1978, and was estimated at $40 billion for fiscal year 1979.) Both of these factors are generally understood to be important causes of inflation. In addition, the energy bill finally passed by the Congress in 1978 did not appear to really address the problem of still-increasing energy usage and rising prices, so that this cause of inflation also seemed to remain unchecked.

In the face of all these conditions, the Carter administration finally acted in November 1978. Employing a combination of monetary and fiscal actions and purely voluntary wage-price "guidelines" (see pp. 55–56 for a general discussion of these policies and their implications), the administration undertook a controversial step. The Federal Reserve Board sharply increased the "discount rate," or basic interest rate charged member banks by the Fed, thereby making credit expensive and slowing economic expansion. The Treasury borrowed extensively overseas to prop up the ailing dollar. The President insisted that the federal government budget would be substantially trimmed to keep spending close to revenues. Perhaps most significantly, the President set specific limits to wage and price increases in the coming period and appointed officials to monitor compliance. Although polls showed that a majority of Americans would support mandatory wage and price controls, the President insisted he did not want to impose them. One reason was that such controls would require legislation by the Congress, and another was that he did not think they would work.

The administration's anti-inflation package was controversial in part because many people simply did not believe voluntary controls would work. Also, many were convinced that the sharp increase in the Fed's discount rate and its probable accompanying reduction in the money supply would so drastically curtail credit and money availability as to bring about another recession and more unemployment in 1979 or 1980. President Carter was clearly viewing inflation as the primary problem, to be countered even at the cost of causing greater unemployment. But he was also gambling that any recession would be mild and/or brief, and that economic conditions would be stable again by the 1980 election. Both he and his inflation-fighting administrators had to walk a narrow and difficult line, however, between assuring people that there would be no recession or depression from such policies and warning them that unless there was voluntary compliance with the guidelines, inflation might proceed to the point where there *would* be.

Even as President Carter sought to rally support for his anti-inflation program, the number of potential problems and opposing considerations seemed to multiply. European and Japanese interests were worried that any slowing of American economic growth would endanger the fragile recovery that some countries were making from the depths of the 1974–1975 recession. Many economists in the United States doubted that inflation could be held below 7 or 8 percent, even with broad compliance with the guidelines, because of forces and commitments already at work in the economy. Very important, and equally delicate and protracted, trade negotiations appeared to be affected by the shifting trends of American anti-inflation policy. If the U.S. Congress sought to protect American industries from foreign competition, five years' efforts to reduce world tariff barriers and promote greater trade (and thus more growth and employment) might be endangered. Widespread resulting protectionism would then threaten stability and pose anew the prospect of world depression—just as it had done in the 1930s.

Unemployment

Focusing on inflation's equally dangerous partner in the same period, we can see that unemployment too is rising in all industrial nations. But in this case the United States leads all other nations. In part, this is a historic condition: Americans normally tolerate rates of unemployment (4–6 percent) that would cause the fall of governments and severe social unrest in European countries. The rapid growth of unemployment in the United States during this period is also the product of government efforts to slow inflation. By the end of 1975, the rate of unemployment was over 8 percent, again the highest it has been since the late 1930s.

In stark terms, an unemployment rate of 8 percent means that about 8,500,000 people are out of jobs. But what *that* really means, in human and large-scale economic terms, is not so easily characterized. To begin with, the official figures drastically underestimate the actual number of jobless people. Such figures include only those people known to government agencies (unemployment compensation and employment offices) to have been searching for work in the previous four weeks. They do not include people who are "underemployed," or working at part-time or other jobs well below their capacities because they cannot locate anything else. They do not include workers who have given up looking for jobs because they have been unsuccessful for so long, or people who are doing other things (such as attending school) because they have no job expectations. The U.S. Department of Labor estimates the total number of people in these latter categories as roughly identical to the number of those officially unemployed. If one includes various other categories of people who might well seek jobs if they were available, such as older people and students and housewives, unemployment rises to around 25 percent.[4]

Next, considering only the official figures for the moment, we must recognize that it is not the *same* 8,500,000 people who are unemployed all year. People find jobs and are laid off throughout the year. Thus the actual number of persons unemployed at some point during a given year is around 25,000,000.[5] The impact of such a rate of unemployment, therefore, is spread widely throughout the population. And for every person who actually experiences some unemployment, many others live in fear of it.

Unsurprisingly, the people who feel the effects of unemployment most acutely, are marginal workers—minorities, the unskilled, many women, and others. One study has shown, for example, that whenever the national unemployment rate rises 1 percent, it really rises more than 2 percent for black heads of poverty-line families and only about 0.5 percent for white heads of families earning $25,000 or more. Nor are such losses made up for by either unemployment compensation or welfare. The same study shows that low-income families recovered only about 31 percent of lost earnings for all assistance programs combined, including food stamps.[6]

The human costs of unemployment are much harder to characterize. Millions of people live on the margins, often without much food or hope; millions more exist just above that level, fearing that at any time they may sink below it. Prolonged high unemployment also has important large-scale economic effects. Consumer demand decreases, which may force cuts in production and more unemployment. Stability and profitability require that unemployment be held roughly constant at a rate that provides for adequate demand and yet keeps workers available and

[4] Bertram Gross and Stanley Moss, "Real Unemployment Is Much Higher Than They Say," in David Mermelstein, ed., *The Economic Crisis Reader* (New York: Random House, 1975), pp. 32–37.

[5] *The Boston Globe*, 10 July 1975, p. 20.

[6] *Monthly Labor Review*, June 1975, p. 30.

willing to work for relatively low wages. Another effect involves the national budget. For each 1 percent increase in the unemployment rate, the federal government suffers the loss of about $1.5 billion in income tax revenue. Because it must simultaneously pay out about $3.5 billion in unemployment compensation and welfare, the net cost per 1 percent unemployment is $5 billion.[7] There remains, of course, the fact—and the fear—that continued high unemployment may lead to serious social unrest. Clearly, nothing could be more "destabilizing" than that prospect.

Governmental Fiscal Crises and Bankruptcies

The close integration of national, state, and city governments' budgets with the rest of the economy is dramatically illustrated by the spread of fiscal crisis in these bodies in the mid-1970s. In the case of states and cities, bankruptcy has become a routine prospect. The reasons for the crisis on the part of all governments are similar, although the federal government has greater and different resources than the states and cities and thus is far less vulnerable.

In all cases, governments' commerce-promoting and service-providing commitments have risen steadily in the past decades. As we have noted, much of this activity seems generated by the needs of the corporate-banking sector and in effect provides the infrastructure for its stability and profitability. The construction of elaborate port facilities, highways, and airports; the guarantee of housing or other loans; and tax concessions to attract business both spur business directly and underwrite the general level of prosperity. Health and educational services help maintain the kind of work force necessary to a technological society. All these services, as well as such direct income-and-consumer-demand-maintaining services as unemployment compensation and welfare, are also desired by the general public or important segments of it. Neither business needs nor public desires alone account for the magnitude of government commitments, which were great and growing up to the mid-1970s. Taxes were seldom sufficient to support such enterprises, and many were financed by extensive borrowing—on the assumption that revenues would continue to rise to cover repayment costs.

By the mid-1970s, however, the condition of the economy had changed drastically, and the impact was immediately felt by governmental budgets. The federal government experienced a sharp decline in revenues and an increase of expenses such that budget deficits began to set new records each year. Lower revenues resulted from reduced individual income and declining productivity in industry; higher expenses resulted from inflation (itself capable of adding $10 billion to expenditures in a single year), new obligations for unemployment compensation and welfare, and another round of new military weapons purchases. A

[7] *The Boston Globe,* 10 July 1975, p. 20.

deliberate economy-spurring income tax cut increased the deficit in 1975–1976, when it reached $50 billion.

But the federal government can always continue to borrow, or simply to make new money by means of its deficits, even though such practices generate new waves of inflation. The states and cities have no such capacity: they must find the money to pay their creditors (employees, vendors, contractors, bondholders) in hard cash. Furthermore, their hard-pressed taxpayers have much greater capacity simply to reject the new taxes that would generate new revenues. As recession shrinks their revenues and inflation raises costs, states and cities approach a point at which only new borrowing can make up the difference. But lenders increasingly doubt their continuing ability to pay, and demand both higher interest rates and greater assurance of state/city determination *to* repay. The result is cutbacks in many public services, layoffs of employees, and the threat or reality of default and bankruptcy.

As states and cities approach this threshold, investing banks and others begin to withdraw from such investments entirely—in effect making bankruptcy, even on the part of cities that could pay their debts under conditions of ordinary investor confidence, a self-fulfilling prophecy. Creditors begin to wrangle among themselves and in court about who gets paid first from the limited available assets. Banks around the world are threatened with the loss of some of their major assets in the form of state and city bonds, and their own stability is in turn called into question.

"And so, extrapolating from the best figures available, we see that current trends, unless dramatically reversed, will inevitably lead to a situation in which the sky will fall."

Source: Drawing by Lorenzo; © 1972, The New Yorker Magazine, Inc.

Worst of all, life in such states and cities becomes more and more austere, and public services steadily decline. Former public employees search fruitlessly for jobs along with thousands of others. And, for every 100 public employees who are laid off, it is estimated that another 75 employees of private businesses lose their jobs as a result of reduced buying power in the area, fewer contracts with governments, and the like.[8] Other job losses result from the generally lower level of business activity throughout the area. These are, of course, only the general trend in the fiscal crisis that stalks the 1970s.

Credit and Capital Problems

Even if the economies of the world were healthy, there would still be cause for concern over the related problems of vast outstanding debts, overextended banks, and the lack of capacity to generate the new capital necessary for future growth. As things stand in the mid-1970s, these factors may be the most threatening of any we have surveyed.

In a special analysis in 1974, *Business Week* surveyed outstanding debt in the United States (a total of $2.5 *trillion,* incurred at an average rate of $200 million a day since the end of World War Two), and concluded:

> It would be an awesome burden of debt even if the world's economic climate were perfect. It is an ominously heavy burden with the world as it is today—ravaged by inflation, threatened with economic depression, torn apart by the massive redistribution of wealth that has accompanied the soaring price of oil.[9]

This is no exaggeration. There is nearly $8 of debt for every dollar of money supply, more than double the figure of the mid-1950s. Corporate debt amounts to more than fifteen times after-tax profits, double that of 1955. Household debt amounts to 93 percent of disposable income.[10] Unless these massive debts continue to be repaid, the whole structure is threatened. Any major default can cause the entire world economy to collapse from inability to pay.

The squeeze is focused particularly sharply on the banking system, the financial core of the nation's and world's economies. Because the ratio of loans to deposits is high, many banks run the risk of insolvency if their borrowers fail to pay promptly. In some cases, banks themselves (such as the Franklin National Bank, the twentieth largest in the country, which failed in 1974) have suffered losses from speculation in currency markets. The Chase Manhattan Bank's real-estate subsidiary lost hundreds of millions in failed real estate loans in 1974 and 1975, prompting concern for the bank's future. As these pressures multiply in the late

[8] *The New York Times,* 9 November 1975, p. 1.
[9] *Business Week,* 12 October 1974, p. 45.
[10] *Ibid.*

1970s, banks become increasingly cautious, making it more and more difficult for borrowers—all but the biggest and safest investments—to find money for expansion and growth.

The inability and/or reluctance of banks to lend to any but the most credit-worthy corporate borrowers poses major problems for the future growth of the economy. And, it cannot grow, of course, if it can neither pay off existing debts nor generate the jobs, profits, and taxes that are necessary to its very existence. *Business Week* estimated in 1975 that $4.5 *trillion* in new capital would be necessary for the U.S. economy to regain and maintain its usual average growth rate of 4 percent per year in the decade 1975–1984.[11] Continued inflation and/or national budget deficits (both of which have since continued) would raise that figure still higher. *Without* such growth, this leading journal argued, there would be no real economic recovery, the biggest companies would survive at the cost of smaller firms, shortages would occur, inflation would continue, and social unrest and conflict would threaten.

But, to understate the matter, the sources of such capital are not readily apparent. The already overextended banking system simply cannot provide it. The Third World is not likely to permit even the present level of drain on its resources to continue. One possibility is drastic curtailment of public services coupled with equally drastic taxation, such that the U.S. government could become the source of loans and guarantees of loans for corporate expansion. Presumably there would be popular resistance to this approach.

In reviewing the dimensions of the economic crisis of the 1970s, we have touched only on those that are most salient and most readily summarized. Nevertheless, it is widely accepted that these four problems constitute a major and unprecedented crisis for world capitalism. There is no reason to assume that this means the collapse of world capitalism. It does, however, strongly imply that we are entering an era of fundamental *transformation* in that system. We shall consider what lies ahead, and what if anything can be done about it, in the final section of this chapter. But first let us turn to a vital factor we have not yet introduced into this analysis: the bearing of energy resources and shortages on the economic future.

Energy: The Economic Aspects

We shall concentrate here on the implications of energy prices and apparent shortages for the world and U.S. economic crisis. Energy is a factor in American foreign policy and national security considerations, and in environmental and ecological problems, matters that will be deferred to Chapter 4. What we shall examine first is a "crisis"

[11] *Business Week*, 22 September 1975, p. 42.

America is treading water.

We seem to be afraid to move. Afraid that if we do move, we will make a mistake. And things will get worse.

Our leadership seems paralyzed, our people dazed. We are told we are running out of resources. Our money is worth less. Our jobs are being threatened. Our water remains polluted. So much has happened to us so fast, that we are overwhelmed. And so we sit. Hoping that somebody, anybody will come along and make it all go away.

Well, this time it looks like the cavalry isn't coming. And if we want something done we're going to have to do it ourselves.

We have already tried doing nothing. Hoping things will right themselves, and it hasn't worked. The time has come to make some decisions. Take some action. Make some hard choices, and some tough sacrifices.

We can start by believing in ourselves again. By believing that the more than 200 million of us can have an effect on our situation.

We can demand action from our leaders. We can give them our ideas. Tell them our problems. And tell them that we are ready to do whatever it takes to solve them.

At Knight-Ridder Newspapers, we believe that this country can find answers to the problems facing it. Because we believe in the people that live here.

And, as leaders in the newspaper industry, we will do everything we can to present the people of America with the issues and the problems as fully and fairly as we can.

And in our editorial pages we will continue to provide a forum for ideas. Ours, yours.

The next few years of American history are going to demand more than a few acts of courage from all of us. The ground is uncharted. But however things turn out, it will be because we did something. Not because we did nothing.

KNIGHT-RIDDER NEWSPAPERS

ABERDEEN AMERICAN NEWS
AKRON BEACON JOURNAL
BOCA RATON NEWS
BOULDER DAILY CAMERA
BRADENTON HERALD
CHARLOTTE NEWS
CHARLOTTE OBSERVER
COLUMBUS ENQUIRER
COLUMBUS LEDGER
DETROIT FREE PRESS
DULUTH HERALD
DULUTH NEWS-TRIBUNE
GARY POST-TRIBUNE
GRAND FORKS HERALD
LEXINGTON HERALD
LEXINGTON LEADER
LONG BEACH INDEPENDENT
LONG BEACH PRESS-TELEGRAM
JOURNAL OF COMMERCE
AND COMMERCIAL
MACON NEWS
MACON TELEGRAPH
MIAMI HERALD
NILES DAILY STAR
PASADENA STAR-NEWS
PHILADELPHIA DAILY NEWS
PHILADELPHIA INQUIRER
SAN JOSE MERCURY
SAN JOSE NEWS
ST. PAUL DISPATCH
ST. PAUL PIONEER PRESS
SEATTLE TIMES
(49.5% of voting stock,
65% of non-voting common stock)
TALLAHASSEE DEMOCRAT
WALLA WALLA
UNION-BULLETIN
(a subsidiary of Seattle Times Company)
WICHITA BEACON
WICHITA EAGLE

DO SOMETHING, AMERICA.

Source: Fortune, May 1975, p. 158.

essentially manufactured, and sharply higher prices thereafter maintained, by the concerted action of the major oil companies—and, to a much lesser extent, by their long-exploited, frustrated, and increasingly assertive junior partner, the Organization of Petroleum Exporting Countries (OPEC).

The oil industry is one of the very few industries in the world in which companies are *integrated*—that is, they perform every function from exploration and the production of raw materials through transportation and refinement to actual marketing at the retail level. Seven such companies dominate the industry: Exxon, Texaco, Mobil, Gulf, Standard of California, Royal-Dutch Shell, and British Petroleum. The first five are all U.S.-based, and rank among the top seven American companies (see Table 2.1). Given such size and market domination, and the international scope of their operations, it is not surprising to find that these companies powerfully influence nearly all the governments of the world. Real competition among them ended long ago with the realization that prices and profits would be higher if production were kept relatively low and under control.

After World War Two, the automotive core of the American economy (oil, steel, automobiles, rubber—representing *fifteen* of the top twenty companies in 1974) mutually promoted a system of highways, car usage, and other oil dependency (heating, utilities' energy production) that was immensely profitable. As the oil companies developed their overseas wells and refining capacities, however, they began to cut back on production and development of oil and other energy resources within the United States. This occurred because the cost of production per gallon in the Middle East, for example, was approximately one-twentieth that in the United States.

By the end of the 1960s, however, several problems had developed. Once-docile Arab and other governments were demanding a broader share of profits and control; price-cutting independent retailers had acquired 25 percent of the market in the United States; and environmentalists were effectively opposing profit-maximizing methods of developing new oil sources. Though the oil industry was still highly profitable, the rate of profit was falling and further declines appeared likely.

In this context, the response of the major oil companies was consistent with their longstanding strategy of limiting supplies and maintaining rising prices. They resisted efforts on the part of OPEC countries to induce them to produce more or, alternatively, to give the OPEC governments larger shares of their profits. In order to overcome environmentalists' objections to inexpensive ways of producing oil from the sea bed and from Alaskan fields, they began to stress the limited supplies of oil available and to join the futurists in projecting an "energy crisis" in the future. To be sure, the supply of oil in now-known wells *is* finite, but its exhaustion even at present rates is literally decades away. By that time, many new sources of oil are likely to be located (again, at current rates of exploration) and alternative sources could be perfected—particularly if oil companies stopped opposing their development.

How much actual collusion occurred in the early 1970s is a matter of some controversy. The historical record is clear enough on the long-term practice of concerted action by the leading oil companies, but cooperation in supply-limiting, price-raising actions may occur spontaneously, without collusion. In any event, reduction of supplies began in the winter of 1972–1973, when the northeast states suffered a fuel oil shortage and prices rose sharply. Gasoline began to be in short supply in the spring and summer of 1973, prices rose, and independent dealers began to go out of business.

At this point the Arab-Israeli War of October 1973 broke out, and eight Arab governments imposed an oil "embargo" on the United States and other countries that supported Israel. The Arabs were indeed seeking leverage against the giant American oil companies, but their action provided those companies with an opportunity that was quite literally golden: massive price increases could be imposed amid the panic of the "energy crisis," and the Arabs could be blamed for it. At the same time, the American public itself could be blamed for consuming too much gas and oil (that is, for doing what people had been urged for decades to do).

The results are instructive as to the real nature of this apparent crisis. To begin with, at the time of the boycott only 13 percent of the oil used in the United States came from the Middle East; 17 percent was from Venezuela and Canada, and over 60 percent from the United States.[12] The share from the Middle East never stopped arriving; instead, many shipments were simply rerouted to the United States after leaving Arab ports, and imports from elsewhere were increased. *Imports for October, November, and December 1973 were actually 32 percent higher than for the same three months in 1972.* In January 1974, several sources reported oil tanks full and tankers lined up to offload along the east coast.

But prices at the gas pump almost doubled. The price of crude oil from American wells, where no change in production costs had occurred, rose at the same time and to the same levels as the price of OPEC crude. The increase in oil companies' obligations to the OPEC countries, negotiated during the "embargo," were substantially less per gallon than the increases at the gas pumps across the country—and prices continued to rise after the "embargo" was lifted in March 1974. Continued restriction of supplies forced more independent retailers out of business throughout 1973 and 1974. Offshore drilling was authorized again, objections to the Alaska pipeline were overcome, and tax concessions were secured.

The biggest achievement of all, however, was the vast jump in oil

---

[12] Data in this paragraph are drawn from Dave Pugh and Mitch Zimmerman's instructive essay, "The 'Energy Crisis' and the Real Crisis Behind It" in Mermelstein, *The Economic Crisis Reader,* which in turn cites the oil industry press for all key figures, pp. 277–278.

company profits. The American oil industry as a whole experienced a gain of more than 80 percent in net profits from 1973 to 1974, the largest gain in the history of *Fortune's* recordkeeping.[13] And the roster of the top twenty companies in the United States was reshuffled more drastically than it had ever been. A look at Table 2.1 will reveal the extent of this change. To the oil industry's explanation that these profits were vital to make new exploration and development possible, their own workers' union responded with national advertisements showing that the profits were being used for (among other things) investments in real estate, entertainment companies, and the purchase of a department store chain. In all probability, they will also help to expand the oil companies' ownership of potentially competing energy sources, already 54 percent of U.S. coal reserves, 73 percent of natural gas supplies, and 45 percent of uranium reserves.[14]

While much has been gained, some problems may have been created for the future. The oil companies in effect jumped ahead of the OPEC governments, giving them a larger share in oil production and profits while increasing their own profits even more. But this may only increase the OPEC countries' leverage in the long run. At some point, they may well decide that they should be in full control of the use of and profit from their resources. As a hedge against this prospect, the companies have apparently increased the proportion of U.S. oil that comes from the Middle East and decreased American production still further.

The international implications of the huge rise in oil prices extend well beyond the oil companies, however. The whole pattern of world balance of payments has been sharply disrupted. Countries whose income from exports used to exceed what they paid for imports, such as Japan, now find that their gold or other reserves are being drained to pay the new oil prices. This phenomenon can have a drastic impact on domestic employment, consumption, and inflation, and may affect the value of a nation's currency. Nations whose finances are shaky to begin with (such as Italy) may be threatened with bankruptcy. In any event, it is clear that a massive redistribution of the world's wealth is underway, *from* oil-consuming people and businesses *to* the oil industry, the OPEC governments, and the international banking system that stands behind both.

The position of the United States' economy is relatively improved by comparison with those of the Western European nations and Japan. Americans depend far less on imported oil than do those countries, and thus the competitive position of U.S. businesses is likely to be stronger in world markets. The American dollar also should be less affected than those nations' currencies by inflation-induced fluctuation, thus giving another edge to American bankers and businessmen. Indeed, some have

[13] *Fortune,* May 1975, p. 208.
[14] Pugh and Zimmernan, "The 'Energy Crisis,'" p. 279.

suggested that the oil price rise was a successful move by the United States to restore its declining position as the world's dominant economy.

What of the role of the United States government during and after the "crisis"? High officials certainly played a leading part in creating the impression that there was occurring a serious crisis that could only be met by national sacrifice. No official question has ever been raised about the extent to which the crisis was and is real, and in what sense it requires reduced consumption and continued inflated prices. Instead, governmental policy has consistently mirrored the needs of the oil companies. Price increases are the means proposed to reduce consumption and promote new exploration and development. New development of alternative energy sources is provided for on the assumption that the oil companies should play a leading role. And American foreign policy in the Middle East simultaneously seeks influence among the Arab states and tries to split OPEC countries so as to reduce their leverage on the oil companies. In the process of redistribution that has heightened world inflation and increased the prospect of economic breakdown, the U.S. government has proved a valuable ally of the international oil industry.

Let us also take note, in our case analysis, of the response of the great bulk of the American people. At least initially, the "crisis" seemed real, and there was considerable willingness to sacrifice. People even policed each other, such as by honking at passing cars to observe the new 55-mile-per-hour speed limit. There were many calls for rationing, and the conviction was widespread that energy conservation was a matter of national survival. Even during the greatest crisis of credibility in American history, Watergate, the American people by and large still accepted their leaders' version of the nature of the "energy crisis"—a version, of course, duly and systematically presented by the news media. Only after the "crisis" was over did a substantial number of people come to question its substance.

Options and Prospects

Let us review the dimensions of the current economic situation, which undeniably merits the term *crisis*. In every category, it is clearly the most threatening economic era since the Great Depression of the 1930s. Of course, economic and other conditions are never quite comparable, and there are clear differences between the circumstances of the 1920s–1930s and our own time. Nevertheless, a comparison will give us some perspective on our own potential future.

A *depression* is (or was) defined as an extended period of decline in the gross national product, industrial production, and employment. The advent of the depression of the 1930s is usually dated as October 1929, when the stock market crashed. Other dates might be more defensible economically, but no single day fully reflects deep and long-term economic trends. The depression did not end, however, until the United States undertook total mobilization for war in 1941–1942. None of the New Deal's then-controversial and now-celebrated measures managed to return production or employment to predepression levels; only the war succeeded in doing so. To be sure, mini-recoveries did occur during the intervening years, but each was followed by a backward slide.

To compare the late 1970s with the early 1930s, some adjustments must be made. The 1970s have seen rapid and continuing inflation, precisely the opposite of the *deflation* that characterized the 1930s and was historically considered a necessary component of a depression. Simultaneous inflation and unemployment are causing working people's overall standard of living to be reduced. Whether this reduction is as severe in the 1970s, with high inflation and 8–10 percent unemployment (the official figures), as it was in the 1930s, when unemployment reached 25 percent but prices were *de*flated by an average of about 5 percent, is probably impossible to tell. Adjustments must also be made for the current availability of demand-and-income-supporting payments from governments to people out of work, and in turn for the fiscal strain and reduced services and employment brought about by those payments.

We would be hard-put to argue that the United States was experiencing a fully comparable depression in the mid-1970s, although some people have so argued. However, a solid case has been made in this chapter for the proposition that the mid-1970s were ominous and in general comparable to the early stages of the Great Depression. In this conclusion, we have plenty of company. The issues of the immediate future, therefore, involve whether—and, if so, how—the actions of the major units of the world economy (great corporations, banks, *and* governments) can prevent a full-scale depression from occurring.

All such actions necessarily distribute unequally the burden of restoring previous levels of profitability, employment, and income. Thus we must ask *how* unequally, and *who* bears the heaviest burdens to restore profitability. While the causes of the present crisis appear structural rather than superficial, capitalist economists have provided no analysis in keeping with conventional understanding of how such economies work. Thus all actions intended to cure current problems must be undertaken in uncertainty as to whether they will work or not. In such circumstances, economic self-interest and ideology are likely to be important factors in choosing among "remedies." We shall now look briefly at three sets of options, considering who the winners and losers are likely to be.

The Post–World War Two Remedies

As World War Two drew to a close, fear of renewed depression was widespread. Full employment had been achieved during the war, and it was feared that popular expectations might lead to serious unrest if millions of veterans returned home to a new depression. Moreover, the success of governmental management of other elements of the economy in wartime led to a new acceptance of its role in the vital stabilization process. This role was performed, of course, in terms of the needs of the major units in the economy and, as we have seen in the case of the Federal Reserve, often by officials associated with the "private" economy. We shall here consider three of government's economy-influencing "tools": monetary policies, fiscal policies, and income policies.

1. *Monetary policies* are basically the kinds of policies the Federal Reserve System applies to the money supply, as well as the Treasury's power to print more or less new money than the total amount that has worn out in a given recent period. One advantage of this type of remedy is that it seems to be impersonal. That is, conscious choices about who is to suffer from efforts to prevent inflation do not appear to be being made. By using only contraction or expansion of the monetary supply as a tool, government in effect lets the workings of the private economy determine who shall bear the inevitable burdens that result from slackening of demand and reduced investment. Normally, of course, this approach translates into unemployment for millions of people at the lowest levels. Another apparent advantage is the limitation on governmental intrusion into the workings of the economy: monetary policies are relatively slight and indirect thrusts, and are felt by various sectors of the economy only after being transmitted by the standard sources of guidance—the supply of and demand for money. But, perhaps for these reasons, monetarists concede that the effects of such policies are not immediate. Under ideal conditions, they take from six to nine months to have measurable consequences, and sometimes longer before their effects are significant. Thus economic or political conditions may make other measures necessary.

2. *Fiscal policies* have somewhat more direct and immediate effects on the economy. The various forms of fiscal policy all have to do with the way the government manages its own finances—that is, how much money it raises in taxes, how much it spends, and for what. The fiscal-policy approach to stabilization and growth was originated by the English economist John Maynard Keynes. Writing in the 1930s, Keynes argued that it is possible for a capitalist economy to become stabilized at low or depression levels of productivity and employment, and that the key to both levels *and* fluctuations lies in the amount of total consumer demand being generated in the economy. Because the budgets of modern governments are primary sources of impact on the private economy, Keynes urged the conscious use of government expenditure-revenue policies to promote or decrease demand and thereby spur or retard the economy.

Such policies could take the form of large budgetary deficits or surpluses, tax reductions or increases, expenditures for new projects such as public works, or cancellation of such projects already under way. The first item in each of these pairs would stimulate demand; the second would contract it. To spur the economy, government should, according to Keynes, cut consumers' taxes, run a budget deficit, and invest heavily in public-works projects. When these ideas were first introduced, resistance to the unorthodoxy of a deliberately unbalanced government budget and to purposeful government intervention in the private economy ran high. But avoidance of a depression since 1946, despite Keynesian rhetoric and practices, has gradually made such policies accepted as part of the role of government. Who gains and who loses from fiscal policy actions depends on the specific actions taken (whose taxes are cut or raised, by what relative amounts, and so on).

3. *Incomes policies* are the third more or less conventional approach, reserved as yet for what are perceived as "emergency" conditions. They assume that circumstances (inflation, profit levels, and the like) require direct government controls over wages and prices to produce the desired economic conditions quickly and effectively. This means that the government must make not only an annual estimate of the direction in which the economy should be guided, as under the Keynesian system, but also a conscious choice of the segments of the economy that should gain or lose proportionally in profits or income during the year. Controls are then applied in such a way as to accomplish the wage and/or price increases or decreases that will bring this about. Clearly, this type of policy involves direct and extensive government management of the economy. Though practiced in wartime, it was unprecedented in the peacetime United States before 1971.

What is distinctive about each of these types of economy-managing policies? We have seen that they reflect increasing degrees of government "intervention" in the economy. They are also distinguishable by the assumptions on which they are based, and by the degree of choice on the part of government as to who will gain and who will lose from their effects. The first two—monetary and fiscal policies—assume the same "package" of economic problems. For example, both see inflation, low unemployment, and active growth as comprising one set of consistent symptoms: of an active, booming economy in which the problem is to dampen expansion so that inflation does not get out of hand. Both see depression or recession, high unemployment, and low growth as typical of the opposite or stagnating end of the business cycle. The problem in such a situation is to get the economy growing again. Each type of policy has a remedy for each package of characteristics or problems, and the remedies differ chiefly in the aggressiveness with which they use government as an instrument for that purpose. Fiscal policies are the more aggressive, but both make major use of the workings of the private economy (properly stimulated by government) for the purpose of bringing about the desired result.

The early 1970s, however, did not conform to the assumptions of monetary and fiscal theory. Inflation was associated with high unemployment and low growth, an unprecedented combination. That it was not a demand-pull inflation was particularly serious because the remedies prescribed by each theory (intended to reduce or stimulate demand) were rendered counterproductive or contradictory. A remedy designed to combat inflation would do so by promoting unemployment and further impeding growth. And a remedy designed to counter unemployment and spur growth would do so only by promoting inflation. Any action by policymakers in accordance with either theory would only make part of the existing problem worse.

An incomes policy, of course, is not necessarily bound to any particular assumptions about the economy. It simply asserts governmental control over the economy. It is a much more direct and complete control system, in which the government's degree of choice about who wins and who loses is much greater. Those who believe, for whatever reason, that a minimum of government control over the economy is desirable tend to be opposed to an incomes policy. But so do those who suspect that, if it is applied at all, it will be applied in the interests of the corporate-banking sector. In 1971–1972, under the Nixon administration's incomes policy, corporate profits surged to a record annual rate. While wages were held down by employers' refusals to pay more, there was no similar restraint on price rises.

Remedy by Government Inaction

Nothing *requires* the national government to do anything to remedy the difficulties of the economy. In our view, government is not an independent choicemaking vehicle, but rather the agent of those who can in any given instance mobilize enough influence to bring about action. And experience tends to show that the corporate-banking sector enjoys the most such influence. A judgment that prolonged recession is relatively desirable could thus make government inaction a deliberate economic policy, involving just as much choice as any of the other more aggressive policies. The losers in such a case would probably be workers forced to undergo extended unemployment and reduced real wages, and the smaller businesses of the competitive sector unable to maintain their prices or borrow money.

At the heart of this issue is the question of a "tradeoff" between inflation and unemployment. Most economists believe that inflation can be controlled by permitting or forcing unemployment. If there is enough unemployment for a long enough time, they say, prices will simply have to stop rising and will level off or even drop. But disagreement is bitter over whether inflation *should* be stopped by letting workers suffer. Conservative economists and businessmen tend to believe that high unemployment is a price that must, when necessary, be paid. Liberal and radical economists, on the other hand, believe that it would be better to live with a certain amount of inflation.

The argument centers on the meaning of the official term *full employment*. Originally, the term referred to workers' jobs and was defined as a proportion of unemployed (say, 3 percent) accounted for by workers normally changing jobs or temporarily displaced by the advent of new technologies. Recently, however, unemployment rates of 4 and then 5 percent have been characterized as full employment, as the definition's focus shifted from workers' jobs to the level of unemployment that would maintain price stability and hold inflation down. Needless to say, this definition is a continuing subject of controversy.

Radical economists tend to see recessions as periodically necessary, and often encouraged by government inaction or pro-recession policies. Periodic recessions are not only inevitable, in their eyes, but also functional for a capitalist economy in that they discipline labor by halting claims for higher wages—thereby reducing labor's share and increasing the corporate share of total output. Because it is always easy for government to do nothing, its actual cooperation is not always recognized as such.

Conservative ideology regards government inaction as the only appropriate "remedy" for economic problems. Those who believe in a *laissez-faire* or "hands-off" role for government, consistent with traditional assumptions about the separation of the economy and the government, insist that the only correct policy is for government to watch the economy work out its own problems. The resulting, perhaps longer, recession may work hardships on workers and competitive-sector businesses, but that outcome is taken as necessary to allow the economy to resume its supposedly self-regulating operation. It is also possible, of course, that government inaction—for whatever reason—may lead to a semi-permanent recession or even a collapse of the sort experienced in the 1930s.

National Economic Planning

At the opposite pole, some liberals and representatives of the largest corporations and banks call for extensive government planning and controls to keep the economy running smoothly. They have proposed a "Balanced National Growth and Economic Planning Act" that would establish a new office in the Executive Office of the President for the purpose of developing such plans and proposing them to the President and Congress. To plan adequately, a great deal of information would have to be collected from businesses, and recommendations would have to be made for harmonizing government taxation, expenditures, and other activities with those intentions. To administer such a plan would require extensive governmental capacity to control the allocation of resources, the availability of labor, and perhaps the kinds of products manufactured, as well as the more familiar wage-and-price controls.

Predictably, there is considerable opposition to proposals for this kind of national economic planning. Some see it as undesirable government intervention into what should be private economic decisionmaking —or, in other words, as the final disappearance of a free-market, private-enterprise system. Others see it as the final stage in the takeover of the state by the corporate-banking sector, or a kind of economic fascism. This unfamiliar but increasingly visible alliance of right and left may be able to prevent more such planning and control. But the advocates of national economic planning argue that there is really no alternative, that the complexity of the economy and the depth of its problems require comprehensive management in this fashion. And among its advocates are the very corporations, banks, and liberal politicians whose alliance has been the source of most government policy for the post-World War Two years.

The issues we have posed are whether—and if so, how—the nation can avoid a depression comparable to that of the 1930s, and which sectors of the economy will pay the price of such efforts. Policy choices in the next several years will play an important (though perhaps not a controlling) part in determining the outcome. And those choices in turn depend on questions of ideology, power, and preference. Before we begin to sort out these factors, however, we need to sketch more of the problems confronting the American political economy, as well as some of the effects of previous policy choices.

4

Economic Security
and Foreign Policy

Economic security and national security are so closely connected that they are in many respects identical. Economic security means steadily expanding opportunities for profitable investment and trade throughout the world, so that constant growth is assured. National security means the assurance, insofar as is possible, of the continued existence of the society and its customary way of life. And there *is* no society or way of life to be preserved except that which is sustained by the success of the economic system. Problems and policies involving economic security thus define the problem and determine the policies of national security-seeking. As the problem of economic security changes character, as it is now doing, new questions arise about the nature and means of achieving national security.

Both the search for economic security and the effort to assure national security are worldwide in scope. They take different forms, however, in the three different "worlds" toward which American policies are directed. One setting is the industrialized capitalist world, including the United States, Western Europe, and Japan. Mutual dependence on closely linked markets and investments does not prevent competition for relative advantage among major sectors of this economy, and the United States is here a kind of "first among equals."

Another arena pits the United States as chief antagonist against the socialist countries (the Soviet Union and the Eastern European nations on the one hand, China on the other). Economic relations, though increasing in light of mutual needs, are still subordinated to enduring suspicions and other vestiges of the Cold War (at least some of whose longevity is due to its domestic purposes).

The rest of the world is usually imprecisely labeled *the Third World* —a term that blurs many vital distinctions including wealth, level of development, culture and history, and past or present relationships with developed countries. We use the term to emphasize the contrast with the United States' relatively well-defined and more equal relationship with countries in the other two arenas. In the Third World, the weight of U.S. economic and political power may be heavy or light, brutal or subtle, depending on a variety of factors. To assure "friendly" governments (stable, willing and able to preserve American trade and investment opportunities), the United States employs a mixture of pressure, economic and military aid, covert manipulation, and military threats and/or actions. Some Third World states, such as much of Latin America, thus become almost U.S. protectorates. Others are able to maintain some leverage through geographic location, possession of key natural resources and/or the availability of Soviet support to counterbalance U.S. power. Still others, such as Israel, Taiwan, and South Korea, are favored clients.

These three analytically useful categories should not be taken as mutually exclusive. Policies are developed with an eye to all three, and their effects are three-dimensional. Furthermore, all three sets of relationships are affected by an increasingly important force with the potential to reorder priorities: the emergence of such worldwide problems as population, food, energy, and preservation of the environment.

We will first examine the problems and policies that characterize the U.S. quest for economic security. We shall see that the current needs and activities of the corporate-banking sector of the American economy, with which the U.S. government is closely associated, run counter in important respects to the interests of many other governments and peoples. To illustrate this point, we next survey the worldwide problems of population, resources, and the like and show how both definitions *and* solutions differ between, for example, the United States and the Third World. An important implication of this analysis is that the crisis of the American political economy involves not only declining profitability and instability, but also potential isolation from the rest of the world.

In this context, the concept of national security takes on new significance. In the immediate post-World War Two period, national security simply meant military supremacy over the Soviet Union. The concept then expanded to encompass the clearly impossible task of maintaining the *status quo* throughout the world. The consequences for other nations of that expanded definition are often noted, but its effects at home are less widely recognized. If decline and isolation indeed continue, the United States' redefinition of its national security needs will become a vital matter for all the people of the world. This issue is taken up in Chapter 5.

Economic Security

The world emerged from World War Two totally dominated by the American economy. No other national economy could come close to matching American wealth or productivity, and thus the power of that economy to design the framework for world economic activity. But because the U.S. economy needed trading partners and investment opportunities, it was in its interest to help other capitalist countries rebuild their shattered economies. One price such nations paid was seeing their former colonies penetrated by American business and made dependent on American rather than European banks and corporate investors. Another price was general American *hegemony* (influence capable of shaping the basic actions of other countries and people): the U.S. dollar became the world's basic currency; multinational banks and corporations sprung up throughout Europe; and the United States insisted on policing the world, particularly by mobilizing forces against the Soviet Union. The United States experienced two decades of prosperity and influence unparalleled in world history.

But then, slowly at first but with rapidly increasing speed, the pillars of American dominance were undermined. American economic and military strength began to wane, in part for self-generated reasons, to the point that by the mid-1970s it was no more than clearly superior—but increasingly vulnerable. The process was probably inevitable, and in any event represents only the prologue to our present context. Its first manifestation was Soviet development of nuclear capability which resulted in a new balance of power. The process continued as newly technological and highly productive economies were built in Europe and Japan. For a while, the key status of the dollar enabled American corporations and banks to operate around the world with a cushion of capital and credit. But by the early 1960s European banks were flooded with dollars. Both European and Japanese products were competing favorably all over the world. And all the industrialized capitalist countries were creeping up on the U.S. lead in total output, income, exports, and other key economic indicators.

The United States' massive but unproductive investment in the Vietnam War, and the simultaneous advent of its intractable inflation, caused it to lose both moral and economic hegemony. The combination of the greater productivity of other economies, the dollar glut in Europe, and U.S. inflation led to effective rejection of the dollar as the basic measure of currency value in the world. Exchange rates fluctuated unpredictably with every change in the soundness of national economies. The newly integrated capitalist world economy was suddenly unstable, both because it had lost its hegemonic cornerstone and because its major units were all suffering from simultaneous inflation, unemployment, and overextended credit. In this context, the quadrupling of oil prices was a major threat. The United States was a relative beneficiary, as a result of its lesser dependence on imported oil, but cracks in the world structure worried the American government and people alike. A new world was clearly emerging, but it was not so clear how basic interests could be served within it.

The Capitalist World: Interdependence and Crisis

In Chapter 3, our analysis noted that serious inflation and unemployment were affecting all the major capitalist countries at the same time. Thus, we have already suggested the two primary characteristics of the capitalist world of the 1970s: interdependence and crisis. The fifteen years between 1960 and 1975 saw the final interweaving of trade, investment, and all other forms of economic activity, such that all these countries now feel the same pressures at the same time. For many years, gross national product rose steadily throughout the capitalist world. To be sure, some nations enjoyed greater success than others, and from time to time one (usually Japan) would spurt ahead in productivity or growth. But for the most part, all moved together. And in 1974, all declined together; by the end of the year, real GNP in the United States, West Germany, and Japan was declining at the rate of 7 percent per year.

The key to both the interdependence and the prosperity generated in the post-World War Two world is the new role of exports. In the case of West Germany, for example, exports represented 23 percent of the entire gross national product in 1974.[1] For the other major nations, this figure was somewhat lower; for such countries as Holland, Belgium, and Denmark it was much higher. Exports represented only 7 percent of the United States' GNP, but even this relatively low proportion amounted to three times the entire value of the production of the U.S. domestic

---

[1] *The New York Times,* 16 November 1975, p. E16. All data in this paragraph are drawn from the same source.

automobile industry, generally considered the cornerstone of the U.S. economy. Two other facts will help to highlight the importance of export trade. First, GNP consists of *both* goods and services, but the latter by their nature cannot be exported. Thus, if we consider only the production of goods, mainly manufacturing and agriculture, exports account for 20 percent in the United States, 45 percent in Italy, and 75 percent in Canada of all that is produced. Second, trade levels fluctuate more widely than GNP, acting to raise it when they are rising and to depress it when they are dropping. The GNP of the advanced countries thus appears to be becoming more and more dependent on trade exchanges.

By 1975, however, trading levels had fallen an ominous 10 percent from the previous year. The crucial policy question was whether various governments, responding to pleas from particular industries and workers, would impose restrictions on the goods that could enter their markets. Such import restrictions could take several forms, including tariffs, quotas, prohibitions, and conditions pertaining to the sending country's acceptance of exports in exchange. The situation was rendered more acute by some governments' practice of subsidizing exports to make them more competitive in foreign markets. All the major capitalist countries pledged not to impose restrictions, but all were under pressure from local businesses to help save them from foreign competition that hurt their sales and profitability. If they yielded to such temptations, of course, retaliation by foreign governments could set off a ruinous trade war. Short of that, certain advantages might be gained by some industries in more powerful countries, such as the United States, by insisting on complete elimination of all restrictions regardless of their importance to another nation's economy.

Another threat to the vital export lifeline is the instability of monetary exchange rates. If the rate of exchange between the currencies of two countries is fluctuating unpredictably, mutual trade is likely to be slowed. If neither buyers nor sellers can be sure of the future value of the currencies they employ, they cannot tell whether a profit will be made on a given transaction. Exchange rates are either *fixed* (set by governments, usually when one nation's currency is accepted as a standard for all and none vary greatly in value) or *floating* (dependent on actual trading in currency markets). During periods of economic instability, such as the 1970s, rates must usually be allowed to float. The alternative is potentially further destabilizing government devaluations of currencies, such as occurred twice in the early 1970s when the U.S. government reduced the international value of the dollar by a total of 17 percent. In both cases, massive speculation by multinational banks or corporations, and even by very wealthy individuals, can cause currency values to rise or fall rapidly—with potentially disastrous results for world trade levels. For all these reasons, the capitalist countries all seek stable monetary exchange rates.

But neither avoidance of all import restrictions nor stable exchange rates, even though they are in the long-run best interest of the entire capitalist world, can automatically be anticipated. The crux of the question is what national governments actually do. And behind that, in turn, is the fact that some sectors of world capitalism stand to gain from every restriction or fluctuation and to lose from their removal or control. The struggle for comparative advantage is reflected in the behavior of national governments, some of which in effect profit from endangering the whole. In general, it is the biggest and most powerful who gain in such circumstances; in the eyes of Europeans, at least, it was the United States that in the mid-1970s was acting on behalf of the comparative advantage of major segments of its economy.

One route the capitalist world might take to cope with the combination of instability and the quadrupling of oil prices is to establish transnational cooperative mechanisms. Such bodies might be able to plan trade and investment patterns for the future, and to induce national governments to act supportively. In this way, future profitability could be assured and conflicts avoided.

Such an organization has indeed been created. Known as the Trilateral Commission, it is composed of leading bankers, corporate executives, politicians, labor leaders, and intellectuals from the United States, Western Europe, and Japan—brought together principally by David Rockefeller of the Chase Manhattan Bank. This group has already conducted and sponsored a number of studies aimed at coordinating the actions of world capitalism and its governments and populations. Inherent in such efforts, of course, is the question of whose interests are to be served—on whose behalf everything is to be coordinated. Smaller units of the world economy, workers, and many others may well wonder if their needs and interests will be served as well as the long-range profit goals of big business and finance.

None of the tensions within world capitalism, however, should be allowed to obscure the contrast between the advanced industrialized nations as a whole and the Third World. This contrast is apparent in the vast gap in wealth and standard of living between the two areas, as well as in the relationship between them. The Third World is in debt to the bankers of world capitalism; its natural resources are for the most part still owned or exploited by foreign corporations; and it is increasingly unable to support itself, chiefly for these reasons. The term *dependence* very considerably understates this relationship, as we shall now see.

The Third World: Dependence and Crises

There are many ways to characterize the difference between the capitalist world and the Third World. One is simply to compare the per capita (per person) gross national product of various countries, in the manner of Figure 4.1. This is a very gross comparison, because there is no assurance that the distribution of income in a country is equal—that is, that

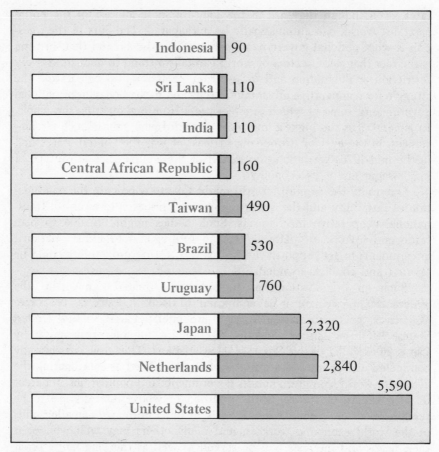

Source: *Christian Science Monitor,* 29 August 1975, p. 13. Data from 1974 *World Bank Atlas* (1972 figures).

FIGURE 4.1

Per Capita Gross National Product (in $/yr)

per capita GNP means anything. All we can say is that *if* the total product were divided equally, these are the sums that would accrue to each citizen. Nevertheless, it is clear that the United States has a long lead over all other countries, a lead only the most industrialized and productive nations even begin to approach.

A more revealing comparison relates several factors, such as per capita income, population, growth rate, and overall prospects. Figure 4.2 does so in three categories, following the World Bank's breakdown. The poorest countries are those in which per capita income is less than $200 per year. In these countries, the period 1969–1973 (for which these figures were compiled) saw almost no growth at all—only 0.5 percent. In other words, more than seventy countries with over 1 billion people

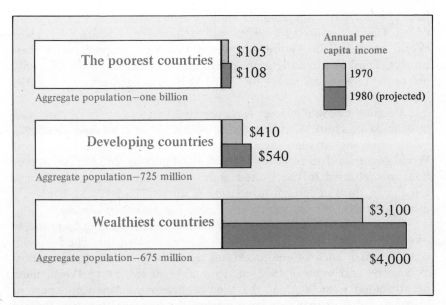

The poorest countries $105 / $108
Aggregate population—one billion

Annual per capita income
1970
1980 (projected)

Developing countries $410 / $540
Aggregate population—725 million

Wealthiest countries $3,100
Aggregate population—675 million $4,000

Source: New York Times, 24 August 1975, pp. 3–13.

FIGURE 4.2

The Distribution of Wealth

made almost no progress whatsoever in these boom times for the rest of the world! People in this part of the world (mostly India and Africa) live in hunger, squalor, and hopelessness about the future.

A second group is the "middle-income" countries, whose populations are somewhat smaller and whose average incomes are more than $400 per year. There are great disparities *within* each country, but the annual growth rate as a whole was over 4.5 percent for this period. These are the countries of Latin America and other specially aided nations, such as South Korea and Taiwan; it is no more than accurate to say that they are the most fully incorporated into the American sphere of world capitalism. According to the World Bank's data, however, even those countries were about to take a step backward in the mid-1970s capitalist/ energy crisis.

The wealthiest countries (here defined as the Western European nations and the United States, but not the socialist countries) enjoy per capita incomes more than seven times as high as those of the middle-income countries. And it is virtually inevitable that the rich will get richer and the poor poorer. In effect, one quarter of the world's population has three quarters of the world's income, investment, and services and most of its research skills. Because these are the essential ingredients of progress, future progress can only expand the gap between nations.

What is the United States' interest, or stake, in the Third World? It may be more subtle, and is certainly less purely economic, than many have alleged. Two quite tangible kinds of interests must first be acknowledged. One is the need for scarce natural resources possessed by Third World countries. In Figure 4.3, which lists vital materials and their sources, Third World nations are prominent. Demand for oil is thus only one of the factors that makes the Third World's allegiances crucial to the capitalist world.

A second tangible interest is represented by the amount of American investment in Third World countries, which by 1975 totalled about $28 billion. Returns on such invested capital are much higher from Third World countries than from the industrialized nations, and higher proportions are returned to the United States each year. Thus, even though less than a third of foreign investment is in the Third World, it plays a disproportionate role in producing profits for American owners.

These two sets of interests—crucial resources and existing investments—account in large part for American policies toward the Third World. But the importance of resources and investments varies from country to country, and some of the American stake in the Third World must be attributed elsewhere. At the time of maximum American effort in Vietnam—an effort that may have marked the threshold between the old and the new world order—little in the way of either resources or investments there could explain American actions. The missing ingredient appears to be a posture toward the Third World as a whole, whose components are the desire for a favorable investment "climate" throughout the world, aspects of basic American ideology, and our conception of national security needs. These factors are often inseparable, and in illustrating one we illustrate the others.

U.S. governmental policies have consistently sought to promote conditions that would render private investment in the Third World profitable and relatively safe. The definition of a good investment climate is stability, determination to repay, and capacity to sell something for dollars so as to be able to repay.

American policies designed to foster such favorable climates have as their central theme the efficacy of private enterprise. In the words of one moderate authority on economic policy:

> To representatives of the less developed nations, it must seem that the United States never tires of citing the advantages—real and imagined—of an economic system based on private enterprise. The main advantages of private investment cited by American policymakers were: first, private investment is more "flexible," presumably referring to the relative absence of governmental "red tape." Second, private investment is "non-political," presumably referring to a supposed absence of interference in domestic affairs by private investors. And third, private investment often carried with it technical knowledge and managerial skill.[2]

[2] David A. Baldwin, *Economic Development and American Foreign Policy* (Chicago: University of Chicago Press, 1966), p. 19.

Mineral	Percentage imported	Major foreign sources
	0% 25% 50% 75% 100%	
strontium	100	Mexico, UK, Spain
columbium	100	Brazil, Malaysia, Zaire
mica (sheet)	99	India, Brazil, Malagasy
cobalt	98	Zaire, Belgium–Luxembourg, Finland, Norway, Canada
manganese	98	Brazil, Gabon, South Africa, Zaire
titanium (rutile)	97	Australia, India
chromium	91	USSR, South Africa, Turkey, Philippines
tantalum	88	Australia, Canada, Zaire, Brazil
aluminum (ores & metal)	88	Jamaica, Australia, Surinam, Canada
asbestos	87	Canada, South Africa
platinum group metals	86	UK, USSR, South Africa
tin	86	Malaysia, Thailand, Bolivia
fluorine	86	Mexico, Spain, Italy
mercury	82	Canada, Algeria, Mexico, Spain
bismuth	81	Peru, Mexico, Japan, UK
nickel	73	Canada, Norway
gold	69	Canada, Switzerland, USSR
silver	68	Canada, Mexico, Peru, Honduras
selenium	63	Canada, Japan, Mexico
zinc	61	Canada, Mexico, Peru, Australia, Japan
tungsten	60	Canada, Bolivia, Peru, Thailand
potassium	58	Canada
cadmium	53	Mexico, Canada, Australia, Japan
antimony	46	South Africa, Mexico, P.R. China, Bolivia
tellurium	41	Peru, Canada
barium	40	Ireland, Peru, Mexico
vanadium	40	South Africa, Chile, USSR
gypsum	37	Canada, Mexico, Jamaica
petroleum (inc. liq. nat. gas)	35	Canada, Venezuela, Nigeria, Saudi Arabia, Indonesia
iron	23	Canada, Venezuela, Japan, Common Market
titanium (ilmenite)	23	Canada, Australia
lead	21	Canada, Peru, Australia, Mexico
copper	18	Canada, Peru, Chile, South Africa
pumice	8	Italy, Greece
salt	7	Canada, Mexico, Bahamas, Chile
magnesium (nonmetallic)	6	Greece, Ireland, Austria
cement	4	Canada, Bahamas, Norway, UK
natural gas	4	Canada
	0% 25% 50% 75% 100%	
	Net Imports	

Source: National Journal Reports, 21 June 1975, p. 917. Data from U.S. Bureau of Mines.

FIGURE 4.3

U.S. Mineral Imports: 1974

Source: Rius-Siempre, Mexico.

The specific techniques by which American policymakers reinforced the priority given to private investment in the early years of the Cold War included outright refusal to make government grants or loans if private funds might be available; referral of requests for capital to the World Bank (which itself declined to make development funds available if they might be "competing" with private investors); and determined diplomatic efforts to open various nations to "fair" treatment for American private investors.

Ranged against the American commitment to private enterprise and the means adopted to further private investment were Third World nationalism and need for central planning and control, as well as the apparent instability of many governments and economies. In the mid-1950s, the U.S. government began to supplement its endorsements of private enterprise by providing "investment guaranty" contracts to American businesses. These guarantees insured them against certain "nonbusiness" risks in Third World investments, such as exchange problems or expropriation, and resulted in increases in the flow of private funds. Investment opportunities in Europe and Canada, however, still attracted much more capital than did those in Third World countries. The efficacy of the guaranty program was undisputable, however, for by the mid-1960s more than $1 billion worth of such insurance for Third World investments had been extended. To some degree, of course, U.S. government willingness to employ military force to maintain stability (and hence a favorable investment climate) in Third World nations must also be counted as a factor in private investment patterns.

The one aspect of investment-relevant policy under complete American control—trade and tariff policy—was *not* brought to bear on this problem in any but marginal ways. Third World nations could only acquire the dollars with which to repay private loans by selling exports, principally in American markets. The executive branch made strong efforts to get the Congress to reduce at least some trade barriers, but no significant reductions were ever achieved. In particular, protections against agricultural products (the most common Third World product) remained fixed at prohibitive levels. In effect, the policies of the U.S. government have focused on promoting opportunities for private investment, but the terms, problems, and consequences involved in following that route have not been attractive to Third World nations. The private investor, on the other hand, could earn substantial profits from Third World investments if he kept ownership or control of the commodities produced and arranged their sale himself. In addition, of course, his investment would be insured by the U.S. government.

This combination of exhortation and policy may be merely ambiguous, or simply self-serving—as the Third World often suggests. But there is undeniably a significant ambiguity in the general ideological posture from which Americans view the Third World. Although procapitalism and anticommunism are paramount, there is also a strand of altruism, of the desire to help others enjoy the good things Americans see themselves as possessing.

This mixture of motives is readily visible in the annual debates over and actual uses of "foreign aid." Each year since World War Two, the U.S. government has extended from $3 to $7 billion in military and economic assistance, much of it to Third World countries. Among the general public and to some extent in Congress, the issue is seen as altruism *versus* "giveaways" that benefit us little in return. Actually, of course, the amount the United States so expends represents a diminishing proportion of the GNP (now less than 0.5 percent); the United States is approximately tenth among nonsocialist countries in the proportion of GNP devoted to foreign aid. In other terms, we spend only about one-third as much on foreign aid as we do on toilet articles and preparations. What we do spend is almost entirely devoted to military assistance to client states (countries whose viability, economically or militarily or both, depends on American assistance), such as South Korea or Taiwan. Thus, in practice, there is little altruism and much anticommunism in the extension of aid. National security interests permeate the policies that are ostensibly intended to promote Third World development.

This sense that national security is at stake in a generalized manner everywhere in the Third World is based on the premise that such countries are either "ours" or "theirs." Needless to say, such a premise is emphatically rejected by the nationalist countries of the Third World. But it remains a factor among American policymakers, many of whom (particularly in the area of foreign policy) either have had or still have close ties to the business world. This posture on the part of "National

Security Managers" of the 1960s is the theme of a major analysis by a former member of that hierarchy:

> The National Security Manager still tends to look at the "Under-developed World" as a vast Gray Area in international politics. No part of it is of intrinsic interest unless, of course, it supplies some vital commodity. Otherwise it can capture the official attention in Washington only if it symbolizes some struggle which transcends the minor turmoil of native politics. To the man of the West, Paris and Berlin are important places in their own right, for they symbolize his own historical heritage. But Danang, Santo Domingo, and Kinshasha penetrate his consciousness, if at all, only as battlefields, and then only if the fight is about something sufficiently important. He has almost no knowledge about such places, their people, or their politics, and little personal commitment to them. They represent either sources of strength, strategic or economic, or points of vulnerability. "Vietnam is not the issue," National Security Managers have frequently confided to critics who question whether systematic bombardment is the best way to secure freedom for the Vietnamese people; "it is the testing ground for the Communist strategy of Wars of National Liberation. If they win here, they will strike elsewhere. If they lose, they will not be so ready to start another."
>
> The National Security Manager is a global thinker. In themselves, local problems of other countries are not worthy of his attention; it is the transcendent importance of local revolutionary struggles that warrants intervention. Interference in purely domestic matters is still unjustified as a matter of law and sound policy. Unfortunately, he hastens to add, the line between domestic and foreign matters has blurred. When political factions struggle with one another in far-off places, their conflict is an expression of a single worldwide struggle. The real contestants remain the same. Only the battlefield shifts. The battle, which takes the form of a series of guerrilla wars, is not about Vietnam or Greece or the Dominican Republic any more than World War II was about Iwo Jima or Sicily. Wherever men struggle for power, one can always find International Communism, the ubiquitous political scavenger, ready to use genuine local grievances as ammunition in a global holy war. Global strategy, more than local conditions, dictates the site of the next engagement between International Communism and the Free World.
>
> At this point let us try to look more closely at the mental set of the National Security Manager as it bears on the U.S. commitment against revolution. The ultimate bureaucratic dream is the perfect freedom of unlimited power. It is the ability to push a button, make a phone call, dispatch a cable, and know that the world will conform to your vision. The capacity to control, or, as he might put it, to have options, is a much clearer objective for the professional statesman than the purposes to which he would put such power. The guiding stars of the working bureaucrat are not cosmic goals. One can find a few expressions of an official eschatology in flowery speeches on National Purpose, or in the negotiated generalities of the Basic National Security Policy papers representing the collective wisdom of the foreign-policy bureaucracy. Usually, however, the

National Security Manager prides himself on avoiding theological and "nonpragmatic" speculation. He has faith in his intuitive grasp of the art of *ad hoc* politics. Yet, in developing official policy on U.S. intervention, he is not quite so free as he thinks. Just as he casts his adversary, the Revolutionary—Castro, Mao, Ho—in the inevitable role of foreign agent, so he has picked out a well-worn part for himself. It is the role of the imperial peacekeeper.[3]

From the perspective of the Third World, the great gap in wealth and the developed world's lack of assistance are the major issues of our times. Despite nationalistic rivalries, racial differences, and vast distinctions in wealth and development, Third World nations as a whole have begun to question the very premises of an international order characterized by the distributions and prospects of the present world. So far, only the most minimal efforts at financial or other assistance have been made by the developed world, except in furtherance of its own profitability or security interests. And conditions of life are steadily worsening.

Two lines of approach to the developed world have recently been taken by Third World countries. One is use of the leverage possession of crucial natural resources provides to redistribute wealth. The obvious example is oil; other such maneuvers may follow. The problem with this approach is that success requires a delicate balance of power between the major world blocs. If the United States had not been weakened by the Vietnam War and the Soviet Union had not been available for support, it is doubtful that the OPEC actions of 1973–1974 would have been so successful. Moreover, as we have seen, there were substantial benefits to be gained by major segments of the capitalist world economy in that situation. And the oil price rise may in time be damaging to Third World nations embarking on energy-utilizing development, far beyond the willingness of Arab governments to compensate through loans.

The other approach is to insist, at the United Nations and elsewhere, on greater assistance—with no strings attached—from the developed world. The drawback of this route is that the industrialized countries can simply refuse, and unless concerted Third World action (such as expropriations or refusal to repay loans) is backed up by Soviet military power, very little can be done about such refusals. Only when the conditions of the Third World are understood as relevant to the conditions and prospects of the industrialized countries is there likely to be serious cooperative effort. Some problems are indeed global, and threaten all nations. But here again, there are great disparities in how such problems are understood, and hence in the solutions sought.

[3] Reprinted by permission of the World Publishing Company from *Intervention and Revolution* (pp. 28–29) by Richard Barnet. A New American Library book. Copyright © 1968 by Richard Barnet.

World Problems: Contrasting Definitions and "Solutions"

The point of this case study is not just to portray the elements of the converging global crisis of population, resources, environment, and human survival; it is also to demonstrate that even the "facts" of a crisis do necessarily impel a solution. Indeed, our basic point is that definitions of the nature and causes of these crises are very different, and thus the solutions offered are equally various and dependent on one's position in the world. The assumptions that are built into definitions are the key to understanding these crises, and what we think should be done about them.

The Elements of Developing World Crises

There is little doubt that conditions in the world are such that the entire world population faces substantial threats to its very survival. The first problem is the sheer number of people in the world and the ever-increasing rate of expansion of that number. If the present rate of increase continues, more people will be added to the world's population *each year* by the middle of the next century than were added in the first *fifteen hundred years* of the Christian calendar. The world's population, 200–300 million in the year 1 A.D., took sixteen centuries to double. It doubled again in the next two hundred years, and again in only one hundred years. The next doubling took less than half a century, making world population in 1975 about 4 billion people. Over 6 billion people are predicted by the year 2000. According to all estimates of available and prospective food supply, the world cannot begin to feed such numbers of people.

And not only food will be in short supply. Other resources are estimated as so limited that dates of probable exhaustion can be calculated. Applying the present rate of usage, and the present rate increased by the usual rate of increase per year, the results are as shown in Table 4.1. New reserves or substitute resources may be found, and price rises may preserve supplies for longer periods than are forecast in the table. But such costs will probably mean hardship, and more likely destitution, for those who depend—as does most of the world—on the products of these resources. Energy resources alone will pose a severe crisis: coal will last only somewhat longer than oil and gas, and new sources simply must be found.

The depletion of natural resources is not limited to certain scarce minerals, however. It extends to the air we breathe, and to the ecological balance of nature itself. Industrial production has led to waste, environmental destruction, and pollution to such an extent that some forms of life have been extinguished, and the means by which nature re-establishes

TABLE 4.1 *Estimates of Year of Depletion for Key Minerals*

Mineral	(1) Constant Consumption Levels	(2) Exponentially Increasing Consumption	(3) With 5X Known Reserves
Aluminum	2070 A.D.	2001 A.D.	2025 A.D.
Copper	2006 A.D.	1991 A.D.	2018 A.D.
Iron	2210 A.D.	2063 A.D.	2143 A.D.
Lead	1996 A.D.	1991 A.D.	2034 A.D.
Manganese	2067 A.D.	2016 A.D.	2064 A.D.
Mercury	1983 A.D.	1983 A.D.	2011 A.D.
Nickel	2120 A.D.	2023 A.D.	2066 A.D.
Tungsten	2010 A.D.	1998 A.D.	2042 A.D.
Zinc	1993 A.D.	1988 A.D.	2020 A.D.
Petroleum	2001 A.D.	1990 A.D.	2020 A.D.
Natural gas	2008 A.D.	1992 A.D.	2019 A.D.

Column 2 = consumption increases at current rates. Column 3 = column 2 if reserves were five times greater.

Source: Dennis C. Pirages and Paul R. Ehrlich, *Ark II: Social Response to Environmental Imperatives* (San Francisco: W. H. Freeman, 1974), p. 20.

itself have been endangered. The prospect is not the loss of amenities by a few wealthy people, but loss of the means of life—air and water—by the many.

Definitions and "Solutions"

A number of "futurist" writers, and particularly the business-and-foundation-financed Club of Rome studies, have articulated world capitalism's definition of these problems. They see a "population crisis" and an "energy crisis," both global in character, which mandate (1) limits on population, (2) stable or reduced standards of living, and (3) worldwide cooperation to manage the remaining resources and their usage. Many people in the developed world have eagerly joined the cause of "Zero Growth," with regard to both population and economic expansion.

But definitions and solutions of this sort present some serious problems. From the perspective of the Third World, for example, the problem is not overpopulation but maldistribution of wealth. To urge limitation of population on people whose infant mortality rates are very high, and whose livelihood depends on labor-intensive means of cultivation or production, is to ignore the basis on which whole peoples now survive. To stabilize their standards of living at submarginal levels is to hand them death certificates; without growth they and their children have no future. To advocate worldwide cooperation sounds very much like incorporating them into a system intended to serve the needs of profitability on the part of the capitalist world's corporations and banks—a system that clearly works for the developed world at the cost of Third World suffering.

What are the assumptions behind the three basic prescriptions of Zero Growth? One basic assumption is that the capitalist world system is desirable, permanent, or both. A "population crisis" exists only to the extent that there are more people than can now be fed by capitalist agribusiness. In other words, food is grown as long as it can be profitably sold under circumstances of multiple profit-taking (fertilizer, mechanized equipment, transportation, and so on). Moreover, food is grown in volumes limited by the need to maintain profit-producing prices. Those who cannot pay such prices must go without. The Third World nations have for the most part been discouraged from engaging in diversified agriculture because it was desirable to keep them focused on one-crop production for sales in world markets—to enable them to repay loans and to keep the developed world well supplied with needed resources. Finally, evidence indicates that rates of population increase are highest in the poorest countries and lowest in the richest countries. The surest route to reduced birth rates is thus not pious exhortation but steadily increasing standards of living.

The prescription for austerity involves a similar number of assumptions—or hypocrisy, as the Third World charges. To limit growth at this stage is to freeze a situation in which the United States, for example, with 6 percent of the world's population, enjoys between 40 and 50 percent of its resources and productivity. Unless Third World economies are not only allowed but encouraged to grow, their populations face mounting starvation. Citing an "energy crisis" as a reason to restrict growth assumes that production of oil and gas must be limited to those levels that maximize prices to those able to pay at all, that the oil industry's monopoly must be preserved and extended to other sources of energy as well, and that alternative sources can only be developed privately.

World organization and cooperation is therefore in the interests of some, and at the expense of others, due to the extremely unequal distribution of wealth. The Third World understandably suspects that its people are considered expendable. And this view is confirmed from time to time by the official publications and discussions of the developed countries. In recent years, the term *triage*, meaning the elimination of those least able to be saved in order to improve the chances of the stronger, has come into general usage, particularly in the works of the Trilateral Commission. Thus even global problems, however staggering in their implications, do not necessarily give rise to agreed-upon definitions or solutions. Instead, they merely exacerbate already tense relations among conflicting interests.

5

National Security:
The Military Aspects

How do the problems and tensions of the emerging future affect American national security? For three decades, national security has been almost synonymous with the maintenance of military supremacy over the Soviet Union and other communist countries. At the same time, its perceived obligation to serve as a world policeman caused the United States to develop and apply non-nuclear force all over the globe. Due to the still dimly understood loss of moral, political, and economic hegemony in the aftermath of the Vietnam War, however, we are entering a period in which the nature and military needs of national security may well be redefined. Whether and how this redefinition will occur, and what its implications may be, are the issues this chapter raises.

To address these questions knowledgeably, we must first examine the assumptions, policies, and consequences that have dominated our past.

National Security as Military Supremacy

Conventional wisdom has it that German aggression prior to World War Two occurred because of the military weakness of potential opponents. Military preparedness, it is therefore assumed, is the key to peace and stability in an uncertain and amoral world. This assumption led to the conclusion that the security of the United States requires maintenance of military strength superior to that of the major communist nations, perceived as expansionist and implacably hostile to the United States. In order to guarantee security, this military superiority would have to be sufficient to cause unacceptable (if not total) destruction of the Soviet Union, and recently China as well, even if such nations should first launch a surprise attack on the United States. Instituted in 1946 in the aftermath of World War Two, the policy of security through military superiority still rests on these basic assumptions.

Security is an elusive and frustrating goal. For several reasons, it can never be finally assured. And, paradoxically, the more it is sought, the more it may recede. At any moment, a potential enemy may reach a scientific breakthrough that enables it to achieve military supremacy through technology. Or such a nation may drastically alter the strategic situation through a sudden diplomatic success, subversion, or other means. The more a nation seeks assurance of security by military means, the more it must commit its resources to weapons, research and development, procurement of multiple attack and defense systems, alliances with the governments of other nations, economic and military support for such governments if necessary, and anticipatory intelligence and subversion activities throughout the world. Every such act, of course, provokes the potential enemy to undertake or expand similar activities, and these in turn reduce the first nation's security and require countering moves. Nearly three decades of Cold War marked by the continuing threat of nuclear annihilation, combined with the fear of communism, have made such commitments almost unquestionable among American policy-makers.

The achievement of security through such means thus presents inevitable and apparently unending difficulties. On the one hand, it may be costly to the point of financial, if not moral, exhaustion. On the other, it may be so provocative that it causes the enemy to do as expected: to attack first in the fear that its survival depends on such a move. One alternative, of course, is to seek nonmilitary means of achieving security. The basic assumptions just reviewed, together with American perceptions of our own and Soviet behavior and intentions, have foreclosed real efforts in such a drastic new direction. A second alternative, however, is regularly argued and sometimes pursued, particularly in times of budgetary stringency. This is the principle of military *sufficiency*, rather than supremacy. In other words, all that is necessary is the sure capability of destroying all possible enemies, even if they strike first and no matter how well they might defend themselves. In addition, of course, policy-makers would have to reach agreement on such matters as the number of conventional weapons and manpower needed to fight lesser wars and maintain domestic security.

The range of options discussed by strategic planners thus tends to be limited to military sufficiency and military superiority. But the difference may be more apparent than real. What is enough? Who will take responsibility for assuring the American people that our military capability is sufficient to deter a Soviet or Chinese attack, when we cannot know for sure what new scientific breakthrough is about to occur or what the Soviet or Chinese planners are up to?

The Strategic Problem

If there is a factual base for resolving this dilemma, it lies in a nation's "second-strike" capability. The principle of deterrence holds that no nation will launch a "first strike," or "preemptive strike," against another if it knows that the attacked nation will still have the capability to retaliate by causing unacceptable levels of destruction. If all major antagonists believe that about each other, mutual deterrence will take effect and relative peace (or a "balance of terror") will reign. Second-strike capability requires that the necessary missiles be located so that they cannot be destroyed by the prospective enemy in a first-strike attack. In practical terms, this has meant intercontinental ballistic missiles (ICBM) in heavy concrete ("hardened") silos and submarine-launched ballistic missiles (SLBM) stationed in undetectable submerged submarines around the enemy's coast. All missiles at above-ground locations, and all heavy bombers not actually in the air, are potentially applicable only to first-strike use, and thus serve to provoke rather than deter. Even ICBM at hardened sites now may be vulnerable to accurate first strikes with heavy new warheads, and deterrence is coming to depend more exclusively on submarine capabilities. In computing second-strike capability, of course, planners must provide for the defensive capabilities of an alert enemy, particularly through its antiballistic missile (ABM) system. Although these have yet to be proven effective, there is always the possibility that some incoming missiles might thus be rendered ineffective.

And so strategic planners must calculate the destructiveness of their second-strike capabilities. Part of the problem for American planners is that the Soviet Union perceives itself as threatened by both the United States and China, and deploys separate sets of missiles in the two directions. Presumably, the United States too seeks deterrence against both potential enemies, even though the Chinese as yet have no second-strike capability. In any event, the rough balance struck in the early 1970s gave the Soviet Union a slight lead in the total number of ICBM in hardened sites and the United States a slight lead in submarine-based missiles. The United States had more than 1000 ICBM in place, however, and the Soviets had almost 600 missiles in submarines; neither side was short. And the United States had a long lead in the number of deliverable warheads, by virtue of the development of multiple-warhead carrying capacity for each missile. Known as multiple independently targeted re-entry vehicles (MIRV), the new warheads can be aimed at different targets. Thus the United States' total delivery strength was raised to about 5700 warheads.

What does this stock of missiles and warheads mean in terms of second-strike capability? According to Defense Department estimates, 200 nuclear warheads landing on major Soviet targets would kill 52 million people (21 percent of the population) and destroy 72 percent of Soviet industrial capacity. In addition, millions would be injured or homeless, the physical environment contaminated, and social organization thoroughly disrupted. We may take this as representing an "unacceptable" level of destruction, sufficient to deter Soviet policymakers from launching a surprise attack on the United States. Assuming that five times the required number of missiles must be launched from protected land sites and from under the sea to assure that 200 missiles penetrate Soviet air defenses and reach their targets, it still appears that the United States possesses enough nuclear armament to destroy the Soviet Union several times over. The reverse is also true, of course. No matter how large the U.S. strategic forces grow, not even an American surprise attack could prevent the Soviet Union from launching a prohibitively destructive second strike from its protected sites and submarines.

The clear capacity to destroy each other several times over, in conjunction with the soaring costs of such weapons, led in 1972 to an agreement to limit future offensive weapons development. In effect, the United States and the Soviet Union agreed in the so-called Strategic Arms Limitation Talks to freeze their respective weaponry at then-existing levels. Only strategic arms were involved, but limits on both offensive and defensive systems were set for a five-year period, and both sides were committed to efforts to extend the limits to other kinds of armaments and for longer periods. The acquiescence of the U.S. military was brought about only by the commitment of vast new sums to research and development of new weapons systems, and thus there was no net saving of money. But the arms race lost some of its momentum, and some form of continuing agreement seemed likely. When the talks resumed in 1975, the major issue was the inclusion of other strategic forces, such as bombers and shorter-range missiles, in the limitations without upsetting the balance between the two sides.

National Security in the Age of Global Hegemony

At a time of national reappraisal, such as the late 1970s, recent events may be seen from a new perspective. The steps by which the United States assumed the role of world policeman, each apparently necessary at the time, may now seem questionable. And at least some of the actions taken on behalf of that greatly expanded concept of national security are now widely and routinely criticized. Let us briefly review some of these steps to see where they lead.

The Truman Doctrine

In March 1947, President Truman announced what has come to be known as the Truman Doctrine: "We cannot allow changes in the status quo by such methods as coercion, or by such subterfuges as political infiltration." This declaration was made in the context of the Greek civil war, in which a highly authoritarian government sought to suppress a revolution that enjoyed considerable popular support but had strong local communist components. For more than two years, British troops had fought on the side of the Greek government they had set up, finally achieving a measure of stability despite continued official corruption and severe inflation. The British, however, were unable to keep up their efforts; their own financial situation was so desperate that they had no alternative but to withdraw their troops. The United States proceeded to take over support of the Greek government's campaign by supplying weapons, military advisers, and substantial amounts of money. The decision to intervene was perceived by the President as essential to American security, given the context of a global struggle between contrasting ways of life, and it has come to be understood in these terms ever since.

The commitment in Greece was a major turning-point in American foreign policy. It effectively marked the beginning of the period when national security concerns led to the use of Third World nations, particularly those on the perimeter of the Soviet bloc, as buffer states, with prevention of the spread of communism seen as more important than the nature of the government or long-term economic development. Ultimately, Greece and Turkey were incorporated into the North American Treaty Organization; but despite massive military and economic assistance, their financial conditions and general economic levels remained low. In the 1960s, continued dissatisfaction led to several changes in the makeup of the government in Greece. Apparently still acting to promote national security, American policymakers tended to support the more conservative factions in each case.

The Korean War of 1950–1953 provides an Asian illustration of this early stage of American policy. South Korea was considered crucial as another testing-ground of what was assumed to be Soviet expansionism. Experts now differ about the extent to which the two crises were instigated or encouraged by the Soviet Union. In the case of Greece, it seems clear that the Soviet Union had declined to help because it considered the revolution a hopeless cause.[1] And it is also apparent that the belligerent threats of the South Korean government to invade the North may have contributed to the North's decision to send its armies south. In any event, this aggressive act triggered American involvement. When the American army appeared to be pushing toward the Chinese border, the Chinese too became involved. The war then settled into a long-term stalemate. Nearly two decades after the end of the war, South Korea had received such massive economic assistance that it was becoming a showcase of economic growth. The government, however, had made little progress toward more democratic organization or operation.

As the perceived communist threat became global, the Eisenhower Administration set about to tie as many Third World nations as possible to the United States through alliance treaties. Alliances modeled on the NATO pact, were formed with Turkey, Iran, Iraq, and Pakistan (CENTO) and, together with Britain and France, with Thailand and Pakistan directly and Laos, Cambodia, and South Vietnam by informal extension (SEATO). Bilateral defense treaties were undertaken with the Philippines and Taiwan. Pursuant to these various treaties, considerable military assistance was extended. Similar help was made available when the key neutralist nation in the world, India, was engaged in border skirmishes with the Chinese. Ironically, the major use of American military assistance occurred not in defense against communist attack but in small wars between nations allied with the United States, such as Pakistan and India.

The Eisenhower Doctrine

When the containment policy was rendered obsolete in the late 1950s by the development of indigenous popular movements all over the world, the United States faced new difficulties in serving its security interests. Any independence movement in an African or Asian colony, or any revolutionary movement in Latin America, might serve as a route to power for communists. Almost without considering the limits of propriety or capability, the global approach to security was extended once again to cover such possibilities: the Eisenhower Doctrine in effect served notice that the United States might see its security at stake, and act accordingly, not only in the internal conflicts of nations with which we had alliances, but also where violence threatened or occurred elsewhere in the world.

The meaning of this commitment is illustrated by the situation in Lebanon in 1958, when Marines landed in and occupied the country for four months. The cause of the disorder was an effort by Lebanon's

---

[1] Based on a quotation from Joseph Stalin reported in Milovan Djilas, *Conversations with Stalin* (New York: Praeger, 1962), p. 164.

incumbent anticommunist president to change the country's constitution in order to serve another term in office. Arab nationalists, supported by aspiring Lebanese politicians, had formed a powerful coalition in opposition. Calls for the violent overthrow of the government came from Egypt and Syria, but U.N. observation groups could find no major foreign sources of arms or men behind the opposition. There was undeniable fighting, however, and it seemed to be part of a trend toward revolutionary disorder throughout the nations of the Middle East. At the height of the fighting, the president abandoned his efforts to succeed himself but nevertheless called for American assistance. The Marines had been alerted for months and landed the next day. Soon the U.S. forces, armed with atomic howitzers, numbered seven thousand men. President Eisenhower told Americans in a television address that the situation was like the Greek civil war and various communist conquests of the early 1950s, and that American troops were required to defend Lebanese sovereignty and integrity. They did so by acceding to the election of a new president, whereupon the fighting died away.

But a precedent had been set for the involvement of U.S. troops in the internal affairs of Third World nations, even in cases where the opposition to the local government came not from communists but from indigenous nationalist forces. This precedent was much recalled in 1965, when American Marines landed in the Dominican Republic. In this instance, there was no solid evidence of communist involvement in the revolution, but the American Embassy thought there was, and President Johnson acted accordingly. The consensus of experts now, however, is that the embassy was either hysterical or acting as the agent of the conservative military forces that were ultimately installed in power with U.S. help. In any event, the United States' commitment to a global view of its security needs, reaching into the internal affairs of Third World nations, began to appear more like a determination to use force to prop up any government that could be induced to request U.S. intervention.

The leading example of American policy under this global definition is, of course, the Vietnam War. Escalating slowly but steadily from the dispatch of the first U.S. advisors in the early days of the Cold War, the American commitment finally became one of maintaining an unpopular government against an indigenous revolutionary movement that enjoyed not only widespread popular support but also the active assistance of a neighboring communist country. To make matters worse for the United States, the site of this insurrection was dense jungle on the Asian mainland, ten thousand miles from the United States. Neither a half million U.S. troops nor bomb tonnages exceeding those dropped by all sides during World War Two succeeded in halting the progress of the revolutionary movement.

The use of military force is often an indication that other forms of power have failed to achieve the ends sought. In the mid-1970s, a seemingly unending series of revelations about covert intelligence operations suggested that the scope of American involvement in other nations' internal affairs was far greater than these relatively isolated military interventions would indicate. The Central Intelligence Agency (CIA) was acknowledged to have undertaken a variety of deliberate efforts to subvert governments and even to assassinate leaders over a thirty-year period and on every continent. Much of the rationale for these interventions was the single unifying concern that unless the United States acted decisively, communist penetration would succeed in gaining control of the government and produce a new ally for the Soviet Union or China. Another factor in all of these bold assertions of American power is the importance of domestic politics in the formulation of foreign policy. Few policymakers have been willing to give their opponents any grounds for charging them with weakness in "standing up to the communists." The dynamics of domestic politics seem to lead decisionmakers to take the strongest possible stances against even remote contingencies that might lead to communist gains. Chagrin at "losing" Cuba is no doubt partly responsible for this bellicosity, but so is an undifferentiated conviction that the security interest of the United States is intimately involved in the domestic difficulties of small nations anywhere in the world.

Consequences of Three Decades of National Security Policies

What have been the effects of the combination of military supremacy and the role of global policeman? To be sure, there has been no nuclear war. Whether this is the case because of or in spite of the American policy of strategic superiority is not so clear. We have approached the brink of mutual annihilation with some frequency—in Berlin and over Vietnam, Cuba, and the Middle East. Perhaps it is only the military might of the United States that has prevented war and preserved the "free world" from communist expansionism. Perhaps other policies would have accomplished the same end with less danger.

With regard to the position of the United States and the Third World, it seems clear that the earlier image of the United States as nonimperialist has been lost. The moral Leadership once accorded the United States by developing nations has simply collapsed in the face of repeated interventions, covert and military, and regular support for the most repressive governments. Some Third World nations are now firmly in the grip of local elites acceptable to (and often educated and trained in social control techniques by) the United States. Many have set out on relatively independent, often nationalist and/or socialist, roads of their own. Would the scoreboard of the late 1970s be more or less favorable to the American cause if we had pursued different policies? This question may be unanswerable, and it is certainly still controversial; its most important implication may be that the nature of American goals—the definition of what we understand as our national security—is really what is at stake.

The foreign intelligence profession.

In international affairs, intelligence is knowledge—accurate, objective knowledge and understanding of men and events throughout the world. The Central Intelligence Agency has a vital role in providing the information our Government's leaders need in making their decisions.

Its interests are broad and the CIA seeks people trained in such fields as:

Information Science	Mathematics	Foreign Languages
Economics	Photo Science	Russian
Electrical Engineering		Eastern European
Foreign Area Studies		Middle Eastern
		Oriental

The Agency also has a Summer Intern Program in foreign studies for students who will be in graduate school in the fall of 1976.

All positions are in the Washington, D.C. area; some offer opportunities for Foreign Travel; U.S. Citizenship is required.

To be considered for a career in the Intelligence Profession, interested senior and graduate students completing work in the above are invited to send a complete resume to:

**Director of Personnel
Central Intelligence Agency
P.O. Box 1925
Washington, D.C. 20013**
An Equal Opportunity Employer

Source: New York Times, 16 November 1975, p. E12.

Report: U.S. Senate Intelligence Committee

The Questions Presented

The Committee sought to answer four broad questions:

Assassination Plots

Did United States officials instigate, attempt, aid and abet, or acquiesce in plots to assassinate foreign leaders?

Involvement in Other Killings

Did United States officials assist foreign dissidents in a way which significantly contributed to the killing of foreign leaders?

Authorization

Where there was involvement by United States officials in assassination plots or other killings, were such activities authorized and if so, at what levels of our Government?

Communication and Control

Even if not authorized in fact, were the assassination activities perceived by those involved to be within the scope of their lawful authority? If they were so perceived, was there inadequate control exercised by higher authorities over the agencies to prevent such misinterpretation?

Summary of Findings and Conclusions on the Plots

The Committee investigated alleged United States involvement in assassination plots in five foreign countries:

Country	Individual Involved
Cuba	Fidel Castro
Congo (Zaire)	Patrice Lumumba
Dominican Republic	Raphael Trujillo
Chile	General Rene Schneider
South Vietnam	Ngo Dinh Diem

The evidence concerning each alleged assassination can be summarized as follows:

Patrice Lumumba (Congo/Zaire)

In the Fall of 1960, two CIA officials were asked by superiors to assassinate Lumumba. Poisons were sent to the Congo and some exploratory steps were taken toward gaining access to Lumumba. Subsequently, in early 1961, Lumumba was killed by Congolese rivals. It does not appear from the evidence that the United States was in any way involved in the killing.

Fidel Castro (Cuba)

United States Government personnel plotted to kill Castro from 1960 to 1965. American underworld figures and Cubans hostile to Castro were used in these plots, and were provided encouragement and material support by the United States.

Rafael Trujillo (Dominican Republic)

Trujillo was shot by Dominican dissidents on May 31, 1961. From early in 1960 and continuing to the time of the assassination, the United States Government generally supported these dissidents. Some Government personnel were aware that the dissidents intended to kill Trujillo. Three pistols and three carbines were furnished by American officials, although a request for machine guns was later refused. There is conflicting evidence concerning whether the weapons were knowingly supplied for use in the assassination and whether any of them were present at the scene.

Ngo Dinh Diem (South Vietnam)

Diem and his brother, Nhu, were killed on November 2, 1963, in the course of a South Vietnamese General's coup. Although the United States Government supported the coup, there is no evidence that American officials favored the assassination. Indeed, it appears that the assassination of Diem was not part of the General's pre-coup planning but was instead a spontaneous act which occurred during the coup and was carried out without United States involvement or support.

General Rene Schneider (Chile)

On October 25, 1970, General Schneider died of gunshot wounds inflicted three days earlier while resisting a kidnap attempt. Schneider was Commander-in-Chief of the Army and a constitutionalist opposed to military coups, was considered an obstacle in efforts to prevent Salvador Allende from assuming the office of President of Chile. The United States Government supported and sought to instigate a military coup to block Allende. U.S. officials supplied financial aid, machine guns and other equipment to various military figures who opposed Allende. Although the CIA continued to support coup plotters up to Schneider's shooting, the record indicates that the CIA had withdrawn active support of the group which carried out the actual kidnap attempt on October 22, which resulted in Schneider's death. Further, it does not appear that any of the equipment supplied by the CIA to coup plotters in Chile was used in the kidnapping. There is no evidence of a plan to kill Schneider or that United States officials specifically anticipated that Schneider would be shot during the abduction.

Assassination Capability (Executive Action)

In addition to these five cases, the Committee has received evidence that ranking Government officials discussed, and may have authorized, the establishment within the CIA of a generalized assassination capability. During these discussions, the concept of assassination was not affirmatively disavowed.

Similarities and Differences Among the Plots

The assassination plots all involved Third World countries, most of which were relatively small and none of which possessed great political or military strength. Apart from that similarity, there were significant differences among the plots:

(1) Whether United States officials initiated the plot, or were responding to requests of local dissidents for aid.

(2) Whether the plot was specifically intended to kill a foreign leader, or

whether the leader's death was a reasonably foreseeable consequence of an attempt to overthrow the government.

The Castro and Lumumba cases are examples of plots conceived by United States officials to kill foreign leaders.

In the Trujillo case, although the United States Government certainly opposed his regime, it did not initiate the plot. Rather, United States officials responded to requests for aid from local dissidents whose aim clearly was to assassinate Trujillo. By aiding them, this country was implicated in the assassination, regardless of whether the weapons actually supplied were meant to kill Trujillo or were only intended as symbols of support for the dissidents.

The Schneider case differs from the Castro and Trujillo cases. The United States Government, with full knowledge that Chilean dissidents considered General Schneider an obstacle to their plans, sought a coup and provided support to the dissidents. However, even though the support included weapons, it appears that the intention of both the dissidents and the United States officials was to abduct General Schneider, not to kill him. Similarly, in the Diem case, some United States officials wanted Diem removed and supported a coup to accomplish his removal, but there is no evidence that any of those officials sought the death of Diem himself.

Findings Concerning the Plots Themselves

Officials of the United States Government Initiated Plots to Assassinate Fidel Castro and Patrice Lumumba

The Committee finds that officials of the United States Government initiated and participated in plots to assassinate Patrice Lumumba and Fidel Castro.

The plot to kill Lumumba was conceived in the latter half of 1960 by officials of the United States Government, and quickly advanced to the point of sending poisons to the Congo to be used for the assassination.

The effort to assassinate Castro began in 1960 and continued until 1965. The plans to assassinate Castro using poison cigars, exploding seashells, and a contaminated diving suit did not advance beyond the laboratory phase. The plot involving underworld figures reached the stage of producing poison pills, establishing the contacts necessary to send them to Cuba, procuring potential assassins within Cuba, and apparently delivering the pills to the island itself. One 1960 episode involved a Cuban who initially had no intention of engaging in assassination, but who finally agreed, at the suggestion of the CIA, to attempt to assassinate Raul Castro if the opportunity arose. In the AM/LASH operation, which extended from 1963 through 1965, the CIA gave active support and encouragement to a Cuban whose intent to assassinate Castro was known, and provided him with the means of carrying out an assassination.

American Officials Encouraged or Were Privy to Coup Plots Which Resulted in the Deaths of Trujillo, Diem, and Schneider

American officials clearly desired the overthrow of Trujillo, offered both encouragement and guns to local dissidents who sought his overthrow and whose plans included assassination. American officials also supplied those dissidents with pistols and rifles.

American officials offered encouragement to the Vietnamese generals who plotted Diem's overthrow, and a CIA official in Vietnam gave the generals money after the coup had begun. However, Diem's assassination was neither desired nor suggested by officials of the United States.

The record reveals that United States officials offered encouragement to the Chilean dissidents who plotted the kidnapping of General Rene Schneider, but American officials did not desire or encourage Schneider's death. Certain high officials did know, however, that the dissidents planned to kidnap General Schneider.

As Director Colby testified before the Committee, the death of a foreign leader is a risk foreseeable in any coup attempt. In the cases we have considered, the risk of death was in fact known in varying degrees. It was widely known that the dissidents in the Dominican Republic intended to assassinate Trujillo. The contemplation of coup leaders at one time to assassinate Nhu, President Diem's brother, was communicated to the upper levels of the United States Government. While the CIA and perhaps the White House knew that the coup leaders in Chile planned to kidnap General Schneider, it was not anticipated that he would be killed, although the possibility of his death should have been recognized as a foreseeable risk of his kidnapping.

The Plots Occurred in a Cold War Atmosphere Perceived to Be of Crisis Proportions

The Committee fully appreciates the importance of evaluating the assassination plots in the historical context within which they occurred. In the preface to this report, we described the perception generally shared within the United States during the depths of the Cold War, that our country faced a monolithic enemy in Communism. That attitude helps explain the assassination plots which we have reviewed, although it does not justify them. Those involved nevertheless appeared to believe they were advancing the best interests of their country.

American Officials Had Exaggerated Notions About Their Ability to Control the Actions of Coup Leaders

Running throughout the cases considered in this report was the expectation of American officials that they could control the actions of dissident groups which they were supporting in foreign countries. Events demonstrated that the United States had no such power.

Excerpts from the Report of the U.S. Senate Intelligence Committee, published 20 November 1975.

A New Definition of National Security?

Several basic conditions in the world are now different from what they were in the 1950s and 1960s, and American attitudes appear to be changing in response to them. The capitalist world is in crisis and disarray, and the United States has no capacity to control it. The Third World is increasingly resistant to exploitation from any source. The pressures of population, resources, and environmental needs place heavy additional burdens on all economies. In short, as we have said, the period of American moral, political, and economic hegemony is over. Many Americans, aghast at revelations about the actions of their government in the previous three decades, have begun to question the nature of our national security needs. But such definitions are not products of deliberate choice alone. They are also outcomes of history, of deeply rooted forces in the world, and of the acts of the most powerful people and groups within the society.

Present trends and conditions promise not a reduction of world tensions, but the reverse. The process of change in both the capitalist world and the Third World seems to be in the direction of socialism. Increasingly, the United States may have to face the prospect of economic and political isolation. The anticommunist commitment appears too deep to be seriously modified, despite our tentative détente with the Soviet Union. The needs of the dominant corporate-banking sector of our political economy must still be served. All these factors suggest a new "fortress America" concept of national security, in which nuclear confrontation may once again hold center stage. No other potential direction for change in our definition of national security seems to square as well with the developing conditions that characterize our immediate present and future.

Levels of Analysis

Why has military supremacy remained the basic definition of national security for thirty years, despite the immense costs and dangers? Many have sought to answer this question, and their differing approaches offer us an important opportunity: we shall demonstrate that people can cast their analyses at any of three *levels,* and thereby consider wholly different factors and relationships, in efforts to understand why things happen as they do in politics. From this point forward, readers should be alert to the level of analysis being offered in support of a conclusion.

The most superficial level of analysis addresses the merits of an issue and decisionmakers' stated reasons for their actions. Seen thus, it appears that military supremacy is the American policy because it is the rational policy; planners have thought the matter through carefully and decided that our interests require it. Or the planners may be seen as wrong, as acting on faulty premises or facts, or as bad people who lack sufficient understanding. In neither case does the analysis consider any factors external to the decision-making act itself. Change in the nature of governmental decisions is thus seen as depending on the advent of new or better decisionmakers; but that is *all* such change would require.

A somewhat deeper level of analysis looks at the institutional setting in which a decision is made. With regard to the issue at hand, this is the "military-industrial complex" explanation. It holds that the relationship between the military in the Pentagon, their supposed overseers in the Congress, and the corporations that supply weapons is so close that they can overcome any opposition to induce the government to continue its profitable policy of military supremacy. To correct such a situation, it clearly would not be enough merely to replace the people who made the decisions. Other factors, such as bureaucratic momentum, economic interest, political advancement, and the like are involved in determining the outcome. The problem is thus seen as residing in the interlocking institutional arrangements; to "correct" the situation it would be necessary to make basic changes in the powers of these or opposing institutions.

The most basic level of analysis, which addresses fundamental societal values or the basic structure and dynamics of the economic system, we shall term the *systemic* level of explanation. Here the sources of a decision are said to be the values of the people or the imperatives of the (capitalist) economic system. The policy of military supremacy is thus explained by the combination of profitability for industry and general anticommunism among the population. Changing the decisionmakers makes nothing come out differently. Nor would breaking the ties between particular military officers, congressmen, and corporations change outcomes. Only fundamental changes in the economy or values of the people would bring about a different policy according to this view.

The two latter approaches dig deeper and are more useful for understanding relationships among disparate facts. Most of the analysis in this book will be undertaken at these levels, both of which are likely—on reflection—to be familiar to the reader. The military-industrial complex argument is undoubtedly part of standard discourse now. But the systemic level of analysis may still require illustration. The economic version is well illustrated by a recent article by economist Michael Reich:

> The growth and persistence of a high level of military spending is a natural outcome in an advanced capitalist society that both suffers from the problem of inadequate private aggregate demand and plays a leading role in the preservation and expansion of the international capitalist system. In my view, barring a revolutionary change, militarism and military spending priorities are likely to persist for the foreseeable future.
>
> In what follows, I shall present three principal propositions on the role of military spending in the U.S. economy. (1) In the period beginning in 1950, if not earlier, the U.S. economy was not sufficiently sustained by private aggregate demand; some form of government expenditure was needed to maintain expansion. Without such stimulus, the growth rate of the United States as well as the international capitalist economy would have been substantially lower. (2) The U.S. government turned to military spending as the outlet for needed government expenditures precisely because it provides the most convenient such outlet; in a capitalist context,

spending on the military is easily expandable and highly attractive to corporations. Military spending supplements rather than competes with private demand, more is always "needed" for adequate "defense," it is highly profitable to the firms that receive weapons contracts, and no interest group is explicitly against it. (3) Federal expenditures on socially useful needs on a scale comparable to the military budget are not a feasible substitute. Massive social expenditures would tend to undermine profitability in many sectors of the private economy, remove potential areas of profitmaking, interfere with work incentives in the labor market, and weaken the basic ideological premise of capitalism that social welfare is maximized by giving primary responsibility for the production of goods and services to profit-motivated private enterprises. In short, military spending is much more consistent than is social services spending with the maintenance and reproduction of the basic social relations of capitalism. . . .

Military spending is acceptable to all corporate interests. It does not interfere with existing areas for profit making, it does not undermine the labor market, it does not challenge the class structure, and it does not produce income redistribution. Social spending does all these things, and thus faces obstacles for its own expansion. . . .

This brings me to a final point regarding the meaning of the question, is military spending really necessary to capitalism? I have tried to frame the answer to this question in the following way. A capitalist economy with inadequate aggregate demand is much more *likely* to turn to military than to social spending because the former is more consistent with private profit and the social relations of production under capitalism. If this military outlet were cut off, say by massive public opposition, it is possible that a capitalist economy might accommodate and transform itself rather than commit suicide. But such reasoning misses the point. Military spending is favored by capitalists and is likely to be defended with considerable vigor, as recent years have shown. Perhaps a parallel with imperialism will clarify this point. It is not essential to a capitalist economy that it be imperialist, for growth can be domestically based. But so long as there are lands to be conquered and markets to be penetrated, it is natural to expect that capitalism will have an imperialist character. Similarly, so long as there is profit to be made in military spending, capitalists will turn to it.[2]

[2] Michael Reich, "Does the U.S. Economy Require Military Spending?" *American Economic Review* LXII (May 1972), pp. 296–297, 302, 303.

6

Income Distribution: Inequality, Poverty, and Welfare

Income and wealth are paramount goals of individual economic and political activity in the United States. It is hardly news that some people are more successful than others. This is due to a variety of factors, including individual talents and opportunities, the systematic effects of government policies, and the nature of economic forces in a highly industrialized capitalist society. In fact, the combination of factors may be different for each individual. *Patterns* of distribution of income and wealth, however, offer a means of analyzing the social consequences of all these factors taken together. Patterns of distribution of income and wealth are a kind of snapshot of the results of many public policies and the way they have combined with "private" forces to shape individual attainments.

As we have seen, many government policies serve to allocate economic benefits and burdens among segments of the population. But some bear more directly than others on who has how much spendable income at any given moment. By focusing on such policies as taxation, subsidies, and welfare—areas in which the actions of government bear directly on the vital income-and-wealth goals of all individuals—we should be able to see clearly for whom government works.

This chapter therefore operates on two levels of analysis. First, and rather briefly, we will sum up the combined effects of public policies and private forces in this crucial area by analyzing the basic patterns of distribution of income and wealth in the United States. Second, we will explore in some detail those government policies that bear most directly on such distribution. In separate sections, we will look at taxation, subsidies to different sectors of the population, and welfare. The larger problem addressed by the chapter is that of income inequality and its sources, but a major subsidiary problem is poverty and its alleviation by various means—chiefly welfare. We conclude with an analysis of the alternatives to, and probable future of, the nation's welfare programs.

Patterns of Income and Wealth Distribution

We begin this analysis with three basic facts. (1) The United States is a sharply stratified society, in which a very few people receive very large proportions of income and wealth, the majority share a relatively modest proportion, and a substantial number receive very little indeed. (2) This pattern has persisted for at least the last sixty years, and has changed only negligibly in the last decades; indeed, recent change has tended to widen these gaps rather than close them. (3) Income inequalities are closely related to *sources* of income (those who gain their income from stocks and dividends and from capital gains are at the top, and wage-earners at the bottom, of the scale), sex (men earn more than women in the same jobs; women are disproportionately concentrated in the lower-paying jobs), and *race* (nonwhites earn less than whites with comparable education in comparable jobs; nonwhites are highly concentrated in the lower-paying jobs). Poverty and racism are so closely linked in the United States that it is very difficult to talk about them separately; we do so chiefly for the sake of analytical clarity.

The Basic Patterns

Table 6.1 presents data on the distribution of income from the most recent national census; the pattern it illustrates has prevailed at least since the early years of this century. Stratification—that is, inequality—is evident, and may be summarized in a variety of ways. The top 5 percent of the population, for example, earns more than twice as much as the bottom

TABLE 6.1   *Shares of National Income (percentages)*

	Bottom 20%	Next 20%	Middle 20%	Second 20%	Top 20%	Top 5%
1969						
Family Income	5.6	12.3	17.6	23.4	41.0	14.7
Unrelated Income	3.4	7.7	13.7	24.3	50.9	21.0
1971						
Family Income	5.5	12.0	17.6	23.8	41.1	15.7
Unrelated Income	3.4	8.1	13.9	24.3	50.4	20.5
1973						
Family Income	5.5	11.9	17.5	24.0	41.1	15.5
Unrelated Income	3.7	8.6	14.4	23.9	49.5	20.0
1974						
Family Income	4.0	12.0	17.6	24.1	41.0	15.3
Unrelated Income	5.4	8.9	14.5	24.2	48.5	19.3

Source: U.S. Bureau of the Census, Current Population Reports Series P-60, no. 97 (January 1975) for 1969–1973 data; no. 99 (July 1975) for 1974 data.

20 percent. And the top 20 percent earns more total dollars than the bottom 60 percent, though the latter group includes more than three times as many people! The data for unrelated individuals reveal even greater disparities. The meaning of these figures in human terms, of course, is that a substantial number and proportion of Americans live in poverty or near-poverty. The precise number depends on a series of definitions and calculations, which we shall explore in a later section; but by any reasonable assessment, at least 27 million persons, or 13 percent of the population, are at or below the poverty level.

Wealth—financial resources not derived from income—is even more concentrated at the top of the social and economic pyramid. The top 1 percent of adult wealth-holders own more than 25 percent of all personal property and financial assets in the country.[1] The top 5 percent of family units hold more than 40 percent of all wealth. Most of this wealth is in the form of financial assets (stocks, bonds, mortgages, and the like), real estate, and business capital equipment. Using data from a survey of American households, one major study found that the top 1 percent held 31 percent of the nation's wealth and 61 percent of all corporate stock; the top 20 percent was found to hold 76 percent of all wealth and 96 percent of all corporate stock.[2]

[1] James D. Smith, Pennsylvania State University, cited in *Business Week*, 5 August 1972, p. 54.

[2] Dorothy Projector and Gertrude S. Weiss, *Survey of Financial Characteristics of Consumers*, Federal Reserve Board, 1962, pp. 110–114.

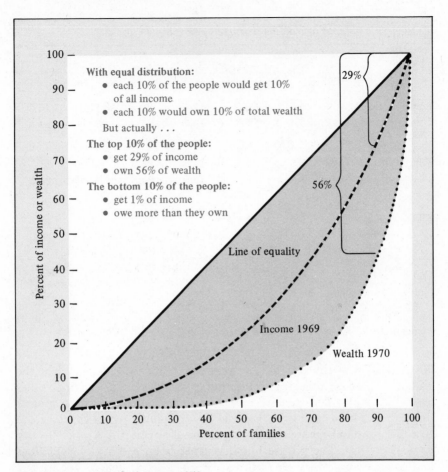

With equal distribution:
- each 10% of the people would get 10% of all income
- each 10% would own 10% of total wealth

But actually . . .

The top 10% of the people:
- get 29% of income
- own 56% of wealth

The bottom 10% of the people:
- get 1% of income
- owe more than they own

Line of equality

Income 1969

Wealth 1970

29%

56%

Percent of income or wealth

Percent of families

Source: Business Week, 5 August 1972.

FIGURE 6.1

U.S. Income Is Shared Unevenly, But Wealth Distribution Is More Unequal. By plotting percentages of income and wealth recipients on the horizontal axis and percentages of income and wealth on the vertical axis, both expressed in cumulative form, it is possible to see at a glance that the bottom 50% of income recipients, for example, drew 23% of personal income in 1969, while the bottom half wealth-holders in 1970 survey accounted for only 3% of net worth.

These distribution patterns are well summarized in Figure 6.1, from *Business Week.* Not known for exaggeration, the editors of *Business Week* nevertheless declare flatly: "Personal holdings of wealth, to a much greater extent than shares of income are dramatically concentrated at the top of the population heap." [3] In the same article, the editors note

[3] *Business Week,* 5 August 1972, p. 54.

that this pattern of wealth-holding persists by virtue of inheritance, and that the rich get richer faster than others can rise by virtue of their headstart. Citing a study of the top 1 percent of wealth-holders—"the rich"—the editors estimated that $326 billion in corporate stock and a total of $753 billion in all was held at this level.[4]

The Permanence of These Patterns

Again in the words of *Business Week*, ". . . income distribution seems to be one of the few real constants in the U.S. system." [5] In the twenty years between 1950 and 1970, the share of the national income received by the poorest 20 percent of Americans rose only from 4.5 to 5.5 percent; and the economic recession of the middle 1970s has again decreased that share by cutting into the family incomes of the poor.[6]

At the same time, the share of national income received by the top 20 percent dropped only 1 percent, from 42.6 percent in 1950 to 41.6 percent in 1970. The middle three income-fifths remained the same during this period. The continuity of these basic patterns could hardly be clearer. Moreover, though all real incomes have been rising, the gap between rich and poor has actually widened in absolute terms. Citing a recent study, *Business Week* reports that, from 1949 to 1969, "the gap between average real incomes of the poorest and richest fifths of the population widened from less than $11,000 to more than $19,000 in constant 1969 dollars." [7]

Nor has there been any closing of the wealth gap. The share of national wealth held by the top 1 percent did drop during the Great Depression and in World War Two, but since that time it has been widening again. Starting at 32 percent in 1922, it dropped to 28 percent in 1933 and as low as 21 percent in 1949; but it was back up to 26 percent by 1956 and is now estimated to be higher than that.[8] On the other hand, the poorest 25 percent of Americans have no net worth at all—their total debts equal or exceed their "assets." [9]

The Sources of Income and Wealth Disparities

The most obvious source of income differentials is the way in which people gain their income. Those who earn their income from wages and salaries, while they are many in number and earn a much larger dollar

[4] *Ibid.*, p. 55.

[5] *Business Week*, 1 April 1972, p. 56.

[6] Irwin Garfinkel and Robert D. Plotnick, "Poverty, Unemployment, and the Current Recession," mimeographed (University of Wisconsin, Institute for Research on Poverty, 1975), p. 2.

[7] *Business Week*, 1 April 1972, p. 56.

[8] Robert J. Lampman, *The Share of Top Wealth-holders in National Wealth* (Princeton, N.J.: Princeton University Press, 1962), p. 24.

[9] *Business Week*, 1 April 1972, p. 56.

total than others, are concentrated at the lower income levels. At the higher income levels, the source of income is much more likely to be stock dividends and capital gains (increases in the value of property held). Of those receiving more than $100,000 per year, for example, 67 percent of all dollars were derived from dividends and capital gains.[10] This is another way of saying that the concentration of wealth (financial assets that give rise to dividends and capital gains) in a few rich people results in sharp income differences.

Income and wealth are related in many and obvious ways, some of which are mutually reinforcing. Theoretically, it is possible that the patterns we have identified could be permanent but that the particular persons or families composing each level could vary over time. In other words, people who were in the top fifth in one period could be in the second or middle fifth twenty years later. Or people whose families were once at the bottom could rise until they reached the top fifth. But the evidence we have examined so far makes this very unlikely. Those who were rich in one time period appear likely to be even richer in the next time period, because the sources of great fortunes are types of wealth-holdings that are handed down within families or transferred only to others with great wealth. Only a few very unusual or fortunate individuals appear likely to rise to the levels of the great incomes within one or two generations, and the amount of mobility between the lower fifths may not be much greater. As we are about to see, other factors also work to hold people at their existing levels of income-earning capacity.

A second major cause of income differentials is the occupations of income-earners. Professionals, managers, and other white-collar workers earn substantially more than blue-collar, service, and farm workers. Both categories tend to be self-perpetuating. The former requires more education; hence a white-collar family is likely to have greater financial resources and the social status or upward identification that makes college education appear appropriate for its children. In other words, white-collar families are likely to produce white-collar children. Conversely, people enter blue-collar occupations in part because their parents held such jobs, were relatively poor, and could offer neither the money nor the social support necessary for further education and occupational mobility.

Recent research casts considerable doubt on some traditional assumptions about the usefulness of education in increasing occupational mobility for the poor. It suggests: that (1) schooling does not go very far toward compensating black children for the educational disadvantages with which they start; [11] (2) schools do not narrow the gaps between

---

[10] U.S. Internal Revenue Service, *Statistics of Income, 1966: Individual Income Tax Returns,* tables 7, 11, and 19. Cited in Frank Ackerman, *et al.,* "Income Distribution in the United States," *Review of Radical Political Economics* III (Summer 1971), p. 28.

[11] James S. Coleman *et al., Equality of Educational Opportunity* (Washington, D.C.: Government Printing Office, 1966).

social classes by enabling the poor to earn more money later in life; [12] and (3) the methods we use to finance public education subsidize higher income groups at the expense of those with lower incomes.[13] Despite a great deal of mythology, occupational mobility remains limited.

Another major cause of income differences is sex. Culturally imposed limitations on educational opportunities and career expectations, and systematic discrimination in both employment and wage or salary levels, have combined to limit severely the income-producing capabilities of women. The result is that women find many jobs closed to them, and are paid less than men for comparable work when it is available.

But the single greatest and most enduring cause of income differentials—one that persists across time and despite individual efforts to fulfill the requirements of mobility within the society—is racism. Nonwhite Americans have always been among the last hired and the first fired; they are systematically excluded from educational and other opportunities; and they are paid less for every job than equally or less well educated whites in the same jobs. The effects of occupation, sex, and race on income are summarized in Figure 6.2. Here we come a little closer to understanding the human dimensions of the discrepancies in income between groups of people. The weekly wages of each group decline as the occupational level declines. The wages of white men are greater than those of nonwhite men in the same job levels. The wages of women trail those of men in the same job levels and within races, so that nonwhite women are the lowest paid of all. Thus race combines with sex and occupation to create a self-perpetuating cycle of income limitation for the majority, while special sources of income provide a vastly greater level of income for the favored minority.

In this context, the question with which we began becomes even more crucial. How do governmental policies affect income distribution? Do they contribute to greater equality, or to increased inequality? Left alone, the private economy appears likely to work toward considerable (perhaps increasing) inequality. But it is not yet clear whether governmental policies accelerate that process, control it, or retard it, and (in either case) how this comes about. It is to these issues that we now turn.

Taxing and Spending

The U.S. government raises and spends roughly $270 billion per year. Nearly all of this amount is raised through taxation, mostly in the form of individual and corporate income taxes. It is spent on a

[12] Christopher Jencks *et al., Inequality* (New York: Basic Books, 1972).

[13] W. Lee Hansen and Burton A. Weisbrod, "A New Approach to Higher Education Finance," University of Wisconsin, Institute for Research on Poverty, Discussion Paper No. 64, 1970, mimeo.

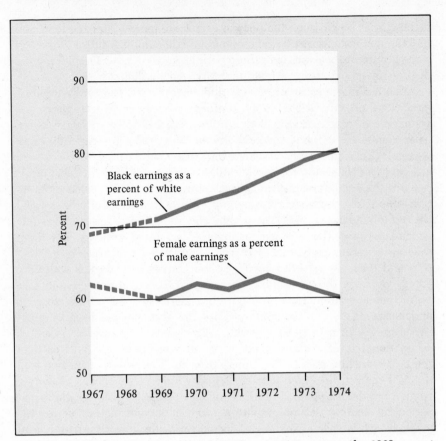

Source: *Monthly Labor Review,* August 1975, p. 26. (Note: Data for 1968 are not available.)

FIGURE 6.2

Black–White, Male–Female Ratios of Median Weekly Earnings, Full-Time Workers, 1967–1974

wide variety of functions, the major items now being national defense, social security, and interest on the national debt. The U.S. government is, in effect, a massive transfer agent, drawing money from certain people and activities and transferring it to other people and activities to fulfill public purposes.

The act of raising and spending sums of this size has profound consequences for the economy as a whole and for the individuals involved at both ends of the process. *It is no exaggeration to say that government taxing and spending policies quite literally determine the income level at which most Americans live.* We do not mean merely that these policies make differences of from $500 to $1,000 in a person's net income, though that is the case for some; in many cases, these policies are the difference between spendable income and no income, or between comfort and hardship or poverty. This is because tax provisions may determine whether a business will be profitable, whether it will be expanded or contracted, whether it will enter a new line of production or marketing, and so on. Spending decisions may create new jobs, terminate others, provide or foreclose educational or economic opportunities of various kinds, and so on.

Stakes this high are likely to arouse sharp value conflicts and much controversy. At every stage of the taxing and spending process, it must be decided who is to pay and on what basis, and who is to receive and for what specific purposes. The result is a vast array of inducements and rewards, penalties and punishments, which have—and are *designed* to have—the effect of shaping the economic behavior, attitudes, and opportunities of nearly everybody in the society. If people fail to see this, it is because they do not look at the totality of the process, the pattern of benefits and burdens, and the values, purposes, and applications of power they represent. We shall survey only a few representative illustrations of the major tendencies of taxing and spending policies.

TABLE 6.2 *Shares of National Income, Before and After Federal Income 1962 ° (percentages)*

	Bottom 20%	Next 20%	Middle 20%	Second 20%	Top 20%	Top 5%
Before Tax	4.6	10.9	16.3	22.7	45.5	19.6
After Tax	4.9	11.5	16.8	23.1	43.7	17.7

° Family units and unrelated individuals combined.

Source: Edward C. Budd, *Inequality and Poverty* (New York: W. W. Norton, 1967), pp. xiii, xvi.

Taxation

How should a tax system be designed? In reality, principles of equity become enmeshed with plain political expediency. The basic principle of equity on which the national tax system is grounded is that of *progressive income taxation*. This means that people are to be taxed in accordance with their ability to pay; it assumes that the people with the most income can afford to pay at higher rates than those with limited incomes. Thus rates vary from zero on the lowest incomes to more than 50 percent on the highest. If the system actually worked this way, the higher income brackets would have their share of national income reduced, and the poorest would gain ground in relative terms.

But this does not happen. Table 6.2 shows that changes in the share of national income received by the various income-fifths as a result of the "progressive" income tax are very slight. The poorest fifth of the population, for example, gains only three-tenths of one percent, while the highest fifth loses less than 2 percent. Another study conducted in the 1970s and aimed specifically at poverty-level people found that those with incomes under $4,000 gained only 1.4 percent of the national income (from 5.0 percent to 6.4 percent) when after-tax income was compared with before-tax income. Those earning over $15,000 dropped 2.4 percent, from 37.7 percent to 35.3 percent.[14] This taxing arrangement clearly has very little redistributive effect, no matter how it is calculated. Other studies show that nonprogressiveness has been characteristic of the tax system since its inception more than a half century ago.[15]

Why does this happen, and what does it mean for the distribution of income and wealth in the country? Essentially, it means that the income tax is progressive in name or image only; people think it is something that in most respects it is not.[16] What then does this system do, and how? One answer is that by means of a package of tax exclusions, deductions, exemptions, credits, write-offs, and reductions—most of which are applicable only to large corporations or the very rich—the privileged are allowed to pay sharply reduced shares of the tax load. The burden must then be shifted elsewhere, and the only alternative is the individual wage- and salary-earning taxpayer. Examples of tax-avoiding exemptions include the opportunity to deduct a proportion of the value of resources drawn from the earth (the oil industry's famous "depletion allowance"), the opportunity to deduct sums invested in new equipment ("investment credits"), and reduced rates on certain kinds of income (such as income gained from the rise in value of stocks and real estates, or "capital gains"). This list could be multiplied at great length. Such selective advantages elicit periodic outcries against "tax loopholes" and calls for tax reform; but new loopholes are created more often than old ones are closed.

The attack on loopholes has produced a number of spectacular illustrations of apparent inequities. In one study, the *real* tax rate was found to be the same for families earning $50,000 per year and for families earning $5,000 a year, because of the variety of deductions open to the higher-income people.[17] An Undersecretary of the Treasury admitted to Congress that people earning between $7,000 and $20,000 per year pay a

[14] S. M. Miller, "Income Redistribution and Economic Growth," *Social Policy* 2 (September–October 1971), p. 36.

[15] Gabriel Kolko, *Wealth and Power in America* (New York: Praeger, 1962), p. 34.

[16] Note that only the federal income tax makes any pretense of being progressive. State and local governments raise more revenue than does the federal government, and do so primarily from the property tax and/or sales tax. Both of these are *regressive*, in the sense that they take about the same absolute amounts from each taxpayer—or, in effect, a much larger proportion from the relatively poor than from the affluent. When state and local taxes are combined with the federal income tax, the effect is to eliminate any vestige of progressiveness from the total American tax system.

[17] Jack Newfield and Jeff Greenfield, "Them That Has, Keep: Taxes" *Ramparts* 10 (April 1972), p. 34.

higher proportion of their incomes to the federal government than do the richest 1 percent of Americans. Each year many taxpayers with large incomes pay no taxes at all. In the fiscal year ending June 1974, the 160,000 Americans with annual gross incomes of at least $100,000 were able to save a total of $7.3 billion dollars as a result of preferential tax provisions; the same loopholes cost the government a total of $52.8 billion that year. And because of the tax advantages granted for home ownership and for certain kinds of business expenses, persons with identical net incomes can bear very different tax burdens. A wage earner who lives in a rented house, for example, pays much more than a person who lives in his or her own mortgaged house and earns the same amount from an increase in the value of stocks.

Another kind of inequity is special opportunities for businesses to reduce their taxes. Some companies making large profits have very low rates. In 1974 the cleaning women who worked for Exxon paid a higher proportion of their incomes in federal taxes than did the corporation, whose first-quarter profits increased 38 percent that year.[18] In the case of the oil industry, this situation is made possible by depletion allowances and generous credit for a variety of business expenses. Other industries benefit from opportunities to deduct new investment from their tax obligations, or to increase their allowable deductions for depreciation of equipment by large sums; in both cases, profits can be large but taxes minimal. In 1971, for example, the Nixon Administration changed certain tax rules for businesses, making it possible for them to "write off" millions of dollars in equipment and greatly reduce their tax liabilities. The administration's tax changes provided $7.5 billion in tax relief to large corporations.

Both types of tax-avoidance advantages are justified by appeal to long- and/or short-range social goals. In the case of individuals, such goals include the encouragement of property ownership and investment, and rewards for hard work, thrift, willingness to take business risks, and the like. In the case of large corporations, the theory is that increased investment and higher profits will lead ultimately to more jobs and faster economic growth. Each type of tax advantage has powerful defenders in and out of government; each network of support normally succeeds in retaining or expanding its particular advantage.

Very little study has been done of the overall effects of the entire pattern of tax advantages. In a major study released in 1972, however, the Joint Economic Committee of Congress introduced the concept of "tax expenditures" or "tax welfare payments." [19] This outlook views tax-avoidance opportunities as costs to the government—money the government would otherwise have raised. One of the Committee's consultants

18 *The Economist,* 6 April 1974, p. 48.
19 U.S. Congress, Joint Economic Committee, *Economics of Federal Subsidy Programs* (Washington: U.S. Government Printing Office, 1972).

estimated that some $73 billion a year was "distributed" by such avoidance opportunities. In other words, loopholes and other tax forgiveness provided some people with untaxed income. The 6 million families whose annual income is $3,000 or less got only $92 million of these benefits, and families with incomes of less than $15,000 per year (more than 70 percent of all families) received only 25 percent. By contrast, the three-tenths of one percent of families with incomes over $100,000 per year received 15 percent of such untaxed money.[20] In effect, the Committee argued, the Congress was voting the nation's richest citizens annual "welfare" payments amounting to tens of billions of dollars.

Spending

Let us focus on the other side of government's activities as a "transfer agent," and ask who gets what the government spends. Once again, principles of equity compete with long- and short-range social goals and sheer political expediency. The broad patterns of expenditure are shown in Table 6.3. Income security outlays grow as more workers qualify for social security benefits. Military expenditures are the second largest item.

Within these classifications by function, of course, government is actually engaging in many different activities. In the case of national defense, it is paying salaries to military and civilian employees, buying supplies, conducting research, and countless other things. In the case of foreign aid, it is transferring money to other countries in the form of grants or loans or export goods. Under commerce and transportation, it is making grants to the states for roadbuilding. Under education, it is transferring funds to local school districts for a variety of purposes. Under social security, it is paying elderly citizens directly from a trust fund created by the payments of working people and their employers over several decades. Under veterans' benefits, it is supplying services and making payments to veterans out of the general tax revenues. It is also paying interest on the national debt, incurred for the most part in World War Two but greatly increased since then, to banks and investors who hold such investments. Under general government expenses, it is paying its own officials and employees and conducting day-to-day business. And, finally, it is simply transferring a portion of its revenues to the states to use as they wish.

The broad totals thus do not reveal the specific uses or, in many cases, the recipients of government money. It is very difficult, as the Congress has learned over and over again, to tell exactly who gets how much from government spending. Frequently, the various operating arms of a single agency do not even know what each other are doing, and the Secretaries of cabinet-level departments can only guess at the real beneficiaries. The

---

[20] William Proxmire, *Uncle Sam: The Last of the Bigtime Spenders* (New York: Simon and Schuster, 1972), p. 181.

TABLE 6.3   *Percentage Distribution of Budget Outlays by Function*

Function	1941	1946	1951	1956	1961	1966	1971	1976 est.
National defense	44.3	75.3	47.8	56.4	47.6	41.5	36.3	26.9
International affairs	1.1	3.5	8.2	3.4	3.3	3.4	1.5	1.8
General science, space, and technology	.1	.1	.2	.2	1.1	5.0	2.0	1.3
Natural resources, environment, and energy	6.4	.9	3.1	1.5	2.2	2.3	2.1	2.9
Agriculture	2.5	1.1	−.7	4.9	2.7	1.8	2.0	.5
Commerce and transportation	4.7	.1	4.8	2.8	5.3	6.7	4.9	3.9
Community and regional development	1.1	.4	.6	.3	.5	1.1	1.9	1.7
Education, manpower, and social services	12.5	.2	.5	.8	1.1	3.0	4.3	4.2
Health	.4	.4	.7	.5	.9	2.0	7.0	8.0
Income security	13.7	4.7	10.2	14.0	21.9	21.5	26.2	34.0
Veterans benefits and services	4.1	4.5	12.1	7.1	5.8	4.4	4.6	4.5
Law enforcement and justice	.7	.3	.5	.4	.4	.4	.6	.9
General government	2.2	1.6	2.3	.7	1.1	1.1	1.0	.9
Revenue sharing and general purpose fiscal assistance	.1	*	.1	.1	.2	.2	.2	2.1
Interest	8.1	8.5	12.2	8.9	8.3	8.4	9.3	9.9
Allowances	....	....	....	....	....	....	....	2.3
Undistributed offsetting receipts	−1.9	−1.5	−2.6	−2.1	−2.5	−2.7	−4.0	−5.8
Total outlays	100.0	100.0	100.0	100.0	100.0	100.0	100.0	100.0

* Less than 0.05%.

Source: Office of Management and Budget, *The Budget of the U.S. Government for Fiscal Year 1976* (Washington, D.C.: U.S. Government Printing Office, 1975), p. 66.

inability or unwillingness to identify systematically the actual recipients of federal funds, of course, may permit more benevolent interpretations than are really justified. If there is no clear evidence to the contrary, for example, we usually assume that the intentions of a funding program have been fulfilled.

But this is often not the case. One area in which some investigation has been conducted is housing and urban renewal.[21] The Housing Act

[21] *Ibid.*, pp. 191 ff.

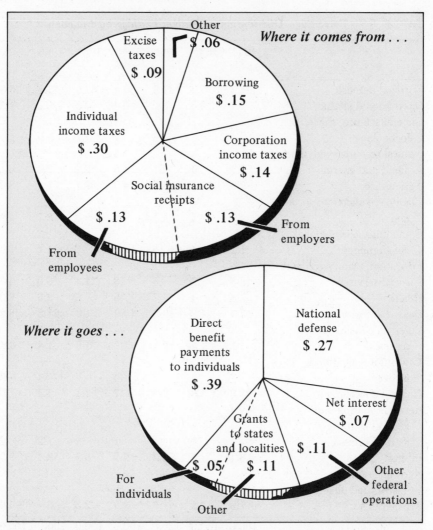

Source: Office of Management and Budget, *The Budget of the U.S. Government for Fiscal Year 1976* (Washington, D.C.: U.S. Government Printing Office, 1975), p. 2.

FIGURE 6.3

The Budget Dollar, Fiscal 1976 Estimate

of 1949 pledged decent housing for all, and more than $10 billion has been spent on urban renewal. Urban renewal has destroyed some 400,000 housing units that once housed the poor, but only 20,0000 units of public housing have been built in their place. More often, urban renewal has meant systematic exclusion of nonwhites and the construction of business or civic center facilities for use by entirely different classes of people. The real beneficiaries must be identified as the construction industry, real estate brokers, downtown businesses, and suburban dwellers—not those in need of housing or the original residents of the area.

It seems likely that similarly tracing the consequences of government expenditures intended to benefit the general public or the poor would show the real beneficiaries to be investors, builders, and other major units of the private economy. Where data are available on the usage of public services provided by government, such as education, health care, research information, and the like, the beneficiaries tend to be middle- and upper-class persons rather than the lower-class or poor people for whom such services are often said to be provided.

Another way to examine the purposes and beneficiaries of federal spending is offered by the Joint Economic Committee of the Congress.[22] Applying its concept of "tax expenditures" to the spending side of governmental fiscal activity, the Committee identified three other kinds of "subsidies" being provided by the government. *Subsidies* are payments or other assistance, *not* for services the recipients do for the government, but for the support of the ordinary and necessary business activities of private (mostly profit-making) companies or individuals. Thus, governmental purchase of military goods would not be considered a subsidy by this definition; only payments and other assistance for which the government got nothing in return would qualify. Even with this limited definition, the Committee found about $25 billion per year being distributed in cash, goods, or services to private businesses and individuals. Each of the three types of subsidies is briefly described and illustrated below.

1. *Cash subsidies.* These are direct payments from the U.S. Treasury, running upwards of $13 billion per year, designed to increase the profits or reduce the losses of various businesses. Cash subsidies also make up for airlines' losses, support construction of merchant shipping, send students to college, and support a wide variety of other activities. The government's program of farm price supports alone now costs nearly $10 billion per year. In order to protect farmers against price drops due to increasing production, the government instituted a program of supporting prices by purchasing some foods and paying farmers *not* to produce others. Once again, however, it is the largest farms that receive the overwhelming proportion of such subsidies; small family farms get very little assistance of this kind. One percent of all farms got 18 percent of all cash receipts in the 1960s, for example, while half of the farms in the country accounted for only 12 percent. In 1969, 396 farms received government checks for more than $100,000; twenty-five giant farms received checks ranging from $360,823 to $4,370,657. For the most part, the big winners from the price and crop-control programs are the cotton, wheat, and feed-grain growers of California, Arizona, and Mississippi.

2. *Credit subsidies.* These are low-interest loans for housing, farming, rural electrification, education, veterans' needs, hospital construction, and purchase of military supplies; and guarantees of privately issued

---

[22] Joint Economic Committee, *Federal Subsidy Programs.*

loans for an even wider variety of business activities. If the government makes a low-interest loan itself, it loses a proportion of the usual interest rate and thus, in effect, subsidizes the recipient by that amount. If the government guarantees or insures payment of a loan that is privately issued, it is using its credit to obtain something for the borrower that he or she could not otherwise obtain.

3. *Benefit-in-kind subsidies.* These are services provided by government to private companies or persons for which they would otherwise have to pay in some way. Grants of public lands, postal subsidies (absorption of much of the cost of running the Post Office or moving certain kinds of mail), airport construction, grants of the use of government-owned machinery, research and development services, information-gathering and other analytical services, and the like are of benefit to some but not to all. In fact, the Committee found, most of the recipients of these services are profit-making firms. If not provided by government, the services would have to be paid for by such firms at the cost of lower levels of profit.

Much of the expenditure we have identified, and all the tax advantages, appear to benefit the wealthier segments of the population. In effect, we have described the relationship between government and the top of the income-and-wealth pyramid. In the next section, which focuses on the problem of poverty, we shall examine the relationship between government and the bottom of the income-and-wealth pyramid.

Poverty and Welfare

A "Revolt" Against Taxes and Welfare

The taxing and spending policies and the welfare developments analyzed in this chapter are closely linked to each other, though not always in obvious ways. A so-called "tax revolt" that seemed to grow intense in 1978 tells a great deal about the nature of the links.

In June 1978, California voters approved a referendum measure known as "Proposition 13" by a 2:1 margin. Its effect was to reduce the state property tax, the chief source of income for local governments, by almost 60 percent. Surveys showed that national support for similar tax cuts was about as strong as it was in California.[23]

At the most obvious level of analysis, the support for such measures is easily explained. Middle class and working class taxpayers have been forced to pay higher and higher taxes, with the property tax one of the most visible. At the same time rising welfare costs and governmental

---

[23] *New York Times*–CBS News Poll, reported in the *New York Times,* June 8, 1978, p. 1.

waste seem obvious reasons for the increased need for revenue. In voting for tax cuts, people are asserting their wish to control government to limit fraud and waste while improving their own often desperate financial situations.

The analyst who looks more carefully at the reasons for the economic squeeze on taxpayers and at who benefits from the "revolt" notices some additional facts that suggest a somewhat different explanation. As our earlier analyses show, the tax system as a whole places its heaviest burden upon middle- and low-income groups; and in the 1970s these same people have been squeezed even harder by prices that have risen faster than most of their incomes. At the same time the welfare system must support two kinds of casualties of the economic system: millions of unemployed people (a 6 percent unemployment level has come to be regarded as "normal") and millions of the working poor. In effect, industry is relying on government, through the welfare system, to compensate for the inability of the economic system to provide jobs for all who are able and willing to work and to provide incomes that are adequate to support a family.

Still, the stark reality to the individual taxpayer is an increasingly tight family budget, higher taxes, higher prices, and constant claims of governmental waste and fraud, especially in administering welfare programs. He or she is understandably troubled, resentful, and easy to persuade that the tax burden is chiefly due to welfare and governmental waste, which are easier targets than price increases for which specific people cannot be blamed or defense expenditures the public is socialized to accept as necessary for national security. In California, conservative groups have played on these feelings, for the affluent are the chief beneficiaries of tax cuts of the Proposition 13 type, while they would be the chief losers if there were serious tax reform that eliminated loopholes.

About two-thirds of the tax savings in California will go to the corporations that own apartment houses and commercial property rather than to the individual homeowners who provided strong support for Proposition 13. Nor will the cutbacks in public services apply chiefly to welfare programs, which are largely funded by the federal government, though there will be some effect on them. Most cutbacks are being felt in the budgets for schools, police and fire protection, health, and recreation: services of great value to the lower class and the middle class. Initially, surpluses in the state treasury will cushion some of the impact.

Changes in federal taxes enacted in 1978 will similarly benefit the wealthy, while modest cuts in the tax rates for middle income groups will be offset or exceeded by steep increases in social security taxes.

The tax revolt and subsequent changes in taxing and spending demonstrate that the anxieties and resentments of people who are financially squeezed can be channelled to the wrong targets, contributing to the very inequalities that created the squeeze in the first place.

Who Are the Poor?

The extent of poverty in the United States depends on the definition used; and the definition always incorporates an arbitrary decision as to how few goods and services people must have available to them in order to be called poor. Since 1964 there has been an official definition of the "poverty line" based on cash income and the number of persons in the family; it is adjusted periodically as the cost of living rises. In 1975, when the poverty line was $5050 for a nonfarm family of four, approximately 27 million people were poor by that standard. Table 6.4 shows that the number of poor people in America, and how far they fell below the poverty line (a concept measured by the "poverty gap") declined somewhat in the decade of the 1960s and began rising again in 1973 as the unemployment rate increased sharply.

By the middle of the 1970s the unemployment rate was between 8 and 9 percent of the labor force, with little likelihood that it would decline very much for at least the next several years. Such severe recession is especially hard on the poor. A 1975 Brookings Institution study proved that every 1 percent increase in the national unemployment figures means a 4 percent increase for low-income groups.[24] But not all the poor are unemployed. In 1970, approximately 6,190,000 people, or 23.9 percent of the American poor, had jobs that did not pay well enough to raise them and their families above the poverty line.

One observer points out that "the Other America" of poor people can be viewed as an underdeveloped nation within the United States. As such, it would be exceeded in population, among the underdeveloped nations of the world, by only six nations. He continues:

> Of 19 Latin-American republics, only Brazil and Mexico were larger than our own "nation" of the poor. In Africa, only Nigeria had more people. All the rest of some 35 underdeveloped African countries had far fewer. There was no country in the Middle East as large; Egypt with 28 million came closest of the thirteen countries in that area. Our own internal "nation of the poor" has twice as many people as Canada. As a matter of fact, a separate nation of American poor would constitute the fifteenth largest nation of the world.[25]

The Bureau of Labor Statistics publishes three levels of budgets for families living in urban areas, imaginatively termed "lower," "intermediate," and "higher" budgets. These budgets are intended to represent the cost of living at these levels. The lower-level budget for an urban family of four in 1974 was $9,200, considerably higher than the Office of Economic Opportunity's "poverty line." By the former standard, between 40 and 50 million people were below the lower level and living in poverty.

[24] *New York Times*, 30 October 1975, p. 39.
[25] John C. Donovan, *The Politics of Poverty* (New York: Western Publishing Company, 1967), p. 96.

TABLE 6.4   *Size of Poverty Population and Poverty Gap and
Unemployment Rates and Median Family Income, 1959–1975*

Year	Number of Poor People (in millions)	Total Poverty Gap (in billions of 1971 dollars)	Unemployment Rate	Median Family Income in 1971 Dollars
1959	39.5	19.0	5.5	$ 7,524
1960	39.9	19.0	5.5	7,688
1961	39.6	19.2	6.7	7,765
1962	38.6	18.1	5.5	7,975
1963	36.4	17.1	5.7	8,267
1964	36.1	16.3	5.2	8,579
1965	33.2	14.9	4.5	8,932
1966	30.4	12.6	3.8	9,360
1967	28.5	12.8	3.8	9,683
1968	27.8	11.5	3.6	10,049
1969	25.4	11.3	3.5	10,423
1970	25.4	12.1	4.9	10,289
1971	25.6	12.6	5.9	10,280
1972	24.5	11.6	5.6	10,766
1973	23.0	10.9	4.9	10,983
1974	25.0 °	11.9 °	5.6	10,684 †
1975	27.1 °	13.6 °	8.7 †	10,273 †

° Figures for the number of poor people and the total poverty gap in 1974 and 1975 are estimated from the relationship of the size of the poverty population and gap to unemployment and average income during the years 1959–1973.

† The unemployment rate for 1975 is the Administration's prediction as of June 1975 of the average annual unemployment rate in 1975. The figures for median family income are our estimates. We assumed that median family income would fall by the same rate as per capita gross national product (GNP) in both 1974 and 1975. Per capita GNP fell by 2.8 percent in 1974 and the Administration as of June 1975 predicts a 3 percent fall in GNP in 1975, which is equal to approximately a 4 percent decline in per capita GNP.

Source: Irwin Garfinkel and Robert D. Plotnick, "Poverty, Unemployment, and the Current Recession," University of Wisconsin Institute for Research on Poverty, *Notes and Comments,* June 1975, mimeographed, p. 2.

The only available data on the poor use the official government definitions, however, and it is on these that our analysis must rest. The characteristics of the nation's poor in the early 1970s are outlined in Table 6.5. More than half the poor are either children or the elderly; of the working-age population, most are women. Thus children, the elderly, and women comprise about 80 percent of all poor persons. Nonwhites account for only about 11 percent of the nation's population, but 33 percent of the poor; nevertheless, almost seven out of every ten poor persons are white.

TABLE 6.5   *Characteristics of the Poverty-Level Population*

	Age				Race		
		Number	%			*Number*	%
Under 16	(1971)	9,917,000	38.8	White	(1971)	17,780,000	69.6
	(1973)	8,665,000	37.7		(1973)	15,142,000	65.9
	(1974)	9,320,000	38.4		(1974)	16,290,000	67.1
16–64	(1971)	10,990,000	43.0	Non-	(1971)	7,780,000	30.4
16–65	(1973)	10,955,000	52.3	white	(1973)	7,831,000	34.1
16–65	(1974)	11,632,000	48.0		(1974)	7,970,000	32.9
Over 64	(1971)	4,652,000	18.2				
Over 65	(1973)	3,354,000	14.6				
Over 65	(1974)	3,308,000	13.6				

Residence (in numbers of families)				Residence (in numbers of families)			
		Number	%			*Number*	%
Northeast	(1971)	916,000	17.3	Central Cities	(1971)	1,781,000	33.6
	(1973)	877,000	18.2		(1973)	1,753,000	36.3
					(1974)	1,827,000	35.8
North Central	(1971)	1,191,000	22.4	Suburbs	(1971)	1,189,000	22.4
	(1973)	1,005,000	20.8		(1973)	1,086,000	22.5
					(1974)	1,246,000	24.4
South	(1971)	2,356,000	44.4	Outside	(1971)	2,333,000	44.0
	(1973)	2,143,000	44.4	Metropolitan	(1973)	1,990,000	41.2
				Areas	(1974)	2,036,000	39.8
West	(1971)	840,000	15.8				
	(1973)	803,000	16.6				

Sources: U.S. Bureau of the Census, Current Population Report Series P-60, no. 98 (January 1975); no. 99 (July 1975).

Some other facts about the poor are worth noting.[26] Only 12 percent of all poor people who did not work were physically able to hold jobs, and most of these were mothers with small children. Only 1.5 percent of all nonworking poor people were able-bodied men. Thus, the poor—even those who are physically able to work—either cannot find jobs for which they are qualified, or are paid such low wages that they are unable to avoid poverty. One study, conducted by the Senate Subcommittee on Employment, Manpower and Poverty in 1971, found that more than 30 percent of all inner-city residents were paid less than the $80 per week

[26] The data in this paragraph are drawn from *U.S. News and World Report,* 14 August 1972, pp. 23–25.

required for a family of four to stay above the poverty line. Many of the families above the poverty line managed by having two or more working members. The Subcommittee identified 22 large cities where at least a third of the inner-city labor force was paid less than $80 per week.

Why are these people poor? Many factors contribute to poverty, but the two major ones are unemployment (or subemployment, which is defined as work at a part-time job or a job that pays less than one is qualified for) and racial discrimination. Unemployment among the poor usually runs well above the national average. Lacking education and skills, they are among the last hired and the first fired as the economy expands and contracts. For blacks the unemployment rate in 1975 was almost 14 percent, as opposed to 7.6 percent for whites. For young non-whites, figures over 35 percent are common in most large cities. As the Senate Subcommittee survey documents, low pay and a shortage of jobs reduce the likelihood that the poor can help themselves. Clearly, much of the explanation for low income and poverty is structural in character: that is, it has to do with the characteristics of the economic system and the racial biases of the society, rather than the personal failures of the poor.

In one sense, low income and poverty are consequences of the combined workings of the private economy and government policies for the last hundred years. For many years, slavery was enforced and defended by governments at all levels. After the Civil War, many public policies defended the rights of employers and promoted the opportunities of various businesses, while only a few aided workers or minorities. The dominant ethos of *laissez faire* ("hands off") in the private economy limited the capacity of government policy to benefit low-income people, though it did not inhibit self-interested actions on behalf of wealthy individuals or large corporations. Not until the Great Depression did federal social welfare programs seek to deal comprehensively with the problems of low-income persons.

Bills Swamp Non-Welfare Couple

Laurie Johnston

Beulah and Ralph Watkins did not know that a pothole lay ahead of their 1965 Oldsmobile as they were driving home through Queens Village after church and Sunday dinner at the home of friends.

"A river of rain was hiding that hole," Mrs. Watkins recalled in her bright, wry manner as she described an incident at Springfield Boulevard and Murdock Avenue. "My head hit the roof of the car twice, and I'm still going to the doctor for neck treatments."

The jolt was enough to break the couple's grasp, once again, on their personal will-o-the-wisp—financial solvency. As with countless blue-collar families who struggle to keep within their meager budgets, such things as a hidden pothole, a leaky roof or a steep medical bill can plunge them into red ink and desperation.

At the age of 59, Mrs. Watkins is not old enough for Medicare or quite poor enough for Medicaid, despite her chronic kidney disease and diabetes. "I have to go and fight with the clinic for some kind of reduced rate," she said.

In addition, the day she missed from work cost her half of the $60 a week she still earns doing part-time housework on Manhattan's Upper East Side—commuting nearly three hours a day.

Mr. Watkins, who is 68, gets a $58.94 monthly union pension as a retired plasterer and $212 in monthly Social Security payments. He needs a hernia operation, but he still owes $60 from three months in the hospital after stomach surgery last year.

"Every month, I think I can pay that bill," he said, "but some emergency always comes up."

In search of "some green and a little space," the couple left Harlem 10 years ago for an $18,500, three-bedroom house near the Queens Village-Hollis boundary. They were the fourth black family on their street.

Mrs. Watkins was making $80 a week as a full-time housekeeper, plus extra for serving at parties. Her husband earned at least $150 a week. Their daughter, Linda, was at Emma Willard Academy, a fairly exclusive girls' school in Troy, N.Y., on a scholarship. They themselves were able to pay for "about $1,000 worth of singing lessons" for her over the years, and she now sings with the Harlem Chorale.

The decade has left the family shaken, still proud and confirmed in a basic blue-collar belief: that society places more potholes in the precarious upward path of the struggling than it does for either the affluent or the indigent.

"We were always trying to better our lot," Mrs. Watkins said. "No gimmicks, just hard work. Welfare is degrading, but the working people who are not on welfare are caught in a tight economic squeeze. We're really being used. They keep us poor to keep others rich.

"Even the clinic says we must be doing all right—don't we have our own house?"

"I helped build the city," said Mr. Watkins, who now has Parkinson's disease, "East Side, West Side, the Bowery to the Bronx. I paid income tax, too." With a short laugh, he added, "I considered myself middle income. Now I'm not even working poor.

"But when the property tax goes up for Mr. Rockefeller, it goes up for me too. Ten years ago we paid $104 a month on this house. Now we pay $150, but I think only about a third of it goes to pay off the mortgage. The rest is for taxes and sewers and all that."

Mr. Watkins, self-supporting since he dropped out of the seventh grade, came to New York in 1926 from Virginia. Mrs. Watkins, who is from Louisiana, finished the ninth grade and "always wished for more."

Linda, 24 years old, attended Barnard College on a scholarship, dropped out

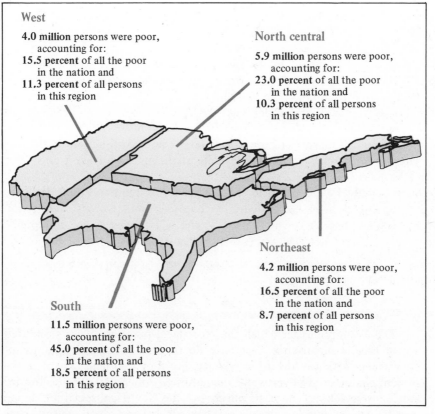

West

4.0 million persons were poor,
accounting for:
15.5 percent of all the poor
in the nation and
11.3 percent of all persons
in this region

North central

5.9 million persons were poor,
accounting for:
23.0 percent of all the poor
in the nation and
10.3 percent of all persons
in this region

Northeast

4.2 million persons were poor,
accounting for:
16.5 percent of all the poor
in the nation and
8.7 percent of all persons
in this region

South

11.5 million persons were poor,
accounting for:
45.0 percent of all the poor
in the nation and
18.5 percent of all persons
in this region

Source: Office of Equal Opportunity, *The Poor in 1970: A Chartbook* (Washington, D.C.: U.S. Government Printing Office, 1972), p. 21.

FIGURE 6.4

Geographic Distribution of the Poor

and now need only complete summer school to get a bachelor's degree in anthropology from Columbia.

"But what can you do with it without a Ph.D.?" she said. "And I'm tired."

In the carpeted living room, on the baby grand piano, a gift from a wealthy employer, an Emma Willard graduation picture shows a very "finishing school" Linda with straightened hair.

Recalling those days, she remarked: "That was a nice interlude—very plush and I wasn't used to that—even though I had to repeat English and history because I was so badly educated in Harlem."

Now Linda wears her hair Afro-style and talks longingly of a future in Senegal. But she has a 4-year-old son, Charles, from a broken marriage to a Columbia student who is now disabled. Charles lives with his grandparents during the week, and the family's most immediate worry is how to keep the boy in a city-sponsored day-care center so his grandmother can go on working.

The day-care center families are convinced that H.R.1, the Federal welfare reform bill passed by the House and now before the Senate, takes aim—as usual—at them, despite proposed Social Security increases.

"The new bill is designed to do away with the kind of center Charles is in," Mrs. Watkins said. "It won't be for community children, only for people on welfare, so the welfare families can work."

As a taxpayer, Mr. Watkins does not grudge pensions for policemen and firemen—"those fellows gamble their lives for us"—but he sometimes wishes he had worked for the city instead of for private contractors. And he wishes the city would come up with some tax relief "to help us maintain and hang on to our property."

He once thought he could sell his house "for a few thousand more than we paid," since he built a patio and added other improvements. Now it needs paint, gutters and leaders, and he can no longer do the work himself. The collapse of the old heating system last year put him $1,000 in debt for a new one.

Source: The New York Times, 2 July 1972. Copyright © 1972 by the New York Times Company. Reprinted by permission.

The assumptions on which the New Deal programs were structured are of crucial importance. Not only do they still shape the pattern of government action in regard to poverty, but they also help to explain the present character of poverty and the nature of American attitudes toward ameliorative action. The basic purpose of the New Deal social legislation was to protect individuals against hazards beyond their control—both natural and biological hazards (aging, blindness) and economic hazards (unemployment, disability through accident on the job). The assumption was that if individuals were given certain minimal assurances of economic security, a revived and prosperous economy would do the rest.

Thus, the basic approach was a series of *social insurance* programs (a federal system of old-age, survivors', disability, and health insurance; and a federal-state system of unemployment insurance) for which working people and their employers would pay throughout their working lives. Men and women in eligible occupations were entitled to benefits, the amounts of which were based chiefly on their earnings while employed.

Supplementing these systems, on what was assumed to be a temporary basis, were *public assistance* or "welfare" programs, assisting the blind, disabled, elderly, families with dependent children, and others; these programs were administered by the states but utilized federal funds to a great extent. They were expected to "wither away" as an expanding economy drew more and more people back to work and social insurance programs were expanded.

Under a strictly temporary program of government employment, many new public works—bridges, highways, public buildings, and the like—were built. The rights to form unions and to engage in collective bargaining were also protected by new laws. The final major component of this package of policies was minimum-wage legislation, which required employers in certain fields to pay at least the specified minimum hourly wage to all employees.

Throughout, the assumption was that the minimum needs of the population could be met adequately by the workings of a reasonably prosperous economy, provided only that some minimum protections were legally established. There was no provision for assistance to those who did not work, except under stringent conditions. Due to fear that the incentive to work might otherwise be weakened, or that moral damage might be inflicted, public assistance programs required that disability or destitution be proven as conditions for receiving aid.

The social insurance programs, chief among which is social security, have for the most part fulfilled expectations. About 138 million people now contribute to social security, and 90 percent of the population aged 65 and over is eligible for monthly social security benefits. In 1973, a monthly average of 28 million people received benefits of $45 billion. A very large proportion of employed people now have protection against loss of income from several important causes. In 1971, 8 million people received $5.2 billion in unemployment compensation. The benefits are not adequate to enable most people to support themselves without further income, and are paid only to those who have previously paid into these funds.

The public assistance programs, however, have not lived up to expectations. Not only has there been no "withering away," but the numbers of people in need of such assistance has steadily increased. And the costs of these welfare programs have multiplied rapidly. The most dramatic rise has occurred in the large cities, and in the category of Aid to Families with Dependent Children (AFDC). Between 1961 and 1973 the number of families receiving AFDC increased from 916,000 to 3,152,000. Most of this increase occurred in the years after 1967, as a result partly of inflation and economic recession and partly of amendments to the law and court decisions that liberalized eligibility and benefits. In New York City in 1975, almost 11 percent of the population was on AFDC; the figure in Boston was 14.5 percent and in St. Louis and Baltimore more than 15 percent.[27] The total number of persons on welfare in the nation in 1973 was over 25 million and the total costs for public assistance exceeded $21 billion.

At the beginning of 1974 a somewhat more generous kind of welfare program went into effect for the aged, the blind, and the disabled—three classes of recipients some conservatives and some legislators regard as more deserving than the women and children under AFDC who are not destitute due to disability. The new Supplemental Security Income Plan (SSI) guarantees an income floor of $2500 for a couple, both federal

[27] Mitchell I. Ginsberg, "New York's Welfare Problem," *The New York Times*, 28 October 1975, p. 33.

and state governments contributing to the payment. If a recipient works, the SSI contribution is reduced by half the amount she or he earns; people earning more than about $6,000 a year are not eligible for SSI benefits. If a recipient has "unearned" income, such as social security benefits, the SSI contribution is reduced by the full amount of such benefits. Recipients do not have to prove inability to work or that no relative could support them (AFDC recipients must prove both, at least in theory). But most people claiming SSI benefits lose their eligibility for food stamps. The makeup of the welfare population is similar to that of the poverty-level population, for obvious reasons. Nearly 60 percent are children, and another 19 percent are their mothers; these stark proportions suggest the contribution of AFDC to the rising costs of the program. Another 16 per-

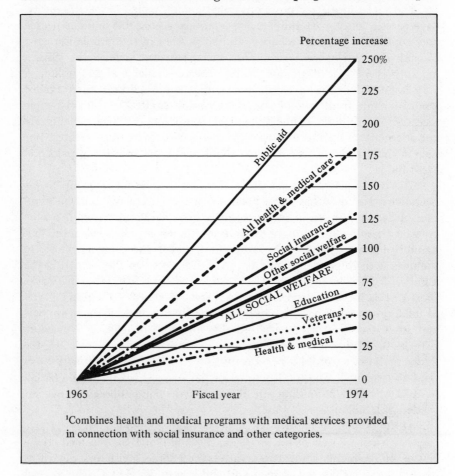

¹Combines health and medical programs with medical services provided in connection with social insurance and other categories.

Source: Alfred M. Skolnick and Sophie R. Dales, "Social Welfare Expenditures, Fiscal Year 1974," *Social Security Bulletin,* January 1975, p. 12.

FIGURE 6.5

Per Capita Social Welfare Expenditures Under Public Programs, in Constant Dollars

cent are aged, and 9 percent are blind or disabled. Less than 1 percent of welfare recipients are able-bodied men.

The costs of welfare shot up in the 1960s for several reasons. One was that the number of eligible families and children increased. Another was that the level of payments increased. Between 1965 and 1970, payments rose 19 percent. According to one set of experts, the most important reason was that welfare was used as a means of reducing discontent and as a direct response to urban rioting.[28] In any event, the greatest increase occurred between 1965 and 1970. During the 1960s the population increased 13 percent, but the welfare rolls went up 94 percent and the number of families receiving AFDC more than doubled. Still, many poor people do not qualify for welfare payments. And the kinds and amounts of benefits vary greatly among the states. In 1973 AFDC benefits for a family of four ranged from $375 per month in Alaska to $60 in Mississippi.

The Current Policy Dilemma

From one end of the political spectrum to the other, there is intense dissatisfaction with AFDC. Some resent its cost and believe that it discourages recipients from working. Others point to its failure to provide aid for many who need it, the inadequate benefits it provides, and the repressive administrative practices that control the number and behavior of claimants and stigmatize them in the process. Its unpopularity and ineffectiveness have given rise to several forms of supplemental "welfare reform." Each of these deserves consideration, for they imply far-reaching change in the whole system of public policy toward low-income people.

One political consequence of the unrest of the 1960s was enactment in 1964 of the Economic Opportunity Act, the so-called "War on Poverty." Chiefly through community action agencies established in approximately 1000 communities, programs providing educational, vocational, medical, legal, and other social welfare services were initiated. But by 1972 it was apparent that this "war" had generated a great deal of talk and political controversy, several programs that had had an impact on small numbers of the poor, but only a relatively small investment of money and other resources—an investment that represented experimentation rather than an effort to eliminate or substantially reduce poverty. Most program funds were cut back sharply or eliminated in the late 1960s. The more important continuing programs offer "in-kind" services to the poor to supplement cash assistance.

Benefits to the poor in forms other than money are justified politically on several grounds: that some recipients cannot be trusted to spend money as they should; that some goods and services can be offered more efficiently in the form of in-kind programs; that these programs benefit the suppliers of the commodities and services offered; and that they are less

---

28 For an elaboration of this point, see Frances Fox Piven and Richard A. Cloward, *Regulating the Poor: The Functions of Public Welfare* (New York: Random House, 1971).

likely than cash grants to discourage the poor from working. Though there is good reason to doubt the validity of most of these arguments, in-kind benefits have increased sharply in recent years.

The least effective in-kind programs have been such "social services" as counselling, family planning, and manpower training. Resented by many poor people as demeaning or pointless, counselling is now stressed less than efforts to prepare the poor for work. Attempts at "rehabilitation rather than relief" have done more to frustrate the poor than to help them, especially in a time of high unemployment.

Other in-kind programs provide necessities. People certified as eligible by a local welfare agency can buy food stamps at a price below their face value; but the food stamp program has never enrolled even a majority of the people eligible for it. A study by a Congressional committee found that 37 million persons had sufficiently meager financial resources to be eligible for food stamps in March 1974, but only 13.6 million actually received the stamps. Even considering the nearly 2 million people receiving food directly under a commodity distribution program, only a little more than 40 percent of the eligible population was benefiting.[29] Though the failure of so many people to claim their rights is due chiefly to ignorance about the stamp program, many simply cannot afford to buy the stamps, even at a reduced rate. In late 1974 and the first half of 1975, the number of food stamp recipients increased rapidly to more than 19 million, due to a liberalization of eligibility and some rise in unemployment; but there were still about as many eligible people not using food stamps as using them.

TABLE 6.6   *Food Stamp Participation Rates for Selected States, 1974*

State	Percentage of Eligibles Using Food Stamps
Illinois	57.0
Kansas	14.7
Louisiana	51.9
Michigan	61.6
Minnesota	37.3
Mississippi	44.3
Wisconsin	24.4

Source: Gary Bickel and Maurice MacDonald, "Participation Rates in the Food Stamp Program: Estimated Levels, by State" *Institute for Research on Poverty Discussion Paper No. 253–75*, Table 1, p. 16.

[29] Gary Bickel and Maurice MacDonald, "Participation Rates in the Food Stamp Program: Estimated Levels, by State," University of Wisconsin Institute for Research on Poverty, *Discussion Paper 253–75*, January 1975, mimeograph, p. 1.

The surplus commodity distribution program requires no cash, but recipients cannot choose what they receive, and balanced diets are hard to achieve. A national school lunch program provides lunches free or at reduced prices to children certified by local officials as unable to pay the full price.

While they unquestionably help, these programs also present problems. Because of the "means test," they stigmatize recipients. Some localities choose not to participate, which is especially likely to hurt the rural poor. A study published late in 1972 found that half of the country's 25 million poor people were still going hungry; 43 percent were getting no federal help with food.[30] Meanwhile, some critics of the food stamp program were concerned in the middle 1970s that it covered too many people; demands were made that the program be cut back to eliminate from eligibility anyone with an income above the poverty line.

Everyone over sixty-five is covered by the Medicare program, which pays some, but far from all, the costs of medical services. The program has been of substantial benefit to the elderly, both poor and middle class, but covers only about 40 percent of their health costs. Far more controversial has been Medicaid, which offers a federal subsidy to the states for medical aid to the poor of all ages. Because of rising costs, Congress has sharply cut back both the quality of Medicaid benefits and the number of people eligible for them. Medicaid has not been an effective program, and has spawned abuses by some physicians who pad their costs and refusals to participate by others because it pays less for their services than does Medicare.

There are other in-kind programs. Federal housing assistance rose sharply in the 1960s, but helped the working poor more than it did welfare recipients and did not go far toward meeting the overall housing need. Legal aid has also been useful, but politically controversial and trivial in comparison to the demand. In some cases it provided the interesting spectacle of lawyers paid by one government agency (the Office of Economic Opportunity) to challenge in court the denial by other government agencies of benefits to the poor. Under such programs as Headstart and Upward Bound, poor children have been given special educational opportunities to try to compensate for the disadvantages with which they start their educational careers.

Though every significant sector of the American public is dissatisfied with the motley set of welfare programs in effect, and especially with the rise in the welfare rolls, there are sharp differences over what to do about it. The effort that has received most attention has been to provide work incentives for AFDC recipients. In 1967 the law was amended to provide small payments for participation in job-training programs and to enable welfare recipients who find jobs to retain some of their welfare benefits if their total incomes remain low. Experience with the WIN (Work Incentive) program was disappointing; it did little

---

[30] *The New York Times,* 27 October 1972, p. 22.

either to encourage job training or to provide jobs for people on welfare. In 1971 the WIN program was made compulsory for every able-bodied person on AFDC aged 16 or over, except some specifically exempted groups such as mothers of children under the age of six. The 1971 amendments also encouraged the states to force recipients to work by providing more federal funding and making funds available for a relatively small number of public-service jobs.

Opponents of this emphasis on "workfare" are convinced it will continue to be ineffective because only a very small percentage of recipients are physically able to hold jobs. Also, research has demonstrated that welfare recipients are already eager to work if they can only find jobs.[31] The basic problems, according to opponents, are high unemployment and the number of jobs paying so little that those who hold them remain poor. It is, they argue, the failure of the economy to provide enough jobs and to pay adequate wages that creates the need for welfare, not individual laziness or the character of the welfare programs. In this view, the chief function served by work requirements is psychological: to create and reinforce the belief that welfare recipients do not want to work.

Those who see the problem as primarily economic, rather than psychological, and who do not like to vest arbitrary power over recipients in bureaucrats, favor automatic "income maintenance" programs under which a minimum income is guaranteed to all American families. An approach winning support from some conservatives, as well as many liberals, would establish a "negative income tax"—an arrangement whereby families with incomes under the poverty line would receive money from the government in amounts sufficient to maintain a subsistence standard of living. As an incentive to work, the grants would be decreased by *less* than a recipient earns so long as his or her total income is under a fixed amount. Some favor allowances to families for the support of children. Another income maintenance proposal would assure government jobs to those unable to find work in the private sector. A public-service employment program was initiated in 1974 in response to the extremely high unemployment rate then prevailing, but it rations relatively few jobs among a very large number of eligible people, and so is largely of token value. Behind all these elaborate proposals, of course, is the stark fact that the transfer of only 1 percent of the national income—$10 billion—would raise *all* of the nation's poor above the poverty line.[32] Meanwhile the very concept of a poverty line that distinguishes the poor from the nonpoor is also under attack. Poverty can be defined as the inability to enjoy goods and services available to many

---

[31] *Cf.* Leonard Goodwin, *Do the Poor Want to Work? A Social-Psychological Study of Work Orientations* (Washington: Brookings Institution, 1972).

[32] Sar A. Levitan, Martin Rein, and David Marwick, *Work and Welfare Go Together* (Baltimore and London: Johns Hopkins Press, 1972), p. ix. For recently published accounts and evaluations of American welfare policy, see this book and also Bruno Stein, *On Relief: The Economics of Poverty and Public Welfare* (New York: Basic Books, 1972).

others, regardless of the absolute amount one has. In this sense it is gross *inequality* that defines poverty, making it a social as well as an economic condition.

Social Policy and Income Distribution

Average family incomes have grown larger in the period since World War Two, even after being adjusted for price increases, but this improvement is partly the result of an increase in the number of workers per family, especially the number of working women. Also, because the growing labor force participation of women (one result of the feminist movement) comes largely from middle- and upper-middle-income families, it will increase the income spread between the rich and the poor.[33] Since the sixties there has been a significant decline in poverty and in income differences based on race, color, and region, due partly to governmentally provided or subsidized medical care, food, housing and other in-kind services. However, the average earnings of women declined relative to those of males in this period because most women entered low-paying jobs.[34]

At the same time, neither the War on Poverty nor other economic policies have significantly reduced *inequality* in income or in wealth. It seems unlikely that any set of antipoverty policies will do that, partly because they have only limited effects in raising the income of the poorest section of the population, partly because they often help the affluent more than the poor. A reduction in inequality is possible only if increased public expenditures that benefit non-elites are financed by tax reforms that impose higher tax rates on people with high incomes. Because public officials typically assume that they must limit expenditures for health, welfare, and education programs and must keep effective tax rates for the wealthy low, a set of policies that would make for greater equality has not been regarded as politically feasible.

[33] Robert H. Haveman, "Poverty, Income Distribution, and Social Policy: The Last Decade and the Next," *Public Policy* 25 (Winter 1977), p. 15.

[34] Sheldon H. Danziger and Robert J. Lampman, "Getting and Spending," *Annals of the American Academy of Political and Social Science* 435 (January 1978), pp. 30–31.

7

The Status of Racial Minorities

Racial minorities—blacks, native Americans (American Indians), Chicanos and Puerto Ricans, Asians, and others—are at the bottom of the American social and economic pyramid. That this is the case because of centuries of often deliberate and systematic discrimination and exploitation by both governmental and private forces can be stated bluntly today, although it would have seemed extreme or provocative only a decade ago. In the last fifteen years, primarily due to the insistence of minorities themselves, there has been growing recognition of the status of minorities in the United States. Some of the many resulting governmental and private efforts to enhance their opportunities have been effective, and in several ways minorities' progress has been significant.

But such progress has also served to bring into focus the depth and complexity of the problem of racial minorities in the United States. Racism is deeply embedded in American culture, and erects barriers far more difficult to surmount than those faced by European immigrant groups in the past. Moreover, governmental undertakings to assist minorities have run up against serious obstacles with roots in the character of American society itself. Even with the best intentions, there is only so much public policies can do in a capitalist and property-conscious society to advance the economic and social status of an entire group promptly and substantially. We have not yet approached those boundaries, but even the modest acts undertaken so far have generated considerable—and sometimes violent—resistance from a great many people. Finally, some members of each racial minority seek not only full participation in the existing American system, but also legitimacy and autonomy for the perspectives, values, and way of life of their culture. In effect, they seek to live in their own way, even though it may be inconsistent with the values and practices of other groups.

This chapter, therefore, will focus both on the conditions of minorities today and on the problem exposed by efforts to improve those conditions —the gap between minorities' needs and goals and what American society offers them. The policies that brought about the present situation will be briefly reviewed first. After we have characterized the conditions, needs, and goals of minorities, current policies and their consequences will be examined.

Four Centuries of Public Policies Toward Minorities

What have governments done with respect to nonwhite races on the American continent—and why? And what have their acts meant, not only for the affected minorities, but also for the dominant society? We will touch only on certain basic policies, to illustrate generalized and long-established practices.

Indians

When Columbus "discovered" America, there were probably about 1 million persons living on the North American continent. Believing himself to have reached India, Columbus mislabelled those he met "Indians"; this was to be the first of many instances of Europeans' failure to understand native Americans except on their own terms. The "Indians" of the time were highly diverse peoples, but they shared the beliefs that land was a resource for all to share, and that man should live in harmony with nature, appropriating only those animals needed for food and clothing. As waves of land-hungry white settlers arrived, the Indian was introduced to the concepts of private ownership of land and the use of nature for commercial purposes (e.g., fur trapping). Indian lands were either "bought," acquired by means of governmental decrees or soon-violated treaties, or despoiled by the hunting and trapping of commercially oriented whites.

By 1840 Indians had been displaced from practically all their lands east of the Mississippi. In some cases, broken treaties were accompanied by forced marches (or "removals") in which thousands of Indians were resettled further west because their remaining lands were wanted by whites. In a series of "Indian Wars," thousands of Indians were killed, injured, or rendered homeless to make first the South and then the West available for commercial and homesteading opportunities. On the Great Plains, millions of buffalo were slaughtered by white hunters for commercial purposes, depriving the Indians of their major source of food and hides. Indians were confined to reservations on then-unwanted lands, and caught between the Army's urge to exterminate them completely and the Bureau of Indian Affairs' preference for simply managing their affairs and making good Americans out of them.

By 1900 displacement, removals, wars, and disease had reduced the Indian population to one sixteenth its original size. Reservation schools enforced the dominant society's customs and religions, preventing Indians from knowing their own heritage. Not until 1924 was the right to vote extended to Indians, and other forms of political redress have been unavailable or ineffective. Many treaties made over the years were broken to serve the needs or desires of governments and private economic interests.

Blacks

The first blacks arrived on the American continent in 1619 and were sold as slaves in Virginia. Slavery was incorporated into the legal structure of the Southern colonies somewhat later in the seventeenth century. Jefferson's proposal to abolish slavery found no place in the Declaration of Independence's glowing language about the rights of men, and the Constitution specifically provided for representation based on slave-holding and for protection of the slave traffic for a period of years. Slavery was too important to the economic and social structure of the Southern states, and too fully in accord with general beliefs in the North as well, to be seen as inconsistent with the assumptions and goals of either document.

The abolition of slavery, accomplished during the Civil War, did little to change the practical effects of previous policies. The war was justified as a means of preventing the spread of slavery to the new Western states—that is, of keeping the territories free for the wage-earning white working man. The Emancipation Proclamation was thus a tactical act of warfare as well as a principled policy. The Fourteenth and Fifteenth Amendments to the Constitution were intended as much to build the political strength of the struggling Republican Party as to assure freedom for blacks. The swift passage of Jim Crow segregation laws, whose constitutionality was confirmed by the Supreme Court in the famous case *Plessy* v. *Ferguson* (1896), officially and legitimately subjected black people to a condition only abstractly better than slavery.

Official segregation continued to be the law of the land until 1954, when a well-orchestrated legal campaign by blacks finally caused the Supreme Court to rule segregated education unconstitutional. The federal government practiced segregation in the armed forces until after World War Two. Aside from these official policies, governments at all levels condoned or practiced systematic discrimination against blacks. Educational systems were not only segregated and unequal, but actually taught that blacks were inferior; other agencies and activities of governments were almost equally "white only."

Chicanos

Spanish explorers, settlers, and missionaries were the first whites to enter New Mexico, Texas, and California, in the late sixteenth, seventeenth, and eighteenth centuries respectively. Contacts with the surrounding Indians of the Southwest and with Mexico, where the Spanish had intermarried with Aztecs and other Indians, led eventually to a mixed Spanish-Indian-Mexican population in these areas. In some cases, vast landholdings existed in relative isolation.

And then came the Anglos, or English-speaking North Americans. The influx of Americans into Texas was followed by the acquisition of the entire Southwest in the Mexican War. The people now known as Chicanos, or Mexican-Americans, owe their status as Americans chiefly to this conquest, and particularly to the Treaty of Guadalupe Hidalgo in 1848. The treaty confirmed all existing land titles as it granted the ostensible subjects of Mexico living in those areas American citizenship, but in the words of one historian, "Mexicans quickly became the Negroes of the Southwest." [1] Although they were not officially slaves, the conditions of peonage and officially condoned discrimination were not far from slavery. Land was taken from them, stock stolen, voting rights denied, and physical violence employed to intimidate and prevent efforts at redress.

The discovery of gold in California led to the rapid Anglicization of that territory, and once again the Mexican-origin population was displaced and reduced to near-peonage. In both law and practice, the Republic and then the State of California aided the rapid private

[1] Paul Jacobs, Saul Landau, and Eve Pell, *To Serve the Devil: Volume 1, Natives and Slaves* (New York: Random House, 1971), p. 237.

exploitation of a captive population while denying them effective redress. Not until the advent of mass farming techniques and the resulting need for cheap labor were Mexican-origin people in demand, and then only as the lowest form of laborers. Whenever they were not needed, Mexicans and Mexican-origin people were uprooted from their homes and deported.

The Mexican-origin population of New Mexico and Arizona was incorporated into the American system somewhat later. Lack of resources or of opportunities for development kept rural areas essentially unchanged until the end of the nineteenth century, and in some cases later. At that time, a somewhat modernized version of the familiar process began. In time family land titles were completely replaced by Anglo ownership, and Anglo forms of organization were imposed on whole communities.

Puerto Ricans

The Puerto Rican population, concentrated principally in major East Coast cities, is the other major, though smaller, group of Spanish-speaking Americans. The island of Puerto Rico was also acquired by conquest, in the Spanish-American War of 1898. Although legally American citizens since 1917, Puerto Ricans have suffered from the same officially condoned and systematic peonage and discrimination as have Chicanos. The lack of economic opportunities on their native island has led many to seek jobs in New York, Philadelphia, and Boston, where until quite recently they were ignored by governments at all levels.

Asians

Asians have been subject to governmental policies that, though inconsistent, have always condoned private discrimination and exploitation. In the nineteenth century, for example, thousands of Chinese were imported as cheap labor to build railroads; when no longer needed (and when white workers' demands that they be prevented from undercutting wage levels led to riots and lynchings), they were excluded by law in 1882. The same exclusion applied to Japanese after 1907. California's land laws prevented Asians from acquiring title to property for many years. And during World War Two, the federal government uprooted American citizens of Japanese descent from their homes and businesses to relocate them in camps in Utah and Nevada, fearing they might be disloyal.

Why has there been a consistent pattern of discriminatory public policies toward racial minorities? Neither economic necessity nor racism is a sufficient answer in itself, though both are major factors—independent but mutually reinforcing. It is not necessary to speculate on which is more important, or whether economic interests lead to an increase of racism. It is enough to see that neither could function without the other. A recent history sums up four centuries of American policy as follows:

The colonizers came to the New World believing that colored people were inferior, and used that ideology to justify the enslavement of blacks, the killing of Indians and Mexicans, and the importation of Oriental labor for work considered unfit for whites. The identification of colored skin with evil, with the devil, with inferiority, infused the entire culture of the Anglo-Saxons during the first centuries of colonization.

In each case, the racism coincided with economic need for slave labor and for land. At the same time, racist attitudes were institutionalized as laws, religion, and everyday practice. Each school child learned, along with the principles of republicanism and democracy, about the inferiority of colored people. Ministers explained to their flocks that slavery was God's will.

Racist law and racist behavior became an integral part of American culture. . . . Racist attitudes not only made whites feel superior by virtue of their skin color; it also made all colored, colonized people feel inferior because of their skin color . . .[2]

As this passage implies, it is not only minorities who experience the consequences of racially discriminatory public policies. Dominant groups are also deeply affected, both in the circumstances of their individual and social lives, and in the ideology and mythology they accept. Belief in the superiority of whites and the "natural" inferiority of other races can come to serve as an underlying principle of social order. Without a myth of this kind, no discriminatory public policy can long persist; and the institutionalization of the myth in such policies serves in turn to sustain it. If today most whites concede that they are not biologically superior to other races, they still tend to believe that they are socially, economically, and/or culturally superior. And some members of racial minorities have also come to believe in the supremacy of whites and white culture. Once established, this myth penetrates all levels of society and serves to justify subordination as well as supremacy. Many in the dominant society do not even realize that their actions reflect such assumptions. They may believe that they are merely "following the rules" or being "realistic" or "practical." Yet their actions are essentially racist because they cannot escape assumptions.

But the effects of racial myths are the least visible consequences of American policies toward minorities. More readily apparent are the actual social and economic conditions of such minorities today.

The Contemporary Circumstances of Minorities

That minorities share low levels of education, income, and employment is increasingly clear from research. We shall not undertake an exhaustive catalogue here, in part because the conditions, atti-

[2] *Ibid.*, p. xxi.

tudes, and behavior of minorities are discussed at appropriate points elsewhere in this book. We shall touch only on certain basic characteristics of the black, Spanish-speaking, and Indian populations, emphasizing in each case those features that are distinctive to each minority. Not all the deprivation experienced by minorities is accounted for by the social and economic gaps visible in these data, however. To concentrate exclusively on these tangible aspects of minority status is to ignore the important point that minorities' difficulties derive partly from less tangible factors, particularly the distinctive way each minority looks at the world. Thus, in a sense, the characterizations that follow are preliminary to the effort to understand the differences in cultures and values that distinguish minorities from the dominant society.

Blacks

As the nation's largest minority, blacks have for many years set the pace in minorities' struggles for recognition and status. In 1973 blacks comprised 11.3 percent of the American population. The black population as a whole is both younger and growing faster than the white population: the black population increased at the rate of 19.6 percent between 1960 and 1970, compared to 11.9 percent for whites. In 1970 blacks accounted for 13.8 percent of the population under fifteen. Increasingly, blacks are concentrated in the cities: in 1970 they comprised 21 percent of all center-city residents, a rise of more than 4 percent since 1960; the same year blacks accounted for 27 percent of all center-city residents under fifteen years of age. Twenty-five major American cities, only seven of which are in the South, have more than 100,000 blacks.

The migration patterns of black people, which constitute one of the major social phenomena of the twentieth century, are characterized by a general movement from agricultural to industrial jobs, and also by a movement away from the South toward the big cities of the North and Midwest. Between 1960 and 1970, as the trend continued, three cities (New York, Chicago, and Los Angeles) all had net gains of more than 100,000 blacks. New York drew a net increase of 435,000 black residents. Other cities had similar increases in black proportions. The dramatic increases in the proportions of blacks are not solely due to black in-migration; they also reflect the exodus of whites from the central cities. This observation does not undermine the basic point, however: the proportion of blacks in the South is dropping steadily and the actual number of blacks outside the South has increased sharply. Between 1960 and 1970, the number of blacks in the Northeast increased by 43 percent; in the North Central states, by 33 percent. There is no escaping the implication that these migration patterns are combining with other factors to concentrate the black minority in the nation's major cities. This fact has profound import for future urban, transportation, and welfare policies.

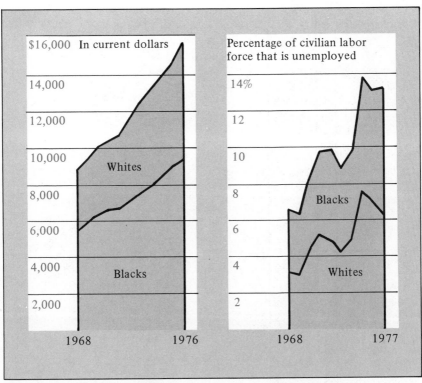

Source: (Left) Bureau of the Census. *(Right)* Bureau of Labor Statistics.

FIGURE 7.1

Median Family Income *(left)* and Unemployment Rates *(right)* Compared.

But perhaps the most distinctive feature of black peoples' lives in the United States is the extent to which they trail whites in income, employment status, and educational attainments. In Chapter 6, we noted the gaps between the median incomes of white and black men, and the extent to which white and black women trailed both. There are many more blacks at the lowest levels, and a substantial number of whites (but almost no blacks) at the very highest income levels. In the case of women, the curves are more similar: most women of both races are concentrated at the lowest pay levels, and only a very few white women are at the highest ranks.

Tables 7.1 and 7.2 provide background information about the non-European American ethnic groups and compare them with the white population. It is apparent that blacks, Indians, and Spanish-speaking Americans are the largest and the poorest of these groups, and so our analysis focuses chiefly on them.

TABLE 7.1 *Population and Distribution of American Ethnic Groups, 1970*

	Popu-lation	% in North East	% in North Central	% in South	% in West	% Urban	% Rural Nonfarm	% Rural Farm
Chinese	431,583	27	9	7	57	97	3	<1
Japanese	588,324	7	7	5	81	89	9	2
Filipino	336,731	9	8	9	74	85	13	1
Hawaiian	99,958							
Korean	69,510							
Mexican	4,532,435	1	8	37	53	86	13	2
Puerto Rican	1,429,396	81	9	4	5	98	2	<1
Cuban	544,600	32	6	52	10	98	2	<1
American Indian	763,594	6	19	25	50	45	49	6
Black	22,549,815	19	20	53	8	81	17	2
White	178,107,190	25	29	28	17	72	23	6

Source: United States Census, 1970.

TABLE 7.2 *Nativity, Education, Income, and Unemployment of American Ethnic Groups, 1970*

	% Foreign Born	% Not U.S. Citizens	Median Years School (25 +)	% High School Graduates	Median Family Income	% of Families Below Poverty Line	Unemployment Rate Male	Unemployment Rate Female
Chinese	47		12.4	58	$10,610	10	3.0%	3.7%
Japanese	21		12.5	69	12,515	6	2.0	3.0
Filipinos	53		12.2	55	9,318	12	4.7	4.7
Hawaiian	1		12.1	53			5.1	5.6
Korean	54		12.9	71			3.6	5.4
Mexican	18	11	8.1	24	6,962	24	6.1	8.9
Puerto Rican	1	< 1	8.7	23	6,165	27	5.6	8.7
Cuban	82	62	10.3	44	8,529	13	4.3	7.3
American Indian	2		9.8	33	5,832	33	11.6	10.2
Black	1		9.8	31	6,067	30	6.3	7.7
White	5		12.1	54	9,961	9	3.6	4.8

Source: United States Census, 1970.

In recent years sexual inequality in employment has been more serious than inequality based upon color. Between 1962 and 1972 both racial and sexual inequalities decreased, but sexual inequality was greater at both the start and the end of the period. It is lower for blacks than for whites.[3]

Black–white differences in educational attainment remain substantial. In 1973, 19.8 percent of all persons between the ages of 25 and 29 had not completed four years of high school; but fully 35.8 percent of blacks in that age bracket had not done so. In the same year, 19 percent of all Americans had completed four or more years of college, but only 8.1 percent of blacks had done so.[4]

Spanish-Speaking Americans (Primarily Chicanos and Puerto Ricans)

The second-largest American minority group is loosely classified as Spanish-speaking. We here treat this group as a racial minority for the powerful reason that it consists primarily of persons who identify themselves as Mexican-Americans or Chicanos, referring to their mixed Spanish, Mexican, and Indian origins. Some Puerto Ricans, too, trace their origins to the mixture of Spanish, West Indian, and black strains. But analysis is rendered difficult by the fact that nearly all Spanish-speaking persons are officially classified by the Census Bureau as white. Their only readily identifiable shared characteristic is the propensity to speak Spanish as their native, home, or family language. And, as we shall see, Spanish-speaking Americans also share a certain level of poverty and deprivation.

Table 7.3, an official Census Bureau table, shows the breakdown of Spanish-speaking people into major categories, of which the Mexican or Chicano is by far the largest. Including those "other Spanish" who are probably Mexican in origin, the number of Chicanos approaches 6.5 million. Puerto Ricans number approximately another 1.5 million, perhaps more. Most Chicanos live in the five southwestern states (Texas, California, New Mexico, Arizona, and Colorado), and to some extent in the Midwest south of and including Chicago. The majority of Puerto Ricans is, as we have said, located in the northeastern coastal cities.

Black and Spanish-Speaking Americans: Some Comparisons with Whites

By undertaking special analyses, the Census Bureau has finally begun to sort out the characteristics of minority groups, certain of which are

---

[3] David L. Featherman and Robert M. Hauser, "Trends in Occupational Mobility by Race and Sex in the United States, 1962–1972." University of Wisconsin Institute for Research on Poverty discussion paper 239–74, November 1974. Mimeographed.

[4] *Statistical Abstract of the United States, 1974,* p. 116.

TABLE 7.3   *"Spanish Origin" Population, 1969 and 1974 (in thousands)*

		United States		The Five Southwestern States		Southwest as % of
		Number	*Percent*	*Number*	*Percent*	U.S.
Mexican	1969	5,073	55.0	4,360	79.2	85.9
	1974	6,455	59.8	5,453	86.3	84.5
Puerto Rican	1969	1,454	15.8	61	1.1	4.2
	1974	1,548	14.3	62	1.0	4.0
Cuban	1969	565	6.1	82	1.5	14.5
	1974	689	6.4			
Central or South American	1969	556	6.0	170	3.1	30.6
	1974	705	6.5		12.8	28.8
Other Spanish	1969	1,582	17.1	835	15.2	52.8
	1974	1,398	13.0	806 °		
Total		9,320	100.0	5,507	100.0	59.7
		10,795	100.0	6,321	100.0	58.6

° Cuban, Central or South American, and Other Spanish are *all combined into one category,* *"Other Spanish,"* for 1974 data on Southwest.

Source: U.S. Bureau of Census, Current Population Reports, Series P-20, No. 267.

particularly worth noting. For example, 51 percent of white workers held white-collar jobs in 1974, while only 32 percent of Spanish-origin workers and 29 percent of blacks held such jobs. The unemployment rates for Spanish-origin persons and for blacks were almost twice those for whites. Spanish-origin families had achieved a median income somewhat above that of blacks but well below whites'. Table 7.4 presents some basic comparative information on incomes. It shows, for example, that the median income of Spanish-origin families, though about $1,000 higher than that of blacks, was still barely 70 percent that of whites. Families with young heads-of-household, however, appeared to trail whites less than did the older generations. At the same time, substantially larger proportions of white families were headed by full-time, year-round workers—suggesting that income differentials are built into many aspects of family and work life.

Table 7.5 shows that whites receive substantially more schooling than do either blacks or people of Spanish origin; sexual inequalities are significant but less marked. In a series of tests of specific accomplishments, such as reading level, black and Spanish-origin children regularly scored below Oriental Americans and those American Indians who were tested. That the former groups averaged three full grades below white

TABLE 7.4 *Median Family Income in 1970, by Age of Head and Ethnic Origin: March 1971*

Age of Head-of-Household	Total Population			Spanish Origin	
	All Races °	*White* †	*Black*	*Total* ‡	*Mexican*
14 to 24	7,037	7,294	5,013	5,697	5,534
25 to 34	9,853	10,187	6,605	7,324	7,567
35 to 44	11,410	11,790	7,569	8,345	8,058
45 to 54	12,121	12,626	7,357	8,146	7,491
55 to 64	10,381	10,737	6,438	7,482	7,997
65 and over	5,053	5,263	3,282	3,756	(B)
Total	$ 9,867	$10,236	$6,279	$7,334	$7,117
Head year-round, full-time worker: Median family income	$11,804	$12,016	$8,880	$9,309	$8,946
Percent of all families	64.1	65.5	51.4	57.4	57.0

B: Base less than 75,000.

° Includes persons of "other races," not shown separately.

† Includes almost all persons reporting Spanish origin. About 97 percent of persons of Spanish origin, about 99 percent of persons of Mexican origin, and 96 percent of persons of Puerto Rican origin were classified white in this survey.

‡ Includes persons of Central or South American, Cuban, and other Spanish origin, not shown separately.

Source: U.S. Bureau of the Census, *Persons of Spanish Origin in the United States,* November 1969. Population Characteristics. Series P-20, No. 213, February 1971, Table 1.

TABLE 7.5 *Educational Attainment of Population by Ethnic Group, Race, and Sex, March 1974 (percentages)*

Years of School Completed	Men			Women		
	Spanish Origin	*White*	*Negro*	*Spanish Origin*	*White*	*Negro*
Less than 4 years of high school	62.2	37.7	60.0	64.0	37.1	55.7
4 years of high school	22.4	32.6	26.1	25.3	40.1	30.1
1 year or more of college	15.5	29.7	13.9	10.7	22.8	14.2

Source: Monthly Labor Review 98 (February 1975), p. 67.

children may indicate that the tests are oriented toward whites, that minority children are badly educated, or both.[5]

Indians

Due to lack of agreement about who qualifies as an Indian, and absence of concern for the question until very recently, it is not possible to say precisely how many Indians now live in the United States. Estimates range from 600,000 to 1 million. The best estimate is probably that of the Bureau of Indian Affairs (BIA), which puts the number of Indians on reservations at about 450,000, with at least another 200,000 or so living in cities. In recent years, there has been substantial migration from reservations to the cities, partly as a result of federal programs aimed at reducing the reservation population (and its landholdings). More than 112,000 Indians, or from one tenth to one sixth of the total Indian population, migrated to the cities in the period 1952–1970, when such programs were in effect. Los Angeles is thought to have the largest number of urban Indians (about 60,000), followed by San Francisco–Oakland, Dallas–Fort Worth, Oklahoma City, Minneapolis–St. Paul, Phoenix, Cleveland, Chicago, and New York.

The economic and social conditions of Indians are probably the worst of all American minorities. The average annual income per Indian *family* is about $1,500 per year; unemployment is very high, reaching ten times the national average in some areas. U.S. Census reports show that about 60 percent of families living on Indian reservations were below the poverty line in 1973. The life expectancy of Indians is one third less than the national average, incidence of tuberculosis among Indians is eight times the national average, infant mortality rates are twice the national average, and the suicide rate is double that of the general population. According to Senator Edward Kennedy, 50,000 Indian families (that is, nearly half of all Indian families) live in unsanitary, dilapidated dwellings; many live in huts, shanties, or abandoned automobiles. Those who migrate to the cities often find that they are untrained for employment and unable to adapt to urban life. The average educational level for all federally educated Indians is under five years, and dropout rates are twice the national average in both federal and local public schools.

A recent Senate subcommittee study examined the history of, and current policies toward, Indian education and issued a scathing indictment of such policies and their underlying purposes.[6] It not only found failures of education to lie at the root of current Indian conditions, but also—far more important—declared the whole approach to education to

---

[5] Tetsuo Okada, *et al.*, *Dynamics of Achievement: A Study of Differential Growth of Achievement Over Time*. Tech. Note No. 53 (National Center for Educational Statistics, U.S. Office of Education, 1968).

[6] U.S. Senate, Subcommittee on Indian Education, *Indian Education: A National Tragedy—A National Challenge*, 91st Cong., 1st sess.

exemplify what is wrong with American policy toward Indians. In a sense, this report is applicable to the dilemma facing all racial minorities; a brief review of it may highlight the problem to be dealt with in the next section.

In its opening sentences, the subcommittee report declares: "A careful review of the historical literature reveals that the dominant policy of the Federal Government toward the American Indian has been one of forced assimilation which has vacillated between the two extremes of coercion and persuasion. At the root of the assimilation policy has been a desire to divest the Indian of his land and resources." [7] Referring to the federal statute dividing reservations into 160-acre parcels so that Indian families would learn about property ownership and become successful farmers—which resulted in the sale or abandonment of much of the acreage because such principles were totally inconsistent with Indian culture—the subcommittee states:

> ... During the 46-year period it was in effect it succeeded in reducing the Indian landbase from 140 million acres to approximately 50 million acres of the least desirable land. Greed for Indian land and intolerance for Indian cultures combined in one act to drive the American Indian into the depths of poverty from which he has never fully recovered.
> From the first contact with the Indian, the school and the classroom have been a primary tool of assimilation. Education was the means whereby we emancipated the Indian child from his home, his parents, his extended family, and his cultural heritage. It was in effect an attempt to wash the "savage habits" and "tribal ethic" out of a child's mind and substitute a white middle-class value system in its place. . . . [8]

The subcommittee's basic points are that racism and economic interests have combined to place Indians at the very bottom of the socioeconomic pyramid, and that the only route by which they are allowed to rise out of poverty and degradation—education—has required that they abandon everything unique to their culture. In other words, the purpose of education has been to make the Indian over into a person whose attitudes and goals are consistent with white capitalist American society. Naturally, Indians resisted such "education," and instead fought a continuing battle to maintain their cultural heritage and integrity.

The situation is not very different for most other minorities, although the process is somewhat less visible. "Progress," in the sense of the increasing capacity to earn income and gain status in the dominant society, has been available only for certain individuals among minorities, and only at the cost of abandoning the distinctive features of their cultures. Unless they give up, at the very least, those values and habits of thought that are inconsistent with competitive individualism and materialistic self-seeking, they will not succeed in American economic life. How much of

[7] *Ibid.*, p. 9.
[8] *Ibid.*

a cost does this represent? Clearly, some minority-group members would gladly pay the price in order to gain the material and other benefits of full participation in American society. But for others the cost is too high. The gap between the values and habits of mind of their cultures and those of the dominant society is too great, or they prize their own values and cultures too highly, to give them up. We shall explore the nature of this gap and the distinctiveness of certain minority views in the next section.

The World-Views, Values, and Goals of American Minorities

We use the term *world-view* here to denote (1) the understanding of the world that is characteristic of a given minority—that is, how it sees the workings of American society—and (2) *the way in which that minority culture thinks*—that is, the concepts, language, and habits of mind that characterize its customary thinking process. The latter is of primary importance. Every culture takes certain things for granted, attaches particular meanings to words, employs specific concepts, and thus tends to think in particular ways. Understandably, these ways of thinking are consistent with the kind of society that has given rise to them; they embody the values that underlie the social order, and provide its members with an understanding of what life is about.

It goes without saying that different cultures do not all employ the same ways of thinking. We shall explore the basic values of the dominant American orthodoxy in some detail in Chapter 8. For the moment, we need only note certain familiar characteristics of the world-view widely shared within American society. It is founded on individualism, and the sense that it is natural for individuals to compete and to seek to satisfy themselves through material gain. It assumes that all people will or should want to amass a certain amount of property, with which to render their economic situation more secure. It takes for granted that human beings have to struggle against nature and other obstacles until they master or are mastered. It analyzes situations and problems by means of tangible evidence, or "hard facts," which must be related to each other step-by-step to "prove" that something is or is not true. And it assumes that white skin, Western culture, and the Judaeo-Christian religious tradition are superior to all other brands.

This world-view is characteristic of nearly all nonminority Americans. It is characteristic also of many members of racial minorities, because they too are subject to the pervasive influences of American culture—its educational system, mass media, public rhetoric, and official practices. But it is *not* shared by at least some members of each of these minorities. Within each minority, there are some who hold to the distinct way of thinking characteristic of their own culture. In a variety of ways, they have resisted assimilation into the world-view and habits of thought of the dominant society. On occasion, this may take the form of an exaggerated attachment to peripheral aspects of the minority's heritage, or even of efforts to rediscover an indigenous culture that has been long forgotten. It may be quite deliberately calculated as a response to the pervasiveness of the dominant culture, and as a means to draw other members of the minority away from the values and ways of thinking that lead to assimilation into the dominant society. For the most part, such adherence to elements of an independent minority culture appears odd or incomprehensible only to those who subscribe fully to the dominant world-view and are impatient with all else. In any event, there are significant numbers of Indians, Chicanos, and blacks who hold world-views and ways of thinking that contrast sharply with those of the dominant culture.

What is distinctive about minority world-views? To begin with, they consciously reject many things—basic values, assumptions, preferences, and the like—that the dominant society simply takes for granted. Individualism, competition, materialism, the concept of struggling against nature, the concept of private property, and many other basic principles of the American social order are completely rejected by some or all of the three minority cultures we have been discussing.

The Indian World-View

The distinctiveness of the Indian world-view is apparent in two excerpts from *We Talk, You Listen,* a major work by Indian spokesman Vine Deloria, Jr. He first points to some basic differences in the ways that Indians and white Americans conceive of the nature of man and of individualism:

> The vital difference between Indians in their individualism and the traditional individualism of Anglo-Saxon America is that the two understandings of man are built on entirely different premises. White America speaks of individualism on an economic basis. Indians speak of individualism on a social basis. While the rest of America is devoted to private property, Indians prefer to hold their lands in tribal estate, sharing the resources in common with each other. . . .[9]

This view of land and the concept of human life as inextricably bound up with nature are major distinguishing features of the Indian world-view. Man is to live in harmony with nature, to preserve and restore it, to be part of its ecological balance—not to struggle against it or exploit it for commercial purposes. Deloria contrasts the Indian view with the white man's developmental mania as follows:

> The Indian lived with his land. He feared to destroy it by changing its natural shape because he realized that it was more than a useful tool

[9] Vine Deloria, Jr., *We Talk, You Listen* (New York: Macmillan, 1970), p. 170.

for exploitation. . . . All of this understanding was ruthlessly wiped out to make room for the white man so that civilization could progress according to God's divine plan.

In recent years we have come to understand what progress is. It is the total replacement of nature by an artificial technology. Progress is the absolute destruction of the real world in favor of a technology that creates a comfortable way of life for a few fortunately situated people. Within our lifetime the difference between the Indian use of land and the white use of land will become crystal clear. The Indian lived with his land. *The white destroyed his land. He destroyed the planet earth.* (Italics in original.) [10]

The distinctiveness of the Indian world-view also extends to ways of knowing. Indian understanding does not depend on logic or evidence, but instead on a sense of wholeness with nature, and on intuitive or mystical insight. Relative isolation has made it possible for some Indians to preserve substantial portions of their indigenous culture, and it stands in sharp contrast to the dominant society in a variety of ways.

The Chicano World-View

In many respects, the Chicano world-view is grounded in similar concepts. This is understandable in light of the close bond between Chicanos and their Indian forbears; the Indian heritage is stronger than the Spanish heritage among Chicanos. And a deliberate effort is being made by some Chicanos to recapture the unique combined heritage and to employ it as a means of uniting "la Raza" into a more effective force. Special emphasis is placed on the sense of brotherhood and community that should and once did exist among Chicanos, and the need to reject Anglo values in order to realize these ideals again. In his *Chicano Manifesto*, for example, Armando Rendon declares:

> Our ideals, our way of looking at life, our traditions, our sense of brotherhood and human dignity, and the deep love and trust among our own are truths and principles which have prevailed in spite of the gringo, who would rather have us remade in his image and likeness: materialistic, cultureless, colorless, monolingual, and racist. Some Mexican-Americans have sold out and become agringados, . . . like the Anglo in almost every respect. Perhaps that has been their way of survival, but it has been at the expense of their self-respect and of their people's dignity.[11]

There is no ambiguity in Rendon's insistence that Chicanos should reject the thought of assimilation into the dominant society:

> The North American culture is not worth copying: it is destructive of personal dignity; it is callous, vindictive, arrogant, militaristic, self-deceiving, and greedy; . . . it is a cultural cesspool and a social and spiritual vacuum for the Chicano. The victims of this culture are not merely the minority peoples but the dominant Anglo group as well; every-

[10] *Ibid.*, p. 186.
[11] Armando Rendon, *Chicano Manifesto* (New York: Macmillan, 1971), p. 46.

thing that passes for culture in the United States is symptomatic of a people so swept up in the profit motive and staying ahead of the Joneses that true natural and humanistic values may be destroyed without their knowing it.[12]

This strong antipathy to Anglo society and its values is in part intended to provide a sense of identity and personal worth to enable Chicanos better to withstand the assimilative pressures of the larger society. But it is also intended as a rallying-point around which several minorities can join forces. The Chicano emphasis on community leads to the idea of a multi-minority cultural pluralism, in which all minorities would have status and legitimacy equal to that of the dominant society. Few steps have been taken to put such an idea into effect, though there have been some tentative overtures, particularly between Chicanos and Puerto Ricans.

The Black World-View

Blacks are obliged to look harder than other minorities for their independent cultural heritage, because they have undergone a longer and heavier exposure to the dominant culture and its social system. But for those blacks who have either rejected or become frustrated by integration, the task is relatively easily accomplished. In many respects, that heritage has been maintained intact but misunderstood as such by whites and by those blacks who accepted white world-views and values; in others, it has been rebuilt out of the life of the ghettoes and the need of millions of blacks for a sense of personal worth and self-respect. In any event, many blacks share a unique understanding of the white world, and of what is necessary to change it in such a way that blacks can live in dignity and comfort.

The "Black Power" era of the mid-1960s, which marked an important stage for the black movement, was partly a result of recognition by many black leaders that the mobilization and ultimate liberation of black people required change at the cultural level. In their eyes, it was necessary for blacks to reject the dominant society's values, and to learn to see themselves as worthy because of, and not in spite of, being black. Blacks were the first to see that integration meant integration *on the white society's terms*. To maintain one's own identity, it is necessary to avoid being subject to another's definitions; this in turn, requires clear understanding and commitment to distinctive values. Stokely Carmichael made these points in 1967:

> ... How much easier it is to keep a man in chains by making him believe in his own inferiority! As long as he does, he will keep himself in chains. As long as a slave allows himself to be defined as a slave by the master, he will be a slave, even if the master dies. ...

[12] *Ibid.*, p. 178.

Black Power attacks this brain-washing by saying, WE WILL DE-
FINE OURSELVES. We will no longer accept the white man's definition
of ourselves as ugly, ignorant, and uncultured. We will recognize our own
beauty and our own culture and will no longer be ashamed of ourselves,
for a people ashamed of themselves cannot be free. . . .[13]

Speaking before Third World audiences, particularly Latin Americans, Carmichael regularly emphasized the role played by independent
cultures in the process of change. In this regard, both language and
symbols become vitally important; a people who would be free must not
subscribe to those of their oppressors:

> . . . When African slaves were brought to this country, the Anglo saw
> that if he took away the language of the African, he broke one of the
> bonds which kept them united and struggling. Africans were forbidden to
> speak to each other in their own language. If they were found doing so,
> they were savagely beaten into silence.
> Western society has always understood the importance of language
> to a people's cultural consciousness and integrity. When it moves into the
> Third World, it has moved to impose its own language. . . .
> The white man hardly needs to police his colonies within this country,
> for he has plundered the cultures and enslaved the minds of the people
> of color until their resistance is paralyzed by self-hate. An important fight
> in the Third World, therefore, is the fight for cultural integrity. . . .
> One of our major battles is to root out corrupt Western values, and
> our resistance cannot prevail unless our cultural integrity is restored and
> maintained. . . .[14]

Certain common themes are evident in these various calls for cultural
independence from the dominant American world-view and values.
Resistance to the overwhelming pressure of the dominant society's values
is urged by all, and all insist that assimilation is offered only at the price
of abandoning what is distinctive and worthwhile in minority cultures.
Each insists that its own culture and world-view has important contributions to make to a reconstructed version of the larger society. Indians
would probably seek merely to be left alone to pursue their own ways,
but the other minorities appear to recognize that their status and
legitimacy depend on changes in the dominant culture and social system.
Chicanos tend to envision a genuine cultural pluralism. Those blacks
who emphasize the uniqueness of black culture tend to do so as a
prelude to more far-reaching change, including revolution itself—which
many see as necessary to eliminate racism.

Thus the dilemma for minorities becomes somewhat clearer. Not
only are the dominant world-view and values promulgated forcefully
and variously; they also pervade the policies that seek to aid minorities.

[13] Stokely Carmichael, "Black Power and the Third World," *Readings in U.S.
Imperialism,* ed. K. T. Fenn and Donald C. Hodges (New York: Herder and Herder,
1971), p. 351.
[14] *Ibid.,* pp. 353–354.

The cost of acquiescence in them is loss of cultural integrity and of the uniqueness of one's heritage. And yet this is the only (though still uncertain) route to "progress" for minorities. The gap that we have been seeking to understand is not just social and economic. It is also a gap in self-definition, between one identity and another. Minority persons must in effect choose between the world-views and values of the culture and communities in which they grew up and those of an alien and often cold society that forces them into a competitive enterprise in which the cards are stacked against them. Thus, deprivation is not measured by mere facts and figures concerning income and employment. Indeed, those are precisely the kinds of measures that are valued chiefly by the dominant society. Important as they are in terms of sheer physical survival, they do not measure the pain and desperation that are felt as one's very identity and way of thinking are cast aside. Nor can public policies conceived within the dominant culture and system go very far toward alleviating such deprivation. As we shall see, such policies can create a better life for certain individuals; but whether they can do so for minorities as a whole, and without exacting the cost of cultural submission, remains doubtful.

Minority-Related Policies of the 1960s and 1970s

We come now to the larger problem posed by the current status of racial minorities in the United States. It involves the sharp contrast between the *limits* set by the dominant culture and econopolitical system and the *needs and goals* of minorities. The limits are defined by the dominant society's perceptions of the "problem" of minorities; its options within the established framework of laws and property rights and the basic premise of individualistic self-help; and the odds against its doing *anything*, given the many powerful defenders of the *status quo* who oppose significant advances for minorities. The needs and goals of minorities involve both vast advances in tangible social and economic conditions of life and, for many, the desire for true cultural pluralism and legitimacy for their values and way of life.

Bases for the Policies

The policies of the 1960s and early 1970s were based on assumptions characteristic of the dominant society. Central among these was the belief that the poverty and low status of minorities was the product of lack of opportunity, and thus could be alleviated by providing better educational and vocational opportunities. A related belief was that discrimination in such areas as housing, employment, and voting operated to reduce individual opportunities. Faith in legal remedies for such discrimination was widespread. Thus one primary response to minority demands and pressure in the 1960s was a series of Civil Rights Acts providing legal remedies for various forms of discrimination against individuals. The other was a set of new educational and training programs (the "War on Poverty") designed to enable minorities to compete more successfully for employment and, hence, income.

The premise underlying such beliefs and programs is that the economic system can and does provide ample jobs and income opportunities, and that if minority-group individuals were only qualified they would be able to raise themselves through their own efforts. But this approach would at best require a long slow process of upgrading skills, finding jobs, and eliminating discrimination on a case-by-case basis. Quite possibly, the jobs might not exist, or only a very few individuals might qualify for them, or broad-scale discrimination might prove impervious to individual attacks. It is even more likely that substantial proportions of minority persons would be unaffected by such programs, or discouraged by the time and effort required for self-help against such entrenched odds.

Not all the burden of bringing about change fell on public policies, of course. The enactment of highly visible Civil Rights Acts and the institution of the much-publicized War on Poverty also had the effect of symbolizing a change in national sentiment. One result was a greater willingness on the part of private businesses to hire at least some minority-group members. Educational institutions developed minority recruitment programs, and various governmental and private agencies initiated hiring and other aid programs specifically directed at minorities. In place of unconcern and lack of interest, there appeared in many instances at least a superficial sensitivity to advancing the status of minorities. At the same time, the new statutes and programs led to greatly increased expectations on the part of minorities in general, and to deep resentment on the part of lower- and middle-class whites of the "special favors" being granted to minority groups, apparently in response to minority pressure.

Thus the dilemma reproduces itself over and over again. Limited public policies do create opportunities for a relatively few individuals. But the process is slow at best, and dependent on the speed with which the private economy is able to absorb new workers. And the fanfare with which the new programs are instituted leads minorities to expect real assistance (and to become frustrated when it is not forthcoming) and creates the impression among whites that massive efforts are being made by their government to raise minorities above them on the socioeconomic ladder.

Consequences of the Policies

It is in this context that the consequences of the programs of the 1960s must be analyzed. That there has been progress cannot be doubted, but it has not been substantial. Nor is it clear whether the visible advances are due to public policies or to broad private response to the militant pressures generated by minorities during that period.

Progress can best be measured in terms of the advancement of blacks, because of their numbers and relatively higher visibility as a deprived minority. Apparently dramatic progress is visible in the ratio of income earned by black families to that earned by white families: [15] in 1959 the median family income of blacks was only 51 percent that of whites, but in 1972 it had jumped to 60 percent. If both husband and wife were working, the median family income for blacks under 35 was 89 percent that of whites.

This sharp overall rise, and the extent of equality among the youngest population, suggests that minority pressures and programs had a substantial impact in the 1960s. It is clear that blacks' share of the higher-paying, higher-status occupations increased substantially, and at a rate well above that of whites.[16] At the highest level—professional and technical positions—blacks showed a 109 percent gain between 1960 and 1970; 8 percent of such occupations are now filled by blacks. During the same period, the number of whites in such jobs increased only 31 percent. The gain in middle-level (clerical, sales, skilled blue-collar) jobs was 64 percent for blacks, compared to 21 percent for whites. At the same time, the number of blacks in the lowest-paid jobs dropped, while that of whites gained slightly. Blacks also narrowed the educational gap, reaching the point in 1970 that young black adults as a group trailed whites of similar age by only a half year of schooling, as compared with a year and a half in 1960. Unemployment among blacks was 8.2 percent in 1970, but the shift toward the higher-paying (and more stable) jobs means that this figure was lower than it would have been in previous years.

Some qualifications must be registered, however. For one thing, the income advances appear to be due in large measure to the fact that more black women are now working. In the North and West, for example, where the greatest advances were made, the number of young black families in which husband and wife both worked almost doubled between 1960 and 1970. Black women were working at considerably higher rates than were white women in 1970: 63 percent of black wives held jobs, while 52 percent had year-round jobs; only 54 percent of white wives worked at any time, and only 36 percent had year-round jobs. Moreover, the earlier figures are drawn from a period of particularly

[15] Data on income in this section are drawn from U.S. Census Bureau, *Differences Between Incomes of Whites and Negro Families by Work Experience and Region: 1970, 1969 and 1959*, Series P-23, no. 39 (Washington: Government Printing Office, 1971).

[16] Data on occupational and educational status in this section are drawn from U.S. Department of Labor, Bureau of Labor Statistics, *Black Americans: A Decade of Occupational Change*, Bulletin 1731 (Washington: Government Printing Office, 1972).

high black unemployment, higher proportions of Southern residence, and lower educational levels generally. Thus, the real advance between 1960 and 1970 was probably less than the data seem to indicate.

How much of this advance should be attributed to governmental policies? At the height of the War on Poverty, less than $3 billion per year—little more than 1 percent of the federal budget—was invested by the federal government. The Civil Rights Acts of the 1960s were enforced by a mere handful of attorneys in the Justice Department, although a series of successfully tried cases constitutionally legitimated the Acts themselves. With the advent of the Nixon Administration, funding for the War on Poverty dropped substantially, and much of the thrust toward school integration was undermined by the President's opposition to busing for racial equality. The steep rise in unemployment in the middle 1970s, in conjunction with a decline in the efforts of the federal government to combat poverty, increased the proportion of the population below the poverty line, as noted in Chapter 6. The recession has been especially hard on minorities, as Table 7.6 makes clear. In March 1974, 10 percent

TABLE 7.6 *Unemployment Rates by Ethnic Origin, Race, Years in School, and Sex, March 1974*

	Men			Women		
Years in School	Spanish Origin	White	Black	Spanish Origin	White	Black
Less than 4 years of high school	8.4	6.7	11.3	12.0	8.9	11.8
4 years of high school	6.0	3.8	9.0	8.5	5.0	9.3
1 year or more of college	4.5	2.5	7.8	5.7	3.5	5.2
Total	7.2	4.3	10.0	9.8	5.6	9.5

Source: Monthly Labor Review 98 (February 1975), p. 67.

of black males who wanted to work could not find jobs. At every educational level there was substantially higher unemployment among blacks and people of Spanish origin than among whites, with the disparities somewhat greater for men than for women. For blacks sixteen to nineteen years old, the unemployment rate in October 1974 was 34.5 percent.

The extent of real progress, even in socioeconomic terms, appears to remain an open question in the mid-1970s. Achievements to date appear fragile and perhaps temporary, and so far limited to the advancement of a relatively few individuals. They appear to depend on the mobilization and militance of minorities themselves, but the massive efforts of minorities in the 1960s may have been a unique and unrepeatable episode. If the various business, governmental, and educational initiatives of the 1960s were merely short-term responses to ghetto riots and other violent confrontations, the costs of "progress" will ultimately be seen as very high. Nor will the situation then appear promising for other minorities, or for those among all minorities who seek legitimacy and equal status for their own cultures and life styles.

PART 3

Contrasting Ideologies

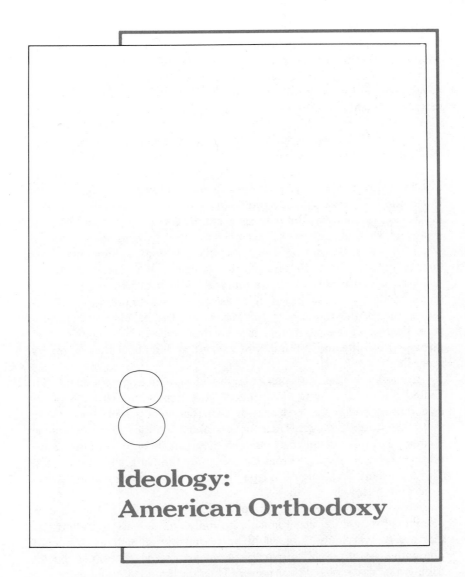

8

Ideology:
American Orthodoxy

We have thus far analyzed a number of problems and examined a variety of consequences of government policies. Patterns of consequences have become apparent: the same people, mostly blue-collar workers and minorities, are at the bottom in every instance. In both the past and the present, and apparently in the future as well, they bear the brunt of inflation control, experience repeated unemployment, make the least income, and (in the case of minorities) suffer the effects of racism. Governmental policies appear to foster or maintain such conditions, while promoting the needs and goals of the corporate-banking sector and its owners and managers. It is trite, but by no means an exaggeration, to say that the rich get richer and the poor get poorer.

What explains these patterns of consequences of government policies? How do such patterns square with our understanding of the United States as a "democracy"? What new policies to address continuing or developing problems are likely, and why will *they* be prescribed? The most fundamental source of both explanation and prescription is often ideology.

Ideology is the collection of beliefs the members of a given society hold about how their government works, or should work, and why. Such beliefs may be articulated fully or merely implicit in the ways people live their lives. They may vary somewhat between the highest and lowest *strata,* or levels, of the population. And they may be held with varying degrees of intensity. But whether factually correct or not, and however expressed, such images in people's minds serve as a kind of lens through which to see, and a set of cues with which to make judgments about, their political world. Both perceptions and values thus contribute to one's ideology, which is normally acquired very early in life from one's family and schooling. It is reaffirmed in a variety of ways as one grows older—by the media, the rhetoric of politicians, and the beliefs and actions of other people. That it fits reality in a sense may be only coincidental, for ideology has a life and continuity of its own, and in effect shapes "reality" accordingly.

In most societies, one particular belief system is predominant. The United States is no exception. Indeed, the depth and strength of the orthodox American ideology are so great that some people do not even recognize it as ideology. Their beliefs about politics and government seem so natural and self-evident that they can imagine no other possibilities; they are convinced that they see only the truth and nothing else. This total short-circuiting of independent analysis is the supreme achievement of an ideology.

American orthodoxy, for example, insists that wealth and income are distributed roughly in accordance with individual talents and effort, and that nearly everybody is or could be reasonably affluent in this highly productive system. Such disparities as may exist do not affect the distribution or usage of political power. Thus the American political system is democratic, works well, and regularly produces policies that are appropriate to the problems in question or at least are the best accommodation possible under the circumstances.

But some Americans reject the dominant orthodoxy. In recent years, the benevolent image of the political system promulgated by American orthodoxy has been challenged in several ways. We shall look first at the functions of ideology generally, and then at the standard values and ideology that make up the American belief system. Then, in the next chapter, we shall examine challenges to the system and what they may mean for both explanation and prescription in American politics.

The Functions of Ideology

        Three primary functions of ideology are worth noting here. First, ideology affects our perception of problems. Because we are used to thinking in certain ways, and because we habitually make certain assumptions, we tend to "understand" new problems only in a particular (limited and narrow) context. Second, ideology not only explains why policies take the form they do, but also justifies (or condemns) these patterns. It may do so on the grounds of the rightness (or wrongness) of the political system that produced them, the structure of power that animates that system, or the basic values underlying it. Third, ideology serves broadly to organize people and to provide them with a coherent sense of the relationship among themselves, their values, and the workings of their government.

1. Ideology and the Perception of Problems

What is a "problem"? Clearly, how we understand the character and causes of problems relates directly to what we regard as acceptable ways to solve them. Is the pollution of air and water, for example, such a drastic threat to the enjoyment of life, or to the long-term ecological balance of nature, that severe measures should be taken to control the industrial sources of pollution? Or is it a necessary price to be paid for the continued expansion of the economy and the provision of jobs for a growing labor force? One's answer depends only partly on objective facts. Part of the "answer," probably some of the "facts," and certainly much of the "solution" depend on one's ideology.

        Thus our understanding of a problem involves much more than its "objective" characteristics; it is a direct outcome of our values and ideology. For example, the American orthodoxy tends to see each problem in isolation, as if it had no roots in our social structure, economic practices, or basic values. Another ideology—a version of radicalism—sees problems as connected to each other and to the underlying conditions and structures of the society and economy. Such divergent ideologies would give rise to very different understandings of the nature of the problem, and thus to very different prescribed solutions.

2. Ideology and Explanation-Justification

Ideology does not just affect what we see and understand in the world around us; it simultaneously implies that what we see conforms to either our hopes or our fears. Things not only *are*, they are also *good* or *bad*, because ideology teaches us to understand them in both dimensions at the same time. By relating newly perceived events to long-established and deeply held convictions, and by insisting that the former are consistent with the latter, ideology filters all events through a particular perceptual screen. In the view of the dominant ideology, for example, the rightness of the American political system and the propriety of our basic political values make it likely that public policies will benefit the society as a whole.

3. Ideology and Organization of People

What does it mean to shape what people see, and whether they see a given phenomenon as good or bad? Clearly, it implies at least organization of, and potentially control over, those people. By providing a coherent understanding of their world, ideology organizes people. It molds them into particular relationships with other people, with government, and with events. They need not be aware of what is happening to them, nor is it as if they were marching in a column of thousands in response to explicit orders from their leaders. But they *are* organized in the sense that they see and think the same things at the same time as do many other people. In the case of the dominant ideology, the experience of most individuals implicitly reinforces (and rewards) acceptance of American orthodoxy, and political leaders explicitly call for behavior in accordance with it. Thus ideology becomes a powerful instrument of social control on behalf of those people or interests served by its teachings. It is easier, and more effective, if people voluntarily behave in ways that are congenial to the existing social order; coercion can then be held to a minimum. A challenging ideology may similarly organize people's lives and serve many of the same functions on behalf of group leaders. In both cases, people perceive and behave in certain ways, and believe in their acts and perceptions, because they consciously or unconsciously hold a particular ideology. And everybody holds *some* ideology, in greater or lesser degree. The only question is *which* ideology, and how it affects understanding and action.

Basic American Political Values

Political values are the most fundamental beliefs that people hold about what is right or wrong in politics. They are the building-blocks for thinking about how political systems should be organized, and why. We shall touch upon five political values that have had major impact on American political thought and practice.

Individualism

The focal-point of political thought in the United States is the individual. From this base, all other relationships and values follow. The individual is the basic unit of politics, and the political system is erected for the individual's benefit. Individuals are viewed as naturally competitive, and their competition as making for personal fulfillment and social progress. The principal goals of political life have to do with providing a suitable context for the individual's satisfaction and happiness. Self-fulfillment is sought, and principles of government are deduced, from assumptions about what is needed to serve the individual's needs. In the mid-eighteenth century, for example, the chief impediment to individual self-attainment seemed (with good reason) to be governmental power wielded by royal or aristocratic authorities. The principal means of assuring individual opportunity, therefore, was a firm set of limitations on the power of government and an equally determined *laissez-faire* approach to the role of government in the society and economy.

The "Natural Rights" of the Individual

As part of their entitlement on earth, due them solely by virtue of their existence, individuals have certain rights. These are (1) the right to property—to be secure in the possession of goods and land, to be able to rely on the value of money, and to be able to collect debts owed; (2) the right to life and liberty, in the sense that one cannot be deprived of either without being granted the due processes of law (hearing, trial, fair procedures, and so on); (3) the right to participate, to some degree at least, in the decisions of government; and (4) the right to equality, whether defined as equal treatment before the law or as equality of opportunity.

Although property rights are only one of several natural rights, political thinkers and practical politicians have frequently tended to elevate them to first priority and sometimes to exclusive entitlement. The problem is, of course, that property rights often conflict with other natural rights, particularly equality; thus the issue of priority is crucial. The deep and bitter conflict over slavery may serve to illustrate this point and demonstrate the power and ascendancy of property as an American political value. None of the Framers of the Constitution seriously doubted that slaves were property, to be provided for as such. The early debates over limited slavery versus emancipation foundered on the appropriate amounts of compensation (the propriety of which was never questioned) for the loss of property. The Abolitionists were bitterly resisted by most Northerners, at least partly because of the antiproperty implications of their position. And when emancipation came, it was as a limited expediency in the course of a difficult war. In this sequence of events, relatively few voices were raised on behalf of granting equality priority over property, and it was only the commitment to preserve the Union that finally mobilized the use of force.

This conflict between property and other natural rights is real and recurrent—in debate over the progressive income tax, social security, the poverty program, and the regulation of the economy generally. But such conflict is anticipated and feared by those who hold property far more than actual inroads on their possessions would seem to justify. The Framers and the early Federalists feared attacks on property and radical redistribution of wealth if majorities were allowed to work their will through the political system. Consequently, they built in a series of restraints on the power of government.[1] In justifying this principle, they developed and promulgated the idea of "majority rule *and* minority rights." By minority rights, of course, they meant property rights. But the two are logically inconsistent: no political system can provide both majority rule and minority rights in the absolute sense. An effective limit on majority rule on behalf of minority rights means that there is no real majority rule. Conversely, if majority rule succeeds in working its will in all cases, the system *cannot* always be protecting minority rights. Nevertheless, most Americans subscribe to both principles and acknowledge such limitations on the power of majorities—testimony, perhaps, to the success of the Federalists in establishing their view as an integral component of American political ideology.

Limited Government

At least as far as eighteenth-century thinkers were concerned, a necessary corollary to individualism and natural rights (in which property rights hold primacy) is the principle of limited government. If individuals possess rights flowing from the laws of nature, then government is their creation. Its powers must be consistent with their natural rights and must have been conferred on it by the collectivity of individuals who together possess all powers. Its sphere of action is defined both by the limited scope of the powers granted to it and by the inviolability of the rights of individuals.

In this view, government is a marginal and semi-illegitimate enterprise. Regardless of the fact that the society (or collectivity of individuals) has no other agent capable of acting on behalf of the whole, each effort to employ government for particular purposes is viewed with suspicion and its necessity and propriety are challenged. To be sure, this principle may be most often invoked to prevent governmental action deemed undesirable, and forgotten when favorable action is sought.

Materialism and the Business Ethic

Since the earliest days of this nation, observers have repeatedly commented on the special disposition of Americans to seek private economic gain. Acquisitiveness and profit-seeking are sometimes related to a so-called "Protestant ethic," based on the belief that ultimate salvation de-

---

[1] For a full presentation of the Framers' ideas, one should examine the *Federalist Papers,* available in many inexpensive editions.

The Capitalist Liberation Front

SOME DAYS, things look bleak. In the worldwide propaganda war our adversaries often seem to steal the headlines. They advance; it seems we decline. They seem to encircle us more tightly.

Except.

Except that the ideas of human liberty and full personal development were never so attractive—or so within the reach of so many human beings—as at present.

Is there a word more exciting to the human race today than "liberation"? Or "do your thing"? Or "individual liberties"? Or "self-determination"? Or "opportunity to be one's self"? Without such conceptions, capitalism would not be possible. These conceptions are the very soul of everything we mean by "free enterprise." These are *our* ideas.

The energy of capitalism is in the human heart. Its name is *liberty.* This is what critics of capitalism have always misunderstood.

In the highest form of flattery, even our enemies embrace our words: in national "liberation" fronts; in "Free" Republics; in "democratic" socialisms. More significant than that, the dreams of the peoples of the world—of billions of individuals—are, at bottom, *our* dreams. Dreams of the fully developed, cooperative, open, free individual.

The critics of capitalism misunderstand. They neglect three features in the human soul.

The number one desire of the human heart is not equality but *liberty.* Equality is an indispensable condition; we are committed to equality. But the further point, the focal point of human aspiration, is *liberty.* No other system, but ours alone, is the system of *liberty:* That deepest human energy of all is ours. Others, as we do, bring equality but we alone deliver *liberty.*

Secondly, the system of free enterprise is *value-giving.* For millenniums, oil lay useless and undesirable beneath the earth. Oil would have no value apart from the industry that capital invented. It was our inventiveness, our exertion, and our creation that in living memory made oil a precious mineral. And so, also, for many other raw materials that today have value. Capitalism is *wealth-creating*—and also *wealth-conferring.* It is true that we "exploited" some nations earlier; but we have also made them wealthy beyond their dreams. Capitalism in its abuses does at times "despoil" the earth. But in its imagination and its practicality it gives humble things values the human race never saw in them before. Capitalism has *enriched* the earth, seeing in it possibilities hidden there by its Creator, evoking marvels and miracles men had never seen before.

Thirdly, capitalism is *transformative.* It has the good of the human race at heart. And so in its unfolding capitalism transforms the world—and in the process transforms itself as well. It has given health to millions who would not have lived before; fed more millions than were ever fed before; built schools and universities for larger proportions of the race than had ever been educated earlier; and distributed higher standards of comfort and amenities, not only for an aristocracy but for ordinary workers and for many of the poor, than the world had ever dreamed of. More precious than all of these, capitalism has taken as its bride—and cherished—political democracy.

If capitalism is surrounded, it is surrounded like the yeast in dough. What capitalism stands for is what is deepest in the human soul. And what eventually, irresistibly, bursts forth: *human liberation,* for the solitary self; for every brother, every sister; and for societies and institutions everywhere.

Rumrill-Hoyt, Inc.

Source: Fortune, May 1975, p. 90.

pends on striving and attainment in this world. National celebration of such motivations reached its height at the end of the nineteenth century, in the days of Horatio Alger and the robber barons. Although it would be little more than caricature to attribute such motivations to most Americans today, it is clear that the United States is a business-oriented society. The underlying value system strongly supports such capitalist principles as the value of consumption by individuals, the measurement of the propriety and desirability of new ventures by their profitability, and the measurement of individual achievement by the accumulation of wealth.

These values and motivations, broadly shared, affect the criteria used to determine the priorities and programs of government. Because private profit and consumption are valued so highly, public expenditure is suspect. Government outlays for such public purposes as schools, hospitals, and welfare may be seen as "spending" and therefore undesirable, while corporate expenditures for new and perhaps unnecessary consumer products are "investments" and therefore good. Government action may be judged from a kind of tradesman's vantage-point, in which short-range questions of profitability dominate. Can the Post Office be run as a business and bring in enough income to balance its costs? Will the proposed bridge earn enough income to pay off the cost of building it in a fixed period of years?

Racism

Almost equally long-lived and pervasive in American society is the assumption of white supremacy. Originating in Western culture centuries ago, the sense of superiority of the white race has been an animating feature of Americans and their governmental policies throughout our history. Neither the American Indian nor the Afro-American was thought fit for full citizenship until very recently. Recent scholarship indicates that nearly all the major leaders at the time the Constitution was framed, as well as in subsequent periods, held white-supremacist assumptions.[2] However unconscious such notions may have been, they were instrumental in shaping policies that massacred Indians, oppressed slaves, and built a sometimes unrecognized racist strain into the American value system.

After centuries of official action in accordance with these premises, it is not surprising that those who seek evidence of the degradation of the nonwhite races are readily able to find it. Efforts to remedy the work of centuries, however, run up against denials of personal responsibility and failure to perceive the racist bases of existing policies, as well as normal resistance to change. Most Americans do not understand the extent to which subtle and not-so-subtle racial barriers have served to

[2] Thomas F. Gossett, *Race: The History of an Idea in America* (New York: Schocken Books, 1963).

prevent the nonwhite poor from rising via the routes taken by the immigrant poor of the nineteenth and early twentieth centuries. Given such widespread and deep-seated racism, it is not difficult to see why the limited governmental steps taken have nevertheless been highly controversial, and why the tangible signs of change are so few.

There are many important factual questions to be asked about all these values, of course. We do not know which groups or strata within the society actually held or hold them, how widely shared or intensely felt they are, or whether people who assert them actually act on them. These are questions we shall attempt to answer later.

The Orthodox Ideology

The dominant political belief system holds that the values just described (with the exception of racism, of course) are realized on a day-to-day basis in American politics. In part, this is the natural function of a nation's political ideology. In effect, ideology is a kind of mental map that tells people how to harmonize what they see with their strongly held convictions about what is good. Because it is simplifying and reassuring, it is also seductive and frequently unconscious. It tends to be strongest among those who have had the most formal education, possibly because their economic interests and social positions act to reinforce what they have heard so often and in so many different forms in the educational process. Others, particularly those who experience more contrast between the ideology and the realities of daily existence, may be less prone to uncritical adoption of it.

But because of such ideology-induced confidence, those few who (however accurately) believe a given policy to have disastrous implications will have great difficulty gaining support from a majority of their fellow citizens. Or ideology may serve to divert or frighten people so completely as to distort consideration of various problems. American anticommunism in the post-World War Two decades was apparently strong enough to dominate policymaking and suppress dissent. We shall illustrate two components of the dominant American political ideology in the paragraphs that follow.

1. The ideology holds that the basic political values of the United States are reflected in the structure of the American government, and that the resulting political system is democratic in character.

The core political values—individualism, limited government, natural rights (with property rights ascendant over equality and other human rights), and procedural regularity—are patently manifest within the Constitution and the government it created. Ideology holds that the institutional forms of these principles will operate as if controlled by an unseen hand, and will deliver the results considered appropriate by those who subscribe to that set of values. The interplay of presidential and congressional power is seen as yielding a mechanistic (and therefore appropriate) product; the decision of the Supreme Court is seen as representing a higher law's mandate, not the preferences of five or more judges. In short, ideology suggests that the translation of values into institutions and powers has achieved a nonpartisan, depoliticized apparatus that works to the benefit of all.

Next, the ideology holds that this structure creates a situation that allows full play to the "natural" workings of human capacities and wants, and of the economic market, which will result in the greatest good for the greatest number of people. Thus, the established political values are seen as manifested in a particular set of institutions; these institutions interact in a mechanical manner; and the result is the furtherance of a natural order in which talent and effort are rewarded and the incompetent and slothful are carried along by the successful.

The teachings of ideology with respect to the structure and operations of government are that all will benefit equally, or at least substantially, from such procedures. But it seems clear that the character of the institutional setup, and the principles on which it frequently operates, neither benefit all equally nor leave results to chance. It works to the advantage of those who are situated so as to be able to seize opportunities for gaining power and influence. Separation of powers, distribution of powers between nation and states, and the protection provided for property rights, for example, make it very difficult to enact laws that change the *status quo*. The principle of *laissez faire* means that people with private economic power are free to use that power as they see fit, and it is difficult (and perhaps wrong in any event) for others to try to use government to control such activities. If government works mechanically, of course, nobody should be aggrieved about its actions, because they are inherent in the (good) design of the American governmental structure itself. Thus, it turns out that nothing is responsible for the advantages secured by those with economic or social power except their own talents in the free and open struggle for individual achievement.

Perhaps even more important than the manner in which basic political values are related to the structure and operations of government, is the way in which the ideology equates the values *and* the nature of American government with democracy. Democracy is good; the United States is good; the United States is a democracy; democracy is what we experience in the United States. Circularity and poor logic are no obstacles for a powerful ideology, and it may be fruitless—perhaps unpatriotic—to try to unravel the relationships here. What has apparently happened is that the ideology has adapted to the powerful appeal of democracy in the last two centuries and interpreted American values and institutions in this light. Thus, the commitment to private property and individualism becomes a characteristic of democratic man. Or, the institution of judicial review, originally designed to frustrate popular will expressed through the elected legislature, comes to be seen as a vehicle for expression of the democratic values of civil liberties. A statute outlawing political participation by people with a particular viewpoint becomes democratic because it preserves the "freedom" of the "democratic" electoral process. A natural tendency to believe that what we have is good, if not ideal, leads to favorable (democratic) interpretations of whatever we have.

We are not arguing that the governmental system of the United States is necessarily *un*democratic, though we may appear to be taking a harsh view of some much-revered things. We are saying that the acts of *assuming* that American institutions are democratic, and of *defining* "democracy" as what exists in the United States, are essentially *ideological* in character. In both cases, "American" and "democratic" become synonymous—testimony to the power of ideology to suggest conclusions rather than leaving them to the judgment of the observer.

It is the social control aspect of American ideology—its capacity to disarm analysis and provide benevolent interpretations—that is so significant to contemporary American politics. Few, if any Americans are fully captured by all the characteristics of ideology we have touched on, but practically everyone is influenced by at least some of them. In the next section, we shall discuss forms of ideology held even by some scholars and students of American politics.

2. The ideology holds that the process of political decisionmaking in the United States consists of negotiation and compromise among many factions and groups, and that the product is a reasonable approximation of both democracy and the public interest. In the next five paragraphs, we shall characterize the generally accepted view of the American political process, sometimes termed "democratic pluralism."

To begin with, the system is considered to be open to all those who wish to take the time and trouble to participate. For the most part, Americans actually do participate through the vehicle of voluntary associations, organized around the ethnic, religious, occupational, social, economic, political, or other interests that are of concern to them. A single citizen may belong to several such groups. These groups articulate the needs and desires of the people at all levels of the society, but particularly with reference to government.

In organizing support among the population and presenting their claims on the government, groups come into conflict with other groups. Each group's efforts to achieve its goals are likely to call into play another group with different or opposing goals in the same field. This is sometimes termed "the principle of countervailing powers." The various interested groups then engage in an elaborate process of negotiation, bargaining, appeals to principle and popular support, pressures on decisionmakers, and finally compromise. Because each group represents a significant segment of opinion and probably has access to some source of power within the governmental structure, it can usually delay if not completely frustrate an extreme demand made by another group. This means that each group is induced to compromise on a solution that falls short of its full goals; if it does not, it may end up with nothing.

Harmonious handling of conflict through compromise is also promoted by the informal rules for group goalseeking. Each group is assumed to be sufficiently concerned with the fairness and openness of the process (because the attainment of its goals depends on getting a fair hearing from the others) to commit itself to defending the procedures of decision-making. Above all, parties to the goal-seeking process should be willing to see each other's problems, and also to compromise at a point not only short of their own goals but also short of absolute disaster for each other. This is also sound strategy, since those who happen to win today may be on the losing side tomorrow, in which case they can expect the same consideration from their new opponents. Thus, the informal rules promote compromise and help to build a shared feeling of mutual approval for the decisionmaking system itself. One's opponents, after all, are people who play the game by the rules and are entitled to respect for their views and for the demands placed on them by their constituencies. Those who do not accept the rules are not playing the right game, or are cheating, and are properly censured by all the regular players. When the regular groups do find themselves in disagreement, or at other moments when major decisions must be made, the basic outlines of national policy are determined by popular elections. In this way, the day-to-day activities of group goalseeking are chaneled; groups devote themselves to working out the details of policies decided on by the mass electorate.

Groups perform many functions within the social and political order. They serve as a major means of representation, providing people with a sense that their voices are heard in the halls of government by means other than the familiar geographical or party systems of representation. Thus, a citizen who belongs to the minority political party in his or her state or congressional district can nevertheless feel represented in government by the efforts of interest groups that seek to further his or her goals. In discharging this representative function, groups also root the citizen more thoroughly in the society—giving him or her a sense of place, status, and fulfillment. And, in a reciprocal manner, groups give public officials a means of knowing what the people want and need, and a way of communicating back and forth that makes for more responsive government.

There are other consequences of the pattern of group activity in politics. People who participate in groups acquire the tolerance for others and respect for fair procedures that help to support a democratic system. They may also belong to two or more groups whose interests are occasionally in conflict. For example, one citizen may belong to both the League of Women Voters and the Catholic Church. If the League seeks to take a position contrary to that of the Church on birth-control issues, the citizen may be "cross-pressured" to take a much less extreme position on the issue than she otherwise would have. At the same time, her influence within each organization helps to lead it to a less extreme position. This "cross-pressured" or cleavage effect, multiplied many times over for many issues, helps to keep the political system on an even keel by reducing the extremity of pressures on it. The process is both democratic and in the public interest. It is democratic because everybody has a chance to be heard, the procedures for "playing the game" are known and observed, and a general consensus based on compromise and tolerance emerges before the decision is cast into final form. It is in the public interest chiefly because it *does* represent a consensus that everybody can accept, and that is therefore very likely to be in harmony with the experience and capacity of the system and responsive to the problem in question.

These five paragraphs sum up a very large body of analysis, interpretation, and self-congratulation by journalists, academics, and the general public. Most of it, however pretentiously set forth, is little more than a restatement of the dominant ideology. Taken together, these two major components of the dominant ideology are characterized by a very strong commitment to the established order. In particular, they emphasize over and over again the necessity and propriety of following the rules. Sometimes insistence on procedural regularity is raised to the level of a basic political value, and given a label such as "legalism." The importance to Americans of formal written provisions, and of the law generally, has often been noted by observers; the major role played by lawyers in the governing of this society also rests on this procedural-legal bias. Beneath the stress on established rules and legalistic procedures, of course, lies a basic conviction that actions taken in the private sphere are best and should take precedence over (if not be protected against) public policies. Thus, the orthodox ideology says in effect that if policies are developed by the established rules of the political system, they must be appropriate. Further, if they maximize people's opportunities to gain their ends by private rather than governmental means, they are good. This view makes it almost unnecessary to examine the actual consequences of policies. Their merits can be determined from the circumstances of their enactment, and from the extent to which they leave people free to gain their ends by private means.

The Implications of American Orthodoxy

So far, we have analyzed the American orthodoxy as a set of specific values and ideological beliefs held by Americans. We have seen how political images and beliefs are rooted in basic values, and have examined the nature of each. Now it is time to note again how fully American beliefs are fused with capitalist values, and to ask what this orthodoxy means for our politics.

How much of our orthodoxy is capitalism by another name? Individualism, materialism, competition, the work ethic and profit motive, property rights, and the primacy of private economic activity are clearly capitalist principles. The concepts of limited government, contractualism, and legalism are applications of capitalist principles to the political system. Some American values may have had other origins and independent support, but have become intertwined with capitalism throughout our history. Racism, a prime example, relegates minority groups to artificially low levels of employment and income, and both divides workers and diverts them from making more effective demands for larger shares of wealth and income. Some early capitalist values are honored only rhetorically by the corporate-banking sector, as a kind of "cover" for its use of government on its own behalf. Perhaps the best way to conceive of the American orthodoxy is as capitalism with certain modifications, ambiguities, and accompanying cultural idiosyncrasies. A capsule characterization, however, would have to emphasize the continuing overlap and parallel with capitalism.

What does this orthodoxy mean for our politics? The *strength* of its influence clearly has several important results. Most Americans are unaware how specific their values and beliefs are, partly because they are rarely challenged effectively. Thus, they consider their values and beliefs natural, inevitable, and self-evident. This stance can lead to failure to understand others' feelings and opinions, and to impatience with or intolerance of those with other views. Because the orthodoxy exists at such a deep level that it is not always recognized, those who depart from it may appear mentally or morally defective. They can then be imprisoned, hospitalized, or otherwise ostracized legally and with general approval.

The *shared character* of at least the major elements of the orthodoxy has other implications. We do not argue that all sectors of the population hold the orthodox values and beliefs to the same degree; as we shall see, there are levels at which only certain basic elements of it are observed, and some where other views predominate. But most Americans share the values and beliefs discussed in this chapter to some degree. This means that prominent public officials can draw support for their actions by manipulating revered symbols. They do not have to justify their acts exclusively, or even primarily, in terms of their merits. Instead, they can claim that their acts conform to the values of individualism or preservation of the economic system. In short, the broadly shared character of the orthodoxy facilitates social control. It causes people to believe in and support their leaders, almost without regard to what they are actually doing.

The *content* of orthodoxy, in conjunction with its strength and shared character, has certain additional implications. Capitalism becomes insulated from critical evaluation, because most Americans do not perceive the economic system in those terms and, in any event, believe it to be both good and inevitable. Nationalism is enhanced, because many Americans come to feel that our system is clearly superior to all others. Some may carry their belief to the point of messianism, a feeling that it is our moral mission to bring the blessings of our (capitalist) system to the rest of the world. Those who willfully oppose and reject our system—for example, communists or socialists—are thus seen as evil and inevitable enemies.

This characterization may seem harsh or exaggerated. We do not believe that it is; at least, it is thoroughly grounded in the interpretations of generations of reputable American scholars. It is more likely that such reactions are the result of a lifetime of uncritical acceptance of orthodox values and beliefs, to a greater or lesser degree. The strength and character of this orthodoxy also suggest one reason why radicalism has not been very successful in the United States. As we shall see, even radicalism has often been unable to extricate itself from the scope of this pervasive belief system.

9

Ideology:
The Radical Challenge

Why do public policies have the character and conse-
quences they do? The radical answer is in clear contrast to the democratic
pluralist-legalist explanation provided by American orthodoxy. It is,
quite simply, that concentrated economic power is, as always, systematically and selfishly exploiting the great majority of the people. Public
policies serve the purposes of the powerful, who use government as a
tool for private profit. At times, when pressure mounts, the ruling class
offers certain pacifying benefits to leading elements among the lower
echelons. The dominant ideology is no more than a facade for manipulation by such corrupting interests.

Radicalism means the belief that drastic change is necessary at the
roots of the social order. The term is applicable to efforts on both the left
and the right that seek such change. We will focus here on the radicalism

of the left, because it is the major source of challenge to American orthodoxy today. The essence of this American radicalism is concern for equality in some form, and for advancing the cause of the "little man" in some fashion. Ever since the nation was founded, radicalism, in one or another of its evolving versions, has periodically risen to challenge the dominant orthodoxy. Tom Paine's early egalitarianism, the Jacksonian movement, the Abolitionists, the women's suffrage movement, the labor movement, and the recent civil rights movement are all manifestations of this deep and continuing stream in American political thought.

Radicalism, in eclipse during the 1940s and 1950s as a result of war, repression, and general social mobilization in support of the Cold War, was reborn in the mid-1960s. Blacks' struggle for basic civil rights quickly reignited similar undertakings by Chicanos, Puerto Ricans, American Indians, Asians, and other minorities. The efforts of white college students, at first directed to the civil rights movement, soon shifted to opposition to the Vietnam War and to the more nebulous "student power" branch of the New Left movement of the late 1960s.

While these highly visible minority and young people's movements were claiming much national attention, two other potentially powerful social forces were emerging. One is the union of poor and other disaffected people from all classes in a loose general movement promptly labelled by the media as populism. The other is the recognition by women of systematic sexual discrimination, and their consequent demands for equal status and opportunity. Populism is more protest than program, adding only depth of support to the existing radical critique of American history. It has no new ideological dimensions as such. The women's movement is still in an early stage, most of its adherents seeking only those rights to which they are already legally entitled (but which are nevertheless systematically denied). Some feminists, however, stress the need for much more comprehensive reconstruction of the social order. But the potential impact of both of these more recent efforts remains in the future.

Perhaps the most significant weakness of the early New Left, whether it addressed its efforts to civil rights or the war or the status of the nation's dispossessed, was its lack of a coherent understanding of what was wrong in the United States and what to do about it—in short, a serious lack of *theory*. In search of an analysis that would indicate some remedies beyond protest and/or the replacement of "misguided" politicians, the new radicals began to undertake a critique of capitalist society. They began to see the Vietnam War and other Third World involvements as imperialist efforts to acquire control over raw materials and markets. Black repression was seen as the product not of idiosyncratic racism, but of a racism partially created and thoroughly encouraged by capitalist values. The upper classes were profiting from the exploitation of the black and other working classes, and thus were quick to defend establishment policies in all essential respects.

For at least some members of this loose coalition, the only solution

Doonesbury

seemed to lie in eliminating the basic sources of racism and injustice at home, and of wars against Third World peoples abroad—in short, in putting an end to capitalism and introducing some form of socialism. Some saw it as essential to build alliances with the working classes, despite the difficulty of reaching a group that seemed in large part satisfied and unsympathetic to middle-class college students, and then to seek to use electoral and other routes to power. Others believed, like some black militants who served as their models, that conditions were so bad that they had nothing to lose from engaging in destructive or revolutionary acts immediately. Still others saw the prospective revolution more in terms of a complete change in life style and values, and sought to make their lives illustrations of those better values. By creating a "counterculture," they hoped to recruit others and ultimately to affect the dominant values of the nation. By the mid-1970s, the number of young whites who considered the termination or drastic transformation of the capitalist economic order to be essential—and by means that included revolutionary violence if necessary—seemed to be still growing. A much larger number, however, dismissed such aspirations as hopeless romanticism but maintained their hopes for equality and democracy and saw these as unattainable without substantial change in the American system.

One way to understand the rebirth of radicalism in the United States and the nature of its potential challenge to the dominant orthodoxy is to see it in terms of its basic elements. There are three major strains of radical thought currently posing serious opposition to American orthodoxy: reformism, anticapitalism, and individualism. These are only labels, of course, and we shall specify what each means in turn. Table 9.1 characterizes these three viewpoints.

Reformism emphasizes opportunity and participation in the evolving American capitalist system. It opposes great concentrations of wealth and privilege, and demands reforms sufficient to allow deprived individuals and groups to enjoy the full benefits available or potentially available in

TABLE 9.1 *Characteristics of the Major Strains of American Radicalism*

Ideology	Attitude Toward Basic American Values	Approach to U.S. Economic System	Major Goals
Reformist	Accepts all; seeks realization in practice, putting equality foremost	Accepts basic structure and dynamics, seeks greater opportunities for all and some redistribution of wealth and income	More humane welfare capitalism, with greater participation by all people
Anticapitalist	Rejects most, particularly individualism, but endorses greatly expanded equality and community	Rejects it as unjust and exploitative	Socialism, usually in decentralized egalitarian form, with all civil liberties
Individualist	Accepts all, but in original form, emphasizing freedom of individual and rights to property	Rejects it as too big, stifling to individuals, bureaucratic, and no longer true free enterprise	Individualist anarchist society via withdrawal or small-scale units

the United States. The anticapitalist strain challenges American capitalism directly, insisting that its inherent nature prevents realization of people's social and personal potential. This strain of radical thought is grounded in the argument that individualism, materialism, and private profitseeking inevitably result in exploitation, misery, and war for the great mass of people in the world. Only a social system in which people cooperate for the fulfillment of the material and human needs of all can provide a decent and morally justifiable life under current world conditions.

A third dimension of radical thought is strictly individualist, or self-oriented, in contrast to the system-orientation of the first two. It holds that no good can be achieved through social action or efforts to reconstruct society as a whole. Instead, people should seek to reconstruct their own thinking and personal lives in ways more truly human and worthwhile. This can be accomplished only alone or in the company of a few other like-minded people.

All three strains have permeated American history. The demand for participation and opportunity is probably the most conspicuous, for it has taken many forms and led to changes in the character of capitalism itself. The Jacksonian, Populist, Progressive, and New Deal periods were all characterized by such protests and by the ultimate transformation of capitalism from one form to another. In effect, the dominant system was able to blunt, absorb, and convert such demands into forms that could serve its own needs because their basic nature was not antagonistic to the principles of capitalism. Direct challenges to capitalism itself were first made by late nineteenth-century socialists and have continued to the present. They have been notably unsuccessful to date, because of the strength of American orthodoxy and attacks on those who hold such views by governments and others. Individualist withdrawal began with the transcendental individualists' attacks on the commercial society in the early nineteenth century. It today takes the forms of a kind of libertarian anarchism and of certan versions of countercultural withdrawal. Because it has never been a serious threat, it has never been repressed as have direct challenges to capitalism.

Thus radicalism is neither a single coherent system of thought nor the rallying-point of a unified social movement. Instead, it is a collection of different (and sometimes conflicting) beliefs, whose adherents chiefly share the conviction that they are deprived, powerless, and victimized by the dominant system. Radicalism begins as a set of reactions against contemporary conditions, and against the values and ideology that rationalize and justify them. Ultimately, it takes the form of an alternative ideology.

People can and do move from one strand of radical thought to another. In the 1970s, radicals have tended to shift from demands for participation and reform to rejection of the existing system. Such rejection takes the form either of calls for the replacement of capitalism or of withdrawal into highly individualistic anarchism or countercultural life styles. At any given moment, of course, some people are sincerely hoping and working for reforms that will make the system more just in their eyes, while others who have despaired of this approach are either attacking capitalism itself or abandoning politics and social life to find solace by themselves. The developing economic crisis spurs *each* of these currents in radical thought.

In this analysis, we shall focus on the distinctions between these three strands of radicalism and orthodoxy, and on the evolving views of some of the major sources of today's rebirth of radical ideology. Throughout, we shall be searching for what is general, or shared, among the different strains of thought that make up radicalism. And we shall emphasize the drift from demands for more equitable distribution of the rewards of the American capitalist system to rejection of the system itself.

Radical Political Values and Ideology

Each strand in radical thought rests on a distinctive response to the political values of American orthodoxy. Individualism plays a particularly central role. The thrust of the major strain of radicalism, as we have said, is toward participation, reform, and re-distribution of rewards within the American system. This form of radicalism accepts all the orthodox values, including individualism, but redefines and reorders them somewhat. The growing trend toward confrontation with capitalism rests on the outright rejection of at least some of these values, including individualism as we understand it, and the substitution of new values. The individualist strand of radicalism raises individualism even beyond its high status among the orthodox values, granting it nearly exclusive standing. It correspondingly reduces emphasis on values that legitimate social or governmental action. Let us briefly characterize what is distinctive about each of these forms of radicalism.

Participation, Reform, and Redistribution of Rewards

This primary strain of radicalism best illustrates the nature and conse-quences of the radical commitment to equality. Much of the history of tension between radicalism and the dominant orthodoxy can be attributed to the conflict between the values of equality and property as they are understood by the respective ideologies. The argument has involved both the *definition* and the *priority* attached to equality. Radicalism of this kind defines equality in broad and steadily expanding terms, proceeding from equality of opportunity to equality in the actual conditions of people's lives. And it gives full priority to equality, elevating it above all other political values when they come into conflict.

But it is easy to exaggerate the "radicalness" of the radical argument. For example, at no time in American history (excepting the period under discussion), did any significant number of radicals call for the abolition of private property as such, or for drastic action to equalize the condi-tions of people's lives. They asked only for somewhat greater emphasis on equality in the context of competitive individualism and respect for property rights. Starting from the acknowledged principle of political equality, in the sense of voting rights and majoritarianism, radicals gradually caused restrictions inconsistent with such principles, such as those involving property, sex, and race, to be removed.

Increasingly, in the 20th century, however, it appeared that sources of power other than government, and other socially produced limitations, prevented individuals from attaining their ends. Radicals, therefore, sought to expand the implications of equality to legitimize government action to preserve opportunity and the provision of sufficient education and social status to enable individuals to compete more equally. Once again, there was strong resistance on the part of those who held to more restrictive definitions of equality. Thus, though equality is symbolically unchallenged, its political and socioeconomic effectuation has been tentative and controversial.

By contrast, attachment to property as a legitimate and paramount value has been widely shared and rarely challenged. No major American thinker, including Jefferson (supposed by some of his contemporaries to have been unsympathetic to the wealthy and propertied), has failed to support strongly the individual's right to whatever land, goods, and money he or she could amass. Hamilton and some other Federalists considered these the central goals of man's motivations and sought to construct a government to serve these ends. Men like Adams and Jefferson believed that property gives people political independence, a stake in the society, and the capacity and right to judge—which in turn leads to wise public decisionmaking.

It should be clear that this strain of radicalism historically affirmed other traditional values, as well as property rights. The concepts of individualism, materialism, natural rights, limited government, and legalism were all taken for granted in the effort to expand and enhance equality. The same is true today: what this form of radicalism seeks is a reality that conforms to orthodox American rhetoric, providing greater opportunity for individuals to compete more successfully and amass larger amounts of the material rewards of the American system.

To some extent, such radicals do see flaws and limitations in the existing values, and would repair these deficiencies. The principle of limited government, for example, though still considered valid in the abstract because people should be free to attain their individual ends, is seen as much violated in practice. In this view, the worst violations are subsidies, price supports, and other financial benefits for those very economic interests most likely to use the principle of limited government as a defense against proposed policies that would benefit ordinary people. Individualism is considered to have humanistic and esthetic, as well as material, dimensions. Material aspirations, however, are still taken to be the primary motivation of "human nature," and the basic dynamic of social life. Racism is acknowledged and condemned, but the chief remedy proposed is laws to prevent discrimination.

Black liberation, however, will not come about solely through the activities of black people. Black America cannot be genuinely liberated until white America is transformed into a humanistic society free of exploitation and class division. The black and white worlds, although separate and distinct, are too closely intertwined—geographically, politically, and economically—for the social maladies of one not to affect the other. Both must change if either is to progress to new and liberating social forms.

From Robert L. Allen, *Black Awakening in Capitalist America: An Analytic History* (New York: Doubleday, 1970), p. 281.

The ideology that flows from these values contains a profound ambivalence. On the one hand, it brusquely rejects orthodoxy's claim that present policies must be appropriate because they are enacted by a system in which rules and widespread participation assure outcomes that reflect a democratic consensus. Economic and social conditions, readily visible to all who are willing to look, completely rebut the claims of American orthodoxy and must be corrected. Concentrations of economic power must be prevented from continuing their exploitation, and ordinary citizens must recapture power over the circumstances of their lives. On the other hand, this ideology holds that these goals can be achieved if more people become involved, reopen the political processes, and "throw the rascals out." By reforming certain aspects of politics, installing better people in office, and thus rearranging the priorities of government and society, the conditions of the mass of the people can be dramatically improved. In short, things are very bad, but it won't take much to set them right.

The fight against this concentration of privilege—open and covert, legal and illegal—is, we believe, the most important political question of this decade. Its goal is a more equitable distribution of wealth and power; its enemy is the entire arrangement of privileges, exemptions, and free rides that has narrowed the opportunity of most Americans to control their own destiny. This fight for fairness is political; it can be won only by organizing a new political majority in America.

From Jack Newfield and Jeff Greenfield, *A Populist Manifesto: The Making of a New Majority* (New York: Warner Paperback Library, 1972), p. 17.

This ambivalence has its roots in acceptance of most of the orthodox political values "as is," and in the effects of orthodox political ideology. Accepting the values of competitive individualism and materialism, this form of radicalism can only say that the "problem" is the unfair distribution of rewards—not the wrongness of the nature or workings of the economy as a whole. Thinking within the framework of American political ideology, and therefore convinced of the rightness and legitimacy of the political system as a whole, it can only say that there must be something temporarily wrong. If corrected through the sincere efforts of the people, the national government could again become the agent of the people and the instrument of economic opportunity for all. For these reasons, this version of radicalism remains principally a protest movement, demanding reform and opportunity *within* the existing system.

Challenges to Capitalism Itself

Though not yet primary, the anticapitalist version of contemporary radicalism has grown in proportion to the failure of reformist radicalism to achieve real success for more than a few sectors of the population. It holds that the traditional American values are not just in need of redefinition and reordering, but are themselves the cause of current problems. In particular, anticapitalist radicalism rejects individualism in the orthodox sense. Human nature is not necessarily competitive and self-aggrandizing, such radicals argue; people can learn to share, and to cooperate for the betterment of their mutual condition. When they do, a true sense of community will emerge. Justice in the form of roughly equal distribution of rewards will be available for all.

The key to achieving such results is seen as abolition of the private ownership of productive machinery and resources, and the profit-maximizing use that necessarily results. As long as such private owner-ship and profit orientation exist, masses of people *must* be exploited. Thus anticapitalist radicalism must reject the value of property rights, not necessarily as to personal property or home ownership, but as to large private holdings of land, capital, securities, and other forms of wealth.

The concept of limited government must also be abandoned, because government must serve as a central planning agency on behalf of the society as a whole. In order to provide enough goods and services for qualitative improvement of the lives of millions of ordinary American citizens, and to discharge obligations to the rest of humanity, it will be necessary to employ the society's productive resources in an efficient manner. Central planning is thus required to determine at least what is to be done where. Local organizations of workers or others may then assume responsibility for deciding how each goal will be reached and by whom.

Materialism is not entirely rejected, for it will be crucial to raise the material standard of living for most Americans, as well as for other people in the world. This is a prerequisite to the opportunity to enjoy other aspects of life, and to develop the creative, esthetic, and other human potential that exists in all persons. But materialism will not be the principal motivating force in people's lives, because they will not seek to amass things for themselves. They will be assured of enough to serve their needs, and instead will work out of a commitment to bettering the lives of others.

Anticapitalist radical values are clearly fundamentally different from those held by most Americans. The ideology derived from such values sees the American system today as fundamentally irrational. Private ownership and the profit motive lead inexorably to exploitation, wide-spread misery, and a sharply stratified class system with a very few powerful individuals at the top. There is a continued need for manipula-tion of the masses by the ruling capitalist class and its agents. Because the ruling class controls the nation's wealth, it also controls the government and, through it, the educational system and the political process generally. The major means of manipulation is inculcation of the ideology we have been calling American orthodoxy. Once fixed in the minds of the people, it makes social control possible with a minimum of conscious effort. Aspiring and competent people are induced to become agents of the ruling class because the ruling class controls the rewards and opportunities they seek.

In this self-reinforcing and self-perpetuating way, the system operates relatively smoothly. The problems that exist arise out of the characteristics of capitalism, but people recognize only their surface manifestations and not their causes. The financial problems of cities, for example, result not from the lack of a tax base or too much spending on education or welfare, but rather from the vast sums being spent to pay the interest and principal on loans from capitalist bankers. Because so many people are seen as hopelessly trapped in the orthodox values and ideology, anti-capitalist radicals face a serious dilemma. Either they must commit themselves to trying to transform the system through revolutionary action with the conscious support of only a minority of the people, or they must await a change of mind on the part of a decisive majority of the people, through events or persuasion or both. Understandably, this issue remains a subject of vigorous debate within this strain of radicalism.

Individualist Rejection of Social Solutions

Reformist radicalism accepts orthodox values and ideology, and asks that rhetoric be made reality. Anticapitalist radicalism requires sweeping value changes and a sharp rupture with orthodox ideology. But both of these strains have in mind an ideal social system, in which aggregations of people do certain things in accordance with specific principles, thereby producing a pattern of rewards for individuals. If the rewards or satisfactions are not just or desirable, the remedy is to change the way the social system operates. But the individualist form of radicalism rejects the idea that a large-scale social system can provide what individuals really need: such nonmaterial things as understanding of life and its meaning, harmony with nature and other people, love, and other forms of personal growth and fulfillment.

—— ■

It is plain that the goal of revolution today must be the liberation of daily life. . . . Revolutionary liberation must be a self-liberation that reaches social dimensions, not "mass liberation" or "class liberation" behind which lurks the rule of an elite, a hierarchy and a state. . . . Out of the revolution must emerge a self that takes full possession of daily life, not a daily life that takes full possession of the self. . . .

If for this reason alone, the revolutionary movement is profoundly concerned with lifestyle. It must try to *live* the revolution in all its totality, not only participate in it.... The revolutionary group must clearly see that its goal is not the seizure of power but the dissolution of power—indeed, it must see that the entire problem of power, of control from below and control from above, can be solved only if there is no above or below.

From Murray Bookchin, *Post-Scarcity Anarchism* (Berkeley: Ramparts Press, 1971), pp. 44–47.

Thus, the individualist rejection of what it sees as a corruptly commercialized and destructive world is a personal, not a social, form of radicalism. Emphasis on individualism is greatly expanded and turned inward, away from material acquisitiveness and from the great mass of other people. The more limited government is, the better, for each individual must seek his or her own solution; real help can come only from the very small number of other persons with whom one has established special relationships.

This form of radicalism can be reached by a direct route from American orthodoxy or from reformist radicalism because it does not require extensive value change. Its emphasis on individualism and withdrawal makes it intellectually accessible to those who tire of struggling against large and impersonal social forces, and to those who conclude that all large-scale social organizations are equally destructive of human freedom and potential. Unless vast numbers of people suddenly embrace the same personalized form of radicalism, it poses no serious threat to the continued operation of the American system or its orthodoxy. Power and its capabilities in a society are unaffected by the withdrawal of a few persons, particularly when their withdrawal is consciously based on the conviction that social efforts toward change are by definition undesirable or impossible. Nevertheless, this form of radicalism is gaining adherents, perhaps because the other two forms of radicalism are frustrating and (in the case of anticapitalism) require greater value change than people can or want to achieve.

The Status and Aspirations of Women

Though women make up about 53 percent of the population, they suffer from some of the same forms of discrimination and bias as racial minorities. Women are typically expected to take care of the housework or to fill low-status low-wage jobs outside the home. Many people have been socialized to believe that women are less creative, less independent, and less capable of exercising independent judgment about business or governmental decisions than men.

In the 1960s and 1970s a growing feminist movement tried to counter these demeaning attitudes regarding the capabilities and roles of women, to work for equality for women, and to raise the consciousness of both men and women about gender roles. This movement for "women's liberation" has registered some successes and encountered some serious obstacles.

The most impressive accomplishments in changing women's roles have come in the economic marketplace. In the 1950s women began working outside their homes in increasing numbers, and in the 1970s the trend became a floodtide. By September 1977, 48.9 percent of women over 16 years old held a paid job, and 41 percent of *all* workers were women. But the median earnings of women were less than $7000 per year, compared to roughly $12,000 for men, and men's incomes were rising at a more rapid rate.[1] College enrollments of women have also spurted, with women outnumbering men in undergraduate colleges and making up one-quarter of the students in law and medical schools. In at least some social circles there is a new awareness of sexism in everyday language and in everyday assumptions about who should do what kinds of work, and many cities and states have made it illegal to discriminate on the basis of sex in hiring or pay.

The more optimistic observers of the women's movement believe that it will continue to make substantial gains because it coincides, as some earlier feminist movements did not, with social and economic trends that favor a more important role for women. During World War Two a severe labor shortage forced industries to recruit women for jobs they had never been allowed to do before, and the experience proved that women could perform well on assembly lines and in administrative positions as well as in the "pink collar" occupations traditionally regarded as women's work. A long-term shift in the labor force from manufacturing to the service industries has markedly increased the economic opportunities for women and the willingness of employers to hire them. In the growing number of technical and office jobs, brute strength is not required. Many families also need two incomes in order to achieve an acceptable standard of living.

Some recent noneconomic trends further encourage women to look for fulfillment, status, and income outside the home. Birth control devices are more readily available than they once were. Educated women are less willing to accept traditional roles. The nuclear family is eroding as the divorce rate climbs and it becomes socially acceptable to live with people without marrying. Sexual exploration is more widely practiced than was the case 20 years ago, giving women a new kind of independence. Finally, the civil rights movement, the youth movement, and the antiwar movement of the sixties helped make women aware that they, too, suffered from discrimination and powerlessness.

Still, the feminist movement has experienced serious setbacks as well as some successes, and it is not clear that significant gains can be ex-

[1] *The New York Times,* November 29, 1977, pp. 1 and 28.

pected in the future. Probably the most publicized goal of the movement has been ratification of the Equal Rights Amendment, an objective it has found extremely difficult to achieve.[2] Although a small number of women have become executives or achieved high status in prestigious professions, the great majority are still finding low-status, low-paying, dead-end jobs. Because childcare facilities are often inadequate or nonexistent, many women cannot go to school or seek work in industry. The opposition to equality has remained strong, and in the late 1970s seemed to be mounting as part of an upsurge of conservative lobbying. Many men also seem immune to the new awareness of sexism, though the feminist movement cannot be successful unless men's consciousness of the inequity and the pathology of inequality in gender roles is also raised.

Implications of the New Radicalism-Populism

Although the New Left has fragmented into such disparate elements as countercultural withdrawal, Christian and Eastern religious sects, anarchism, terrorism, community control movements, and others, new groups of serious radicals and revolutionary socialists are joining the general thrust toward change. This movement has gained considerable depth due to the growth of populism, which has drawn poor people and many other protest-minded individuals to the point of readiness to act against established practices and interests. The populist surge has little independent theory or ideology, and some elements in it could probably be readily mobilized to attack minorities and the left. But its traditional critique of "economic royalists" and the establishment generally, as well as its demand for a larger share of income and opportunity, ally its numerous followers with the radical movement.

These nontraditional, change-oriented ideologies are important because of what they *stand for* (alliances among the lowest classes to bring about fundamental change in the *status quo*); and because of the kind of reaction their beliefs and tactics may *provoke* (rigid policies, repression, a police state). Their reactionary counterparts, increasingly visible and certainly both more numerous and more powerful, seem likely to act in essentially similar ways if and when the radical groups approach success.

If and when the economic crisis worsens, the protests of frustrated workers may make the upheavals of the 1960s seem tame. It is, of course, possible to overestimate the likelihood of social unrest resulting from unemployment and reduced standards of living. Sometimes people merely blame themselves, or believe even more strongly in the capacity of established leaders and institutions to solve such problems. Or they may

[2] See Chap. 13, pp. 263–264.

seek a deeply authoritarian social order that promises to right all wrongs immediately. But the basic feeling aroused is rejection of things as they are, and that can lead in many directions—most of which involve fundamental change.

Contrasting Ideologies and the Nature of Social Problems

It should be clear that the orthodox values and ideology lead to a disintegrated view of the nature and causes of problems. Individualism's "every man for himself" approach, and the premise that economics is distinct from politics and should remain so, serve as barriers against seeing problems as interconnected and grounded in both basic values and the fundamental characteristics of the economic and social systems. Not all problems are, of course; but the longer a problem endures, in one form or another, the more we may suspect that its sources lie at these deeper levels. Problems are certainly easier to deal with politically if they are seen as discrete and superficial, but they may not be easier to *solve* permanently. This too is characteristic of the dominant ideology, in that it stresses accommodation and compromise and seeks to avoid basic conflict at all costs.

Is radical-populism distinctively different in its analysis of the nature and causes of problems? Again, we must be careful not to attribute too much consistency or unity to that loose ideology, but the answer would appear to be a qualified yes. A progression can be traced from relatively superficial analysis toward a view of problems as rooted in basic values and the nature of the economic system. Problems are seen as the combined product of social, economic, and political factors, implying rejection of the compartmentalized approach of the dominant ideology. Problems are also seen as aspects of a social totality, not isolatable from each other.

But some features of the radical outlook suggest that certain qualifications are in order, and that it should not be seen as the precise opposite of the dominant ideology. Radical-populism is very different from orthodoxy, but is by no means its opposite. For one thing, many of its allegations appear to be facile oversimplifications. Often neither evidence nor logic connects visible issues or problems with the alleged underlying "causes." Also, many of the remedies that radicalism urges presuppose the continuity or efficacy of the very values, systems, and processes that it purports to be attacking as corrupt or fraudulent. To argue that economic exploitation by a callous American ruling class is the central cause of worldwide misery, and then to urge community organizing and electoral campaigns as a remedy, is at best inconsistent and confused, and perhaps hypocritical.

Finally, and perhaps most important for our purposes, radicalism and populism both still operate within the confines of American political consciousness, broadly conceived. American radicals and populists project the future from what they see around them today, and from readings in American history, data on social conditions, and attempts to understand what people actually want. They consider and select alternative courses of action based pragmatically on existing conditions and on what they think others can be induced to accept. Their values are only modestly different, mostly in terms of priorities, from those of most other Americans. In these and other ways, their style of thinking is pragmatic, empirical, and distinctively American—and therefore distinguishable from orthodox values and ideology only in a limited fashion. Nevertheless, this is sufficient to cause great tensions and the potential for drastic change in the United States in the next decade.

Though it is not vital to our analysis, we should perhaps note the beginnings of a fundamentally different political consciousness that may achieve real significance in the future. These new beginnings lie in some aspects of minority thinking, and in some versions of socialist thought. In no case do they embody elements of mainstream American thought. Nor is this world-view built on the rejection or correction of specific aspects of the dominant values and ideology. In this way, it avoids the problem of so many radicals—unintentionally falling back into an orthodox frame of reference by focusing exclusively on it.

The political consciousness and world-view of American Indians, for example, rest on wholly different premises and values, and on a cultural milieu so distinct as to be unrecognizable to most Americans. The rational, empirical, logical approach of the capitalist-liberal American mind is absent. In its place are intuitive, communal, traditional, holistic thought processes. The same is true of certain segments of the black and Chicano movements. Wholly distinct world-views reflecting sometimes-distant cultural heritages are taking contemporary forms and serving as the basis of self-contained enclaves within the larger society. In all of these cases, the ultimate goal is self-determination, a kind of multicultural pluralism in the United States in which each minority is free to live in accordance with its own standards and principles. Whether this is practical or not, or even attractive to a substantial proportion of each minority, remains to be seen.

But there can be little doubt that, for the present, the focus of political conflict in this country is the tension between the established orthodoxy and its radical-populist offspring. The former may evolve gradually and grudgingly, or the latter may recede in the face of change and coercion. Far more likely, however, in light of the continuing convergence of problems into a deepening crisis, is an exacerbation of this conflict. In that event, the differences between these positions may come to seem very real indeed. We shall note the implications of these differences repeatedly throughout our analysis, and then return to a head-on confrontation with prospects for the future in Part 6.

The Unresolved Questions

A number of questions remain, and some have barely been touched on. We have not yet determined why American public policies have the forms and consequences they do. The ideological answers are, after all, only that—ideology. They tell us what some people believe to be the answers, but they have no necessary relationship to reality. Only evidence about who does what to bring about which results —and why—can satisfactorily answer this key question. But we *have* raised a series of questions in this analysis of contrasting ideologies. Is power in the United States dispersed and held mostly by the people, as the orthodoxy insists, or is it concentrated in such a manner as to leave the people powerless in most cases, as radicalism argues? What is the relationship between economic power and political power: is it direct, as radicalism claims, or are they separate worlds, as the orthodoxy maintains?

In short, we have before us some clear patterns of policy consequences, and some conflicting "explanations" of them. We shall use both to frame our approach to the study of power and decisionmaking in American politics. From the evidence gathered and analyzed in all the ways suggested by these two types of inquiries, we should be able to reach some conclusions.

PART 4

Institutions
and Processes:
The Role of Elites

10

Managing the
Political Economy

We now begin a series of seven chapters devoted to analysis of the *institutions* and *decisionmakers* that produce policies and address problems such as those we have explored. We shall look first at the general subject of managing the overall political economy, and then at the more specific question of how its governmental sector is managed. In Chapters 12 through 16, we examine the workings of the components of government: the Constitution, the Congress, the courts, the presidency, and the bureaucracy.

In Chapter 2, we articulated the basic conceptual framework of an integrated political economy composed of a dominant corporate-banking sector, a competitive business sector, and government. Their integration was analyzed chiefly in economic terms; even the case study of combined public-private decisionmaking concerned money and its control. In this chapter, we shall explore other dimensions of that integration, particularly the social process by means of which the total political economy is held together and given direction. But before we can do so, we must consider a preliminary issue that is central to political analysis. What are the goals of our inquiry? What questions are to be asked in these next several chapters, and what sorts of evidence or reflection are necessary to answer them?

The Basic Questions

The questions basic to political analysis are: Who holds power? How do they employ it to sustain themselves and to manage the society? What difference do such uses of power make to people and problems? Answers to these questions are necessary both to understand how a given system works *and* to consider the desirability and probability of various kinds of change. But, as is true of most really important questions, the available answers conflict sharply due to different ways of posing the questions and looking for answers.

We shall here assess three very different approaches to these questions, not for the purpose of choosing among them, but merely to point up their distinctive features and relative potential. No one approach is necessarily "better" than another, except in terms of the premises and purposes of the analyst. Our intent is to provide materials that permit the use of any or all of these approaches. We shall employ each where and when useful in search of convincing answers to the basic questions. Our final answers are set forth in Chapter 19, after evidence on elite decision-making and non-elites' impact on such decisions has been reviewed in this and the next part.

1. The Systemic Approach

We have already introduced the essential components of this approach. It begins with the comprehensive conceptualization of an integrated political economy. Next it sees certain dominant imperatives (maintenance of profitability and expansion of sales and investment opportunities) as creating enduring internal dynamics (tensions produced by inequalities, economic pressures, and the like generate a continuing need to preserve social support). Together these imperatives and dynamics set the agenda for governmental action. This approach asserts that government, *no matter who the people holding office may be,* has no alternative but to act in ways that serve the needs of the dominant units of the economic system. Whatever the social origins and political beliefs of officeholders, they *must* act to defend investments and open up markets abroad. At home, they *must* encourage profitability, defend inequality of wealth and income, and prevent social unrest—whether by diversion, manipulation, or coercion.

According to the systemic approach, the answer to the question "Who holds power?" is not to be found by analyzing government office-holders or even their policies. Instead, it lies in the structure of ownership and control of the major units of the corporate-banking sector, identification of those whose interests are served by the workings of the total system. One version of this approach also conceives of the social order in terms of classes of people, dominated by a tiny ruling class made up of the major owners of the key banks and corporations. This ruling class need not actually direct events on a day-to-day basis, for the ideas and practices that are considered "realistic" and that predominate in the society are those that reflect and effectively serve its interests. If an analyst understands the long-range interests of the ruling class, according to this view, nearly all political economic actions become comprehensible.

One weakness of the systemic approach is that it may seem to explain things too mechanically. After all, there is much conflict about proposed government actions, and at times the policies implemented appear to be at odds with the interests of the corporate-banking sector. Three observations need to be offered here. First, much of what government does is not of fundamental importance to the maintenance of the economic system itself, to its major imperatives, or to the basic pattern of burdens and benefits that it generates. Such non-fundamental isues may well be subjects of controversy between components of the corporate-banking sector, or between groups emerging from the competitive business sector and the population generally (consumers, environmentalists, and the like).

Second, the shared commitment of all sectors to the maintenance and continued profitability of the total system should not obscure the existence of continuing rivalries among component elements. The oil industry's success in increasing its profitability in 1973–1975, for example, cost other major industries. They may in turn be expected to resist policies intended to consolidate the oil industry's gains and/or to seek ways of passing their new costs on to others; inevitably, considerable political conflict will result.

Finally, policies that appear to be contrary to the immediate interests of dominant elements of the corporate-banking sector may actually serve their long-range interests. The federal income tax is a celebrated example: rather than redistributing wealth, it appears to serve the function of assuring people that the tax system is progressive and fair while actually preserving the pre-existing pattern of unequal distribution. The Marshall Plan, through which the United States invested tens of billions of dollars in the reconstruction of European industries after World War Two, is often cited as an example of American generosity. But U.S. industries *required* export markets and trading opportunities, and the only possible market of the necessary size and scope was a revived Europe. Moreover, the investment of vast public funds provided many opportunities for profitable investment of private funds. And the American investment was provided by tax revenues from the entire population, not just from the corporate-banking beneficiaries of a revived Europe.

These observations make the systemic approach appear less mechanical and more open to contending forces whose efforts often succeed in shaping particular outcomes. All such conflict, however, can be seen as occurring within the basic framework created by the structure and imperatives of the total political economy. Where fundamental questions are concerned, the range of choice is very narrow; and whoever occupies positions of responsibility (in government, the corporate banking sector, the media, schools, foundations, and the like) must act to preserve the mutual enterprise, the American economic system and its associated social structure.

2. The Policy-Consequences Approach

We have also laid the groundwork quite explicitly for this approach to characterizing power. No particular elegance of conceptualization is required, nor need the analyst amass a great deal of detailed evidence about who makes decisions and on what basis. All that need be done is to specify who gains—and who either gains *less* or *loses*—from the actions of government over time. If regular patterns of consequences can be identified, and if such patterns are found to recur in various areas, one may plausibly infer that those who benefit most have played a part in bringing about such results. Constant and recurring patterns are highly unlikely to *be* the result of sheer coincidence; their sources are to be found in structural factors or the power and influence of those who benefit most. People who are regularly on the losing side undoubtedly do not *seek* or *prefer* to be; something or someone has caused them to be losers. And where the majority of people appears to be systematically less favored, analysis points to a relative few as the key holders of power.

What is difficult about this approach is to say exactly what the consequences of particular government policies are. It is often hard to tell what has resulted from which government actions, and how the operation of the "private" economy may have affected final outcomes. This problem is partially solved by looking at large-scale and aggregate patterns of consequences over long periods of time. And where, such as here, "public" and "private" sources of power are seen as related parts of one coherent whole, the problem is minimized still further. Patterns of consequences—the conditions that people experience, such as the continuing impact of taxation on the distribution of income—can serve as the basis for locating power and understanding the workings of the system.

3. The Nature-of-Governing-Elites Approach

We consider this approach last for two important reasons. First, the other two approaches are simpler, more direct means of locating power in the integrated political economy we have been portraying. And we have already done much of the preliminary conceptualization and factual presentation appropriate to their use. Second, although it is much more familiar among social scientists and journalists as a method of locating power, the nature-of-governing-elites approach is one of the most controversial subjects in all social science. (The differing positions on this issue will be considered with special care in the next chapter.) And, most importantly, this approach focuses with varying exclusivity on government institutions and the people who make decisions within them.

Application of this approach tends to lead analysts to one of two conflicting conclusions: the "power elite" viewpoint and the "democratic pluralist" viewpoint. The first school of analysis looks almost exclusively at the social backgrounds (family origin, income level, education, occupation, and the like) of key decisionmakers—chiefly in government, but also in the economy, media, and elsewhere. It finds them representative almost entirely of the upper class, and concludes that government actions reflect the interests and preferences of that class. Adherents of the other viewpoints, limiting their inquiry still more narrowly to government itself, claim that analysis of actual *decisions*—rather than social backgrounds—reveals many sources of influence, an arbiter's role for public officials, and results that generally reflect compromises in the public interest.

Because we see government as only one aspect of the total political economy, we believe that analysis confined to or even primarily focused on that sector can be misleading. One runs the risk of tunnel vision: of overestimating the importance, independence, and discretionary choices of government decisionmakers, as well as the involvement of the general population. And yet government and politics are not only the focus, but the very *purpose*, of our inquiry in this book. Once the appropriate context has been established, therefore, we shall be eager to take up this phase of our analysis. It cannot alone reveal who holds power in the society but, carefully done, elite analysis can tell us much about how and why government does what it does.

In distinguishing these three approaches, we again emphasize that "facts" may have very different meanings depending on the premises and purposes of the analysts who marshal them. Each of these approaches looks for a particular kind of evidence, but all also employ much of the same evidence. The latter circumstance enables us to develop a large body of data without becoming exclusively committed to any one approach. As our analysis proceeds, the pieces we assemble may be applicable to one or more of the three approaches. Such is surely the case with the following survey of the process of social integration, for all three approaches stress its importance.

Social Integration: Institutions and Process

The core of our integrated political economy is the network of economic interdependence and mutual impact we described in Chapter 2. But much of the glue that holds this massive entity together, enabling it to operate as a coherent whole, is a social product. It is generated by the basic values and beliefs we learn from family and schools; the selection and interpretation of the news we see, hear, and read in the communications media; the reports and recommendations of prestigious persons and groups; and the actions of leaders in various fields. A variety of more or less deliberate uses of power combine to create a complex and subtle process in which general acquiescence, support, and even anticipatory responses play a part.

Much of the coherence that characterizes the actions of this political-economic system is thus provided by the apparently voluntary behavior of millions of people. They may be thoroughly conditioned to such behavior by external phenomena; the outcome is roughly the same as if there had been direct and forceful coordination. But the process is generally peaceful and routine—the "natural" way to do things. Many institutions contribute to this process. The elementary schools insistently stress the benevolent and competent nature of our economic and political institutions. Foundations such as the Ford Foundation and the Carnegie Foundation commission studies documenting how much the country needs the things they espouse. The communications media select the news we receive, or even make the news by asking certain kinds of questions; in both cases, the result reflects the fact that the media themselves are big business. Prestigious businessmen's organizations such as the Committee for Economic Development, the Council on Foreign Relations, and the Business Council advise their colleagues in government on a day-to-day basis and develop long-range plans for governmental action.

In all these cases, studies have shown (or could show) how people with wealth, status, and power effectively shape the attitudes and behavior of other people. We shall focus on only one institution—higher education—because it is both representative of all the others and a process in which we are all engaged. In this case study, we shall see how the combination of public and private institutions, and their control by particular types of people, leads to opportunities for managing the society. There are more than 2,200 institutions of higher education in the United States, ranging from junior colleges to institutions with 30–49,000 students and an equal number of faculty, staff, and administrators, which offer a variety of Ph.D. and other professional degrees. They are not usually seen as involved in the ongoing political processes, except as recipients of large proportions of state budgets or sites of student outbursts. But they are an integral part of the configuration of power in the United States and serve some vital functions for it. Any analysis that seeks to locate sources of elite influence or to trace uses of power must make a point of analyzing the political role of institutions of higher education. We shall sketch the outlines of this political role briefly, using the major universities as our principal source of illustration. In general, our thesis is that elites dominate these institutions more fully than most other institutions within the society, and use them to serve their own needs and to influence both rising near-elites and the mass public toward support of established structures, policies, and practices.

The parameters of the university's functions are determined by four factors: the people who govern it, the sources of its financial support, the purposes these and other forces encourage it to serve, and the people who execute these tasks—that is, the faculty. A recent study by the Educational Testing Service, the well-known and authoritative testing arm of American higher education, sheds considerable light on who trustees and regents of colleges and universities are, and what they think about higher education.[1] Table 10.1 highlights some major aspects of the socio-economic backgrounds of these trustees, categorizing the institutions they serve as selective private universities (selective with regard to admissions, such as the Ivy League and similar schools) and public universities. It suggests quite simply that the governance of universities, more than any other institutions we have examined, is in the hands of persons belonging to the uppermost strata of our society.

University Trustees as Elites

Nearly two thirds of all college and university trustees in the nation are in the top 1 percent in income level; in the case of the selective private universities, 43 percent earn over $100,000 per year. The occupations of trustees are nearly all the highest-status ones, with business executives making up 35 percent of the total. The prevalence of businessmen helps to explain the fact that 20 percent of all trustees—including all the trustees or regents of junior colleges, community colleges, and small private colleges—are members of the boards of directors of one or more corporations whose stock is traded on a stock exchange. A total of 46 percent of the trustees of the selective private universities overlap with

---

[1] Rodney T. Hartnett, *College and University Trustees: Their Backgrounds, Roles, and Educational Attitudes* (Princeton, N.J.: Educational Testing Service, 1969).

TABLE 10.1   *Socioeconomic Backgrounds of Members of College and University Governing Boards, 1967 (in percentages)*

	Total, Trustees of All U.S. Colleges and Universities	Trustees of Selective Private Universities	Trustees of Public Universities
Age			
under 40	5	1	3
40–49	21	11	20
50–59	37	42	34
Over 60	36	46	40
Annual Income			
below $10,000	8	2	2
$10–$19,999	18	3	13
$20–$29,999	15	6	15
$30–$49,999	19	18	27
$50–$99,999	20	26	24
Over $100,000	16	43	16
Occupation			
Lawyer	10	13	20
Merchandising executive	7	3	7
Manufacturing executive	17	27	18
Bank or insurance executive	11	14	12
Professional	32	21	19
All Other	23	22	24
Number of corporations, traded on a stock exchange, for which trustees served on board of directors:			
None	78	53	76
One	10	15	11
Two	5	13	5
Three or more	5	18	6

Source: Rodney T. Hartnett, *College and University Trustees: Their Backgrounds, Roles and Educational Attitudes* (Princeton, N.J.: Educational Testing Service, 1969), pp. 57–59.

boards of directors of these major corporations, and 18 percent serve on three or more such corporate boards. In general, the selective private universities tend to have the wealthiest, highest-status trustees, perhaps partly because board positions are filled chiefly by the boards themselves on a kind of self-perpetuating basis. The typical board member of a public university is a lawyer, perhaps because open positions are filled chiefly by the governor, who may tend to pay political debts in this way.

Trustees' political attitudes may be determined from their political party identifications and self-described ideological orientations. Of all trustees, 58 percent were Republicans and 33 percent Democrats; 21 percent described themselves as conservatives, 15 percent as liberal, and the remainder as "moderate." [2] The proportion of each was roughly constant among the various types of institutions. But of perhaps more immediate relevance are their attitudes toward issues likely to arise in the university's context. Responses on several such issues, posed in the form of statements, are given in Table 10.2. It is clear that trustees believe

TABLE 10.2   *Trustees Attitudes on University Issues (percent agreeing or agreeing strongly)*

	Total, Trustees of All U.S. Colleges and Universities	Trustees of Selective Private Universities	Trustees of Public Universities
Attendance at this institution is a privilege, not a right.	92	98	80
All campus speakers should be subject to some official screening process.	69	45	68
Students who actively disrupt the function of a college by demonstrating, sitting-in, or otherwise refusing to obey the rules should be expelled or suspended.	81	71	83
Students involved in civil disobedience off the campus should be subject to discipline by the college as well as by local authorities.	49	29	46
The requirement that a professor sign a loyalty oath is reasonable.	53	33	52

Source: Hartnett, *College and University Trustees*, p. 60.

higher education to be a privilege and not a right, and that one of the functions of the university is to train faculties and students in accordance with established standards and procedures. In response to other questions, the trustees made clear their determination to maintain control over all major decisions within their universities. Beyond doubt, the structure of

[2] *Ibid.*, p. 65.

university governance indicates firm guidance and charting of basic directions.

Links to Government in University Funding

The financing of most institutions of higher education is a major link to the more formal governing structures of both federal and state governments—and, presumably, to those dominant in such circles. Public institutions, of course, receive most of their financial support from state (or, in some cases, local) governments. They characteristically charge relatively low tuitions, with the deficit made up from public tax revenues. (A provocative and carefully detailed analysis of the sources of revenue and actual recipients points out that, overall, this process amounts to working-class financing of low-cost educations for middle-class youth.[3]) The dependence of these institutions on the largesse of state legislatures makes them especially anxious to serve the needs and preferences of individual state legislators and the interests dominant in the state generally. Thus, there is a strong desire to be "useful," as defined by key businesses and industries, and to avoid the taint of unorthodox political ideas or behavior that might antagonize established powers in the state. Despite these pressures, of course, tensions between the larger state universities and their legislatures are frequently high.

Both public and private universities also rely heavily on financial assistance in various forms from the federal government. Public universities such as the University of Michigan and the University of California receive about 50 percent and 40 percent respectively of their annual budgets from the federal government. At private universities such as the University of Chicago and Harvard, the totals were roughly 65 percent and 40 percent respectively in the late 1960s. Table 10.3 lists the ten universities that received the most federal support in 1974. Federal assistance takes many forms, from loans and grants to students, buildings, and equipment to performance of research and teaching functions (ROTC, for example) on the campus and provision of contract services. In the latter case, the university in effect acts as a direct arm of the United States government, whether in experimental programs of crime control or poverty amelioration in the United States or in the development of agriculture or training of police and bureaucrats in developing countries. In every case, these funds are valued by universities, and a major university must place and keep itself in a position to compete successfully for such grants if it is to retain its status. Not only does the capacity to hire and provide research opportunities for well-reputed faculty members depend on funds of this type, but a substantial share of the operating budget of the university is also contributed in this way. Some university

[3] Lee Hansen and Burton A. Weisbrod, *Benefits, Costs and Finance of Public Higher Education* (Chicago: Markham, 1969).

TABLE 10.3   *How They Stand: American Universities Ranked by Amount of Federal Support, 1974*

Rank	University	Amount (millions)
1.	University of Washington	$81.89
2.	University of California, Los Angeles	73.68
3.	University of Wisconsin	73.6
4.	Harvard University	72.5
5.	University of California, San Diego	71.1
6.	Massachusetts Institute of Technology	69.5
7.	University of Minnesota	68.06
8.	Howard University	67.02
9.	Stanford University	66.78
10.	University of Michigan	63.87

Source: National Science Foundation, *Federal Funds for Research Development and other Activities* (Washington, D.C.: NSF, 1975).

administrators see this process as a welcome opportunity to be of service to the society, others are less enthusiastic, but none deny the reality of the pressure.

Purposes of the University

The purposes of the university are much less concretely demonstrated than the last two parameters, but we can begin to identify the kinds of pressures that contribute to defining them. Three basic purposes may be identified, though how most universities rank them in terms of priority may be disputed. First is the purpose of providing social mobility for students and well-trained functionaries for the economy and society. These goals are complementary: students and their parents visualize college education principally as a means of getting a good job, and the economy and society require alert, aspiring, adaptable men and women to perform a multitude of tasks. The result is a vocationally oriented program of instruction whose chief criterion of success is the student's acquisition of a job offering prospects of income and status. To prepare students for such jobs, the current structure of the economic and social order must be taken as a given, its needs assessed and extended into the future, and students shown how to adapt to and fulfill those needs.

Second is the purpose of providing knowledge that will help solve problems facing the society. To be of assistance, the definitions of such problems must be similar to those of the relevant policymakers; otherwise the results of research will not be used and this purpose will not be served. Thus much research effort is devoted to finding ways for those who are currently dominant to carry out their policies. In seeking to solve problems of social disharmony, this perspective may lead to defining those who for one reason or another do not accept orthodox standards of behavior and life styles as "maladjusted" or "criminal," and to developing techniques for better controlling such "deviants." In the case of problems perceived by private industry, university efforts amount to socializing the sometimes high costs of research and development, while benefits accrue chiefly to the user industries.

Third is the intellectual purpose of the university—to transmit the culture and wisdom of the past, to adapt it to the needs of the present and the future, and to help students develop the capacity to think critically and independently about themselves, their society, and the world. This is the most difficult, least accepted, and least accomplished of the university's purposes. To think critically and evaluatively about oneself and one's surroundings requires severe effort and self-discipline, and the destruction of a lifetime's complacent assumptions. It provokes sharp reaction from an insecure but financially vital outside world. And so it does not often occur, and if it does, it is not often sustained long.

Standards for the Faculty

The faculty must operate within the context defined by these various factors. Men and women who teach, let us assume, seek advancement and security as much as do others in society. To be well regarded in one's own institution and profession, to do the research that makes for visibility and mobility, and to avoid the controversies that spell an end to advancement, faculty members must accept the basic standards that trustees, financial sources, and accepted university purposes have set for them. The real deviant soon becomes uncomfortably visible, pressures focus on them, and they either return to their accepted role or lose their university status. Nor is this established role uncongenial to many university faculty members. Their class origins; identification with a prestigious profession; need for access to people of knowledge, money, and power; and current positions of authority lead them to adopt the perspective of the "is." Their task is to explain, rationalize, and project the present into the future.

What is the impact of these various forces on the students who pass through American institutions of higher education? In general, survey evidence suggests that the long-term effect has been to induce them to trust and support the acts of government more fully than do ordinary citizens. College graduates are better informed, take part in politics more, and are more fully imbued with orthodox ideology than those of comparable age and life experience who do not attend college. To some extent, the effects of college education may be mistakenly attributed to the effects of either youth (the proportion of college-educated people is higher in each new generation and age group) or economic status (college students come from wealthier families and earn more income after college). The autonomous influences of these separate factors are seldom made distinct. College education has repeatedly been shown to have an independent effect, aside from the fact that it usually coincides with both youth and wealth. Taken by itself, it correlates with greater confidence in the established political system and its current policies. Nor is the reaction to the Vietnam War really an exception to these general propositions. College graduates at first supported the war more strongly than others, and only shifted to greater conviction that the United States had made a mistake *after* President Nixon began to withdraw troops. The campus-based dissent against the war began as a very small movement; its escalation took several years and repeated provocations, and even then seemed in many cases to be limited exclusively to opposition to the single policy of war in Southeast Asia.

It is clear, therefore, that the universities serve elites as a major means of developing long-term influence, both by shaping vocational orientations and skills and by instilling the political ideology and broad behavioral cues that will lead to later support. Nevertheless, some universities, some faculty members, and some students do not fit these general descriptions.

The Nature and Implications of the American "Establishment"

What follows is a frankly speculative commentary on patterns extracted from the foregoing evidence, many exhaustive case studies and biographies, and our own political experience and intuition. We think that the character of leadership in the American political system may fairly be characterized as an "establishment," if the proper definitions are used, and that this situation has profound implications for both the structure of power and the process of change in the United States.

The concept of an *establishment*, though vague and subject on occasion to overtones of conspiracy, has an expressiveness that justifies its use. For us the term encompasses individuals holding positions of power (in government *and* private affairs) who have come to share roughly the same values, interests, political ideology, and sense of priorities about what government should be doing. Most of all, it denotes a shared proprietary concern for the continued success of the enterprise—meaning the American system, in its familiar social, economic, and political dimensions. Admission to the establishment is not easy, and it is never automatic. It is contingent first on possession of some distinct power resource, such as institutional position (in politics, business, education, or other fields), talent, money, family status, and so forth. Among the many men and women with such resources, some are distinguished by their concern for the success of the enterprise, their willingness to play by the familiar rules, and their talent for finding and articulating the compromise or making the sacrifice that insures conflict reduction. These are the crucial attributes. It is such people whom established leaders will invite into the loose and highly informal establishment. Members recognize each other not by labels or lapel pins, but by the orthodoxy they share—for example, the readiness with which they can negotiate with each other, even across class lines or occupational boundaries. Establishment types are "regular guys" who try to understand the other fellow's problems, avoid "rocking the boat" publicly, and instead do what they can to reach accommodations in which all end up better off than when they started. Mutual trust, mutual support, and mutual advantage knit the establishment together; but it is never so self-conscious and coherent as when challenges arise to the very system that has made possible this relaxed and congenial arrangement.

The establishment recognizes its antagonists on both left and right, uses their complaints to demonstrate its own middle-road propriety, but acts against them only when they "go too far." In part, this is because the establishment has loose margins at either side, some useful part-time members moving back and forth, and it prefers to act only at such late stages that practically all its members and supporters will concur that "something must be done." (This was true, for example, when conservatives took the lead in the late stages of undermining Senator Joseph McCarthy in the 1950s, and again when liberals formed the cutting edge of prosecution of radicals and peace movement leaders in the 1960s.) Within the establishment itself, consensus is highly valued. Members may disagree on occasion, particularly over the *best* means by which to preserve the system in times of crisis, without risking their membership unless their convictions lead them to take anti-system instead of system-preserving actions.

Public Conception of the Establishment

Thus, our concept of establishment does not suggest that a unified upper social class dominates the nation's political structure, though great wealth and upper-class connections serve many as platforms from which they can achieve such a status. Nor do we see economic imperatives as the sole or even prime determinants of establishment actions, though in the absence of compelling reasons to the contrary they will often be the "natural" principles of behavior. We do not even envision much explicit consultation among establishment members about positions on issues, partly because none is necessary. Our concept of an establishment is, therefore, not the tight ruling group of some elite theories, but neither is it the benevolent representative statesmen envisioned by some democratic pluralists. Our establishment ranges between the two, depending on the type of issue involved. On most routine issues and decisions, it may function much as the latter view suggests. But on fundamental questions, or when the system itself is threatened, it acts in ways characteristic of the former.

Nor is our model of an establishment intended as a final characterization of the American structure of power. It is no more than a working hypothesis, grounded in a substantial but not conclusive body of evidence. But it has vital implications for the process of political change in the United States.

We do not imply that there is necessarily anything sinister about this establishment. We do not even suggest that this group is doing anything conspiratorially, or even contrary to the public interest. But the clear evidence that governmental decisionmaking is dominated by a small circulating elite—consisting chiefly of the upper echelons of big business, banking and investment, and the law—most of whom share many characteristics of social and economic background, lends credibility to the idea of an establishment. We asserted our belief that individuals in government share certain orthodox values and ideology with those at the top in private affairs, and that such views lead them to mutual support for the established rules of the game of politics and to a shared concern for the preservation of the basic outlines of the economic and political systems. We have not "proved" this assertion, nor can we from the evidence available. But the similarity of background and interest implies strongly that shared ideology and shared concern for defense of the system are likely to exist at this level. Of fundamental questions, in other words, we expect nearly all members of the establishment to be of one mind—that the American system as it now operates should be preserved in all its essential characteristics.

But social background and shared responsibility for the management of public affairs are not the only factors operating to cause decisionmakers at this level to see issues from a single perspective. Most people in key positions are of roughly the same generation, and thus became politically "aware" at the same period in American history. All of us tend to be structured permanently by what was happening in politics at the time we happened to tune in to such matters. For one generation, Vietnam has meant opposition to a callous and wasteful foreign policy. For many of their teachers, however, political socialization occurred during the early days of the Cold War or the late years of World War Two, when one did not question the need to defend the "free world" and resist the spread of communism. For those who made up the establishment in the 1960s, the structuring experiences dated back to pre-World War Two failures to contain Hitler; and they showed that they remembered those lessons. The analogy to Munich and the inevitable failure of appeasement was offered again and again as a rationale for American policy in Vietnam.

The image of international communism as a unified, monolithic force was shared by most decisionmakers. Thus, wherever trouble broke out in the world, including the United States, the guiding hand of Moscow was discerned. An oft-cited classic example is the allegation by Dean Rusk, made two years after the Chinese Revolution while he was in charge of Far Eastern operations for the State Department, that Mao Tse Tung was a Russian agent. Mao's regime, he asserted, was "a colonial Russian government—a Slavic Manchukuo on a large scale—it is not the government of China. It does not pass the first test. It is not Chinese." [4] The point is not that any man can be wrong on occasion. It is that each generation shares a basic image of what is going on in politics, and what is likely to happen, largely created by the lessons they have drawn from experiences at the outset of their careers. As such, the establishment of the 1960s and 1970s shares an understanding of the world derived from the 1940s and before.

The Establishment View of the World

The convergence and rigidification of beliefs and principals of action among the top echelon of decisionmakers is further aided by some characteristic features of large-scale organizations. Once a position has been taken and the organization has become committed to it in terms of allocation of resources and the career investments of personnel, it is very difficult to modify its methods, purposes, or actions. Many large agencies of the national government, such as the FBI and the State Department, are now committed to a view of the world, a set of procedures, and an understanding of how things should work that reflect and support the establishment's principles. They see, and report to their superiors, what is consistent with their expectations and career aspirations. One classic example of the triumph of organizational commitments over evidence is the experience of strategic bombing during World War Two.[5] The Air Force and its supporters had insisted for years that bombing alone could destroy German war production, cripple the armed forces, and eliminate the German people's will to fight. The U.S. Air Force accordingly had been designed and trained for strategic bombing, which was carried out with high optimism and massive loads of explosives. But, according to the careful postwar Strategic Bombing Survey undertaken by the Air

---

[4] Dean Rusk, as quoted in Ronald Steel, *Pax Americana* (New York: Viking, 1967), p. 129. In 1961 Rusk became Secretary of State, serving in that capacity until 1969.

[5] This account is drawn from Herbert Wilensky, *Organizational Intelligence: Knowledge and Policy in Government and Industry* (New York: Basic Books, 1967), pp. 24–34.

Force itself, strategic bombing never seriously affected war production, had little or no effect on the capacity of the armed forces or the will of the population, and incurred heavy losses in the bargain. Intelligence failures, equipment failures, and faulty analysis of the German economy and society were also to blame, but the chief explanation was simply the incapacity of bombing to accomplish the goals set for it. The same conclusion was arrived at by a similar official study in Japan at the end of hostilities there. But the Vietnamese experience suggests that lessons about the limited capabilities of air power have still not been learned.

An establishment of relatively small size thus receives many self-confirming and supporting messages from its environment. Its approach to politics and its view of the world are validated by almost every trusted source—in bureaucratic memoranda, in the communications media, and at the country club. Attitudes and practices may, under such circumstances, become hardened. Supported by belief in the rightness of their actions, and even in the sacred nature of their responsibility to defend the system against those who would undermine it, members of the establishment may become highly resistant to basic change.

But this does not mean that they are insensitive or inflexible. Indeed, long-term stability is promoted by short-term flexibility (within limits) and adroit channeling of thrusts toward change—in part through judicious use of available coercive power. Although one major characteristic of the establishment is its shared basic beliefs and principles of political action, it would be a gross misinterpretation to see such agreement extending to rigidity of *membership* or of *specific policies*. Indeed, one of the most stability-producing features of American ideology and practice—of the American system, in other words—is its flexibility. By opening itself to new members, new ideas, and new policies, the American system incorporates thrusts toward change into its upper-level consensus. *Such new members, ideas, and policies must, however, accept the basic framework of political values, ideology, structure, and style on which that system is based.* To the extent that they do, of course, extra-systemic movements for change are effectively blunted. Popular movements lose their leaders and their platforms. New governmental policies include enough of their proposals to give the appearance of progress—and reasons for unusual political activity no longer exist.

Co-optation

The process by which rising leaders with new ideas or programs are drawn into the establishment is known as *co-optation*. Many aspiring young men and women seek leadership positions and try to display their ideas and talents in such a way as to make themselves candidates for co-optation. Others find that their efforts on behalf of a particular constituency gain attention and produce opportunities to take on governmental responsibility and carry out some of the programs they have been urging. In both cases, establishment-arranged appointments to offices or aid in electoral advancement lead to rises in stature and responsibility. The sobering consequences of responsibility then combine with the real difficulties of achieving goals through the complex political process to induce the candidate to practice the skills of accommodation and mutual support that are the hallmark of the establishment. A candidate who demonstrates these skills and concern for the maintenance of the essential outlines of the system will rise further; one who does not will soon decide to leave government, thereby losing prospective establishment status.

Co-optation does not mean that the new leader gives up his independence, ideas, or program entirely. He retains substantial proportions of each, but learns to adapt them to the framework of the established system so that they are compatible with it. He frequently does succeed in changing things, if he is a skillful advocate of his causes, but not as much as he might originally have wished (and for reasons that he—and we—might rightly consider fully persuasive). The directions of public policy may shift in response to such initiatives after strenuous efforts by the new leader, his supporters, and the new allies his establishment status has made available to him. When the process has run its course, some new policies have been instituted; the basic complaints against the system have been reduced; the establishment has absorbed new members; and the system has acquired new defenders. The basic outlines of the system have against survived. Flexibility in the short run, in other words, means permanence in the long run.

Other types of flexibility also contribute to the stability of the American political system. Many layers of government make for many alternative ways to achieve particular goals, and people who seek ends unacceptable to those in power may be directed from one government to another, from one type of approach to another, or from one branch, committee, or department to another. Demands that at first seem indigestible or extreme may be converted into another form and thereby rendered satisfiable. A minority group's demand for status and recognition may be salved by appointing a prominent leader to a visible position, or by naming a public monument or park in their honor. Or, if not quieted by such costless tactics, they may be diverted by channeling their claims into aggression against another minority religious or racial group. Some claims can be converted into economic demands or largely settled on such terms.

The materialistic orientation of the people and the abundance of the economy have made this a recurring tactic throughout American history. By merely increasing the size of the total economic product and directing the new surplus toward the demanding group, their claims could be satisfied without depriving those who were already advantaged of any of their possessions or expectations. In the history of labor-management conflicts, for example, an increase in total production and therefore total profits (or an increase in price to the consumer) made it possible to grant higher wages without reducing owners' returns. Workers, for their part, tended to be satisfied by higher wages and to abandon other goals, such as control over the means of production.

Flexibility is thus a means of absorbing, blunting, and deflecting thrusts toward change. But flexibility does not operate alone to promote stability. It functions in tandem with other factors to induce or compel behavior into the established channels. American political ideology emphasizes procedural regularity, and insists on working through the means provided for the attainment of political goals. The "law-and-order" ethic legitimates action against those who do not follow such prescribed procedures. And, under the conditions of the late twentieth century, the official agencies of law enforcement have a vast monopoly over the power that is necessary to compel obedience. Thus, there is a considerable array of inducements at work to direct political activity into forms that can be dealt with by the established order without serious threat.

The Stability of the System

In effect, the political system offers many routes by which to seek one's goals, most of which lead to conversion of those goals into forms compatible with the basic outlines of the system. Its flexibility tends to absorb both leaders and goals, and to result in incrementally modified elites and policies. Many pressures channel political action into these approved forms, and when they fail there remain both accepted grounds for legal compulsion and the requisite power to prevent disobedience. Against this resourceful complex of containing forces and the broad support they apparently evoke from wide segments of the population, it is very difficult to generate fundamental change.

Over the years, these factors have helped to render the American system stable—in itself a desirable characteristic for a political system to enjoy. Most people probably would assess the costs of this stability (in terms of lost opportunities, unfulfilled aspirations, poverty for some, and the like) as entirely tolerable. To many, stability is the highest priority in politics. Whether stability continues to be equally desirable today, measured against possibly greater costs and more challenging conditions, is a more acute and more controversial question. After an extended period of stability, unabsorbed pressures for change may build to explosive potential. Or issues may arise that even the most flexible system will have difficulty containing.

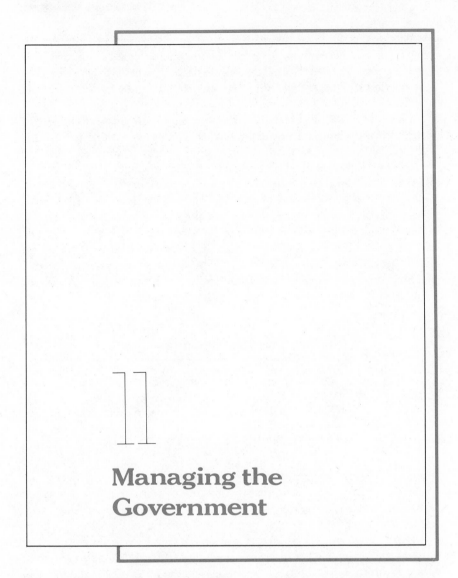

11

Managing the Government

Continuing to narrow our focus (and in effect adopting the nature-of-governing-elites approach), we now address our inquiry to the governmental sector of the political economy. Recognizing that many forces outside of government play a part in shaping decisions, we nevertheless have a range of questions to ask about who makes those decisions, and how, and what difference it makes. Let us first consider some definitions, then some more carefully framed questions, and then the evidence.

Elites are those people who hold more of the resources of power than others, whom we term *non-elites* or, to avoid repetitiveness, *masses*. Where one draws the line between elites and non-elites is not crucial, as long as there is a clear basis for this necessarily arbitrary distinction.

Everybody has *some* power, of course, but at some point the disparity between a congressman, corporation president, or newspaper editor and a steelworker, welfare mother, or student becomes quite obvious.

Elite status may flow from the mere possession of disproportionate wealth, status, knowledge, or any other power-yielding resource, held as *a personal attribute*. Persons in this general category are more capable of exercising influence over public policy than is the ordinary citizen, if they choose to so apply their resources. Or elite status may be bestowed on a person who holds an *institutional position* that confers the capacity to control or affect the lives of others, such as an officer or director of a major corporation or an official of government. In the latter case, both the voluntary compliance granted to legitimate authority and the availability of means of coercion contribute to the official's potential power. Thus most of our analysis will be directed at governmental elites.

The Key Questions in Elite Analysis

All important questions have several parts. Evidence must be addressed to each component, and the links between them established logically and evidentially, to constitute an answer. The first step in our analysis is a careful formulation of our questions, understanding why they are important (that is, what is at stake in the answer) and how they might be answered.

The problem before us—who holds power *in government*—is important because it is connected to the larger question of who holds power in the political economy as a whole. In whose interests do the people who hold power in government act? Their own, in the corporate-banking sector's, the general public's, or some (what?) combination of all these? What can the available evidence tell us about who these people are, how they achieved their positions, and how they make their decisions? By subdividing the larger question in this manner, we might move toward some inferences that could lead to answers.

What is at stake in such an inquiry? What assumptions about our politics would be affected if we were able to find answers to the questions posed? Two major interpretations were outlined in Chapter 10: the "power elite" school argues that elites represent the upper classes and act in their interest; the "democratic pluralist" school argues that elites respond to shifting group and public pressures that in the long run add up to a representative policymaking process. Behind this debate lies the question of whether and how our political process lives up to its claim of being democratic. How much impact do non-elites have on the decisions of elites in government, and what form does it take?

To answer these questions, we have data on the social makeup of governmental elites, but only incomplete evidence about their behavior.

By looking at their age, sex, race, education, income, and occupation, we shall gain a sense of the kinds of people who staff and manage the government. We can also characterize the route by which they obtained their elections or appointments, which will help determine whether elite positions are owed to the choices of already existing elites and/or how much they depend on non-elite actions. We shall also consider how elites actually make decisions, on the evidence of their own explanations and the reported observations of others. Unfortunately, such sources are often only the tip of the iceberg, and can be misleading when they are not simply incomplete.

These data should be reviewed, therefore, with some caution and continuing concern for corroboration. Proof of the upper-class social origins of government decisionmakers, for example, is not proof that they act accordingly; the latter is only an inference. Perhaps they actually respond to non-elite preferences or interests; we need to know what those preferences or interests were on a given issue, if and how they were expressed, and what happened. Thus we must undertake several steps and examine a variety of evidence before we can reach conclusions. We must look not only at who elites are and how they act in the various institutions of government, but also at the *relationship* between elites in government and non-elites outside. This will be the task not only of this and the next five chapters, but of all of Part Five on non-elite attitudes and behavior as well.

Probably the most important evidence we need pertains to mass or non-elite values and attitudes. In particular, we want to know how mass values and attitudes compare with those of elites and with the policies actually adopted by government. If they are substantially the same, we need to ask next about the sources of such mass values and attitudes. As best we can tell from admittedly sparse evidence, are they genuinely self-generated by masses themselves, or are they the product of elite action or indoctrination? If mass values and attitudes are truly self-generated, and similar to elites' and to governmental policies, we have grounds for inferring at least that the political system does not ignore mass goals.

But if mass desires are not similar to those of elites, or are not expressed in public policies, or are essentially the product of elite manipulation, we must infer that the system is elite-dominated. If elites in effect produce the mass values and attitudes to which they later generously respond, initiative rests with elites. If they fail to enact mass values and attitudes into effective policy, the same conclusion is even more inescapable. If elites hold dissimilar values and yet act according to masses' preferences—an unlikely combination—we have a system whose official management at least is in the exclusive hands of elites.

Power involves a kind of transaction between two or more people, in which the greater resources of one cause the other(s) to act in certain ways. Similarly, leadership implies followership; one cannot be a leader unless others more or less willingly follow. Institutional elites and masses thus have a reciprocal relationship; initiatives and constraints flow back and forth between them. The actions of elites, taken with a view to probable mass reactions, are perceived by masses, whose responses in turn either suggest new actions to elites or cause them to recognize new limits on their action. Or mass demands, conceived in a context of perceived limits, are acknowledged by elites, who act to contain or promote them as their own interests and expectations of probable mass responses dictate.

Let us reiterate what is at stake in this inquiry. Neither masses nor elites are powerless. We know that each can initiate change, and constrain the other, under particular circumstances. Our question presses further: how much power of initiative and constraint characteristically lies on each side, and under what conditions is the normal balance disrupted? When and how can elites impose their preferences on unwilling masses? When and how can masses force elites to change their policies or institute new ones? This phrasing of the question lacks subtlety, but it will serve to guide us on the path toward greater understanding of the real structure of power in the United States.

Elites in Government

The social backgrounds of people in major governmental positions have always been highly unrepresentative of the population as a whole.[1] Despite notable exceptions, the historical pattern has been for key governmental positions to be filled by upper-status people. This assertion is confirmed by a variety of empirical studies. They show that political decisionmakers are quite disproportionately white Anglo-Saxon Protestants with high incomes, many of whose families have been active in politics for generations. Their occupations are almost entirely the upper-status ones, principally the law. Although they account for less than 1 percent of the adult population, lawyers usually constitute about 60 percent of the two houses of Congress and the entire Supreme Court. Lawyers constituted 70 percent of all Presidents, Vice-Presidents, and Cabinet members between 1877 and 1934. And such lawyers are far from representative even of their own profession: in most cases, wealth, family political involvement, or a large corporate law practice (or some combination of these) also prefigure high political position. Nearly half of all decisionmakers were educated in Ivy League schools—chiefly Harvard, Yale, and Princeton—or in the small elite eastern colleges modeled on them. What emerges from this body of research is a composite picture of government conducted by a narrow slice of the population—and reflecting the very characteristics of income, status, and education we have described as elite.

[1] The major source of the data in this paragraph is Donald Matthews, *The Social Background of Political Decision-Makers* (New York: Random House, 1955).

Source: By permission of John Hart and Field Enterprises, Inc.

The Wizard of Id

A particularly good analysis illustrating these general propositions is Donald Matthews' study of members of the U.S. Senate during the period 1947–1957.[2] Matthews found that 84 percent of the 180 senators had attended college (at a time when only 14 percent of the white population over twenty-five had done so) and that 53 percent had been to law school. Sixty-three percent of the Democrats and 45 percent of the Republicans were lawyers; 17 percent of the Democrats and 45 percent of the Republicans were businessmen. The other occupations represented were those of farmer, professor, and such other professionals as minister and physician. There were no representatives of any blue-collar occupation, only one woman, and no blacks. The senators came from upper- and middle-class families, as measured by their fathers' occupations; Matthews notes that "the children of low-salaried workers, wage-earners, servants, and farm laborers, which together comprised 66 percent of the gainfully employed in 1900, contributed only seven percent of the postwar Senators." [3]

The implications of such a pattern of origins and occupations for the operation of the Senate as an institution is apparent in Table 11.1, which shows the occupational makeup of Senate committees. All proposals for constitutional amendments and all nominations for the Supreme Court, for example, must pass the scrutiny of the Judiciary Committee, 81 percent of whom were lawyers. Businessmen accounted for more than half the membership of the Banking and Currency Committee, even though they constituted only about a quarter of all senators. The pattern is that each occupational grouping asserts control over governmental action in the areas of special concern to it. We shall see further implications in a later chapter.

[2] Donald Matthews, *U.S. Senators and Their World* (Chapel Hill: University of North Carolina Press, 1960). Page citations are from the Vintage Books edition (New York: Random House). The educational and occupational data are from pages 26–36.
[3] *Ibid.,* p. 19.

TABLE 11.1 *Occupational Distribution of Members of Senate Committees*

Committees	Occupations (in percentages)					
	Lawyers	Businessmen	Farmers	Professors	Other Professionals	
Foreign Relations	59	16	6	16	4	= 100 (38)
Appropriations	55	27	12	0	5	= 100 (31)
Finance	46	36	11	4	4	= 100 (28)
Armed Services	55	32	6	3	3	= 100 (31)
Agriculture & Forestry	50	19	27	4	0	= 100 (26)
Judiciary	81	6	6	6	0	= 100 (31)
Interstate & Foreign Commerce	60	29	6	0	6	= 100 (35)
Banking & Currency	28	55	3	10	3	= 100 (29)
Interior	52	27	14	0	7	= 100 (29)
Public Works	50	35	6	3	6	= 100 (34)
Labor & Public Welfare	50	25	4	14	7	= 100 (28)
Government Operations	53	26	8	3	10	= 100 (38)
Rules & Administration	51	29	8	3	8	= 100 (38)
Post Office & Civil Service	56	20	13	4	7	= 100 (45)
District of Columbia	62	27	4	2	4	= 100 (48)
All Senators	54	27	7	5	7	= 100 (167)

Note: Data represent the 80th through 84th Congresses. Committee assignments of less than one year's duration are omitted.

Reprinted from Donald Matthews, *U.S. Senators and Their World* (New York: Vintage Books, 1960), Appendix E, p. 290. Copyright © 1960 by the University of North Carolina Press.

The Senate, of course, is only one institution of government. Its counterpart, the House of Representatives, is somewhat—but only somewhat—less aristocratic in origins and occupations. Although it normally includes a few low-status occupations, it frequently has a higher proportion of lawyers. In general, it displays essentially the same income, status, and occupational characteristics as the Senate. The Supreme Court reflects a greater preponderance of high-status backgrounds, in part because it is made up of the upper echelons of the legal profession.

The executive branch, which most analysts see as possessing the important initiative and decisionmaking capacity within the federal government, displays some variations of the same basic characteristics. A major study of 1,041 individuals who held 1,567 executive appointments from March 1933 through April 1965 was published in 1967 by the Brookings Institution.[4] The study reports that 39 percent of these leaders had gone to private school; the total for the Department of State was 60 percent. Upper-status origins are also indicated by the fact that 26 percent of all appointees were lawyers and 24 percent were businessmen at the time of appointment. Sixty-three percent of all Cabinet secretaries (86 percent of the military secretaries), 66 percent of all undersecretaries, and 50 percent of all assistant secretaries were either businessmen or lawyers at the time of appointment.[5]

Patterns of Circulation

Other studies, focusing on smaller numbers of strategically located decisionmakers, have produced findings that shed more light on the social backgrounds of executive officials. For one thing, a pattern of circulation appears to be developing in which decisionmakers are neither pursuing lifelong careers in government service nor close associates of the President. Instead, they are people who move back and forth between the upper echelons of business or law and government. Historian Gabriel Kolko studied the backgrounds and career patterns of 234 major decisionmakers in the foreign policy field during 1944–1960.[6] He found that individuals whose career origins were in big business, investment banking, or law held 60 percent of the positions studied. Table 11.2, drawn from this study, shows that individuals with such origins held many more foreign policy positions than did those who rose through the ranks of government service. Kolko concludes that an overlap of attitudes and interests can hardly fail to arise under circumstances of circulation back and forth between business, law, and government.

Nor is the convergence of upper-echelon personnel in government,

[4] David T. Stanley, Dean E. Mann, and Jameson W. Doig, *Men Who Govern* (Washington: Brookings Institution, 1966).

[5] These are apparently recalculations by Gabriel Kolko, in *The Roots of American Foreign Policy* (Boston: Beacon Press, 1969), note 6, p. 141.

[6] *Ibid.*

TABLE 11.2 *Occupational Origin of Individuals, by Number of Government Posts Held, 1944–60*

Occupational Origin	Individuals with Four or More Posts				Individuals with Less Than Four Posts			
	# of Individuals	% of all Individuals	# of Posts Held	% of all Posts Studied	# of Individuals	% of all Individuals	# of Posts Held	% of all Posts Studied
Law Firms	12	5.1	55	8.1	33	14.1	72	10.6
Banking and Investment Firms	18	7.7	94	13.9	24	10.3	24	3.5
Industrial Corporations	8	3.4	39	5.8	31	13.2	49	7.2
Public Utilities and Transportation Companies	0	.0	0	.0	4	1.7	4	.6
Miscellaneous Business and Commercial Firms	7	3.0	32	4.7	17	7.3	35	5.2
Nonprofit Corporations, Public Service, Universities, etc.	7	3.0	37	5.5	7	3.0	12	1.8
Career Government Officials (no Subsequent Non-Government Post)	15	6.4	85	12.5	11	4.7	19	2.8
Career Government Officials (Subsequent Non-Government Post)	8	3.4	38	5.6	12	5.1	13	1.9
Career Government Officials (Subsequent Non-Government Post and Return to Government Post)	8	3.4	45	6.6	6	2.6	15	2.2
Unidentified	1	.4	5	.7	5	2.1	5	.7
Totals	84	35.8	430	63.4	150	64.1	248	36.5

Reprinted by permission of the Beacon Press, copyright © 1969 by Gabriel Kolko. From Gabriel Kolko, *The Roots of American Foreign Policy* (Boston: Beacon Press, 1969), p. 18.

business, banking, and law at any point a product of electoral decisions. In another study of top political decisionmakers, it was found that only 28 percent of the more prominent politicians in 1933–1953 rose largely through elective office; 62 percent were *appointed* to all or most of their political jobs before reaching top positions.[7] These findings imply that the executive branch represents an even higher-status echelon than does the Congress, and one that is even further detached and insulated from popular electoral control. This situation may in part be due to the increasing need for expert knowledge in the generation and implementation of governmental programs. But the apparent circulation of decisionmakers between government and high-status specialized occupations in the corporate, legal, and financial worlds occurs under both political parties, and seems to imply at least an opportunity for certain "private" preferences to exert significant influence.

What have we gleaned from this analysis of the social backgrounds of elites? The existence of a relatively small group of people especially favored with the resources of power seems undeniable, as does the fact that those in the major positions of government are drawn chiefly from this group. We may infer, though it has by no means been established, that people in the general category of elite share some values and interests that are distinct from those of the majority of the people, and that governmental elites may also have such commitments or unconscious perceptions. A shared high level of income, wealth, and status—and, most likely, family histories of similar standing—does not necessarily mean that even governmental elites will hold similar views on all matters. Indeed, at times their economic interests or conceptions of the public interest may be diametrically opposed. The occasions and nature of the conflicts that result constitute one of the crucial issues of political analysis.

The Pluralist View

The pluralist view holds that conflicts among institutional elites are frequent, and that the basic directions of public policy are determined by the people in elections. Supporting this view is evidence of distinctive social backgrounds among subgroups of elites. For example, Andrew Hacker surveyed the backgrounds of the presidents (as of 1959) of the 100 largest industrial corporations, and compared them with the backgrounds of the 100 senators in 1959.[8] Presidents were somewhat more likely to have gone to private school (28 percent to 15 percent) and an Ivy League college (29 percent to 15 percent) than senators, and to have exchanged their town and state of origin for metropolitan residence and

---

[7] C. Wright Mills, *The Power Elite* (New York: Oxford University Press, 1956), p. 230.

[8] Andrew Hacker, "The Elected and the Anointed: Two American Elites," *The American Political Science Review* 55 (1961), pp. 539–549.

national mobility. Hacker concluded that these and other similar findings helped to explain the existence of significant tensions between the major economic and political institutions. Without denying that conflicts do arise, the opposing view holds that such differences in origins and life experience, and in current institutional responsibilities, do not give rise to fundamentally conflicting perceptions or preferences. Both groups of people, for example, would strongly defend orthodox political values, the present distribution of wealth, and the basic structure of the economic system. In this context, their differences would be over the shares to be distributed among established claimants, or over the means of more effectively serving such agreed-on ends.

The extent to which values and interests are in fact shared among elites, and the differences between such values and interests and those of the masses of non-elite people, are empirical questions. Inference from the existence of similar and distinctive social background characteristics, while suggestive, is not conclusive. Similarly, the existence of internal conflicts between subgroups of elites can only be inferred from differences in social background. On larger questions, their essential homogeneity and difference from the mass public may be more determinative. In the next section, we shall begin to analyze potentially more conclusive attitudinal and behavioral evidence.

Elite Values and Attitudes

The utility of socioeconomic background analysis lies in the gross comparison of the characteristics of two groups of people (here, elites and non-elites). Extreme differences in background may lead to situations in which values and attitudes may differ consistently between the groups—as aggregates, at least. But within such general confines, many other factors contribute to shaping values and attitudes. For example, specialized family or personal experience, loyalty to a political party, occupational role orientation, individual personality or ideology, or the characteristics of particular issues may lead to a wide variety of specific priorities and preferences within each group. There may thus be many different configurations of political values and attitudes among members of even such a relatively small group as our general category of elites. The influence of resources and life style may in some cases be overcome by such factors, so that an individual's political perceptions and orientations may resemble those of subgroups of the general population more than those of objectively elite persons. Unfortunately, little is known about the extent to which these apparently reasonable possibilities are actually borne out in practice.

Understanding of elite values and attitudes is inhibited by two types of problems. One is the inherent complexity of human belief systems and cognitive and perceptual processes. The impact of apparently clear objective circumstances is apparently very different on different people; for some, it is direct and consistent, while for others it may seem to be just the opposite. The concept of socioeconomic status—class—illustrates this lack of "fit" between objective and subjective "reality." Subjective class identification is probably more relevant to attitudes and behavior than such objective factors as income, education, and status. And Americans are known to hold subjective class identifications at odds with their actual socioeconomic circumstances. Before their values and attitudes can be understood, the presence and relative importance of such factors must be sorted out and characterized, along with the effects of such other factors as political party loyalties, occupation, and ideology. The complexity of the problem is obvious.

The second problem has to do with the kinds of analytical tools and efforts that have been applied to the task. Very little survey analysis has been done on elite values and attitudes. We know much more about mass sociopsychological processes than we do about those of elites, perhaps partly because of access problems. Values—commitments to abstract but fundamental principles such as individualism or equality—are hard to explore in brief questionnaire surveys. For such information, there are only impressionistic accounts by the chroniclers of the upper class.[9] Survey-oriented social scientists tend to concentrate on more easily pinpointed attitudes toward specific issues. But even in this area, information is very scarce. Surveys of cross-sections of the national population do turn up a proportionate number of people with high income, education, and status, and to an extent such data can be used to describe the attitudes of our general category of elites. But our category is relatively limited, and its members would be a very small number of even the highest-income, -education, and -status national survey respondents. Better survey evidence is available at the community level, where researchers have more deliberately sought out the relatively wealthy. Here too, however, the number of those who would fit into our general category of elite is very few.

With regard to institutional elites, the lack of reliable quantitative data is no less acute. Again, the best sources are the more or less impressionistic accounts of informed observers of particular institutions, processes, or individuals.[10] There are some careful survey studies of the attitudes (and, to some extent, the values) of specialized subgroups of elites, such as delegates to national presidential nominating conventions, corporation presidents, and community officials and leaders. Except for

---

[9] See, for example, Ferdinand Lundberg, *The Rich and The Super-Rich* (New York: Lyle Stuart, 1968), or E. Digby Baltzell, *Philadelphia Gentlemen: The Making of a National Upper Class* (Glencoe, Ill.: The Free Press, 1958).

[10] The biographical and case-study literature is vast; a particularly good example of perceptive revelation of values is Alpheus T. Mason, *Harlan Fiske Stone, Pillar of the Law* (New York: Viking Press, 1956).

the corporation presidents, however, these institutional elites are at subordinate, rather than decisive national, levels of decisionmaking. For the values and attitudes of major national governmental elites, the best sources are case studies, memoirs, and biographies. The product of their views and actions—the public policies adopted by the government—may also shed some light on their values and attitudes. But, for many reasons that we shall explore in later chapters, it is a very gross and uncertain means of characterization.

In the paragraphs that follow, we shall use the evidence available to sketch briefly the values and attitudes of elites and of institutional elites. In the final section, we shall extract some frankly speculative interpretations about elite orientations and styles from the great body of qualitative research and journalistic observation.

1. The General Category of Elites

According to a large body of national attitude research and studies of voting behavior, people of high socioeconomic status may be broadly characterized as more informed, more ideologically oriented, and more involved in politics than others.[11] They are also distinguished by greater orientation to issues, greater support for the political system, and a greater sense of capacity to affect action in politics. In general, they tend to hold conservative views on both domestic and international issues, although an identifiable minority is decisively liberal with regard to governmental services and civil rights.

To what extent do they conceive of themselves as a class distinct from others? In a national study made through the facilities of the American Institute of Public Opinion (Gallup Poll) in 1964, Lloyd Free and Hadley Cantril sought to explore class identifications.[12] They asked a cross-section of the population, "In the field of politics and government, do you feel that your own interests are similar to the interests of the propertied class, the middle class, or the working class?" The responses were as follows:

Propertied class	5%
Middle class	37%
Working class	53%
Don't know	5%
	100%

But this self-identification was not consistent with the respondents' other characteristics. The authors note:

[11] Unless otherwise noted, characterizations are drawn from Angus Campbell, Philip Converse, Donald Stokes, and Warren E. Miller, *The American Voter* (New York: John Wiley, 1960).

[12] Lloyd A. Free and Hadley Cantril, *The Political Beliefs of Americans: A Study of Public Opinion* (New Brunswick, N.J.: Rutgers University Press, 1968), p. 18.

. . . more than one-fourth of those with incomes of $10,000 a year or more identified their interests with the "working class," as they defined the term, while more than one-fifth of those with incomes under $3,000 associated themselves with the "middle class." Similarly, three out of ten of the professional and business group identified with the "working class," while more than one-third of the blue-collar workers saw themselves as members of the "middle class." [13]

The question nevertheless reveals some matters of importance. Very few people associate themselves with a "propertied class," but those who do display some distinctive characteristics. For example, the people who saw themselves in the propertied class were only 40 percent "liberal" on the authors' scale of support for various types of governmental assistance to ordinary people, while middle-class people were 57 percent liberal and working-class people were 74 percent liberal. Of the propertied class, 57 percent characterized themselves as either moderately conservative or very conservative, compared to 35 percent of the middle class and 31 percent of the working class. Table 11.3 correlates attitudes toward the

TABLE 11.3 *Class Identification, Attitudes Toward Government Power, and Political Party Identification*

	Propertied Class	Middle Class	Working Class
Government power:			
Has too much	53%	33%	18%
About right as is	30	39	39
Should use more	16	25	34
Don't know	1	3	9
Political party:			
Republican	54%	33%	16%
Democrat	22	38	62
Independent	23	26	21
Other, don't know	1	3	1

Source: Free and Cantril, *Political Beliefs of Americans,* pp. 218 and 234.

use of governmental power and political party identification with the various self-described class levels. Given the thorough blurring of subjective class identification in the United States, and the enduring but frequently cross-cutting pull of long-established political party loyalties, these distinctions are fairly sharp. When we recall that this national sur-

[13] *Ibid.,* pp. 17–18.

vey could include only a small sprinkling of those high enough in income and status to qualify for our general category of elites, the implication is that class-based and distinctive policy orientations do in fact exist.

Greater insight can be gained from focusing on certain subgroups of elites, even though there is considerable risk in generalizing from small and possibly unique populations. One of the few studies that deliberately sought to include a large enough number of very wealthy people to be able to analyze their attitudes responsibly was conducted by two sociologists in a medium-sized (100,000) Michigan city.[14] Together with a random sample of the community, they included a special group of people whose incomes in 1960 (over $25,000) placed them in the top 1 percent of wage-earners and, for comparison, a special group of poor people with incomes ranging from less than $2,000 upward, depending on the number of dependents. Among other queries, they asked all respondents which interest groups in the country ought to be most powerful in shaping government policy. Many people (44 percent of all respondents) volunteered that all should be equal. Sixty-four percent of poor blacks said that all should be equal, while 14 percent nominated labor unions and 8 percent suggested some other group. Only 39 percent of rich whites, however, endorsed equal status for all groups, while 30 percent nominated big business for supremacy and 27 percent favored some other group. No poor black suggested priority for big business and no rich white endorsed priority for labor unions. The authors concluded tentatively that rich people are less egalitarian than the lower classes, preferring government by their own kind.

A more specific and tangible comparison is provided by answers to three questions about government assistance to poor and black citizens. Table 11.4 shows these results. The first question had to do with providing temporary incomes for poor people who would undertake job training, the second was a general inquiry about all forms of assistance to the poor, and the last concerned the open-housing provisions of recently enacted civil rights legislation. In each case, opposition rose with income. Rich whites were decisively more opposed to all three forms of government assistance, in stark contrast to black attitudes and substantially distinct even from middle-income whites' attitudes. It is possible to attribute too much significance to one study of a single city, of course, but the implication of distinctiveness again seems clear.

Other studies based on national surveys show distinctive attitudinal characteristics among the best-educated echelons. Because education generally correlates with pre-existing family income, these results are suggestive of at least the general direction of elite orientations (though not of the specific causal origins of particular attitudes). Higher educa-

[14] William H. Form and Joan Huber (Rytina), "Ideological Beliefs on the Distribution of Power in the United States," *American Sociological Review* 34 (1969), pp. 19–31. The data in this paragraph are from p. 26.

TABLE 11.4   *Opposition to Federal Help for Disadvantaged (in percentages)*

Income	Race	Government should not pay poor to go to school	Government has done too much for poor	Government should stay out of open occupancy
Poor	Negro	30	8	8
	White	46	23	62
Middle	Negro	17	15	8
	White	64	32	73
Rich	White	78	72	96
Total, analytic sample	%	52	31	57
	Number	350	351	344

Reprinted from William H. Form and Joan Huber (Rytina), "Ideological Beliefs on the Distribution of Power in the United States," *American Sociological Review* 34 (1969), p. 28.

tion usually leads people to have greater confidence in and support for governmental action, possibly due to faith in the capabilities of technical experts or of people like themselves—or perhaps to the fact that educated people are more likely to read or hear about and absorb the explanations of government officials. At the same time, events and pronouncements by government officials tend to have greater effect on highly educated people. An example of both aspects of this phenomenon is the trend of opinion on whether or not it was a mistake for the United States to become involved in the Vietnam War. Less educated people were more dubious at the start, while college people denied that an error had been made. As time went on, however, college people responded much more drastically, and by 1969 they believed that a mistake had been made in larger proportions than did less educated people.[15] The same sequence of opinion change is apparent in many other policy areas: it is usually the most highly educated people who are most supportive of government action and most ready to change their minds in response to shifts in government policy or new events.

2. Institutional Elites

Understandably, institutional elites are distinctly well-informed, issue-oriented, ideological, and self-confident about their ability to influence political outcomes. Although most of the available survey evidence deals with subgroups of institutional elites, this finding is characteristic of

[15] This evidence is reviewed in detail in Chapter 18.

practically all research on such elites. Their basic values are also explored in some subgroup analyses. One major study contrasted the responses of delegates to the 1956 presidential nominating conventions of both the Democratic and Republican parties with those of a national cross-section of Democratic and Republican voters.[16] In an effort to probe the extent to which both sets of respondents understood and were committed to the value of equality, they were asked to agree or disagree with statements thought to be indicative of political, social and ethnic, and economic egalitarianism.

The political equality statements turned out to measure chiefly political cynicism, and the political "influentials" (delegates) proved to be considerably less disenchanted than the voters. On matters of social and ethnic (racial) equality, the two groups were very similar. But on economic issues, the "influentials" were much less likely to feel that "labor does not get its fair share of what it produces" (21 percent agreement, versus 45 percent for voters); that "the government should give a person work if he can't find another job" (24 percent to 47 percent); and that "the government ought to make sure that everyone has a good standard of living" (34 percent to 56 percent).[17] These contrasts are the more remarkable because they reflect the combined consensus of both Republican and (presumably more liberal) Democratic delegates, suggesting strong economic conservatism among this subordinate level of elites.

Economic conservatism on the part of convention delegates may be explained in part by their high degree of politicization and absorption of orthodox ideology, which may cut through party loyalties and otherwise relevant liberalism. It is also, we may assume, rooted in their highly atypical income levels. According to one study, almost 39 percent of the Republican and 30 percent of the Democratic convention delegates had incomes over $25,000, and thus were among the top 1 percent of American wage-earners.[18] The nominating conventions, moreover, are usually seen as one of the areas of political decisionmaking where lesser elites predominate. If this is true, it suggests that the higher elites may be even less representative in background and attitudes.

Another institutional elite for which attitudinal data are available is the upper echelon of businessmen, bankers, and other executives. Detailed studies of business ideology have been made by analysis of the speeches of corporate presidents, and by long-term examinations of corporate reports, advertising, and public statements. Even in an era of large-scale organization and technological complexity, these studies find that top businessmen laud individualism, materialism, the work ethic, the

[16] Herbert McClosky, "Consensus and Ideology in American Politics," *The American Political Science Review* 58 (1964), pp. 361–382.

[17] *Ibid.*, Table 5, p. 369.

[18] Kevin L. McKeough and John Bibby, *The Costs of Political Participation* (Princeton, N.J.: Citizens Research Foundation, 1966), p. 84.

free market, profit orientation, and the other elements of classic capitalism. This stance is tempered somewhat by the recognition, particularly at the highest levels of the Eastern corporate and financial world, that some governmental assistance to the less advantaged is permanent, desirable, and eminently preferable to what might happen if the economic system operated without such support. One excerpt from a speech by the president of IBM displays not only this general attitude toward the government but the tension between the Eastern managers of large businesses and the more conservative business elite:

> Much as we may dislike it, I think we've got to realize that in our kind of society there are times when government has to step in and help people with some of their more difficult problems. Programs which assist Americans by reducing the hazards of a free market system without damaging the system itself are necessary, I believe, to its survival. . . .
>
> To be sure, the rights and guarantees that the average man believes in and insists upon may interfere, to some degree, with our ability to manage our enterprises with complete freedom of action. As a result, there are businessmen who either ignore or deny these claims. They then justify their views by contending that if we were to recognize or grant them, the whole system of free enterprise would be endangered.
>
> This, it would seem to me, amounts to an open invitation to exactly the kind of government intervention that businessmen are trying to avoid. For if we businessmen insist that free enterprise permits us to be indifferent to those things on which people put high value, then the people will quite naturally assume that free enterprise has too much freedom.[19]

Survey evidence about the same institutional elite is also available. *Fortune* magazine's 500 survey is a continuous sampling of more than 300 chief executives of the 500 largest industrial corporations, plus the 50 largest banks, insurance companies, retailers, transportation companies, and utilities.[20] It demonstrates that such top businessmen are alert to, and to some extent concur with, contemporary definitions of problems in the society. Confronted in 1969 with the flat statement that "we are a racist society," for example, 15 percent of these executives agreed strongly and another 31 percent agreed with reservations; the comparable figures for a sample of college youth were 38 percent and 40 percent, and for all youths 18–24 years of age, 28 percent and 46 percent. When the issues are economic, however, the gap is much greater. Two-thirds of top businessmen saw fears of the military-industrial complex as greatly exaggerated and opposed shifting funds to domestic uses; at exactly the same time, 52 percent of respondents to a national Gallup Poll said that too much was being spent on defense and only 8 percent said that such

---

[19] Thomas B. Watson, cited in Robert Heilbroner, *The Limits of Capitalism* (New York: Harper and Row, 1966), p. 34.

[20] *Fortune* 80 (September 1969) contains a description of the sampling procedure and all the data reported here with the exception of those comparing executives attitudes with youth attitudes, which are from the October 1969 issue.

expenditures were too low. The general pattern of similarity and differ-ence between corporation presidents and national cross-sections is apparent in a comparison of their respective definitions of the greatest problems facing the United States in 1969. The presidents were asked for the "most pressing and critical problems" and the national sample was asked for the "most important problems."

Despite some problems involving the comparability of categories and respondents' propensity to give multiple responses, the top business-men take a broader and more proprietary overview, in which economic problems receive special attention. And their orientations toward solu-tions are also distinctive. When asked what level of unemployment they regard as unacceptable under today's social and economic conditions, more than half of the responding executives gave answers of 5 percent and up. By contrast, national samples regularly rank economic security and insecurity as crucial factors in their lives. These differences in view-point are exactly what we would expect, given the institutional respon-sibility of the top executives. But this is just the point. Decisionmakers can only act on their perceptions—on the problems they understand to exist and to require solution. If governmental actions are shaped by the circulation of elites back and forth between top levels of business and government, or by government officials who take their cues from business-men's definitions, such actions will be in keeping with public views on some issues but not on others. Whether they *should* be on any given issue, of course, is another question entirely.

The top businessmen also appear to be distinctively concerned about communism. Asked in 1969 whether the communist threat was greater or less than a decade earlier, 31 percent said it had increased, 41 percent said it was the same, and 26 percent said it had decreased.[21] Those who saw it as having decreased based their views chiefly on the decline of Soviet hostility and relative power on the international scene. Those who saw it as increasing, however, were thinking chiefly in terms of an internal threat; two-thirds of such respondents traced the rising danger to com-munist involvement in student and black protest movements.

Confirmation that institutional elites tend to be more fearful of the dangers of communism is available in the major study of American atti-tudes toward communism and tolerance of unorthodox political behavior, Samuel Stouffer's *Communism, Conformity, and Civil Liberties.*[22] Con-ducted at the height of Senator Joseph McCarthy's anticommunist activity in the 1950s, this study sampled a national cross-section and selected community leaders in small cities across the country. The community leaders, local rather than national institutional elites, nevertheless saw communism as a more pressing problem and a greater threat than did

21 *Ibid.*
22 Samuel A. Stouffer, *Communism, Conformity, and Civil Liberties* (New York: Doubleday, 1955). Page citations are from the Science Editions paperback (New York: John Wiley, 1966).

ordinary citizens, very few of whom considered it a threat at all. By a nearly two-to-one majority, they expected communism to be rooted in the lower classes and the less educated. And they were much more likely than average citizens to view communists as "crackpots," "queer people," or "warped personalities." [23]

But the most salient finding of the study, and one that is reinforced wherever a similar investigation is made, is that institutional elites appear more tolerant of unorthodoxy and more supportive of the democratic liberties of free speech and assembly than do ordinary citizens.[24] This finding may be attributable merely to a quicker recognition of the relation between hypothetical situations and standards of civil liberty, more elaborate ideology, greater confidence in their capacity to manage events, or a sense of responsibility as public officials. Or it may be that education and socialization in the life of politics have promoted genuine respect for the rules of the game of democratic politics. In any event, elites uniformly endorse the traditional civil liberties more emphatically than do non-elites; what they *do* in particular circumstances is, of course, another question.

These findings about the values and attitudes of institutional elites substantially exhaust the available evidence. They suggest a generally conservative class-altered attitudinal posture that emphasizes economic problems and priorities but encompasses such civil liberties as racial equality and established procedures as well. We may have what is sometimes called an "activist subculture," in which wealth and status are high, ideology is well-developed, and both interest and confidence in managing government are marked. This does not suggest insensitivity to what others in the society want, but rather the rudiments of consensus on how, when, and to what extent such desires should be served.

[23] *Ibid.*, pp. 172–175.
[24] *Ibid.*, Chapter 2. Also see McClosky, "Consensus and Ideology."

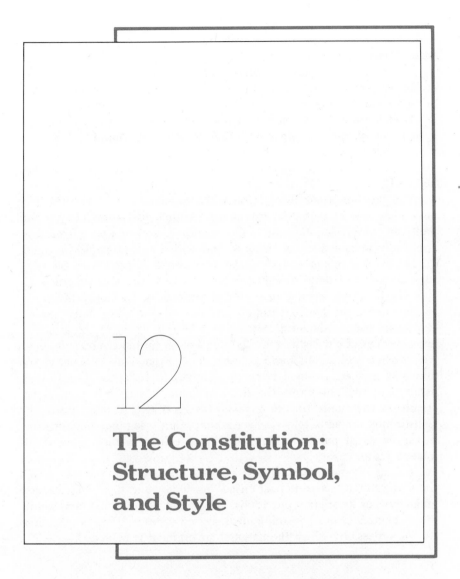

12

The Constitution: Structure, Symbol, and Style

In a general sense, the American government functions within the broad legal and institutional context established by the United States Constitution. Many acts regularly performed by people in government, however, are not explicitly authorized by the Constitution. And some apparent requirements are routinely ignored. None of these practices are challenged, nor would there be legal support for such a challenge if it were made. The fact is that the provisions—and even the spirit—of the original document are not self-executing. Power must be brought to bear to provide for interpretation and enforcement. This in turn means that the values and preferences of people with power determine the actual impact of the Constitution. Our task, therefore, is to understand *when* and *how* the Constitution affects our politics, and what such patterns imply.

The Constitution itself is disarmingly brief. The first three articles create, empower, and specify limits on the Congress, Presidency, and Supreme Court respectively. The next three articles, setting forth the legal relationships between the states and between the states and the nation, the process of amending the Constitution, and the legal supremacy of the Constitution itself, are even briefer. (Readers are urged to study the entire document and its twenty-six amendments in Appendix II.)

But the document itself is only the beginning, and a potentially misleading one at that. It is too easy to assume that these powers and limits are self-explanatory and fully operative, and/or that government is actually managed in this manner and with these principles in mind. People in government actually have very broad discretion to do what they choose, and then to legitimate their acts in the eyes of others by claiming that they are authorized or prescribed by the Constitution.

But neither is the Constitution a mere tool of whoever holds power. Its impact can be demonstrated in a variety of ways: in the structure and practices of our institutions, in our ideology, in the symbols to which we respond, and in our basic political style. From time to time, as the power of various political forces is brought to bear, the Constitution assumes a tangible form: the Supreme Court voids a Congressional statute, or the House tries to impeach the President. At other times, the Constitution amounts to a partly enabling, partly legitimating construct in the minds of political elites, with some echoes in the minds of the general public.

In this chapter we shall first examine some of the ways in which the Constitution has an impact on politics today, and then work back to an analysis of its original provisions. Thus we shall develop a more subtle understanding of our governing ideology and style, and their implications for the process by which the national government is managed.

The Impact of the Constitution Today

One of the most noteworthy characteristics of the Constitution is the division of powers between the states and the nation. There are some things the national government has no delegated power to do, such as to make a purely local act (murder, theft, and the like) a crime punishable by the United States government. Such acts are punishable only by the state in which they are committed, in accordance with the criminal law and procedure of that state. The U.S. government has only those powers delegated to it, and those necessary and proper to their implementation. Over time this arrangement has led to some awkward situations, and to some severe straining of the Constitution to enable the national government to do the things people wanted it to do. As the saying goes, however, "where there's a will there's a way"—as we shall now see.

Auxiliary Means to Agreed Ends

One of the conclusions emerging from the celebrated crime investigations of the early 1950s was that the individual states were unable and sometimes unwilling to cope with organized local betting rings, and that federal support would encourage or embarrass them into action. But the Constitution has always been understood to deny the federal government power to make purely local acts (murder, robbery, etc.) crimes punishable by federal authorities. In this instance, however, there was a will to act, and so a way was found. The constitutional authority to raise revenue was used to levy a $50 tax on all bookmakers in the country. Those who paid the tax and filed an address to which to send the revenue stamp were promptly reported to the local police, and a follow-up was made to see whether the local police had acted or not. If a bookmaker elected not to pay the tax, of course, he was in default of a legal obligation to the federal government. He could then legitimately be made the subject of direct FBI investigation, and ultimately prosecuted—not for bookmaking but for failure to pay the tax and obtain the stamp.[1]

Although the means are somewhat awkward, the national government enables itself to do many things by similar types of rationalization. In the early years of the twentieth century, for example, one of the major goals of social welfare advocates was the elimination of child labor. Efforts to obtain prohibitory laws from the states, which had clear constitutional power to legislate such statutes, were generally unavailing. Some state legislatures were under the influence of the very industries over which regulation was sought. Others were reluctant to put their industries at a competitive disadvantage by forcing them to pay higher wages than companies in other states.

The movement therefore turned to the national government, but found that the only pertinent federal power was that of regulating interstate commerce. Under then-current Supreme Court definitions of "interstate commerce" (the Framers having failed to provide any clues to the meaning of the term), the mere production of goods was *not* sufficient to define a factory as "in commerce"; the issue was therefore outside the scope of federal power. But a resourceful Congress nevertheless enacted a law forbidding the *shipment across state lines* of any goods made with child labor, thereby achieving nearly the same ends as if it had possessed the power to eradicate child labor in the first place.

[1] *United States v. Kahriger,* 345 US 22 (1952), is the Supreme Court decision that upheld this arrangement.

An equally resourceful Supreme Court, however, held that the statute was too palpable in its intent—that is, a subterfuge intended to achieve prohibited ends—and was therefore void as being in excess of congressional powers.[2]

And so the matter rested [3]—the political system being legally powerless to eliminate the practice of child labor—until a new and bolder Congress enacted an analogous statute to regulate labor relations in factories. A newly chastened Supreme Court then reversed past precedent and upheld such regulations as a legitimate aspect of the power to regulate commerce.[4] Since then, the congressional imagination and the Supreme Court's acquiescence have enlarged the definition of commerce to the point that Congress can now constitutionally require little luncheonettes in the backwoods of Georgia to serve blacks, even if the luncheonette never sees a person traveling in interstate commerce and never buys supplies from another state. The supporting argument is that even though the luncheonette itself is not "in commerce," it has "an effect" on commerce because people who eat in the luncheonette do not go to eat in restaurants which *are* in commerce.[5]

If this sounds like an elaborate way to say that the Supreme Court is currently unwilling to limit congressional power to regulate commerce, consider the case that provided the basis for the decision just described. A farmer who was growing his full quota of grain under federal crop limitations (an exercise of the power to regulate commerce) decided to grow more, solely to feed his chickens and not for sale. He was nevertheless held to be in violation of the limitations on growing, because the grain he grew himself he would not buy in commerce; he thereby had "an effect" on commerce and was subject to congressional power.[6]

The States and the Nation

The Constitution divides between the states and the national government the power to tax various types of goods and activities. A brief outline of the consequences of these allocations suggests another way that constitutional provisions can have an impact on contemporary politics. Since the states have the power to tax all objects within their jurisdictions except imports, the national government was effectively kept from tapping the most lucrative source of income—property, including both land and personal property. But as the need for govern-

[2] The case was *Hammer v. Dagenhart,* 247 US 251 (1918).

[3] A constitutional amendment to authorize child labor laws was passed by the Congress, but it was not ratified by a sufficient number of states to become effective.

[4] *National Labor Relations Board v. Jones & Laughlin Steel Corporation,* 301 US 1 (1937).

[5] *Heart of Atlanta Motel v. Maddox,* 379 US 241 (1964).

[6] *Wickard v. Filburn,* 317 US 111 (1942).

mental revenue grew, and the states encountered severe resistance from property-taxed citizens, the national government's end of the bargain began to look better. The income tax provided a means for acquiring revenue sufficiently remote from the taxpayer to be relatively immune to resistance. Further, the national government ran none of the risks a state did when it sought access to taxable resources within its boundaries. States, on the other hand, were constantly faced with a situation in which tax benefits were offered by competing states to encourage industries to move from one state to another. Many states, therefore, were naturally reluctant to take full advantage of the available resources lest a company move elsewhere. Thus, a provision originally designed to prevent the federal government from garnering enough revenue to overawe the states ultimately had the reverse effect, due to changed economic conditions.

By the mid-twentieth century, the federal revenue-raising capacity was so much greater and more efficient than that of the states that some form of centralization was practically necessitated. Even with grants-in-aid to the states and other more drastic revenue-sharing practices, it was clear that revenue-raising capacity alone would make possible federal involvement in (if not control over) the activities of state and local governments for the foreseeable future. What had begun as a deliberate scheme to promote decentralized government had become a powerful inducement to centralization. In this and other ways, economic developments have outdated and reversed precise constitutional provisions. The provisions themselves are faithfully observed, but the consequences are far from what the Framers intended.

The Constitution's Effect on the Character of Party Politics

Observers of American politics are fond of characterizing the two major political parties as decentralized, locally oriented coalitions of divergent elements that coalesce only in the few months before a presidential election. Thus the American party system is capable of promoting intra-party compromise and moderation, but is less effective at providing a coherent link between the wishes of majorities and government action. These characteristics of party politics are caused by some very basic structural provisions of the Constitution: federalism, separation of powers, and the electoral college.

Federalism is the division of powers between constituent units (the states) and a single central unit (the national government) such that each has defined powers and is supreme in its own allotted sphere. It implies a balance and a certain amount of tension between the two, with the deliberate purpose of permitting local majorities, or other interests not dominant in the central government, a base of power from which to seek their own ends. Although the Constitution does not expressly provide for federalism as such, it does confirm it as a fact of life (indeed, the Framers had no choice, given the independence and power of the states in 1787) and specifies the powers and obligations of each level of government to the other.

That is all the Constitution needs to do, however, for several natural effects immediately follow: the existence of real power to do important things at the state level means that those who seek the benefits of governmental action, as well as those who seek power, must focus on the states. Those who successfully control or influence the actions of a state government for their own ends have a strong vested interest in maintaining and defending that control. Therefore, the political parties in each state may well become more concerned with state affairs than national affairs. State elections and the subsequent uses of state patronage (both jobs and contracts) are frequently more vital to political party activists than are national issues, candidates, or policies.

Because each state party has a distinctive set of interests and priorities, the national party is not much more than a very loose coalition of fifty state parties, each with a unique view of what the national party should do and why. Party activists, accustomed to a local struggle for control of their major source of rewards and benefits, retain their localism and private-interest attitudes even when they enter the national political arena. Federalism almost by itself mandates internal divisions and conflict within the major political parties, and assures a decentralized and locally oriented ethos as well.

Separation of powers is the division of specific national governmental powers among the institutions of the national government. A more accurate description of the American system is "separated institutions sharing powers,"[7] since the separation is not accomplished precisely according to the nature of powers; instead each type of power (legislative, executive, judicial) is distributed among the major institutions. The President, for example, has the (legislative) power of veto, and the Senate has the (executive) power of confirming appointments of ambassadors and department heads. Of course, most of the legislative powers of the national government are located in the Congress, most of the judicial powers in the Supreme Court, and so on.

What the separation of powers does is to assure that the power of government is placed in several hands, each with a distinctive constituency. The probability is high that the several constituencies represented will not share the same values or priorities, and that conflict will result over all but the most innocuous questions. Although many people in government belong to the same political party, the fact that they are associated with different institutions and respond to distinctive constituencies leads them to disagree with each other.

Thus the party is divided again, and not even its national office-

---

[7] This apt phrase was coined by Richard Neustadt in his *Presidential Power: The Politics of Leadership* (New York: John Wiley, 1960).

holders share a clear position on its programs. Instead, each fragment of the party claims that its views are representative of the entire party, and then proceeds to seek allies within the other party who share its views on a given issue. Separation of powers in effect assures internal conflict among both majority and minority officeholders in the national government, and encourages attempts at temporary alliances between like-minded elements across party lines.

The Electoral College

The *electoral college* is one of the Framers' peculiar compromises, a device that allots ballots for President and Vice-President among the states according to the size of the state's total congressional delegation (two for each, representing the two senators, plus an additional number equivalent to the number of representatives from that state in the House of Representatives). In order to maximize its influence in national party circles, each state has provided that all of its ballots will go to the winner of the popular vote for President in that state. This procedure means that the heavily populated states (such urban and industrial states as New York and California) represent very critical prizes in the eyes of any presidential candidate. The gain or loss of a few votes in those states could mean the difference between gaining and losing large blocs of electoral ballots, while the smaller states represent much lower risks and opportunities. Consequently, presidential candidates usually become specially attuned to the needs and goals (and ethnic minorities) of the urban states; this circumstance has important effects on both the character of the political parties and the government itself.

Because the electoral college works on a winner-take-all basis in each state, it benefits the two major parties by making it difficult for a new third party to compete successfully for the single most important prize in politics, the presidency. To have a chance to win the presidency, a party must seek a majority of votes in the electoral college for its candidate. This means that the new party must try to build a base in *all* the states, not just a particular region in which its candidates might be very popular; no region has enough electoral votes to make up a majority of the electoral college ballots. In trying to compete in all the states, however, the new party encounters difficulties getting on the ballot, great financial burdens, and the prospect that one or the other of the two established parties has a majority in most states anyhow. Thus the electoral college preserves the established two-party structure and discourages the development of third parties.

However sketchy, these illustrations point up some important consequences of the provisions of the Constitution on American politics and public policy. We have seen that the words of the Constitution in and of themselves contain few imperatives and do not normally determine the outcome of specific issues. Instead, constitutional provisions are a kind of a starting-point, which political activists use as their values, interests, and relative influence dictate. The lack of constitutional power to perform a particular act may be decisive if enough strategically located individuals oppose it and those who do support it are not willing to make a special effort to see it succeed. But a similar lack of power in other circumstances may be successfully (though awkwardly and perhaps inconsistently) circumvented, if enough individuals and other interests strongly desire particular goals.

This is not to say that the provisions of the Constitution are *merely* instruments, to be used by various political activists as they see fit. There are traditions and expectations surrounding many specific provisions; and these traditions and expectations are felt very strongly by political elites, whose careers and prospects are deeply committed to the need for consistent and predictable behavior on the part of other men and women in government. As a result, many provisions take on an independent status and meaning, which *in the absence of compelling reasons to the contrary* will probably control the outcome in any given case. When determined and powerful people or groups seek particular goals, however, constitutional words are not likely to prevent them from attaining their ends. In time (if they are successful), their preferences will become the new and accepted interpretation of the Constitution's meaning, and new generations will begin their political goalseeking from this new point of departure.

The most vital single point to be made when considering the implications of the American Constitution is thus implicit in these illustrations: there is simply no mechanical inevitability about American politics inherent in the Constitution. Nothing *necessarily* follows because of the wording of the document, and *everything* depends to a greater or lesser degree on the preferences and priorities of the more powerful political activists of the period. This realization lends crucial significance to the process by which the Constitution is interpreted and applied to contemporary politics. Whoever manages to affix a preferred interpretation to the Constitution acquires the aura of legitimacy and traditionalism the Constitution evokes from others in government and the general public. It is not a matter of indifference to most people whether the Constitution is or is not interpreted to permit abortion, busing, or sex discrimination.

Who interprets the Constitution is therefore a more important issue than *what the document says*. Nor is it clear in any given instance which institution or other participant will win the battle to establish the authoritative constitutional interpretation. There are many participants in the grim and sometimes invisible struggle within the national government for power to determine what the Constitution "requires" on any particular issue, and much is at stake in each of these contests. As we examine this struggle and the stakes involved in it in succeeding chapters, it will become clear that the Supreme Court is an intensely politicized organ of government—and by no means the only interpreter of the Constitution.

But the values, standards, and procedures written into the Constitution by its Framers have given it an important power to shape American legal and political practices. Indeed, the original document can be read as a catalogue of orthodox American political values, and as a major instrument by which those values are projected into the present.

The Original Constitution: Limited Government, Property Rights, and Antimajoritarianism

Limited Government

The underlying theory of the American Constitution fully embodies commitments to the values of limited government and contract. The document prescribes all the powers and limitations of government, and as such is the complete contract between the collectivity of individuals who compose the society and the governmental agent. Legalism—the belief that a neutral mechanism called "law" is a complete and self-executing set of answers to all problems—is inherent in the so-called "supremacy clause" in which the Constitution declares itself to be the supreme law of the land, binding on all governmental officials at all levels.

Against this general background of shared political values, the Constitution reflects several compromises between divergent interests that existed among the Framers. Men from small states resisted exclusively population-based representation in the legislature, and managed to secure equal status in the Senate. Southerners extracted a prohibition against interference with the importation of slaves for a fixed period of time. And the electoral college was constructed to balance the respective weights of the small and large states in selecting the President. Because of these and other differences between some of the Framers, the document is not logically consistent or precisely symmetrical, and it has often been called a "bundle of compromises." But it is easy to overestimate the extent of conflict and the scope and difficulty of compromise at the Constitutional Convention. Much was shared in the way of political values, and the Framers had very definite convictions about certain critical principles of government—all of which made compromise on the limited differences of interest among them more attainable.

Generations of historians have battled over the proper interpretation of the Constitutional Convention and the goals and purposes of the men who attended. To some, it was a conservative counterrevolution in reaction to the excesses of liberalism inherent in the Declaration of Independence. To others, it was a far-sighted, bold experiment in expanding the frontiers of democracy. Politicians disagreed from the very moment the veil of secrecy was lifted from the proceedings of the Convention, Patrick Henry, for example, declaring that he had "smelled a rat." James

Madison, the chief notetaker at the Convention, did not publish his records until more than fifty years later, and he has been accused of polishing them to assure that they lent support to his changing views.[8]

Nineteenth-century historians, perhaps sympathetic to Federalist principles, tended to be specially struck by the Framers' accomplishments, occasionally implying that they were divinely inspired. In reaction to this school of Constitution-worship, Charles Beard lent support to Progressive Movement realism in 1913 with the publication of his *An Economic Interpretation of the Constitution.*[9] Beard very nearly turned American history upside down by arguing that the Framers were men who had acquired vast holdings of bonds and scrip (issued by the Continental Congress during the Revolutionary War) at low values, to which they had fallen because of the inability of the Congress to pay its debts. He implied that they then constructed a powerful government that could raise revenue and pay off the bonds at full value—to their great personal profit. This debunking was viewed by some as in very bad taste, but it helped others to look at the Constitution as a value-laden document with quite human strengths and weaknesses. Not for four decades did scholars seek to verify Beard's allegations, and when they did it appeared that he had at the very least overstated his argument.[10] But few now deny that there was at least a shared upper-class ethos among the Framers and that economic interests played some part in shaping the Constitution. Thus, although we cannot expect to achieve a final interpretation of the Framers' purposes, it is possible to analyze what they wrote into the document and to point to two very broadly shared principles of government evident in it. The two themes that apparently united most of the men present at the Convention of 1787 were the need to protect property rights and a wish to prevent rampant majoritarianism.

Protection for Property Rights

Much of the motivation for the Annapolis Convention, which preceded the call to revise the Articles of Confederation, and for the latter s well, was dissatisfaction on the part of businessmen with the protectionism of the states and the tendency of some state and lower units of government to promote both inflation and the avoidance of debts. For financial and creditor interests, the Constitution was a triumph. They gained:

1. prohibitions on state import restrictions and taxation.

2. a prohibition on state impairment of the obligations of contracts.

---

[8] For a thoroughly revisionist view that is very hard on both Madison and Marshall, see William Crosskey, *Politics and the Constitution in the History of the United States* (Chicago: University of Chicago Press, 1953).

[9] Charles Beard, *An Economic Interpretation of the Constitution* (New York: Macmillan, 1913).

[10] The leading counter to Beard is Robert Brown, *Charles Beard and the Constitution* (Princeton, N.J.: Princeton University Press, 1956).

3. a single central agency to coin money and regulate its value.

4. a prohibition on state use of paper money or other legal tender.

5. a system of courts operated by the central government, so that they did not have to take chances with locally run courts in states to which their debtors had fled.

6. a guarantee of full faith and credit in one state to the acts and judgments of another, so that they could pursue their debtors more effectively.

7. a guarantee of a republican form of government for the states, as well as provisions for suppressing domestic insurrections, so that they need fear no further incidents such as the celebrated Shays' Rebellion of 1787–1788 in western Massachusetts.

In all these respects, the Framers acted consistently to promote the enforcement of contracts, the collection of debts, the maintenance of stable valuation for money, and the promotion of a national economy. These are surely economy-building goals, at least under the conditions of the times, but they were implemented in the new Constitution at the expense of many small farmers and artisans. In this respect the Constitution favored the interests of one class over those of another. Nor was the desire of some small farmers to promote inflation, avoid debts, or protect their local industries merely an ungrateful rejection of contractual obligation. In their eyes, and perhaps objectively, the Eastern financiers and businessmen were profiting unconscionably from exorbitant interest rates and other forms of economic exploitation of the hapless and frequently penniless farmers and artisans. Shays' Rebellion, and such other west-east tensions as the Whiskey Rebellion, grew out of the perception by Western workingmen that they were being exploited by urban financiers. In their eyes, the Constitution was another means of furthering this exploitation.

Antimajoritarianism

Consistent with the desire to protect property rights, but drawing more specifically on their anticipation of redistribution of property by the masses, the Framers built into the Constitution layer upon layer of obstacles to simple majority rule. It may be instructive to see how fully almost every one of these restrictions has been moderated in subsequent years. If it had not been possible to find ways around these limitations, the Constitution would probably have aroused more criticism in recent decades.

The major limitations on majority rule, and the means found to circumvent them, are as follows:

1. Amendment to the Constitution is very difficult, requiring a vote of two-thirds of both houses of Congress and ratification by

three-quarters of the states. But informal means of amendment have been developed, such as the shifting interpretations of the Supreme Court.

2. The electoral college is a device designed to give discretionary power to the elected delegates and deny the people direct choice of the President. But delegates to the electoral college run on a pledged basis, and virtually never violate their pledges; ballots list the names of the presidential candidates, and most voters do not realize that an intermediate step is involved at all.

3. Separation of powers prevents the people (supposedly represented in the Congress) from working their will on the government as a whole. But the President and the Court have both become virtually representative of majority will, while the House has fallen into the hands of its senior members from chiefly rural safe districts. And the party system cuts across the separation of powers to induce some degree of cooperation between the branches.

4. Senators were originally selected by the state legislatures. But direct election of senators was accomplished by constitutional amendment in 1917, and for decades before that state legislators had run for election on the basis of pledges to vote for one or another senatorial candidate.

5. Judicial review is a means of applying restraints to the legislature, supposedly the representatives of the people. But Congress and the President together have shown imagination in pressuring the Court or avoiding the implications of its decisions.

6. The division of the legislature into two houses was an attempt to introduce institutional jealousies and constituency rivalries into the popular branch, and thereby to reduce coherent action. But the party system and presidential leadership have promoted some degree of unity between the two houses.

This catalogue might be expanded, but the point should be clear: this impressive list of conscious efforts to fragment, divide, and neutralize the will of the people cannot be coincidental, nor is it likely that a government thus paralyzed in practice could have long endured. What has sustained the American political system is perhaps not so much the quality of its Constitution as the capacity of political elites to generate a style of political behavior that satisfies the different demands of the major economic and social interests *and* of the masses of average citizens.

What has transpired over the years in the United States is a commentary on *both* the Framers and the flexibility of the American politician. Somehow, amidst this complex process, political activists have apparently found it convenient and practical to perpetuate reverence for the Constitution as the embodiment of wisdom and justice in government. Perhaps we should examine the other side of this vital equation—perceptions of the Constitution in the minds of the American people.

The Constitution: Continuity and Symbolism

As an instrument of government, the Constitution appears to have immediate behavior-conditioning effects on political elites and to serve a more general legitimating function for the general public. Officials in government internalize the precedents and traditions surrounding particular provisions and so enable each other to understand and predict official behavior. People outside of government revere the Constitution and apparently desire the sense of continuity and propriety it radiates; and so they seek assurance that new actions are consistent with it. Officials in government compete with each other for the power to interpret the Constitution as favoring their own positions in political controversies, and thereby to gain the acquiescence of those less involved. To all political activists, apparently, there is a potential payoff in promoting and sustaining the idea that the Constitution contains all necessary answers to public problems if we only adhere to its principles.

In one important respect, the Constitution itself promotes this continuity-symbolizing role. Some of its provisions are eminently precise, leaving little to chance. But in other respects it is almost unconscionably vague and indeterminate ("the President shall take care that the laws be faithfully executed . . ."). Careful analysis indicates that the *precise* provisions have to do principally with the manner in which elections are to be conducted, and with the question of who is to hold office. The *vague and ambiguous* provisions, for the most part, have to do with the powers of officeholders, or, in other words, with what they are to do with their powers once they are in office. Political elites, therefore, may have confidence that officials are duly elected, for there is very little uncertainty about such matters. But the directions in which officeholders may lead the nation are very marginally circumscribed (except for a few specific prohibitions); they are practically free to do whatever they can justify by their political mandate and circumstances.

Continuity and symbolic reassurance are also furthered by the fact that contention over the meaning of particular phrases in the Constitution translates political controversies into the less heated arena of legal debate. It also simultaneously reminds both participants and the public of what they share—acceptance of the same Constitution and the accumulated political association it represents. The stifling of political controversy in this fashion has not led to later upheavals, perhaps because differences over division of the economic product were more frequent than differences over such fundamental matters as how the political or economic systems should be organized. Indeed, the reduction of tensions by translating them into legalistic debates has probably contributed to the tradition of nonfundamental political debates that is now part of the American political style. Let us look more systematically at the ways in which constitutional provisions merge with established values and ideology to create a distinctive American political style.

Ideology, Constitution, and Political Style

The Constitution, as we have seen, scatters official power across a wide spectrum of positions within the governments of the United States. First, it divides power between the national government and the various state governments, and further fragments the power of the national government among the three major branches. Subsequent developments have extended this fragmentation well beyond the Framers' intentions, so that significant portions of the capacity to govern are today located (due to a combination of tradition, necessity, and aggrandizement) in, for example, the committees of the Congress, the Joint Chiefs of Staff, and the middle ranges of the executive bureaucracy.

As has often been noted, this pattern of power distribution creates a multitude of pressure points (sometimes less neutrally characterized as veto points) scattered across the map of American government. Not surprisingly, what results is a political system highly sensitive to the *status quo*—one that does not readily produce new policies that would tend to destroy established relationships. Usually, it takes a wide-ranging and determined effort to neutralize all these veto points, to reach some form of accommodation with their preferences, so that a broadly supported new policy can be instituted.

There is nothing casual about the *status quo*—enforcing consequences of the Constitution's dispersal of power. It is entirely consistent with the Framers' antigovernment biases. It conforms completely to their (and their successors') views on the need for private freedom of action: the only way that individuals can be sure of complete freedom to pursue their own ends as they see fit is through the reduction of governmental action to a "lowest common denominator." Moreover, it follows the more fully articulated political principles of James Madison, often termed the "father of the Constitution," in every basic feature.

The Madisonian Approach

Madison, perhaps the most scholarly of the Framers and at the same time completely attuned to their concern for the threat of majoritarian redistribution of property, provided an intellectual framework for the simpler value preferences of his colleagues. He argued that the dangers of a rampant popular majority could be effectively checked by enlarging the scope of the republic to create so many special interests within the potential "majority" that no single coherent majority could stay united long enough to do real damage to the *status quo*. By giving each special interest within the potential "majority" a selection of possible power points within the governmental structure at which to aim, their cross-pressuring and mutually containing potential would be realized.

The Constitution thus not only facilitates the realization of the pluralist (many groups, many veto points) image of how government does and should work; it is itself based on a belief in the desirability of such a process. It should be clear that the creation of substantial and necessary units of power at a multitude of points within the political system invites (if it does not impel) various groups to seek to control those that happen to be most available or vulnerable to them. This inducement to group activity is not coincidental. It is instead the fruition of Madison's hopes for institutionalizing the social process, which he believed would permit the people to take part in government but assure that the government was still able to do the right thing (that is, what the better informed and generally wealthier people thought was best).

Madison's thesis is sometimes known as the principle of "natural limits to numerical majorities." This means that when a majority in favor of an action reaches a size sufficient to have a chance of achieving its goals, its internal diversities will be so great as to fragment it. This prospect is made more likely by districting systems that require a very large (and nationwide) majority and result in election of its most moderate representatives. It is aided by multiple power points within the governmental structure that enable each divergent interest to make its opposition felt. And it is supplemented by division of the national government into branches, providing a further level of opportunity for opposition and disabling internal tensions. In this manner, argued Madison, ill-intentioned majorities would be held in check. So would "well-intentioned" majorities, of course, but Madison was arguing to and on behalf of the propertied upper classes of his day. His readers were not democrats but aristocrats (or plutocrats) who favored more direct and explicit limitations on popular influence over governmental policies. Madison carried the day because he convinced some of them that he had devised a subtler and less provocative means to their goals than they had thought possible.

The pluralist characterization of politics and government in the United States thus has a long and respectable intellectual history. It begins with the intentions and achievements of the Framers of the Constitution, and is carried into effect today by the provisions of the document they produced. It is little wonder that this image should have such ideological power by now, or that it should be effective in shaping the American political style. Madison's thesis, and the Framers as they constructed the new government, sought to preserve the capacity of the wealthy, propertied aristocracy to shape the nation's policies. These purposes lay behind the origin of the pluralist interpretation, though of course they may not hold true today. But it is not unreasonable to think that some of the consequences the Framers sought still inhere in their combined ideological and constitutional achievement. These underlying assumptions, for example, lead to some distinctive characteristics of politics in the United States.

Politics: The Rules of the Game

For one thing, American politicians tend to engage in a balancing act, in which they measure the weight, determination, and potential governmental access of groups that seek something from government, and act according to this calculus rather than on the merits of the claim. Office-holders assume the posture of referees, despite the fact that they are products of the system's power equations themselves. As referees, they uphold "the rules of the game," which are the specified ways in which groups seeking influence are supposed to go about their efforts. Theoretically at least, fairness, hearings, due process, and tolerance of opposing positions are part of these rules of the game.

Concentration on the rules of the game, however, may obscure two crucial aspects of the process of politics. The nature of the rules is to allow certain kinds of competition among certain established players, and also to foreclose and illegitimize some other kinds of conflicts. Bargaining, negotiation, compromise—the leading characteristics of the American political style—are possible only when the "antagonists" share certain assumptions about what the game is about and how it should be played. Management and labor can agree to submit issues to arbitration only when the issues at stake are sufficiently confined within shared value premises to be soluble by factual analysis or compromises that do not deprive either side of its essential holdings. Wages or specific assembly-line grievances have this potential, but the nationalization of the factory or the workers' right to hire the company president do not. Similarly, the rules of the game of politics allow only those types of disagreements that acknowledge shared value premises. These are disagreements within the basic framework of the *status quo*—disagreements about who gets how much of a particular economic product, for example, or the application of an accepted rule. To play by these rules, in other words, is to acknowledge the premises and continuity of the basic economic and political structure of the American social order.

Not only the validity of those premises, but also the kinds of results that can be obtained, are shaped by the rules. Behind the rules lies a particular *status quo,* not an ideal form of political order. When the rules limit the scope of challenge, they eliminate much of the possible range of alternatives and specify that the *status quo* can only be changed a certain degree. Thus, if only limited changes are possible, the rules become part of the means of maintaining the *status quo;* and to defend the rules as if they were neutral is really to defend the substance of the *status quo.* This gives new significance to the American penchant for concentration on procedure—how things are done—rather than substance. It is as if it were more important that all the established procedures were followed than that the right thing was done. Countless tragedies have been written about this dilemma, from classic drama to contemporary works, but the issue has not yet been widely recognized as relevant to American political principles.

The inducements to engage in politics under the essentially pluralist rules of the game are very strong. The Constitution's structure and intentions and current political styles all militate in this direction. Just as there are strong attractions, however, there are strong auxiliary coercions for those who do not comply. The widely shared popular commitment to the established rules—which usually overlooks the fact that such rules shape what can be done—first creates a social support for such behavior. Next, a reputation for breaking the rules may lead to social or economic sanctions—ostracism from established society, exclusion from economic opportunities, loss of a job. If deviant behavior persists, legal reprisals are likely to be followed (or perhaps augmented) by physical coercions such as jail or other injuries. Those who seek substantial change in the policies of government may thus appear to be nothing but rule-breakers, and may well suffer serious punishments in the bargain.

It should be clear that this discussion of the rules of the game and the American political style only superficially confirms the pluralist characterization of the American political process. That the rules promote, and the style endorses, such an image of the political process does not remove it from the realm of hypothesis and/or ideology. The function of ideology, after all, is to explain, rationalize, and promote behavior in accordance with an established structure. Such group conflict as does occur may be over marginal matters, such as who gets how much of the economic rewards of a plentiful economy, and not over fundamental questions. In the latter case, all groups may concur and hew to a single line; or superior sources of power may channel their actions so fully that the result is the same. Thus, the chief consequence of their interaction for our purposes may be that they serve as an effective barrier to efforts toward change generated by new groups or segments of the general public.

Conflict and the "American Way"

We cannot conclude this discussion without commenting on the way the rules and the American political style have labelled conflict as a social process. We have seen how the rules and the style combine to discourage behavior inconsistent with the premises behind the rules. Action at odds with the rules—in short, provoking serious conflicts of values or challenging behavioral norms—is deplored as violating "the American way." But there is nothing inherently immoral or socially reprehensible about conflict as such. Conflict of a fundamental kind (that is, conflict over ends and not just over means) may sometimes be essential to release constructive forces in a society and to remove restraints that simply will not eliminate themselves.

Nor is the distinction between nonviolent and violent conflict sufficient to permit moral or historical judgments. To take a very obvious example, slavery would not have been eliminated in the United States without violent conflict—unless one wishes to argue that blacks should have been willing to wait another two centuries until white plantation owners were persuaded of their own immorality so strongly as to overcome their economic interests. Conflict, in short, must be judged not on the basis of its existence, and not on the basis of its nonviolent or violent nature, but in light of the entire context in which it takes place. If, on balance, it serves to further social and humanitarian progress, and if other means toward these ends are blocked by dominant forces within the society, disapproval of conflict is essentially a vote on behalf of one's private interest in maintaining the *status quo*. Widespread consensus within a society may be similarly good or bad, depending on what the consensus supports and how general are the interests that profit from it. If consensus maintains conditions or policies that are in the special interest of a few and not in the general interest, it is surely undesirable. A broadly shared consensus on either goals or methods that most of the society conceives to be in its interest would be valuable.

This argument is not intended as an unequivocal call for conflict instead of consensus. It is meant simply to point up the fact that political systems can find both functional at different stages in their development, and that too much of either is likely to be destructive. In the American case, at least for the past decades, both the rules of the game and the general political style have strongly insisted on consensus and denigrated or repressed conflict. We may, and perhaps should, be en route to redressing that balance in the 1970s. Soon, perhaps, the validity of *avoidance* of issues may again be open to debate.

The American style of not facing issues, of insistence on following the rules and letting the results fall where they may, has the merit of reducing conflict. Some conflicts may be potentially disastrous: they may be of such a fundamental nature as to be insoluble without mass violence. Where this is the case, the prospect of seriously self-destructive mass violence may suggest that the avoidance of issues and deflection of attention is morally and politically preferable. The crucial variable is the nature of the context: neither conflict nor consensus has meaning except in terms of goals and existing conditions, and what is useful and desirable in one setting may be disastrous in another. For the present, of course, we operate with the political style and the rules we have been describing.

13

Law and the Courts

Law takes many forms, from constitutional and statutory provisions through regulations and ordinances to court decisions. Law originates in a variety of institutions: legislatures, administrative bodies, executives, the people, courts, and accumulated social practices. It serves multiple functions at various levels. These range from resolution of the most fundamental (or *constitutional*) questions to the day-to-day management of thousands of routine economic and political transactions between individuals, corporations, and governments. All are politically significant, for in many respects law is merely politics by another name.

We shall examine the law and the courts in terms of their political significance, starting with the major problems of constitutional interpretation and working our way through the court systems to some current

241

issues and the part played by law in the process of social control. In general, we shall see that the workings of law are closely bound up with the values and goals that are dominant within the society, normally those of its more powerful members. Law and the legal order are the vehicles by which the relatively powerful effectively establish their values and priorities as controlling factors within the society. Almost by definition, law must be non-neutral—it is a conserving force that works in a wide variety of ways to sustain the established social order. Its principal task, after all, is to maintain order—that is, continuity of the existing structures and procedures, which has the effect of helping some people far more than others. But both the law and its applications are usually strongly supported by the great bulk of the people, for whom they may also serve important though different needs.

Interpreting the Constitution

Law plays a larger role in organizing the basic structures and procedures of government in the United States than it does in most political systems. This is so because the Constitution is a written document, and by its own declaration the supreme *law* of the land. Fundamental—constitutional—issues are thus removed at the start from the realm of open value choices made according to their merits and the felt needs of the times. They are translated into the language and procedures of the law as *it* exists at the time. Thus, issues must be articulated in terms of the concepts and forms the law happens to make available, and trusted to a particular (generally upper-class) skill group, lawyers. In the American system, this means that a powerful role is played by pre-existing contractual obligations, property rights, and precedent—the decisions and practices of a perhaps irrelevant past. It also makes for a contest over the right to say what the law "really means"—a contest which, however vital to all, must be decided only by the backward-looking professionals and methods of the law. In particular, as we noted earlier, this contest focuses on the capacity to authoritatively interpret the Constitution. Whoever succeeds in doing so gains real advantage in shaping the future policies and practices of government.

Most Americans, if pressed, would probably say that the Supreme Court is the proper vehicle for interpretation of the Constitution. Moreover, it would be difficult for them to imagine a basis for challenging the right and power of the Court to do so. Such is the triumph of Alexander Hamilton's argument, written into constitutional doctrine by the adroit opportunism of Chief Justice John Marshall. The complete acceptance of Hamilton's argument today, however, should not obscure the bitter clash of values and competing philosophies between Hamilton and Jefferson over the question of who was to interpret the Constitution. Hamilton's total victory brought with it mixed costs and benefits, and has had fundamental consequences for the nature of the American system of government. We shall first review the stakes in the conflict and then examine the effects of Hamilton's victory.

The Hamilton-Jefferson Positions

Hamilton had argued for a limited monarchy at the Constitutional Convention, but supported the final product as acceptable for the economy-developing purposes he had in mind. Together with John Jay and James Madison, he authored several essays designed to promote ratification of the Constitution in New York and known by the collective title *The Federalist Papers*. For the most part, Hamilton stressed the utility of union and the need for a strong central government as reasons for accepting the document. But he saved his special enthusiasm for two innovations in the Constitution that improved on the old Articles of Confederation: a strong and vigorous executive to administer the laws with force where necessary, and an independent judiciary with the power of judicial review (the power to declare acts of Congress unconstitutional).

In arguing for judicial power to declare acts of the other branches unconstitutional and therefore void, Hamilton employed the legal analogy of the relationship between principal and agent.[1] The people (the principal) having granted the agent (the national government) certain powers and not others, Hamilton argued, any act in excess of those granted powers must be void. But this position raised the problem of how invalidity was to be determined: how does anybody know when an act of a legislature is in excess of the powers granted to it? Certainly sincere and knowledgeable legislators had decided that the act *was* within their powers, or they would have chosen another means of attaining the end they had in mind. Hamilton argued that these determinations were questions of law (again, the Constitution conveniently *declares* that it is the law of the land) and as such ought to be decided by the Court. Jefferson insisted that the question of whether the principal had delegated a particular power to the agent ought to be decided by the principal himself, and certainly not by the agent. In other words, he wanted the people to determine in every instance whether the act of the legislature was authorized or not. The Constitution itself does not specify by what means its provisions are to be interpreted, and so the issue evolved into a test of logic, persuasiveness, and power between the two positions. Analysis of the debate suggests that two major disagreements divided the parties, and that both of these disagreements were rooted in the same conflict of values.

First, Hamilton and Jefferson had quite different views of the nature of a constitution. To Jefferson, it was a fundamental allocation of the people's powers, superior to the ongoing acts of government. For these reasons, it was not law in the ordinary sense of a statute or code, but

[1] See essay number 78 of the *Federalist Papers*.

Some perplexity respecting the rights of the courts to pronounce legislative acts void, because contrary to the Constitution, has arisen from an imagination that the doctrine would imply a superiority of the judiciary to the legislative power. It is urged that the authority which can declare the acts of another void, must necessarily be superior to the one whose acts may be declared void. . . .

. . . The interpretation of the laws is the proper and peculiar province of the courts. A constitution is, in fact, and must be regarded by the judges, as a fundamental law. It therefore belongs to them to ascertain its meaning as well as the meaning of any particular act proceeding from the legislative body. If there should happen to be an irreconcilable variance between the two, that which has the superior obligation and validity ought, of course, to be preferred; or, in other words, the Constitution ought to be preferred to the statute, the intention of the people to the intention of their agents.

Nor does this conclusion by any means suppose a superiority of the judicial to the legislative power. It only supposes that the power of the people is superior to both; and that where the will of the legislature, declared in its statutes, stands in opposition to that of the people, declared in the Constitution, the judges ought to be governed by the latter rather than by the former. . . .

Alexander Hamilton, *Federalist Papers* Number 78, 1788.

It is emphatically the province and duty of the judicial department to say what the law is. Those who apply the law to particular cases, must of necessity expound and interpret that rule. If two laws conflict with each other, the courts must decide on the operation of each.

So if a law be in opposition to the constitution; if both the law and the constitution apply to a particular case, so that the court must decide that case conformably to the law, disregarding the constitution; or conformably to the constitution, disregarding the law; the court must determine which of these conflicting rules governs each case. This is the very essence of judicial duty.

If, then, the courts are to regard the constitution, and the constitution is superior to any ordinary act of the legislature, the constitution, and not such ordinary act, must govern the case to which they both apply. . . .

Chief Justice John Marshall in *Marbury v. Madison* (1803).

. . . The Constitution and the right of the legislature to pass the Act, may be in collision. But is that a legitimate subject for judicial determination? If it be, the judiciary must be a peculiar organ, to revise the proceedings of the legislature, and to correct its mistakes; And in what part of the Constitution are we to look for this proud pre-eminence? Viewing the matter in the opposite direction, what would be thought of an Act of Assembly in which it should be declared that the Supreme Court had, in a particular case, put a wrong construction of the Constitution of the United States, and that the judgment should therefore be reversed? It would doubtless be thought a usurpation of judicial power. But it is by no means clear, that to declare a law void which has been enacted according to the forms prescribed in the Constitution, is not a usurpation of legislative power. It is an act of sovereignty. . . It is the business of the judiciary to interpret the laws, not scan the authority of the lawgiver; and without the latter, it cannot take cognizance of a collision between a law and the Constitution. . . .

Chief Justice Gibson of the Pennsylvania Supreme Court, in *Eakin v. Raub* (1825).

. . . I ask for no straining of words against the General Government, nor yet against the States. . . .

But the Chief Justice says, "There must be an ultimate arbiter somewhere." True, there must; but does that prove it is either party? The ultimate arbiter is the people of the Union, assembled by their deputies in convention, at the call of the Congress, or of two-thirds of the States. Let them decide to which they mean to give an authority claimed by two of their organs. And it has been the peculiar wisdom and felicity of our constitution, to have provided this peaceable appeal, where that of other nations is at once to force.

Thomas Jefferson, in a letter to Justice William Johnson, June 1823.

---

rather the people's instructions to their government about the goals and purposes it should pursue. These goals and purposes would be changeable over time, of course, as circumstances changed, and Jefferson insisted on the right of the people to change their Constitution regularly. Hamilton, on the other hand, saw the Constitution as a technical legal document with more or less fixed meaning, requiring legal expertise for interpretation. He argued that the Court was more likely than the people to possess the expertise and wisdom necessary to divine the meaning of the document's words. Although he acknowledged that the Constitution flowed from the people, he insisted that their ratification had carried with it authorization of the Court as interpreter.

Second, the two men disagreed over the nature of the act of interpretation. Since Jefferson viewed interpretation as requiring value-based choices, it followed that the choice should be made by the people themselves. If that was not feasible, it should be made by the institution closest to the people—normally their elected representatives in either state or national legislatures. He was particularly unwilling to be subjected to the value choices of a body of judges not elected but appointed (and for life terms) by members of the very national government whose exercise of powers was being questioned. Hamilton blandly declared that there was no act of choice involved in interpretation of the Constitution. He argued that it was simply a matter of comparing the statute with the words of the Constitution and registering the mechanical judgment that would be apparent from the comparison. He expressed confidence that the independence and life terms of judges would enable them to rise above the petty strifes of the day and render decisions true to the basic intent of the document.

What really divides the antagonists in this debate is their respective value premises and priorities. Jefferson feared the self-serving tendencies of the financiers and businessmen represented by Hamilton and the Federalist Party. Thus he sought to prevent them from staffing and using the Supreme Court to legitimate their aggrandizing schemes. His trust in the people was by no means complete, but he preferred their judgments to those of any self-selected elite. Hamilton feared the property-redistributing tendencies of the masses, and so sought to keep control over the scope of legislative powers in the hands of a trustworthy body sympathetic to property rights. Lawyers, already accustomed to reverence for the traditions and practices of the past, would be—particularly if well selected—another bulwark in defense of the Constitution's protections for the established order.

In principle, Jefferson's position appears the more logical and democratic. If, as seems evident, the act of interpretation involves value choices, then choice by the people or their recently elected representatives seems more democratic than choice by an appointed body that is not accountable to the people in any way. But Hamilton's view was made into authoritative doctrine by Chief Justice John Marshall in the case of *Marbury v. Madison* in 1803.[2] To add insult to injury, Marshall accomplished his feat while Jefferson was President, with a Republican majority backing him in the House of Representatives. He did it by declaring that an act of Congress was contrary to the Constitution. The institution restrained by the declaration of unconstitutionality was the Court itself, so Marshall faced no problem of failure to comply.

Despite some wavering in the face of Jefferson's pressures, Marshall stuck to the principle of the Court's power of judicial review throughout the remaining thirty years of his term on the Court. He had the political sophistication not to exercise the power, however, and it was not until 1857 and the *Dred Scott* case [3] that the second test of judicial review occurred. This too met with strong political reaction, and the principle of judicial review did not become firmly established in practice until after the Civil War. By then, the Court had proven to be an effective defense against the experiments of several states with social legislation, but the acceptance of the Hamiltonian position was nevertheless widespread.

The Hamilton Victory

Why did Hamilton win the argument so fully that it is now difficult to convey the significance of the choice that was unconsciously made?

---

[2] *Marbury v. Madison,* 1 branch. 137 (1803).

[3] *Dred Scott v. Sanford,* 19 Howard 393 (1857).

Surely the American penchant for legalism and the law is both cause and effect here. Americans were a receptive audience for Hamilton's legalistic approach to political problems. Further, the group to which Hamilton first appealed was made up chiefly of the upper and upper-middle classes of propertied people. They may have perceived the same advantages in the prospective role of the Court as he did. Business and wealthier interests consistently supported the Court's power of judicial review right up through the famous Court-packing conflicts of the New Deal period.

The latter event suggests another reason why Hamilton's argument may have succeeded in the long run. There is nothing inevitable about the Court's decision in any given situation, for the real determinant of a decision is less the power of the Court than the preferences of the judges who happen to be sitting on the Court at the time. The presence of liberal judges leads to liberal decisions, as the Warren Court era demonstrated; thus the Court may become a Hamiltonian instrument that acts on behalf of Jefferson's ideals. This realization may lead to acceptance of the Court's power of judicial review by *all* political activists, each of whom hopes to control the presidency and thus appointments to the Court. Careful choice of appointees to the Court—and longevity on their part—may permit greater impact on the directions of public policy than some Presidents generate in four years in the White House.

There seems little doubt, however, that the bestowal of the power of judicial review on the Supreme Court adds an important dimension to the character of American politics. For one thing, it tends to depoliticize some issues and convert them into a form in which only some people —lawyers and their clients—rather than the entire citizenry, are the relevant decisionmakers. Taking some of the great value conflicts of the society to the Supreme Court for resolution probably siphons off some tensions and bitterness from our politics and perhaps renders the nation more stable. But this can be a mixed blessing, for people probably *ought* sometimes to become engaged in vital questions affecting their futures.

The Supreme Court is not the final authority on any question about which a large number of people care strongly. There are many ways to combat or circumvent a single decision. It is nevertheless, even as a contingent decisionmaker, able to structure public understanding of some issues and to resolve many others without much public attention. Again, the desirability of this situation depends on one's attitude toward popular participation and the need for a preliminary decisionmaker in a large society with many public issues of considerable complexity.

Nonjudicial Factors in Interpretation

In any event, the Supreme Court does not perform the task of constitutional interpretation by itself. Many other institutions and political participants take part in shaping the meaning of the Constitution in any particular situation. The Court is, after all, an essentially passive institution, requiring several prior decisions by a variety of interested parties before a case even reaches it. Why and under what circumstances do some people or interests decide to sue others? Litigation is not the most direct and sure way of gaining one's political ends, and therefore must be utilized because other routes appear blocked or unpromising. The courts thus become a kind of supplementary political level—a means of impelling other institutions to action, or occasionally a route to limited specific ends. Other choices within the legal arena include decisions to or not to appeal, decisions by the Department of Justice as to the position it wishes to take on cases appealed to the Supreme Court, and all the decisions of trial and lower appellate court judges on aspects of a case both before and after the Supreme Court decides it.

The many participants in the legal process are not allowed to decide important questions through interaction alone. Neither the Congress nor the President has been submissive to the Supreme Court in American history. Both have reacted strongly to decisions they considered inappropriate or undesirable. Congress can pass a new statute only marginally different from one ruled unconstitutional. It can initiate constitutional amendments to overrule decisions. And it can and does express its displeasure by modifying the Court's jurisdiction or severely challenging and perhaps rejecting confirmation of newly appointed justices.

Because the President's cooperation is usually necessary to enforce Court decisions, he is often in an even stronger immediate position to prevent the Court's interpretation of the Constitution from becoming definitive or final. Presidents have ignored the Court, flatly refused to obey its decisions, or simply nominated judges with totally different views from those that previously prevailed. Thus, even when the Court does receive and decide a case in such a way as to assert a particular interpretation of the Constitution, the other institutions may reverse, modify, or ignore its determination.

Much of the time, questions about the Constitution's meaning are resolved without the involvement of the Court at all, such as when the President, the Congress, the political parties, and others establish precedents and traditions that are unchallenged or unchallengeable in courts. For example, the President is solely responsible for determining when the Constitution's guarantee to the states against domestic insurrection should be invoked. The political parties decide in light of their accumulated years of practice how the electoral college shall work, and so forth. Thousands of lower court opinions generate a wide variety of constitutional interpretations. In addition, statutes and regulations specify the jurisdictional boundaries of courts and agencies, particularize the generalities of the Constitution in an infinite number of ways, and authorize or preclude the bringing of claims to enforce constitutional "rights."

The history of interactions among the many participants in American politics suggests that interpretation of the Constitution is considered too important an act to be left to the Supreme Court. Even if it were capable in practice of hearing cases on all the disputed aspects of the Constitution, the other political participants are too vitally concerned about gaining their ends to defer to the preferences of the judges. The contest over whose preferences shall be asserted as the established meaning of the Constitution involves great stakes—perhaps the winning or losing of major prizes of politics—and so is on occasion bitterly fought. The final, authoritative meaning of the Constitution (assuming one ever finally emerges) is thus more a product of relative political power than of legalistic analysis alone.

Even if the Supreme Court is only a preliminary, or contingent, authority on the meaning of the Constitution, its role remains a powerful one. In analyzing the Court as an institution, we shall interpret it in political terms. For example, we shall examine the internal distribution of power and influence in order to come to grips with the reality of its operation.

The Supreme Court as a Political Institution

After two decades in which the Supreme Court has had major impact on a wide range of public matters—segregation, political freedoms, defendants' rights in criminal cases, and state legislative and congressional districting, to mention only a few—it hardly seems necessary to stress that it plays a major policy-making role within the national government. Although it can make decisions only on cases brought before it, the Court's powers to interpret the Constitution and judge the acts of other branches render it an integral part of the political process. In order to decide what a statute or an executive regulation means, whether an act by a government official is consistent with authorizing legislation, or whether either is consistent with the Constitution, the justices must make choices. These choices are inevitably based, at least in part, on their personal values, preferences, and goals. It is no coincidence that the same issues that have been before the Congress or the executive branch are also brought before the Supreme Court. Thus, the Court is different from the other institutions in form, but not in political character or impact on the society.

The Supreme Court consists of only nine persons, each of whose votes is of equal weight. It has no committees, and (with rare exceptions) all the justices personally hear arguments on, discuss, and vote on every case. Nevertheless, there are ways in which influence becomes concentrated within the Court. Not all justices are equally determinative of the Court's policy positions. Official status; the division of labor among the justices; and their reputations, personalities, and styles as individuals are the chief reasons for sometimes sharp differences in their real power.

The Chief Justice

The position of Chief Justice offers the principal opportunity within the Court to affect the nature of its decisionmaking. In nearly two centuries under the present Constitution, there have been only fifteen Chief Justices, as compared with thirty-nine Presidents. A politically astute Chief Justice who assumes his position at a relatively early age and enjoys a long life may leave a more lasting imprint on the public policies of the nation than some Presidents. Chief Justice John Marshall (1801–1835), for example, probably had considerably more effect on the development of the United States than several of the Presidents who held office during the nineteenth century. Not all Chief Justices have left the mark of a Marshall, a Hughes, or a Warren. Some have found the tasks of the office, the strongmindedness of other justices, or the issues of the times to be more than they could manage. To be effective, a Chief Justice must employ the political skills of bargaining and accommodation. He must develop and use the formal powers of his office in harmony with the more personal techniques of small-group leadership in order to bring a majority of the justices into agreement with the positions he favors.

The formal powers of the Chief Justice are few. But tradition and practice have combined with an increasing caseload to make them important sources of leverage within the Court. For example, the Chief Justice presides over the conferences at which the justices select the cases on which they will hear arguments and write opinions expressing new or clarified rules of law. Of the many thousands of cases appealed every year, the Court must of necessity decline to hear the great majority and allocate its time to the 150–200 cases involving what the justices see as the most important issues. Although each justice has the right to review all these potential cases, the Chief Justice has a larger staff and therefore makes it his responsibility to see that all appeals are reviewed. He suggests the cases that should be selected for further hearings and those that should be rejected. Discussion at these conferences thus proceeds according to an agenda and a preliminary selection set by the Chief Justice. If he has done his work carefully, the cases actually chosen for the Court's subsequent calendars will closely resemble his original list.

The Court's practice is to hear oral arguments on cases for two-week periods and then to devote the next two weeks to research, decisions, and opinion-writing. Decisions on cases are made at regular conferences of all justices, again presided over by the Chief Justice. At these conferences, the Chief Justice normally articulates the issues for resolution in each case, and then opens the floor for discussion among the justices. Voting on the case, however, proceeds from the most junior justice (the most recent appointee) up to the Chief Justice. Because he votes last, the Chief Justice has the decisive vote in closely divided cases. Although each vote in a 5–4 majority is of equal importance to the outcome, the final vote cast gains a trump-card status by virtue of its conclusive effect.

Perhaps more important than casting the last vote is the Chief Justice's power (when he is in the majority) to decide who will write the majority opinion in the case. If the Chief Justice wants to state the rule of law applicable to the case in terms consistent with his own policy preferences, he may write the opinion himself. Or he may assign it to another justice of similar views. In some cases whose outcome has been decided before the Chief Justice's turn to vote, he may decide to vote with the majority even if he does not wholly agree with them. Doing so gives him control over the writing of the opinion, and thus prevents the dissemination of an extreme statement that he would oppose.

Writing the Majority Opinion

The writing of the majority opinion is a crucial stage in the Court's work. Through this opinion, other political activists and the public will learn of the Court's position and its reasoning, and a new bit of substance will be added to the body of law and precedent that supposedly guides or controls behavior in the nation. The scope and nature of the rule asserted by the Court in an opinion is normally more important than who wins or loses the case itself. The opinion exercises the justices' broad discretion as to whether their decision will be grounded in a new, perhaps drastic, interpretation of the Constitution, or in a narrow interpretation of a statute or minor omission by one of the figures in the case. Further, the author of the opinion can write it in such a way that the reasoning behind the decision appears to apply to many similar or analogous situations. Or he can confine it so strictly that no other cases or behavior need be affected.

The justice who is chosen to write the opinion in a crucial case thus acquires substantial influence within the Court, at least in that subject area. (He also achieves public and professional visibility and the satisfaction of the judicial ego, a fact that gives the politically astute Chief Justice a kind of patronage to bestow on associate justices who vote with him.) There are limits to this power, of course. If an opinion writer seriously misrepresents the views of the other justices who voted with the majority, one or more of them may decline to join in the opinion. In some cases, this may mean loss of the vote(s) necessary to make up a majority. Drafts of the opinions are circulated within the Court for comments by the other justices, and the process of negotiation and compromise over the wording may take weeks. In some instances, the majority-uniting solution is an opinion in which conflicting or ambiguous positions are taken—in effect, postponing precise formulation of new rules of law to some future time or other institution.

The Chief Justice has other powers, mostly of a housekeeping nature, which he can use to make the daily routines of the other justices relatively more pleasant. He also serves as head of various bodies having administrative responsibilities over the lower federal courts, which gives him an opportunity to influence the opinions of lower federal court judges in a number of issue areas. Within the Supreme Court, however, he must rely for further influence on the personal support and regard he generates from the other justices.

The only other institutional positions of importance within the Court derive from seniority relationships among the associate justices. When the Chief Justice votes with the minority in a case, the senior associate justice in the majority chooses the writer of the opinion. The justice with the longest tenure on the Court may acquire some added prestige, particularly because he is most likely to select opinion-writers when the Chief Justice votes in the minority, but he rises above his fellows only slightly by virtue of such prerogatives.

Influence of the Justices

This analysis is not intended to suggest that the other Supreme Court justices are without means of developing significant influence as individuals. Instead, we stress that power within the nine-member Supreme Court is very much the product of individual reputation, effort, personality, and style. There are many ways in which justices can maximize their influence. By developing expertise in difficult subject areas, for example, or earning a reputation for hard and effective work on the Court, a justice may end up writing far more than his share of opinions. Or by joining with other justices through pre-conference "caucuses" or simple logrolling, a justice may help form coalitions that establish Court policy positions of great significance. Four votes are required to select a case to be heard on appeal, for example. Justices convinced that particular aspects of existing law should be changed may simply vote to hear any cases raising such issues, regardless of the Chief Justice's suggestions. The history of the Court's decisions shows that justices have frequently coalesced to form blocs for or against certain national policy developments. During some such periods, one or two "independent" justices have shifted back and forth between the blocs, casting the deciding votes first on one side and then on the other.

Extra-Court prestige, such as intimacy with a President, may contribute to a justice's capacity to exercise influence on the Court. More often, his real power depends on the persuasiveness with which he argues cases among his fellows and the personal esteem in which they hold him. If he is almost always accurate, incisive, and unabrasive in intellectual discourse; if he is tolerant of the views and mistakes of others; if he is able to combine disagreement over policy with personal friendship; and if he understands what is possible and practical for the Court and does not seek decisions that are inconsistent with the underlying nature of the system, he may become highly influential. In short, the Court places a premium on an accepted political style in much the same way as do the two houses of Congress. Though here it is much influenced by the lan-

TABLE 13.1 *Supreme Court Justices, 1978 (in order of seniority)*

Name	Year of birth	Home State	Law School	Prior Experience	Appointed by	Year of Appointment
Warren Burger	1907	Minnesota	St. Paul College of Law	Assistant Attorney General, Federal Judge	Nixon	1969
William Brennan	1906	New Jersey	Harvard	State Judge	Eisenhower	1956
Potter Stewart	1915	Ohio	Yale	Federal Judge	Eisenhower	1958
Byron White	1918	Colorado	Yale	Deputy Attorney General	Kennedy	1962
Thurgood Marshall	1908	Maryland	Howard	Counsel to NAACP, Federal Judge	Johnson	1967
Harry Blackmun	1908	Minnesota	Harvard	Federal Judge	Nixon	1970
Lewis Powell	1907	Virginia	Washington & Lee	President, American Bar Association, Federal Judge	Nixon	1972
William Rehnquist	1924	Arizona	Stanford	Assistant Attorney General	Nixon	1972
John P. Stevens	1916	Illinois	Chicago	Federal Judge	Ford	1975

guage and techniques of legal scholarship, it is as well formed and as institutionally defensive as elsewhere in government. The maverick who challenges the long-established operating procedures of the Court, who fails to do his share of the work, or who advocates actions that are "far out" in the eyes of his fellows is not likely to be effective.

Because of the relatively small number of men who have served as Chief Justice, or even as justices of the Supreme Court, it is difficult to generalize about the types of men and political preferences that have been dominant. All of the justices have had legal training, and most have been prominent in the law or in political life. The President consistently nominates men likely to share his policy preferences, and senators just as consistently resist confirmation when a nominee holds views contrary to *their* preferences. Republican Presidents tend to nominate men from the ranks of the federal and state judiciary or from large private law firms, while Democrats are more likely to nominate from political life, such as the Congress or the Cabinet. Presidents have occasionally guessed wrong about a nominee's probable actions on the Court, or have paid political debts instead of seeking policy support. Eisenhower's nomination of former Chief Justice Warren and Kennedy's appointment of Justice Byron White are only the latest in a series of such examples. But by and large, the best cues to the political preferences of the Chief Justice and the other members of the Court are the goals of the Presidents who appointed them. Since Roosevelt appointees gained full control of the Court in 1941, it has been generally liberal, with the exception of a short period of Truman-appointee dominance in the late 1940s and early 1950s. The character of several Nixon Administration appointees, however, indicates clearly that the next decades will see a much more conservative Court.

The Federal and State Court Systems

One of the most conspicuous illustrations of American federalism is the dual court system. The national and state governments each maintain distinct and complete court systems with separate jurisdictions and powers. Both are hierarchically organized—that is, trial courts are superseded by a series of appeals courts rising to a single authoritative highest court. Each set of courts has both civil and criminal jurisdictions —that is, they hear and decide cases involving disputes between private persons, corporations, and governments *and* prosecutions by governments of those who are alleged to have violated criminal statutes.

The Federal System

The federal court system consists of more than 90 District Courts, at least one in each state. These are the trial courts of the federal system, and they hear both civil and criminal cases. The kind of civil cases that are brought to such courts involve federal laws, such as antitrust issues, or suits between citizens of different states. The criminal cases in their jurisdiction involve violations of federal statutes, in which the federal government is the prosecutor, such as income tax fraud or transporting narcotics across state lines. A single judge presides in such District Court trials, although many judges are normally assigned to each District to keep up with the volume of business. Juries are a regular feature of such trials only in criminal cases. In roughly two-thirds of all civil trials the litigants waive their right to a jury trial, while only one-third of criminal defendants do so.

The federal government also has several specialized trial courts to hear income tax questions, claims against the federal government, and customs or patent cases. For certain constitutional issues involving state or federal statutes, three judges are convened to form another special kind of court. This procedure is designed to speed the hearing of important constitutional questions; direct routes of appeal to the United States Supreme Court are available after their decisions.

Above the District and specialized courts in the federal system are the federal Courts of Appeal. Eleven such courts exist in the country, each in a separate geographic "circuit," from which trial-court cases may be appealed to them by losing litigants. Not all issues may be re-examined at this level; only matters of law that have been specifically raised at the trial-court level may be raised on appeal. This means, for example, that a question of fact (such as whether the defendant performed a particular act or not), once decided by a jury, is forever conclusive except under very special circumstances. The kinds of questions that can be raised involve such issues as whether the judge correctly instructed the jury as to the applicable law in the case, whether certain evidence was or was not lawfully admitted into the case, and so on. No new evidence may be presented on appeal, nor does an appellate court listen to any of the parties to the case. It may not even hear their attorneys, but may limit itself instead to reading the "briefs" they are required to file on the disputed points of law.

The highest federal court is, of course, the United States Supreme Court. It exercises supervisory authority over all federal courts, seeking to standardize their actions and procedures across the country. It also hears appeals from losing litigants in the Courts of Appeals. It should be obvious that several screening procedures operate to make it unlikely that any given case will ever reach the Supreme Court. First, only losing litigants can appeal, and then only on points of law they have explicitly raised at the trial-court level. Second, it is a very costly process to appeal, because skilled attorneys must be retained and expensive briefs prepared; only wealthy or broadly supported litigants can normally afford to carry an appeal to the Supreme Court. Finally, as we have already noted, the Supreme Court does not have to hear every case appealed to it. It uses its right to choose the cases it will consider to select those involving serious constitutional questions or interpretation of key sections of federal statutes or of the powers or procedures of federal administrative bodies, or those in which two federal Courts of Appeal have ruled differently on the same issue.

The State Systems

Each state's court system has certain distinctive features; very few are alike. In general, however, they parallel the federal system. At the trial-court level, states tend to maintain a great variety of courts with varying names. In some cases, local magistrates or Justice of the Peace Courts handle such minor matters as traffic offenses. Another set of trial courts hears more serious matters, such as felony cases (violations of the criminal laws involving possible jail sentences of more than a year). In some states, civil and criminal courts are combined, as in the federal system; in most states there are separate courts and judges for the two types of cases. Specialized courts for such matters as domestic relations also exist in many states.

Only 22 states have intermediate appellate courts similar to the federal Courts of Appeal. In the majority of cases, appeals from the major trial courts go directly to the state's highest court. Generally, the criteria for the right to appeal are the same as in the federal court system—only losing litigants can appeal and only on matters of law they raised at the trial-court level. Each state's highest court fully controls all matters of state law, just as the U.S. Supreme Court does in the federal system. In other words, once the highest court of the state has declared the proper interpretation of a state statute, no other court (including the U.S. Supreme Court) can modify that interpretation. The judgments of such courts are therefore *final*, and all matters of state law are solely determined within the legal system of that state. As a result, the laws and practices of the 50 states vary greatly; acts that are crimes in some are not in others, and the rights of defendants or others also differ greatly.

If a question of federal law or a constitutional issue is raised in a state case, however, there is a possibility of an ultimate appeal to the U.S. Supreme Court. In these areas only the U.S. Supreme Court is superior to the highest courts of the states, since there must be a single authority to interpret the meaning of federal laws and of the Constitution. Once again, however, the Supreme Court decides whether the constitutional or other federal question raised in a case appealed to it is important enough for it to hear. If it does decide to hear the case, it only considers federal questions. Of course, state statutes or practices may be alleged to be contrary to the Constitution; if the Court agrees and declares them void, there is considerable opportunity for conflict between the Court and the state or states involved.

Issues of the Late 1970s

The State of Political Freedom

Citizens' basic political rights are set forth in the first ten amendments to the Constitution, known as the Bill of Rights, and particularly in the first six. They provide that the United States government shall not do certain things. In particular, it "shall make no law . . . abridging the freedom of speech, or of the press; or the right of the people peaceably to assemble, and to petition the Government for a redress of grievances." This sounds absolute—it seems to say that there can be *no* law abridging the freedom of speech or assembly, and thus no instance in which government could legally prevent speech or assembly, of any kind. But, in a series of decisions from the early days to the present, the Supreme Court has interpreted the First Amendment to guarantee only the limited form of freedom of speech and assembly protected by law in 1789 when the Amendment was adopted. Thus, the Congress is free to adopt such limitations as it sees fit, provided they meet the Court's standards of reasonableness—which the Court derives from its view of the proper combination of eighteenth-century precedent and current circumstances and necessities. In practice, the Court has only twice in its history declared a Congressional statute void on the grounds that it violated the First Amendment.

Notice that these political rights exist only as limitations on the United States government. In other words, they do not protect citizens against each other's actions. If a gang of hoodlums prevents a person from speaking in a private auditorium, for example, no constitutional rights have been violated; the crimes of assault or trespass may have been committed, but the Constitution provides guarantees only against the acts of government. As originally written, the Constitution did not provide these protections against state governments: in an early case the Court held that citizens must look to their state constitutions for such protections. In the 1920s, the Supreme Court decided that at least some of these guarantees *do* apply to the states, and since that time it has in a series of decisions added one after another of the guarantees of the Bill of Rights to the list of individual rights that are protected against state action. The Court did so on its own initiative, holding that the Fourteenth Amendment's provision that the states not deny their citizens "due process of law" made the guarantees of the Bill of Rights applicable to the states. Not all of them are thus applicable, the Court has held, but only those that the Court deems fundamental to the concept of due process.

In practice, the protection of political rights presents serious problems for many elements of the judicial process. The Supreme Court has declared that speech is to be protected up until the time it presents a "clear and present danger of bringing about an act which government has a right to prevent." This means that if armed insurrection or rioting is about to break out, policemen may legally restrain a speaker and/or

---

... the character of every act depends upon the circumstances in which it is done.... The most stringent protection of free speech would not protect a man in falsely shouting fire in a theater and causing a panic.... The question in every case is whether the words used are in such circumstances and are of such a nature as to create a clear and present danger that they will bring about the substantive evils that Congress has a right to prevent. It is a question of proximity and degree....

Justice Oliver Wendell Holmes, in *Schenck v. United States* (1919).

---

the speaker may be prosecuted for such words and/or action. The operative principle is that no one should be prevented from speaking or publishing something, no matter how unpopular it might be, but that he or she must bear responsibility for such acts afterwards, such as in suits for libel or slander.

But afterwards may be too late, from the perspectives of both governments and dissenters. Police may unreasonably foresee riots resulting from provocative speeches; licensing authorities may fear that granting a parade permit will make demonstrators vulnerable to attack by a hostile crowd, and either or both may act to prevent speech or assembly. Those who seek to exercise their rights in such circumstances must find an attorney willing to suffer public disapproval for representing their cause, and must try to convince the courts to order the authorities to permit them their rights. Local judges do not willingly expose themselves to popular disapproval either, and so appeals to higher courts may be necessary. By the time all these procedures are concluded, of course, the occasion for exercising one's political rights may be long past. Thus, important discretion remains with local authorities who are often subject to popular pressures—and perhaps only too willing to support or help generate such pressures themselves.

The court's record in defense of the exercise of the political rights supposedly guaranteed by the Bill of Rights has not been particularly aggressive or distinguished. Most of the time, courts side with legislative or administrative authorities. They typically consider claims made by unpopular people, parties, or causes only to conclude that the established authorities were exercising their constitutional powers in imposing limitations on political activity. Rights to dissent, assembly, and the like for purposes not favored by governments are far more firmly established in legal theory than in actual practice.

A similar pattern is apparent among the general public. When contrasted to the theory of the Bill of Rights, popular support for political freedoms seems low. This may be attributable to the continuing barrage of criticism and condemnation directed by political and other opinion-makers at "deviants," "extremists," and others who do not think and act in orthodox ways. Or it may represent recognition by ordinary people that leaders' endorsement of political freedoms is more rhetoric than reality, and hence may be a more honest response.

In any event, one of the interesting developments of the 1970s was a distinct rise in political tolerance and support for political liberties relative to the 1950s. This contrast is shown in Table 13.2. The questions

TABLE 13.2   *Willingness to Grant First Amendment Rights*

Type of Freedom	Year	Admitted Communist	Against Religion	For Governmental Ownership	Homo-sexual
To speak	1954	27	37	58	
	1972	52	65	77	
	1974	58	62	75	62
To have book in library	1954	27	35	52	
	1972	53	60	67	
	1974	58	60	69	55
To teach	1954	6	12	33	
	1972	32	40	56	
	1974	42	42	57	50

Source: Hazel Erskine and Richard L. Siegel, "Civil Liberties and the American Public," *Journal of Social Issues* 31, no. 2 (1975), The questions were as follows: "There are always some people whose ideas are considered bad or dangerous by other people. For instance, somebody who is against all churches and religion. If such a person wanted to make a speech in your city (town, community) against churches and religion, should he be allowed to speak, or not? Should such a person be allowed to teach in a college or university, or not? If some people in your community suggested that a book he wrote against churches and religion be taken out of your public library, would you favor removing this book, or not?" The same questions were asked about the other "extremists."

asked (listed below the table) were the same in both cases. Levels of support for political freedoms may not seem high, but they are clearly rising in significant ways.

Observers might well have seen this development as a welcome step toward greater freedom and a more open political process. But, instead, the major issue of the late 1970s was the extent of official governmental violation of political freedoms. In a series of lawsuits, citizens' demands for information, and subsequent Congressional investigations, an extensive pattern of provocation and promotion of crimes, surveillance, wiretapping, burglaries, and other crimes on the part of governmental agencies was steadily documented. Many agencies, up to and including the National Security Council, the Defense Department, and the White House itself were shown to have condoned, authorized, and participated in theft, burglaries, and wiretapping. The FBI acknowledged an extensive program of infiltration of legal organizations, use of informers and provocateurs to instigate or commit crimes, and a general pattern of harassment of civil rights leaders. The CIA had an analogous program of surveillance, provocation, and disruption. All of these and other acts were extensively documented in the official reports of both House and Senate investigating committees.

Each revelation was matched by a sober report from the admittedly guilty agency that the illegal activities in question had been terminated. In some cases, however, agencies used such occasions to suggest "guidelines" that would authorize heretofore illegal activities at their discretion; Attorney General Levi, for example, proposed in 1976 to impose just such a set of guidelines on the FBI. And at the same time the Congress began considering a revision of the federal criminal law that would, in its draft form at least, make legal many previously illegal actions, including many of those for which Watergate-related defendants were convicted. In the aftermath of the Watergate confessions and convictions, there remained a serious question as to where trustworthy support for political freedoms could be found. Clearly, executive agencies themselves had been the lawbreakers, and elected officials in all branches had inspired, authorized, or condoned their activities for a long time. The new Supreme Court indicated in a series of 1975 and 1976 decisions that it would not stand by the principles of constitutional law established by the Warren Court of the 1950s and 1960s. In one case, for example, it held that not even a demonstrated pattern of violation of constitutional rights by the Philadelphia police department created any right of redress for citizens. In another, it drastically cut back limits on the power of police to arrest people without warrants.

Crime and Punishment

The incidence of crime in the United States in the late 1970s was very high. Crime statistics are notoriously unreliable, both because the numbers reported can be manipulated in various ways and because people often fail to report crimes that are embarrassing or that they believe the police unable to do anything about. But crime was undeniably increasing, and fear of crime was rising even more sharply. Crime most often victimizes poor people in large cities, but fear radiates out to grip middle-class people—the people who have the most to lose, and more political power to do something about it.

One manifestation of such dissatisfaction was hostility toward the

Supreme Court. Many advocates of "law and order" alleged that the Supreme Court and other judges were "coddling criminals." The observance of defendants' constitutional rights may make convictions of guilty persons more difficult; but it may also protect the innocent and serve as a measure of a humane civilization. It is easier to condemn the courts, however, than to create a social order in which crime is not necessary or encouraged, or even to pay for adequate policing and corrections facilities. In any event, the net result in the 1970s was a distinctly unfavorable attitude toward the Supreme Court, and a strong desire for more conservative judges in the future.[4]

There is considerable controversy in the United States over the effectiveness and uses of punishment. Some argue that crime is caused by an unjust society, whose reform should be the primary goal of social efforts. Others believe in the rehabilitation of individual criminals, to help them adapt to the society as it is. But many people, perhaps the majority, resist both these strategies, preferring instead to increase punishment for crimes as a means of deterring all future crimes. Despite considerable historical evidence that even such drastic punishments as torture and death did not prevent crime, moves have been made in several states to restore the death penalty and impose harsher sentences. Such arguments received support from some arithmetically inclined economists, one of whose correlations indicated that every execution prevents seventeen murders. These findings were disputed by others, who stressed that the period of the study (the mid-1960s) was a time of social unrest, and that the validity of any gross correlation characterized by so many other variables is questionable.[5]

Both the issues we have been examining involve social control. Preservation of the *status quo* is one of the major goals of any governing elite. So is the use of the criminal law to enforce the present (unequal) distribution of wealth, property, and other benefits of the society. Let us grant immediately that any society must have some means of restraining people who wantonly assault or endanger others. But from that point forward, the values and characteristics of the society shape the nature of its approach to restraint. What acts are to be defined as crimes? If it is "legal" to charge 20 percent interest rates for necessities of life, why should it be "criminal" to keep such goods after missing an installment payment? What shall be done to those who break such rules—should they be helped in any of several possible ways, or should the society exact retribution by killing, confining, or otherwise punishing them? In every case, judgments are made consistent with the values of those who are favored by the existing system, and those who are not favored are limited (or perhaps, in their own eyes, exploited) by the provisions of the criminal laws.

Thus, the enforcers of these laws may come to be viewed as the

[4] *Gallup Opinion Index,* August 1973, p. 16.
[5] *Business Week,* September 15, 1975, p. 97.

MY HANDS ARE TIED, RIGHT? · MY FEET ARE SHACKLED, RIGHT? · MY EYES ARE BLINDFOLDED, RIGHT? · M'MOUF'S GGGD, RRT? · WHEN DO YOU BREAK FREE? · WHAT DO YOU MEAN BREAK FREE? · I LIKE IT.

Feiffer

agents of a repressive or exploitative system. Where it also appears that they enjoy broad discretion, serious tensions may result. This is particularly true in the case of minorities, who are likely to feel the restraint of criminal laws far out of proportion to their numbers or to the actual incidence of violation of such laws. Most large-city police forces are quite disproportionately made up of members of the dominant society. In no major city does the proportion of nonwhite police officers approach the nonwhite proportion of the population. It is not surprising, therefore, that in some cities the police are looked on as an occupying army by ghetto residents.

The arbitrariness and variability that characterizes the protection of political freedoms and the enforcement of criminal law create demonstrable patterns of injustice and serious tensions within American society today. Dominant groups are clearly advantaged by the character and actual uses of the law and the courts. The reasons for this situation include the makeup and backgrounds of those who apply the law, unequal access of legal services, and the exaggeration of certain structural characteristics of the law itself by the American emphasis on legalism as a political value. In the courts as well, a number of factors assure that elite interests will be accorded great weight in decisionmaking. The nation's judges and lawyers are drawn disproportionately from the prosperous and high-status groups in the population. Law school education, like public education generally, consists in part at least of the inculcation of elitist values. Accused persons with money and social status are far more likely than those without these advantages to benefit from competent legal advice and defense. Finally, the elaborate legal code and the established processes for interpreting and enforcing it work in the interests of the advantaged.

The last of these factors is both more subtle and more potent than the others, and in turn underlies and bolsters them. Americans have always been proud to say that we have "a government of laws, not men." That belief stems from our development of an elaborate code of legal rules that are relied on to settle conflicts and to determine guilt or innocence, with a theoretical minimum of human arbitrariness and a maximum of impersonal "equality before the law." Justice is portrayed as blind: blind, it is alleged, to differences among litigants in income, color, race, education, social position, and so on.

In a crucial sense, this very blindness to real differences means that the legal code repeatedly offers justifications for dealing harshly with the disadvantaged and leniently with the elite. In the trenchant words of Anatole France: "The law in its splendid impartiality prosecutes both the rich and the poor for stealing a loaf of bread or sleeping under bridges."

Two Other Issues: The ERA and Some New Judges

The problems of political freedom and crime control are continuing problems of social order that regularly spark disagreements among people. In 1979, however, two different kinds of issues were at the center of controversy, and they demonstrate both the wide range of issues involving law and the differences between such issues. The question of ratifying the 27th Amendment to the Constitution, the "Equal Rights Amendment," was one that engaged millions of people in often heated debate. It took on powerful symbolic meaning for people on both sides of the debate, far beyond any actual consequences it was likely to have. The other issue was almost unknown to the public at large, although the manner of its resolution might have profound effects for years to come. It involved who would be appointed by President Carter to fill the record number of new federal court judgeships created by the 95th Congress shortly before its adjournment in 1978. For most political activists, such questions were much more important than the ERA. Let us look a little more deeply at each of these distinctive law-related issues.

The Equal Rights Amendment is a short, simple statement declaring that there shall be no discrimination on the grounds of sex. It was sought as one of the early goals of the National Organization of Women, part of the mainstream of the women's movement. In March 1972, the Congress passed it and referred it to the states, with the usual stipulation that ratification by the necessary two-thirds of state legislatures must occur within seven years or the amendment would be void. Several states immediately ratified the amendment, some in such a hurry to be among the first to do so that there would be grounds for later charges that they had not carefully considered its implications. But then a reaction set in, an active group of women began to oppose ratification, and the approval by states came only slowly and after protracted debate. In some states, the amendment was defeated.

The reasons for the opposition reflected some misconceptions, some consequences of changes and tensions within American society, and a good deal of symbolism. In what would have fit well with Justice Holmes' famous description of a "parade of imaginary horrors," opponents of the amendment dreamed up all manner of possible changes and disruptions of social life that would follow upon ratification. It was said that women would be forced into military combat roles, that all bathrooms would have to be "unisex," that alimony and child support would be abolished, the traditional role of housewife altered beyond recognition, and so forth. What lay behind these exaggerated fears in many cases were feelings of pressure from changes in social values and practices, and particularly a sense of threat to the family from a variety of sources. The ERA seemed to its opponents to be a symbolic endorsement of all these changes and threats. To its supporters, on the other hand, it seemed like simple justice.

The campaign for ratification was hard-fought for several years. Supporters of ERA sought to get professional and other organizations who hold annual conventions to boycott states refusing to ratify the amendment, hoping that economic pressure involved in lost revenues from convention-goers would work where moral persuasion had not. Opponents sought to have states that had previously ratified act again to rescind their ratifications, which would have thrown the whole process into chaos. Supreme Court precedents and Congressional opinion, however, seemed to be clear that once a state had ratified it could not later change its mind.

By mid-1978, three more states' ratifications were still needed to make the ERA part of the Constitution. But the time limit would expire in March 1979, before some state legislatures would be able to consider ratification (in some cases, for the second or third time). Supporters therefore mounted a campaign to get the Congress to extend the deadline for another three years. Marches were conducted in localities around the nation and in Washington, and a lobbying group made up of nearly 80 sons and daughters of members of Congress issued an appeal to their fathers to extend the time limit. In October, the Senate joined the House in a three-year extension, and supporters of ERA began a renewed campaign for ratification.

The issues involved in staffing the 152 new federal judgeships created by the 95th Congress (117 in District Courts, 35 in the Circuit Courts, both records for expansion) were intensely political *and* vital to the insiders who sought to influence the appointments. This group of judges would make up about 25 percent of the sitting judges in the two levels of courts when all the appointments were complete, and all those who cared about the kinds of decisions to be made in these courts were intimately concerned with who was to be appointed. In one sense, President Carter had been handed a vast "patronage plum" with which to reward those who cooperated with him. However, such patronage powers would be shared with Democratic Senators from the states involved, despite some vague language about merit criteria for selection. All signs pointed to some lively conflicts over specific appointments.

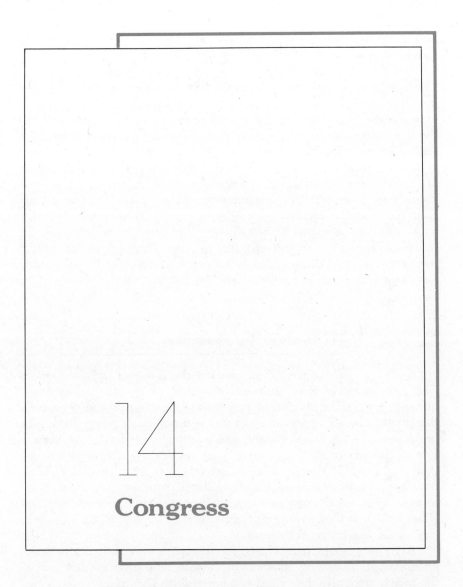

Congress

The Constitution appears to envision the Congress as the nation's chief policymaking body, the arena in which national issues would be debated and basic decisions made. The Congress is created and empowered by Article I of the Constitution, which is nearly three times the length of the next longest article (that regarding the presidency) and alone accounts for more than half of the Constitution. All the legislative powers of the United States government are given to the Congress; among them are the powers to tax and spend, to regulate commerce, to declare war and maintain the armed forces, and to "make all laws which shall be necessary and proper" to exercise the various powers granted to the national government. This is a sweeping grant of power and authority, and one might expect the Congress to be the decisive source of policymaking within the government.

But it has not worked out that way. At least in the twentieth century, Congress is much more of an after-the-fact critic and modifier of policy initiatives taken by the other branches, particularly the President and the executive bureaus. Not even the crucial power to tax and spend enabled the Congress to assert independent policymaking capacity over the vast federal bureaucracy. The reasons for this situation have been the subject of much debate, and answers range from the visibility and decisiveness of the presidency in an age of emergencies to the character and internal procedures of the two Houses themselves. In any event, the tragic Vietnam War and the revelations of Watergate and its aftermath led to a major effort on the part of the Congress to reassert its policymaking powers in the 1970s. In this chapter, we shall first look closely at the personnel and procedures of the two Houses, and then at the steps they have taken to regain initiative within the government.

The House of Representatives

There are 435 members of the House of Representatives. This fact, no doubt familiar from sixth-grade civics, has profound significance for the distribution of power and operating procedures within the House. The 435 representatives face a bewildering array of complex problems, a vast national budget, and a sprawling federal bureaucracy. Few of them come to Congress with any special expertise or experience that would enable them to cope effectively with such problems. Their time to acquire such knowledge is limited, both by the demands of service to their constituents and by the imminence of the next election. What little staff they have must devote most of its time to mail, errands, and, again, the forthcoming election.

Even, or perhaps particularly, for representatives with the sincerest intentions of translating constituents' wishes into governmental action, the task is extremely difficult, if not impossible. They must develop two types of capabilities: a subject-area expertise in order to know what should be done, and administrative sophistication to enable them to recognize whether or not executive-branch employees are acting (and spending authorized funds) to administer congressional policies in the manner prescribed. In both areas, they can act as independent policymakers only if they are able to acquire knowledge on their own, and not if their knowledge depends on inevitably self-serving voluntary disclosures by the executive branch or private power centers.

For all these reasons, they have little choice but to divide their governmental responsibilities among individuals or committees formed out of the House membership. Through specialization, at least some of the members will have a chance to develop the expertise and managerial capacity to make independent policymaking possible. Presumably, members will exercise such capabilities in accordance with the will of the majority of the House. But when there is a division of labor, a stratification of power results. Special knowledge or responsibility in a subject area gives the possessor the tools and prestige to cause others to go along with his or her views. Formation of a task group implies leadership within it, and the chairman of a committee may come to exercise disproportionate influence over its work. To a considerable extent, these are the inevitable costs of a necessary division of labor.

It is a mistake, however, to take for granted that the members of Congress with the greatest knowledge of an area necessarily have the greatest influence on policy. Values play at least as great a part as facts; indeed, the two are not really separable. If a particular set of values or ideology dominates a committee or a house of Congress, it is likely to be a more important shaper of policy than is expertise.

Before the reforms of the 1970s, the House of Representatives evolved a unique manner of dividing its labor, such that most of its capacity to act lay in the hands of about 25 individuals occupying its key positions. Moreover, such individuals were chosen solely by virtue of their "seniority" (length of service). Although this may appear a mechanical, and therefore politically neutral, means of selection, it in fact placed power in the hands of older, usually more conservative, individuals: longevity in the House depends on having a relatively "safe" electoral district. Many such districts are found in the rural South and Midwest, usually the more conservative parts of the nation. Some districts in the more liberal large cities regularly return candidates of a single political party, but the availability of alternative political careers and the volatility of city districts tend to eliminate any given representative before he or she reaches the higher levels of seniority.

The overall effect of this House system was to create a highly structured game. In this "game," only the oldest members actually held power; members on the next level had invested many years in moving up the ladder and were more or less patiently awaiting the death or retirement of their elders; and the newest and youngest members were close to impotent. The House has roughly co-equal hierarchies of leadership positions, both reflecting this principle clearly; this pattern has survived the recent reforms. The first type of position involves leadership of committees, each of which has responsibility for the actions of the House in a particular policy area; the major position is that of chairman, with secondary status for the ranking member of the minority party. The second type is leadership in the management of the House itself; these positions include the Speaker of the House, the majority and minority leaders (and their "whips," or assistants), and the Rules Committee. Let us briefly examine the powers of these offices and the characteristics of their occupants.

Policy Area Committees

There are 20 standing committees in the House, ranging in importance and prestige from Civil Service and Post Office to Armed Services, Ways and Means, and Appropriations. Most committees have 20–25 members (Appropriations has 50), appointed from each party roughly according to the partisan ratio then prevailing in the House. Each representative usually serves on two committees. Although they naturally seek assignment to committees whose work will be of importance to their home districts, representatives have no way to assure this. There are only so many choice assignments, and it takes a certain amount of seniority to lay claim to them. The two most sought-after policy committees are those dealing with money matters—Ways and Means (taxation, social security, and Medicare, for example) and Appropriations (all expenditures). Raising and spending money is absolutely crucial to the operation of the government, and is the route by which Congress has the greatest chance to influence the conduct of the rest of the government.

Though, as we have said, the key position on a committee is that of chairman, the recent reforms have parceled out some authority to the chairmen of subcommittees. The division of power between the chairman of the full committee and the chairmen of subcommittees tends to vary with each committee, depending in part on the political skills and personalities of the incumbents. These powers include setting the agenda for the committee or subcommittee, controlling hearings and executive sessions, choosing witnesses, managing the actual drafting of legislation, and shepherding a bill through floor debate and possible later conferences with a Senate committee to work out the bill's final version. In all these actions, the chairman's personal preferences can play a crucial role in determining the final provisions of laws.

Chairmen are not autonomous, of course. The President, and the House or party leadership, may bring pressure on them, and members of the committee may bring concerted influence to bear. But chairmen have defenses at their command. Neither the President nor the leadership wants to incur their opposition, for they know that chairmen can cause delay, drastic revision, or even destruction of legislation they dislike. Nor do the members of committees wish to lose either opportunities to obtain special provisions in legislation that chairmen can grant them, or the public visibility that their goodwill makes possible. At all times, chairmen also have on their side the traditions of the House, which call for action only in accordance with duly established procedures—in this case, with the recommendations of the standing committee having jurisdiction over the subject area of the bill. The House almost never considers, and even more rarely enacts, legislation that is completely opposed by the chairman of the applicable committee. In part, this is because alert chairmen know when to join a majority position; but even when they do so, they leave the clear mark of their preferences on the final product.

The ranking member of the minority party on a committee gains some leverage from representing his or her party and mobilizing other party members on behalf of specific positions. He or she becomes the chairman of the committee when the party wins control of the House. Frequently, this prospect generates a friendly *modus vivendi* with the chairman, for both have served on the committee for a long time and know that they may be destined to rotate with each other for the rest of their political careers. Having served together for some time, the two probably also share a strong concern for the "proper" working of the House itself, and for the efficient discharge of their committee's responsibilities to the House. In many ways, therefore, the two positions complement each other, rather than serving as opposing correctives.

House Leadership Positions

The major leadership positions within the House itself are filled by the majority political party, usually through application of the seniority principle. The key position is that of Speaker of the House. The Speaker presides over House debates on bills, recognizing speakers he considers appropriate by prearrangement or preference. He shapes the House agenda, deciding which bills will receive priority. He designates the members of the "conference committees" who will represent the House in negotiations with the Senate. He makes public visibility possible for, or ignores, members as he chooses. And he is privy to the President's preferences and intentions regarding the legislative program for that session of Congress, and can (if he wishes) work in harmony with the President to schedule and obtain passage of desired legislation.

The majority and minority leaders within the House are party leaders. In both cases, seniority is a major factor, but policy views representative of the mainstream of the party are also influential in determining election by the party's caucus. The duties of these leaders, assisted by their elected "whips," are to mobilize party members behind legislative positions the leadership has decided to be in the party's interest. Members of the House are often under pressure to support the position of the President when he is of their party or to join with other members of their party in opposition to a President of the other party. (Many measures before the House are not made matters of party discipline, of course, and in such cases members are free of all pressures to vote with the leadership.)

Another group of positions of crucial importance to the management of the business of the House is membership on the Rules Committee. These are perhaps the most coveted committee positions in the House, and are filled, predictably, with its most senior members. All proposed legislation must go through the Rules Committee en route to the floor of the House. The function of the Rules Committee is to set specific rules for debate and voting on each piece of business, in order to conserve the time and order the transactions of that unwieldy body. In practice, this means that the Rules Committee exercises an important influence over the form in which a given bill will be presented and the real prospects for its passage. Particularly at the close of congressional sessions, the Rules Committee (frequently in the person of its chairman) may prevent legislation from reaching the floor. Or it may attach rules for debate and voting calculated to assure its defeat, such as permitting unlimited amendments to a tax bill that represents a number of delicate compromises. At other times, the Rules Committee may content itself with making clear to the chairman of a policy-area committee that certain provisions must not be included in prospective legislation.

The formal powers of the party leadership in the House have been reduced by recent reforms, but it remains capable of making a member's political life much easier or more difficult—depending on his or her willingness to abide by the informal rules and traditions of the House. For those who "go along" and demonstrate the proper respect for the institution and its elder members, there are special opportunities for public visibility and status, which are often the keys to reelection. The party leadership is also one of the major sources of information for ordinary members, most of whom would otherwise have no better sources than the daily newspapers. Party leaders provide knowledge about the President's plans and make arrangements for joint action by all party members in response to those intentions. Representatives cannot be successful by themselves; they must have the support of many other representatives, and the political party machinery is the most promising means to secure it. Thus, the party leadership gains an important kind of leverage within the institution.

Why do the other members acquiesce in the dominance of these two types of leadership positions? The simple answer is that, as a practical matter, there is very little they can do about it. Communication among the balance of the 435 members is very difficult, and it is inhibited by party and ideological differences. Even if they could agree on measures to redirect or unseat the leadership, the total control of the parliamentary machinery by the established leaders would make such action very complicated, requiring a degree of perception, trust, skill, and discipline not likely to exist in any large body. If they did replace the leadership, moreover, the new leaders might be even less desirable than the old ones.

A more sophisticated answer would point out that most members do not even want to extricate themselves from the web of seniority-based leadership and management. Representatives depend for reelection on achieving visibility in the home district, preferably by accomplishing some tangible benefit for constituents. They can do so in their early terms in the House, when need is greatest, only through the assistance of established members—such as the chairmen of committees and subcommittees, or the party leadership. Almost before they realize it, they have incurred debts to senior colleagues. And as soon as they acquire a degree of seniority themselves, the system begins to look better. Representatives find that there are payoffs in the established operating procedures, and begin to identify with the House as an institution and the accommodating, bargaining system to which it is committed. Some naturally begin to give higher priority to maintaining harmonious relationships among members than to the merits of the great issues of national policy.

Table 14.1 provides some basic data about the incumbents of the major positions in the House of Representatives of 1979–1981. In addition to the personal backgrounds of these men, it is noteworthy that most of them are relatively older people who have been in Congress for some time. This does not necessarily mean that they are conservative or out of touch with current thinking, but it does raise such questions. We shall explore the matter of age, ideology, and committee/subcommittee chairmanships further when we examine the progress of reform efforts in our final section.

The Senate

The Senate has only 100 members, and prides itself on dispensing with the many formal rules and procedures that characterize the House. In contrast to what it views as "the lower house," the Senate tries to operate with a minimum of organization and a maximum of gentlemanly agreement, which allows for the objection of one senator to prevent or delay the transaction of crucial business. In fact, the Senate has evolved an elaborate set of rules and traditions governing the behavior of members. These standards are maintained by an institutional establishment—an informal group of usually senior senators distinguished principally by their commitment to the Senate as an institution. This group asserts authority not only over internal procedures but also on occasion over the policy positions assumed by the Senate as a body. Membership in the inner circle of the Senate is personal rather than institutionally based. Supplementing this form of leadership is a division of labor characterized by many of the same benefits and costs as is that of the House of Representatives. Again, the types of positions may be divided between policy areas and Senate leadership.

Policy Area Committees

The differences between House and Senate committee structure and operation are minor, reflecting chiefly the difference in size of the respective houses. The Senate has fewer, smaller committees, ranked somewhat differently in terms of prestige. Finance and Appropriations, which deal with revenue and expenditures respectively, are (despite the Senate's secondary role in House-initiated money matters) probably the most im-

TABLE 14.1 *Biographical Survey of Political Leaders and Key Committee Chairmen of the House of Representatives, 96th Congress (1979–1981)*

Position	Name	Age (as of 1979)	Occupation or profession	Year entered Congress	State
Political Leadership					
Speaker	Thomas O'Neill	66	Insurance	1953	Massachusetts
Minority Leader	John J. Rhodes	63	Lawyer	1953	Arizona
Chairmen of Major Committees					
Agriculture	Thomas Foley	50	Lawyer	1962	Washington
Appropriations	Jamie Whitten	69	Lawyer	1941	Mississippi
Armed Services	Melvin Price	74	Journalist	1945	Illinois
Banking and Currency	Henry Reuss	67	Lawyer	1955	Wisconsin
Education and Labor	Carl Perkins	67	Lawyer	1948	Kentucky
International Relations	Clement Zablocki	67	Teacher	1948	Wisconsin
Judiciary	Peter Rodino	70	Lawyer	1949	New Jersey
Rules	Richard Bolling	63	Teacher	1948	Missouri
Ways and Means	Al Ullman	65	Businessman	1957	Oregon

portant committees. Foreign Relations, because of the Senate's special powers in that field, is a more visible committee that attracts many senators, but its impact on policy is not great. Judiciary, because of its power to confirm or reject Supreme Court nominees and the Senate's special concern for proposed constitutional amendments, is also a high-status committee. Armed Services and Agriculture follow, and the remainder are reserved for specialists and newcomers.

The formal powers of the chairman of a Senate committee are much the same as those of a House chairman, but in practice they fall short of the autocracy of the House model. Operating with smaller numbers and a more relaxed, gentlemanly ethos—perhaps abetted by the relative length of their six-year terms—the Senate chairmen tend to consult more with their members, grant them more visibility and influence within the committee, and proceed on the basis of a general consensus. The chairman is clearly the leader, and no junior senator would be unaware of or dare to ignore that fact; but the operation of the committee is normally more harmonious.

The Senate's traditions of elaborate courtesy among members extend to the manner in which pressure is applied to chairmen to consider legislation, and to the relationship between the ranking minority member of a committee and its chairman. Rising to the chairmanship of a Senate committee implies not only substantial seniority, but also commitment to the Senate as an institution and to its "proper" functioning within the system. No President or party leader would insult the dignity of the Senate by making brash or blatant attempts to coerce a committee chairman. And party differences ordinarily play a small part in the deliberations of senior members of a committee. In short, in the Senate there is at least the appearance of greater consideration of the merits of issues, and a smaller organizing role for the political party.

Senate Leadership Positions

Although the position of President Pro Tem of the Senate corresponds in form to that of Speaker of the House, it is in practice no more than an honorific title bestowed on a very senior member. The actual managerial functions performed by the Speaker in the House are in the hands of the Senate Majority Leader. This officer is elected by the senators of the majority party at the outset of each session; once chosen, of course, a senator usually retains his position as Majority Leader until he dies, retires, or is defeated for reelection. The choice is influenced, but not controlled, by relative seniority among senators of the majority party. But more important is a reputation for commitment to the protection and furtherance of the Senate as an institution, a mainstream position within the party on major issues, adherence to traditional rules and procedures, a sense of fair play, and parliamentary skills. Choice of the Minority Leader by the minority party is based on similar criteria.

The Majority and Minority Leaders serve informing, scheduling, and unifying functions for their respective parties, in effect combining the duties of Speaker, party leader, and Rules Committee in the House. The Majority Leader coordinates the activities of Senate committees, seeking to bring bills to the floor in accordance with his view of the proper priorities for that session. He selects members of the conference committees that negotiate differences between House and Senate versions of enacted legislation. He is the chief source of information for other senators, as well as the dispenser of public visibility, additional institutional responsibilities, and improved committee status. He consults regularly with the Minority Leader so that most of the Senate's business can proceed with the support of a broad consensus. Both Leaders are normally consulted and kept informed of major developments by the President, although matters of party strategy or program are reserved for the Leader of the President's Party.

Behind the two Leaders of the Senate is the inner "establishment," or "club," of generally senior senators. This group has no precise boundaries, but some senators are clearly inside and some just as clearly outside. Membership is personal, based in part on acceptance of the Senate's traditional ways and in part on the senator's political skills and style. The senator who works hard and effectively on committees and other tasks assigned by the leadership, thereby contributing to the work of the Senate, is soon marked as a potential member. If he continues to show tolerance and respect for other senators, demonstrates a strong concern for the harmonious transaction of the Senate's business and the preservation of its reputation, and is not too "far out" on issues, he may be consulted more and more often about important matters of Senate policy. In time, he will be fully socialized and eventually integrated into the social grouping within which most of the major decisions of the Senate are made.

The individual senator, whether a member of the inner group or not, is somewhat more capable of making himself felt within the institution than is a member of the House. He is no more likely to be able to redirect or unseat the leadership, nor is he likely to want to try. But he can count on being able to gain the floor and address the Senate, which a representative may not be able to do. Further, the Senate's tradition of operating on the basis of unanimous consent means that the objection of a single senator can delay or, in some cases, prevent action on matters to which one senator is opposed. The Senate's famous filibuster rule, for example, permits any senator or group of senators to talk for as long as they are physically capable, and some have held the floor in excess of twenty-four hours. Toward the close of a legislative session, a filibuster or even the threat of one by one or more senators can result in a leadership decision to abandon proposed legislation. Thus, the individual recourses of a senator are substantial, though it is questionable whether he can have any greater ultimate impact on policies than his counterpart in the House. In both cases, the leadership's grip on the machinery of the institution is very strong.

Table 14.2 shows the backgrounds of the leadership of the Senate during the 96th Congress (1979–1981). These Senators are somewhat older than their counterparts in the House, and many of them were once members of that body. The chairmanships of the key committees are held by men whose terms in the Senate average 27 years (as of 1979, not counting House service). Not surprisingly, lawyers predominate among the leadership, even more completely than in the Congress as a whole (see Table 14.2).

What do these patterns of power distribution and incumbency mean for the overall operation of the Congress? Clearly, the most powerful individuals are far from representative of the nation's population. They are much older, probably much more conservative, and motivated by long-established traditions that impose additional restrictions on what they can seriously consider or hope to accomplish in the way of legislation. Because such individuals are rarely challenged effectively in elections, they do not feel pressures for change within the society unless the interests and people with whom they have close contact happen to present such problems to them. Under these conditions, the Congress is normally likely to be responsive to developments in the economy or society chiefly in arbitrary, unpredictable, and conservative ways. Further, what appear to be challenges to the system itself are likely to be met with lack of understanding and severe reaction. On such matters, nearly all men and women of power are likely to be of a single mind.

A second major consequence of the existing pattern of power in the Congress is its great dependence on effective leadership. Unless the President and the party leaders within the two houses establish clear and agreed priorities, and work effectively to coordinate committee actions and floor debates, very little legislation will be produced. At best, the Congress is an institution that operates on a fits-and-starts basis; the number of powerful individuals who must be convinced of the necessity of a particular action, the difficulty of persuading them, and with the multitude of public problems on which action of some kind must be taken, mean that a given subject comes before the Congress for serious consideration only once every few years. Unless the leadership does its job well, the opportunity for action will pass having given rise to the enactment of a halfway or patchwork measure that makes conditions worse instead of better.

Finally, the decentralization of power in the hands of a relatively few congressmen means that many veto points are created from which the positions and prerogatives of well-established groups can be defended even against the wishes of a large majority. Because it is so easy for one or two key congressmen to block legislative action, and so difficult

TABLE 14.2 *Biographical Survey of Political Leaders and Key Committee Chairmen of the Senate, 96th Congress (1979–1981)*

Position	Name	Age (as of 1979)	Occupation or profession	Year entered Congress and/or year entered Senate	State
Political Leadership					
Majority Leader	Robert C. Byrd	61	Lawyer	1952 & 1959	West Virginia
Minority Leader	Howard H. Baker, Jr.	54	Lawyer	1966	Tennessee
Chairmen of Major Committees					
Appropriations	Warren Magnuson	74	Lawyer	1937 & 1944	Washington
Armed Services	John Stennis	77	Lawyer & farmer	1947	Mississippi
Finance	Russell B. Long	60	Lawyer	1948	Louisiana
Foreign Relations	Frank Church	55	Lawyer	1956	Idaho
Judiciary	Edward Kennedy	47	Lawyer	1962	Massachusetts

for the leadership to mobilize support at all the necessary points in the legislative process, inaction (and advantage to those favored by the *status quo*) is a frequent result. The other likely result is legislation of the "lowest common denominator" kind—legislation that offends few, usually because it has no serious effect on the *status quo*. One may well ask, of course, whether such legislation is capable of solving problems.

The Legislative Process

The legislative process has two major parts: the authorization process and the appropriations process. At the authorization stage, a bill proposing a new policy or activity for the national government is submitted; if ultimately passed in some form, it becomes in effect a commitment by the government to execute that policy. If new funding is required to launch such a program, as is often the case, all its costs must be inserted in the budget proposed to the Congress the next year, which in effect subjects the matter to a second consideration. If it successfully emerges from the latter (appropriations) stage, during which an entirely different set of committees and interest groups is able to affect the outcome, the new program takes its place among the activities of the national government.

Both stages are long and difficult. Thousands of bills are submitted during each session of the Congress, and only a relative handful are enacted into law. If a bill is to be taken seriously, special attention must be called to it. This usually comes about because it is part of "the President's program" (the list of legislation the President tells the Congress is desirable that year) or by decision of the majority party leadership in the Congress.

The first step in the passage of a bill is referral to the appropriate policy area committee, and then to the relevant subcommittee, in each house. After several weeks or months of hearings, lobbying, bargaining, compromising, and the like, the subcommittee addresses itself to the task of drafting the actual provisions of the bill. Formal votes are not usually taken until the final draft is considered by the committee as a whole, by which time many tradeoffs and amendments have already been made. When the bill has finally been passed by the standing committee, it is ready for consideration on the floor of the House or Senate. In the House of Representatives, as we have said, the Rules Committee determines when and how the bill will be debated.

If the bill is passed in both houses, a conference committee is ordinarily required to iron out the differences in the bills passed by the two houses. Usually made up of key members of the relevant policy area committees of each house, the conference committee is the real source of the final version of the bill. In some cases, influential members wait until this point to shape the bill to their liking. Often the final bill only vaguely resembles the earlier versions. In any event, both houses must pass the bill in the same final version.

If the President signs the bill, it becomes law. If the President vetoes it, but both houses pass it again by two-thirds majorities, it becomes law. The influence of the threat of a presidential veto can be substantial: all it takes is one-third of the votes in one house plus one vote, to thwart the work of weeks or months by both houses. This threat and the use of the news media to put public pressure on the Congress enable the President to shape legislation.

But enactment into law may be only the beginning. Relatively few statutes are "self-executing" in the sense that they can immediately be put into effect by existing agencies. Many require funding, if only in the form of new personnel to perform the investigation, services, or enforcement called for in the statute. In such cases, the appropriations process following submission of the next year's budget serves as the second consideration of the issues addressed by the statute; the arena is not the policy area committees but subcommittees of the Appropriations Committees. When a budget has been passed by each house, differences are settled by an appropriations conference committee.

The allied processes of logrolling and coalition-building are basic to legislative policymaking. Only a rare issue, such as a declaration of war or a strong civil rights bill, arouses a fairly strong interest, pro or con, in virtually all members of the legislative body. When this happens, it is because there is widespread concern or controversy over the issue in the country at large. Only a relatively small proportion of the members take an active interest in most issues that come before a legislative body. Most have a mild concern or none at all, largely reflecting the degree of interest or lack of it among their constituents. A proposal to raise the tariff on foreign coal imports will certainly evoke strong interest in the coal-producing areas of Pennsylvania, West Virginia, and Illinois, and thus in legislators representing these areas. But most other members of Congress are not likely to be strongly aroused, even though some of their constituents use coal to heat their homes or factories. A proposal to appropriate federal funds to redirect the flow of the Colorado River will certainly awaken hopes or anxieties in legislators from the states bordering the river, but will probably not deeply stir legislators from Georgia, Alaska, or New Jersey.

Where this combination of strong interest among a few legislators and apathy among most prevail, conditions are ripe for bargaining, logrolling, and coalition-building. The congressman from Pennsylvania who wants support for a higher tariff on coal knows he can probably get supporting votes from unconcerned colleagues in return for his goodwill and the resulting expectation that he will support them in the future on some issue on which *they* badly need support. He may have an understanding with congressmen from cotton-growing states that he will vote for higher price supports for cotton: an issue in which he and his Pennsylvania constituents have relatively little interest. It is more likely that there will be no such explicit understanding about vote-trading at all, but rather a gentlemen's recognition that a favor rendered today deserves a return favor in the future.

Appropriations in Action: The Military Orchestrates Pressure

Each year the President submits to the Congress a budget that reflects his judgments and preferences on national priorities for the coming fiscal year. The Congress then reviews the proposed funding for each department and activity of the government, and modifies allocations in accordance with its own priorities before appropriating the money. Underlying this formal description, of course, are some hard realities: each year bitter contests take place, first within the executive branch and then in the Congress, among the armed services themselves and also between the military and its supporters and those seeking other priorities for governmental action. Each service naturally believes that its needs are paramount and that with new weaponry it can make an even greater contribution to national security. The cumulative effect of sincere and persuasive arguments for the pressing needs of the Air Force, Army, Navy, and Marine Corps is to force other governmental departments and functions to defend themselves or be content with what is left over. In this competitive process, three factors work to the advantage of the military services.

1. As large and complex organizations, the military services constantly need increased funds merely for self-maintenance. Over the years, they have perfected tactics for effectively influencing the Congress and the public. In this, they have been aided by a general aura of patriotic necessity and selfless sacrifice in the struggle against communism. Not surprisingly, generals and admirals in testimony before Congress, in speeches, and in books consistently endorse the doctrine that only superior military power can keep the peace and assure the security of the United States and the free world. When budget-cutting pressures build, they are likely to report new advances by Soviet military forces and to predict dire consequences unless our own appropriations are increased. We may be sure that they are sincere in reporting conditions as they perceive them. They believe that it is part of their job, if not their duty, to proceed in this fashion. At some point, however, natural enthusiasm and confidence in the importance of one's lifework are likely to produce claims that are, from the broader perspective of *all* national needs and resources, out of proportion. But it is not easy for either a citizen or a congressman to resist when confronted by a high-ranking military officer's expert testimony that national security will be endangered unless another

$5 billion is provided for a new defense system. Nor do congressmen relish hearing their opponents at the next election attack their records on the ground that they have been "penny-pinching with the nation's security" or "advocating unilateral disarmament."

Below the level of patriotic publicity and exhortation, the military services make effective use of the pressure tactics familiar to American politics. They regularly lobby supporters and potential supporters in the Congress, explaining in detail the economic benefits to districts and regions that can result from new defense contracts and rewarding their friends with free air transportation or round-the-world trips. Because the Armed Services Committees and Appropriations Committees of the two houses are so crucial to approval of new spending programs, the military services pay special attention to them. They lobby on behalf of their friends for appointment to these cherished positions, and they build new bases in, and direct defense contracts toward, the districts represented by such members.

The armed services are also able to call on powerful allies in their efforts to influence decisionmakers. Private associations closely aligned with each service bear much of the burden of lobbying, particularly in ways that might seem improper for military officers on active duty. These associations are made up of former military officers and reservists, contractors and suppliers who do business with that service, and some interested citizens. By holding conventions, issuing statements, visiting congressmen, and otherwise engaging in pressure tactics, these associations serve as nongovernmental extensions of the various services. A second and growing body of allies is that segment of the scientific community that is engaged in research-and-development work for the military services and NASA. Some scientists have left universities to set up businesses to provide skills and products for the services, while others retain their university positions. In both cases, their prestige and seeming independence lend useful support to the military argument.

2. The military services can count on powerful and closely coordinated support from major defense suppliers who stand to gain or lose large sums as a result of budgetary decisions. It seems fair to conclude that these companies have a vital interest in the outcome of military appropriations controversies, some because of near-complete dependence and others because of the profitability of this portion of their business. Nor are these companies reluctant to press their efforts to acquire contracts: frank statements of determination to secure shares of this business lie behind extensive lobbying, contributions to the services' associations, and institutional advertising in national magazines and scientific and engineering journals. Coordinated lobbying campaigns, as well as close contacts for the purpose of securing contracts and administering them smoothly, are achieved through the contractors' well-established pattern of employing high-ranking retired military officers with procurement

experience. Senator William Proxmire of Wisconsin released figures in 1970 showing that, as of February 1969, 2,124 former high-ranking officers were employed by the 100 largest military contractors.[1] The ten largest suppliers employed 1,065 of these retired officers: Lockheed had 210; Boeing, 169; General Dynamics, 113; North American Rockwell, 194; and General Electric, 89. As a group, the top ten suppliers employed about three times as many ex-high-ranking officers in 1969 as they had a decade earlier. The same rate of increase applies to the top 100 defense contractors.

3. The key members of Congress are strong supporters of the military services, and most others are vulnerable to the economic opportunities for their districts represented by military contracts. The members of the Armed Services Committees of the two houses, and their counterparts on the Appropriations Committees, enjoy a virtual monopoly of influence over the substance of military authorizations and appropriations. They have the time and opportunity to become informed about the details of military activities and expenditures. In past decades, they have usually been willing to appropriate *more* than the services requested. The ordinary member of Congress is habituated to take the word of colleagues who are specialists in a subject area, unable to acquire the inside knowledge that permits informed challenge or preparation of sensible alternatives, and vulnerable to the economic needs of his or her district. This dependence on the evaluations and recommendations of others has several implications.

The geographic concentration of defense business creates both strong defensiveness on the part of members of Congress who want to maintain business for their districts, and strong acquisitiveness on the part of others who want to share it more widely. As we saw in Chapter 5, defense business is monopolized by a few states. Others, chiefly in the Midwest, are especially low in defense business. Although the lack of any real opposition to military budget appropriations makes analysis of congressional voting patterns on this issue meaningless, it is clear that what opposition exists comes quite disproportionately from the Midwest and urban areas where the level of defense business is particularly low.

For many congressmen, defense contracts have become another (and larger) "pork barrel" like public works. A politician's constant need to be able to show his constituents that he is working effectively on their behalf is fulfilled by the announcement of new defense contracts, even if he had little or nothing to do with securing them. The military and the White House have contributed to the gamesmanship and spoils-system aspects of defense contracting by helping to make congressmen "look good" in this respect—by arranging for them to make public announce-

---

[1] William Proxmire, *Report from Wasteland* (New York: Praeger, 1970), pp. 153–154.

ments of contract awards, for example. The question of who has done or who can do most for the district by obtaining contracts is regularly an issue in many congressional campaigns.

What does this mean? To what extent can it be said that Congress controls the appropriations process, let alone the various other activities of the far-flung federal government? In effect, the division of labor into committees that is necessary to transact business at all has caused the Congress to parcel out vital power to a few members—who then become as much advocates as overseers of the agencies under their jurisdiction. Only rarely does the Congress rise to the level of independent policy-maker. For the most part, the sheer volume and complexity of issues force it into secondary modifying-ratifying roles. And, as we have just seen, it has difficulty performing even these functions rationally and consistently.

Congress Seeks to Reclaim Its Role: The Developments and Reforms of the 1970s

The Vietnam War, followed by the Watergate scandals, led to demands, and resultant opportunities, for efforts to check the President's steadily increasing power and discretion. The most obvious means of providing for such a check is to restore the power of Congress to establish the policy it believes to best serve the national interest and to exercise constant oversight of the acts of the executive branch. But this outcome requires that the Congress itself be ready and able to act, which would represent a major deviation from past experience.

The prime movers toward regeneration of the Congress from within have been the Democratic members of the House. An unusually large number of new Democratic members entered the House in the 1960s, and they began to use the Democratic party caucus as a vehicle for pressuring standing committee chairmen and party leaders to share power more broadly. Between 1958 and 1970, for example, 293 new Democrats entered the House; between 1971 and 1975, another 150 came to the House for the first time. In late 1974 and early 1975, the advent of 75 new "freshmen" tipped the balance and enabled these generally younger and more liberal members to institute several reforms.

A series of changes in House rules and positions adopted by the Democratic caucus have brought about the following changes:

1. No House member can be chairman of more than one legislative subcommittee. Adopted in 1971, this rule resulted in the rise to subcommittee chairmanships of several younger Democrats.

2. Subcommittee members have a kind of "bill of rights" that assures them of real influence and consideration throughout the commit-

tee process. The power of committee chairmen has been reduced, and is now more broadly shared with subcommittees. In the larger committees, the formation of subcommittees was mandated and subcommittees were authorized to hire their own staffs.

3. Committees were required to have written rules, again reducing the capacity of chairmen for arbitrary action.

4. In late 1974, the Democratic caucus limited senior Democrats to two subcommittee positions, effectively diminishing conservative power on the Appropriations Committee. It also required that the chairmen of such subcommittees be approved by the caucus, and subsequently unseated the chairmen of three key committees, replacing them with younger and presumably more active members.

Working in favor of the reinvigoration of Congress are the turnover in membership and the increasing dissemination of power by means of these reforms. At the same time the new Democrats were entering the House, an unusually large number of older and senior members were retiring. This trend began in 1972 and 1974, with 35 and 44 members retiring, and peaked (to date) in 1978, when a record 49 members did not run for re-election. One result was that fewer members of the House held high seniority and there was thus greater opportunity for newer members. But the large proportion of junior and inexperienced members also led to concern for the capacity of Congress to work its will amidst the more permanent bureaucracy and the more powerful President. Indeed, in 1978 much attention was drawn to the fact that members of the House seemed to be retiring out of frustration with their inability to get things done and the growing demands of their constituents.

Turnover in the Senate, initially slower than that in the House, also began to pick up in 1978. A total of 20 new Senators entered the 96th Congress that convened in 1979: 10 were due to retirements, the most in the post World War Two era; three incumbents were defeated in primary elections, the most in a decade; and seven more were defeated in the November general election. The latter figure was exceeded only once in 20 years, and then in 1976 when 9 incumbents lost. There has been nothing comparable in the Senate to the rules changes accomplished in the House, but some of the same forces seem to be at work. That is, committee chairmen act less arbitrarily, power is more decentralized, increasing proportions of new Senators make for inexperience, and frustration among members runs high.

Observers differed sharply as to what the significance of the Watergate aftermath, rules changes, and membership changes actually were for the Congress. According to *Business Week,* for example, the Congress of the 1970s was engaged in a "Great Congressional Power Grab," particularly noticeable in 1977–1978 when "The overwhelmingly Democratic 95th Congress has wrested policy control from the executive over energy and taxes, interferes more than ever in foreign policy, and is

---

TABLE 14.3

The Senate (Dem. 59*, Repub. 41; net change Repub. +3)

Summary of Results

Incumbent Senators defeated	6	(Dem. 4, Repub. 2)
Seats Dem. to Repub. 8		
Seats Repub. to Dem. 5		
Total new Senators	20	(Dem. 9, Repub. 11)
(second largest total in history)		

Special features

Newcomers include the first woman ever elected who was not preceded by her husband (Nancy Landon Kassebaum, R-Kansas); the first Republican Senator elected in Mississippi since 1875 (Thad Cochran); and a former professional basketball player in his first try for office (Bill Bradley, D- New Jersey.) Defeated was the only black Senator, (Edward Brooke, R-Massachusetts.)

The House of Representatives (Dem. 276, Repub. 159; net change Repub. +12)

Summary of Results

Incumbent Representatives defeated	19	(Dem. 14, Repub. 5)
Seats Dem. to Repub. 21		
Seats Repub. to Dem. 10		
Total new Representatives	77	(Dem. 41, Repub. 36)

Committee Chairmanship Changes

Senate

3 Committee Chairmen retired; none were defeated.

Major committees: Kennedy (D-Mass.) replaces Eastland (D-Miss.), *Judiciary;* Church (D-Idaho) replaces Sparkman (D-Ala.), *Foreign Relations.*

House

4 Committee Chairmen retired; one was defeated in primary.

Major committees: Whitten (D-Miss.) replaces Mahon (D-Texas), *Appropriations;* Bolling, (D-Mo.) replaces Delaney (D-N.Y.), *Rules.*

---

* Includes Harry F. Byrd, Jr., of Virginia, elected as Independent.

openly contemptuous of executive leadership."[2] But the Congress, because of turnover, lack of party discipline, the dominance of special interests, etc. has been unable to exercise its power constructively. Instead, it essentially blocks Presidential leadership while falling more out of touch with the need for decisive action every day.

[2] *Business Week,* September 11, 1978, p. 90.

Others disagree with the idea that Congress is newly powerful, at least as far as exercising continuing purposeful control over the national government is concerned. In a series of post-election articles in November 1978, for example, the *New York Times* stressed the new emphasis among Congressmen on "service to the District" and the increasingly powerful role of special interest groups.[3] Both of these developments suggest less sustained, policy-oriented power in Congress as a whole, and more specialized efforts by various members toward self-interested ends.

The issue seems to boil down to the question of what one thinks the Congress *should* be doing. It clearly has not shown the capacity to provide steady or sustained direction for the basic course of American public policy, but it has on occasion blocked important Presidential or other policy initiatives, and it reserves its systematic attention to the needs of local interests—or at least those represented by Congressmen or Senators with power in their respective Houses. Reform has not worked to achieve the former capability, but it probably has enhanced the latter.

[3] *The New York Times,* November 13, 1978, p. B9.

15

The Presidency

Presidential Power

In the early 1960s Americans accorded the presidency "great respect," and most children regarded the President as a "benevolent leader."[1] In 1968 President Lyndon Johnson, who had won a landslide victory four years earlier, was forced to withdraw from office without seeking reelection because the public distrusted him and his Vietnam War policies. Six years later President Richard Nixon was forced to resign

[1] Fred I. Greenstein, "What the President Means to Americans," in *Choosing the President,* ed. James David Barber (Englewood Cliffs, N.J.: Prentice-Hall, 1974), p. 125.

the presidency under threat of impeachment for abuses of power and serious violations of the law. Americans had lost much of their earlier confidence in the presidency.

Was it just personal defects that led two successive Presidents into serious trouble? That is part of the story, but only a small part. The President stands at the head of a rapidly growing executive branch, employing more than 2 million people, that affects the lives of Americans and other people all over the world. As the powers of the office increase, opportunities for mistakes and abuse grow. A late twentieth-century President can act without public knowledge in ways that earlier Presidents could not; and he can take advantage of the attention focused on him to *create* public opinion in ways that were impossible before the advent of television and radio networks and instantaneous worldwide communications.

The modern presidency is a very different institution from what it was forty-five years ago, before World War Two and the Great Depression. In 1932 there were three people on the White House staff; in 1975 there are 540. In 1930, 601,319 people administered all the functions of the federal government; in 1975 the number was 2,835,348. Throughout most of American history, including the first third of the twentieth century, Congress dominated the government, though an occasional "strong" President was able to have his way for a short time. Now every President is "strong," suggesting that the office has changed more than the personalities of the men who occupy it.

Though the powers of and checks on the President specified by the Constitution have hardly changed, what he can do with his powers has changed enormously. To understand the place of the President in American government today, we must look not only at the man who lives in the White House, but also at power centers and tensions in the society as a whole, what he can do to shape them, and what *they* can do to shape *him*. In a sense, therefore, this entire book describes the forces that make the presidency what it is; in this chapter we focus directly on what the President can do and how he does it.

The Sources of Presidential Power

The President's power is of a kind that no other government official has at his or her disposal: that power derives from his position as the executive head of the nation and the symbol of the United States to Americans and to citizens of other countries. The Constitution, the laws, and court decisions confer particular powers on public officials: a general can decide where to attack; the Secretary of Agriculture can ban contaminated wheat from the market. The most important powers of the President, by contrast, depend less on specific provisions of the laws than on his influence over public opinion. No citizen can have direct knowledge of more than a tiny fraction of the thousands of issues on which the

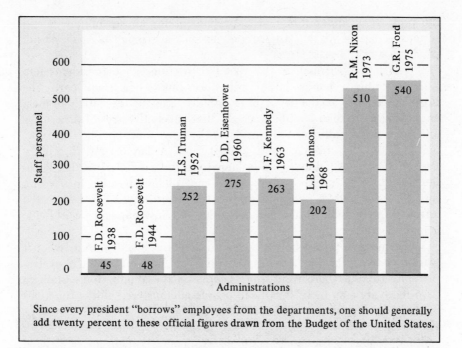

Since every president "borrows" employees from the departments, one should generally add twenty percent to these official figures drawn from the Budget of the United States.

Source: Thomas E. Cronin, *The State of the Presidency* (Boston: Little, Brown and Company, 1975), p. 119. Adapted from Howard E. McCurdy, "The Physical Manifestations of an Expanded Presidency," paper delivered at the 1974 Annual Meeting of the American Political Science Association, Chicago, September 1, 1974. Reprinted by permission.

FIGURE 15.1

Growth of the White House Staff, 1938–1975

government acts every day, and few can or want to spend all their time keeping informed. It is chiefly what the President and his staff say publicly and tell reporters that causes the average citizen to worry about a military threat from Russia or Vietnam, to believe that the steep increases in food bills are due to union pressure for higher wages, or to conclude that it is patriotic to save oil by driving more slowly. The President, far more than anyone else, can make large numbers of people worry about alleged threats to their welfare, lead them to accept sacrifices for what he tells them is the common good, or reassure them that the government is solving the problems that concern them. By shaping people's hopes and fears, the President can usually do a great deal to influence what people support and what they oppose.

This is especially true of issues of foreign policy, internal security, and other matters that have a deep impact on our lives but depend on actions over which most of us have little control. When President Lyndon Johnson told the country in August 1964 that the North Vietnamese had fired on two harmless American ships in the Tonkin Gulf, he immediately created overwhelming public and congressional support for sending American troops into Vietnam. No one was in a position to question his claim, and the President himself may not have known he was distorting the facts, though it later became clear that he had. Johnson had been planning for at least several months to ask the Senate for a resolution that could be used to authorize military intervention, and his administration helped create an incident that would arouse public opinion in support of such intervention.

Members of trade associations, labor unions, and other organizations that try to influence many policies are less likely than other citizens to be influenced by the President on such issues. They have strong interests in profits or wage increases regardless of what the President says. But even in such cases he can exercise a great deal of power over public opinion generally by linking economic interests to national security—by urging, for example, that wage restraint or limits on prices are necessary to keep the United States strong.

Most countries have a head of state (like the English queen or the President of Israel), who symbolizes the nation, and a prime minister, who is the executive in charge of day-to-day affairs. Combining both roles, the American President is in a unique position to shape his own powers by creating and guiding the very public opinion to which he responds.

The President can increase his powers by *ignoring* the public, as well as by influencing what it believes. During Harry Truman's presidency the CIA apparently provided arms for Chinese Nationalist troops in Burma, and under Dwight Eisenhower it helped bring down governments in Iran and Guatemala. Richard Nixon ordered the secret bombing of Cambodia, a country with which the United States was not at war. Lyndon Johnson received FBI reports on secret telephone taps of the conversations of public officials and political opponents. Nixon or his staff did the same, and also brought pressure on the Internal Revenue Service to be especially severe in auditing the tax returns of opponents of the Vietnam War. The White House pursued these and similar actions for long periods without the knowledge or approval of the public, the Congress, or the courts. In most cases they would certainly have met with far more popular disapproval than support.

The President's Formal Powers

The Constitution and hundreds of laws Congress has enacted over the years confer formal powers on the President. What such provisions mean is never fully apparent from the legal language in which they are stated; their meaning resides in the actions of particular Presidents and court decisions interpreting them—which is another way of saying that such meanings change continuously, and usually in the direction of wider presidential powers.

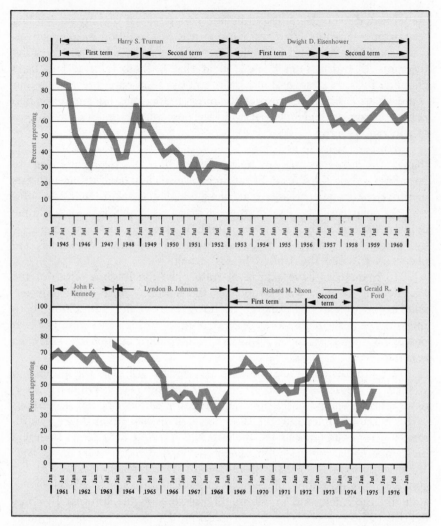

Source: Thomas E. Cronin, *The State of the Presidency* (Boston: Little, Brown and Company, 1975), pp. 110–111.

FIGURE 15.2

Presidential Popularity (assessed at 3–5 month intervals, June 1945–1975). Question: "Do you approve of the way _____ is handling his job as president?"

According to the Constitution the President is Commander-in-chief of the armed forces, while Congress has the power to declare war. But many Presidents have waged wars without congressional approval, and some created situations that left Congress little choice. During the first 25 years of American history, Presidents waged three undeclared naval wars. In 1846 President James Polk ordered troops into territory claimed by Mexico, provoking a war which Congress then had to declare. Presidents Johnson and Nixon later waged wars in foreign countries without formal declarations by Congress.

The Constitution also authorizes the President to make treaties, which must then be ratified by a two-thirds vote in the Senate; but recent Presidents have increasingly evaded the requirement of Senate approval by entering into "executive agreements," in effect making treaties without regard for the "advice and consent of the Senate" provision of the Constitution.

The most general grant of power in the Constitution directs the President to "take care that the laws be faithfully executed," a provision whose meaning depends on what Presidents actually do as well as on occasional reviews of their authority by the courts. After America's entry into World War Two, President Franklin Roosevelt imposed far-reaching economic controls by *executive order*, without waiting for Congress to pass laws authorizing such controls. These measures included nationwide price, wage, and rent ceilings; limits on the use and export of raw materials; and curbs on employment practices that discriminated against blacks.

A great many laws also confer powers on the President. The Communications Act of 1934, for example, authorizes the President to allocate radio frequencies for use by federal government agencies in their own operations—a matter of considerable importance to the armed forces, the Commerce Department, the Civil Aviation Agency, manufacturers of communications equipment, and commercial radio and television stations, who get *their* licenses to broadcast from the Federal Communications Commission. In allocating frequencies, the President relies on an Interdepartment Radio Advisory Committee; but he can intervene personally when the agencies concerned do not agree among themselves. Another example is the tariff laws, which allow the President to raise or lower tariffs on some imported goods within specified limits; this power strengthens his hand in negotiations on trade matters with foreign countries.

Restrictions on the President

Sensitive to the abuse of power by eighteenth-century European monarchs, the Framers of the Constitution were careful to provide for curbs on the President. The courts and the Congress can check some of the President's actions, and his need to maintain broad political support imposes other restraints. As we have seen, these checks worked well for about a century and a half. Some historians believe they worked too well, often creating impasses among the three branches of the government that prevented effective governmental action. They are far less effective now, and the predominant criticism of the "balance of powers" among the branches of government in the 1970s is that the presidency has grown too powerful, "imperial," and capable of the kind of abuse of executive power the delegates to the Constitutional Convention of 1787 tried to prevent. Developments in the next several decades will reveal just how effective the checks still are; meanwhile, it is impossible to understand the presidency without knowing what they are and how they are being weakened or ignored.

Legal restrictions on the President, in which the Founding Fathers and early constitutional lawyers placed most of their faith, today seem to be in jeopardy. Determined Presidents have found ways to circumvent some of the most important Congressional powers, including the power to declare war and the power to approve treaties. And, as we shall see, Presidents have found devices to evade other powers of the Congress, including its powers to direct the President to carry out particular laws and to override presidential vetoes by a two-thirds vote of both Houses. Even the power of Congress to act as the chief legislative branch is no longer clear-cut, for recent Presidents have devised programs and made policy themselves. Yet Congressional prerogatives remain important as long as Presidents are subjected to criticism for bypassing them and forced to justify actions some see as exceeding their powers.

The requirement that the Senate confirm presidential appointments of federal judges and high officials in the executive branch of government is not easily evaded. The occasional rejection of a nominee makes Presidents think twice about ignoring popular values (or ignoring senators from the nominee's home state, who are usually supported by their Senate colleagues if they ask for rejection on the grounds that the nominee is "personally obnoxious" to them). President Kennedy's nomination of Francis X. Morrissey to a district judgeship and President Nixon's nominations of Clement F. Haynsworth and G. Harrold Carswell to the Supreme Court were rejected because the nominees' competence or fairness were in serious doubt.

In all but the rare case, however, presidential appointments win routine approval and are the White House's major means of exerting influence on the executive and judicial branches. Occasionally a President uses the power of appointment for ends that would be politically harmful if he avowed them openly or asked for legislation to accomplish them. John Kennedy won wide support from liberals for his strong stand on civil rights, but as President he appointed a large number of district judges in the South whose decisions crippled much of the civil rights legislation Kennedy initiated or publicly supported. In this way the President paid debts to powerful Democrats in the South who were less than enthusiastic about his rhetorical stance on civil rights. Richard Nixon appointed a Director of the Office of Economic Opportunity, Howard Phillips, who disapproved of the programs to help the poor that agency was administering. Phillips virtually succeeded in killing the agency by dismantling its programs and replacing or firing many members of the staff who tried to take their duties seriously.

Informal Restrictions on the President

Though it is supposed to be subject to his orders, the federal bureaucracy is a tough obstacle for every President. The bureaucracy, which is considered in detail in Chapter 16, restricts the President simply because agencies develop their own ways of doing things, beliefs about what is desirable or not, and devices for ignoring or sabotaging directives from above that they do not like. The prevailing attitude is that Presidents, Cabinet secretaries, and assistant secretaries come and go, while the real work is done by experts who will still be around after the political guard has changed. For this reason, Richard Neustadt has argued that the only way for a President to be influential is to persuade others to go along.[2] Otherwise, he may issue orders only to realize later that little or nothing has happened in spite of them.

The power of the bureaucracy to drag its feet is important chiefly with regard to long-established domestic programs supported by influential pressure groups. Franklin Roosevelt's effort to make the Federal Trade Commission and the Antitrust Division of the Justice Department effective watchdogs of business by means of appointments to their top positions did not succeed, for the permanent staffs of both agencies and organized business groups proved more effective in defending established postures than did the unorganized consumers who would benefit from revitalized regulation, even when the consumers were supported by the President of the United States.

A President has much less reason to fear this form of restraint from subordinates when he is launching new programs or dealing with foreign policy or national security. In these cases public opinion and patterns of pressure are more volatile and easier for him to manipulate through actions and rhetoric that make people fear foreign or internal threats.

No list or chart of influences and restrictions on the President can present a sufficiently *dynamic* picture of how these pressures operate. In areas of policymaking in which prosperous industries have built close alliances with administrative agencies and congressional committees, the most eloquent and popular President can do little except go along. But it must be remembered that some of the most affluent industries achieved wealth and power in the first place due to government contracts, subsidies, and tax breaks that were publicly supported because a President helped arouse such support. The Cold War psychology that all the Presidents of the 1950s and 1960s did their best to promote led to a level of spending on armaments that made corporations like Lockheed, General Dynamics, and McDonell-Douglas formidable political forces. Allied as they are with the congressional military affairs committees and the Defense Department, no President can ignore them. Kennedy's touting of space exploration helped create a potent aerospace

---

[2] Richard E. Neustadt, *Presidential Power* (New York: New American Library, 1960), pp. 42–63.

industry, and Nixon and Ford did a great deal to expand the nuclear energy industry by playing on fears of oil shortages. The Congress, the courts, the political parties, the press, public opinion, and foreign governments all influence the President; but such influence flows in both directions. The astute analyst of public affairs must calculate under what conditions and in what policy areas the President has the advantage. If he either reflects the interests of powerful groups or wins over a supportive public, other elites usually go along with the President rather than serving as checks and balances.

The Organization of the Presidency

The presidency is a group of organizations rather than an individual person. The thousands of agencies, bureaus, and other subunits of the federal government represent the interests of many different and often conflicting groups, some with enormous economic and social power and others with very little. Because the President must try to prevent open and serious conflict among the complex set of interests in American society, he cannot rely only on the established departments of the government for information or estimates of the extent of public support for their programs. Increasingly, Presidents have had to create organizations under their own control, partly duplicating the functions of many of the regular administrative agencies, such as defense, foreign policy, telecommunications, and energy. As is so often true in politics, the same conflict expresses itself in several forms and can be interpreted in alternative ways. The competing interests of unions and employers, for example, may take the form of conflicting policy recommendations from the Departments of Labor and Commerce; the same conflict may also be reflected in personal infighting between the secretaries of those departments or between other officials responsive to the two interests. The student interested in personal sparring for position will find it, and so will the student interested in conflicts over value allocations; they will typically be seeing different aspects of the same battle.

To collect reliable information and to exercise control, the modern President works through a set of concentric organizations with himself at the center. A White House Office of trusted assistants channels information to the Oval Office, where the President works, but shields him from far more information than it transmits. In this respect presidential styles have differed. Franklin Roosevelt liked to know about serious conflicts, was relatively open to reports from the various agencies, and appointed trusted people to subordinate positions in key departments as sources of information and advice. Roosevelt sometimes assigned two different agencies overlapping responsibility for the same controversial program. Thus, if serious problems arose, conflict between the two organizations would make him aware of such problems and allow him to step in if he chose to do so. At the other extreme, Lyndon Johnson and Richard Nixon tended to be isolated by their staffs, who shielded them from unwelcome information and advice. Screening is obviously necessary, but the temptation every White House staff feels to minimize criticism reaching the President and to tell him what he wants to hear can hurt the President and the country, as was the case with both Johnson and Nixon.

The White House Office is part of the Executive Office of the President, whose composition varies somewhat depending on prevailing national problems. One of its key units is the Office of Management and Budget (OMB), which carries out the responsibility of the President to prepare the federal budget. Its staff of more than 600 people reviews the annual budget requests of all executive departments and agencies, and all legislation such agencies would like to recommend to Congress. This is a critical form of presidential control, since an agency's effective-

"And put in a higher fence too."

Source: *Herblock Special Report* (W. W. Norton & Co., Inc., 1974).

ness depends on its appropriation and the statutes that pertain to its policy area. The OMB typically trims agency appropriation requests somewhat. Some agencies have enough private backing and influence in Congress to push legislation through (surreptitiously) even if the OMB refuses to make it part of the President's program. Such occasional "end runs" around the OMB in effect tell the President that he has underestimated the current strength of the interest group that accomplishes them.

Other agencies in the Executive Office—notably the Council of Economic Advisers, the Council on International Economic Policy, and the Council on Environmental Quality—help the President keep abreast of economic trends. In conjunction with the budgetary and legislative powers of the OMB, these agencies contribute to a trend toward White House coordination of the broad policies of the entire executive branch. It is important to remember, however, that an organizational structure that permits the President to coordinate the policies of other agencies does not free him from the need to be sensitive to politically powerful groups. Neither does it allow him to do whatever he pleases on behalf of the poor, consumers, or other groups with little political power of

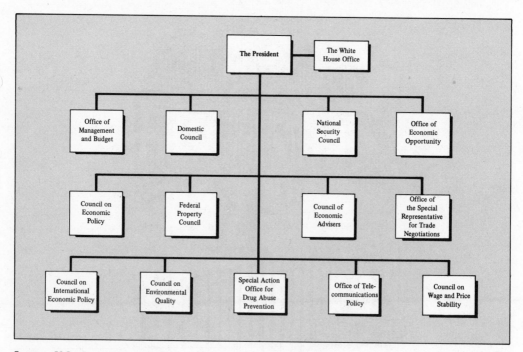

Source: U.S. Government Manual 1975–1976 (Washington, D.C.: U.S. Government Printing Office, 1975), p. 80.

FIGURE 15.3

Executive Office of the President

their own, though liberal Presidents are expected to try to, and usually do, advance measures advantageous to such groups in symbolic or short-term ways. Legislation to protect environmental quality, for example, lost presidential support in the 1970s when widespread belief in an energy shortage allowed oil and automobile companies to claim that the country had to choose between clean air and adequate heating and transportation.

The Cabinet

The term *Cabinet* has been used since George Washington's administration to refer to the heads of the large executive departments, whom the President appoints and can remove at his pleasure. Though the term implies that these officials collectively plan broad national policy, the Cabinet has never done so regularly; and it engages in less and less joint policymaking as pressures build for presidential coordination through the agencies in the Executive Office that are under direct White House control.

Cabinet members can be useful to the President in highly various ways. Some are appointed because of their political appeal to a wing of the President's party or a segment of the public. Because Presidents Hoover, Eisenhower, and Nixon had few ties to the labor movement, all of them appointed labor leaders as their Secretaries of Labor during at least part of their administrations; Presidents Roosevelt and Kennedy, who had prolabor reputations, did not feel it necessary to make that gesture. Some Cabinet members have reputations as experts on the matters for which their departments are responsible. Some have done political favors for the President. Others have followings in regions of the country where the Administration is politically weak. Several recent Presidents have appointed women to Cabinet posts, with at least one eye on the fact that more than half the eligible voters are women.

The same qualities that make Cabinet members valuable politically give them some independence from the President and incline them to represent particular interests rather than to work together. So do the pressures on them to promote the objectives of the groups that influence the departments they head, whether farm organizations, defense contractors, or advertisers interested in low postal rates for "junk mail."

One student of the presidency makes a useful distinction between the "inner" Cabinet—the heads of the Departments of Defense, State, Justice, and Treasury and a few high-level White House staff members—and the "outer" Cabinet—the heads of the departments dealing with domestic affairs: Interior, Agriculture, Commerce, Labor, HEW (Health Education and Welfare), HUD (Urban Development), and Transportation.[3] Members of the inner cabinet, as individuals if not collectively,

[3] Thomas E. Cronin, *The State of the Presidency* (Boston: Little Brown, 1975), pp. 190–191.

enjoy closer ties than ever to modern Presidents, for their departments deal with matters that enable Presidents to appeal powerfully to broad public opinion by invoking national security and internal security.

Increasingly, Presidents pay little personal attention to the outer Cabinet members, delegating this function to White House aides and to the Director of the OMB. The departments they head deal primarily with the problems of groups possessing few political resources (welfare recipients, students, Indians, railroad passengers) and with the interests of organized groups whose well-established influence the President could not change substantially even if he wanted to try (large manufacturers, corporate farmers, organized labor, cattle grazers). Because these circumstances leave little room or reason for dramatic maneuvering, the problems addressed by these departments tend to involve relatively small changes in existing policies and conflicting demands that are often politically embarrassing. Understandably, tension is constant between Cabinet secretaries under pressure to make concessions to one or another group and White House aides eager to minimize domestic spending and avoid politically harmful publicity. In the Nixon White House the authoritarian style of the President's chief assistants, H. R. Haldeman and John Ehrlichman, exacerbated relations with the inner Cabinet, but such conflict transcends personalities in that it involves basically incompatible roles: the White House is subjected to a wider range of political pressures than is the secretary of a Cabinet department, and so must resist his demands and recommendations much of the time.

How To Become President

Presidential Elections: A Constraint or a Springboard to Power?

The Framers of the Constitution thought that providing for presidential elections every four years was a useful device to assure that no President could abuse his powers without being called to account for it. Yet, like most efforts to limit the President, this has been a two-edged sword: our system of presidential nominations and elections has also served to insure that only people with certain social characteristics can become President and to enable incumbent Presidents to dominate their parties, future elections, and public opinion.

Nomination

The choice of presidential nominees by the two major political parties is more critical than the general election since it eliminates all but two people from any chance of becoming President. And though millions of people meet the constitutional requirements for serving as President— native-born citizens at least 35 years old—only a very small number are ever seriously considered as nominees who might attract a large popular vote. In the 36 years between 1936 and 1972, only 62 Democrats and 47 Republicans won the support of as much as 1 percent of members of their own parties in Gallup polls on candidate preferences.

The narrowing-down process is neither a lottery in which everyone starts with an equal chance nor a rigorous screening to find the best or most popular candidate. Only aspirants whom newspapers and television news programs have mentioned frequently are regarded as serious contenders, and publicity as a serious contender in turn gives an aspirant a public following.

This kind of self-fulfilling prophecy seems to pervade the nominating process. An aspirant who makes a good early showing in the polls and the primaries finds it much easier to raise the millions of dollars necessary to continue to look popular. Even the "fat cats" and corporations that make large contributions, directly or indirectly, want a winner as well as a candidate who will support their interests. Names familiar from previous contests for the nomination are most often mentioned in conjecture about future ones. Because past winners have virtually all been male, white, Protestant, Anglo-Saxon, public officeholders, fairly wealthy, and fairly old, the overwhelming majority of the eligible population has little chance of being taken seriously. A rigid barrier confronts women, blacks, Jews, people whose ancestors emigrated from any part of the world other than Northern and Western Europe, and probably Catholics as well, even now; it is assumed large numbers of voters are prejudiced against these groups.[4]

There are other limits on eligibility for the nomination. A first-term President can normally have his party's nomination for a second term if he wants it; and he usually does, since he is virtually a sure winner. Victorious generals are the chief exception to the practice of nominating only individuals who have held elective office before, especially as Vice-President or Senator. An impressive military record has helped nominate and elect seven Presidents, though it is hardly likely that the same qualities make for success in both jobs.

The tests that are all-important in choosing nominees come partly from presidential primary elections held in a number of states in the early months of election years and partly from the preferences of local party officials and activists. About a third of the states conduct primaries in which voters may express a preference for one of the aspirants or actually select delegates to their party's nominating convention; approximately one-third of the convention delegates are chosen in primaries. The presidential primaries receive a lot of publicity, but their chief consequences are to encourage intra-party competition and divisiveness, to increase the cost of the election process substantially, and to cre-

---

[4] Donald R. Matthews, "Presidential Nominations," in *Choosing the President,* ed. James David Barber (Englewood Cliffs: Prentice-Hall, 1974), pp. 39–40.

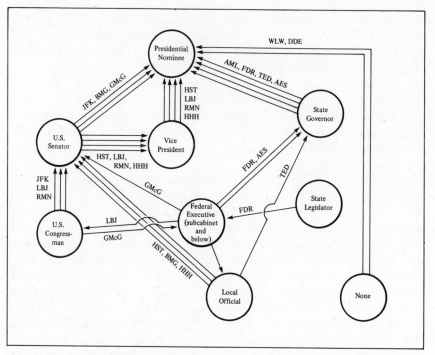

Source: James David Barber, ed. *Choosing the President* (Englewood Cliffs, N.J.: Prentice-Hall, Inc., 1974), p. 46.

FIGURE 15.4

Pattern of Public Office-Holding by Presidential Nominees, 1936–1972

ate the often illusory impression that "the people" have a major voice in the selection of nominees. Convention delegates often fail to support the candidate who won their state's primary; and the convention may choose a candidate who did not even enter the primaries, as the Democrats did when they nominated Hubert Humphrey in 1968. The aspirant who leads the field in the early polls almost always wins. Presidential nominating conventions serve more as occasions for hoopla, party propaganda, and the *legitimization* of choices made earlier than for key decision-making.

Let us consider some features of election campaigns that are distinctive to presidential elections. The general account of elections in Chapter 19 is also pertinent. Incumbent Presidents are usually reelected. Of thirteen incumbent Presidents who have run for second terms in the twentieth century, only two have been defeated, both in exceptional circumstances. Why does an incumbent President enjoy so great an advantage? For one thing, he can use press releases and other reports by the entire executive branch to create an impression of accomplishment and help for citizens with all sorts of problems. Recent Presidents have increasingly done so. During the Nixon Administration approximately 60

"We're interested in prime time—you know what we mean?"

Source: Herblock's State of the Union (New York: Simon & Schuster, 1972).

people in the White House and 6,144 people in the executive branch worked on public relations, at a cost of $161,000,000 a year.[5] An Associated Press survey in 1975 found 6,391 full- and part-time officials of the federal government dealing with public relations and information.[6]

The needs of news reporters make it all the easier for the incumbent regime to tout its activities—and to manage the news, if it wants to do so. Public affairs are so wide-ranging that even the wealthiest and most conscientious newspaper, television network, or wire service must rely on official releases for most of its information. Table 15.1 shows that *The New York Times* and *The Washington Post* do so, even though they have far better means of independent news-gathering than do most newspapers, which draw heavily on them as sources and as models of how to treat current news stories.

Psychological needs on the part of the public also help the incumbent

---

[5] David Wise, *The Politics of Lying* (New York: Random House, 1973), pp. 188–213.

[6] *Wisconsin State Journal,* 5 October 1975, section 4, p. 6.

TABLE 15.1   *Sources of Information in the* Times *and the* Post—*All Stories*
(N = 2,850)

	% of Total Sources
U.S. officials, agencies	46.5
Foreign, international officials, agencies	27.5
American state, local government officials	4.1
Other news organizations	3.2
Nongovernmental foreigners	2.1
Nongovernmental Americans	14.4
Not ascertainable °	2.4

Source: The table, reprinted by permission of the publisher, is taken from Leon Sigal, *Reporters and Officials* (Lexington: D. C. Heath, 1973), p. 124. It is based on a count of a sample of stories in the two newspapers over the years 1949 to 1969.

° Not ascertainable includes stories in which the channel was a spontaneous event or the reporter's own analysis.

President. People who are worried about foreign or domestic threats they cannot deal with themselves tend to want to believe that the President *can* cope with them, and so they cooperate with him in creating an image of competence. Asked in one study what they looked for in a President, people seemed concerned primarily with strength and toughness. Compassion was hardly mentioned.[7] It is also striking that every landslide presidential victory since Roosevelt's in 1936 was won by an incumbent who had coped or seemed to cope resolutely with a major crisis: Roosevelt with the Great Depression; Eisenhower in 1956 with the ending of the Korean War; Johnson in 1964 with the War on Poverty and the aftermath of the Kennedy assassination; and Nixon in 1972 with the ending of the Vietnam War and detente with Russia and China. Their opponents, by contrast, were reputed to be indecisive or inconsistent (Landon, Stevenson, McGovern) or wild, trigger-happy, and therefore unreliable (Goldwater). In the very close elections of the same period (1960, 1968), on the other hand, no incumbent was running and neither candidate had built a reputation for toughness and decisiveness.

Until 1940 no President ever sought a third term, though no Constitutional provision prevented it. Franklin Roosevelt ran for a third term that year and was elected to a fourth term in 1944. This precedent might have enhanced the advantages of incumbency considerably, but the Twenty-second Amendment, ratified in 1951, now forbids election to the

[7] Doris A. Graber, "Personal Qualities in Presidential Images: The Contribution of the Press," *Midwest Journal of Political Science* 16 (February 1972), pp. 54–55.

"I'll tell you everything you need to know."

Source: *Herblock's State of the Union* (New York: Simon & Schuster, 1972).

presidency more than twice.

A presidential candidate or incumbent is supposed to be the leader of his political party, and such Presidents as Thomas Jefferson, Abraham Lincoln, both Roosevelts, and Woodrow Wilson certainly were that. From the point of view of local leaders of the Republican and Democratic parties, the main use of the name at the top of the ticket is to carry into office hundreds of candidates for lesser offices from the same party; even so, this "coattail effect" often does not work, and there is some question whether any candidate can lend popularity to others.

Some recent Presidents and candidates have paid little attention to their regular party organizations. Many local Democratic leaders refused to cooperate with George McGovern, the presidential nominee in 1972, because they resented his attempts to weaken their positions by bringing higher proportions of young people and women into party and campaign activities. In the same campaign Richard Nixon, virtually ignoring the regular Republican party organization, set up a separate Committee to

Reelect the President (CREEP) dominated by White House aides loyal to him personally but uninterested in the party as a whole. The regular party workhorses found this arrangement frustrating because it denied them both funds and presidential cooperation. They liked it even less when Republican candidates for governorships and Congress did quite poorly on election day while Nixon won reelection by an enormous majority, and still less when it became known that CREEP had engaged in unlawful activities and "dirty tricks" that hurt the Republican party badly in the 1974 Congressional election. In the 1976 campaign Gerald Ford took care to work through the Republican National Committee, as part of an effort to heal the wounds in the party caused by Watergate.

A President can take advantage of his newsmaking resources and of popular trust in his office to create exaggerated or misleading impressions of his competence and achievements. Presidents would be more than human if they failed to do so, though some have shown far more interest in and skill at news management than others. A favorite device is the "pseudo-event," an incident that seems to occur naturally but is deliberately contrived to make an impression on an audience: the "crowd" that is concentrated at one point so as to appear large on television as the candidate drives by; the crowd recruited to insult a candidate or act violently in order to win sympathy for him; the planted question or the planted group of "representative Americans" who chat with the candidate on TV, enabling him to display his rapport with many elements in American society and his knowledgeable treatment of complex issues. Trips to foreign countries, and especially to trouble spots, are a classic strategy by means of which presidential candidates display their interest in and mastery of foreign affairs.

The Vice-President and Succession

The Vice-President is a key figure in the federal government, but only because he has a very good chance of becoming President either due to the death of the President or by election in his own right.

The Twenty-fifth Amendment, ratified in 1967, insures that there will be no lengthy period without a Vice-President by authorizing the President to respond to a vacancy in the Vice-Presidency by nominating a candidate, who then takes office if confirmed by majority vote of both houses of Congress. Vice-President Spiro Agnew's resignation in 1973 brought this provision into play, and President Nixon appointed Gerald Ford to the office. Ford became President upon Nixon's resignation in August 1974, and in turn invoked the Twenty-fifth Amendment to appoint Nelson Rockefeller Vice-President. This exceptional sequence of events meant that for several years neither the President nor the Vice-President had been elected to their offices, a state of affairs that has aroused some criticism of the Twenty-Fifth Amendment.

Another part of the same Amendment provides for the Vice-President to serve as Acting President if the President is unable to perform his duties. In case of the death or disability of the President and Vice-President, the Speaker of the House of Representatives is next in line, followed by the President Pro Tem of the Senate (a senator elected by the other senators to that post), and then by the members of the Cabinet in the order in which their Departments were established historically.

The Vice-President is formally the presiding officer of the Senate. He may vote only on the rare occasions when there is a tie vote, though this sometimes constitutes an important power. Vice-Presidents have traditionally not been given important functions in the executive branch, though most Presidents make some pretense of doing so. John Nance Garner, who served as Vice-President during Roosevelt's first two terms, considered the administration much too liberal and was hardly on speaking terms with the President. President Eisenhower, asked near the end of his term to name a key administration policy in which Vice-President Richard Nixon had played an important role, replied, "Give me a week and maybe I'll think of one." As Gerald Ford's Vice-President, Nelson Rockefeller tried very hard to exert some influence on domestic energy policy, but had to employ a large private staff and the resources of the Rockefeller family in the effort.

Watergate

Through most of American history, as we have noted, Congress has blocked a great many presidential initiatives, especially during the frequent periods in which different political parties dominated the two branches. Such impasses always involved highly publicized proposals openly advocated by some and resisted by others and reflecting conflicting interests among different groups of people. It is also true, however, that on many of the most long-range and critical issues, presidential proposals were *not* blocked. Throughout the latter half of the nineteenth century, for example, all three branches of the federal government pursued policies conducive to the growth of large corporations. In the Great Depression of the 1930s, both the executive and legislative branches effectively encouraged the organization of workers into labor unions. And the branches have almost always supported each other in declaring and waging wars.

Since World War Two a drastic reordering of relations among the three branches has taken place. The executive has acquired a new independence and primacy, which is likely to continue because it is based on far-reaching changes in the objectives of powerful interest groups and in the ability of the President both to marshal popular support for his public actions and to act secretly when he wants to *avoid* a public reaction.

Concentrations of economic power flow more directly than' before from public policies, as described in Chapters 8 and 9. The President, through the Office of Management and Budget, serves as the coordinating instrument for elite power, and is therefore in much closer touch with key decisions and private and public decisionmakers than Congress or the courts can be. And in the years after World War Two, the secrecy that had long characterized some aspects of the conduct of foreign affairs became far more pervasive in that field and began to creep into some domestic governmental activities. It is always the alleged need for se-curity—from criminals, subversives, and foreign foes—that justifies secrecy, abroad and at home. The creation of an expanded intelligence establish-ment went hand-in-hand with the Cold War against communism that dominated American foreign policy from the late 1940s until the 1970s, the suspicion of internal subversion that characterized "McCarthyism" in the 1950s, and the hot wars in Korea (1949–1952) and Southeast Asia (1965–1972). Secrecy, public concern for national security, and presi-dential oversight of intelligence feed each other and together make it easier for Presidents to extend their controls over public and private life, with public support and sometimes without it. But the ability of the President and of executive agencies to conceal much of what they do also permits them to act on behalf of powerful economic and social in-terests without arousing public criticism or the threat of political chal-lenge.

This is the institutional background of the series of events in the Nixon Administration we know as "Watergate." The institutional back-ground did not make those particular events necessary: the personal fears, ambitions, and ideology of Richard Nixon and his close associates in the White House led them to try to expand their power by means of many kinds of unlawful acts and then to conceal their illegal actions, itself a serious offense. Watergate is an instructive example of the con-junction of personality traits and a conducive organizational and political environment. It is unlikely that any previous President, however am-bitious or insecure, could have done the same thing.

What did the Nixon White House do? It tried to insure its own con-tinuation in office and to weaken political opposition by means of various unlawful actions and attempts to politicize a number of key federal agencies to cause them to act in the political interests of the President. The unlawful acts included a break-in at the office of a psychiatrist whose patient, Daniel Ellsberg, the administration wanted to discredit for having made public the "Pentagon Papers," a set of documents that raised serious questions about the justification for waging the Vietnam War. Break-ins were also staged at the headquarters of the Democratic National Com-mittee as part of a more general plan, approved by the President in 1969, for widespread spying and harassment of people the Administration dis-trusted. During the 1972 campaign the White House supervised "dirty tricks" against Democratic aspirants the Administration feared, planting embarrassing phony letters and disrupting some campaign appearances. And fundraisers for the President put strong pressure on corporations to make large secret campaign contributions of doubtful legality.

The Administration also brought pressure on the Internal Revenue Service to make special audits of the income tax returns of leading political adversaries and opponents of the Vietnam War, and encouraged the FBI to spy on the same kinds of domestic "enemies."

Most of these activities became known in the spring of 1973. A "cover-up campaign" directed by the White House had been strikingly successful throughout the 1972 political campaign, and might well have continued to work except for the efforts of enterprising reporters on the *Washington Post*, and, later, *The New York Times*. In the summer of 1974, nationally televised hearings by a special Senate Committee riveted national attention on Watergate, and elicited startling information from a number of high officials seeking lenient treatment, notably John Dean, who had been Counsel to the President. The Committee learned that President Nixon had secretly taped all conversations taking place in his office.

From that point on, Watergate became a battle in which the Senate Committee, a special prosecutor, and later the House Judiciary Committee tried to gain access to the tapes and other White House documents, while the President and his close associates tried to avoid disclosing them by claiming that they were protected by the doctrine of "executive privilege" inherent in the presidency. Public pressure forced the release of transcripts of many of the tapes, though the White House first issued them with many deletions and some distortions.

In July and August 1974, the House Judiciary Committee held hearings on the impeachment of Richard Nixon. *Impeachment* is a formal resolution by a majority vote of the House of Representatives accusing a federal official of "treason, bribery, or high crimes and misdemeanors," to use the language of the Constitution. The House resolution names the specific offenses, and the Senate, acting as a court, then holds a trial; a two-thirds majority is required to convict.

A bipartisan majority of the House Judiciary Committee ultimately recommended to the full House that Nixon be impeached on three counts. One charged the President with helping to obstruct the investigation of the break-in at Watergate by making false or misleading statements, withholding evidence, advising others to commit perjury, and approving payments to witnesses to silence them. A second article charged that the President had used the FBI and the Internal Revenue Service to violate citizens' rights and to interfere with their lawful operations. The third Article of Impeachment accused the President of failing to honor the Judiciary Committee's subpoenas of evidence.

While the President was losing his fight in the Judiciary Committee, he also lost in the Supreme Court, which held that the claim of "executive privilege" did not justify withholding tapes. One result was the release of a tape revealing that Nixon had helped plan the cover-up within four days of the break-in at the Watergate—an extremely damaging development, especially in that it proved that the President had repeatedly lied when he denied taking part in the cover-up. The President's staunchest supporters in the Congress now abandoned him, and on August 8, 1974, he announced his decision to resign—the first resignation of a President in American history.

Three members of Nixon's Cabinet, his two top White House aides, his former legal counsel, and a large number of other former White House and CREEP officials were convicted of crimes, chiefly perjury and obstruction of justice in connection with the cover-up. A federal grand jury cited Nixon himself as a "co-conspirator," but because Gerald Ford pardoned him shortly after succeeding to the presidency, he was never indicted or tried.

Does Watergate demonstrate that constitutional checks on presidential wrongdoing "work," or that it is altogether too easy for a powerful cabal in the White House to harass opponents illegally; act without congressional approval; and use governmental tax, police, and intelligence agencies for their own ends? Critics have drawn both these conclusions from the events that took place between 1969 and 1974. That it is possible to do so is another example of the way in which our personal values influence the meanings we read into political actions.

Enough facts came to light to force a President from office and to send many of his subordinates to prison, and thus there is an important sense in which the system of justice worked. On the other side it is argued that a great deal of harm was done before any checks were brought to bear, and that it was sheer accident that brought them into play at all. Before the public or Congress became aware of what was happening, many people's rights had been violated, the course of a presidential election had been illegally interfered with, and key governmental agencies had used their powers unlawfully or unethically.

It is even more disturbing, some argue, that confidence in the office of the President is such that most of the public, the press, and Congress refused to admit the possibility of serious wrongdoing until long after strong evidence of it had been made public: until, by a chance not likely to occur again, the President's secret tapes provided indisputable proof of his guilt. During the 1972 election campaign the efforts of George McGovern, the Democratic candidate, to draw public attention to early evidence of a White House connection to the Watergate break-in failed. For many months during and after the campaign, American news reporters, with the exception of two on the *Washington Post*, ignored the story almost completely. And long after damaging admissions on the tapes had been widely publicized, a large portion of the public and many members of Congress refused to believe that the President himself was implicated because the evidence was based on inference rather than a "smoking gun." It seems quite unlikely that Nixon would have been seriously threatened with impeachment or forced to resign had the incriminating tapes not been available and ultimately made public. And it is equally unlikely that the matter would even have drawn widespread public attention until after Nixon had served out his second term if two newspaper reporters had not been suspicious when others were not and shown remarkable ingenuity and perseverence in pursuing the story. In either case, the subversion of governmental institutions and of public confidence in democratic government might well have reached a dangerous state.

Most important of all, it is unlikely that Watergate has significantly changed the structure of institutional power that produced a threat to democratic control in the first place. The impeachment hearings served chiefly to focus attention on the personal vices of Nixon and his associates, and so to divert attention from the powerful institutions and elite interests they served. And once Nixon had been publicly discredited, it was to the advantage of precisely those groups to have a new President responsive to similar values; Nixon had become a liability. The aftermath of Watergate—secret American support for a war in Angola, strong administration efforts to defend the power of intelligence agencies to act covertly and harass dissenters, and continued expansion of the part of the budget that benefits large industries—suggests that the institutional background has not changed. Historians will probably see Watergate as a symptom of underlying power relationships that it did little to change.

The Crisis in the Presidency

Changes in economic and political institutions and the President's increased ability to define issues so as to muster public support seem to justify widespread concern that the presidency as an institution may again threaten the rights and interests of citizens who lack the resources to learn what is happening or to resist. At the same time *some* device for coordinating and directing the federal government is plainly necessary. We suggest that any remedy that confines itself to electoral and governmental reform is likely to be ineffective, since the presidency reflects power in the economy and society, and not in the formal government alone.

The Carter Presidency

Jimmy Carter's style, his promises and programs as a candidate and as President, and his performance in office illustrate many of our conclusions about American politics today. A President must win public support, but he must also respond to the groups that have the economic and political power to shape the country's economy, to block presidential programs they oppose, and to influence public opinion.

TABLE 15.2 President Carter's Inner Cabinet, September 1978

Name	Position	Age	Occupation	Previous Governmental or Political Positions
Cabinet Members				
~~Cyrus R. Vance~~ Edmund Muskie	Secretary of State	61	Lawyer	General Counsel, Department of Defense 1961–1962; Secretary of the Army, 1962–1964; Deputy Secretary of Defense, 1964–1967; Special Representative of the President in Cyprus crisis, 1967–1968; U.S. negotiator at Paris Peace Conference on Vietnam, 1968–1969
Harold Brown	Secretary of Defense	51	Research scientist and Physics lecturer	Scientific adviser to several defense-related offices; Delegate to the Strategic Arms Limitation Talks in Helsinki, Geneva, and Vienna 1969; Secretary of Air Force 1965–1969
Griffin B. Bell	Attorney General	60	Lawyer	Chairman and member, Board of Directors, Committee on Innovation and Development of the Federal Judiciary; Judge, U.S. Court of Appeals, Fifth Circuit, 1961–1976
W. Michael Blumenthal	Secretary of the Treasury	52	Economist and Businessman	None
James R. Schlesinger	Secretary of Energy	49	Professor and Economist	Acting Deputy Director of Office of Management and Budget, 1969–1970; Assistant Director, OMB, 1970–1971; Chairman, Atomic Energy Commission, 1973; Secretary of Defense, 1973–1975; Director, Central Intelligence Agency, 1973
Executive Office Staff				
Robert J. Lipshutz	Counsel to the President	57	Lawyer	Treasurer, Jimmy Carter Campaign Committee 1976; Vice-Chairman, Georgia Board of Human Resources, 1977

Name	Position	Age	Profession	Background
Hamilton Jordan	Assistant to the President	33	Political adviser	Executive Secretary to Governor Carter Manager, Jimmy Carter Campaign Committee
Zbigniew K. Brzezinski	Assistant to the President for National Security Affairs	50	Professor	Member, Policy Planning Staff, Department of State, 1966–1968
Joseph L. (Jody) Powell	Press Secretary to the President	35	Political adviser	Personal aide to the Gubernatorial Campaign of Jimmy Carter, 1970; Press Secretary to Governor Carter, 1971–1975; Press Secretary for Jimmy Carter Campaign Committee, 1975–1976
James T. McIntyre	Director of the Office of Management and Budget	37	Lawyer	Director, Georgia Office of Planning & Budget, 1974–1976; Deputy Director, Office of Management & Budget, 1977
Charles L. Schultze	Chairman, Council of Economic Advisers	54	Economist	Staff Economist, Council of Economic Advisers 1952–1953; Assistant Director, U.S. Bureau of the Budget, 1962–1965; Director, Budget Bureau, 1965–1968
Stuart E. Eizenstat	Assistant to the President for Domestic Affairs & Policy	35	Lawyer	Political adviser to Carter Gubernatorial and Presidential campaigns; Political adviser to political campaigns of Andrew Young, 1970–1976; Member, Democratic National Committee, 1973
James M. Fallows	Chief Speechwriter	29	Writer	None

Rather more obviously than most Presidents, Carter won the presidential nomination and election and has tried to maintain public confidence in his administration through promises and actions that were largely symbolic, with broad appeal to low-income groups, minorities, and the middle class. At the same time he has supported the military and economic programs that are most vital to capitalist industry, though this focus has sometimes meant he could not carry out his promises. Such a contradictory mix of promise and performance may nonetheless be a practical political strategy. It permits government-industry collaboration to continue, though it may also mean that incumbent Presidents will be more expendable after one term in office than they have been through most of American history.

In the way he presents himself in his speeches, in his justifications for his programs, and in his personal style, Jimmy Carter is a populist: a politician who identifies himself with the common people against the establishment and the bureaucrats. This vision of the outsider, the farmer, who would take on entrenched interests in Washington and in the big corporations was the key theme of his campaign. He has rarely been specific in his promises, and so has appealed to many different groups because they could read different meanings into his words and acts. The populist note has continued to appear in many Carter statements as President, as have related declarations that he would deal resolutely with the national "crises" he claimed the country faced: an energy crisis, an urban crisis, and a crisis created by "a confused and bewildering welfare system."

Another theme Carter and his aides have often stressed is the importance of administrative and technical practicality, narrow limits on what government can accomplish, and the need for public sacrifice. Though this emphasis usually points in the opposite direction from the populist theme, it also carries a strong popular appeal, even to many who are also attracted by the populist promises; for this second focus conveys the message that the administration is practical, knowledgeable, able to deal in a toughminded way with do-gooders at home and with potential foes abroad. The Carter who presents himself in this way is not the peanut farmer, but rather the Annapolis graduate and the engineer. He is also a member of the Trilateral Commission, an international group of bankers, industrialists, high-level public officials, and labor leaders whose major concern lies in maintaining the freedom of these groups to make the industrial and governmental decisions that will promote profitability and cooperation with one another. The Commission's statements oppose those demands of the poor, the minorities, and the Third World that they see as incompatible with the existing international system of industrial and governmental cooperation; so the Trilateral Commission has deplored what some of its spokesmen call the "ungovernability" of mass publics who make too many demands.

In line with this second theme of his administration, Carter has de-

TABLE 15.3 *The Presidency: The First 15 Months*

	Rating at Beginning of Term	Rating After 15 Months
Truman	87%	43%
Eisenhower	68	68
Kennedy	72	77
Johnson	79	71
Nixon	59	56
Ford	71	41
Carter	66	39

Source: Surveys by American Institute of Public Opinion (Gallup), latest that of April 14–17, 1978.

cided not to implement his populist promises in some crucial areas and has declared that people should not expect government to do much for them: that too many public demands impair governmental efficiency and detract from the ability of political leaders to act in the public interest:

> government cannot eliminate poverty, or provide a bountiful economy, or reduce inflation, or save our cities, or cure illiteracy, or provide energy . . .[9]

On many issues, the Administration's record shows few accomplishments, for issues have rarely been resolutely confronted or resolved. Much of the record consists of recommendations Congress has failed to accept or accepted only in small part; on some other issues the administration has pulled back from the promises made during the election campaign.

During the campaign, Carter called the federal tax code a "national disgrace" because of its loopholes for the affluent and its burden on the middle class, but as President he proposed only a few changes; these would not touch most of the injustices and would make some worse. He later concluded that no serious tax reform is feasible in the next few years.

The unemployment rate dropped about a percentage point, to close to 6 percent of the labor force (or approximately six million people out of work) in the spring and summer of 1978, due partly to statistical manipulation of the method of computing the rate, but the decline represented some success for Carter. In another respect as well the administration resorted to symbolism to allay fears of unemployment. It promised support of the Humphrey-Hawkins bill which, in its original form, would have committed the government to keep unemployment

[9] State of the Union Address, January 19, 1978. Quoted in Sheldon Wolin, "Carter and the New Constitution," *New York Review of Books,* XXV (June 1, 1978), p. 16.

down to 3 percent and would have given unemployed workers a legal right to bring court action for public jobs. As revised by the administration, the Humphrey-Hawkins bill merely sets a goal of a maximum 4 percent unemployment rate, to be reached by 1983, but provides no machinery for actually reducing unemployment; and only 200,000 public service jobs were funded. The administration has regarded inflation as a more serious problem than unemployment, but in 1978 prices began climbing at a much more rapid rate than they had done.

President Carter placed more emphasis on legislation to deal with the "energy crisis" than on any other domestic issue, though he had little success in his first two years in office either in arousing public concern about the issue or in securing Congressional action to implement his goals. The Carter energy program was designed to reduce the consumption of oil and natural gas by making them more expensive: partly through the elimination of controls on the price of natural gas and partly by placing taxes on oil, the proceeds of which would be used to subsidize conversion of houses and factories to other fuels, especially coal and solar heat. To reduce consumption of any commodity by raising its price is in effect to ration its use by the poor. Subjected to very heavy lobbying by oil companies, Congress has provided for gradual deregulation of the price of natural gas, but has not imposed the taxes on oil that Carter requested.

In the fall of 1977 the administration proposed a package of programs to help the nation's cities, many of which were fast running out of funds to meet their obligations, especially in welfare, health, education, and transport. The key proposal was a program of fiscal aid to localities with high unemployment levels. There were also provisions for expanded federal purchasing to stimulate business in depressed areas; for loans to private business to expand or locate in depressed areas; for a public works program that would provide 60,000 jobs over a three-year period; for low-cost housing rehabilitation loans; and other measures. Though the list of proposals made the Carter urban program sound impressive, it was sharply limited in scope and in funds. It involved little money not already going to the cities, and immediately brought charges that the program would not help the areas that were most in need. Congressional opposition was strong, and the program made little progress in the House or the Senate.

The administration's welfare program has been similarly cautious in key respects and similarly unlikely to win Congressional approval without long delays and major changes. In May 1977, the President proposed abolishing the existing AFDC, food stamp, SSI, and other welfare programs[10] and replacing them with a simple cash payment that would vary only with the cost of living in different parts of the country. There would be pressure on recipients to work, and public jobs would be provided as

[10] See Chapter 6.

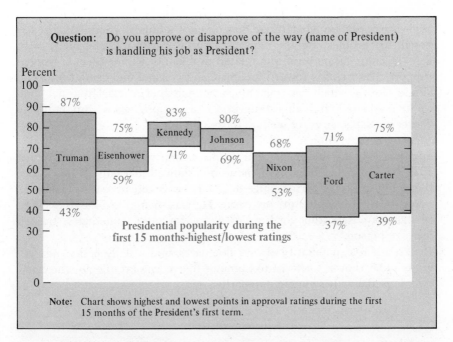

Question: Do you approve or disapprove of the way (name of President) is handling his job as President?

Presidential popularity during the first 15 months-highest/lowest ratings

Note: Chart shows highest and lowest points in approval ratings during the first 15 months of the President's first term.

Source: Surveys by American Institute of Public Opinion (Gallup), latest that of April 14–17, 1978. Chart prepared by *Public Opinion* (May/June 1978), p. 34. Copyright 1978 American Enterprise Institute. Reprinted by permission.

FIGURE 15.5
Swings in Presidential Popularity

a last resort. Because Carter continued to give top priority to a balanced budget, there would be little or no additional money, however, and Carter no longer supported his campaign pledge of a federal takeover of the welfare function from local governments.

In foreign affairs Congress has been more willing to support administration initiatives, but Carter's promises and actions have often been equally divergent in this field. He has talked a great deal about bringing pressure on repressive governments to support human rights, but has applied the pressure selectively, chiefly on the Soviet Union, while giving increased arms and moral support to some highly repressive regimes, especially that of the Shah of Iran. During the campaign Carter promised a five to seven billion dollar reduction in defense expenditures, but has in fact increased them, from about 105 billion to 119 billion dollars in his first two years in office. The major successes in this field have been Senate ratification of an administration-backed treaty restoring the Panama Canal to Panamanian ownership, with provision for American intervention under certain conditions; and some provisional agreements between Israel and Egypt reached with Carter's good offices at a summit meeting near Washington in September, 1978.

Forgotten promises are not new in politics; in this regard the Carter record may not be worse than that of most administrations. As already noted, the problem for the administration is partly its determination to keep business support and the related problem of winning Congressional support. The trend is toward greater Congressional independence of the White House, which can sometimes put together a legislative coalition for a single bill, but almost never for a comprehensive program like Carter's urban, energy, or welfare proposals.

At the same time a public that once rated Carter highly largely disapproved of his performance during his second year in office. In August 1978, an Associated Press–NBC news poll showed that only 25 percent of the public gave his performance a "good" or "excellent" rating, while 73 percent called it "only fair" or "poor." He was seen as not tough enough, though many who thought little of his performance nonetheless trusted him as a person.[11]

Presidential popularity always fluctuates, and usually it declines. As Figure 15.5 shows, Carter ranks among the recent Presidents who have experienced a wide swing in popularity.

[11] *Denver Post,* August 12, 1978, p. 7.

The Bureaucracy

The Nature, Growth, and Influence of the Bureaucracy

Though the President, congressmen, senators, Cabinet members, and Supreme Court justices often appear in the headlines, what they do rarely has a direct effect on people's everyday lives. It is policemen, income tax auditors, welfare department caseworkers, field examiners for the National Labor Relations Board, customs officers, FBI agents, army sergeants, wheat inspectors for the Department of Agriculture, and thousands of other public employees, often in relatively lowly positions, who decide whether individuals and groups of individuals will be helped or hurt by the statutes, court decisions, and executive orders they apply and interpret. Not even a congressional declaration of war, to take an especially dramatic example, affects the daily lives of citizens until draft boards decide whether they can remain civilians; a rationing board decides how much meat, sugar, and ketchup they can buy; wage and price boards determine how well they can afford to live; and a war production board determines which industrial products will be manufactured and which will be scarce. It is at the level of administration that the political system pays off for the man and woman in the street.

Bureaucrats Make Public Policies

Nor is it true, as primary-school textbooks sometimes assert, that administrators only "carry out" decisions made at the higher levels of the government. It is seldom possible for a President, legislature, or high court to make policies that take effect automatically and do not need to be interpreted in the course of application to a specific case. For example, Congress has directed the Federal Communications Commission (FCC) to grant and renew radio and television licenses so as to promote "the public interest, convenience, or necessity." But this legal phrase hardly specifies who gets licenses or what types of applicants are favored in grants of a scarce, influential, and very lucrative public resource. The real policymakers include FCC accountants, who decide whether applicants have adequate financial resources; FCC engineers, who decide whether a proposed station will interfere excessively with other stations; FCC lawyers and other employees, who decide whether proposed programs meet standards of fairness and balance, and so on.

A 55-mile-per-hour speed limit posted on a highway does not mean what it says if the highway police never issue tickets to anyone travelling less than 60 miles per hour, as is often the case; it means whatever the policeman chooses to do about it. An applicant for welfare benefits who is turned away by a caseworker at the welfare office does not benefit from the words in the law, even though a different caseworker might have interpreted those words in her favor.

Public administration, in short, involves discretion; and it involves politics as well, for administrators have a great deal to do with determining who gets what, when, and how. Administrators' decisions reflect the conflicts of interest that divide people. Should TV and radio licenses be awarded to applicants with ample financial resources to insure the use of good equipment, or should they be awarded to applicants who represent diverse economic and social groups and diverse ideologies? How much weight should a draft board give to the value of letting a student finish his college education, and how much to the value of making young people from middle-class families just as susceptible to the draft as young people who cannot afford to go to college? In deciding thousands of such matters, administrators are making critical choices on politically divisive issues.

Bureaucrats are embroiled in politics in another way as well: their actions and the language in which they describe their policies *create* public opinion at least as much as they reflect what the public already thinks. Citizens are typically unaware of a given issue until news media bring it to their attention. It is often news about administrative actions that shapes what large numbers of people recognize as a problem and what they then think about it. A welfare administrator quoted as declaring it necessary to clear the chiselers off the welfare rolls is obviously creating the belief in many people's minds that many welfare recipients have no legal or ethical right to their benefits. He or she is intensifying conflict between resentful taxpayers and those who need or favor the current level, or higher levels, of welfare payments. What the public statement implies may be accurate or inaccurate; but few who hear and react to it have access to any source of information other than the statement of a supposed authority on the subject. Nor is their attention directed to related public issues: whether, for example, people legally entitled to benefits are being denied them, and whether welfare payments amount to a significant or a minimal drain on the public treasury relative to other politically controversial costs, such as armaments or space research.

Administrative *actions* often create public beliefs even more effectively than does language, since their effect is more subtle. The sudden mobilization of troops or a military alert awakens fears that a hostile country is about to attack, and so musters support for a larger armaments budget and greater influence on the part of military experts in foreign policy decisions. When the Department of Labor undertakes retraining programs to help the unemployed, its action encourages the belief that unemployment is due largely to the failure to match vacant jobs with those who have the skills to perform them. Though this belief is partly valid, it points to a relatively minor cause of unemployment and so awakens false hopes in many trainees and false beliefs in the public generally.[1]

There is still another reason that administrative actions are a form of politics: they are closely linked to outside pressure groups and to the opinions and demands of influential people. In favoring radio and TV license applicants with large financial resources, the FCC is taking a position that pleases the National Association of Broadcasters. When a state public utilities commission allows gas and electric companies to raise their rates several times in a single year, as have many in recent years, it is responding to pressure from the utilities and recognizing that the people who must pay the higher bills are neither organized to protect their interests nor able to refuse to pay. Decisions on controversial matters made inside a public administrative agency reflect the political clout of groups outside the agency who are helped or hurt by what it does; and its policies often *contribute* to the political power or weakness of outside groups in turn.

[1] See Chapter 21.

The result is that administrative agencies are bound to reflect and also to *strengthen* the interests of groups that are already powerful. Though public bureaucracies maintain public support by claiming impartiality and expert knowledge, they use that support—with few exceptions—to further the goals of elites. That is the common theme of analyses of bureaucratic growth, structure, decisionmaking, and impact. Administrative agencies' claims that they simply "carry out" policies made by representatives of the people can be understood largely as a way of legitimizing administrative actions that further the goals of the economically and politically powerful. It will be clear from our analysis that many of the actions of the most controversial administrative agencies are taken without the knowledge or direction of legislative or executive superiors. In some cases they violate the law. To understand and predict such actions, a realistic analysis must focus on the groups with the power to influence the thinking, careers, and budgets of the agencies.

The Growth of the Bureaucracy

Throughout most of the nineteenth century American federal, state, and local governments dealt chiefly with foreign relations and national defense; the prevention of crime; delivery of the mail; public schooling, especially in the primary grades; and the use and disposal of public lands. Governmental functions were few and simple relative to today, costs were relatively low, and the number of people needed to administer the laws was small.

The big increases in the number of people employed in government occurred in the second third of the twentieth century, when all levels of government acquired new functions made necessary by the development of an extremely complex industrialized economy, sharp increases in population, and a large shift of population from rural areas to cities. These changes brought about pressures on government to help both those who were benefiting from such changes and those who were suffering from the social problems that had become serious and chronic in the twentieth century: poverty, health problems, emotional disturbance, bad housing, and monotonous and unsatisfying work.

As a result, public employees today perform just about every kind of work found in private industry, as well as some types only governments undertake. Every professional, scientific, and managerial skill is represented, as is every form of unskilled labor. Public administrative activities include regulating and aiding industries; fighting wars; performing scientific research; running hospitals, prisons, and schools; building roads, and many other functions.

Employees of the federal government account for only a small fraction of the number who perform these diverse governmental functions: there are close to 2.8 million civilian federal employees and well over 11

TABLE 16.1 *Paid Civilian Employment in the Federal Government*
1816–Jan. 31, 1975

Year	Total	Executive Branch	Legislative Branch	Judicial Branch
1816	4,837	4,479	243	115
1851	26,274	25,713	384	177
1881	100,020	94,679	2,579	2,762
1901	239,476	231,056	5,690	2,730
1921 [1]	561,142	550,020	9,202	1,920
1930	601,319	588,951	10,620	1,748
1940	1,042,420	1,022,853	17,099	2,468
1945	3,816,310	3,786,645	26,959	2,706
1950	1,960,708	1,934,040	22,896	3,772
1955	2,397,309	2,371,462	21,711	4,136
1960	2,398,704	2,370,826	22,886	4,996
1965 [2]	2,527,915	2,496,064	25,947	5,904
1970	2,921,909	2,884,307	30,715	6,887
1975 [3]	2,850,448	2,803,678	36,851	9,919

[1] As of July 31.

[2] Includes 33,480 appointments under Youth Opportunity Company.

[3] As of January 31.

Source: U.S. Bureau of the Census, *Historical Statistics of the United States: Colonial Times to 1957* (Washington, D.C.: U.S. Government Printing Office, 1957), p. 710; *Statistical Abstract of U.S., 1975*, p. 243.

million employees of state and local governments. An additional very large number work for private firms hired by governmental agencies to build highways and public buildings, manufacture equipment for the armed forces and space exploration, undertake research, and execute other public contracts.

The Structure of the Federal Bureaucracy

Organizational charts, like Figure 16.1, call attention to the many different kinds of organizations in the executive branch and also depict legal and formal lines of authority; they tell us who can give orders to whom. Such charts are useful as long as the reader remembers that formal legal authority sometimes has very little bearing on real influence in the day-to-day operations of a governmental bureaucracy. As we have already noticed, an outside pressure group is often the key influence on a particular administrative agency, though it does not appear on the organization chart at all. And, as we will see in more detail later, subordinates often wield more real power than their superiors.

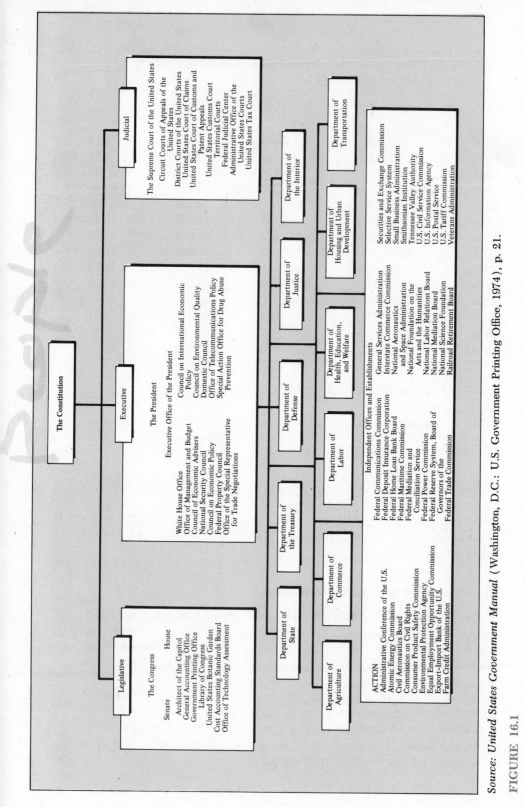

Source: *United States Government Manual* (Washington, D.C.: U.S. Government Printing Office, 1974), p. 21.

FIGURE 16.1

The Government of the United States

Organization charts also oversimplify by making it look as though each governmental function is neatly assigned to a particular agency or subunit within an agency.

In practice, governmental organizations' functions often overlap. Consider, for example, responsibility for keeping track of the activities of labor unions in foreign countries. The labor attaché assigned to each major American embassy, though formally under the authority of the State Department, is chosen largely by the Department of Labor, with the understanding that the AFL-CIO can veto choices it does not like. The attachés have frequently been CIA agents as well, and their reports and activities are often influenced by the concerns of the Department of Commerce, the Department of Labor, the Department of Defense, or the Council on International Economic Policy in the Executive Office of the President. When the British Labour party won an election in 1946 and unexpectedly came into power, the Labor Attaché in our London Embassy was for a time the most influential member of its staff: he had already developed close ties with key people in the new Clement Atlee government, many of whom had trade union backgrounds, while senior Embassy officials hardly knew them. Organizations must have formal and legal structures, but it is necessary to examine each situation to learn who calls the shots and how often.

Links to the President and Congress

Administrative agencies have various sorts of formal ties to the President and Congress. The President can remove heads of the Cabinet departments at will, but members of independent regulatory agencies, like the Interstate Commerce Commission, can be dismissed only for such specific causes as misuse of their official positions. The Federal Bureau of Investigation is a subdivision of the Justice Department, but its popularity and strong support on Capitol Hill have rendered it quite independent of its nominal superior, the Attorney General, and to some extent even of the President. The Army Corps of Engineers, though officially subject to the Defense Department, enjoys similar independence because of the strong support of localities in which it can create jobs by building bridges, dredging rivers, and granting other favors that also win it independent Congressional backing.

Some executive-branch agencies are corporations owned by the government; one such is the Tennessee Valley Authority, which generates and sells electric power, guards against flooding by means of an intricate system of dams in seven Southeastern states, manufactures fertilizers, and demonstrates good farming practices. Some are service organizations, like the General Services Administration, which performs housekeeping jobs (purchasing, building, storage of equipment) for other agencies. And there are large research organizations such as the National Institutes of Health.

The Civil Service System

Government jobs can be dispensed to serve a number of different purposes. Until late in the nineteenth century, federal jobs were awarded to people who had actively supported victorious political parties and candidates. Jobs were part of the spoils of office; but the spoils system also encouraged people to work for political parties, which play an important part in any government. In 1882 Congress passed the Pendleton Act, which was intended to make ability rather than party or personal loyalty the criterion for choosing federal workers. The Act established a Civil Service Commission to draw up detailed rules and regulations, and Congress gradually extended the merit system to cover more employees. By 1938, 80 percent of all federal employees were covered; in 1940, 95 percent were covered.

The top officials in each agency and those on whom the President relies for general policy advice are not regarded as part of the civil service. They are ordinarily chosen because the President likes their political beliefs or because their appointment to high posts is politically advantageous for the administration—not necessarily because of skill or expertise and certainly not because they score high on a competitive examination. Cabinet secretaries and assistant secretaries, commissioners in the regulatory agencies, top White House aides, ambassadors, and some other leading figures in the executive branch fall into this group.

There have been exceptions to the merit principle. Veterans receive preference for federal employment as a result of lobbying by the American Legion. Some agencies, such as the CIA, are exempt from hiring by civil service criteria because they claim to have special requirements. The National Labor Relations Board, established in the 1930s to prevent employers from interfering with labor unions, was allowed in its early years to discriminate in hiring in favor of people who believed in the principle of union organization. A trend toward more comprehensive application of the merit principle has been apparent, however, even in many state and city governments.

Decisionmaking in Bureaucratic Organizations

Each administrative agency is formally charged with achieving some goal the legislature has decided the people want: regulating public utility rates, assuring that food and drugs are not contaminated, defending the nation, protecting citizens against crime, protecting lakes and air against pollution, helping cities build airports, assuring farmers fair incomes, protecting the interests of Indians, and thousands of comparable objectives. Most of the tasks public administrative organizations undertake involve assembling complicated facts and deciding among the claims of people with diverse personal interests and conflicting values.

Such agencies are organized in a pattern we call "bureaucratic," and are basically similar regardless of field of operation. For one thing, they are *hierarchical,* which means that staff positions are ranked so that occupants of lower positions are formally subject to the authority of those in higher positions. The Army, characterized by ranks running from Commander-in-Chief to private, is an especially clear example of a hierarchy.

The subunits into which a bureaucratic organization is divided are grouped so that each can devote its attention to a given topic and employ a staff qualified to deal with that topic. The Federal Communications Commission, for example, maintains a law department and an engineering department because every application for a broadcasting, telephone, or other communications license involves legal and engineering questions. Sometimes an agency's organization reflects the variety of people or clients with whom it deals; thus a welfare department may have separate subunits for the elderly, children, the handicapped, and so on. Specialization makes it possible to bring together staff members who supposedly have the skills to find the necessary facts and interpret them.

But administrative decisions depend on more than facts. Values—judgments about what is good or bad, desirable or undesirable—also shape choices. It is commonly assumed that the laws an agency administers give it its values and that officials make judgments that will achieve those values in the particular policy areas for which they are responsible.

As an example, consider a typical National Labor Relations Board case in which an employer is charged with having fired a worker for taking an active role in a labor union. The law prohibits such a dismissal as an unfair labor practice. The employer admits firing the worker, but says he did so because he was a poor worker, not because of his union activities. A relatively low-level NLRB employee, called a field examiner, is sent out to find the facts. The field examiner probably interviews the employer, the discharged employee, and other workers; examines the past history of labor relations within the company; compares the work record of the fired employee with those of other workers; and looks into any other evidence he can turn up. He then files a report containing his "findings of fact." Other NLRB offices review the report and add their own comments. If the case is not settled by informal agreement, as are more than 80 percent of unfair labor practice charges, another NLRB official presides over a hearing at which all interested parties testify and are cross-examined. He or she then files a report, including a decision on the legality of the firing. This report is reviewed by the five-man Board, which may uphold it or overturn it. Finally, the Board issues a legally binding finding and order. It may, for example, find that the employer did indeed commit an unfair labor practice and order him to give the worker his job back, with or without retroactive pay. Or it may find that the firing was for incompetence and therefore did not violate the law.

Decisionmaking procedures vary in other kinds of NLRB cases and in other agencies. Some administrative decisions result not in judgments on the rights of particular individuals but in general rules, such as a Department of Agriculture regulation specifying the proportion of adulterated matter allowed in grain intended for export. Both forms of administrative policymaking are based on the interpretation of facts in light of the values of those who make the decisions.

A realistic student of bureaucratic decisionmaking must realize that the values of an agency's staff members influence its policies no matter how high or low they rank in an organization. This is true even when administrators are supposed to limit themselves to finding facts. In the case just discussed, it is impossible for an NLRB field examiner to cast aside his own beliefs about unionism in deciding whether a complex set of acts in a plant amount to anti-union discrimination; his conclusions are presented as facts and are bound to influence higher NLRB officials, who cannot reexamine every complaint themselves. Similarly, decisions by relatively low-level officials in American embassies are usually decisive in determining whether aliens wishing to come to the United States may do so. In making such decisions the officials are supposed to consider the moral character of the applicant and any prior political activity potentially harmful to the United States. Obviously, no one can make such decisions except in the light of his or her own value judgments; and the precedents of many such judgments influence general State Department rules about which aliens may be admitted to America and which must be kept out.

Facts are never completely objective; the values of the people who perceive them shape their meanings. Thus administrative decisionmaking is never the wholly impersonal, expert, professional process bureaucrats often claim it is. The claim itself, however, is a way of mobilizing public opinion to support administrative policies. For example, people dislike paying higher rates for telephone service; but a public utility commission that lets the phone company increase its charges can assume that few citizens will seriously challenge its "findings of fact" about the company's need for higher earnings to cover higher production costs or future investments in equipment.

Though administrative agencies are therefore relatively free from strong pressures by consumers and unorganized clients, they must be responsive to pressures from interest groups whose resources give them political influence. Bureaucrats are in constant contact with the organized groups that have a stake in their policies. Many agency employees either begin their careers in such industries or are later employed by them. A congressional study released in September 1975 shows that 350 officials of federal regulatory agencies had once worked for the industries they were regulating. In the previous five years at least 41 high-level officials had accepted higher-paying jobs in companies they had previously regulated.[2] For these reasons it is only natural that the same goals and values are usually dominant in both the government agencies and the regulated industries, whether they are commercial airlines, television licensees, gas and electricity companies, railroads, or whatever. Such sharing of values and interests will be examined at greater length in the discussion of pressure groups in Chapter 19.

The typical result is that agency staff members come to see issues from the point of view of the groups they are supposed to regulate. It is never clear exactly how much such "regulation" is benefitting consumers and how much it simply authorizes industries to do what they would do anyway, legitimizing their actions with a governmental stamp of approval. Many studies of administrative regulation of business conclude that the second result is more common than the first.

Some bureaucratic organizations are established to help large groups of people who are politically and economically weak, rather than to regulate relatively small groups of people who are politically and economically strong. Welfare departments are set up to help the poor, public hospitals to help the sick, and education departments to help people get educations. The Bureau of Indian Affairs is supposed to protect the Indian population. These agencies do help, but they also *control* the politically powerless, making sure they will not offend the economic interests, morals, and *norms* of the middle class.

Welfare agencies, for example, provide money to some who need it, offer counselling services that may assist people, and help clients find other governmental and private services that might be able to alleviate their problems. Most children acquire a basic education in school. Yet the helping agencies regulate their clients as well. Welfare agencies are under constant pressure from conservatives and groups purporting to represent taxpayers to *limit* the money they give welfare recipients and to pressure them to take jobs, often on terms other workers will not accept. Welfare counselling consists largely of pressure on the poor to adopt middle-class patterns of living, raising children, keeping house, and working industriously. Some schools provide liberating education; but virtually all schools indoctrinate their students to play the social roles that employers, the government, armed forces, and/or the middle class expect of them: to work hard, to be loyal to superiors, and if necessary to sacrifice for the benefit of the state or the corporation. Hospitals and health departments help cure sick people, but in dealing with what they call "mental illness" they also regulate unconventional behavior, especially on the part of poor people, and drug or lock up nonconformists who resist efforts to make them conform.

This is, at least, the view of many critics. That supporters and critics of organizations to help the powerless see them so differently is itself an

<hr>

[2] *Wisconsin State Journal,* 28 September 1975, p. 1.

important political phenomenon: these agencies respond both to the groups they are established to help and to more powerful groups who want to be sure that such help is limited and accompanied by controls on unconventional and uncooperative behavior and rebelliousness. An agency head who is not sufficiently sensitive to such pressures becomes a target of public criticism and of budgetary cuts; he is charged with coddling lazy people who refuse to work or failing to train students for practical work. Here again, the political analyst must be sensitive to the actual effects of administrative actions on people's lives, regardless of the formal goal of the agency in question.

Organizational Effectiveness

Every organization must adjust to the pressure groups concerned about its policies. This fact raises some important questions about administrative agencies' "effectiveness," suggesting that such judgments depend as much on the values of the student or observer of such organizations as they do on the agencies' acts. The Civil Aeronautics Board seems to be fairly effective at protecting the interests of the scheduled airlines, but there is dispute about how much protection it offers the airplane passenger and shipper. Whether it is judged a useful agency depends, therefore, on which of these goals is more important to the observer. In the same way, evaluations of a typical welfare agency depend on the relative importance to the observer of the various policies such an agency enforces. Administrative organizations reflect the values of the more powerful groups in the community, and cannot survive for long if they try to do otherwise.

Bureaucratic organizations fall short of total effectiveness for another reason: they can almost never acquire enough information to make the best possible decision, no matter whose interpretation of "best" is applied. Consider the problem facing the Secret Service, which is charged with protecting the President. Such an objective is much more specific, more widely supported by public opinion, than those of most governmental organizations; thus it ought to be relatively easy to make the necessary policy decisions. But is it? The only way to give the President virtually complete protection from an assassination attempt is to prevent him from appearing in public at all. But all Presidents resist that, and so does much of the public. So the Secret Service must adopt other strategies, all of which involve far more guessing than knowledge. How can people likely to try to shoot the President be identified in advance? How much public support and opposition will there be for detaining such people as a preventive measure when they have not committed any crime? In what cities and situations are assassination attempts most likely? What qualities are most desirable in Secret Service agents? In choosing among strategies, none of which is foolproof, which will minimize public criticism of the agency if it fails? These questions are a sample of those Secret Service policymakers must ask themselves; and they must make policies without ever having definite answers. About complex issues involving economics, military planning, and social policy, the uncertainty is far greater.

Bureaucratic Budgets and Policy Choices: Routines or Reassessments

Officials of any given administrative agency typically take it for granted that in the coming year the agency will continue to do as it has been doing, with minor changes that justify a somewhat higher budget. The previous year's appropriation is almost always the benchmark for deciding how much money the government will spend on the agency's programs. There seldom takes place any reassessment of an established program to determine whether it ought to be drastically expanded, reduced in size, or eliminated entirely. To do so would require time and effort that is seldom available. Furthermore, administrators do not want to challenge the policies that give them their roles, jobs, and senses of accomplishment; and they know that there is rarely any chance of winning executive and legislative support for drastic expansion. At best they can make a case for more funds to handle an increased workload, rising costs, or other relatively small additions—a budgeting strategy known as *incrementalism*.

The interest groups concerned with an agency's field of operations are a known political force with which the agency has established a more or less stable relationship; but some of these groups can be counted on to resist reductions in its program, while others are just as certain to resist expansion of its program. A proposal to halve the budget of the Food and Drug Administration, for example, might be welcomed by drug and food manufacturers, but would quickly elicit charges of a sellout from consumers and the opposition political party. Interest-group concern is therefore another reason why major changes in the scope of an ongoing program are rare. The expedient course for everybody concerned is to treat most budgetary decisions as routine.

That strategy is safe, easy, and almost always adopted, but it is by no means neutral with regard to who gets what. Supporters of incrementalism make the following kind of case for it. First, it is an efficient way of making most decisions because it builds on past decisions; it would be wasteful—in fact, impossible—to reassess past decisions about the importance of each program every year or two. Second, it minimizes conflict. To accept last year's appropriation as generally appropriate means that conflicts over the basic worth of the program are not raised or fought repeatedly. Political argument is limited to marginal issues: whether, for example, the Federal Aviation Agency should be allowed to increase its spending somewhat for the improvement of electronic landing devices at commercial airports. Whether the government *should* be subsidizing commercial airlines by providing them with electronic landing devices is not raised as an issue. Decisions, in short, are made relatively easily, and usually without divisive, bitter, or ideological disputes.

The opponents of incrementalism use the same observations to criticize it. It is, they say, a strategy for ignoring critical political issues while focusing on the relatively trivial ones with which incremental change is concerned. For this reason it is undemocratic and conservative in its consequences, while pretending to be democratic and liberal in its procedures and forms. Incrementalism also makes it likely that ineffective programs will continue and even expand so long as no powerful group has reason to attack them. And budget drafters' systematic focus on minor changes rather than basic programs makes it unlikely that administrators will evaluate their effectiveness either.

Regardless of the opposing arguments, incrementalism continues to be the characteristic strategy of the great majority of programs. The exceptions are chiefly emergency policies, such as those adopted in response to wartime needs, steep inflationary surges, or major depressions.

Even deliberate efforts to abandon the incremental strategy seem to have a way of flickering out. In the middle 1960s, for example, President Lyndon Johnson ordered that a system of evaluating administrative programs called Program Performance Budgeting (PPB) be adopted in all federal agencies. PPB emphasizes evaluation of the contribution of every expenditure to the achievement of specific objectives. It is designed, in short, to force administrative staffs to consider everything they do in a systematic way, rather than relying on routine incremental increases. But within a few years PPB was judged a failure and largely abandoned. It did require agencies to present their budgets in a new form, but the language used to present and justify such budgets changed more than did the agencies' acts or the care with which they assessed their goals and achievements. Here is added evidence that political pressures and values continue to influence administrative policies despite commands from on high.

Conflicts Among Powerful Interests

Agencies sometimes clash with each other over policy. The Department of Labor, for example, is traditionally sensitive to the concerns of unions and of the AFL-CIO leadership; the Department of Commerce, which maintains close ties with the National Association of Manufacturers and the U.S. Chamber of Commerce, can be counted on to reflect the concerns of businessmen. When the President is considering measures to curb inflation, therefore, it can be taken for granted that the Secretary of Commerce will favor effective controls on wages, while the Secretary of Labor will be more sensitive to the political problems arising from the unions' distaste for tight wage controls; but the latter will be more willing than Commerce Department officials to support controls on industrial prices.

The Labor Department can do little to promote unions' interests with regard to many issues of grave concern to workers, because it has no jurisdiction over these issues. In a time of high unemployment, for example, the Department has no power to expand the credit and money supply or otherwise encourage an upturn in business activity that would mean more jobs for the unemployed; and the Federal Reserve Board, which does have such powers, includes no representatives of unions, though the law specifies that industry, banking, and agriculture must be represented on the Board. The Federal Reserve Board is therefore bound to be more sensitive to businesses' and banks' concerns about inflation and decline in the value of the dollar than to workers' concerns about unemployment, especially since the policies that cut unemployment sometimes promote inflation.

An especially dramatic example of infighting between administrative agencies responsive to conflicting interests was the War on Poverty in the 1960s. The Office of Economic Opportunity, established in 1964 to help the poor, was staffed largely by people dedicated to pursuing that goal with considerable zeal. In many cities, agencies established by OEO aroused the opposition of local welfare departments, mayors, and other units of city and county government by bringing legal actions to force the latter to put more people on the welfare rolls and to end long-established policies that allegedly discriminated against the poor. Opponents of OEO eventually succeeded in dismantling some of its programs and transferring others to different agencies.

The Department of Defense

Since World War Two the Defense Department has grown so large that it dominates the federal bureaucracy, is the largest single influence on the American economy, and strongly influences public opinion. In size and influence it is hardly typical of other administrative agencies; but it *is* typical in its hierarchical organization, its close links to private interest groups, and its power to arouse popular fears and hopes.

The Department of Defense employs more than 1.3 million civilians; this figure represents about 40 percent of *all* federal government employees, and substantially more workers than the largest private employer, General Motors, has on its payroll. The Department spends about three-fifths of the budget of the entire executive branch, and additional large military expenditures are made by the CIA, the National Security Agency, the National Aeronautics and Space Administration, and the Atomic Energy Commission. American military spending remained fairly low throughout the nineteenth century; the sizeable increases occurred at the time of the World War One and especially during and after World War Two.

Critics of government spending often pay little attention to the defense budget, concentrating instead on reducing appropriations for such functions as welfare and education. The fact is that a great many federal expenditures represent fixed obligations that cannot be con-

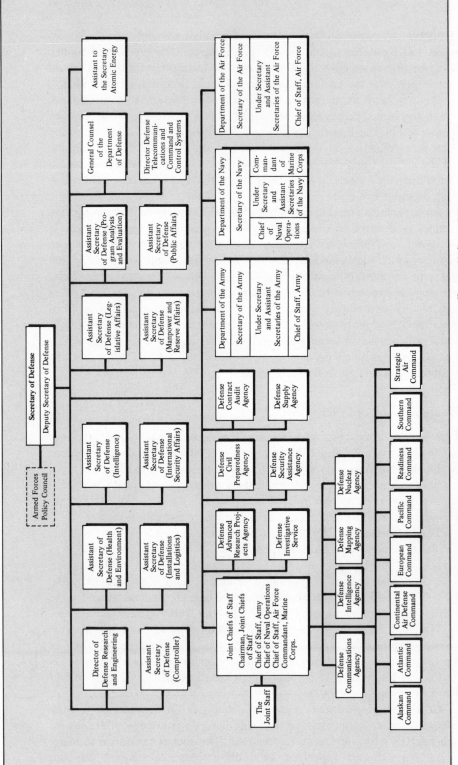

FIGURE 16.2
Department of Defense

Source: United States Government Manual (Washington, D.C.: U.S. Government Printing Office, 1974), p. 151.

trolled or changed. The people who have paid taxes into the social security system all their lives are legally entitled to the benefits they were promised. Interest on the national debt cannot be reduced by failing to appropriate it. If we focus our attention on *controllable* government outlays, it turns out that more than 60 percent of them are military expenditures, as Table 16.2 shows.

In 1947 Congress reorganized the old Departments of War and Navy into a new Department of Defense, though the Secretaries of the Army, Navy, and Air Force remain members of the President's Cabinet along with the Secretary of Defense, who overshadows them.

This organizational change occurred at a time when domestic shifts were also taking place in the nature and frequency of American involvement in wars and in the importance to the American economy of the production of goods for military use. Fear of attack from abroad and preparation for war are, of course, the justification for having a Department of Defense and the basis of popular support for the Department and the armed forces. Since World War Two American involvement in

TABLE 16.2 *The Controllable Portion of the Federal Budget, Fiscal Year 1973 (departmental shares of the controllable budget)*

Department, Agency, or Branch of Federal Government	Percent of Controllable Budget
Defense-Military	62
Health, Education and Welfare	8
Agriculture	5
Treasury	4
Housing and Urban Development	3
Labor	3
Transportation	2
Veterans Administration	2
Commerce	1
Justice	1
State	*
Legislative	*
Judiciary	*
All other	8
Total	100

* Less than 1 percent.

Source: M. L. Weidenbaum and D. Larkins, *The Federal Budget for 1973* (Washington, D.C.: American Enterprise Institute, 1972), p. 52.

wars has been more frequent, and such wars have lasted longer. Equally importantly, the definition of Russia, China, and other foreign countries as ideological threats to the United States has accustomed the American public to the idea of "cold war"—to the belief, that is, that very high levels of armament, tough military postures, resistance to diplomatic concessions, and readiness to go to war at any moment are necessary to prevent a communist takeover of the free world. The Cold War, interrupted by frequent shooting wars and American intervention in wars in various parts of the world, keeps the public anxious and supportive of the large defense budget and gives military considerations a dominant place in the formulation of all governmental policies. The Department constantly publicizes foreign threats, and many charge that it helps create them by frightening potential adversaries into increasing their own military budgets so they will not fall too far behind the United States.

But the influence and policies of the Defense Department cannot be understood only as a response to military threats from abroad. The American economy has come to depend so heavily on military orders that they represent a major influence on economic prosperity and public economic policy. The armed forces annually buy weapons and equipment priced at an average of more than $40 billion dollars, or about 15 percent of the goods manufactured in the United States.[3]

A number of the largest companies depend very heavily, or entirely, on military contracts, and the orders are highly concentrated. In 1971 the 100 largest defense contractors accounted for 72 percent of the defense business.[4] Thousands of smaller firms also depend heavily on subcontracts for military goods; at least 20,000 firms do some manufacturing for the Pentagon.

Some sections of the country are especially dependent for their economic well-being on military orders. The South and California have been especially successful at attracting military orders and military bases, and the Middle West has been least successful at securing military contracts; this configuration may help explain the prominence of Southerners among Pentagon supporters and of Wisconsin Senators and congressmen among Pentagon critics.

Foreign arms sales also cement the bond between the Pentagon and arms manufacturers, for there are both political and economic reasons to expand that trade. To the extent that a foreign country, such as Iran, is dependent on American arms, it becomes a more reliable ally of America. And this political consideration is strengthened by several economic factors. The U.S. economy is increasingly dependent on military exports to improve its balance of trade and to provide a market for

---

[3] Tom Christoffel, David Finklehor, and Dan Gilbarg, *Up Against the American Myth* (New York: Holt, Rinehart, and Winston, 1970).

[4] Murray L. Weidenbaum, *The Economics of Peacetime Defense* (New York: Praeger, 1974), p. 42.

the aerospace industry. The Defense Department itself has a stake in expanding the foreign market because American arms manufacturers can afford to keep more types of weapons in production and to sell them to the Pentagon more cheaply if they can sell the same weapons abroad. Little wonder, then, that U.S. foreign military sales amounted to $9.5 billion in the fiscal year ending 30 June 1975, having jumped from $3.9 billion two years earlier. These sales now account for almost a tenth of all American exports.[5]

Probably the most salient fact of all is that truly awesome amounts of money have been invested in the pursuit of military supremacy: during the decade ending in the mid-1970s, the United States invested more than $800 billion in direct military expenditures. One critic of military spending summarized the situation this way:

> Each year the federal government spends more than 70 cents of every budget dollar on past, present, and future wars. The American people are devoting more resources to the war machine than is spent by all federal, state, and local governments on health and hospitals, education, old-age and retirement benefits, public assistance and relief, unemployment and social security, housing and community development, and the support of agriculture.[6]

The military budget, partly due to continuing inflation and partly because the new weaponry is increasingly expensive, began to exceed $100 billion per year in 1976.

Expenditures of this size cannot help but have powerful effects throughout the economy. For one thing, an entire new industry has been created since the end of World War Two. New companies, some of which do all or nearly all their business with the government, have been created to supply these needs. Fewer than thirty such companies received more than half of all defense dollars awarded in the mid-1970s. The major defense contractors are located in two sections of the country: the aircraft and missile manufacturers and their related subcontractors tend to be centered in the Southwest and Florida, while the electronics industry is chiefly located in the Northeastern states. In 1972, for example, the three states of California, Texas, and Florida received almost 34 percent of all defense expenditures. The five Northeastern states of New York, Connecticut, Massachusetts, New Jersey, and Pennsylvania received almost 20 percent. The other 42 states shared the remaining 37 percent of the defense budget, none of them receiving as much as any one of the five leading companies doing business with the Defense Department. This concentration of expenditures in a few regions means that the impact of defense spending is greatly multiplied in those areas. One estimate holds, for example, that 43 percent of the economy of the Los Angeles area depends on direct defense expenditures and the jobs

[5] Emma Rothschild, "The Boom in the Death Business," *New York Review of Books* 14 (2 October 1975), pp. 7–12.

[6] Richard J. Barnet, *The Economy of Death* (New York: Atheneum, 1970), p. 5.

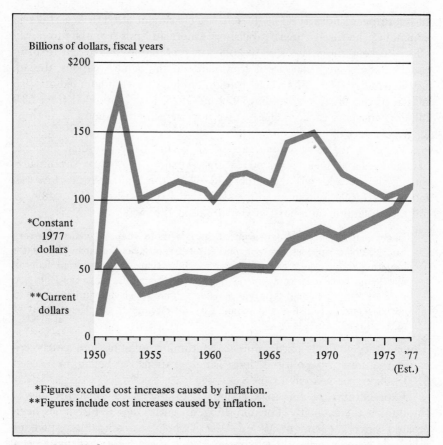

Source: *New York Times*, 22 January 1976. Data from Office of Management and Budget.

FIGURE 16.3

Military Spending: The First Real Increase in Seven Years. Although defense spending has gone up almost steadily in total dollars over the years (bottom line), fiscal 1977 will be the first time in seven years that it will show a real increase by rising faster than inflation (top line).

and other services they generate indirectly.[7] Cutbacks in Boeing's prime contracts in the 1969–1970 period led ultimately to unemployment levels approaching 20 percent in the Seattle area.

Nearly 7 percent of all American workers hold jobs directly dependent on defense expenditures. Probably an equal or larger number owe their jobs to the indirect or "multiplier" effects of this spending. Although many engineers and scientists are included in this work force,

[7] Murray Weidenbaum, "Defense Expenditures and the Domestic Economy," in *Defense, Science, and Public Policy,* ed. Edwin Mansfield (New York: W. W. Norton, 1968), p. 25.

the proportion of blue-collar workers is higher in defense-related industries than in the rest of the American labor force: nearly 10 percent of skilled and production workers in the United States are engaged in defense work.

It is hard to imagine a more solid political base for a governmental organization than the Defense Department. The general public counts on it for security from foreign foes and ideologies, and the Department maintains and intensifies that wide base of support each time it calls attention to a foreign threat, deploys troops to a "danger zone," or justifies a decision to develop a new weapons system. Underlying public opinion of this kind are politically powerful groups with economic incentive to press for a large Defense budget: the largest corporations, the high proportion of the labor force whose jobs depend on military spending, and roughly two-thirds of university researchers. Few members of Congress are in a position to criticize the power generated by such an impressive bureaucracy, and every President in the last quarter-century has made it part of his political appeal to support high levels of defense spending and expansion of Defense Department activities, even in some cases while decreasing federal appropriations for education, health, welfare, and other domestic governmental functions. Dwight Eisenhower, speaking in 1960, was the last President even to warn that dangers might be inherent in the "military-industrial complex" the Defense program has brought into being as a political and economic force. In the face of a bureaucracy whose staff, budget, economic influence, and political power are this large, the notion that administrative agencies only administer policies assigned to them by the Congress and the President becomes untenable. It is probably true enough that most people support the budget and activities of the Defense Department to the extent they are aware of both. But it is also true that such support is largely elicited by the symbolism, public relations activities, and economic clout of the Defense Department itself. And, as was the case during the last four years of the Vietnam War, it is sometimes doubtful that there really is wide public support. Empirical research shows that most Americans opposed the war,[8] though the Nixon Administration continued to claim it was supported by a "silent majority."

Personnel, Personality, and Ideology

The Defense Department and the industries with which it does business constitute a "complex" for still another reason: many key staff members move back and forth between them, working as civilian employees of the Department or officers of the armed forces for part of their careers and as officials of large defense contractors after—or sometimes before—

[8] John E. Mueller, *Wars, Presidents, and Public Opinion* (New York: Wiley, 1973).

their stints in government. A number of Secretaries of Defense, Army, Navy, and Air Force previously worked for major military suppliers. In 1974, 499 former Defense Department employees filed reports declaring that they were employed by major defense contractors.

An even more basic personnel link makes the boundary line between the Defense Department and the defense industry unclear. We noticed earlier that within any organization operating in a controversial policy area the administrative staff tends to share common values and a common ideology: the values and ideology of the outside groups whose interests they reflect. This pattern is especially conspicuous in organizations responsible for military policy, a subject that elicits especially clear and strong ideological differences in the general population.

To take an extreme example, a pacifist is not likely to look for work in the Department of Defense or in a company that manufactures munitions; and an employee of either organization who voices pacifist ideas will soon be made to feel unwelcome and will very likely be fired if he or she does not quit first. In the day-to-day course of a job in the Defense Department (involving, for example, planning military reactions to possible foreign threats; choosing weapons systems; lobbying Congress for higher defense appropriations; ordering equipment for the armed forces; maintaining housekeeping facilities and post exchanges at foreign and domestic military bases; or coordinating plans with the CIA), the bureaucrat's basic commitment to the ideology of military preparedness and the possible need for military solutions to foreign problems is likely to be reinforced. People who work in defense industries, especially at the managerial level, are likely to be sympathetic to the same beliefs; if they were not, they would find it hard to live with themselves and to work industriously at their jobs. The Defense Department is therefore the center of a defense community that reflects the society's concern with military defense and resists criticisms of militarism and of the concentration of power in a military-industrial complex.

For the same reason, the employees of any organization are typically called on to make use only of those skills and forms of thinking that contribute to the achievement of the organization's task. A lawyer for the Defense Department is expected to use his legal skills to make it possible for the Department to do what its top officials want to do, not to criticize them. An Air Force Deputy Secretary for management systems, A. Ernest Fitzgerald, was fired for calling public attention to the contracting procedures by which the Pentagon had paid Lockheed $2 billion more than its initial estimate because costs had skyrocketed. The case was an example of *cost-plus contracting*, an arrangement under which the government pays the costs of manufacturing a product it has ordered plus a fixed profit, regardless of how high the costs turn out to be. This formula clearly rewards inefficiency. The Fitzgerald case illustrates one of the problems of bureaucracy: the pressure on people to play a narrow role in the interests of the organization, even if doing so means

The All-Purpose Cover

Source: *Herblock's* State of the Union (New York: Simon & Schuster, 1972).

making inadequate use of their talents and suppressing their moral qualms. Such pressure is not always present, but it is a constant danger.

Intelligence, Spying, and Underground Operations

Like the Defense Department, the intelligence organizations became a major—and unique—feature of the federal bureaucracy only in the middle decades of the twentieth century. And like the Defense Department, they differ from conventional departments and agencies in their functions, relative freedom from congressional controls, and power.

The Federal Bureau of Investigation (FBI) was created in the Department of Justice after World War One to guard against threats to internal security from criminals and subversive political movements. Its long-time Director, J. Edgar Hoover, achieved an early reputation for incorruptibility and dedication; but the FBI first won general popularity in the 1930s with its dramatic capture of John Dillinger and other colorful desperadoes. Continuous publicity for such operations and for the FBI Director made the Bureau a political force that was virtualy untouchable on Capitol Hill and even by the President. The Cold War and fear of subversion that characterized the 1950s further enhanced the FBI's political influence and budget, which has continued to grow in spite of recent criticisms.

The FBI has been charged with doing little to combat organized crime or white-collar crime, which are far more damaging to the country than the individuals on its widely publicized list of the "Ten Most Wanted Criminals." The Bureau has interfered with the civil rights of lawful dissenters, destroying reputations by reporting unverified rumors to employers and government agencies, taping tapped telephone conversations, and preventing people from exercising their rights of free speech and assembly by making them afraid of FBI harassment. It was learned in 1975 that over a period of 26 years the FBI had illegally broken into several hundred houses in an effort to find evidence of subversion; these burglaries produced almost no evidence of the kind.

For the political observer or critic, such bureaucratic actions pose a question of values. In the minds of people for whom crime and subversion are overriding concerns, an agency that fights these evils deserves support even though it deprives some people of their civil rights. Many also take the position that a national police agency is justified in breaking the law in order to combat others who allegedly break the law. In the minds of those for whom civil liberties and the rights of the individual are overriding concerns, on the other hand, law enforcement as an end does not justify resorting to illegal means, especially when such tactics hurt the innocent and are typically ineffective.

While debate goes on, the FBI has continued to enjoy public, congressional, and presidential support well in excess of that given most agencies. Fear of crime and subversion runs strong and deep, and an organization widely believed to be curbing both is allowed a great deal of moral and legal leeway. Indeed, such an agency must justify its existence by discovering, or even creating, subversives.

Similar fears have given intelligence agencies a role in foreign policy that is even more powerful and independent of congressional control than that of the FBI at home. Congress created the Central Intelligence Agency in 1947 to gather and evaluate foreign intelligence for the President under the direct supervision of the National Security Council (NSC). Almost at once the CIA also undertook actual operations to influence the makeup, policies, and officials of governments in Western Europe, Iran, Guatemala, Greece, Cuba, Laos, Vietnam, and many other countries.

The annual budget for the CIA and for Defense Department intelligence activities is close to 10 billion dollars. With agents in virtually every foreign capital, the CIA gathers information from public sources; operates secretly to buy information; tries to shape the activities of foreign labor, business, student, and other organizations; strengthens some foreign regimes and political parties and weakens others; and influences elections in foreign countries. It has helped overthrow lawfully chosen governments in a number of foreign countries, including Chile,

"It's frightening the way some of these congressmen want to pry into our affairs."

Source: Copyright © 1975 by Herblock in *The Washington Post.*

Iran, and Guatemala, and has been accused of doing so—and even of plotting the assassination of foreign leaders—in many other countries. To accomplish its ends, the CIA has bought influence in foreign newspapers, circulated false rumors to embarrass political figures it opposes, and engaged directly in military operations.

Though the CIA is limited by law to foreign operations, it has for many years illegally spied on Americans at home, maintained files on U.S. citizens, opened their mail, infiltrated protest groups, tapped telephone conversations, and broken into homes.

The CIA is largely free to choose its own activities; there has been little oversight of its operations, and it is doubtful that effective limitations can be imposed on an agency that is allowed to engage in covert activities and to draw on a massive secret budget. The NSC gives the CIA formal instructions, but these inevitably allow for a great deal of discretion. And the same leeway applies within the CIA: former agents allege that even relatively low-level agents sometimes ignore limits and instructions from the Director when they are convinced a given action would be in the national interest.

The CIA's budget is hidden in that of other federal agencies, especially the Defense Department. A "watchdog committee" of congressmen has been able to exercise little surveillance or control, though it does serve as an assurance to the public that somebody is on the alert.

Though the CIA gathers a great deal of information, most of it from public sources, it is impossible to evaluate its overall effectiveness. It failed to learn about the surprise installation of Russian ballistic missiles in Cuba in 1962 until after they were in place, failed to give adequate advance warning of the construction of the Berlin Wall in 1961, failed to warn of the impending outbreak of several wars of serious concern to U.S. interests, and was caught by surprise when a coup overthrew the Portuguese government in 1973. In 1975 the Chairman of the House Select Committee on Intelligence declared that the CIA could not be counted on even to warn against a surprise military attack on the United States, a charge the CIA Director vehemently denied.[9]

As is true of the FBI, people's evaluations of the CIA and other foreign intelligence activities are influenced by their values, fears, and knowledge of the facts. For some, the paramount consideration is the danger of foreign attack and damage to American interests: it happened, they remind us, at Pearl Harbor in 1941. It is argued that the Russian KGB and other foreign intelligence agencies engage in dirty tricks, espionage, and violence, and that such measures can only be fought with similar tactics. Espionage is as old as mankind, and any government that neglected to learn everything it could about foreign threats would be failing in its obligation to its citizens—especially in an era in which nuclear attack, internal subversion, and electronic eavesdropping have vastly increased the stakes in the international power game. The means employed are not always gentlemanly, pleasant, or even legal, but the protection of the country justifies their use. In any case, the argument continues, covert operations account for only a small fraction of CIA activities. Public knowledge and criticism of the CIA keeps the Agency from accomplishing its objectives, and closer surveillance by the congressional watchdog committee, the President, and the National Security Council can be counted on to assure that it acts responsibly.

Different values lead to different fears and a different assessment. People who worry about the accountability of bureaucratic organizations take the view that the CIA is no longer an instrument of the American government people know, elect, and support. In fact, if not in theory, it has become an "invisible government" that is free from effective controls, justifies anything it does in the name of national security, pursues policies that many find highly questionable or odious, and is answerable to nobody. Nor do the results justify this dangerous grant of power. The

[9] *New York Times,* 29 September 1975, p. 1. For some of our data on the CIA, we have relied on Harry Howe Ransom, *The Intelligence Establishment* (Cambridge: Harvard University Press, 1970), and Philip Agee, *Inside the Company: CIA Diary* (Penguin Books, 1975).

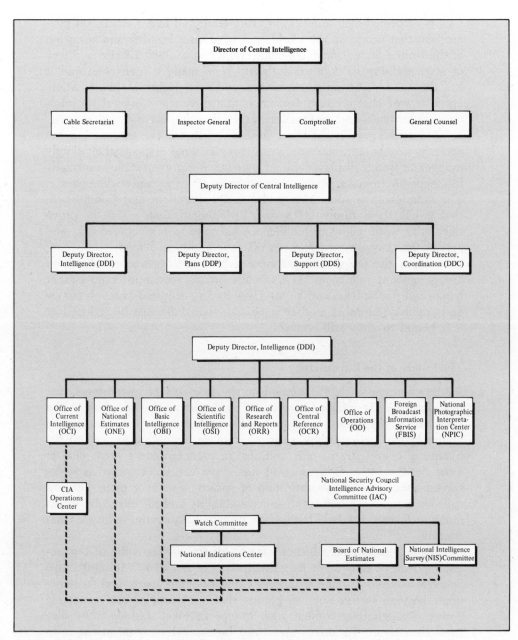

Source: Philip Agee, *CIA Diary* (London: Penguin Books, 1975), Appendix 3.

FIGURE 16.4

Organization of the CIA and the DDI

CIA is suspected of interfering in every coup and major change of government that occurs in the world, and so arouses hostility and suspicion of the United States, making enemies rather than allies. Its size and lack of accountability to political authority have made it ineffective and it has damaged democratic institutions and civil rights at home. Many argue as well that secrecy, espionage, and dirty tricks exacerbate international tensions, and so threaten rather than protect national security.

Regardless which view an observer adheres to, the intelligence agencies are extraordinary organizations. In some respects they simply exaggerate trends displayed by all bureaucratic organizations, especially the tendency to make policy while claiming that they only administer it. The same claim is sometimes useful to the President and Congress, in that it lets them disown CIA and FBI actions that misfire or prove unpopular while allowing intelligence agencies to take covert risks and actions the government could not officially admit or defend.

In sum, the Defense Department and the intelligence establishment are paramount influences on tensions abroad, economic conditions at home, and public fears and hopes. Once having acquired as much money and popular sentiment as they have, can their influence be reduced or is it bound to grow still larger?

The Future of the Bureaucracy

Public attention is chiefly focused on the branches of government that have traditionally wielded power and made the key policy choices: the President, Congress, and the Supreme Court. But day-to-day decisions by administrative organizations seem to have an increasing impact on the quality of every citizen's life, and also to predetermine a great deal of what the President, Congress and the courts can do. Concern is widespread about the bureaucratization of society, and ever more insistent calls are heard for administrative accountability and for means by which individuals can insulate themselves from bureaucratic influence and controls.

Nonetheless, there is little reason to expect any lessening of bureaucratic power or slowing of its growth, short of holocaust. Administrative agencies have to respond to interests that can hurt them, and so sometimes become instruments of groups that wield social and economic power. Though they combat such groups in token fashion, they also strengthen them. To survey American bureaucratic organizations is to identify the centers of power and the interests of Americans with influence; it is also to identify both the cutting edge and the cement of the contemporary governmental process.

PART 5

Institutions
and Processes:
Non-Elite Roles

17

The Political
Context of Non-Elites

The next three chapters deal with issues and relationships that stand in stark contrast to those examined in the last six chapters. Here we deal with *non*-elites, the overwhelming majority of relatively powerless people who have little or no wealth and no institutional positions. What are their lives like? How do their lives affect their beliefs, attitudes, and actions? How and where do the felt needs of non-elites have impact on public policy? In short, what is the meaning—the political implications—of the *context, attitudes,* and *actions* of non-elites?

In a sense, we shall now look at the meaning and consequences of capitalism at the mass level, where before we analyzed the workings of the major power units in the system. Immediately, we face the issues of (1) a satisfactory definition of the concept of social *class,* and (2) the political relevance of class and class consciousness in American politics. Our analysis begins in this chapter with an exploration of the objective conditions of non-elites' lives and certain of their subjective reactions, from which we conclude that many of the requisites of "class" and "class consciousness" are fulfilled in this country. In Chapter 18, we examine the values, ideology, and other attitudes of non-elites, and tentatively conclude that the dominant orthodoxy has diverted attention from objective circumstances and blunted thrusts toward redress of those injustices that are perceived. Finally, in Chapter 19, we analyze the ways in which non-elites seek fulfillment of their perceived needs. For the most part, the orthodox channels—such as political parties—are managed by elites, and non-elites have only limited choices among their offerings. But alternative channels, such as strikes and demonstrations, also influence policy. Although their use is costly, their effects can often be broad and far-reaching.

The overall thesis of these chapters is that (1) non-elite conditions give rise to real and unfulfilled needs, but orthodox values and ideology inhibit recognition of the depth, scope, and shared nature of such needs ("class consciousness"), and diffuse or deflect efforts made to fulfill them; and (2) that the orthodox channels available to non-elites to seek their ends are managed by elites, and tend to absorb non-elites' thrusts or to convert them into harmless or mutually cancelling forms. Thus the *status quo* persists, and non-elites appear to generate little explicit or effective action to change it. Some observers are quick to say that they are satisfied, and that the system has fulfilled all their real wants and needs. Let us examine this question step-by-step.

Social Context and Social Class

What is the political significance of the kinds of lives non-elites lead? In this chapter, we shall try to understand what such lives are like, and how they shape non-elite political ideas and actions. For example, one of our focal points will be the economic status of non-elites. It is sometimes said that non-elites are becoming predominantly affluent and middle-class in income and life style, and that this accounts for the lack of political militance on the part of working and lower classes. The weight of the evidence, however, suggests that non-elite economic status is insecure and marginal, and that we must look elsewhere for explanations of this apparent quiescence. This issue leads to another set of questions: what needs really *do* exist at this level? How fully have non-elite needs actually been satisfied, and what kinds of wants that might be served through public policies still remain unfulfilled?

We shall also be examining the extent to which non-elite life conditions justify conceptualization in class terms, and searching for indications of present or potential class consciousness among such non-elites. In Chapter 11, we saw that the concept of class was meaningful for elites (that is, those who identified themselves as members of the "propertied class"). But the problem of giving concrete meaning to the concept of class in the case of the much larger and less cohesive body of non-elites is much more difficult. If class and class consciousness were found to be realities at this level, of course, the political implications would be vast: a powerful and cohesive force would exist in the American political arena, potentially capable of significant impact on public policy.

Definitions of Class

What do we mean by "class"? There are many definitions, some with long and emotional histories. Each definition carries a particular set of implications. Some refer only to *objective* characteristics of people, such as their income, education, occupational status, or relationship to the means of production (as owners or non-owners). Others define class in *subjective* terms, arguing that classes exist only to the extent that people think of themselves as members of social classes, or are "class-conscious." The first type of definition often amounts to no more than a set of convenient categories in the mind of the observer: such categories frequently have no meaning for the people involved, and thus do not say anything about their real thoughts or actions. The second type of definition suggests that a class can come into existence only if people see themselves in such terms, but does not connect such perceptions to any objective factors in their lives. According to this view, quite casual shared perceptions might be enough to create a "class," or "classes" might never exist; in either case, the concept becomes practically meaningless. In other words, each of these two types of definition requires supplementation by the other before it acquires real utility.

A useful definition of class for purposes of political analysis adds to these two a third dimension—present or potential political power. The concept of class we shall use posits three conditions. First, a number of people are objectively affected in similar ways by some fundamental dynamic of the socioeconomic system. For example, wealth distribution is a fact of life, and it is caused by that fundamental dynamic, the economic system. But the income of professional athletes is not linked to such a structural pattern, and thus does not locate football or basketball players in the upper class.

Second, groups of people develop similar values, attitudes, and orientations toward the world, which are related to the objective conditions of their lives and distinguish them from those outside the group. For example, they have, and understand that they have, certain patterns of access to education, certain probabilities of future income or job levels, and certain cultural experiences or interests, related to amounts of wealth. If these first two conditions are met, a class exists; its members need not be explicitly conscious of how fully they share their particular situation with other people, or of other factors to be noted.

Third, for a class to have real political significance, its members must become aware that they share their situation *and that the reason for their shared status is that they are similarly affected by the same fundamental dynamic of the economic system.* The realization that their status is systematically caused becomes the primary factor in their political orientation. It leads them to define their political goals and mobilize their political power in order to defend or improve their relative positions. No other goals, interests, or loyalties take precedence over the desire to serve the class' needs in this manner. And people must (correctly) believe that political power can be mobilized and applied, so that they are not, and do not see themselves, engaging in an empty or self-deluding exercise.

Political Class Consciousness

The third condition is what we mean by class consciousness in the political sense. It requires four elements: (1) recognition of significant status shared with identifiable others, (2) identification of the systemic cause of this shared status, (3) primary commitment of one's political goals to group action with respect to this status and cause, and (4) perceived access to (real) sources of political power sufficient to make the group an effective force in politics. It is thus possible for a class to exist without class consciousness, though such a class would not have much political significance as an independent force. But it is *not* possible for class consciousness in the real sense to exist without the objective and subjective components of classhood to give it reality and substance. Women will not constitute a class or its equivalent, for example, even if they all become conscious of what they share as women, unless they also perceive such characteristics as the most significant defining forces in their lives, define themselves politically exclusively in such terms, and find and apply political power toward systemic reconstruction.

We shall use this concept of class as a means of analyzing the situation of non-elites and its political potential. If a class exists, of course, there is always the possibility of class consciousness. But many forces intervene between the two phenomena. If such forces are strong enough, and sustained enough, class consciousness may never develop. If conditions contribute to the development of class consciousness, however, dramatic political consequences may follow. One of the continuing arguments in American politics, as we shall see, is over the existence and consciousness of an American "working class." Recently, this debate has centered on the existence of a "new working class" made up of professional, technical, and other higher-level white-collar workers, and students—and on the possibility that such a class might take over the historical role of the working class as an agent of change. Let us begin by simply describing some of the characteristics of non-elite life, and work our way toward these more complex issues.

American affluence is much celebrated and, in aggregate terms, it is real. Per capita gross national product and real income are the highest in the world. Per capita personal income in 1970 was about four times higher than it was in 1900. But these figures represent averages, not actual patterns of distribution. When the actual incomes of all families are examined, it becomes clear that the majority of Americans are either poor or economically marginal—that is, likely to drop into the ranks of the officially poor in the event of a layoff, illness, or accident.

Monetary and Occupational Circumstances

The measurement and exact characterization of economic marginality presents continuing difficulties of definition and data. One method is to compare income levels with the Bureau of Labor Statistics' regularly published family budgets.[1] These are calculated for families of four living in urban areas, and set at "lower," "intermediate," and "higher" levels according to prices of food and other goods and living standards thought to be common or appropriate to families at these levels. The intermediate budget (formerly termed the "modest but adequate" budget), for example, assumes careful shopping, modest apartment rental, and other frugal habits. And yet, at no time since these budgets were first prepared in the mid-1960s has the income of any category of blue-collar worker except certain skilled craftsmen and foremen reached this level. Characteristically, the incomes of nearly all blue-collar and several categories of white-collar workers fall below the "modest but adequate" standard in their cities, sometimes by as much as $2,000 per year. These facts take on added significance when they are related to occupational patterns. Forty-six percent of all employed males in 1974 were in either manual or service work, the typical blue-collar jobs. Nearly 80 percent of all employed women are at these levels or in low-paid clerical or sales positions. Thus, almost half of all employed males and the great majority of employed females earn incomes that do not provide them modest but adequate standards of living. Life is far from affluent at this level, and those whose regular earnings do keep them above this line are faced with the prospect of dropping below it in the event of a recession or other financial reverse.

[1] The basic source of data in this passage is Bureau of Labor Statistics, *Employment and Earnings,* January 1970, p. 67.

Some recurring myths about changes in the American occupational structure and about the identity of those who are poor or economically marginal might well be addressed at this point. Table 17.1 summarizes many of these changes, comparing the proportions of workers in each of the major categories in 1900, 1940, and 1970. It shows clearly, for example, that blue-collar workers are *not* disappearing as a category: the proportion of males in manual work occupations has actually risen since 1900! In 1970 there were only half as many people in the independent, entrepreneurial category of managers, proprietors, and farm owners as in 1900. In other words, more and more people are working for wages and salaries and fewer own their own businesses. Long-term changes have drawn workers away from the farms and toward professional-technical and clerical-sales occupations. Women workers in particular have been concentrated in clerical positions. Black workers, who make up 12 percent of the labor force, are still most numerous in service jobs. They are only slightly disproportionately manual workers.

These data, and other facts about the makeup of the officially poor, demonstrate that both the poor and the economically marginal are predominantly white. The myth that poor means black is simply inaccurate, even though it is both long-lived and probably partly responsible for the lack of effective action to raise the standard of living of people at these levels. Sixty-four percent of *all* employed whites in 1973 were in blue-collar, service, or clerical occupations, and thus earning low incomes. Of the officially poor in the nation as a whole, only 25 percent are black.[2] The figure rises to one-third in metropolitan areas and one-half in central cities, but this means only that the white poor are disproportionately rural. Nor are the poor unemployed: one-third of the heads of families listed as officially poor work full-time, and others work part-time. In other words, most of the poor and the great bulk of the economically marginal are white and hold jobs.

Financial standing is also measurable in terms of accumulated assets and liabilities. Annual surveys that measure both regularly report very limited funds on hand and extensive debts for the purchase of cars and appliances.[3] For example, an average of about 70 percent of all families have less than $500 in checking or savings accounts—and are thus only two or three paychecks away from public assistance of some kind. Installment debts are steadily climbing, and the great majority of all families with incomes under $10,000 have debts requiring regular payments from current earnings.

Many other factors enter into economic and occupational status. A major one is the prospect of unemployment. Manual workers and other lower-paid workers are most likely to be laid off during recessions or to

[2] George Katona, James N. Morgan, Joy Schmiedeskamp, and John A. Sundquist, *1967 Survey of Consumer Finances* (Ann Arbor: University of Michigan, 1967).

[3] Gus Tyler, "White Worker, Blue Mood," Dissent (Winter 1972), p. 190.

TABLE 17.1 Occupations of the U.S. Labor Force (*percentages*)

	1900			1940			1970			
	Male	*Female*	*All*	*Male*	*Female*	*All*	*Male*	*Female*	*All*	*Nonwhite % of all*
Managers, officials, proprietors, farm owners	30	7	26	22	5	18	17	5	13	4
Professional-technical	3	8	4	6	13	8	14	15	14	7
Clerical & sales	7	8	8	12	29	16	13	42	24	7
Service workers	3	36	9	6	29	12	7	22	12	23
Manual workers	38	28	36	46	22	40	47	16	35	14
Farm workers	19	13	18	8	3	7	3	1	2	12
Total	100	100	100	100	100	100	100	100	100	100

Source: Historical Statistics of the United States; Statistical Abstract, 1970. (Figures may not total 100% due to rounding.)

work only intermittently at the best of times. Less educated and less skilled workers, particularly minorities, are likely to be the last hired and the first fired; economic fluctuations thus have exaggerated effects at these levels. Technological change works particular hardship on older workers, who may not be able to find alternative employment for which they are qualified. All workers who suffer intermittent unemployment risk losing such fringe benefits as medical and hospitalization insurance. In most cases, of course, the economic ups and downs of business firms occur for reasons unrelated to workers' efforts or competence, but they nevertheless feel the effects.

Working conditions among the working class and the lower-middle class are also distinctive. In many cases, employment means hard and exhausting physical labor. Some work on an assembly line, where speed is essential and the number of units produced is the measure of income or the criterion of further employment. Loud noise and danger may be constant. For others, safer and more comfortable settings may mean highly routinized, tedious work requiring intense concentration. Nor are white-collar workers insulated against undesirable working conditions: routine work, highly bureaucratized rules and requirements (and, for women, menial and subservient roles) are characteristic of many low-paid positions. For most working-class people, travel conditions also contribute to insecurity and frustration: public transportation systems are crowded, inconvenient, expensive, and time-consuming; but the cost and upkeep of a car may be a serious drain on family income.

Social Circumstances

Despite national affluence, the United States as a whole does not enjoy a particularly high level of social welfare. In many Western nations, for example, family allowances (payments to help support children) are a common means of sharing this financial burden and marginally redistributing income. Most have broader manpower training and reemployment assistance programs than the United States, and none either experience or (apparently) would tolerate the levels of unemployment that are standard in this country.

The general health conditions of Americans are not commensurate with national affluence either, and hardships are concentrated in the lower socioeconomic levels. Americans have lower life expectancies at birth than do the citizens of 15 other nations of the world; infant mortality rates are higher than in 14 countries, and rates of death from a variety of diseases are higher than in several other countries.[4] The lower classes, and particularly blacks, experience a higher incidence of infant

---

[4] U.S. Department of Health, Education, and Welfare, *Toward a Social Report* (Washington: Government Printing Office, 1969), pp. 6–10. The data apply to the mid-1960s.

mortality and higher death rates from infectious disease than do the middle and upper classes. For example, among employed males aged 45–64, those with incomes of less than $2,000 have three-and-a-half times as many disability days as those who earn over $7,000.

People at lower income levels tend not to make use of preventive services or to visit doctors for medical care, no doubt chiefly because of their cost. More than 20 percent of members of families with incomes under $3,000 have *never* visited a dentist, compared to 7 percent of those in families with incomes over $10,000. Fifty-four percent of children under 17 in families with incomes of more than $10,000 had had physical checkups, in contrast to 16 percent of those from families earning less than $2,000. Medical care prices have risen at a rate 50 percent higher than the cost of living in the last decade, and the costs of hospital services have climbed even faster. Medicare covers only about 35 percent of total medical expenses, and then only for those over 65. Nearly half of the remaining population is covered by some form of private health care insurance, but these plans pay, on the average, less than half the costs of medical care. Poor health and its costs, it seems clear, are an acute aspect of lower classes' economic and social circumstances.

The living conditions of the working and lower classes also differ from those enjoyed by the more affluent. The most drastically substandard housing in the country is found in rural settings inhabited chiefly by the poor—and, again, principally by the black poor. Large city neighborhoods are normally crowded, and the cost per square foot of living space is frequently higher than in the suburbs. Blacks in particular have little choice over where they will live, however, as the nation's sharply (and in many cities, increasingly) segregated city ghettos attest.

Moreover, the incidence of crime is far higher in lower-class areas, and particularly in black neighborhoods, than elsewhere. Despite all the concern about crime expressed by middle-class suburbanites, it is the poor—and, again, the black poor—who experience most of the nation's personal crimes. We saw a comparison of the incidence of crime by race and income in Chapter 13. Except for the theft of property, which naturally occurs more often among those who have property, the lower income levels experience more incidents of every kind of crime than do the higher levels. Whether due to the surroundings in which they live or the lack of effective police protection, crime is a condition poor people must live with to a degree unknown to the middle and upper classes.

Mobility Opportunities

We may well ask to what extent real opportunity exists for individual members of the lower classes to escape from these circumstances. Table 17.2 presents an important overall summary of social mobility opportunities in the United States. It uses responses to a U.S. Census Bureau survey to compare the occupations of working-age men with their *fathers'*

TABLE 17.2 *Mobility from Father's Occupation by Race for Civilian Men 25 to 64 Years Old, March 1962 (in percentages)*

Race and fathers occupation	1962 Occupation*						
	Higher white-collar	Lower white-collar	Higher manual	Lower manual	Farm	Not in experienced civilian labor force	Total
Negro							
Higher white-collar	10.4	9.7	19.4	53.0	0.0	7.5	100.
Lower white-collar	14.5	9.1	6.0	69.1	0.0	7.3	100.
Higher manual	8.8	6.8	11.2	64.1	2.8	6.4	100.
Lower manual	8.0	7.0	11.5	63.2	1.8	8.4	100.
Farm	3.1	3.0	6.4	59.8	16.2	11.6	100.
Not reported	2.4	6.5	11.1	65.9	3.1	11.1	100.
Total, percent	5.2	5.4	9.5	62.2	7.7	10.0	100.
Non-Negro							
Higher white-collar	54.3	15.3	11.5	11.9	1.3	5.6	100.
Lower white-collar	45.1	18.3	13.5	14.6	1.5	7.1	100.
Higher manual	28.1	11.8	27.9	24.0	1.0	7.3	100.
Lower manual	21.3	11.5	22.5	36.0	1.7	6.9	100.
Farm	16.5	7.0	19.8	28.8	20.4	7.5	100.
Not reported	26.0	10.3	21.0	32.5	3.9	6.4	100.
Total, percent	28.6	11.3	20.2	26.2	6.8	6.9	100.

* Combinations of major occupation groups. *Higher white-collar:* professional and kindred workers, and managers, officials, and proprietors, except farm. *Lower white-collar:* sales, clerical, and kindred workers. *Higher manual:* craftsmen, foremen, and kindred workers. *Lower manual:* operatives and kindred workers, service workers, and laborers, except farm. *Farm:* farmers and farm managers, farm laborers, and foremen. Classification by "father's occupation" includes some men reporting on the occupation of a family head other than the father.

Source: Unpublished tables, survey of "Occupational Changes in a Generation."

Reprinted from U.S. Department of Health, Education and Welfare, *Toward a Social Report* (Washington: Government Printing Office, 1969), p. 24.

357

What Does It Mean? The Subjective Side of Non-Elite Life

occupations, as a means of measuring relative improvement or decline in status. The left-hand column lists fathers' race and occupations, and the horizontal rows represent the respondents' present occupations. In general, white children tend to remain in the same occupations and status levels as their fathers. Today's higher white-collar jobs are filled by people whose fathers had similar jobs. For whites, however, there is some net upward mobility. For example, 36 percent of whites whose fathers were in the "lower manual" occupations are themselves in the same category; but 23 percent have moved up to the "higher manual" level, and 21.3 percent of such children have attained high white-collar status.

But for blacks, there is much heavier initial concentration in the lower occupations, less mobility, and little retention of higher status once gained. Children of lower-manual fathers move up at much lower rates than do whites; children of higher white-collar fathers tend to *drop back* into the lower manual category! In analyzing these data, of course, we must keep in mind that the general structure of employment in the nation has shifted toward white-collar jobs and away from those classified here as lower manual or farm. Thus, some of this apparent "mobility" is due to broad structural changes and not to the relative striving and achievement of individuals. This realization leads to the sobering conclusion that mobility for lower-status people has been modest at best, and for blacks practically nonexistent.

These aspects of the socioeconomic situation of the great majority of American people are the context of their political behavior. Economic hardships and insecurity are constant; it takes very substantial effort to maintain existing levels of income and status, and prodigious effort or good fortune to move ahead. There is a substantial lack of health and medical services, educational opportunities, neighborhood and work-place amenities, and protection against crime. What is taken for granted at middle-class levels does not exist for the majority of the population.

The political implications are several. Unfulfilled needs exist, and might be satisfied by elite action or by non-elite mobilization. But non-elites have very little time readily available for political action; the demands of daily living tend to exhaust both time and psychic and physical resources. And a number of external barriers, some already examined and others to be discussed shortly, operate to discourage or deflect mass assertion of group demands. Finally, there is no way of knowing that mass goals would be attainable even if a concerted effort were made, and good reason for predicting that they might well be denied.

What Does It Mean? The Subjective Side of Non-Elite Life

The preceding brief characterization of the major socioeconomic facts of non-elite life is only part of the story. It says nothing about the feelings of people at this level about their lives, their jobs, and their prospects. And the latter may be more crucial to the actual life styles and potential class consciousness of such people than are the bare facts of income and job status. Let us turn from data analysis to listen to a steelworker talking about his job and his world. This excerpt is from a collection of similar interviews with ordinary people conducted by a Chicago journalist. What are the political implications of Mike LeFevre's view of the world? In what ways is he class-conscious?

Mike LeFevre

It is a two-flat dwelling, somewhere in Cicero, on the outskirts of Chicago. He is thirty-seven. He works in a steel mill. On occasion, his wife Carol works as a waitress in a neighborhood restaurant; otherwise, she is at home, caring for their two small children, a girl and a boy.

At the time of my first visit, a sculpted statuette of Mother and Child was on the floor, head severed from body. He laughed softly as he indicated his three-year-old daughter: "She Doctor Spock'd it."

I'm a dying breed. A laborer. Strictly muscle work ... pick it up, put it down, pick it up, put it down. We handle between forty and fifty thousand pounds of steel a day. (Laughs) I know this is hard to believe—from four hundred pounds to three- and four-pound pieces. It's dying.

You can't take pride any more. You remember when a guy could point to a house he built, how many logs he stacked. He built it and he was proud of it. I don't really think I could be proud if a contractor built a home for me. I would be tempted to get in there and kick the carpenter in the ass (laughs), and take the saw away from him. 'Cause I would have to be part of it, you know.

It's hard to take pride in a bridge you're never gonna cross, in a door you're never gonna open. You're mass-producing things and you never see the end result of it. (Muses) I worked for a trucker one time. And I got this tiny satisfaction when I loaded a truck. At least I could see the truck depart loaded. In a steel mill, forget it. You don't see where nothing goes.

I got chewed out by my foreman once. He said, "Mike, you're a good worker but you have a bad attitude." My attitude is that I don't get excited about my job. I do my work but I don't say whoopee-doo. The day I get excited about my job is the day I go to a head shrinker. How are you gonna get excited about pullin' steel? How are you gonna get excited when you're tired and want to sit down?

It's not just the work. Somebody built the pyramids. Somebody's going to build something. Pyramids, Empire State Building—these things just don't happen. There's hard work behind it. I would like to see a building, say, the Empire State, I would like to see on one side of it a foot-wide strip from top to bottom with

359

What Does It Means? The Subjective Side of Non-Elite Life

the name of every bricklayer, the name of every electrician, with all the names. So when a guy walked by, he could take his son and say, "See, that's me over there on the forty-fifth floor. I put the steel beam in." Picasso can point to a painting. What can I point to? A writer can point to a book. Everybody should have something to point to.

It's the non-recognition by other people. To say a woman is *just* a housewife is degrading, right? Okay. *Just* a housewife. It's also degrading to say *just* a laborer. The difference is that a man goes out and maybe gets smashed.

When I was single, I could quit, just split. I wandered all over the country. You worked just enough to get a poke, money in your pocket. Now I'm married and I got two kids . . . (trails off). I worked on a truck dock one time and I was single. The foreman came over and he grabbed my shoulder, kind of gave me a shove. I punched him and knocked him off the dock. I said, "Leave me alone. I'm doing my work, just stay away from me, just don't give me the with-the-hands business."

Hell, if you whip a damn mule he might kick you. Stay out of my way, that's all. Working is bad enough, don't bug me. I would rather work my ass off for eight hours a day with nobody watching me than five minutes with a guy watching me. Who you gonna sock? You can't sock General Motors, you can't sock anybody in Washington, you can't sock a system.

A mule, an old mule, that's the way I feel. Oh, yeah. See. (Shows black and blue marks on arms and legs, burns.) You know what I heard from more than one guy at work? "If my kid wants to work in a factory, I am going to kick the hell out of him." I want my kid to be an effete snob. Yeah, mm-hmm. (Laughs.) I want him to be able to quote Walt Whitman, to be proud of it.

If you can't improve yourself, you improve your posterity. Otherwise life isn't worth nothing. You might as well go back to the cave and stay there. I'm sure the first caveman who went over the hill to see what was on the other side— I don't think he went there wholly out of curiosity. He went there because he wanted to get his son out of the cave. Just the same way I want to send my kid to college.

I work so damn hard and want to come home and sit down and lay around. *But I gotta get it out.* I want to be able to turn around to somebody and say, "Hey, fuck you." You know? (Laughs.) The guy sitting next to me on the bus too. 'Cause all day I wanted to tell my foreman to go fuck himself, but I can't.

So I find a guy in a tavern. To tell him that. And he tells me too. I've been in brawls. He's punching me and I'm punching him, because we actually want to punch somebody else. The most that'll happen is the bartender will bar us from the tavern. But at work, you lose your job.

This one foreman I've got, he's a kid. He's a college graduate. He thinks he's better than everybody else. He was chewing me out and I was saying, "Yeah, yeah, yeah." He said, "What do you mean, yeah, yeah, yeah. Yes, *sir*." I told him, "Who the hell are you, Hitler? What is this *"Yes, sir"* bullshit? I came here to work, I didn't come here to crawl. There's a fuckin' difference." One word led to another and I lost.

I got broke down to a lower grade and lost twenty-five cents an hour, which is a hell of a lot. It amounts to about ten dollars a week. He came over—after breaking me down. The guy comes over and smiles at me. I blew up. He didn't know it, but he was about two seconds and two feet away from a hospital. I said, "Stay the fuck away from me." He was just about to say something and was pointing his finger. I just reached my hand up and just grabbed his finger and I just put it back in his pocket. He walked away. I grabbed his finger because I'm married. If I'd a been single, I'd a grabbed his head. That's the difference.

You're doing this manual labor and you know that technology can do it. (Laughs.) Let's face it, a machine can do the work of a man; otherwise they wouldn't have space probes. Why can we send a rocket ship that's unmanned and yet send a man in a steel mill to do a mule's work?

Automation? Depends how it's applied. It frightens me if it puts me out on the street. It doesn't frighten me if it shortens my work week. You read that little thing: what are you going to do when this computer replaces you? Blow up computers. (Laughs.) Really. Blow up computers. I'll be goddamned if a computer is gonna eat before I do! I want milk for my kids and beer for me. Machines can either liberate man or enslave 'im, because they're pretty neutral. It's man who has the bias to put the thing one place or another.

If I had a twenty-hour work-week, I'd get to know my kids better, my wife better. Some kid invited me to go on a college campus. On a Saturday. It was summertime. Hell, if I have a choice of taking my wife and kids to a picnic or going to a college campus, it's gonna be the picnic. But if I worked a twenty-hour week, I could go do both. Don't you think with that extra twenty hours people could really expand? Who's to say? There are some people in factories just by force of circumstance. I'm just like the colored people. Potential Einsteins don't have to be white. They could be in cotton fields, they could be in factories.

The twenty-hour week is a possibility today. The intellectuals, they always say there are potential Lord Byrons, Walt Whitmans, Roosevelts, Picassos working in construction or steel mills or factories. But I don't think they believe it. I think what they're afraid of is the potential Hitlers and Stalins that are there too. The people in power fear the leisure man. Not just the United States. Russia's the same way.

What do you think would happen in this country if, for one year, they experimented and gave everybody a twenty-hour week? How do they know that the guy who digs Wallace today doesn't try to resurrect Hitler tomorrow? Or the guy who is mildly disturbed at pollution doesn't decide to go to General Motors and shit on the guy's desk? You can become a fanatic if you had the time. The whole thing is time. That is, I think, one reason rich kids tend to be fanatic about politics: they have time. Time, that's the important thing.

It isn't that the average working guy is dumb. He's tired, that's all. I picked up a book on chess one time. That thing laid in the drawer for two or three weeks, you're too tired. During the weekends you want to take your kids out. You don't want to sit there and the kid comes up: "Daddy, can I go to the park?" You got your nose in a book? Forget it.

I know a guy fifty-seven years old. Know what he tells me? "Mike, I'm old and tired *all* the time." The first thing happens at work: when the arms start

361

What Does It Mean? The Subjective Side of Non-Elite Life

moving, the brain stops. I punch in about ten minutes to seven in the morning. I say hello to a couple of guys I like, I kid around with them. One guy says good morning to you and you say good morning. To another guy you say fuck you. The guy you say fuck you to is your friend.

I put on my hard hat, change into my safety shoes, put on my safety glasses, go to the bonderizer. It's the thing I work on. They rake the metal, they wash it, they dip it in a paint solution, and we take it off. Put it on, take it off, put it on, take it off, put it on, take it off . . .

I say hello to everybody but my boss. At seven it starts. My arms get tired about the first half-hour. After that, they don't get tired any more until maybe the last half-hour at the end of the day. I work from seven to three thirty. My arms are tired at seven thirty and they're tired at three o'clock. I hope to God I never get broke in, because I always want my arms to be tired at seven thirty and three o'clock. (Laughs.) 'Cause that's when I know that there's a beginning and there's an end. That I'm not brainwashed. In between, I don't even try to think.

If I were to put you in front of a dock and I pulled up a skid in front of you with fifty hundred-pound sacks of potatoes and there are fifty more skids just like it, and this is what you're gonna do all day, what would you think about— potatoes? Unless a guy's a nut, he never thinks about work or talks about it. Maybe about baseball or about getting drunk the other night or he got laid or he didn't get laid. I'd say one out of a hundred will actually get excited about work.

Why is it that the communists always say they're for the workingman, and as soon as they set up a country, you got guys singing to tractors? They're singing about how they love the factory. That's where I couldn't buy communism. It's the intellectuals' utopia, not mine. I cannot picture myself singing to a tractor, I just can't. (Laughs.) Or singing to steel. (Singsongs.) Oh whoop-dee-doo, I'm at the bonderizer, oh how I love this heavy steel. No thanks. Never hoppen.

Oh yeah, I daydream. I fantasize about a sexy blond in Miami who's got my union dues. (Laughs.) I think of the head of the union the way I think of the head of my company. Living it up. I think of February in Miami. Warm weather, a place to lay in. When I hear a college kid say, "I'm oppressed," I don't believe him. You know what I'd like to do for one year? Live like a college kid. Just for one year. I'd love to. Wow! (Whispers) Wow! Sports car! Marijuana! (Laughs.) Wild, sexy broads. I'd love that, hell yes, I would.

Somebody has to do this work. If my kid ever goes to college, I just want him to have a little respect, to realize that his dad is one of those somebodies. This is why even on—(muses) yeah, I guess, sure—on the black thing . . . (Sighs heavily.) I can't really hate the colored fella that's working with me all day. The black intellectual I got no respect for. The white intellectual I got no use for. I got no use for the black militant who's gonna scream three hundred years of slavery to me while I'm busting my ass. You know what I mean? (Laughs.) I have one answer for that guy: go see Rockefeller. See Harriman. Don't bother me. We're in the same cotton field. So just don't bug me. (Laughs.)

After work I usually stop off at a tavern. Cold beer. Cold beer right away. When I was single, I used to go into hillbilly bars, get in a lot of brawls. Just to explode. I got a thing on my arm here (indicates scar). I got slapped with a bicycle chain. Oh, wow! (Softly) Mmm. I'm getting older. (Laughs.) I don't explode as much. You might say I'm broken in. (Quickly) No, I'll never be broken in. (Sighs.) When you get a little older, you exchange the words. When you're younger, you exchange the blows.

When I get home, I argue with my wife a little bit. Turn on TV, get mad at the news. (Laughs.) I don't even watch the news that much. I watch Jackie Gleason. I look for any alternative to the ten o'clock news. I don't want to go to bed angry. Don't hit a man with anything heavy at five o'clock. He just can't be bothered. This is his time to relax. The heaviest thing he wants is what his wife has to tell him.

When I come home, know what I do for the first twenty minutes? Fake it. I put on a smile. I got a kid three years old. Sometimes she says, "Daddy, where've you been?" I say, "Work." I could have told her I'd been in Disneyland. What's work to a three-year-old kid? If I feel bad, I can't take it out on the kids. Kids are born innocent of everything but birth. You can't take it out on your wife either. This is why you go to a tavern. You want to release it there rather than do it at home. What does an actor do when he's got a bad movie? I got a bad movie every day.

I don't even need the alarm clock to get up in the morning. I can go out drinking all night, fall asleep at four, and bam! I'm up at six—no matter what I do. (Laughs.) It's a pseudo-death, more or less. Your whole system is paralyzed and you give all the appearance of death. It's an ingrown clock. It's a thing you just get used to. The hours differ. It depends. Sometimes my wife wants to do something crazy like play five hundred rummy or put a puzzle together. It could be midnight, could be ten o'clock, could be nine thirty.

What do you do weekends?

Drink beer, read a book. See that one? *Violence in America*. It's one of them studies from Washington. One of them committees they're always appointing. A thing like that I read on a weekend. But during the weekdays, gee . . . I just thought about it. I don't do that much reading from Monday through Friday. Unless it's a horny book. I'll read it at work and go home and do my homework. (Laughs.) That's what the guys at the plant call it—homework. (Laughs.) Sometimes my wife works on Saturday and I drink beer at the tavern.

I went out drinking with one guy, oh, a long time ago. A college boy. He was working where I work now. Always preaching to me about how you need violence to change the system and all that garbage. We went into a hillbilly joint. Some guy there, I didn't know him from Adam, he said, "You think you're smart." I said, "What's your pleasure?" (Laughs.) He said, "My pleasure's to kick your ass." I told him I really can't be bothered. He said, "What're you, chicken?" I said, "No, I just don't want to be bothered." He came over and said something to me again. I said, "I don't beat women, drunks, or fools. Now leave me alone."

The guy called his brother over. This college boy that was with me, he came nudging my arm, "Mike, let's get out of here." I said, "What are you worried

363

What Does It Means? The Subjective Side of Non-Elite Life

about?" (Laughs.) This isn't unusual. People will bug you. You fend it off as much as you can with your mouth and when you can't, you punch the guy out.

It was close to closing time and we stayed. We could have left, but when you go into a place to have a beer and a guy challenges you—if you expect to go in that place again, you don't leave. If you have to fight the guy, you fight.

I got just outside the door and one of these guys jumped on me and grabbed me around the neck. I grabbed his arm and flung him against the wall. I grabbed him here (indicates throat), and jiggled his head against the wall quite a few times. He kind of slid down a little bit. This guy who said he was his brother took a swing at me with a garrison belt. He just missed and hit the wall. I'm looking around for my junior Stalin (laughs), who loves violence and everything. He's gone. Split. (Laughs.) Next day I see him at work. I couldn't get mad at him, he's a baby.

He saw a book in my back pocket one time and he was amazed. He walked up to me and he said, "You read?" I said, "What do you mean, I read?" He said, "All these dummies read the sports pages around here. What are you doing with a book?" I got pissed off at the kid right away. I said, "What do you mean, all these dummies? Don't knock a man who's paying somebody else's way through college." He was a nineteen-year-old effete snob.

Yet you want your kid to be an effete snob?

Yes. I want my kid to look at me and say, "Dad, you're a nice guy, but you're a fuckin' dummy." Hell yes, I want my kid to tell me that he's not gonna be like me . . .

If I were hiring people to work, I'd try naturally to pay them a decent wage. I'd try to find out their first names, their last names, keep the company as small as possible, so I could personalize the whole thing. All I would ask a man is a handshake, see you in the morning. No applications, nothing. I wouldn't be interested in the guy's past. Nobody ever checks the pedigree on a mule, do they? But they do on a man. Can you picture walking up to a mule and saying, "I'd like to know who his granddaddy was?"

I'd like to run a combination bookstore and tavern. (Laughs.) I would like to have a place where college kids come and a steelworker could sit down and talk. Where a workingman could not be ashamed of Walt Whitman and where a college professor could not be ashamed that he painted his house over the weekend.

If a carpenter built a cabin for poets, I think the least the poets owe the carpenter is just three or four one-liners on the wall. A little plaque: Though we labor with our minds, this place we can relax in was built by someone who can work with his hands. And his work is as noble as ours. I think the poet owes something to the guy who builds the cabin for him.

I don't think of Monday. You know what I'm thinking about on Sunday night? Next Sunday. If you work real hard, you think of a perpetual vacation. Not perpetual sleep . . . What do I think of on a Sunday night? Lord, I wish the fuck I could do something else for a living.

I don't know who the guy is who said there is nothing sweeter than an un-finished symphony. Like an unfinished painting and an unfinished poem. If he creates this thing one day—let's say, Michelangelo's Sistine Chapel. It took him a long time to do this, this beautiful work of art. But what if he had to create this Sistine Chapel a thousand times a year? Don't you think that would even dull Michelangelo's mind? Or if da Vinci had to draw his anatomical charts thirty, forty, fifty, sixty, eighty, ninety, a hundred times a day? Don't you think that would even bore da Vinci?

Way back, you spoke of the guys who built the pyramids, not the pharaohs, the unknowns. You put yourself in their category?

Yes. I want my signature on 'em, too. Sometimes, out of pure meanness, when I make something, I put a little dent in it. I like to do something to make it really unique. Hit it with a hammer. I deliberately fuck it up to see if it'll get by, just so I can say I did it. It could be anything. Let me put it this way: I think God invented the dodo bird so when we get up there we could tell Him, "Don't you ever make mistakes?" and He'd say, "Sure, look." (Laughs.) I'd like to make my imprint. My dodo bird. A mistake, *mine.* Let's say the whole building is nothing but red bricks. I'd like to have just the black one or the white one or the purple one. Deliberately fuck up.

This is gonna sound square, but my kid is my imprint. He's my freedom. There's a line in one of Hemingway's books. I think it's from *For Whom the Bell Tolls.* They're behind the enemy lines, somewhere in Spain, and she's pregnant. She wants to stay with him. He tells her no. He says, "if you die, I die," knowing he's gonna die. But if you go, I go. Know what I mean? The mystics call it the brass bowl. Continuum. You know what I mean? This is why I work. Every time I see a young guy walk by with a shirt and tie and dressed up real sharp, I'm lookin' at my kid, you know? That's it.

Mike LeFevre has said a great deal, both implicitly and explicitly, about his feelings toward work and life—probably more effectively than any collection of surveys could. Most of his basic reactions and attitudes are widely shared, according to a number of recent studies. Almost all of his feelings have political significance, but we shall defer analysis of his most explicitly political attitudes until we have reviewed reactions to work among today's blue-collar workers.

To begin with, Mike is not alone in finding little meaning in his work. His fruitless search for pride in his work and his compensatory insistence on self-respect are paralleled by the feelings of other manual and assembly-line workers. In a national survey conducted in 1969 by the

365

What Does It Means? The Subjective Side of Non-Elite Life

Michigan Survey Research Center,[5] for example, workers ranked "having interesting work" first among all their job-related desires. Three other dimensions of work-pride (enough help and equipment to do a good job, enough information to get the job done, and enough authority to do the job) were ranked above "good pay." Levels of job satisfaction are also indicated by the data in Table 17.3, which shows the proportions of vari-

TABLE 17.3 *Proportions in Various Occupations Who Would Choose Same Kind of Work If Beginning Career Again*

Professional Occupations	Per- cent	Working-class Occupations	Per- cent
Mathematicians	91	Skilled printers	52
Physicists	89	Paper workers	52
Biologists	89	Skilled automobile workers	41
Chemists	86	Skilled steelworkers	41
Lawyers	83	Textile workers	31
Journalists	82	Unskilled steelworkers	21
White-collar workers, cross section	43	Unskilled automobile workers	16

Source: Work in America: Report of a Special Task Force to the Secretary of Health, Education, and Welfare (Cambridge: MIT Press, 1972), p. 16.

ous kinds of workers who would choose the same work if they could begin their careers again.

Such working conditions, and workers' resulting dissatisfaction with them, can hardly fail to carry over to life outside of work. Mike LeFevre's sense of being trapped by marriage and children, his frustrations, and his occasional outbursts of violence are clearly linked to his work. The same is true of other workers, though their outlets may take a wide variety of forms. Sabotage is commonplace in some large plants; sometimes it is organized, but often it is simply the result of private resentment against speed-up, monotony, and harsh work. Here is one worker's description of quitting time at an auto plant:

> With a feeling of release after hours of monotonous work, gangs of workers move out from the side aisles into the main aisles, pushing along, shouting, laughing, knocking each other around—heading for the fresh air on the outside. The women sometimes put their arms around the guards at the gates, flirting with them and drawing their attention away from the men who scurry from the plant with distributors, spark plugs, carburetors,

[5] Neil Q. Herrick, "Who's Unhappy at Work and Why," *Manpower* 4 (January 1972), p. 3.

even a head here and there under their coats—bursting with laughter as they move out into the cool night. Especially in the summers, the nights come alive at quitting time with the energy of release: the squealing of tires out of the parking lot, racing each other and dragging up and down the streets. Beer in coolers stored in trunks is not uncommon and leads to spontaneous parties, wrestling, brawling, and laughter that spills over into the parks and streets around the factory. There is that simple joy of hearing your voice loudly and clearly for the first time in 10 or 12 hours.[6]

Neither Mike nor other workers want their children to spend their lives at similar jobs, or indeed in a factory of any kind. Although Mike himself has little respect for college graduates, he sees education as a route of escape for his children. He wants them to enjoy whatever it is that the higher-ups in society have, such as self-confidence in the plastic surroundings of the Playboy Club.

Mike's reactions are shown to be valid on a nationwide basis by the Michigan survey mentioned above.[7] Of a national sample of *all* categories of workers, *one out of every four workers under thirty* expressed dissatisfaction with his or her work situation. The proportions dropped with age, but a total of 17 percent of all blue-collar workers and 13 percent of all white-collar workers expressed such dissatisfaction. Young black workers were the least satisfied, and workers in retail and service jobs were also highly dissatisfied. Among many of the most dissatisfied groups, negative attitudes carried over into their lives generally; nearly 25 percent of those with grade-school educations, in service jobs, or in low income brackets expressed dissatisfaction with their lives as a whole.

Analysis of this pattern of dissatisfaction with work yields some further findings relevant for our purposes. There was no difference between blue-collar and white-collar workers in the under-thirty group: in both cases, 24 percent declared themselves dissatisfied with their work. Nor did college education make a difference at this age level: those with degrees were just as likely to be dissatisfied as those with only limited education. This suggests that job dissatisfaction is not just a blue-collar phenomenon, but a growing characteristic of younger workers in all kinds of jobs. And mere income does not seem likely to make people much happier: the kinds of satisfactions sought tend to be related to the quality of work rather than its wage levels.

Elements of Class and Class Consciousness

Not only socioeconomic characteristics—the objective conditions of life—distinguish Mike LeFevre from more advantaged

---

[6] Bill Watson, "Counter-Planning on the Shop Floor,' *Radical America* 5 (May–June 1971), p. 7.

[7] Herrick, *op. cit.*

Americans. He clearly has a subjective sense of "we-they," of the "average working guy" (with whom he sees himself having much in common) versus more favored people in the society. He has no difficulty seeing a hierarchy of status superiors above him. But he does not believe that their relative status is a product of innate superiority. Instead, he considers people similar in intelligence and capabilities (and, presumably, in other human qualities as well) as distinguished only by their relative opportunities. He insists, for example, that only lack of time distinguishes working people from rich people intellectually and politically. His own conversation supports his outlook; he has literary awareness, historical sense, and political insight. In sum, he believes his status and that of others like him to be due to the workings of *social structure*—the larger system, and the lack of opportunity it provides for such people—and not to their *personal attributes* or shortcomings.

This is an important element in our analysis of the extent of class and class consciousness. If people see themselves at the bottom, in relatively less favored situations, *along with other people and because of characteristics of the socioeconomic system rather than through their own personal faults,* we have the beginnings of potential class consciousness. No national data exist on this matter, but some useful findings are available from a study of a midwestern city in the late 1960s.[8] People of different races and income levels were asked a series of questions about why the rich were rich and the poor poor. Table 17.4 shows the proportions of each group that attributed such differences to personal characteristics (individual strengths or weaknesses) rather than to the social structure. Rich people, it is clear, believe that personal qualities account for their wealth and others' poverty. They are more likely to believe that being on relief is due to personal failings, and that the poor don't work as hard and don't want to get ahead, than are poor or middle-income people. The poor, and particularly the black poor, are much more likely to attribute their status to nonpersonal or structural factors. The accuracy of this judgment is less important for our purposes than is its prevalence—for the latter phenomenon is the root of class and class consciousness as we have defined them.

Nor are such interpretations dependent entirely on the *proportions* in which the respective groups give particular answers. Qualitative statements confirm their significance. The authors of the study, for example, report a rich man explaining why the rich are rich and the poor poor: "... If you have to generalize, it's the self-discipline to accumulate capital and later to use that capital effectively and intelligently to make income and wealth." On the other hand, a poor black is quoted as saying in answer to the same question, "The rich stole, beat, and took. The poor

---

[8] Joan Huber (Rytina), William H. Form, and John Pease, "Income and Stratification Ideology: Beliefs About the American Opportunity Structure," *American Journal of Sociology* 75 (Chicago: University of Chicago Press, January 1970), p. 713.

TABLE 17.4 *Personal Attributes as a Cause of Income by Income and Race*
(*in percentages*)

Income and Race	Wealth (a)	Poverty (b)	Being on Relief Last Six Years (c)	Poor Don't Work as Hard (d)	Poor Don't Want to Get ahead (e)
Poor					
Black	17	17	28	3	0
White	34	30	46	13	19
Middle					
Black	29	19	45	4	6
White	35	41	59	30	29
Rich					
White	72	62	78	39	46
Total, analytic sample					
%	37	36	54	21	23
N	(350)	(341)	(347)	(343)	(347)
Total, systematic sample					
%	31	40	57	25	25
N	(183)	(177)	(185)	(186)	(180)

The percentages in the wealth column represent those who saw favorable traits as a "cause" of wealth; in the poverty columns, those who saw unfavorable traits as a "cause" of poverty. In columns (d) and (e), the percentages are those agreeing with the statements indicated.

Source: Huber (Rytina), Form, and Pease, "Income and Stratification Ideology."

didn't start stealing in time, and what they stole, it didn't value nothing, and they were caught with that." [9] That difference, we suggest, is the essence of class consciousness.

Views of Power Distribution

Another way of exploring the extent and character of class-grounded thinking is to look at people's images of power distribution within the society. Mike LeFevre has a clear sense that a few people on top control things, and that they are afraid of the people like him down below. He acknowledges that there may be grounds for that fear, but makes obvious his own distaste for rule by self-selected intellectuals. Similar atti-

[9] *Ibid.*

tudes are often expressed by workers at this level. In a study made in the 1960s of skilled and semi-skilled auto plant workers in New Jersey, Lewis Lipsitz found that all categories of workers shared images of vast power disparities in the society, and saw key initiative as in the hands of big business.[10] They believed that power was used exploitatively, and exclusively for purposes of maximizing profit, in the context of a society devoted to profitmaking. They also saw government and the mass media manipulating people, partly in the interests of business but also in keeping with the "inherent" selfishness of human nature.

A somewhat more systematic impression of attitudes toward the distribution of power in the United States can be obtained from the survey of a midwestern city noted earlier.[11] In this inquiry, people were given three "models" of power distribution from which to select. One was pluralism, the view that power is widely dispersed and that shifting coalitions of groups and individuals shape the outcome of governmental decisions in each issue area. Another was the elitist model, which holds that a continuing coalition of the same families, corporations, and interests makes most basic decisions and orchestrates popular acceptance of them. The last model was derived from the Marxist image of a ruling class, and termed "economic dominance." According to it, the biggest owners and stockholders control all decisions, either directly or through their agents.

Table 17.5 shows the responses, broken down by educational levels. There is, of course, a close correlation between educational level and income, and so to an extent both factors are represented here. Given that the pluralist image is a major ingredient in the orthodox American ideology, it is significant that the proportion who subscribe to it drops sharply with educational level. Moreover, the least educated people are the most likely to hold the Marxist ruling-class view; this outlook becomes less prevalent as the level of education rises, until only 8 percent of college graduates profess it. Does this pattern suggest that the less educated (who are also the lowest in income) have such views for class-grounded reasons? Or is it just that they have been exposed to less education—or, perhaps, less indoctrination? In any case, their outlook is distinct from that of the better educated, wealthier people—and that is what counts for our purposes.

It appears that we have identified at least the outlines of class and the beginnings of class consciousness among American non-elites. Their lives share systematically caused characteristics. The life situations, opportunities for mobility, and access to amenities of people at this level

---

[10] Lewis Lipsitz, "Work Life and Political Attitudes: A Study of Manual Workers," in *The White Majority: Between Poverty and Affluence,* ed. Louise Kapp Howe (New York: Random House, 1970), pp. 160–162.

[11] William H. Form and Joan Huber (Rytina), "Ideological Beliefs on the Distribution of Power in the United States," *American Sociological Review* 34 (January 1969), p. 23.

TABLE 17.5 *Selection of Societal Models of Power Distribution, by Years of Education* (*in percentages*)

Years of education	Models of Power Distribution			Total	
	Economic dominance	Elitist	Pluralist	%	(N)
0–7	40	26	33	99	(42)
8–11	28	16	57	101	(141)
12–15	14	19	67	100	(108)
16 or more	8	20	73	101	(40)
Total %	22	19	59	100	(331)
Total (N)	(74)	(62)	(195)		

Source: Form and Huber (Rytina), "Ideological Beliefs on the Distribution of Power."

are simply not what they are for people at the top of the socioeconomic pyramid. Values and basic subjective reactions appear to be similiar: Mike LeFevre is not isolated or unique, but typical of a large segment of Americans. He and others like him see themselves as *down here,* below the few people *up there,* because of the social system and not because of personal talent, effort, or qualifications.

A New Militancy

How does the "new working class" thesis accord with these tentative findings? The thesis holds that changes in the occupational structure of American life from manual and service jobs toward professional and technical employment, coupled with the growing middle-class attainments of the formerly lowest echelons, have drained the traditional working class of its militancy and created a new grouping of better educated people who must now be recognized as the principal agent of social change. In effect, this argument says that thrusts toward change must now grow out of the rejection by middle-class (and relatively affluent) people of materialism and acquisitiveness. It is perceived as a kind of revolt of the intelligentsia, in which the young and better-educated may lead the way to new standards and practices for all.

Several facts support this thesis. Table 17.1 showed a distinct reduction in the proportions of people who are self-employed, and a commensurate rise in the numbers and proportions of people who work for others. These people do not have much control over the conditions of their work, and may thus be resentful of their job situations. Professional and technical employment has risen substantially, from 3 percent of the labor force to 13 percent. The greatest increase in all job categories has occurred in government services—particularly among teachers, office workers, and other semi-professional white-collar workers. It is also true that many white-collar jobs are poorly paid. It is no longer possible to rank all white-collar jobs above all blue-collar jobs in terms of income potential; many skilled blue-collar jobs pay more than routine office work, and are more satisfying as well. The data we examined on job dissatisfaction showed that as large a proportion of young white-collar as young blue-collar workers were unhappy with their work.

But only the last of these findings even begins to address the key subjective dimension. The real question is whether, in the context of American orthodoxy, such middle-class and relatively affluent people can and will develop a sense of shared deprivation—fundamental, systemically caused—equivalent to class consciousness. Individualism is probably stronger at this level than at higher and lower levels, where class feelings have historically been more potent. It will be very difficult for such people to submerge their individualism in favor of shared class sensitivity.

In the meantime, it seems too soon to dismiss the traditional working class as a potential force for change. The manual worker has not disappeared, although the proportions of skilled workers are increasing. Blue-collar workers are still the largest single group in the society, and they are for the most part poor or economically marginal. If the "new working class" has political significance at this point, it appears to be because it is becoming more like the working class—and not the reverse. The pay levels and standards of living of most of this group are dropping, and have been since at least 1966. Inflation is rising, taxes are increasing, and little has been done to ease the burden on either blue- or white-collar lower-middle- or working-class people.

But again, the basic issue is the extent to which people see their fundamental interests as shared and their plight as systemically caused, and commit themselves to seeking remedies as a group. And it is at this point that the dominant orthodoxy enters in. Let us turn now to the meaning of that ideology as it finds expression in the attitudes of non-elites.

18

The Political
Attitudes of Non-Elites

In this chapter, we shall first examine some of the American people's most basic beliefs and attitudes, and how Americans compare with some other peoples in their attitudes toward government. We shall see close ties with the pattern of class-related beliefs noted in the last chapter. Confidence in government, and indeed in established leaders in most areas of life, has been declining in the past decade. Government has done little to provide for basic needs and wants. And yet most people still believe in the orthodox values, and want also to believe in and defend their government.

The second focus of this chapter will be an attempt to understand this ambivalence—this mixture of dissatisfaction and apparent support for the *status quo*. We shall see that channels of communication are dominated by elites, and that in many respects people have to depend on cues from above before they can respond to events. The Vietnam War was a classic case of the slow process of attitude change, and we shall trace the combination of dependence on elites and reaction to events as it gradually undermined orthodox support for the government. In the final section, we shall examine some of the major trends of opinion in the middle and late 1970s.

Basic Attitudes: Wants and Needs

In analyzing the political attitudes of such a large group of people, we must be sensitive to several principles of interpretation. Although opinion polling is a sound social science tool, its users must exercise care. The form of the question is important, for it may shape answers in several ways. For example, a long checklist of possible answers may result in the impression that people have many strong opinions. A "free-answer" question, which requires the respondent to come up with his or her own answer, may come closer to measuring real knowledge and concerns. Behind this caution lie some even more important facts about the distribution of opinion in a heterogeneous society. People differ greatly in the subjects about which they are concerned, the information they possess, and the intensity with which they hold preferences about particular subjects or issues. In many cases these differentials reflect the relevance of an issue to matters of personal or economic interest to the respondent. This is another way of saying that attitudes are often related to respondents' class status, race, religion, occupation, place of residence, ideology, and/or political party identification. Some issues appear to touch people primarily in terms of their income, occupation, and education. Others seem to activate loyalties or perceptions along racial or religious lines. Sometimes the same issue strikes different people differently, some seeing it as a simple matter of group economic benefit while others understand it as a question of religious or ideological principle.

On any given subject, therefore, there may be wide variations in interest, information, and preferences—with conflicts of opinion existing not only between groups but also within the same individuals. Further, opinion may shift over time, sometimes steadily as events or campaigns bring new facts or interpretations into focus, sometimes sharply after a single dramatic event or governmental action. Understanding complex and fluid opinion in detail at any given moment may be very difficult or even impossible. But it is not difficult at all to identify and describe the enduring values and attitudes that form the basic structure of non-elite political beliefs. Semipermanent assumptions and preferences are what we examine here. Similarly, we shall point out some consistent features of subgroup attitudes (such as the higher levels of information and support for government among the more educated) as occasions arise.

Some basic wants and needs are so fundamental that they barely change over time. For example, in nearly three decades of polling Americans on their personal hopes and fears, the same two responses regularly prevail. The two dominant personal hopes are good health for oneself and a better standard of living; the two dominant fears are ill health and a lower standard of living. War and peace usually rank next in each sequence. When the question is phrased in terms of hopes and fears for the country as a whole, war and peace far outdistance all others. Only economic stability ever challenges these responses.

These basic concerns seem to underlie broad support for governmental action in the social welfare field. Since responsible public opinion surveying began in the 1930s, large majorities have favored the basic social security and social assistance programs that were ultimately enacted. Public support often preceded enactment by several years or even decades, as in the case of medical care. The federal social welfare programs of the 1960s enjoyed no less support, two-thirds of the population favoring most aspects of the poverty program, aid to education, housing, the reduction of unemployment, and so forth. There can be little doubt about the strength of public demand and support for these "welfare state" policies.

But this desire for government to be of service in coping with the problems of daily living in an industrial society does not transcend some basic practical and ideological limits. Nearly equal majorities say that taxes are too high, and the lower income levels are usually most resistant to taxation. The latter fact is sometimes cited as an inconsistency on the part of those who are the probable beneficiaries of much of the social legislation to be funded by such taxes. But it may represent an insistence that those who can better afford the burden of taxation should carry a larger share.

An interesting example of the enduring strength of the work ethic, a central element of the American value structure, may be seen in attitudes toward government's role in assuring adequate incomes. When talk of income maintenance plans, negative income taxes, and guaranteed annual wages became prevalent in early 1969, a national sample was asked their views on a governmental guarantee of at least $3,200 per family per year. In the same survey, respondents were asked their reactions to the idea that government should guarantee enough *work* to assure a family at least $3,200 a year. The questions were posed consecutively, so that respondents did not have to choose between them. Nevertheless, their answers show clearly that people seek only governmental assistance to enable them to do what they feel they should do—that is, work. Table 18.1 presents the totals which range from nearly two-thirds majority rejection of the guaranteed income plan to nearly two-fifths majority support for guaranteed work. If previous experience holds true, however, support for guaranteed income plans will rise as their desira-

TABLE 18.1　*Attitudes Toward Guaranteed Income and Work, 1969*
　　　　　　　(*in percents*)

	Income			Work		
	Favor	*Oppose*	*No opinion*	*Favor*	*Oppose*	*No opinion*
National	32	62	6	79	16	5
Education						
College	26	71	3	75	23	2
High School	31	64	5	77	18	5
Grade School	40	50	10	83	9	8
Occupation						
Professional						
and business	26	68	4	75	20	5
White collar	26	66	8	80	17	3
Farmers	21	74	5	73	23	4
Manual	36	58	6	82	14	4
Income						
Over $10,000	24	72	4	76	16	8
Over $7,000	27	69	4	78	15	7
$5–6,99	33	62	5	81	14	5
$3–4,999	40	54	6	77	17	6
Under $3,000	43	44	13	77	11	12

Source: Gallup Opinion Weekly (January 1969), pp. 20–21.

bility is publicly argued and people become more familiar with them. Assuming governmental support for and eventual enactment of such a program, public support would probably reach majority levels by the time it went into effect and continue climbing thereafter.

The distribution of support for these two types of programs is also significant. The divisions reflect differences of class, rather than race, region, religion, age, or sex. Lower-status persons tended to be more supportive of both, which is understandable (and consistently true for almost every piece of social legislation that is proposed). But not even manual workers, or those earning under $3,000 per year at the time of the survey, gave majority support to the guaranteed income. Even those who stood to gain immediate economic benefits preferred work to an assured income without work. It seems clear that the work-ethic aspect of traditional American ideology is still viable, even at the lowest levels of the economic order.

When the public's attention is drawn to its hopes and fears for the United States as a nation, war and peace far outdistance all other issues.

Only in times of economic instability, when economic anxieties vie with this dominant preoccupation, is its status challenged. People also generally believe the national government should be spending much less money on defense, space exploration, and foreign economic and military aid; however, this finding may be attributable to the previously noted resistance to taxation, and simply represent a preference for funds to be used to solve domestic problems.

Thus we see that people *do* have wants and needs, particularly with regard to health and social welfare, and that they want their government to help them to provide them. People are far from satisfied with their living conditions or the performance of their government. In a subtle and revealing study of 82 poor men in a Southern city, Lewis Lipsitz sought to probe these grievances in greater depth than is possible in national surveys. He found that, of those who thought the government spent too much money, 79 percent identified the space program, military expenditures, or foreign aid as projects for which too much was spent, and *none* named domestic welfare programs. Conversely, of those who thought that government was not spending enough money, only 5 percent said that more should be spent for space exploration, the military, or foreign aid, while 95 percent thought that domestic welfare programs should receive more funds. Summing up his analysis, Lipsitz concludes:

> ... The dominant theme is the sense of being cheated: one's government is not concerned enough with one's well-being; one's government is willing to spend money on what appear to many of these men as frivolous or illegitimate enterprises while it fails to meet their own deeply felt day-to-day needs.
>
> In keeping with this sense of deprivation, we also found a desire among the poor for some sort of assistance from the government, and a series of dissatisfactions with the kind of work the government was engaged in .... we should acknowledge that poor people have many grievances concerning both what the government does and does not do ...[1]

Lipsitz adds that, in his view, one of the reasons such grievances are not expressed more forcefully in politics is that political activists do not always take them up—that is, the elites who frame grievances into issues have not been concerned with these matters. Nor do poor people with grievances necessarily know how to carry them into the political arena by themselves, Lipsitz argues.

The American View and Others

We can gain some perspective on the nature of American orientations toward politics and government by comparing them with the views of

[1] Lewis Lipsitz, "On Political Belief: The Grievances of the Poor," in *Power and Community: Dissenting Essays in Political Science,* ed. Philip Green and Sanford Levinson (New York: Random House, 1970), pp. 165–167.

other populations toward their governments. Such a comparison was made in the mid-1960s in a five-nation study by Gabriel Almond and Sidney Verba, entitled *The Civic Culture*.[2] This analysis explores the orientations of samples of the general population in the United States, the United Kingdom, West Germany, Italy, and Mexico. The extent to which Americans are distinctive in their conviction that their political institutions are right and good is evident in Table 18.2. Whether as a

TABLE 18.2   *Aspects of Nation in Which People Take Pride*

Percentage who say they are proud of:	U.S.	U.K.	Germany	Italy	Mexico
Governmental, political institutions	85	46	7	3	30
Social legislation	13	18	6	1	2
Position in international affairs	5	11	5	2	3
Economic system	23	10	33	3	24
Characteristics of people	7	18	36	11	15
Spiritual virtues and religion	3	1	3	6	8
Contributions to the arts	1	6	11	16	9
Contributions to science	3	7	12	3	1
Physical attributes of country	5	10	17	25	22
Nothing or don't know	4	10	15	27	16
Other	9	11	3	21	14
Total % of responses*	158	148	148	118	144
Total % of respondents	100	100	100	100	100
Total number of cases	970	963	955	995	1,007

* Percentages exceed one hundred because of multiple responses.

Source: Almond and Verba, *The Civic Culture*, p. 64.

consequence of political ideology or not, Americans professed pride in the Constitution, political freedom, democracy, and similar items much more often than respondents in other nations. Although Americans were proud of their economic system, Germans outdid them in this respect. On the other hand, Americans were distinctively unlikely to volunteer answers having to do with the arts, sciences, or attributes of the country's environment.

Americans also felt more engaged in the continuing political processes

[2] Gabriel Almond and Sidney Verba, *The Civic Culture* (Princeton, N.J.: Princeton University Press, 1963). Reprinted by permission of Princeton University Press.

of their country, and drew more satisfaction from voting. Given the criteria employed for measuring the "democraticness" of the political values and expectations of the population, the United States emerged ahead of the other four nations. Great Britain did frequently equal or exceed the United States in some categories. Some of these responses may be only reflections of dominant ideology. In some cases not encompassed by such ideology, both Germans and Britons saw more democratic conditions in their countries than Americans did in theirs. Table 18.3 compares the five nations' population samples' expectations of "serious consideration for your point of view" when dealing with either administrative officials or police. Americans, it is clear, are less confident of such treatment than either Britons or Germans; the differences with respect to Great Britain are particularly sharp. Also of interest is the fact that Americans manifested a class-based variation in expectations of consideration for one's point of view. Those with some university education have more confidence in receiving consideration than do those with less education. In Britain, by contrast, higher proportions of the least educated respondents expected consideration from the police than did people with university educations.[3]

We should note immediately that these surveys were conducted in the early 1960s, and that events and circumstances since that time might have caused changes in these beliefs. But we doubt that, on such a fundamental question as the general legitimacy of one's society's institutions, much relative change would occur. Instead, we think that we are beginning to get at the underlying ambivalence of most Americans—dissatisfaction with the government's performance, coupled with a desire to believe in and be proud of those very institutions. Let us continue inquiry along these lines, in the larger context of the opinion-forming and -changing process.

Key Characteristics of the Opinion Process

We know that Americans have a variety of attitudes and beliefs that more or less add up to an orthodoxy. What we are interested in here is the way in which these basic beliefs (unevenly distributed among different strata of the population, as we have seen) *interact* with events, perceptions, and experiences to generate a *process* of attitude formation and change that has political importance. We shall examine some characteristics of the way in which people learn about events, and then try to explore the ambivalence generated as existing ideology and media-communicated cues interact with peoples' feelings.

One image of the communications process is that the media keep citizens informed and enable them to exercise influence over public

[3] *Ibid.*, p. 73.

TABLE 18.3 **Consideration Expected from Bureaucrats and Police, by Nation**

If you explained your point of view to the officials (police), what effect do you think it would have? Would they give your point of view serious consideration, would they pay only a little attention, or would they ignore what you had to say?

Percentage who expect:	U.S.		U.K.		Germany		Italy		Mexico	
	bureauc.	*pol.*	*bureauc.*	*pol.*	*bureauc.*	*pol.*	*bureauc.*	*pol.*	*bureauc.*	*pol.*
Serious consideration for point of view	48	56	59	74	53	59	35	35	14	12
A little attention	31	22	22	13	18	11	15	13	48	46
To be ignored	6	11	5	5	5	4	11	12	27	29
Depends	11	9	10	6	15	13	21	20	6	7
Other	0	—	—	—	1	2	6	6	—	1
Don't know	4	2	2	1	8	11	12	14	3	4
Total percentage	100	100	98	99	100	100	100	100	98	99
Total number	970	970	963	963	955	955	995	995	1,007	1,007

Source: Almond and Verba, *The Civic Culture,* p. 72.

policy. Another is that the media are a means by which elites derive support for their actions. There are ways in which the first image is correct, of course. Without information from newspapers, magazines, radio, and television, most people would have little chance of exercising influence on government at all, or even of knowing when an issue of concern to them arises.

At the same time, studies of opinion formation and opinion change point unmistakably to a number of mechanisms through which mass publics are placed at a disadvantage and subjected to both deliberate and unconscious influence by elites.[4] First, a substantial proportion of the people have relatively little interest in news of public affairs and do not especially try to expose themselves to it. One study, which questioned people about their knowledge and opinions on eight different public issues, found that from 22 percent to 55 percent of the population, depending on the issue, either had no opinion or had one but did not know what the government was doing.[5] Also relevant is the finding that much political information is "retailed" by opinion leaders to large audiences. Such a two-step flow of messages in the media gives elites, who are somewhat better educated and have somewhat higher status than the recipients of the messages, a disproportionate influence.[6]

Influence of the Media

People get most of their political information from television and radio stations that rely chiefly on a few networks to supply their news programs and from newspapers that rely heavily on a few wire services. Understandably, there is concern both about the possibility of mass manipulation and about the concentration of influence. As the late A. J. Liebling once remarked, "To have freedom of the press, you have to own one."

On this issue, as on others we discuss, different levels of analysis yield somewhat different conclusions. Many of the major studies of mass communications conclude that the media can have only limited effect on opinions regarding political issues.[7] The human mind is not a blank slate on which those who control the media can write whatever they like. Female secretaries who are demeaned in the office will not be impressed

[4] Philip E. Converse, "The Nature of Belief Systems in Mass Publics," in *Ideology and Discontent*, ed. David Apter (New York: Free Press, 1964), pp. 206–61; see also Robert E. Lane and David O. Sears, *Public Opinion* (Englewood Cliffs, N.J.: Prentice-Hall, 1964), pp. 57–71.

[5] Lane and Sears, *Public Opinion*, pp. 59–60.

[6] Elihu Katz and Paul Lazarsfeld, *Personal Influence* (New York: Free Press, 1955).

[7] Some studies that emphasize this conclusion are: David O. Sears and Richard E. Whitney, *Political Persuasion* (Morristown, New Jersey: General Learning Press, 1973); Lee Becker *et al.*, "The Development of Political Cognitions" in Steven H. Chaffee (ed.), *Political Communication* (Beverly Hills: Sage, 1975), pp. 21–64; Joseph T. Klapper, *The Effects of Mass Communication* (New York: Free Press, 1960).

by a television program proclaiming that the feminist movement has dramatically improved the status of women. A dedicated Republican is unlikely to change his vote even if he sees a Democratic spot commercial repeatedly. People's loyalties to other fellow workers, their professions, their ideologies, their political parties, their religions, and their other beliefs are often stronger than the persuasive power of political rhetoric or drama. Studies of election campaigns typically find that they change the voting intentions of a relatively small proportion of the electorate (though that may be enough to change the result).

At another level, however, the mass media do have substantial effects: by publicizing and legitimizing established institutions, including the major political parties; by justifying inequalities in power; and by predetermining the political issues that people will regard as important. In other words, the very stability in opinion that some studies see as *limiting* the effects of the media is itself a significant result of media influence.

Those who want to influence the public go to great lengths to win media coverage for their points of view. The kidnapping of political figures and other violent actions of political dissenters are a dramatic way of ensuring media attention to their grievances. Opposition groups see desperate measures of this sort as sometimes necessary to win public notice, largely because the media so consistently reflect the positions of officials and other elites.[8]

In election campaigns, media attention is similarly prized, and it is won increasingly by the efforts of professional campaign management firms who contrive impressions, events, and the candidates' personalities when they can. Most people, especially those with relatively low incomes and limited education, get most of their news from television. A recent study concluded that television news teaches viewers little about the issues and has no effect on voters' images of the candidates; but the same study found that viewers do learn about the issues from television commercials, including spot commercials, which therefore encourage rational voting.[9] Another study concluded that the 1976 television debates between the presidential candidates also contributed to informed and issue-related voting.[10] These findings were based on interviews with voters. Some critics do not accept either the findings or the authors' interpretations.

Some other studies of the media analyze their long-term and more subtle effects, and raise some questions about the findings just discussed. Television does have considerable influence on which issues people discuss and worry about, as Table 18.4 makes clear. They therefore also

---

[8] This point is discussed on pp. 308–309.

[9] Thomas E. Patterson and Robert D. McClure, *The Unseeing Eye* (New York: Putnam, 1976).

[10] Jack Dennis, "Impact of the Debates upon Partisan, Image and Issue Voting," in Sidney Kraus (ed.), *The Great Debates 1976: Ford versus Carter* (Bloomington: Indiana University Press, forthcoming 1979).

TABLE 18.4   *Responses to Three Salience Measures: Fall 1974*

	Issue important personally	Issue talked about most	Issue in the news
Inflation	68	67	63
Watergate	8	8	21
Other	24	24	17
Total (n = 339)	100%	99%	101%

Source: Steven H. Chaffee (ed.), *Political Communication* (Beverly Hills: Sage, 1975), p. 45.

Note. Respondents could select only one issue for each measure.

influence which issues people forget or ignore. While crises, economic and social problems, and scandals are always in the news, the class distinctions and chronic inequalities in wealth and power that produce probblems and crises are not likely to be. The media play an important part in perpetuating established conditions by shaping people's consciousness about what is inevitable, what is fair, who are meritorious, and who are incompetent or immoral. This result is not usually consciously planned and it is not wholly effective; but it may well be the most important impact of the media in the second half of the twentieth century.

a few striking black advances in employment or housing shape people's thinking even if the cases are not typical.

Public Simplification of Issues

Because controversial public issues are typically highly complex, and it is hard or impossible to sort out causes and effects, people have to simplify them in order to think about them at all. Thus such issues come to be perceived in terms of a metaphor or a simple model. Urban riots may be attributed to outside agitators who stir up basically satisfied blacks in the ghettos. Or they may be viewed as the actions of aggrieved poor people finally demanding through militance and violence what they deserved long before. Political speeches and public policies help shape the particular simplified view that people adopt, and so do newspaper and television reports. Once a person adopts a metaphor to define a complex situation, he or she tends to fit later developments into the same mold and to see them as offering further support for the view already adopted. People have to make some sense of complicated and threatening situations, and so they perceive selectively in order to bolster the view that serves some emotional function and reassures them.

When people are anxious and have no way to be sure what will help and what will hurt, they are especially willing—even eager—to receive and believe cues from authoritative political leaders that alleviate their doubts and their fears. This is exactly the situation that usually prevails in many fields of public policymaking. Typically, citizens who see a great deal of unemployment around them and fear it will increase do not know how to restore prosperity. They are therefore eager to believe that the President of the United States and the economists on whom the President depends for advice *do* know. It is relatively easy in such a situation for a President to win popular support for spending, credit, or public employment policies that he says will solve the problem.

Similarly, citizens must rely very heavily for their beliefs on what the government tells them about the friendly or hostile intentions of foreign governments. And the existence of regulatory commissions to protect consumers against unfair prices or other unfair business or labor practices serves to reassure people that they are in fact protected. They have no direct way of learning what prices or rates are fair and whether the business firms with which they must deal are making excessive profits or exploiting them in other ways. Ambiguity about what is fact and what is fair is characteristic of the complicated issues with which government deals. Thus the susceptibility of mass publics to the influence of leaders is all the greater.

But there are also forces operating in precisely the opposite direction. The upheavals of the 1960s, followed by Watergate and other revelations of the 1970s, have apparently initiated a period of profound transformation in the underlying values of the American people. For one thing, confidence in the leaders of most social institutions and occupations is dropping. Table 18.5 documents this trend, and reveals that it is broadly applicable to almost all aspects of American society.

Ambivalence re-emerges, however, when people are asked whether others should be allowed to criticize the government. Perhaps this finding is attributable to hope that if criticism is muted, problems will disappear —or to adherence to traditional values and virtues *because* they appear so threatened and the future so uncertain. In any event, a study conducted in 1970 found that the majority of a cross-section of Americans believe people should not be allowed to publish books "attacking our system of government." The margin was 53 percent to 35 percent, a clear majority. The same sample voted against allowing people to make "speeches against God" by a margin of 62 percent to 32 percent.[11]

The best way to make sense of the conflicting trends in contemporary non-elite attitudes is to see the United States as a nation in transition. Substantial value change is taking place, many traditional beliefs are being modified, and people feel threatened. Consequently, they try to hold on to something, and adapt only partially or in stages to new values and beliefs as they become clearer and firmer. As ideology conflicts with perceived needs or visible changes, however, contradictions develop and behavior may take on diversionary, violent, or unusual forms. Let us look at examples of each of these parts of the process.

[11] W. Cody Wilson, "Belief in Freedom of Speech and Press," *Journal of Social Issues* 31, no. 2 (1975), p. 71.

TABLE 18.5 *Confidence in Leaders of Social Institutions (in percentages)*

Institution	1966	1971	1974
Medicine	72	61	50
Military	62	27	33
Education°	61	37	40
Major U.S. Companies	55	27	21
U.S. Supreme Court	51	23	40
Congress	42	19	18
Organized Religion	41	27	32
Federal Executive Branch	41	23	28
Press	29	18	25
Television†	25	22	31
Organized Labor	22	14	18

Note. Question: "How much confidence do you feel in the people who are running [institution]: a great deal, only some, or hardly any?" Entries are percentages responding "a great deal."

° For 1974 the question specified "colleges."

† This question was asked about television news.

Source: Hazel Erskine and Richard L. Siegel, "Civil Liberties and the American Public," *Journal of Social Issues* 31, no. 2 (1975), p. 23. Notes in the original.

The Basic Ideology

One interesting illustration of the tension between felt needs and received ideology is provided by Lloyd Free and Hadley Cantril, professional students of American opinion, in a major book entitled *The Political Beliefs of Americans.*[12] Using the responses of a national cross-section to a series of questions in 1964, they constructed two "spectrums" of opinion. One, called the "operational" spectrum, was composed of answers to questions regarding specific governmental actions or proposals in the areas of Medicare, poverty, housing, and aid to education. The other, labeled the "ideological" spectrum, was made up of answers to more abstract, less tangible questions about how problems ought to be solved and whether the government is interfering too much in private and economic affairs. Those who consistently favored governmental assistance in the specific issue areas were labelled either strong liberals or predominantly liberal, depending on the number of affirmative responses they gave. Opposition to governmental assistance led to classification as predominantly conservative or strongly conservative. The same approach

[12] Lloyd A. Free and Hadley Cantril, *The Political Beliefs of Americans* (New York: Simon and Schuster, 1968). The analysis in the following paragraphs is drawn from Chapter 3.

was applied to the ideological spectrum, with endorsement of governmental solutions and denial that the government was interfering too much characterizing the liberal category.

When the two spectrums were compared, some very interesting and revealing findings emerged. In *operational* terms, 65 percent of respondents were completely or predominantly liberal. But in *ideological* terms, only 16 percent were. Fully 50 percent of respondents were *ideologically* conservative, compared to only 14 percent who were *operationally* conservative. This suggests that when it comes to a question of what government should do in a specific situation, people want action to solve problems. But when issues are cast in the form of abstract philosophies or basic values, people endorse the conservative and more traditional assumptions. In other words, the grip of ideology remains strong even in the face of specific needs and desires to the contrary. The questions that gained such support for the conservative side of the ideological spectrum involved standard American nostrums: the federal government is interfering too much, it is regulating business and interfering with the free enterprise system, social problems could be solved if government would keep hands off and let people handle them themselves, anybody who wants work can find it, and we should rely more on individual initiative and not so much on welfare programs. No doubt some people can cheerfully voice such beliefs and then endorse governmental action to solve problems; 46 percent of ideological conservatives were operational liberals. But people of conservative ideology gave only half as much support to liberal measures as did those of liberal ideology. And those who were conservative ideologically accounted for almost all of those who were conservative operationally. Thus, the conservative nature of the ideology, and its continuing strength, appear to contribute importantly to resistance, even among the general public, to governmental social legislation.

Implications of the Findings

What are the implications of these findings? For one thing, they suggest a gap between rhetoric and performance. For another, they suggest that the ways in which people focus on politics, and what they see as important, may coincide with those differing dimensions. Those who think and perceive in ideological terms may care most about the abstract principles and rhetoric surrounding government. Those who are operationally oriented may be more concerned with solutions to concrete problems. This conjecture is confirmed by Free and Cantril's analysis of their respondents' ranking of public concerns. Ideological conservatives ranked such intangibles as preserving economic liberties and states' rights at the top of their list of concerns, while liberals gave first place to specific actions such as aid to education and ending unemployment. Thus, in addition to the familiar divisions among people along class, racial, religious, and other such lines, we must distinguish between them on the basis of perceptual orientation. This phenomenon is related to class status, but is not identical with it.

Diversions by Means of Racial Conflict and Scapegoating

Several kinds of diversions operate to deflect non-elites from making efforts to fulfill their wants and needs through coherent political action. War, which causes people to forget their differences and unite in patriotic support for their government, is the classic example. Even if the war is unpopular, it serves as a focus for conflict that aligns people in different ways than do the class-based contests that could bring fulfillment of non-elite wants and needs. Space programs, races to the moon, and other forms of international competition—particularly against communism—serve many of the same functions.

Other diversions divide groups of non-elites. Ethnic and religious conflicts and sex discrimination are examples. But the single most important diversion for all Americans is racism. Outbursts of racist violence have served to vent non-elite resentments throughout American history. Continuous systematic denigration of minority groups has provided satisfactions for those just above such minorities on the social ladder. In part, such continuing tensions are kept alive by the natural tendency of employers to seek the lowest possible labor costs. Historically, this has meant the use of minorities as cheap labor and as strikebreakers, to the detriment of white working-class wage levels. Aid to the poor has also been interpreted as aid to minorities, particularly blacks; as a result, whites have been less supportive than they might have been had they understood the potential recipients to be people like themselves.

Racism and racial tensions remain prominent focuses of non-elite attention today. Whites blame blacks for wanting too much too fast, and for not working hard enough to get it. Blacks see whites as unresponsive and racist. The more blacks seek equality, the more whites resent it, and the less either group sees its problems as caused by anything but the other. How rapidly white resistance stiffened in the 1960s is apparent in the shift in whites' opinions about whether blacks "have tried to move too fast":[13]

	Yes: Too fast	No: Not fast enough
1964	34%	32%
1965	49	19
1966	85	3

[13] *Public Opinion Quarterly* 32 (Fall 1968), p. 522, citing a Louis Harris survey.

The differences of opinion that separate whites and blacks in the 1970s remain at the high levels to which they rose in reaction to the riots of the late 1960s. A Louis Harris national survey in 1972 showed, for example, that much of the gap still (or again) focused on integration of schools and the use of busing for the purpose.[14] Blacks wanted schools integrated by a 78 percent to 12 percent margin, compared to a 46 percent to 43 percent margin among whites. But whites opposed busing for that purpose by an overwhelming 81 percent to 14 percent margin, while blacks favored it by 50 percent to 36 percent. Similar but less dramatic differences were found in a series of other social welfare areas. Blacks also demonstrated lack of confidence in the Nixon Administration's record on racial matters, while whites approved it solidly. The overall impression was one of dogged white resistance, and black conviction that whites simply had no real interest in racial equality.

Other forms of scapegoating also frequently occur in American politics. Youth, protestors, and unorthodox or dissenting people have served from time to time as objects of such scapegoating. We shall see the strong disapproval of demonstrations and support for the police that developed after the Chicago Democratic Convention clashes in 1968. Hostility to protestors, and to black demands, tends to be highest among the lower echelons of non-elites. In 1971, one study found that twice as many blue-collar people expressed high hostility toward student demonstrators and black demands as did professional white-collar persons.[15]

Intolerance of dissent or unorthodoxy is a familiar feature of non-elite attitudes. It is sometimes argued that this finding means that non-elites are "undemocratic" or that elites' support for free speech and due process is the main pillar of democracy in the United States. We think it is better understood as evidence of a tendency to scapegoating, brought about by the unfulfilled wants and needs and other ambivalences we have explored.

The Process of Attitude Change: The Case of the Vietnam War

The dominant attitude of the American public changed from prowar to antiwar between 1965 and 1969. But more significant than the fact attitudes changed may be (1) the way they did so, (2) the length of time it took for them to do so, and (3) the many events, acts of leadership, and other governmental maneuvers necessary before real attitude change occurred. Let us review the process by which attitudes changed during this period.

In some important respects, of course, the political setting of the war in Southeast Asia was distinctive. As a matter of foreign policy in

---

[14] Louis Harris survey (November 1972).

[15] H. Edward Ransford, "Blue Collar Anger: Reactions to Student and Black Protest," *American Sociological Review* 37 (June 1972), p. 339.

which the armed forces were involved, it fell within an area of presidential discretion and initiative in which the Congress has not sought to assert itself. Given this traditional deference to the President, in part suggested by the Constitution's conferral of substantial power on the President as Commander-in-Chief, there were few ways to enforce limits on his actions. Moreover, neither Congress nor the general public had any reliable information on the situation in Vietnam. In a context of uncertainty, the natural tendency is to accept what the apparent experts decide is necessary; once commitments were made and the necessity for them repeatedly emphasized to the public, policy and events were seen in these terms. Not to trust one's elected leaders in an ambiguous situation would have been a drastic departure from traditional patterns of behavior. Finally, the subject of Vietnam raised issues of patriotism, national prestige, and anticommunism. Once national honor was committed and troops deployed, many of these symbols became activated. The presentation of the issues by the Johnson Administration emphasized these concepts strongly as a means of mobilizing support for its policies.

The Beginnings of Dissent

Dissent from these policies began on the campuses as early as 1963, but was still relatively limited in 1964. During that election campaign, the aggressive language of the Republican candidate, Barry Goldwater, made Johnson's policy and assurances about not sending troops to Vietnam sound moderate indeed. The war was not highly salient for the general public, with more than a third of the voters unable to answer survey questions about policy preferences for U.S. action in Vietnam. Of those who had preferences, nearly four times as many preferred "taking a stronger stand, even if it means invading North Vietnam" to "pulling out of Vietnam entirely."[16]

In February 1965, the United States began bombing North Vietnam. This was to be the first in a series of acts which campus dissenters perceived as escalations of the war and by which they were provoked into greater activity. The "teach-in" stage of antiwar activity that then ensued was characterized by many debates staged on campuses between supporters or members of the administration and prominent dissenters. It is even possible that the Johnson Administration sought to legitimize dissent in this fashion as a means of defending itself against what it expected to be the major pressure in the country—toward greater (and more dangerous) military action in the war.

As the commitment of American forces grew throughout 1965, and the draft began to cut more heavily into American life, the war became

---

[16] Philip Converse, Warren Miller, Jerrold Rusk, and Arthur C. Wolfe, "Continuity and Change in American Politics: Parties and Issues in the 1968 Election," *American Political Science Review* 63 (1969), p. 1086.

much more salient to the general public. In the fall of 1965 it was strongly supported, however, particularly by the better educated and higher-status people.[17] The first major round of campus outbursts occurred in 1966, with disruptions of speeches by administration members and demonstrations and sit-ins directed at the draft. The dissenters were still a tiny minority, and the troop commitment in Vietnam was growing.

By mid-1967, there were half a million American troops in Southeast Asia, a series of urban riots had swept the country, repeated campus outbreaks were occurring, a balance-of-payments problem was developing, and mounting budget deficits indicated growing inflation ahead. Not all of these phenomena were related to the Vietnam War, of course, but they combined to create a context of turmoil and tension. Most of the campus dissent was directed at the war and the draft, and public opposition to the war was rising. Nearly half of the population now said that U.S. involvement in Vietnam had been a mistake, but college graduates continued to express support for the administration, and self-characterized "hawks" outnumbered "doves" by 5–3 ratios.

A chiefly student-sponsored movement that sought to reach adult voters and affect the course of the war was generated in 1967 as a move to "dump Johnson," and in early 1968 it evolved into a campaign to win the Democratic nomination for Senator Eugene McCarthy, a prominent dissenter. In February 1968, the so-called "Tet offensive" by the Viet Cong shocked Americans into the realization that military matters were proceeding less satisfactorily than most official accounts had indicated. The proportions of voters declaring that the Vietnam War had been a mistake rose to equal the number who still supported the administration's rationale.[18] In the first Democratic primary, in New Hampshire in early March, Senator McCarthy's student compaigners succeeded in winning 42 percent of the Democratic vote for their candidate, while President Johnson's write-in campaign secured 48 percent. The result was interpreted as indicating widespread antiwar sentiment among Democrats, and set in motion a train of events that had immeasurable impact on the election in November. First, President Johnson announced that he would not seek renomination, declaring that this had been his intention all along. Peace talks with the North Vietnamese were undertaken in Paris. Senator Robert Kennedy entered the campaign for the Democratic nomination, after much hesitation.

Subsequent analysis shows that the McCarthy victory in New Hampshire was only partially due to "dove"-style antiwar sentiment. The Michigan Survey Research Center found that New Hampshire McCarthy voters were indeed unhappy with the Johnson Administration, but that a whole range of problems was on their minds. On the issue of Vietnam itself, those who wanted a *stronger* prosecution of the war outnumbered

---

[17] *Gallup Opinion Weekly* (October 1969), p. 15.
[18] *Ibid.*

those who wanted to end it by a nearly 3–2 margin.[19] Among all Democrats interviewed in the national phase of the Center's survey before the Democratic Convention, more McCarthy supporters eventually favored Wallace than any other candidate considered in 1968.[20] Thus it seems clear that many observers overestimated the extent of antiwar feeling within the electorate in 1968. Well over half by then agreed that involvement in Vietnam had been a mistake, but these totals must have included many who were simply frustrated at not being able to win the war faster.

Chicago, 1968: The Turning-Point

The Democratic Convention of August 1968 was the next major event in the expanding student-based movement against the war. Those who went to Chicago probably represented only a relatively small proportion of all students at that time, but the result of the events in Chicago again had powerful effects on the nature of public opinion and on the election itself. Public reaction against the demonstrators and in favor of the police was very strong, as we suggested earlier. Not even those who took "dove" positions on the war expressed significant support for the demonstrators.[21] Only one in six or seven whites believed that the United States had made a mistake in getting involved in Vietnam and that the best course would be to pull out entirely. But even within this group, almost 70 percent denied that "too much force" had been used by the Chicago police, and the main body of opinion was that "not enough force" had been used against the peace demonstrators. Those who were against the war and sympathetic to demonstrations were a tiny minority of the population, about 3 percent. Most other people were adamantly opposed to the demonstrations. It is impossible to tell whether the violence that occurred in Chicago actually gained or lost support for the antiwar cause, but it is clear that it promoted much support for "law-and-order" candidates.

By the time of the 1968 election, much of the indecision of 1964 had of course dissolved, and the voters had clear preferences on Vietnam. Table 18.6 shows, however, that there had not been a great reduction in the proportion of people who wanted a stronger stand. In three of the four categories, the proportion even went up. Higher proportions favored pulling out entirely, but they still represented only about half the number of those wanting stronger action. The electorate, in short, did not turn against the war. The signs of revulsion at violence and of trust in established officials and practices, suggest that the actions of campus-based dissenters had the opposite effect.

[19] Converse *et al.*, "Continuity and Change," p. 1086 ff.
[20] *Ibid.*, p. 1093.
[21] Data in this paragraph are all drawn from Converse *et al.*, "Continuity and Change," pp. 1087–1088.

TABLE 18.6   *Attitudes on Vietnam Policy, 1964 and 1968, Whites Only*

"Which of the following do you think we should do now in Vietnam?
1. Pull out of Vietnam entirely.
2. Keep our soldiers in Vietnam but try to end the fighting.
3. Take a stronger stand even if it means invading North Vietnam."

	Pull out	Status quo	Stronger stand	Don't know, other	Total
Northern Democrats					
1964	8%	25	29	38	100%
1968	20%	39	35	6	100%
Northern Republicans					
1964	8%	19	38	35	100%
1968	20%	39	36	5	100%
Southern Democrats					
1964	8%	25	28	39	100%
1968	17%	36	38	9	100%
Southern Republicans					
1964	10%	18	42	30	100%
1968	15%	29	48	8	100%

Source: Converse *et al.,* "Continuity and Change," p. 1086.

Nevertheless, the proportions of the adult population who said that the Vietnam War had been a mistake continued to rise. As we now realize, this group is composed of both "doves" and "hawks," the latter presumably feeling that it is better not to become involved in wars we are not prepared to do everything possible to win. Figure 18.1 shows the trend in attitudes toward American involvement. By late 1968 there was strong consensus that it had been a mistake, and this sentiment continued into the first year of the Nixon Administration. President Nixon's own ratings remained high for the first year he was in office, showing particular strength after his November 1969 announcement of slow but apparently assured troop withdrawals. His expressed commitment to this goal was actually made earlier in the year, and may have accounted for the rise in proportions believing the war was a mistake. In mid-1969, 29 percent of the adult population favored immediate withdrawal from Vietnam, but this figure fell to 21 percent after Nixon's November speech and rose to 35 percent in February 1970.[22]

[22] *Gallup Opinion Weekly* (March 1970), p. 9.

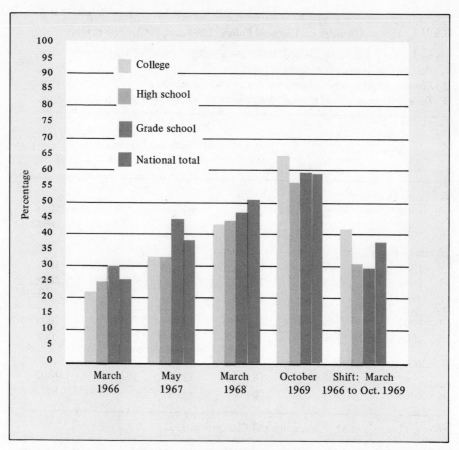

Source: Gallup Opinion Weekly (October 1969), p. 15. By permission of the American
Institute of Public Opinion (The Gallup Poll).

FIGURE 18.1

Agreement That U.S. Involvement in Vietnam Was a Mistake, by Education Levels

but this figure fell to 21 percent after Nixon's November speech and rose
to 35 percent in February 1970.[18]

Perhaps the most important finding reflected in Figure 18.1, however, is the difference between better-educated (and, presumably, higher-
income) people and less-educated, lower-income people. College-educated people were consistently *less* likely to believe the war had been a
mistake than were grade-school or high-school people *until 1969, when
it became the official policy of the President and the United States
government to pull out of South Vietnam.* In other words, opposition to
the war was stronger among the lower classes and less educated; college

[18] *Gallup Opinion Weekly* (March 1970), p. 9.

graduates were apparently readier to trust their government, and to assume that what it was doing must have been right. This is indeed a high level of confidence in one's government, and indicates continued broad discretion for the President in foreign affairs.

In conclusion, it seems clear that most members of the general public continue to trust the established officials of government, and particularly the President, in such a situation. They are strongly opposed to dissent and particularly strongly disapprove of violent dissent, even when it is not initiated by the dissenters themselves; and they are subject to appeals based on patriotism, nationalism, and anticommunism.

Area of Student Influence

But these findings do not mean that the campus-based dissent of the 1960s was without consequence for the character of governmental policy. Quite the contrary; students had considerable influence, but on elites and opinionmakers, not on the general public. College students are vaguely near-elites, and people in power seek the approbation of rising generations and their prospective leaders. Highly conspicuous and continuing opposition in the citadels of culture and learning in the nation is embarrassing, if nothing else, for government officials. The issue of the Vietnam War might never have been framed in moral and ethical terms if such terms were not emphasized on the campuses, and governmental policymakers would have found it much easier to gain support for escalation of the war if it had not been for the student movement. The McCarthy candidacy, the Johnson withdrawal, and even the relatively moderate public posture assumed by President Nixon are traceable in important ways to this movement. Its failure to sway most political spectators should not obscure its significant intra-elite effects.

So, too, the mere fact that a segment of the population is engaging in violent actions assumes the stature of a serious threat in the eyes of national elites, both in and out of government. They see danger not in the capacity of the dissenters to bring about their goals, but in the prospect of social chaos and the possibility that other groups will respond similarly endangering the structure of order and civility they consider it crucial to maintain. Even if elites cared little about Vietnam, therefore, it was preferable to them to end the war than to have business endangered, inflation rampant, and repeated violence in the streets.

Trends in the Mid-1970s

As the 1970s began, there was marked fear of instability and disorder in the nation. A substantial proportion—47 percent—of a national survey sample expected "a real breakdown" as a result of social tensions. Those at the upper educational and occupational levels tended to blame the system itself, while the lower classes and farmers blamed individual failures and protesters. In conjunction with the declining levels of confidence in leaders of various institutions, this seemed to represent a significant malaise.[23]

By the mid-1970s, however, fear of instability had been replaced by economic worries. More than half of all respondents in one national sample named the high cost of living as the most serious problem facing the country in 1975. As many people expected things to get worse as thought they would improve, and around 40 percent believed in 1975 that the United States was heading for another depression.[24] One particularly revealing study found that people not only saw themselves as less well off than they had been five years before with regard to the quality of life, but also had lower expectations of improvement in the future than they had previously had. For some time, researchers have worked with a ten-step scale that reflects respondents' estimates of their own standing on "the ladder of life." The prevailing pattern had been for people to rank themselves at higher and higher levels each year, and to indicate optimism about their futures by saying that they expected to rise about half a step in the next five years. But this pattern was sharply reversed in 1974, when people began to rank themselves lower than before on the ladder. By 1975, they were averaging a full half-step lower. At the same time, their expectations of improvement in the future were also reduced.[25]

These economic preoccupations were accompanied, as we have seen, by continued lack of confidence in established leaders and widespread cynicism about politicians and government generally. No doubt the events of the Watergate years and the repeated documentation of governmental secrecy and outright lying contributed significantly to such attitudes. But they probably also reflect the scope and importance of the value transformations taking place in the United States. Under such conditions, ambivalence, scapegoating, and a deep desire to believe in something—perhaps almost anything—seem likely to persist.

[23] Albert H. Cantril and Charles W. Roll, Jr., *Hopes and Fears of the American People* (New York: Universe Books, 1971), p. 31.

[24] *Gallup Opinion Index,* August 1975, pp. 5, 17, 19.

[25] *The New York Times,* 26 October, 1975, p. 1.

19

Participation:
Voting and
Alternatives

There are many forms of political participation. Most of the more effective forms—personal contact with decisionmakers, large contributions to political parties, lobbying, test cases before the Supreme Court, and extensive campaigns for or against contemplated legislation—are open chiefly to elites. Non-elite participation may take these forms, but it is for practical purposes limited to those activities in which a citizen may engage near home and with limited resources and time. Non-elite participation is distinctly low, whether measured in terms of the resources brought to bear by individuals or groups, the proportion of the people who actually use officially authorized channels, or the proportion who engage in other types of participation. Participation in the established channels, such as political parties and elections or interest groups, rises sharply with class status and varies directly with income, occupation, and education.

Political parties and interest groups both tend to be hierarchically organized and bureaucratic. Not surprisingly, stable and self-perpetuating leadership elements develop arrangements for conducting business with each other. Often they pay more attention to their own needs, or those of their leading supporters, than they do to the interests of the mass of non-elites.

Alternative forms of participation—such as demonstrations, petitions, and *ad hoc* campaigns for particular goals—do arise from time to time, revealing demands for change that have gone unheeded within the established channels. But even participation in these informal processes is infrequent and low, and often reflects the same class biases as do the official channels.

The Electoral Process

The reasons why non-elite political participation is both low and relatively ineffective have aroused much speculation since survey evidence first called attention to the problem. It may be that the lower classes are satisfied with the upper classes' management of the political system, that they have more economically productive uses for their time, or that they are simply uninformed or too apathetic to care about public affairs. Or they may have been convinced that their role is to accept what their betters achieve for them and that all works automatically for the best in this ingenious system. Perhaps they are too busy trying to make ends meet amid economic hardships, or they may know from past experience or intuition that it will do no good to press their goals through the established system because it is designed to permit elites to deflect, delay, and ultimately deny them. It is worth trying to resolve some of these issues. In this chapter we shall first explore the orthodox channels, looking particularly at the incidence and nature of participation and its meaning for the system as a whole. Then we shall examine some of the ways in which elites are able to manage these orthodox channels so that non-elite interests do not predominate. Finally, we shall look at some of the unorthodox means that have been used to express non-elite desires and demands more directly—and at some of the mixed reactions they have aroused.

In general, about 60 to 65 percent of adult Americans vote in presidential elections, despite (a cynic would surely add "or, perhaps, because of") all the publicity and campaigning that urges participation. This level of participation is lower than those of all other major industrialized nations, and of many small, rural, and otherwise "developing" nations as well. In off-year congressional elections, the proportion drops to about 50 percent, and in many state, city, and local elections it falls still lower. Only about 10 percent of the adult population ever performs any more strenuous electorally related act than voting, such as attending rallies, campaigning, contributing, or taking part in primaries.

Voting Patterns

The act of voting is closely related to intensity of preference for one or another candidate or party, and in turn to class level and membership in active political groups. Nearly 90 percent of college-educated persons and nearly 80 percent of high-school graduates vote in presidential elections, but only a little over half of the eligible population with grade-school educations does so. The dropoff in voting is constant all the way down the status ladder. Skilled workers, for example, vote with greater regularity than do unskilled workers. Union members vote with distinctly greater consistency than similar workers who do not belong to unions. In general, members of organized groups are much more likely to vote than people who are not members.

Other *demographic* characteristics are also associated with the disposition to vote. Men are more likely to vote than women, a circumstance that almost certainly reflects widely held beliefs about the "proper" role of women in society; this is the case in almost all countries. The young are less likely to vote than are older people, partly because of residency requirements that discriminate against the mobile and partly because older people more often feel they are part of the political system. Blacks are much less likely to vote than whites, even when they are not legally barred from doing so or informally intimidated. People who live in urban areas vote more frequently than rural residents, probably because political life in the cities is more stimulating and there is more social pressure to vote. Voting participation rates are far lower in the South than in other regions, chiefly because of the higher proportion of the Southern population that is poor, black, and lacking much formal education.

The turnout of voters depends not only on these socioeconomic factors but also on people's interest and involvement in party politics. That high-status voters go to the polls more often chiefly reflects their greater belief that it matters how they vote and who wins. Anyone who feels strongly that it makes a difference is obviously more likely to vote than those who do not.

For some, nonvoting is an expression of their rejection of that belief —of their assumption that the major parties present no real choice and that the voters have little influence on what government does. The proportion of nonvoters who consciously reject the electoral system in this way has probably always been small, but this phenomenon may be particularly significant because it occurs in the face of such an intense barrage of pressure and propaganda to take part. This pressure is, of course, intended to integrate people into the political system and give them a greater stake in it. The extension of the right to vote—first to propertyless males, then to women, blacks, and finally to the 18 to 21-year-old age group—has never had any significant effect on government policy. But it does seem to have lessened the protests of such groups, and to cause them to believe that remedies for their problems can be found within the orthodox political processes. The right to vote thus helps to commit people to the system and to legitimize governmental actions. Not to exercise that right requires strong resistance to American orthodoxy.

Turnout and participation patterns are clearly fundamental to the outcome of the political process. The sharp disparities in levels of participation that we have seen contribute to the extension of upper-class influence. One leading scholar suggests conceiving of political participation in terms of three types of people: "apathetics" (persons who are uninvolved in any way), "spectators" (people who seek information, vote, talk about politics, and the like but are not themselves active), and "gladiators" (people who go to meetings, become active in a party, etc.).[1] If we then imagine the gladiators (perhaps 3 to 4 percent of the population) battling in a stadium half full of spectators (about 60 percent of the people), while a third or more of the population (the apathetics) simply stay home and ignore the battle, we have a rough characterization of the American electoral process in operation. It might be desirable to add to this characterization that in some cases the spectators are prevented from becoming gladiators, and that the "apathetics" may include some who tried to take part and lost. Thus modified, the characterization is not inappropriate.

The Meaning of Elections

What significance do elections have in the American political system? The answer depends on whether we are talking about the system itself (in the sense of stability, or national integration, as they are affected in part by political parties and elections), about the impact elections have on mass beliefs about politics, or about their actual influence on governmental policies. A brief exploration of the role of political parties and the meanings of elections will lend some perspective to our analysis of contemporary changes in voting and party identification.

---

[1] Lester Milbrath, *Political Participation* (Chicago: Rand McNally, 1963), p. 20.

The Two-Party System

For nearly 150 years, the United States has maintained the same basic two-party system. This means that, with rare and temporary exceptions, only two parties have had any serious chance of winning the presidency or even a substantial minority in the Congress. A great many "third parties" have existed over the course of American history, and one of these, the Republican party, even managed to become a major party. Most American third parties (Know Nothing, Prohibition, Populist, Greenback, Socialist, Communist, Progressive, Liberal, American Labor, Peace and Freedom, and others) have had relatively short lives. They have chiefly espoused policy positions regarded in their times as more or less deviant or "extreme," though many of these positions gained broad popular support and eventually began to look quite conventional. The chief function of these parties for the political system has been to introduce policy innovations: to make it clear that a course of action earlier thought deviant was in fact widely supported, and so to induce one or both the major parties to espouse that position itself. Universal compulsory education for children, the progressive income tax, prohibition of the sale or use of intoxicating beverages, the Tennessee Valley Authority, governmental guarantees of the right of workers to organize labor unions, and many other policies first became live issues because a third party made them campaign issues.

Though third parties have occasionally elected candidates to public offices at every level of government except the presidency, the two-party system has remained intact throughout American history. That it has done so tells us something fundamental about mass political belief patterns. It indicates that the American people have never been divided for a long period of time into two well-defined groups that basically and intensely differed on the whole range of public issues regarded as most critical. In Italy and in France since World War Two, there has been such a division of the mass public into those with a rightist-center ideology and those with a leftist orientation. People in these two ideological camps have quite consistently differed on foreign policy, economic policy, church-state relations, and educational policy. Within each camp, there are additional differences, and seven or eight distinct political parties have sprung up to compete for the various shadings of the rightist, center, and leftist vote. One can readily understand from these examples that a multiparty system is likely wherever such a "bimodal" pattern of mass political beliefs exist—that is, wherever the voters form two distinct ideological coalitions that take contrasting positions on the range of basic political issues.

Unimodal Political Beliefs

In the United States, and in other countries with two-party systems, mass political beliefs, by contrast, are *unimodal*. While people differ on particular issues, they have not formed clearly defined ideological blocs that maintain differing stances on all central policy issues consistently over time. Because people who differ on one issue may agree with each other on others, politics is often less intense emotionally. Given this pattern of mass political beliefs, a political party that wants to win elections is well advised to take a stand near the center of the belief spectrum on the major issues and to remain vague about those matters on which public opinion is seriously divided.

This is precisely the strategy major parties do pursue in countries with unimodal patterns of mass beliefs. In such a system, parties that take clear ideological positions different from the centrist one obviously limit their appeal to a minority, and often a rather small minority, of the voters. On ethical grounds such a stand may be the only tenable one for supporters of these parties; but it has the effect of limiting third parties to an experimental and educational role. Because parties chiefly interested in winning elections must adopt a centrist position, the major parties do not often differ significantly on issues. They each want to elect their own leaders to public office. Sometimes, when it is unclear what most of the public wants, the major parties do differ on specific issues. But often they differ more in rhetorical tone and style than in the policies they actually put into effect.

Both major parties in the United States embrace within their ranks a gamut of policy positions ranging from far right to moderate left—which further underlines the relative unimportance of issues as a determinant of party membership or support. With two parties competing for the center track, where the votes are, still another party trying the same strategy would have little chance of success; it is bound to be absorbed by the major parties in their efforts to broaden their support. Hence, a unimodal or unclear pattern of mass beliefs encourages a two-party system.

Power of the Vote

For most people, voting is the most potent of all symbols of popular rule and therefore a powerful ingredient in the legitimacy of a regime that holds public office. Whether a group of political participants wins or loses an election, the fact that it has supposedly been consulted evokes its support for the government. It may not like some policies the government pursues, but it is far less likely to challenge its right to pursue them than would be the case if the government had not been elected. In this critical sense, elections lessen social tensions and inhibit potential civil strife. This is frequently, perhaps usually, the chief function they serve in the political system, though that hypothesis is debatable and not easily susceptible to rigorous testing. Provisions for compulsory voting in some countries, as well as social pressures to vote in order to prove one is a "good citizen," doubtless reflect an awareness that people who vote are psychologically inoculated against fundamental resistance to the state.

It is even more clear that the use of elections in nondemocratic states reflects the same awareness. Some forms of election, such as the plebiscites of totalitarian countries, do not even offer the *possibility* of defeating unpopular candidates or policies, amounting only to ratification of actions already taken. It is in such rigged elections, nonetheless, that legal and social pressure to vote has been strongest. The citizen who fails to vote is suspect as a potentially disloyal person and can expect the kind of ostracism that would await a member of a primitive tribe who refused to participate in a communal fertility rite or war dance. Sometimes elections are rigged to eliminate candidates who stand for a genuine alternative on controversial issues, as is true of many elections in the deep South, some in the North, and virtually all elections in one-party states. The results are nevertheless publicized as mandates for the government and fervently accepted by many as exactly that.

Apart from their uses in promoting and symbolizing social solidarity, to what degree do elections provide policy guidelines for public officials to follow? On the occasional major issue on which the two major parties disagree, they apparently do furnish a clear mandate, though historical examples warn against making this logical assumption without empirical evidence. In 1928 the Democratic platform favored repeal of the Eighteenth (Prohibition) Amendment, while the Republicans were "dry." A Republican victory did indeed delay repeal for four years, even though public sentiment increasingly favored repeal, and in 1932 both parties' platforms reflected that sentiment. In 1964 escalation of the Vietnam War, certainly a major issue, was favored by Barry Goldwater, the Republican candidate, and opposed by Lyndon Johnson, his Democratic opponent. Though Johnson won by a wide margin, he moved quickly after the election to escalate the war. Though this is by no means the only instance in which a major party disregarded what appeared to be a clear popular mandate, elections do in such instances provide a means for evaluating the performance of a regime. This can be an important factor in the following election, as it evidently was in 1968; but there is no guarantee that it will be.

Permanence of the Election Mandate

Even when elections do offer a real choice, however, they are not a sufficient condition of democracy. Election mandates are almost always unclear, and it is always possible to justify departures from them on the ground that conditions have changed since election day. Even when elected officials have every intention of heeding the voice of the people as they understand it, election mandates typically furnish only the vaguest kind of guide to administrative officials and judges who have to make decisions in particular cases. Does the fact that the winning political party promised to hold down prices mean that it should institute wage-

and-price ceilings when some economists forecast rising prices and others disagree? Should officials elected on such a plank institute price controls after prices have risen 2 percent? 4 percent? 10 percent? What difference should it make if the winning political party also promised to avoid unnecessary governmental intervention in the economy?

Dilemmas like these face modern governments all the time. The decisions taken to resolve them are bound to reflect a complex set of group interests and guesses about the future political and economic effects of one or another course of action. They cannot be predetermined, or even guided very far, by the votes people cast in election campaigns.

Because of the American parties' avoidance of clear stands on issues, and the tendency of candidates (once elected) to act as they consider necessary under the circumstances, it is very difficult to say precisely what elections mean in the United States. We have no doubt that it sometimes makes a difference which party or candidate wins an election, at least in the general approach to problems of governing, if not in specific policies. But the permanence of the basic social coalitions underlying the parties, and the arbitrariness of both parties' internal processes preceding nominations, preclude exact definition of the role of elections. Events can split the basic social coalitions; indeed, such a process may now be under way. But in the past, only the Civil War and the Great Depression of the 1930s were of sufficient magnitude to realign the major social blocs and redirect the party system. After the Civil War, the Republicans were dominant for nearly 70 years, with only two Democratic intrusions (Cleveland and Wilson). After the Depression the Democrats took over and remained in office, with the exception of Eisenhower, until 1968.

Exhaustive electoral analysis has led experts at the University of Michigan Survey Research Center to distinguish three broad types of American elections.[2] The first and most frequent type of election is the "maintaining" election, in which the party with the numerically larger social coalition is returned to office. The second and least frequent type of election is the "realigning" election or "realigning era" of elections, in which events of cataclysmic proportions succeed in rending the majority coalition and installing a new coalition in power through the vehicle of the other party. Third is the dual category of "deviating" and "reinstating" elections, in which for some reason the minority party wins a particular election without altering the basic underlying social coalitions and is subsequently replaced by the permanent majority party. The Wilson and Eisenhower elections are cited as deviating elections, and the elections of Harding and Kennedy represent the return of the dominant social coalition.

This is a low-level estimate of the quality of popular impact on government policy directions, of course. It implies that policymakers can

[2] Angus Campbell, Philip Converse, Donald Stokes, and Warren Miller, *The American Voter* (New York: John Wiley, 1960).

count on support for practically anything they wish to do, at least in elections. Mass impact, however, may simply be more subtle than the very gross policy preferences that can be expressed through the instrument of elections. Or more recent elections and contemporary changes may suggest that these characterizations are obsolete. We shall keep these possibilities in mind as we examine recent events.

Party Identification and Party Disarray

The 1960s and 1970s have been marked by social tensions, economic insecurities, governmental flouting of widely held values, and bitter controversy over military policies. These developments have been accompanied by major changes in Americans' political party loyalties and voting behavior, changes that reveal a great deal about the connections between what people get from government and how they express their political preferences.[3]

Until the middle 1960s most Americans who voted at all developed attachments early in life to the Republican or the Democratic party; such "party identification" was the best single predictor, though not the only one, of how a person would vote. Since the 1964 election, however, this has no longer been true. A study of the proportionate influence of party identification and people's stands on public issues showed that in 1964 and 1968 issues were substantially more influential on voting than political party attachment.[4]

A growing proportion of Americans identify themselves as Independents, rather than political party members. More voters under 30 years old call themselves Independents than call themselves Republicans and Democrats combined; among all voters there are more Independents than Republicans, according to a 1972 election survey.

One result is a strikingly greater inclination to abandon straight party voting in favor of split tickets on election day; this is true even of voters who still identify with a major party. Figure 19.1 shows that ticket-splitting has been growing ever since the end of World War Two; far more Americans have been voting for a congressional candidate of one party and a presidential candidate of the other party.

As we noted in Chapter 15, an incumbent President is almost sure to be reelected if he runs, and in recent years incumbent congressmen have been enjoying a similar, though not quite as certain, advantage. More than three-quarters of the 435 congressional districts are fairly sure to reelect the incumbent. Even if defeats in primaries and general elections

---

[3] Our discussion of these changes relies in part on the exposition of them in Richard W. Boyd, "Electoral Trends in Postwar Politics," in *Choosing the President,* James David Barber, ed. (Englewood Cliffs, N.J.: Prentice-Hall, 1974), pp. 175–202.

[4] Norman N. Nie, "Mass Belief Systems Revisited; Political Change and Attitude Structure," *Journal of Politics* 36 (May 1974), pp. 40–41.

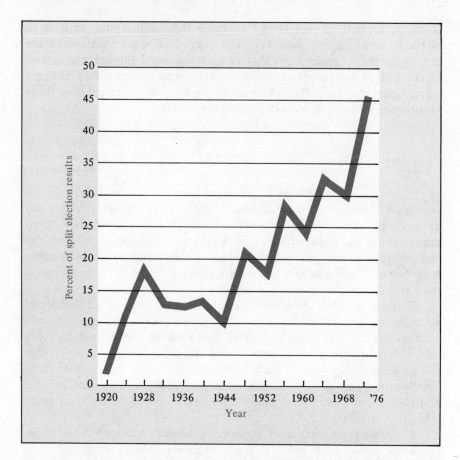

Sources: James David Barber, ed. *Choosing the President* (Englewood Cliffs: Prentice-Hall, Inc., 1974), p. 185. Data for 1920–1964, Milton C. Cummings, Jr., *Congressmen and the Electorate* (New York: Free Press, 1966), p. 32. For 1968, Walter DeVries and V. Lance Tarrance, Jr., *The Ticket-Splitter* (Grand Rapids: Eerdmans, 1972), p. 30. For 1972, the data are provided by Pierre M. Purves, director of statistical research, National Republican Congressional Committee, Washington, D.C., and by Michael Barone, Washington, D.C.

FIGURE 19.1

Trends in Split Ticket Voting for President and Congressmen, 1920–1972. The figure is the percentage of congressional districts carried by presidential and congressional candidates of different parties in each election year.

are combined, only 10 percent of incumbent congressmen lose their bids for reelection.[5] In elections from 1966 to 1970, 80 percent of incumbent Senators who ran were reelected.

Attachment to incumbents obviously means it is no longer *party*

[5] Charles O. Jones, *Every Second Year* (Washington, D.C.: Brookings Institution, 1967), p. 68.

attachments that are decisive. In part at least, this trend reflects the growing ability of elected officials to use the news media and favors for key interests to shape opinion and raise campaign funds.

Many people who used to vote regularly for the same political party have become deeply distrustful of government and do not vote at all. The events and revelations of the 1960s and 1970s, unsurprisingly, have been accompanied by growing cynicism: by beliefs that political leaders are crooked or unintelligent, that government benefits big interests, and that taxes are wasted.[6]

At the same time a smaller proportion of the electorate is bothering to vote, though the trend was in the opposite direction in the 40 years following World War One. Between 1960 and 1972 the proportion of the electorate that voted fell from 63.1 percent to 55.6 percent.

Issues

Incumbents' relative invulnerability to electoral challenge, together with large-scale voter disaffection and a dropoff in voting, have further insulated elected officials from adverse public opinion, since the people who are most critical are also the most likely to stay away from the polls. Concern about policies and issues is having a marked effect on voting in one basic sense: dissatisfaction with what government does is discouraging millions of people from engaging in even the conventional means of trying to influence policy, voting. But among many of those who do vote, concern about issues is also more important, and has a different impact than was the case before 1960.

A higher proportion of voters began in the 1960s to develop consistent sets of beliefs about political issues that were logically linked to each other and mutually reinforcing.[7] Those who favored civil rights at home, for example, were also likely to oppose a Southeast Asian war they saw as a form of racism abroad and to support economic and welfare policies to reduce inequalities in wealth. Such consistent patterns of belief may seem only natural, but studies of the 1950s indicate that at that time they were characteristic of only a small proportion of the electorate.[8] It seems that public policies that offend or shock a large part of the public force attention to issues, as well as creating distrust of government.

This increased concern for issues has also meant that Republican voters are more consistently conservative than Democrats, at least in their

---

[6] *Cf.* Arthur H. Miller, Thad A. Brown, and Alden S. Raine, "Social Conflict and Political Estrangement," paper presented at the 1973 Midwest Political Science Association Meetings, Chicago. Mimeograph, p. 7.

[7] Norman N. Nie, "Mass Belief Systems."

[8] Angus Campbell *et al.*, *The American Voter*, p. 240.

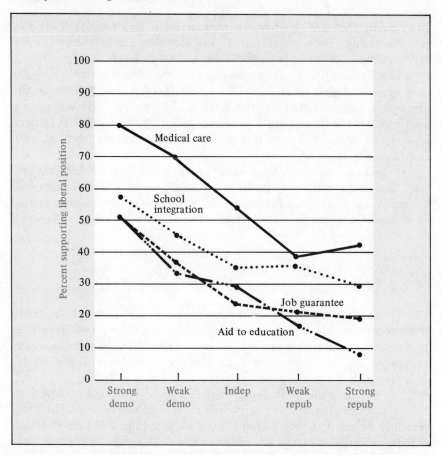

Source: James David Barber, ed. *Choosing the President* (Englewood Cliffs: Prentice-Hall, Inc., 1974), p. 193. Based on a table by Gerald M. Pomper, "From Confusion to Clarity: Issues and American Voters, 1956–1968," *American Political Science Review* 66 (June 1972), p. 417.

FIGURE 19.2

Party Identification and Policy Beliefs, 1968

responses to opinion polls. In the 1950s supporters of the two major parties were equally inconsistent. Now, as Figure 19.2 demonstrates, Democrats are more likely than Republicans to say they favor governmental support of medical care, school integration, governmental guarantees of jobs for the unemployed, and federal aid to education.[9] For reasons discussed in the chapters on Congress, the bureaucracy, and symbolic politics, however, it is far from certain that such voter preferences will be translated into tangible policies.

The new emphasis on issues is also creating strains *within* the parties.

[9] Gerald M. Pomper, "From Confusion to Clarity: Issues and American Voters, 1956–1968," *American Political Science Review* 66 (June 1972), p. 417.

The Democratic party relies in part on people chiefly interested in policies friendly to labor unions and in social security benefits; and these people often disagree with another component of the Democratic party's constituency: those favoring the encouragement of diverse life styles; rejection of racism and economic inequality; and a foreign policy that de-emphasizes militarism, cold war, and support of despotic foreign governments. The party's 1968 presidential standardbearer, Hubert Humphrey, chiefly reflected the values of the first group; George McGovern, its 1972 nominee, more closely reflected the concerns of the second group.

For some of the same reasons, there have been recent geographic realignments in party support. The Deep South, which was solidly Democratic for a century following the Civil War, has now become a bastion of Republican strength due to Republican emphasis, since Goldwater's 1964 campaign, on opposing welfare benefits and civil rights for blacks and on identifying cities with crime and disorder. These themes have also cut heavily into Democratic strength among European ethnic groups and Catholics.

Issues and Volunteer Campaign Help

People whose interest in politics springs chiefly from their concern with specific issues have in recent years been willing and eager to do volunteer work in campaigns: canvassing prospective voters, soliciting signatures on nominating petitions, delivering literature to homes, and working in campaign headquarters. Such work has been a highly significant form of campaign contribution, and it has been especially conspicuous in the campaigns of such issue-oriented aspirants as Eugene McCarthy, Barry Goldwater, George Wallace, and George McGovern.

The 1974 Federal Elections Law Amendments

The Watergate scandals involved serious abuses of the electoral process, including large, illegal, secret corporate contributions; "dirty tricks" to discredit opposition candidates; misuse of the FBI, CIA, and Internal Revenue Service to harass political opponents; and break-ins at the Democratic National Headquarters. Partly in response to these revelations, Congress changed the election law in 1974.

The new law limits campaign contributions by an individual to $1000 and by an organization to $5000 for each campaign, and sets an aggregate limit on contributions to all federal candidates of $2500 annually for an individual; there is no aggregate limit for organizations.

For the first time in American history, government money is being used to fund election campaigns. For presidential general elections and nominating conventions, political parties that received at least 25 percent of the vote in the previous election campaign are fully funded; others are not eligible. In practice, therefore, the Republican and Democratic parties are funded from the public treasury and minor parties get nothing; independent candidates are eligible for some retroactive public funding only if they win more than 5 percent of the total vote. A candidate becomes eligible for federal money in a primary if he or she raises at least $5000 in gifts of $250 or less in each of 20 states. The federal subsidy increases as private contributions do, to a maximum of $5 million.

The law also creates a bipartisan Federal Election Commission to interpret and administer the election laws.

On the face of them, the 1974 amendments are an effort to clean up federal election campaigns, assure that they are fairly conducted, reduce candidates' dependence on large contributors, and strengthen the positions of candidates and parties through partial public financing.

Critics concerned about civil liberties and the rights of political independents and minorities charge, however, that in practice the new law will do precisely the opposite of what it is supposed to do: it subsidizes the major parties while denying public money to minor parties. Nor does this legislation reduce the influence of wealthy contributors, in spite of its limits on contributions by individuals and special interest groups. The American Civil Liberties Union explains how the law is likely to be flouted:

> Ten executives at an oil company, for example, each contribute $25,000 to a voluntary political fund. The fund can then distribute $5000 apiece to the re-election campaigns of fifty favored congressmen and senators. If ten oil companies each do the same thing, then those fifty congressmen and senators would receive a total of $50,000 each in perfectly lawful contributions from the oil industry, or a total of $2,500,000. However, if one well-to-do backer of a minority party wanted to give $1500 to its congressional candidate, the law makes that a crime.[10]

The ACLU further charges that the law will discourage small contributions and make it easy to harass dissenters. Contributions of less than $100 cannot be a corrupting influence, but by requiring that they be disclosed the law subjects small contributors to penalties from employers or others who may not like their politics.

There is no question that money and the expectation of governmental favors can corrupt the political process. But the careful analyst of government must also consider the role of free public services, the free publicity available to incumbents, the ability of the major parties and public officials to reward big contributors with governmental favors, and the fact that those who challenge such actions are limited in their contributions. It is often the case in politics that the actual impact of a policy is quite different from what it promises to accomplish.

[10] American Civil Liberties Union, *Civil Liberties* 308 (September 1975), p. 6.

The 1976 Election

A climate of distrust of government, political parties, and presidential candidates dominated the 1976 campaign, coloring the party infighting, the issues, and the result: a narrow victory for Jimmy Carter over the incumbent president, Gerald Ford. Carter carried 23 states and the District of Columbia with 297 electoral votes, winning 51 percent of the popular vote. Ford carried 27 states with 241 electoral votes, winning 48 percent of the popular vote.

The presidential primary campaigns were especially divisive in the Republican Party, where party workers and voters were polarized in a bitter contest between Ford and Ronald Reagan. Reagan appealed especially to Republicans who wanted a strong rhetorical statement of right-wing principles. Ford, while about as conservative as Reagan in his policies, relied rather less on the conservative slogans of earlier decades, seemed to many a more viable standard bearer in the general election, and so won the nomination. But the Republican platform rang with the statements of the Reaganites in an effort to keep them in the fold, and the "moderate" Republicans remained unrepresented in their own party.

A rather large field of aspirants, ranging from conservative to liberal, entered the Democratic presidential primaries, many of them familiar faces from previous campaigns. Jimmy Carter, a relatively unknown former governor of Georgia and one of the more conservative of the aspirants, did surprisingly well in some of the early primaries, thereby became the "front runner" and most often "mentioned" in the press, and so managed to turn his opponents' rivalries to his own advantage.

"The opinions expressed by the candidate are not necessarily those of this station . . . or the candidates, either, for that matter."

Source: DUNAGIN'S PEOPLE by Ralph Dunagin; courtesy of Field Newspaper Syndicate

"I said, sir, you *do* have your hearing
aid turned on, don't you?"

As neither presidential candidate displayed much flair for evoking popular enthusiasm, and as their differences on the issues were rarely sharp or clear, a large part of the electorate remained undecided or vacillating in their leanings throughout the campaign. On foreign policy, both candidates favored strong military force and a tough stance with respect to Russia. Carter criticized Ford for allegedly condoning Soviet domination of Eastern Europe, for insensitivity to human rights in some countries receiving American aid, and for abuses in the intelligence agencies; while Ford defended his record and claimed that past faults had been corrected.

A high unemployment rate and declining economic indicators enabled Carter to attack the administration's economic record, while Ford defended his view that inflation is a more serious problem than unemployment. The two major "style" issues were abortion and amnesty for Vietnam deserters and draft evaders, on both of which the public seemed divided and the candidates fudged, though they differed in emphasis. Carter favored a "pardon" for draft evaders, but refused to call it "amnesty" in order to avoid admitting that opponents of the war may have been right. At the same time he said he would refuse to grant even a "pardon" to service people who had deserted. Ford claimed credit for a scheme tried in 1974 that permitted evaders and deserters to return and receive an "amnesty discharge" after they had worked for two years in a hospital or in similar work symbolizing contrition. Relatively few had taken advantage of this program. Ford, and the Republican platform, opposed abortion. Carter said he personally opposed it, though he refused to endorse legislation prohibiting it.

Three television debates between the presidential candidates and one between the vice-presidential candidates (Republican Robert Dole and Democrat Walter Mondale) did not markedly clarify positions, serving chiefly to convey an impression of the candidates' personalities and to test their ability to avoid political traps.

Developments in the months preceding election day certainly influenced the results and chiefly hurt the Ford candidacy. Economic activity declined significantly in the two months before the election, fueling concerns about recession and a high unemployment rate. Organized labor, which had refused to help McGovern four years earlier, worked hard for Carter and was especially helpful in turning out a large Democratic vote in the industrial states. The new Election Reform Law also helped Carter by limiting the funds the Republican organizations could raise and spend. As Republicans had long outspent Democrats by a wide margin in presidential campaigns, these limits reduced an important advantage. Though the law permits additional spending on behalf of a candidate as long as it is done independently of the party organizations, uncertainty about what spending the courts might later hold illegal apparently worried contributors. Though Watergate was not stressed as a Democratic theme, Ford's association with Nixon and his pardon of his predecessor rankled many voters.

Doubts about Carter persisted to the end of the campaign. As a Southerner and a "born-again" Baptist, Carter apparently seemed an enigma and a risk to many traditional northern Democrats and independents.

Carter nonetheless rebuilt something like the Roosevelt coalition, winning considerable support from the South, organized labor, low-income groups, blacks, and some European ethnics. A CBS News poll[11] of voters indicated that Carter had won these levels of support from some critical groups:

blacks	83 percent	farm areas	43 percent
Catholics	55 percent	cities (above 500,000)	60 percent
Protestants	46 percent	Democrats	80 percent
Jews	68 percent	Republicans	11 percent
union members	62 percent	Independents	48 percent

Only 53 percent of the eligible voters cast ballots, marking the fourth successive presidential election in which there had been a decline in voter turnout.

[11] *New York Times,* November 4, 1976, p. 25.

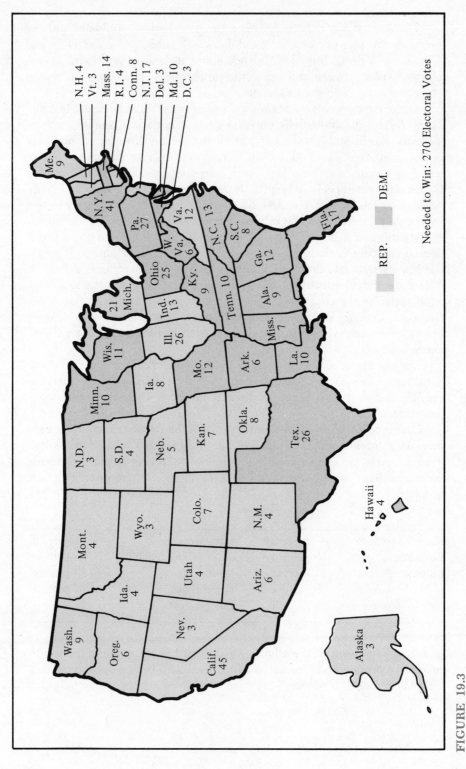

FIGURE 19.3

State-by-State Electoral Vote in the 1976 Presidential Election

Labels on map:

N.H. 4
Vt. 3
Mass. 14
R.I. 4
Conn. 8
N.J. 17
Del. 3
Md. 10
D.C. 3

Me. 9
N.Y. 41
Pa. 27
W. Va. 6
Va. 12
N.C. 13
S.C. 8
Fla. 17
Mich. 21
Ohio 25
Ky. 9
Tenn. 10
Ga. 12
Ala. 9
Ind. 13
Ill. 26
Mo. 12
Ark. 6
Miss. 7
La. 10
Wis. 11
Ia. 8
Minn. 10
N.D. 3
S.D. 4
Neb. 5
Kan. 7
Okla. 8
Tex. 26
Mont. 4
Wyo. 3
Colo. 7
N.M. 4
Ida. 4
Utah 4
Ariz. 6
Wash. 9
Oreg. 6
Nev. 3
Calif. 45
Hawaii 4
Alaska 3

REP.

DEM.

Needed to Win: 270 Electoral Votes

The 1978 Election

The 1978 elections produced little change in the makeup of the House and Senate, and only modest change among state Governors. Normally, the party out of power expects to gain substantially in the House and somewhat in the Senate. Republican gains of 12 and 3 seats, respectively, although more than had been predicted a year before the election, were still far less than "normal." In all respects, voters appeared to be voting along traditional lines (people with higher income and education vote Republican, and the opposite, for example). Perhaps the most significant fact about the election was that only 36 percent of the total eligible electorate actually turned out to vote for House candidates. This was the lowest proportion since World War Two, when many voters were away from their residences at war or at work. It was the culmination (to date) of a continuing nonvoting trend, and (together with the fact that presidential voting turnout has also been steadily decreasing) gave rise to concern about the continuing legitimacy and democratic claim of national institutions. It also gave special opportunity to the efforts of special interest groups, such as the gun lobby and the right-to-life movement, which succeeded (sometimes together) in defeating or seriously threatening several targeted incumbents.

Party labels were not uniformly synonymous with liberal or conservative policy preferences (in some cases, Republicans appeared more liberal than their Democratic opponents, or vice versa), but observers agreed that the new Republicans (and chastened Democrats) in the House and Senate meant a somewhat more conservative Congress. In the statehouses, Republican victories went more often to the moderate wing of the party. They ensured that the party would go into the 1980 presidential election in control of 5 of the 10 largest and most important states.

Looking ahead, the *New York Times* and CBS News sought to compare the policy preferences of candidates and voters on some key issues of the next Congress. As before, the results showed that political activists/candidates were more decisive in their positions than voters, and along predictable lines.[12] For example, the following percentages favored each of these two prominent issues:

	Dem. Cand.	Dem. Voters	Repub. Cand.	Repub. Voters
Large cut in federal income tax	24	46	45	97
Government-financed national health insurance	64	61	32	10

[12] *The New York Times*, November 8, 1978, p. A21. Based on a national sampling of voters leaving polling places and all but a handful of incumbents and candidates for the House.

TABLE 19.1 *The 1978 Elections and National Politics*

	1976		1978		Net
	Dem.	*Repub.*	*Dem.*	*Repub.*	Change
U.S. House of Representatives	288	147	276	159	R, +12
U.S. Senate	62	38	59	41	R, +3
State Governors	38	12	32	18	R, +6

    (States Dem. to Repub.: Minnesota, Nebraska, Nevada, Oregon,
Pennsylvania, South Dakata, Tennessee, Texas.
States Repub. or Ind. to Dem.: Kansas, Maine, New Hampshire,
South Carolina.
Newcomers: 20 out of 36 elected—Dem. 11, Repub. 9).

Traditionally, voters cluster towards the middle, while activists take up polar positions.

In a series of post-election articles, *The New York Times* summed up what many observers thought they saw evidenced again in the 1978 election, perhaps now more ominously than ever. This was a kind of on-going disintegration of the established political parties, the rise of special interests, a deepening voter malaise, and a crisis of governability. Cynicism and skepticism about the sincerity and capacity of politicians to do *anything* constructive appeared to be at all-time highs. In this situation, veteran observers questioned whether the national governing system itself might be endangered.[13]

Interest Groups

It is often said that the United States is a nation of "joiners," and that the voluntary associations to which Americans belong in such numbers serve as a kind of auxiliary representation system. Thus, whether or not one feels "represented" by a congressman or senator, one can always find a group that represents one's interests and become effective in politics through its organized activities. Once again, however, it is middle- and upper-middle-class people who are most likely to join such interest groups. And, as Table 19.2 shows, the incidence of membership is *not* particularly high in the United States. Only 57 percent of Americans belong to *any* voluntary association, compared with 47 percent in Great Britain and 44 percent in West Germany. If it were not for the distinctive American tendency to belong to church organizations and fraternal bodies (such as the Elks, Moose, Masons, Rotary, Kiwanis, and the like), the United States might not rank ahead of the other countries at all.

[13] *Ibid.*, November 12–14, 1978, pp. 1ff.

TABLE 19.2   *Membership in Various Types of Organizations, by Nation*

Organization	U.S.	U.K.	Germany	Italy	Mexico
Trade Unions	14	22	15	6	11
Business	4	4	2	5	2
Professional	4	3	6	3	5
Farm	3	0	4	2	0
Social	13	14	10	3	4
Charitable	3	3	2	9	6
Religious°	19	4	3	6	5
Civic-political	11	3	3	8	3
Cooperative	6	3	2	2	0
Veterans'	6	5	1	4	0
Fraternal†	13				
Other	6	3	9	6	0
Total percentage of members	57	47	44	30	24
Total number of respondents	970	963	955	995	1,007

° This refers to church-related organizations, not to church affiliation itself.

† U.S. only.

Source: Reprinted from Gabriel Almond and Sidney Verba, *The Civic Culture* (Princeton, N.J.: Princeton University Press, 1963), pp. 246–247.

People tend to join groups to express interests that are stable and fairly strong. The doctor who joins the county medical society, the worker who joins a union, the factory owner who joins a trade association, and the hunter who joins the National Rifle Association all have other interests that do not give rise to organizational membership, chiefly because they are not as important or continuous as these. Many people do not join organizations, in spite of stable and strong economic interests, because they reap the benefits of relevant pressure groups' activities anyway. Businessmen benefit from the pro-business lobbying of the Chamber of Commerce whether or not they are members; and workers often win higher wages because employers want to *discourage* them from joining unions. One astute analyst has suggested that membership in interest groups is often dependent either on coercion (such as a requirement that lawyers join the state bar association in order to practice law) or on incidental benefits (such as a union pension plan or a malpractice insurance plan available only to members of a medical association).[14]

In any case, it is chiefly people with solid economic and social roots

[14] Mancur Olson, *The Logic of Collective Action* (New York: Schocken, 1968).

who become members of interest groups. If people have strong common interests, but are not brought together by those interests in a way that makes organization likely, groups acting on their behalf rarely emerge. This is true of the poor, the unemployed, the workers who work intermittently or are very poorly paid, and consumers. It cannot be taken for granted, therefore, that every interest will have its organized "watchdog." The oil and natural gas companies will lobby effectively through their trade associations, but the people who buy heating oil and gasoline are unlikely to organize at all.

Legislative and Administrative Lobbying

Pressure groups that lobby for favorable legislation are most effective when they can be helpful to the legislators they try to influence. Buttonholing a congressman at a cocktail party is not likely to be very useful to a lobbyist, nor is an organized letter-writing campaign. The most effective lobbyists are those who regularly provide useful information to legislators, and so come to be trusted. A congressman often needs accurate information, about both technical matters and the strength of various groups' feelings about an issue; thus the lobbyist who gains a reputation for accurate reporting on such matters wins goodwill and influence for his group.[15] Needless to say, a large campaign contribution from a pressure group signals an expectation that the recipient will continue to support the group or will be sensitive to its needs in the future.

Most pressure groups devote more attention to administrative than legislative bodies, though these efforts are usually less widely recognized or publicized. To the National Association of Broadcasters, the rules and decisions of the Federal Communications Commission are usually more critical than changes in the Communications Act; thus the NAB maintains close ties with the FCC through formal recommendations regarding rules and cases and through personal ties to commissioners and staff members.

In general, pressure groups try to avoid publicity and to work through on-going contacts with an agency's staff when they are getting what they want from the agency and the issues are technical or complex. This strategy prevents potential opposition from being awakened to action. Groups that are losing under existing arrangements, on the other hand, usually gain more by publicizing an issue in the hope that a larger public will support them. Paper mills in Wisconsin are not likely to appeal for public support of their right to pollute rivers with contaminating chemicals as long as they are allowed to do so without interference; but environmental groups are sure to try to arouse as wide a public as possible to the dangers of pollution. "Fellow travellers" who are not themselves members of pressure groups often make a critical difference in determining policy outcomes.

[15] For a good account of legislative lobbying, see Lester Milbrath, *The Washington Lobbyists* (Chicago: Rand McNally, 1963).

TABLE 19.3 **25 Top Spenders of the Organizations that Filed Lobby Spending Reports for 1973 and 1972**

Organization	1973	1972
Common Cause	$934,835	$558,839
International Union, United Automobile, Aerospace and Agricultural Implement Workers	460,992	no spending record
American Postal Workers Union (AFL-CIO)	393,399	208,767
American Federation of Labor-Congress of Industrial Organizations (AFL-CIO)	240,800	216,294
American Trucking Associations Inc.	226,157	137,804
American Nurses Association Inc.	218,354	109,642
United States Savings and Loan League	204,221	191,726
Gas Supply Committee	195,537	11,263
Disabled American Veterans	193,168	159,431
The Committee of Publicly Owned Companies	180,493	no spending record
American Farm Bureau Federation	170,472	180,678
National Education Association	162,755	no spending record
National Association of Letter Carriers	160,597	154,187
National Association of Home Builders of the United States	152,177	99,031
Recording Industry Association of America Inc.	141,111	88,396
National Council of Farmer Cooperatives	140,560	184,346
American Insurance Association	139,395	82,395
The Farmers' Educational and Cooperative Union of America	138,403	113,156
Committee of Copyright Owners	135,095	no spending record
National Housing Conference Inc.	125,726	77,906
American Petroleum Institute	121,276	38,656
American Medical Association	114,859	96,145
Citizens for Control of Federal Spending	113,659	no spending record
American Civil Liberties Union	102,595	73,131
National Association of Insurance Agents Inc.	87,422	50,924

Source: Congressional Quarterly, *The Washington Lobby,* 2nd edition, 1974, p. 38.

Crosspressures

Neither members of pressure groups nor other people necessarily have singleminded, fixed opinions on controversial issues. An individual's various concerns often conflict with each other, producing what are sometimes called "overlapping interests" or "crosspressures." A member of the United Automobile Workers who is prejudiced against blacks, for example, may be "crosspressured" about his union's official stand in favor of fair employment practices. In an influential book, David Truman[16] has argued that such overlapping interests moderate social conflict and promote stability; people who are divided on some issues are allies on others, and such crisscrossing divisions of opinion help cement the society together. If people who disagreed on foreign policy also disagreed on economic policy, educational policy, civil rights, and everything else, the society would be divided into two hostile camps and civil war would probably be inevitable; because disagreements are moderated by cross-cutting agreements, we have moderation and stability.

This is a reassuring view, and overlapping interests often do have that result; but the United States is in fact characterized by frequent outbreaks of violence, deep polarization of opinion, and occasional instances of riot and civil war. Critics of Truman's argument make several important points. First, it is not justifiable simply to assume that a person who holds membership in two groups with conflicting goals is in fact crosspressured and therefore inhibited from taking a strong position. Crosspressuring is a *subjective* condition, and can only be shown to exist by empirical examination of people's actual behavior when pressured to act in inconsistent ways. Often they simply ignore one of the pressures. Furthermore, it is argued, people do not necessarily try to reduce tension in their lives; they often *seek out* tension-producing situations, including those produced by conflicting political pressures. There is evidence, for example, that voters often seek out conflicting opinions, rather than selectively exposing themselves only to congenial views.[17] The implication of this finding is that crosspressuring is not necessarily a moderating influence on pressure groups or on political conflict. It is also compatible with intense feelings, social tension, and the outbreak of political violence.

Elite Dominance of the Orthodox Channels of Non-Elite Influence

The management of interest groups is, as we have noted, often the private preserve of those with higher status and other skills and resources of leadership. There are also patterns of association be-

[16] David Truman, *The Governmental Process* (New York: Alfred A. Knopf, 1951).

[17] Peter W. Sperlich, *Conflict and Harmony in Human Affairs: A Study of Cross-pressures and Political Behavior* (Chicago: Rand McNally, 1971).

tween groups that tend to create a structural advantage for elites and their interests. One is the tendency of people engaged in making or selling the same product or service to form an organization to promote and protect their interests. Steel manufacturers, broadcast station licensees, trucking companies, physicians, stockbrokers, real estate brokers, cotton farmers, and hundreds of other groupings of people with the same production or sales interests have organized into associations to win favorable governmental policies and sometimes to influence private economic policies as well.

Such interest groups typically represent economic or social elites. Usually, though not invariably, the people who ultimately *buy* their goods or services do not find it natural, easy, or even possible to organize themselves into interest groups. The consumers of manufactured or grown products, the patients who pay physicians' bills, and the viewers of television programs and commercials rarely organize to promote their interests politically or economically. They find it hard or impossible to do so, for some obvious reasons—their large numbers, their lack of face-to-face contacts or facilities for communicating with each other, and, above all, people's tendency not to define themselves as consumers. They find themselves politically divided by their other interests: economic, ethnic, regional, religious, ideological, and so on. This pattern can be summed up in the generalization that people's interests as producers, for which they are paid, are typically seen as primary and are intensely pursued. People's interests as consumers are typically perceived as secondary and are hard to pursue in an organized and effective way.

The Consumer's Problem

Some exceptional groups of consumers do organize effectively. But these groups are themselves elites, rather than part of the mass public. Companies that ship their products by truck or rail are organized into interest groups, and the consequence is that their interests, like those of the truck and railroad carriers, are politically protected. But the ultimate buyers of these products, who do not form interest groups, pay for the protection accorded to these elites both in higher prices and in taxes, which often go for governmental subsidies to various businesses. Similarly, management groups, which are consumers of labor, are organized into effective interest groups. Here again the outcome is often that organized labor and management groups are able, through political and economic agreements, to pass the costs of their price and wage gains onto a mass public of consumers that is not organized—at least not as consumers.

The difficulty of organizing interest groups made up of consumers is especially burdensome to the poor—that large part of the mass public least likely to be represented and helped by any kind of interest group of producers or sellers, including labor unions. Fewer poor than affluent people vote, and they do not vote as a bloc in any case. Their main eco-

U.S. TREASURY

FREE
HANDOUTS TO BIG OPERATORS

LECTURES ON
ENTERPRISE
TO LOWEST-INCOME PEOPLE

OIL

LOCKHEED

PENN-
CENTRAL
BANKS

FOOD STAMPS

©1975 HERBLOCK

"The system of free enterprise . . . has fired the imagination and determination of our people."—*Sec. William Simon*

nomic resource is their labor, and because they are largely unskilled, intermittently employed, or unemployed, and not attached to the mass production industries, they are for the most part not organized into labor unions. What political power they do have derives chiefly from the support of sympathetic liberals and others who have political resources. For reasons already considered, however, such support frequently produces largely symbolic benefits for the poor and the disadvantaged: laws declaring their right to vote in a social setting that makes it unlikely they will use that right massively and effectively; laws purporting to protect them from economic exploitation when the agencies administering the laws are influenced chiefly by the economically powerful; civil rights laws that reassure liberals their values are being advanced but that actually make only token housing, credit, jobs, and social status available to those who suffer from social discrimination.

Interest groups, therefore, serve chiefly to institutionalize and formalize the exercise of political resources deriving from wealth, social status, and the ability to organize effectively—that is, they operate for the benefit of the elite. They are not generally and widely efficacious as a resource for the mass public.

Elite Influence Through Political Parties

To some extent, though not as clearly or consistently, the same must be said of political parties. Two central characteristics of the major American political parties make it easier than it would otherwise be for elite groups to use them to mobilize support for their interests. Party discipline is minimal or nonexistent; and the locus of power in both major parties is local and decentralized. The implications of each of these characteristics for elite maneuverability are worth attention.

The lack of party discipline in the major American parties means that an elected representative is usually entirely free to support or oppose particular policies regardless of his or her party's stand on the issues. In disciplined parties, such as those in England, a party member who fails to support the party position on a major issue can expect to be disciplined, or even expelled from the party. In the United States discipline is extremely rare, and Republican and Democratic legislators at all levels of government constantly cast votes inconsistent with their parties' platforms or caucus decisions.

One effect of this state of affairs is that the values of those who command political resources are reflected in legislators' votes even when they conflict with the party's formal positions or rhetorical appeals. Southern Democrats consistently vote against civil rights bills even when their party's platform has endorsed them. A congressman from Pittsburgh is likely to vote for a high protective tariff to keep out foreign steel even if his party favors fewer restrictions on foreign trade.

The net effect of such lack of discipline is that American voters have no assurance that the party they support will in fact work for the policies or principles it has promised to support in order to attract their votes. On the contrary, they can be quite certain that, as a party, it will do nothing of the kind. In fact, the lack of party discipline makes every candidate and officeholder more vulnerable to pressure from powerful interests in his or her constituency. In a disciplined party system, pressure groups have to concentrate on influencing the party's platform, for that is what determines the subsequent behavior of party members. In an undisciplined system, the platform becomes largely symbolic, as we have already noted; the individual candidate or officeholder becomes the focus of pressures. It is not surprising, therefore, that there may exist a "senator from Boeing Aircraft Corporation" or that many candidates and legislators from diverse areas should be offered large campaign contributions by conservative Texas oil interests. Elites can take advantage of undisciplined parties to maximize their impact on individual policymakers. The second characteristic of the major parties—decentralization of power to the state and local level—makes the kind of pressure and bargaining just described even easier and more effective.

Interest Group Spending in Elections

For many years business and labor groups have contributed substantial funds to candidates for public office, easily evading prohibitions or legal limits on contributions by forming "political action committees," each of which can spend up to the legal limit. This device has been especially useful to labor unions.

In the later half of the 1970s new and militant conservative organizations began to form political action committees and to spend larger sums than the established labor and business groups. Of the five biggest spenders in legislative election campaigns in the first half of 1978, four political action committees were linked to the far right. The fifth was the American Medical Association, long a supporter of conservative causes. The top five were:

Citizens for the Republic (Ronald Reagan's organization)	$2.1 million
National Conservative Political Action Committee	2 million
Committee for the Survival of a Free Congress	1.5 million
American Medical Political Action Committee	1.4 million
Gun Owners of America	1.2 million

During the same period the National Association of Realtors spent almost $1.2 million and the AFL–CIO $735,000.

Political action committees have been springing up at a fast rate. At the end of 1975 there were 722, but by the middle of 1978 there were almost 1500.[18]

Alternative Forms of Political Participation

The alternative forms of participation span a wide range of activities. Some are as authorized and accepted as, though less formalized than, elections or interest-group actions. Others are discouraged or forcefully repressed, but nevertheless represent means by which segments of non-elites participate in politics and may influence policy. In the latter case, of course, many consequences may ensue, some quite different from those sought by the participants. In general, although the alternative

[18] The data cited in this section were reported in the *Chicago Sun-Times*, September 8, 1978, p. 16.

forms are frequently efforts to bypass the established channels, they exhibit many of the same class biases as do parties, elections, and interest-group activity.

One of the most obvious and accepted modes of communication and "pressure" from non-elites to decision-making elites is the simple act of writing a letter, or signing a petition, to be sent to an official or a newspaper. Congressmen are sometimes said to "wait for the mail" before making up their minds how to vote on an issue. There are several problems with this assumption, however. One is that people tend to write or petition those they have reason to believe are on their side or at least on the fence. This means that letterwriters favoring a proposal write to decisionmakers who favor it, and those against write to those who oppose it. The net result, even if the decisionmakers take their mail seriously, is no change in positions. Another problem is that decisionmakers become impervious to pressure campaigns organized by very small interest groups.

Even more important is the fact that writing letters, and to a lesser extent carrying and signing petitions, is more likely to be undertaken by people who are relatively well-educated and upper-class. Moreover, even within class and education levels, it is an act more likely to be undertaken by conservatives than by liberals. In an effort to find out why the 1964 Republican strategists thought there was a "hidden" conservative vote, the Michigan Survey Research Center compared the political preferences of those who wrote letters to officials or newspapers with those who did not.[19] The researchers found, first, that only 15 percent of the population had *ever* written a letter to a public official, and that two-thirds of *all* letters were written by a total of 3 percent of the population. The 3 percent was distinctly conservative in every ideological dimension; by "vote" of letter writers, Goldwater would have been elected by a comfortable majority. Thus, if decisionmakers took guidance, or if officials sought to measure the mood of the country, from the views expressed in the mail to officials and newspapers, they would acquire a very skewed image.

"Citizen Participation"

Some alternative forms of participation are built into the process of administering and implementing laws. Juries, for instance, place a significant function in the hands of citizens, and might well serve as means of communicating to higher levels citizens' dissatisfaction with law or with their circumstances. But juries are drawn from lists of voters or property owners (or, in the case of grand juries, from "blue-ribbon" panels), and thus reflect class orientations. Nevertheless, juries in many cases involving political figures and issues (Black Panthers, draft resisters,

---

19 These data are drawn from Philip Converse, Warren Miller, Jerold G. Rusk, and Arthur C. Wolfe, "Continuity and Change in American Politics: Parties and Issues in the 1968 Election," *American Political Science Review* 63 (1969), p. 333.

the Chicago 7 trial, and others) have refused to convict or been relatively lenient, suggesting that some potential prosecutions may have been discouraged by these results.

In many areas of governmental activity, advisory boards of citizens are required by law. Urban renewal, Selective Service, and other agencies deliberately engage citizens in the implementation of their programs. But they accomplish relatively little on behalf of the preferences of ordinary citizens, because participants in these programs are drawn from the higher echelons of non-elites. Businessmen, local leaders, and higher-status people generally dominate these positions. Only in the Community Action Agencies of the poverty program has there been a real contest over who is to shape a governmental program. Lower-class citizens did begin to take part, and the result was first an amendment to the law that gave local governments control over the local aspects of such programs, and then such controversy that the funding for many local units was sharply cut back or eliminated.

In general, formal participation by non-elites in policy-making bodies is bound to be largely ritual unless it is accompanied by a form of power non-elites can assert, such as a strike, boycott, or disruption of programs important to elites. The chance to participate is often regarded as a concession, but it is more often a way of making sure a low-status group will not resort to effective protest or resistance. Participation is so effective a way of diverting discontented people from disorder that it is often *required* of low-status groups in totalitarian settings: in prisons, mental hospitals, schools, and totalitarian states, where it serves as a form of pseudodemocracy.

A much less institutionalized form of participation that has arisen from time to time in American history, and particularly during the 1960s, is the protest demonstration, sit-in, disruption, or deliberate refusal to obey rules. Those who have been unable to make themselves heard through the established channels have resorted to these tactics, often with great success, when their claims were consistent with generally shared values and not at extreme odds with the basic features of the political system. But when they have been unable to find allies, or have been seen as dangerously at variance with established values or familiar political practices, rejection and repression have been very harsh. Successful protest-type activity requires allies, or at the very least inaction on the part of those who might oppose the protesters. It involves risks of a personal kind for the participants, and is difficult to keep up for a long period of time without a supportive environment. Thus it depends on achieving some tangible goal, usually from an existing political structure.

Another, even less institutionalized alternative form of participation is the spontaneous riot. Although clearly grounded in the circumstances of ghetto existence, the riots of the 1960s were spontaneous, in contrast to deliberate obstructive sit-ins or other protest tactics. Touched off by one or another form of provocation, they often engaged thousands of participants for days at a time. The immediate consequences were destruction of millions of dollars' worth of property and the deaths of many ghetto residents at the hands of police and National Guard forces. Subsequently, governmental assistance to ghetto residents and other poor people increased, but so did strong popular support for future repressive measures and political candidates who stood for such action.

Riot and Demonstration Patterns

Patterns of participation in both riots and student demonstrations offer some insight into these alternative forms of participation. In the case of the ghetto riots of 1967, for example, it is clear that substantial proportions of each community were involved. Supplemental studies undertaken for the National Commission on Civil Disorders estimate that participants represented from 11 to 35 percent of residents of the riot areas in major cities (Detroit, Newark, New Haven) where riots occurred.[20] The composition of the rioters was roughly representative of the occupational makeup of the ghetto population, with a slight emphasis on the less skilled and the unemployed. Nearly all of those arrested during the riots were residents of the neighborhood involved.[21] The riots were thus fairly broad-based actions by cross-sections of the area populations. They were not caused by the "criminal element," by "outside agitators," or by a tiny minority of militants. They were, it seems fair to say, genuine expressions of community protest of an essentially political kind. Certainly they were perceived as such by most blacks; and several surveys have shown that, while most blacks do not approve of rioting, they see it in many cases as necessary and helpful toward achieving black goals.[22] Younger blacks in particular tend to believe that violence will be necessary before such objectives are attained.

But the same riots were perceived quite differently by whites. We have already seen the electoral consequences of these riots and other race problems. National elites, with limited exceptions, tended to emphasize theories that outside agitators, a few militants, or habitual troublemakers had caused the riots. The Kerner Report alone blamed "white racism"; it went largely unheard. Table 19.4 lists the causes identified by six key groups within fifteen major cities of the country in 1968. Merchants, employers, and the police saw the riots as primarily the work of criminal elements and nationalists or militants; educators, social workers, and political workers came closer to the explanation offered by blacks

---

[20] Robert M. Fogelson and Robert B. Hill, "Who Riots? A Study of Participation in the 1967 Riots," *Supplemental Studies for the National Advisory Commission on Civil Disorders* (Washington: Government Printing Office, 1968), p. 231.

[21] *Ibid.*, pp. 236, 237.

[22] Opinion data in this section are drawn from Angus Campbell and Howard Schuman, "Racial Attitudes in Fifteen American Cities," in Fogelson and Hill, *Supplemental Studies,* pp. 48–52.

TABLE 19.4 *"Theories" of Riot Causation Among Six Occupations*
(*in percentages*)

Proportions rating "theory" as "main reason" or "largely true"

"Theory"	Police	Educa-tors	Social workers	Political workers	Mer-chants	Em-ployers
A. Unheard Negro complaints	31	70	72	72	48	47
B. Criminal elements	69	33	27	27	65	42
C. Nationalists and militants	77	46	38	39	65	62
D. Riots as political acts	27	26	25	20	23	24
E. Police brutality	9	33	37	53	21	7
F. Negroes basically violent	28	8	4	8	23	11

Source: Campbell and Schuman, "Racial Attitudes," p. 96.

themselves. Only small minorities in any category saw the riots as political acts. Consistent with these impressions on the part of local elites, white residents of the same cities perceived the riots entirely differently than their black neighbors. Table 19.5 presents these contrasts very clearly. It is as if the two groups of people had seen totally different events—which, of course, they did. Most whites surveyed saw the riots as opportunities for looting, and a substantial minority said that even orderly marches to protest racial discrimination were unjustified; two-thirds believed that sit-ins were unjustified. In the aftermath of the riots, there can be little doubt that white opinion hardened firmly against further advance by blacks. By comparison, the actions of (essentially white) national elites may well seem generous.

The Aftermath of the Riots of the 1960s

Eruptions in the black ghettos of a large number of major cities in the 1960s almost certainly helped keep welfare rolls high by frightening the middle class into liberalizing eligibility and benefits, at least for a time.[23] But it is already clear that the riots have not significantly changed the social or economic conditions of the poor and/or black population. Each wave of riots in American history has produced commissions and recommendations for reform in employment practices, city services to the poor, housing, transportation, and racist attitudes; but such recommendations

[23] Frances F. Piven and Richard A. Cloward, *Regulating the Poor* (New York: Random House, 1971).

TABLE 19.5 *Have Riots Helped or Hurt the Negro Cause?* (in percentages)

"On the whole, do you think the disturbances have helped or hurt the cause of Negro rights, or would you say they haven't made much difference?"

	Negro		White	
	Men	*Women*	*Men*	*Women*
Helped	37	30	13	14
Hurt	22	24	69	59
Helped and hurt equally	12	11	7	7
Made no difference	21	28	9	17
Don't know	8	7	2	3
	100	100	100	100

"Why do you feel that way?"

	Negro		White	
First reason given	*Men*	*Women*	*Men*	*Women*
Helped:				
Tangible gains (e.g., more jobs)	19	20	8	8
Whites understand Negroes' problems better	14	10	8	8
Show of Negro power	9	5	2	1
Hurt:				
Destruction, injury	8	8	2	3
Increased anti-Negro sentiments	16	19	64	54
Made no difference:				
No tangible gain	19	23	5	12
Negroes are still not satisfied	0	1	7	10
Don't know	15	14	4	4
	100	100	100	100

Source: Campbell and Schuman, "Racial Attitudes," p. 49.

yield few lasting results. The accompanying account of the situation in Watts—a black suburb of Los Angeles that experienced one of the earliest, most publicized, and most studied riots of the 1960s—is typical: it describes a relapse into acceptance of high unemployment, endemic crime, poverty, and hopelessness.

Nor did unrest on university campuses bring about any lasting change in curricula or increase in student power. In the middle 1970s student political activism was slight compared to what it had been five years earlier, though this passivity reflected defeatism more than the smugness that had typified the campus scene in the 1950s.

The disorders of the 1960s did teach law enforcement officials more effective methods of crowd control, and federal money is now more freely available for police equipment to suppress popular demonstrations: tear gas, armored vehicles, sophisticated communications equipment, and firearms.

When resort to resistance is unorganized and short-lived, and when its suppression by police forces is effective, this form of nonelite participation seems to bring about only temporary and token reform at best.

In Watts a Decade Later:
Poverty in Ashes of Riots

By Jon Nordheimer

LOS ANGELES, Aug. 6.—Ten years after the fires of the era of the long hot summer were kindled in Watts, the black ghetto on the south side of Los Angeles has lapsed into a cold autumn of desperation.

Watts, for a while, became a workshop for new ideas and bold invention—a laboratory for social theory and strategies financed by the foundations and the universities and the Federal Government.

But the money and manpower dried up, so did the programs and the will of those who felt that individual risk and sacrifice could make the difference. Like a great wave that surged forth in full flood, it eventually retreated under resistance, carrying away with it the elements not irretrievably rooted there.

Compared with the economic and spiritual desolation that exists today, the conditions that sparked six days of looting and burning a decade ago now seem almost salubrious.

For Watts today is a community that has been left behind in the advancement of those who by luck or pluck were able to take advantage of the gains won by black Americans in the intervening years.

Watts today, in the view of those inside and outside the community, is a compendium of urban failure, a nesting place of the social and racial ills that represent the nation's retreat from the challenge of finding effective measures to deal with its most intractable problems.

Like scores of other black, central-city ghettos, Watts in the summer of 1975 has been further devastated by high unemployment and other ills of the national recession, yet so far there has been no sign of a renewal of mass violence.

It is an area stripped of stable leadership, for those who can escape Watts depart at the first opportunity, leaving behind a paralyzed society of welfare mothers, street gangs and the elderly. Unemployment is running about 50 per cent among those who can work, breeding hard-core social dependence and crime.

The white-owned shops and small plants that were burned out or closed by the rioting have never reopened. Houses that were removed by renewal projects were not replaced. Economic conditions that created a recession elsewhere fell with a hammer blow here.

"This whole environment is designed for failure," says Gregory Welch, a 25-year-old ex-convict, as he stands at the intersection of Central Avenue and 103d Street, the epicenter of the 1965 riots. "Watts is all negative with very few positives."

There are few who dispute that assessment. "What we are seeing today is an overwhelming mental depression, particularly among the young, that life holds no promise of opportunity for them," says Dr. Roland Jefferson, a black psychiatrist who is a consultant at the Watts Health Center.

Consequently, Dr. Jefferson notes, ghetto youths in recent years have moved deeper into self-destructive pursuits, turning aggression inward through a variety of forms such as drug addiction, alcoholism or suicide, a pattern he describes as "ominous."

"The increase in the number of black alcoholics, particularly among the young, is phenomenal," he says. "Even more frightening is the sharp rise in young black suicides, where black males under the age of 25 now have the highest suicide rate of any group in the country."

Technically, Watts is a three-square-mile community of about 28,000 residents in the southwestern corner of Los Angeles, a palm-lined ghetto of one-family cottages and sun-splashed public housing projects that appear benign compared to the festering tenements of New York's Harlem or the Chicago South Side.

But emotionally Watts represents the broader, predominantly south-central corridor of the city that fell under curfew during the 1965 riots that resulted in 34 deaths, more than 1,000 injured, and property damage estimated at $40 million.

Median family income in Watts is about $6,000, a figure that includes welfare benefits. Increasingly, it has become a community of welfare mothers and children, unemployed young blacks and the elderly. The group between 25 and 50 has become the vanishing generation of Watts.

Since the riots, Watts has become one of the most analyzed communities in America, yet the only tangible product of all the research and all the reports is a dust-gathering pile of paperwork and the corrosive emotion of failure.

Watts today is not typical of anything except a community where the cycle of poverty, promises and a new decline has exhausted the energy of change and hope. Conditions are not quite that bad for poor blacks in other areas of Los Angeles, but some other areas come close to Watts.

The city of Compton to the south, for example, is a community with black political control where conditions were recently described by a recent special report of the Los Angeles grand jury as "worse than at the time of the Watts revolt."

As in Watts, unemployment in Compton is running above 50 per cent, and an estimated 60 per cent of the population there is receiving some form of public assistance, compared to 24 per cent in Watts 10 years ago.

And almost no one knows what to do about these conditions. For the most part—with few skills, money or other resources—there is little that the people of Watts can do outside of trying to survive one day at a time. Even the threat of rioting has little support, though each summer day still holds the potential for a spontaneous outburst.

"The cops got all the power," says Robert Searles, a lounger outside a Central Avenue barbecue stand. "Rocks ain't much good against tanks."

The Impact of Non-Elites on Policy

Elections are an uncertain vehicle of political participation. Interest groups are highly specialized. The alternative forms of participation are erratic and even counterproductive. And yet needs, claims, and demands *are* introduced into the political arena by the actions of segments of non-elites. At least to some extent, elites feel obliged, or are forced, to respond. Their response may be merely symbolic, negative, or marginal; but there is nevertheless often *some* response, and sometimes one consistent with non-elite demands.

Frequently, a fully satisfactory "solution" is impossible because of perceived conditions, opposition from other segments of non-elites, or elites' priorities and preferences. These determinations are made by elites, of course. Their power, status, and legitimacy enable them to decide how to fit demands that are strongly pressed and supported by established values into the mix of policy and practice that characterizes the political system. Other demands can normally be deflected or dismissed. In this process, elites are aided by the screening effect of the greater participation and efficacy of the better-educated and higher-status members of non-elites. They cushion or absorb much of the thrust of deviant, minority, or lower-class demands before such demands emerge into the national political arena and begin to induce elite response.

In many instances, at least some members of elites *want* to respond; they may even have been waiting for a chance to do so. Elites may support mass demands because they expect to benefit from doing so. Free universal public education is a case in point. Before the Industrial Revolution, free public education was an issue that divided Americans along economic class lines. It was a major plank in the platform of one of our earliest third parties, the Workingmen's Party, which gained considerable support among wage-earners in Philadelphia between 1828 and 1832. The issue grew less and less controversial as industrial technologies required that a larger proportion of the work force be literate and possess elementary skills in arithmetic and what were called the "agricultural, industrial, and mechanic arts." Indeed, many states began establishing normal schools, state colleges, and universities around the middle of the nineteenth century, and in the Morrill Act of 1862 the federal government helped them to do so. As industry and agriculture have required work forces with increasingly complex skills, elite support for education at all levels has also increased. To some degree, this trend has been further bolstered by the fact that methods of financing state universities provide a direct subsidy to the largely middle-class students who attend them.

Sometimes elites have even more pressing and immediate economic reasons to support mass demands. In the early years of the twentieth century, a growing number of states enacted minimum-wage laws. It was widely acknowledged that if workers were unable to live on their earnings, they should be entitled to a wage that would at least support their families at a subsistence level. This policy was supported both on a moral basis and because it was recognized that people could not work efficiently when undernourished. A chief reason for the enactment of the first federal minimum-wage law in 1938 was its support by some powerful industrial groups, especially New England textile manufacturers. Forced by unions of their workers to pay higher wages than their unorganized Southern competitors, the New England mill owners saw in the minimum wage a device to increase their competitors' labor cost to the level of their own, thereby improving their competitive position.

Social security legislation, certainly a significant benefit to a large part of the public, has also enjoyed substantial elite support, for economic and other reasons. Growing worker demands for industrial pension plans, backed by the right to strike, put employers under strong pressure to make some concessions. Governmental old-age benefits, financed by regressive payroll taxes paid chiefly by the workers and by consumers, represented an economical solution. In consequence, frequent improvements in the benefits and coverage of American social security legislation have been relatively uncontroversial since the basic federal law was enacted in 1935.

Elite Fear of Public Restiveness

This discussion has deliberately moved from a consideration of such routine channels of influence as voting and legislative bargaining to those some regard as illegitimate, such as civil disobedience. The analysis and illustrations should make it obvious that there is no clear dividing-line between legitimate and illegitimate tactics. Similarly, there is no clear empirical distinction, but only an analytically useful one, between people who feel relatively gratified and those who feel relatively deprived. It is the relatively deprived who are most likely to support political strikes, boycotts, riots, civil disobedience, or civil war as channels of influence.

It is tempting but misleading to classify people neatly as content or dissatisfied, as exhibiting a sense of gratification or a sense of deprivation, as perceiving the political system as legitimate or illegitimate, or as believing they are efficacious or politically powerless. Test results do, of course, categorize people in these ways; but there is also clear evidence, some of which we have already cited, that people's feelings may vary over time, by issue, and according to the social context in which the question is presented to them. How stable and how consistent any individual or social group is in these respects is an empirical question, to be answered by observation and research. To take stability and consistency for granted is to underestimate the complexity of the human being and to guarantee that some of the most significant political phenomena will not be investigated or fully understood.

In spite of great inequalities in wealth, power, and dignity, the mass of the population rarely make demands for basic changes in who gets what. People usually accept their lot, partly because of the legitimizing and symbolic actions discussed in Chapter 21 and partly because it is rarely clear how to organize common action among people who share the same grievances. Only when conditions become desperate or intolerable is common protest action likely, not simply when people come to expect a better life. Rising expectations alone do not bring serious political restiveness.

Sometimes public officials and the general public fail to recognize protest activities for what they are. A sharp increase in delinquent rent or tax payments, in truancy from school, or in welfare applications signals massive discontent, but because it is usually not organized or publicized, people see it only as individual delinquency, not as political action, so that it is more likely to result in repression than in responsiveness to people's grievances.

In the face of disorder or civil disobedience, however, there is sure to be some kind of elite response. Sometimes there are significant concessions. All industrialized countries, for example, have established social security systems, almost all of them instituted earlier and extending wider protection than the American system does. In Germany, Bismarck's highly elitist and authoritarian government provided extensive social security protections as early as the 1880s.

Fear of mass restiveness or violence has been a major reason for the enactment of other governmental programs benefitting non-elites. Large-scale strikes, rural violence to protest the taking of land from farmers who could not make payments on their mortgages, and the spread of radical ideology helped win wide support for the New Deal reforms of the 1930s. In Chapter 7, we noted that widespread civil disobedience and urban riots helped mobilize support for civil rights laws to protect the rights of blacks to vote and for an antipoverty program.

Though mass defiance is one of the few ways the poor and the disadvantaged have been able to achieve some political impact, the gains this tactic has won for them have usually been quite limited. While such legislative victories as those just mentioned are seen as major break-throughs, their administrative enforcement tends to become half-hearted after a time, and symbolic results are more common than tangible ones. As protest fades, established inequalities often reappear and concessions may be withdrawn.

The rise and demise of the National Welfare Rights Organization (NWRO) offers some insight into the uses and limits of disruption as a political strategy for disadvantaged groups. Founded in 1966 to promote the rights of welfare applicants and recipients, the NWRO relied during its first few years on mobilizing the poor to demonstrate against specific grievances. Though it had little money in its treasury and only a skeletal organization, NWRO repeatedly forced welfare office staff members to grant applicants the benefits to which they were legally entitled by in-forming them of their rights and helping them file claims, by staging demonstrations outside and inside the offices, picketing, demanding hear-ings, and encouraging a national compaign for special grants for hardship cases. This militancy not only won welfare rights for individuals and groups but also contributed to support for the antipoverty program in general by reminding officials and the general public of the risks of dis-order. The very success and prominence of the NWRO began to bring it legitimacy, substantial funds from private foundations and from the public treasury, and formal representation on governmental committees. By the early 1970s it was functioning largely through the conventional lobbying channels of bureaucratic and legislative politics and abandoning its earlier reliance on demonstrations and disruption of established rou-tines. As it became respectable, the NWRO, paradoxically, lost its effec-tiveness and gradually faded from the scene. Its demise was due not only to its change in tactics and status but to the ebbing of black protest generally.[24]

Militance and Popular Support

The efficacy of civil disobedience and militance in winning benefits for the masses depends ultimately on how much popular support these tactics stimulate for their cause. When they serve dramatically to call attention to deprivations widely regarded as shocking and unfair, they are effective in rallying such support. Until the civil disobedience cam-paigns of the early 1960s and the riots of the middle 1960s, a large seg-ment of the American people was blissfully unaware of the "other America" living in poverty and denied basic civil rights. Increasingly militant demonstrations against the Vietnam War awakened many Ameri-cans to the dubious grounds on which the Johnson Administration had

[24] Cf. Frances Fox Piven and Richard A. Cloward, *Poor People's Movements* (New York: Pantheon Books, 1977), pp. 264–362.

justified escalation of the war, its high toll in civilian and military casualties, and the corruption and unpopularity of the Saigon regime.

Civil disobedience and violence do, as we have seen, create a "backlash," and so damage the political position of those who engage in them. Militance unquestionably antagonizes some people and evokes repression. The historical record leaves no doubt, however, that it also wins support for righting genuine wrongs. If such real deprivations can be dramatically brought to public attention, militant tactics are the most potent political device in the meager arsenal of tactics available to non-elites.

PART 6

Political Change

Power Structure:
Contrasting
Interpretations

Before we can assess the prospects of various forms of political change in the future, we must reach some conclusions about today's structure of power. The task of this chapter is to synthesize the separate analyses of problems, policies, ideology, structure, and decisional processes that have been offered in earlier chapters. Do they "add up," so that one or two consistent themes of power and its usage may be formulated? If so, what are these themes? Or are policies, values, and processes so disconnected that the American political system responds unpredictably and unsystematically to shifting, *ad hoc* coalitions of officials, interests, and forces? Each of the many potential answers to these questions implies a particular spectrum of possibilities

437

for the future. Each suggests a distinctive set of prospects and tactics for political change.

We know that government cannot be neutral. It acts in response to the interests of those with the greatest power resources in the society. Who are these wielders of power? There is ample evidence about the holders of the largest private power resources in our society, and this evidence can be used to show that they run the government. From readily available proof of sharp disparities in economic possessions and social status between classes, one might infer government by an upper-class elite. Many studies do just this.[1]

But there are some important intervening questions to be asked, and those who are most determined to view the United States as an operating democracy do not think they have been satisfactorily answered. (1) What proof is there that upper-class elites, despite their comparatively vast power resources, actually *can* and *do* apply that power to control the government? (2) *Even if they do* (assuming, for example, that their members or agents hold most of the key positions in government and dominate its policymaking), how do we know that their actions are not consistent with the preferences of the people? In other words, these analysts would argue, there need be no inconsistency between elite governance and democracy.[2] The people may freely choose these leaders in elections, or the leaders (however chosen) may in fact accomplish what the people want, or should want, or both. These are demanding questions, perhaps born of ideological resistance to the idea that the United States might be controlled by an upper-class oligarchy. It is extremely difficult to find the evidence necessary to prove elite motivation one way or another. But these questions do point to the fact that those who reach the latter conclusion are making an inference, namely that social background and economic interests control behavior. This inference seems plausible to many scholars, but totally unjustifiable to others. The conflict has raged for decades, sometimes politely but sometimes with real emotion, as befits a fundamental question of power and its implications.

We have tried to circumvent this scholarly controversy, and the real evidential problem it highlights, by the approach we have taken in this book. We did not try to identify power in the private sphere and then trace its possible merger with control of, or pressure on, the institutions of government. Instead, we reversed the process entirely. We started with actual governmental policies and their consequences, and then looked

[1] G. William Domhoff, *Who Rules America?* (Englewood Cliffs, N.J.: Prentice-Hall, 1967).

[2] For a full discussion of these problems, see Peter Bachrach, *The Theory of Democratic Elitism* (Boston: Little, Brown, 1966). See also Jack L. Walker, "A Critique of the Elitist Theory of Democracy," *American Political Science Review* 60 (1966), pp. 285–295, and Robert A. Dahl, "Further Reflections on the Elitist Theory of Democracy," *ibid.*, pp. 296–305.

at the characteristics of the political system in search of explanations for these consequences. With sufficiently precise description of the beneficiaries and losers from governmental action over time; the priorities actually operative in shaping these patterns; and the manner in which values, ideology, structure, and decision-making processes cause or reinforce them, we emerge with a viable characterization of how power is used and for whose benefit. If this characterization shows that power is used for the principal benefit, and consistently in the exclusive interest, of the upper class, whose members occupy most governmental offices, *then we are close to resolving the crucial question of whether or not they use their power in accordance with their own needs and preferences.* In other words, we have characterized their *actions,* from which we can much more safely infer their motivations. Comparison with popular needs and preferences is the only remaining step, and one that presents relatively little difficulty.

Our purpose is thus to identify the power structure of the United States by linking a description of the consequences of governmental policies to the goals, interests, and power of a definable segment of the society. In our eyes, these phenomena *do* form an integrated whole.

Policies, Goals, and Decisionmaking: A Coherent Picture

We have already identified visible patterns in the consequences of public policies, examined the principles urged in support of such policies, and reviewed characteristics of power distribution and decisionmaking. Now we must try to bring all these issues together. The basic theme running through them, it seems to us, is this: *Governmental policies assume that the existing organization, operations, motivations, and perceived needs of the American economic system must be preserved and furthered in every practical way.* No other premises or motivations evident in U.S. public policies effectively displace this basic assumption. Nor can any goal, however desirable in the abstract, be implemented effectively if it conflicts with this presupposition. Given this basic premise, governmental actions and their consequences may be *understood* as a coherent, integrated, and purposeful package. Without such recognition, they can only be *described* with puzzlement at apparent contradictions and chagrin at the mixture of successes and failures, hopes and frustrations.

The needs of the economic order are expressly addressed in the area of economic stability and growth. They are evident in development policies, and again in military expenditures. The military establishment and the space program are also vital to such foreign-policy goals as limiting communist expansion and inducing developing nations to adapt their economies to ours and reach more harmonious long-term relationships. Anticommunism itself rests heavily on the desire to protect the existing economic order and the values surrounding it. Policies to combat poverty encounter resistance because they conflict with values that bolster the economic system (such as self-reliance and rewards according to effort and talent) and because they threaten the distribution of wealth and power that system creates. Racism lingers in part because stronger measures to enforce desegregation and equal opportunity would run counter to economic values (such as freedom to sell property or hire workers) and perhaps disrupt the current operations of the economic system. In short, although the policy areas we have examined were chosen only because of their diversity and continuing social importance, actual governmental policies in each area seem to flow from the same economic premises. What appeared to be isolated, independent problem areas, each with a distinctive set of characteristics and relevant political forces, now appear to be overlapping, integrated extensions of a single set of priorities and limitations.

Value Priorities in Policy

Can we formulate a rough priority ranking of the values and goals that dominate policymaking in these areas, and perhaps in other apparently "independent" areas as well? Clearly, economic values and property rights are central. The rights to a return on invested capital, protection of that return by armed force if necessary, and the unrestricted use and secure enjoyment of one's property converge to impose imperatives for governmental action abroad and to create imperatives for, and erect barriers against, governmental action in domestic affairs. The United States must stand firm against communism and in favor of an open door to developing nations. It must maximize economic growth but tread lightly in combating poverty and racism because of these strong commitments. Associated with property rights are the allied economic values of materialism and profit maximization, and the exaltation of productivity as a sufficient measure of societal achievement. Below this upper echelon of values are some with lower priority but more general applicability, such as anticommunism and the tendency to resort to military force if the dominant economic values are not being adequately served by other means. Still lower on the scale, and subject to a strong general commitment to the existing distribution of wealth and racial status, is the value of equality. Centuries of much rhetoric and some action have given equality real stature as a principle, though it remains subject to the higher priority of other values.

This rough ordering is an operational (as distinguished from historically received, rhetorical, or symbolic) ranking of American political values and goals. The central economic values we have identified and ranked as paramount need not have been explicit in the minds of policymakers. But they are evident in several apparently independent policy areas and over lengthy time periods. Whether implicit or explicit in the minds of policymakers, they seem to have been prime factors in the shaping of policies.

These chiefly economic values and goals may serve as an initial framework for understanding the relative weights given to other political values. The latter must be assigned lesser status in the hierarchy, according to the extent to which they are in harmony with and serve to further the paramount values and goals. Ultimately, we emerge with a serviceable and historically grounded image of the priority ranking of political values that currently animates the American political system. In brief, it amounts to the protection and promotion of the American economic system and the distribution patterns it has established by various means, culminating in military force.

Political Structure as Support for the Basic Values

Just as patterns of policy consequences reveal an identifiable hierarchy of political values, both of these phenomena show consistent links with characteristics of the political structure and processes. The constitutional structure and institutional arrangement of American government, for example, limit the legal capacities of national, state, and local governments and disperse the total governing power across a wide landscape of levels and branches. The effect is to assure primacy for the private sphere on most questions. Those who are able to generate the greatest power out of private sources can shape basic patterns of thought and behavior, because government is unable to act coherently in majoritarian interests. Instead, government is open to penetration by major private interests, which use its many veto points to establish defenses against the threat of change in economic and social life. Majorities of people are delayed, if not prevented, from achieving their common goals by their internal divisions and by the complex procedures and limitations that must be transcended. For decisive governmental action to occur, it must be entirely consistent with the limits and goals of external powerholders, or there must be some highly unusual organizing force (such as an extreme emergency or a charismatic leader, or both) operating to unify its dispersed powers.

Similarly, decision-making persons and processes operate with a set of imperatives and constraints that combine to reinforce the economic priorities. To begin with, many offices are filled by persons who have previously risen to high positions in the legal, banking, or business communities. Their orthodoxy seems assured. Even persons who achieve high official status from extra-establishment positions experience powerful inducements to adhere to accepted priorities. They are normally appointed to governmental offices only because they have acted out their commitments to established values in some way. After doing so for some time, they may find it natural and congenial, and a way to avoid a rash of complaints from others in high places. More important, nearly every officeholder shrinks from the prospect of national unemployment or depression, and thus becomes committed almost by default to maintaining the growth and prosperity of the existing economy as a (if not *the*) major priority of government.

Many officeholders are thoroughly familiar with the need for good relations with major sources of wealth. Both political parties, and nearly all candidates for nominations within them, are able to compete effectively only with the support of large contributors. Major senatorial nomination and election campaigns now involve sums approaching $5 million per candidate, and the presidential nomination-and-election process requires hundreds of millions of dollars. Access to the mass media, if not the official support of those who own them, is essential to winning office. Officeholders thus learn the importance of economics early, and in a multitude of ways. Under these circumstances, their decisionmaking cannot help but reflect the priorities of the established economic system. In short, neither structures nor processes are neutral, in the sense of giving rise equally to any number of different patterns of policy. Instead, they contribute to reinforcement of the standards that yield this particular set of results.

At every major stage of analysis, this review suggests that the policy consequences we have examined are not the product of accident or coincidence. They reflect a consistent relationship between policies, values, institutional structures, and the officials and processes by which decisions are made. Each of these political factors independently contributes to, and in effect reinforces, the primacy of property rights and the protection and promotion of the economic system as the basis of policymaking.

Alternative Interpretations of Power Distribution

This pattern of consequences and of operative values may flow from quite different structures of power. We shall pose, and critically examine, three alternative interpretations: (1) power is located chiefly in governmental offices, whose incumbents respond to a mix of public and interest-group pressures; (2) power is extracted from both public and private resources by an establishment that seeks to shape popular preferences into forms that can be used to support its own basic goals and the system itself; and (3) power is derived from private economic resources by a relatively few persons who influence government in their interest, using it to promote popular acquiescence, discourage resistance, or both. Shorthand terms for the first and last models would be "pluralism" and "ruling-class."

Each of these interpretations seems to us capable of explaining the pattern of consequences described, if certain other conditions are taken to be true and other specific assumptions are made. None of them, of course, is likely to be entirely accurate. They are merely abstractions (not caricatures, we trust). But they serve to suggest the directions interpretations may take and the nature of the questions that must be resolved before final conclusions can be reached.

1. Pluralism: Competitive Pressures in the Governmental Arena

The pluralist interpretation denies that there is either a deliberate purpose or a unified power structure behind the making of national policy—except for those instances when practically the entire population is of a single mind on an issue. It holds that each area of public policy involves distinctive problems and separate sets of political agents and forces, such that each action undertaken by government is the result of a unique process of interaction. Accordingly, each action can only be understood by focusing on the particular circumstances and idiosyncratic features of the policy-making processes and individuals involved. In other words, policies vary unpredictably in substance, depending on what the people in office perceived, sought, and did, and on the complex of forces and circumstances that happened to exist at the time. By implication, if the public had strong preferences otherwise, or if the officeholders were different, or if the institutional mechanisms of government were different, the end results would also be different. This interpretation contains at least six major elements, each of which makes some necessary assumptions about the economic and social setting in which American politics takes place.

a. The political system is sufficiently separable from the economic and social systems of the United States that it may be understood chiefly through analysis of the behavior of individuals in governmental offices and in the electoral processes by which they acquire such offices. This premise rests on an especially narrow definition of politics, which considers it nothing more than activity in and bearing on governmental institutions. Further, politics is seen as self-contained, in the sense that practically all important factors influencing it exist in its immediate surroundings. Analysts need never look beyond decision-making processes and elections, for nearly everything else is irrelevant, not amenable to scientific study, or the province of some other social science.

But this restrictive definition itself flows from an image of *boundaries* around distinct systems of relationships—"economy," "society," "polity"—each largely independent of the others. It is this notion of detachment and separation that leads to images of "politics" as no more than the internal machinations of government and the official channels immediately surrounding it. Moreover, it leads to analysis of politics exclusively in its own terms. For example, it becomes difficult to distinguish major issues from minor ones except in "political" dimensions. Either all decisions appear equally significant, or the "important" ones are those on which the voters most often express themselves or on which the Congress debates longest.

b. Government's independent resources give it the decisive balance of power within the society and make it the mechanism through which all other spheres of activity may be managed. Government responds principally to popular preferences expressed in elections, and secondarily to the pressures of organized interests. Thus, it can become an arbiter between conflicting interests or an agent of the general will, essentially in accordance with the people's wishes. This is the case partly because of the prominence and efficacy of the electoral process, in which all people have equal power—in the sense of one vote. But it is also because the equal-power principle spreads further: the American economic and social systems either do not produce serious inequalities of power between individuals or groups, or those inequalities are not translated into effects on governmental decisionmaking. In short, relevant private power is distributed roughly equally throughout the society. All groups have about the same capacity and opportunity to shape governmental action, and politics becomes a contest (nearly always decided by votes) for the right to shape the direction of governmental policies.

c. The power of government is parceled out into so many component branches, agencies, committees, and offices that every significant interest within the society is able to gain access and affect the course of government action. Each locus of power within the framework of government is capable of delaying or preventing action. Government becomes in effect a much-elaborated system of checks and balances in which opportunities to veto action are broadly distributed, and affirmative action can be taken only when practically everybody concurs in the form it should take and its necessity. The society, instead of being a vast aggregation of individuals, is actually organized into a large number of distinct interests, most of which are represented by groups or associations. All of these have or can gain access to one or more of the many "veto points" among the institutions of government. Thus, there develops a harmonious linkage between governmental and societal structures, the divisions in one paralleling divisions in the other.

d. Government is an arena within which the various interests in the society contend with each other for often conflicting goals. Public officials, because they control the use of decisive (governmental) power, must be at the center of these conflicts. They serve as brokers, mediating the differences between competing interests and helping them to find the necessary compromises. This is a broadly representative process because practically every citizen is or can be represented by one or more groups and can thereby have his or her interests weighed in the process of policymaking. Conflicting pressures are applied to officials in roughly the same proportions that they are felt within the society. Divisions within the society are in effect translated into negotiable claims and adjusted; officials certify the accommodations through their authoritative support for one or another public policy.

e. These accommodations are reached through a set of well-established procedures that assure fairness and opportunity to all; all groups share a commitment to making such a process a continuing reality. Compromises that are just and acceptable to all do not occur by accident; they develop because of strict adherence to principles of procedural due process. These procedures call for full and fair hearings, consideration for others' points of view, and self-limitations if the larger system might otherwise be endangered. Each interest has an investment in preserving a setting in which it can be confident of receiving fair treatment; therefore all act to protect the fairness and openness of the procedures by which decisions are made.

f. The brokerage role played by public officials in reaching accommodations, and the residual choice-making role the situation permits them, means that the public exercises meaningful control over the general direction of public policy through elections. Further, the system as a whole amounts to a stable, satisfied equilibrium of groups and individuals. The officials who serve as mediators of conflicting claims are either elected or directly responsible to those who are. The wide availability and equal weighting of the vote therefore allows the people to choose at least the broad priorities of the government. The entire political system, though with some acknowledged imperfections and time lags, is thus tuned to popular preferences. And it is certainly controllable by the people if they care enough to exert themselves. If they do not, it must be because they are satisfied with its operations. The latter conclusion is also supported by the fact that the many conflicting pressures within the society (both between opposed interest groups and within an individual who belongs to two or more perhaps opposed groups) apparently operate to hold the entire society to the middle of the road. Extremes are avoided in this way, as the great majority of people insist successfully on continued compromise and accommodation. In such a setting, faith in the workings of the established political system is likely to be and remain high.

These six components of the pluralist model make up a familiar and in many ways persuasive image of power in the United States. We can all point to many areas in which there is conflict between interest groups and others, and in which governmental power is wielded by public officials to mediate and thereby further the public interest. Policy outcomes frequently do favor first one group and then another, and elections indeed often set policy directions for the future.

But there are several barriers to acceptance of this interpretation. One has already been suggested explicitly: it employs a very narrow, tunnel-vision definition of politics, which excludes much of the usage of power in the world (particularly that which determines what can become a political issue, and in what form) and fails to discriminate between more important and less important issues. Others are implicit in our presentation: it rests on the extra-empirical conviction that the United States is an open, democratic political system in which all citizens play roughly equal parts in shaping governmental policy, and it strains to interpret events to conform to this optimistic assumption. It never asks, for example, to what extent the American political parties actually present the electorate with the full range of possible policy choices at elections, nor to what extent both parties are controlled by factors other than popular preferences.

We shall consider two major criticisms of this interpretation. First is the charge that nearly every major assumption it makes about the economic and social structures of the United States is wrong. And second, it is argued that this view fails to explain why a consistent pattern of policy consequences and operative values exists—unless one makes some very agile intellectual leaps or some very unlikely assumptions about the society we live in. The latter criticism interests us more, for the former has been made often and with little effect on those who choose to adhere to this interpretation. But let us consider each in turn.

First, there seem to be solid grounds for challenging almost every assumption about the American social and economic structure that underlies this interpretation of the structure of power. The social and economic systems are not separate from, but intimately integrated with, the political system. One cannot rise to the top in the former without both acquiring the capacity to, and experiencing the necessity of, exerting power in the latter.[3] Inequalities of social status and economic possessions (and hence of the major resources of power) in the United States are too obvious and too widely documented to require much elaboration. Wealth, whether measured by income or by property holdings, is heavily concentrated in the upper twentieth of the population, with severe deprivation in the lowest third. Vast accumulations of economic power in the great corporations are under the control of a relative handful of owners and managers.

The social structure clearly represents these facts of economic life:

---

[3] In part, this is a matter of defining what constitutes "power" and what activities are "political." The reader should recognize by now that we are committed to broad definitions of both, and should choose the definitions that strike him or her as most reasonable under the circumstances. But we do not stand solely on our definition: the empirical verification is also extensive, and we think persuasive.

a small upper class dominates the major institutions and controls the corporate economy, while a large middle class takes its cues from them. More than half of the population, however, consists of blue-collar workers, low-salaried office personnel (particularly women), and the unemployed and unemployable. This large proportion of the society is divided against itself, whites resisting the progress of blacks and men defending their "prerogatives" against women, so that the upper echelon's preponderance of effective power is even greater than its share of wealth and official positions would suggest. Although each system—economic, social, and political—is "open," in the sense that some members of each rising generation are able to penetrate or be co-opted into the upper reaches, the general patterns are *continuity* (those on top stay there) and *concentration and overlap* (those on top in one system merge with those on top in the others). "One man, one vote" thus evokes a democratic illusion: power flows from many sources other than votes, and concentrations of power of various kinds regularly move into government and work their will through it.

Readily documentable social and economic realities suggest much less benign and self-congratulatory *value judgments* about its operation than those implied by the pluralistic interpretation. At the very least, there are substantial grounds to doubt the propriety of terming this system "democratic." More important for our analysis, the crucial assumptions of the pluralist model about social and economic structure seem seriously to lack *empirical accuracy*. And if it is factually invalid in these important respects, as well as dubious in its accompanying value judgments, the model itself appears to be undermined.

The second criticism of the pluralistic interpretation is that the consistent pattern of policy consequences and operative values we have identified is left completely unexplained. This is a crucial point, with profound implications for the validity of the pluralist model. The first criticism, examined above, has been made regularly, exhaustively, and with considerable evidential support. But it has not been accepted by most political scientists, because the link between social and economic inequalities of power and the actions of government has not been demonstrated to their satisfaction. It is not enough, in the eyes of those who subscribe to the pluralist model, to show that inequalities result in concentrations of power in the upper echelons of the population, and that these same people hold a very high proportion of the key positions in government. It must also be shown that such people (a) *actually use their power* to cause government to act in ways that are (b) *not only in accordance with their own interests, but also opposed to the public interest*. This is a high standard of proof, perhaps insisted on out of the deep desire to believe in a relatively democratic interpretation of power. It is not an illogical standard, but is a very difficult one to meet given the understandable limitations on acquiring accurate evidence about the motivations of decisionmakers.

The evidence we have developed, however, circumvents this difficulty and addresses the issue of whether governmental action is shaped according to the preferences of private powerholders. We have seen the consequences of government policies, and we have extrapolated the value priorities that actually dominate governmental action. The central theme is action on behalf of the preservation and promotion of the economic order, frequently at the cost of personal deprivations for many millions of people and denial of values that are rhetorically exalted. Such actions are, however, entirely consistent with the interests and power of the upper echelons of the overlapping social and economic structures of the United States.

In the light of such evidence, it seems fair to infer that the patterns we discerned were brought about by *some* consistent and purposeful force operating through the government. We may then demand that alternative interpretations attempt to explain *how* this consistent pattern may have been produced. The pluralist model offers only happenstance, coincidence, or determinism by way of explanation. We think there must be more plausible explanations. Accordingly, we shall reject the pluralist model *except with regard to minor decisions,* and concentrate on the search for more plausible interpretations of the structure of power as it applies to the fundamental issues of politics.

If we assume that some consistent and purposeful force is shaping governmental policies, and that there is unequal power inherent in the existing economic and class structure that overlaps into politics, what interpretations of the structure of power follow? We think there are two major ones, which we shall evaluate after presenting each briefly.

2. Power as a Social Process: Establishment Orchestration of Econopolitical Life

This interpretation accepts the pluralist model for minor decisions, though with less optimism about government mediating group conflict in the public interest and more emphasis on special interests' success at achieving their goals. On major issues, however, involving the basic structure of the economic and political order and the permanence of the established patterns of distribution of wealth and social status, a more unified power structure comes into being. Various holders of power coalesce to form a coherent and nearly singleminded force capable of managing major sources of private power, the government, and the general public alike.

The "glue" that holds this coalition together and enables it to work so effectively in defense of the *status quo* comes from two primary sources. One is the class-originated shared values and interests of the establishment, itself consisting of a circulating group of persons moving freely among the upper echelons of the economic, social, and political systems. These people are accustomed to holding and exercising power from their "command post" positions. Their life experiences and current interests have bred in them a strong commitment to orthodoxy and defense of the integrated economic and political structure. They see these values as synonymous with the public interest, not as self-serving.

The other source is the willingness of the general public—or at least the majority of its visible, audible, and active members—to endorse and support the actions of the major officials of their government. This acquiescence has many sources: faith in the institutions established by the Constitution, lack of alternatives, apathy, political party loyalties, hopelessness, fear of coercion. One of its major sources, however, is the wide dissemination of effective inculcation of the familiar American political values and ideology—itself one of the major achievements of the establishment. From twelve or more years of schooling to patriotic rituals and media messages, the individual lives in a context of symbolic assurances, materialism, racism, and benevolent rationalizations about how the government does and should operate. Embedded in this body of myth are the clear grounds of establishment dominance. At least some fragments of this belief system become implanted in people's minds, available to be drawn on in times of stress by the status- and legitimacy-exuding establishment.

Under ordinary circumstances, few major issues arise. Most public policies and private practices fit snugly within the approved contours of the established economic, social, and political systems, and special interests are free to seek their narrow ends within this context. When conditions change, and more basic questions are forced to the fore, the establishment begins to rally to the defense of the systems that have served it so well. Despite some disagreements about the best way to preserve the basic framework of the *status quo* (by yielding in the direction of greater equality or by "standing firm"), a consensus usually emerges without much direct consultation. Action then occurs on many fronts simultaneously to mobilize public support for particular forms of governmental action to meet and "solve" the crisis. Taking their cues from the actions of the uppermost echelons, many lesser officials and associated elites (mayors, policemen, Chambers of Commerce, and the like) institute similar (or more drastic) policies and manifest their support for the system-preserving program.

What looks like a consciously synchronized and coordinated movement may be no more than an elaborate follow-the-leader game. And what appears to be slavishly ideological mass support may be no more than silence. But the establishment seems to have managed the situation, and by so doing it improves its chances of succeeding again the next time—unless the social situation reaches a point at which open opposition destroys the harmonious image. Then the issue becomes the capacity to apply coercion to some without losing the public acquiescence and cooperation necessary to make the system operable.

3. Power as a Tool: Economic Dominants Manage the System

This interpretation views power as tightly concentrated in private hands and public impact on policy as negligible. It holds that economic resources are the paramount sources of power, and that those relatively few persons who own or control them are in a virtually unchallengeable position of power. They set the operative values and priorities in their own private interest. They can direct the actions of people in government and, through control of the foundations, universities, and mass media, shape the attitudes of the general public. Normally they provide only general direction, but when necessary they can and do assert specific control over governmental action. A principal tool for thus managing the society (and in some respects, the world) for their own benefit is physical coercion. Although efforts are made to present this use of power publicly as necessary and desirable, the lower classes in particular are kept aware of the ready availability of police and other military forces frequently used against them.

There is in this view a distinct structure of power—a more or less definable and self-conscious group of individuals, sometimes labeled "the ruling class." This group uses its extragovernmental resources to control nominations, elections, and governmental decisionmaking, not necessarily by dictating specific decisions but by maintaining boundaries within which action may proceed unrestricted and beyond which rejection is swift and drastic. The motivations of this group are almost exclusively economic: maximization of the profits of the corporate economy. All areas of governmental activity are subject to that overwhelming goal. Nor is the need for governmental support limited to a desire to defend established domestic prerogatives. Because of the pressing need of the economy for new opportunities to invest surplus capital, this economic class exerts control over government to assure profitable opportunities in the developing nations.

Selecting Among Alternatives: Questions and Implications

In at least one important respect, the two latter interpretations are in complete agreement: on all fundamental questions, a unified power structure is ready and determined to defend the *status quo* in drastic and effective ways. But in most other respects, they are quite distinctive. The economic dominants model in effect abstracts one dimension—the economic—out of the establishment orchestration model and makes of it a simpler, harsher characterization of the structure of power. The economic dimension is surely central to the establishment orchestration model, and the proper one to build on if only one theme is to dominate. But doing so posits not only a different basis of power but also a distinctive set of implications for the prospects and tactics of change.

Extensions of the Economic Dominants Model

The economic dominants model sees power arising from economic holdings, tightly concentrated in private hands, and using government as a tool. The establishment orchestration model sees power flowing from several resources (of which economic strength is a major one), and thus spread more broadly within the upper echelons of the society. Decisive power in any situation may rest with an *ad hoc* coalition of establishment members, depending on the subject area, the dynamics of specific events and social conditions, the skills of strategically located individuals, and the particular configuration of popular attitudes toward the government and the issue. Private power merges subtly with government's independent powers after an exchange in which people at the top act and elicit symbol- and ideology-induced support for that action from key segments of the general public. Again, the result may be the same, but the process is different. The establishment orchestration model envisions a somewhat more open process, characterized by interchangeable roles for a larger number of top figures, greater mutual dependence between individuals in and out of government, and greater reliance on more or less "voluntary" popular support.

The economic dominants model emphasizes economic sources of power and economic motivations on the part of the ruling elite, with capitalism as the source of the values and ideology that facilitate their management of the system. The establishment orchestration model is not only multicausal, but also sees an independently generated set of values as more important than economic interests on at least some decision-making occasions. This belief system, perhaps originally influenced quite strongly by the nature of the economic system, is seen as now self-perpetuating. Although it has a strong economic component, it is made up also of the heritage of Anglo-American legal thought; Judaeo-Christian religious postulates; and such values as nationalism, patriotism, and equality. When the establishment acts, it does so on the basis of one or a combination of these received values and beliefs. There is thus more room for uncertainty on its part, and greater need for confidence that key segments of the population concur and support it. To state the point from the perspective of non-elites, the establishment is more vulnerable to popular demands.

The economic dominants model assumes a greater divergence of interests between upper and lower classes and a more distinctive set of values and ideology among those lower classes. Accordingly, although it too sees ideology-based manipulation as a convenient means of managing the masses, physical coercion plays a greater part in maintaining elite governance. In part because coercion is employed so regularly, the lower classes are kept aware of their different interests. Of course, the middle and upper classes are not normally cognizant of such violence and would probably assume it to be necessary and justified if they were. The establishment orchestration model tends to see lower classes as more fully captured by the values and ideology promulgated by the establishment, so that they do not clearly recognize the divergence of their interests from the middle and upper levels. Thus, management of popular preferences is easier. The underlying value system contributes massively to the stability of the economic and political order because it teaches the population to "genuinely" want, accept, and defend what is in the establishment's interest. Physical coercion, though necessary at times, is a last resort. Further, indiscriminate use of physical coercion raises the risk of loss of support (and bestowed "legitimacy") by a people who have been taught to revere due process.

The economic dominants model has the virtue of zeroing in on the central theme of power and presenting a clear and coherent interpretation of the American power structure. It permits clearer assignment of motivation and much greater apparent predictability of future elite behavior. The establishment orchestration model, although it posits the same results in crisis situations, envisions those results as flowing from a distinctly more complex structure and process. The differences are not insignificant, in light of our concern for the prospects of change. Stated briefly, the most crucial issues are: (1) the relative solidarity and single-mindedness of decisive elites and the extent to which they are able to command, as opposed to being obliged to seek to acquire and develop, the power resources of government; and (2) the extent to which their management of the polity is accomplished through consent or quiescence manipulated or coerced from the lower classes, as opposed to drawing more on apparently "voluntary" support. These are open questions, for which conclusive evidence is still lacking. And much is at stake in the answers tentatively chosen.

Implications for Change

The implications for change may already be obvious. If the economic dominants model is correct, elites are largely impenetrable by non-elites; nor is government a significant means of non-elite access to a share of power. But, at the same time, there is greater consciousness of divergence of interest and deprivation among the lowest classes. Under these conditions, there may be a continuing tension between the desire for change below and the rigid structure of power above. For change to occur, however, drastic reconstruction of the social order from below—by forceful means—may be the only route. However unlikely, and perhaps unattractive to contemplate, no other method of change is in keeping with this interpretation.

If the establishment orchestration model is correct, elites' incomplete domination of government, and their need for its legitimating power, opens an aperture for non-elite penetration. If representatives of such non-elites are successful at acquiring key offices and resisting co-optation as establishment agents, they may succeed in short-circuiting accepted practices or even in introducing new priorities. Because the underlying values generate broad and "voluntary" support for the existing economic and political order, and the establishment is genuinely dependent on this support for effective management of the system, two paradoxical results follow. The establishment recognizes that it must at least appear to satisfy changing demands among the major segments of the population, and may even be led by such changes to adopt new policies. But changes in values and ideology require long periods of education, among the principal devices for which is the behavior of leading establishment figures themselves. One implication of this mutually reinforcing situation is that power relationships may remain apparently stable for some time, while shifts in underlying values are actually steadily eroding the bases of that power. When a dramatic event or condition sparks bold action by some establishment figure, he or she may encounter widespread approval and acceptance, much to the surprise of all who remain steeped in the conventional wisdom.

Thus with the establishment orchestration model relatively peaceful change seems somewhat more possible. It does require a special convergence of people, events, and conditions, and even then it is likely to proceed only to modest lengths before enough popular demands are satisfied to reduce the situation to a manageable level again. Further, it requires a period of value change to bring broad segments of the population to the point where their desires induce some establishment members to act boldly in unprecedented directions. The few truly change-oriented representatives of non-elites who penetrate the establishment and remain unco-opted are not able to do more than raise issues. Although this is a major means through which segments of the public can adopt new priorities, only determined mass insistence on doing so will cause the establishment to agree to the wholesale modification of governmental policies.

Which of these two interpretations of the structure of power is the more accurate? As may be clear from our analysis, we tentatively accept the more complex establishment orchestration interpretation. We acknowledge the revealing thrust of the economic dominants version, and view it as an often accurate portrait; and we are aware of the utility of clear and direct answers to "Who rules?" But there seem to us to be more currents of power at work, greater uncertainty in the ways power is mobilized and applied, and more (though by no means direct) influence by popular attitudes. For these reasons, our image of the American power structure is essentially that of the establishment orchestration model. Perhaps we are also affected by the contrasting implications for the nature and prospects of change; discouraging as it is, the establishment orchestration model nevertheless holds out some hope for a process of change that falls short of full-scale revolution. In Chapter 21, we shall look more systematically at different forms of change and the conditions necessary to each, accepting as our premise that the basic structure of power in the United States is that described here as the establishment orchestration model.

21

Symbolic Politics
and Political Change

Politics is not simply, or perhaps even primarily, a series of rational decisions and purposeful actions to produce intended results. Neither the powerful nor the powerless can fully calculate or control the actions of others. Many actions are unforeseen or unintended, and so are many results. What seems logical or likely often simply does not occur. One of the most powerful reasons why this is true is discoverable in the part played by symbols in politics. In particular, symbolic processes and effects go a long way toward explaining the sporadic, erratic, and generally unsuccessful nature of thrusts toward change in the United States.

In this chapter, we shall explore the nature of symbols and the part they play in our politics. Once again, we shall approach our subject comprehensively, examining many aspects of symbolic politics. But our primary purpose is to understand how symbolism diverts people, reassures them, and thereby deflects or undermines thrusts toward change. There is no direct relationship between the *fact* or even the *perception* of deprivation and rationally calculated action to change that situation. Even if people accurately understand the causes of problems, they may not even consider acting to solve them. Politics is simply not that logical or rational. But it *is* potentially understandable, nevertheless, and a clear sense of the role symbols play will help greatly. We shall consider first the scope and importance of symbolism in our politics, and then some of the ways symbols are created and used. Then we shall move to our major task: an assessment of the effects and implications of symbolism for politics and political change.

The Scope and Importance of Symbolism

The Nature of Symbolism

Government does not just reflect the will of some of the people. It also *creates* public wants, beliefs, and demands, which have powerful impact on who gets what in politics. If some of the major demands and beliefs of mass publics are evoked by what the government does and by what public officials say, talk of responsiveness to the will of the people means less (or more) than meets the eye.

Governmental actions and rhetoric can reassure people and make them apathetic, or it can arouse them to militant action. And the messages that reassure or arouse can be either accurate or misleading. Because controversial policies always hurt some people, the temptation is strong for public officials to be reassuring; officials are naturally eager to be reassured themselves and to believe that what they do is in the public interest. Even if political symbols are misleading, therefore, they need not be *deliberately* deceptive. Indeed, the most powerful political symbols are disseminated by people who believe in them themselves.

Public officials can win mass support for actions that would elicit protest and resistance if undertaken by private groups. If private gas and electric companies could raise their rates whenever they pleased without any pretense of governmental supervision, any company that substantially raised its rates every year or two would certainly evoke massive protests and demands for public ownership or tight regulation.[1] But few people protest publicly when state public utilities commissions permit precisely the same rate rises. The blessing of a government agency reassures consumers and wins support for actions that would otherwise be resented.

---

[1] This is precisely what happened in the late nineteenth century, giving rise to the existing state and federal regulatory laws.

If the wealthy, as private individuals, forced the poor or middle-class to give them a substantial part of their earnings, resistance would be massive and immediate. Yet governmental tax and subsidy policies that have exactly this effect are perceived as reasonable, even though particular taxes or subsidies are criticized by scattered interests. If private individuals forced millions of young men to leave home, submit to strict discipline, kill others, and be killed themselves, such "slavery" would be regarded as intolerable. But when legitimized by duly enacted draft laws, it is not only tolerated by most, but regarded as highly desirable and even necessary.

The point is that official governmental acts and statements are rarely *simple* in their impacts or their meanings. Almost never are their consequences clear and certain. Economists conclude that public utility laws typically do little to keep gas and electricity rates low. But it still seems likely to most people that the rates would be even higher without governmental regulation. Low tax rates for oil producers force other taxpayers to subsidize an affluent group, but the subsidy is justified on the grounds that it enlarges a vital national resource—and it probably does. In such cases the financial costs to large numbers of people are high (though they are largely or completely hidden), the method of calculating them is complex, and their fairness is hard for most people to judge. By contrast, the symbolic benefits—protection of the consumer, promotion of national security—are easy to see and to understand even though they often turn out to be trivial, misleading, or nonexistent when carefully studied.

The legitimacy of government—the belief that public officials represent the will of the people—therefore confers a mystique that can reassure people even when they have reason to be wary or alarmed. And it can arouse people to endure severe sacrifices due to wars or regressive taxes even if they have little to gain. In such cases the facts are hard to recognize or analyze, and anxious people want very much to believe that the government knows how to handle the economic, military, and other threats they fear but cannot cope with as individuals.

Not all public policy is symbolic or based on deliberate or unintended mystification, of course. The impacts of many governmental acts on people's everyday lives are so clear that there is little question whether they help or hurt. People in a slum neighborhood who want a playground or a traffic light know when they are getting what they need. The farm corporation that gets several hundred thousand dollars in "price support" subsidies knows precisely how public policy boosts its profits. To the taxpayer, of course, this same public policy may be invisible or perceived as an aid to the small family farmer or a desirable way of enhancing the nation's food production.

The key question, then, is under what conditions the acts of government become symbolic and help *create* beliefs, wants, and demands in mass publics. The question is both a highly practical one for the citizen or lobbyist and an intriguing one for the student of government; public policies have symbolic effects under conditions that we can identify, at least within rough limits. Because political symbolism is a *systematic* phenomenon, we can learn to understand and perhaps control it.

Symbol Analysis

Analysis of political symbolism allows us to see some things that are not otherwise obvious and to evaluate or judge them in a new way. People's satisfaction or dissatisfaction with government does not depend only on how much they get. It depends even more on what society, and especially the government itself, cues them to expect, want, and believe they deserve. Corporate farm interests made rich by a price support program are often dissatisfied if they do not also get tax breaks, such as rapid depreciation allowances. Most of the poor, taught by schools, welfare workers, and governmental policies to feel inadequate for not having made money in a "land of equal opportunity," docilely accept meager welfare benefits and sometimes degrading "counseling" on how to live their lives. They may feel lucky if their benefits are raised ten dollars a month. In both these cases it is people's *expectations*, rather than how much they get, that chiefly influences how satisfied or how demanding they are. In both examples, and in thousands of others, government helps shape expectations rather than simply responding to them. Indeed, government acknowledges "the voice of the people" largely by influencing what that voice says.

The study of political symbolism necessarily focuses on *change* and the attitudinal and behavioral conditions of change. Symbols evoke either *change* or *reinforcement* of what people already believe and perceive. It becomes essential to know, for example, how a governmental action or statement may change beliefs or perceptions. A poll may show that virtually all Americans are convinced that the Chinese People's Republic is their eternal enemy and its people enslaved and hostile. But these poll results reflect a response to particular stimuli, and not necessarily to a stable state of affairs. More important than such a snapshot poll is the way such results change after the President of the United States visits China and the television networks broadcast pictures of beautiful Chinese cities and friendly-looking people. Statistics on support or opposition to the President are less important than what kinds of *change* in support will take place if unemployment rises or prices decline. Statistics on attitudes, in short, are not "hard data," important in themselves. They are, rather, a way of learning something about how governments and other social groups evoke changes in the direction, intensity, or stability of attitudes. The symbolic perspective is a dynamic one.

Every mode of observing and interpreting the political scene has normative implications. It crudely or subtly suggests that the system, and particular aspects of it, are good or bad, right or wrong. Here, too, the symbolic perspective makes a difference. The conventional view of the political process sees public policy as reflecting what the people want—as expressed in their votes and responded to by legislatures and by the administrators and judges who carry out legislative policy. Systems theory, the most fashionable metaphor for explaining government, portrays public demands and support as the "inputs" of the system and legislative, executive, and judicial policy as the "outputs." Both systems theory and the traditional outlook are highly reassuring and justify the *status quo*, for they tell us that governmental action reflects what the people want.

The student of symbolism knows that this is often true, but does not avoid the less reassuring aspect of the political process: that government can often shape people's wants before it reflects them. To the extent that governmental actions create popular beliefs and wants, the political process is not democratic but potentially antidemocratic, for policies are not always based on the people's will even when they seem to be. It is tempting to take the appearance for the reality. This is true whether the manipulation of public opinion by governmental officials is deliberate or unintentional. For this reason the symbolic perspective often raises questions about the legitimacy of political regimes, the obligation to support them, and the desirability of their policies.

Symbols and Their Creation

Some Characteristics of Symbols

How is it that on controversial public issues people come to hold conflicting views of the facts, the nature of the problem, and the proper course of action to solve it? Consider some recent public issues. Will antiballistic missile installations increase national security or actually decrease it by intensifying the international arms race? Will busing to desegregate public schools improve the quality of education or ruin the schools? Does a wage-price freeze help stop inflation or simply allow employers to keep the money they would otherwise pay their employees?

All these issues have been hotly fought in recent years, and it is obvious that both sides cannot be right about the facts and impacts of proposed policies. The first step toward understanding this kind of conflict is to notice that the facts about such questions cannot be fully known and understood. Thus there is a large element of uncertainty, or ambiguity. Whenever ambiguity exists about matters that concern or threaten large numbers of people, public policies become "symbolic" in the sense that they evoke intense feelings and beliefs about a range of issues that may be quite different from the one that is publicly debated. Support for the ABM (antiballistic missile) may be based, perhaps subconsciously, on deepseated inclinations to be tough with enemies or strong fears of unemployment in the aerospace industry. But both feelings are expressed as concern for protection against foreign enemies. To its opponents, on the other hand, the ABM may arouse strong emotion not only because they think it unnecessary and economically wasteful but because it "symbolizes" a violent or aggressive posture they find repulsive. Such symbols are sometimes called "condensation symbols" because they condense into one event or act a whole range of anxieties, attitudes, memories of past victories or defeats, and expectations of future glories or catastrophes. To the extent that something serves as a condensation symbol, reactions to it are not based on observable facts that can be verified or falsified. Responses are based, rather, on social suggestion—that is, on what other people cue us to believe. They may turn out to be perfectly reasonable and appropriate responses, but often they are not.

Not all political acts, terms, or events are condensation symbols, of course. They may be only partly symbolic. We react to many political events as observable reality, as a part of our everyday lives with which we realistically cope. Such phenomena serve as "referential symbols." Often a political event is dealt with both as part of the factual world and as an expressive symbol. It may serve both functions for the same person or it may be chiefly referential for some people and chiefly expressive for others. And it may express quite different things to different groups of people.

When social workers refuse to give destitute people their welfare checks unless they agree to "counseling" on how to spend their money, raise their children, and run their homes, the social workers see counseling as help for the unfortunate. They refer to themselves as members of a "helping profession." Many of their clients, however, see "counseling" as demeaning and repressive interference in their private lives and as coercion to make them live by middle-class standards and values. The same phenomenon symbolizes very different things to the two groups most directly involved with it.

What counseling symbolizes for the general public determines which group has power, status, and public support. Because social workers have been able to get their perspective on this issue widely accepted by the general public, they wield the greater power. Their clients are generally perceived as people who have much more wrong with them than lack of money. The notion that they need counseling evokes a view of the poor as personally inadequate and incompetent, unable to cope with life in the way other people do, and in need of guidance and even coercion to behave well. Most people do not even perceive counseling as a political issue, so completely are they "socialized" to see social work as a helping profession. Indeed, convincing the public to perceive the exercise of authority and the allocation of values as a "professional" rather than a political issue is one of the most common and effective political techniques in contemporary society.

It is therefore the meanings of governmental actions and rhetoric to specific groups of people that are important to the analysis of political symbolism. The key issues are (1) how actions and words come to mean different things to different people and in different situations, and (2) the impact of such meanings on the distribution of power and on the inclination of people to be either militant, aroused, and violent, or willing to accept governmental action with satisfaction, apathy, or quiescence.

The Creation of Political Symbols: Language and "Information"

People underestimate the pervasiveness of political symbols partly because they are largely shaped and maintained unconsciously—through the language used to describe events and through unconscious emphasis on some kinds of information and disregard of other kinds. The nonobvious meanings of everyday activities are nowhere more striking than in analysis of the subtle meanings of the language we speak, hear, and read every day. What messages, for example, are conveyed by the appeals of politicians to vote for a particular candidate or to support policy A rather than policy B? There is, of course, an obvious level of meaning: a plea for support for the political cause or candidate.

It is equally clear, however, that this kind of political exhortation also tells the masses that what they support matters, that they do have an influence on how government works. People easily grow skeptical about the obvious message. They often question or resist specific appeals for support. But the subtle, nonobvious message is far harder to question or resist. To be asked for support is to be told that your support counts. In this way the *form* of political rhetoric shapes thought and belief more powerfully than can its content. Hortatory political language is only one example of the symbolic level at which language influences us. The legal language and administrative jargon to which we are constantly exposed also convey latent messages that reassure us that the political system functions so as to realize the will of the people.[2]

The metaphors we use, usually unconsciously, to describe political events and issues also subtly shape our political thought. A metaphor describes the unknown by comparing it to something that is well-known, and in doing so it highlights some features and conceals others. "A crusade for freedom" and "legalized murder" are two metaphoric descriptions of war that place it in quite different perspectives. A wage control program can be viewed either as "a battle against inflation" or as "a subsidy to employers." Every controversial political development is described and perceived by the use of conflicting metaphors, not necessarily because of a deliberate effort to influence or to mislead (though that, of course, happens too), but because we cannot speak or think about any complex matter without resorting to metaphor. It permeates our language whether or not we are aware of it.

The particular metaphor that describes a political issue for a per-

---

[2] For a discussion of their symbolic meanings, see Murray Edelman, *The Symbolic Uses of Politics* (Champaign: University of Illinois Press, 1964), ch. 7.

son reinforces the other symbolic processes. A person who works in a defense industry and fears Russian aggression is likely to adopt the political role of defender against a foreign enemy and to see the Cold War as a crusade for freedom. Those who call war "legalized murder" will look to him like dupes or traitors. His beliefs, his self-concept, and his language reinforce each other and are, in fact, components of a single pattern of thought and behavior. They can be fully understood only as aspects of each other, and this is the important function of political language. It is always a vital part of a larger pattern of thought and action.

Political metaphors help shape both what we see as fact and how we *evaluate* political developments. Some think of abortion as a form of murder and some think of it as a form of freedom. Whichever metaphor is in a person's mind influences what he or she imagines when reading a news story about an abortion clinic or about legalization of abortion. And, obviously, it influences whether he or she favors or opposes legal abortion.

The metaphoric mode in which people perceive complex political issues and events is an obstacle to complete understanding and to changes in perception and belief as new information becomes available. New information is ordinarily screened to conform to the metaphor, rather than allowed to change it. Two people with opposing views can read the same news about abortion clinics and each find that it confirms their earlier opinions. In this way metaphors become self-perpetuating. They are the patterns into which we fit our observations of the world. If army communiqués describe the bombing of "structures" in Southeast Asian villages, people feel better than they would if they were told that our bombs were destroying people's houses or huts. For those who want to believe it, the word "structures" evokes an image of military installations rather than homes.

Statistics about governmental activities can readily create misleading beliefs and are an especially common form of impression management. In this case there is often a deliberate attempt to mislead, which is not typically true of other symbolic processes. But misleading statistics also depend for their effectiveness largely on the willingness, or eagerness, of the public to be convinced. In a society that puts a high premium on science and precision, and in which we are socialized to believe that "figures don't lie," statistics are usually highly persuasive. They are a form of information we are strongly tempted to accept and believe.

Nonetheless, figures often do lie, and it sometimes requires considerable sophistication to recognize their falsity. Unemployment is invariably understated in the statistics when it is high. This may occur, for example, because people who would like to have jobs but are convinced (often accurately) that there are none to be had are not counted as unemployed unless they actively seek work. A decline in the unemployment statistics often means, therefore, that a lot of people have become discouraged about the economy. But it is accepted as evidence of an upturn in the economy. "Body counts" showing far more enemy than American soldiers killed can easily create an impression of progress toward "victory" in a population eager for hard evidence. The impression is dubious. Such figures are supplied by field commanders who can seldom actually count enemy bodies but know their promotions depend on supplying statistics pleasing to their superiors; and even if the statistics were accurate, of course, they would not have much to do with which side is winning. Even accurate figures can create quite misleading impressions. If crimes increase by exactly the same number each year, a government can claim, quite accurately, that there has been a drastic decline in the rate of increase and so win credit for an effective fight against crime.

There is, then, a very strong temptation to accept or invent information that confirms what we already believe, gives events the meanings we want them to have, and serves our interests. The tendency to accept myth is sometimes virtually unrestrained. Where the temptation to accept it is less strong, empirical observation and reality-testing can offset or overcome it. Political belief and behavior cannot be understood without recognizing that there are severe limits on how well the human mind accepts and takes account of pertinent information.

Symbols and Reality

Fortunately, beliefs and perceptions about the world and about ourselves are also often realistic and based on accurate observation. When people are directly and critically affected by readily observable political events, they are likely to base their beliefs on what they see rather than on symbolic cues. The poor in eighteenth- and nineteenth-century Europe rioted when food shortages occurred.[3] Peasants in Southeast Asia ment of civil rights laws.[5] In none of these cases is there much doubt or today riot or rebel when their patrons stop providing them with at least a subsistence level of food, clothing, and shelter.[4] Blacks in American urban ghettos typically base their beliefs about progress toward racial equality on what happens to them in their daily lives, not on the enactuncertainty about what is happening, and those most affected are realistic, though other groups may not be.

It is in ambiguous situations that evoke strong fears or hopes that symbolism becomes a powerful influence on what people believe and what they think is happening. To upper middle-class whites, the enactment of civil rights laws is an encouraging signal that the lot of the

[3] George F. Rude, *The Crowd in History* (New York: John Wiley, 1954).

[4] James Scott, "The Erosion of Patron-Client Bonds and Social Change in Rural Southeast Asia." Mimeographed.

[5] For a discussion and documentation of this point see Murray Edelman, *Politics as Symbolic Action* (Chicago: Academic Press, 1971), pp. 19–20.

ghetto black is improving, especially if there was a bitter struggle in Congress over passage of the law. Their evidence is news stories about the legislative outcome, not experience of life in the ghetto. In some lower-middle-class whites, the same news stories create a belief that blacks are progressing too fast and threatening their jobs. When hopes or fears are strong and political events cannot be observed directly, governmental acts become especially powerful symbols. But every political belief involves some mix of direct observation and symbolic cuing, though in greatly varying proportions. The hungry food rioter is close to the realistic end of the realism-symbolism scale. Close to the other end of the scale is the German in the 1930s who followed and obeyed Hitler because he or she believed Hitler's claim that the Nazis would create a glorious thousand-year empire.

Even this formulation understates the marvelous complexity of the human mind. The same person rarely retains exactly the same beliefs about a political issue over time; he or she responds to new events and new cues. In the wake of news of a particularly brutal crime, a person may take the position that fewer civil rights and longer prison terms for criminal offenders are necessary to reduce the crime rate. Shortly afterward, the same person may read a study of the effects of imprisonment that persuasively argues that prisons rarely "rehabilitate," often force the person who has violated the law once to adopt crime as a way of life, and therefore create more criminals than they cure. On controversial political issues, many people's beliefs and perceptions are likely to be consciously or unconsciously ambivalent and often quite unstable. Realistic observation keeps us from straying too far into fantasy most of the time. But given sufficient uncertainty about the facts and sufficiently strong fears or hopes, large groups of people indulge in mythical thinking about political issues. Let us now examine some of the effects and implications of such thinking.

Symbolic Politics and Political Quiescence

Legitimacy and Support

Why is there so little resistance to, and such overwhelming support from all strata of the population for, a political system that yields the substantial inequalities in wealth, power, status, and sacrifice examined in the earlier chapters of this book? Support for the system and belief in its legitimacy is all the more striking in view of the fact that Americans are taught early that all men are created equal, and that they live in a land of equal opportunity.

Many governmental processes inculcate both generalized support for the political system and acquiescence in particular policies. Such pro-

though most of the middle class remains relatively affluent. Racial conflict is exacerbated by such conditions, and class consciousness is commensurately retarded. Social tensions multiply, there appear to be many severe problems but no solutions, and no clear moral or spiritual principles seem applicable. Amid this general social fragmentation and purposelessness, various militant populist-type protest movements gain adherents. Some call for a general redistribution of wealth, others for a "return to fundamentals"; all are impatient with the continuing claims of minorities for equal status and opportunity. Governing elites, particularly those with roots in the corporate and financial world, grow alarmed at the obviously decaying social situations and worsening condition of the economy. They make a private alliance, tentative at first, either with incumbent politicians or with major populist leaders, enabling them to remain in or rise to power on this combination of elite and mass support.

A disorganized left offers little serious resistance, manifesting itself chiefly in isolated strikes and occasional terrorism. The new government uses the latter to justify exaggerated public attacks on minorities, the left, and all forms of unorthodoxy and un-Americanism. Infiltration and surveillance are used in a broad campaign of intimidation. The general public, genuinely alarmed by the apparent reality of the alleged threat to national security, supports vigorous repression as necessary and justifiable.

Swept along by the hysteria, courts and juries find the means to jail people suspected of unorthodox actions or intentions. The Supreme Court, staffed by the nominees of the same elites, approves (and thereby legitimates) such uses of the police and judicial systems. The acknowledged vulnerability of the society appears to justify far-reaching supervision and control over behavior to prevent outbreaks.

At the same time, established elites recognize the necessity of promoting economic well-being, by which they mean serving the needs and preferences of various segments of the economy as fully as possible. Accordingly, they proceed much further than in the preceding scenario, regimenting the domestic working population, actively insisting on opportunities for American investment and trade in various parts of the world, and employing American military power freely on behalf of both ends.

Political opposition begins to fade at the same time. Because of their similar perceptions of social conditions, and trends among those in authority and among voters, few recognized political leaders seriously dispute the propriety of existing public policy. Elections thus become contests between candidates who share a commitment to repression of dissent and promotion of the needs of the economy at practically any cost. Regardless of the winning political party, and because of the widespread inability to perceive any alternative to surveillance and repression, such policies once undertaken become fixed, and can only intensify. In this manner—by the steady erosion of fixed standards of due process and fair procedures, coupled with rigid insistence on the *status quo*—a police state evolves. The American version of fascism, well grounded in popular support, is complete.

3. *Marginal reformist change, culminating in welfare capitalism.* This scenario posits visible and continuing economic dislocation sufficient to convince a sizeable segment of the population—not just intellectuals and leftist organizers—that something is wrong with the economic order. It could be a mild depression or a continued recession that affects more than the lowest levels of workers. What is crucial is that it provide a basis for some degree of class consciousness or other shared consciousness of joint deprivation sufficient to overcome the divisiveness of group or racial conflicts. The latter, though unlikely to mellow substantially, could become somewhat less divisive if black/brown/red leaders began to interpret their plight in class-based or economic, rather than exclusively racial, terms. Young people would continue to be a source of new, more egalitarian, and humanistic values. For ever-increasing numbers of them, the older priorities would simply lack validity. Vitally important to the convergence of these conditions is the absence of war, for war would inject new obstacles into the path of a growing but fragile coalition seeking to span class, age, racial, and sexual divisions.

Considerable value change, gaining momentum continually as new waves of young people enter the society's mainstream, would make for a temporarily severe "generation gap." Before very long, however, elites themselves would be penetrated by the new standards, and key personnel at middle-management levels would begin to see like-minded persons permeating their areas of activity—including politics. Organizations of change-seeking persons would proliferate, venting their impatience with the stubbornness of the established procedures in repeated outbreaks of violence. Unions in particular would regain their old militance as younger workers reinvigorated them, and waves of strikes demanding greater control over the conditions of work (not just higher wages and benefits) would take place.

Widening agreement among both elites and the general public on the justice of such causes would inhibit, but not entirely preclude, elite repression. Elites, perceiving themselves as severely threatened, would seek to undercut the new thrust by making marginal concessions to demands. In time, as each adjustment granted new legitimacy to the rationale underlying the demands, and more and more elites became committed to the new values, a major turning-point would occur. The most likely would seem to be a sweeping victory for the more progressive political party in an election posing clear-cut alternatives between the new and the old values. After that, major institutional changes (such as the elimination of conservative rules in the Congress) would be possible, and fundamental change could then ensue.

The change would involve implementation of new value priorities:

22

Political Change

This chapter addresses the most crucial questions about the future of the American political system. Will there be change? What kind? What kind of change *should* there be? How may such change come about? These questions force us to develop a very crude theory of how political change does and can occur, given the current political power structure and associated social and economic order of the United States. Applying this general framework to circumstances as they develop, we can generate some sense of the types of change that are most likely and ways to bring about changes we may consider desirable.

We shall first construct a crude theory describing when and how change occurs, and what determines the form such change will take. In practical terms, our theory will be little more than a set of analytical categories that facilitate thinking about change. In some respects, however, we shall be specifying factors and relationships among factors that make change of various kinds *more,* or *less,* likely. Then we shall apply this framework to contemporary events in the United States, in an effort to assess the probable outcome of the forces now operating in this country. Finally, we shall suggest what seem to us to be some imperatives for the process of change in the United States. Once again, readers are reminded that our analyses are necessarily permeated with our value perspective, and that they should evaluate our work in the light of their own critical judgment.

Analysis of Political Change: A Framework

When is change likely to occur in the structure or policies of the American political system? What circumstances determine the form it will take? Our approach is based on the premise that certain preconditions cause pressure to be exerted on the fundamental aspects of the political system. If they are strong enough, modifications of both mass and elite behavior follow, and—depending on the particular configuration of factors, forces, behavior, and events—political change of various kinds and directions then occurs. We shall take up three areas in which the preconditions of change are likely to be generated and then identify some of the major factors that determine the degree and kind of effect such conditions will have on the political system. We shall then consider four alternative types of political change possible in the United States, and the prerequisites and processes associated with each of them.

The Preconditions of Change

In one sense, political change is continuous. Governing elites regularly make adjustments in established policies, or undertake major policy initiatives, in response to changing conditions. Such changes may and often do result in alterations in domestic economic or social relationships or in international affairs. One example is the emergence of Cold War foreign policy and the related evolution of massive defense and space programs. Another is the decision to institute a "war on poverty." But these changes we term *marginal* because their essential effect is to defend and promote the established economic and political structures and the existing patterns of distribution of wealth and status within the society. We shall reserve the term *fundamental* for instances of substantial alteration in the economic or political power structures or in key governmental policies bearing on distribution of wealth and status. Fundamental change is drastic in character; it may come about, however, through either violent or relatively peaceful means.

Our approach to the analysis of political change should permit us to distinguish between these two types of change, and acknowledge the relative improbability of the more fundamental type. *Marginal* change is frequent, requiring few preconditions. But *fundamental* change is infrequent and unlikely to occur without severe pressures on the central concerns of politics that are widely perceived and acted on by masses and elites alike. We would expect fundamental change only when the preconditions begin to disrupt or seriously threaten the basic organization and operation of the economy, the class structure, existing control over the uses of government's coercive powers, or the established patterns of distribution of wealth and status. The more preconditions generate such effects, the more probable are changes in the structure and uses of political power, the character of political institutions, and the key policies of government. In short, the severity of dislocations in closely related policy areas determines the probability of fundamental *political change*; we shall consider three such areas in the order of their importance for political change.

1. *Changes in the level and distribution of economic prosperity.* The most powerful source of pressure on the political system is the state of the economic system, for the obvious reason that it affects first the very survival, and then other avidly sought goals, of people in all social settings. Despite its image of stability, American politics has always been highly sensitive to fluctuations and dislocations in the economy. When the economy is stable and unemployment limited, the political system is normally free of strain even though distribution of economic rewards is very unequal. But if either inflation or recession occurs, pressures begin to build up and distribution differences become salient and provocative. If a depression develops, pressures may become truly explosive.

2. *Social tensions and underlying value changes.* A second—and potentially quite independent—major source of pressure on the political system is the rise of tensions and open conflict between major segments of the society. Such conflict is often associated with, and normally exacerbated by, rapid changes in the level and distribution of economic prosperity or other major technological changes. But it can also be generated by noneconomic factors and culminate in deep and widely felt animosities even during periods of economic affluence.

Deep social divisions exist within the United States, rhetorical calls for solidarity and assertions of consensus notwithstanding. The most visible, long-standing and deeply-rooted of these is race. The extent to which racism is entrenched in the psychological makeup, political values, and institutional practices of white America may never be fully understood. But white-black/brown/red tensions escalate with every new assertion of the right to equal status.

More likely to produce fundamental change than the tensions created by the demands of relatively small and containable racial minorities are those grounded in class consciousness. Suppose most blue-collar workers and other wage-earners—black and white, men and women— should come to perceive themselves as jointly exploited for the benefit of a small group of owners and managers who already hold the vast majority of the nation's wealth. Justice, in their eyes, entitles them to a much larger share of the economic product. Their numbers alone would assure great impact, if their power could be organized and applied— though that is difficult.

Other sources of tension exist, though none compare with race and class as long-established antagonisms with continuing raw edges. Religious, regional, and rural-urban conflicts remain real, and could exert pressure on the political system if particular issues again raise perceptions of deprivation or create frustrations. But new forms of tension unrooted in old divisions also exist. One is the general lack of a sense of personal satisfaction that seems to pervade the United States in the 1970s. Despite such achievements as moon landings and the highest standard of living in the world, many observers see Americans as lacking contentment, self-confidence, and a sense of purpose. Work seems to be providing a less meaningful rationale for life, and to be less a source of pride, than in previous decades. Individuals seem to be aware of their apparent powerlessness to affect the course of events, or even matters that touch their own lives.

Perhaps the most striking new tension-producing feature of American social life, however, is the new set of values developed by young people. Contrasting sharply with the materialism, nationalism, conformity, and support for the economic and political *status quo* of their elders, the new value system has been termed a "counterculture." Its priorities are egalitarianism, humanism, participation, and self-fulfillment through a wide variety of individual activities. A growing women's liberation movement is pressing for substantial change, reaching deep into the personal relationships and public roles of men and women, and potentially into basic societal values and assumptions.

3. *International tensions and events.* The obvious interdependence of international and domestic affairs means that events overseas often spark economic and social tensions at home. Such developments may serve either to generate massive new pressure on the political system or to deflect already powerful pressures away from it.

The most obvious source of restructured domestic relationships is war, or the immediately perceived threat of war. A relatively small, festering war in a distant place, such as Korea or Vietnam, is likely to create new social divisions or exacerbate tension between left and right; at the same time it promotes economic well-being and then inflation. A full-scale war, or even a small war close to home, tends to draw wider support and to eclipse all other issues that might otherwise divide people. More complex effects derive from the threat of armed conflict and from a posture and ideology that support constant readiness for nuclear war, such as the Cold War, anticommunism, and defense expenditures of the 1950s and 1960s. This atmosphere creates underlying tensions while it legitimates many actions, and diverts attention from others, in the name of patriotism and national security.

But war and the threat of war are only the most obvious sources of disruptive tensions and the prospect of political change. Sharp changes overseas—such as an oil embargo, nationalization, or severance of trade relations—may reverberate throughout segments of the U.S. economy and induce shortages, diplomatic pressure, or military intervention to restore American advantage. International developments of a non-economic nature may also have an impact on American life. The increasing militance among American blacks during the 1950s and 1960s was due in part to the example of newly independent African and Asian nations, whose nonwhite leaders acquired power and led their countries effectively and with great pride.

This brief analysis of some sources of intrasocietal tensions and conflicts sufficient to raise the possibility of fundamental political change is merely illustrative, and not comprehensive. No doubt there are many other causes of pressure on the political system. But our point is that substantial pressures must be generated from *some* source before established econopolitical relationships are likely to undergo change of a fundamental kind. If there are several such pressures, and if they converge or overlap in such a way as to be mutually reinforcing (rather than pitting different groups against each other in a self-canceling and immobilizing fashion), the prospect of such change is greater.

The Political Impact of the Preconditions of Change

Preconditions are thus necessary, but not sufficient, causes of fundamental change. What is crucial for our purposes is the manner in which such preconditions become translated into effects on the political system. Multiple sources of tension clearly exist, some of them deep and others worsening. But there have always been some such tensions, and fundamental political change has not occurred in more than a century. Depressions and severe social tensions have given rise to militant parties and movements seeking fundamental change, but they have failed to achieve their goals. Social tensions must not only produce converging and mutually reinforcing perceptions of deprivation; they must also be translated into politics in particular ways before they are likely to generate fundamental change. We may identify several prerequisites that, if fulfilled, will make fundamental change more likely. Again, we do not see it as necessary or inevitable that all these political effects be present in order for change to take place, but the prospect of change will increase as each is fulfilled. We shall frame the conditions as three basic questions.

1. How fully do existing dislocations, tensions, and underlying value changes disrupt established patterns of distribution and detach masses of people from their previous commitments to the dominant political values, ideology, and behavior? *For fundamental change to occur, there must be a decrease in the supportive attitudes of people toward their government; its legitimacy must be eroded, and a vacuum of authority must develop.* This is a long-term process, of course, and must be deep-seated enough to counteract the best efforts of the major socializing and interpreting agents (schools, mass media) of the existing system. It also requires visible, legitimate leadership; but leaders are not likely to arise until the trend of popular change is already underway. Thus, the impetus toward change in values must be self-generated. Social and economic conditions, international events, or personal experience must create perceptions of serious personal deprivation that call into question the legitimacy or propriety of established political values and practices. Such perceptions of contradiction or unworkability in the present system must be strong enough to survive such explanations and diversions as the alleged failure of individuals, racial antagonisms, symbolic appeals, anti-communism, and so forth. Not just one or two such perceptions, but an extended and cumulating series of them, are probably necessary to drive people to develop new priorities for political action and seriously consider alternatives to the present system. Without deep doubts about established values, at the very least, proposals or movements for change will be ignored, dismissed, or resisted by the very people who constitute an almost irreplaceable component in the process.

2. How much (and what kind of) power can be mobilized by change-oriented elements within the society, and how does such power relate to elites' power resources? Almost by definition, those who feel personal deprivation in such a way as to commit themselves to fundamental change do not possess large or immediately effective power resources. A few wealthy, well-connected, or strategically located persons may identify with the causes of the deprived, and serve as leaders or key supporters. But most persons with access to major power resources are probably either already members of the establishment or at least persuaded that the basic structures and values are acceptable and that only marginal change is required. *Fundamental change thus normally requires the mobilization of the latent power resources of the currently powerless.* Numbers become crucial. Regardless of how slight their individual power, if a substantial segment of the population becomes committed to unified action in support of fundamental change, their joint power is immense. Strategic location within the economy or society is also important. Effective strikes in vital service-providing fields (governmental functions, transportation, and the like) greatly multiply the power of relatively small numbers of people.

But the most crucial factors for mobilizing the powerless into a potentially successful force for fundamental change are *organization* and *communication*. Organization means the emergence of groups of people whose commitment is so complete that they subordinate all economic and other personal goals, and make single-minded efforts to awaken numbers of other people to the need for (and prepare them for the action necessary to) achieving fundamental change. Organization-building requires a supportive environment for group members, so that their commitments are regularly reinforced and new members are recruited. And it requires substantial agreement on (or at least only limited conflict over) the basic strategy by which change is to be accomplished.

The need for communication has both internal and external dimensions. There must be regular exchanges of information and effective coordination between the geographically (and perhaps in some ways ideologically) separated units of the growing organization. And there must be communication between the organizers and the people whom they seek to mobilize. Unless numbers of people can be brought to support the organized movement, or at least detached from their support for established ways and thus neutralized, the movement has little real prospect of success. It will either gradually become aware of its failure and dissipate, or be forced into isolation and resort to indiscriminate terrorism or other desperate and self-destructive measures.

The task of mobilizing numbers of people into a unified, change-seeking force is very difficult. Previously inert individuals must acquire a sense of political efficacy and hope strong enough to impel them to action. Various means of attracting attention and reaching people in terms they can readily identify with and understand are necessary: action, deliberate self-sacrifice, rational persuasion, and blatant propaganda all play parts at various stages. As organization progresses, a series of minor skirmishes in which victories over established institutions or procedures are scored probably contributes to awakening self-confidence and determination. The bases of solidarity among people must be developed over time and against a background of deep-seated suspicions, divisions, prejudices and misunderstandings. Without the development of such organization and its promotion of broad support, fundamental change seems unlikely.

3. How do established elites react to forces seeking fundamental change? Because they hold the initiative and have a responsibility to act in response to events, existing elites' behavior plays a vital role in the evolving process of change. They may act to promote divisions and hostility within the population, and/or to isolate and discredit groups seeking change, thereby making mobilization difficult or impossible. They may appear to institute, or actually make, marginal changes in policies in order to reduce popular perceptions of deprivation, thereby undercutting (or, in some circumstances, promoting) the thrust toward fundamental change. They may introduce wholly new issues or appeals, such as

space exploration, war, or the threat of war, which redirect attention or mobilize support for the existing order. They may also engage in active repression of change-seeking groups. If done with sophistication and restraint, this may help to solve their problem. But if crudely handled, it can provide the movement with substantial new constituencies.

In each case, it is clear that elite response shapes the opportunities and problems of change-seekers. What determines how elites act? In part it depends on which segment of the establishment is currently dominant within the executive branch. The Eastern upper class, the managers of the great corporations, and welfare-state liberals tend to react with modest policy changes, deflection, and sophisticated repression. Those newer to real power and more steeped in the ideology than the practice of American government, such as the Southern and Southwestern individualist-conservatives, are more likely to react by exaggerating the threat, appealing to popular fears and prejudices, and escalating open repression.

Neither set of behaviors by itself determines whether the movement for change will gain or lose momentum as a result. What it does, essentially, is to shape the degree of polarization in the society. When accompanied by the disaffection, tensions, and loss of legitimacy described earlier, and when there is a cohesive organization ready to act with substantial popular support, a highly polarized situation ripe for fundamental change may be created. What is then required is a spark—the fortuitous event that creates the opportunity for the movement to cross the threshold to real and sweeping impact of some kind. Then, if the existing organization has the skill (or the sheer determination, which may often overcome lack of skill or the absence of some important conditions) to apply its power decisively, the whole structure of power may be sharply altered. Violent revolution need not occur, although violence undoubtedly plays a major role in promoting change of a fundamental nature. Established elites are quite unlikely to release their grip on governmental power unless convinced that it is necessary or inevitable that they do so. Often the escalation of the stakes that results from serious and repeated mutual violence has created such conviction. A relatively low level of violence, if sustained and accompanied by credible threats of more to follow, has sometimes induced elites to acquiesce in, or even to institute, major changes sought in a relatively peaceful manner. Once the process of change has reached this point, developments are no longer even crudely predictable. The outcome depends on such factors as key individuals' personalities and chance.

We can summarize these general observations about the politics of change in terms of a contrast between top-down and bottom-up processes of change. Thus far, we have been speaking chiefly of fundamental change and its prerequisites; marginal change is almost always possible, at the almost exclusive option of establishment elites. To be sure, there are limits within which such elites must select their policy options, but these are chiefly of their own making and only partially subject to popular preferences. In a fundamental change situation, however, elites have lost their predominance. They are either fragmented and beginning to contend with each other, or struggling to maintain themselves against the demands of a newly powerful antagonist arising from outside their ambit. Clearly, we are dealing with two contrasting levels and processes of change. Change initiated from the top down by established elites occurs because of their perceptions and needs, or perhaps through gradual changes in their membership. Such changes are likely to affect only minor policies, well within the established power systems—or, in short, to be *incremental* changes. Only when a thrust from outside the establishment (that is, from below) begins to have an impact on elites' power and status does fundamental change become a possibility. The agency of change must be created by the previously powerless, and must build on deep social tensions and/or value changes to force its way into the political arena. The more such thrust is generated from below, the more the system itself is the target, and the more likely is fundamental change.

Levels and Directions of Change: Four Scenarios

We have said nothing about the *direction* that either marginal or fundamental change may take. Clearly, either may go to the *left*, in the direction of wider distribution of power, wealth, and status within the society, or to the *right*, toward rigid insistence on the *status quo* or even narrower and more restrictive distribution. A nearly infinite number of combinations of possible factors in the total political context could give rise to either marginal or fundamental changes in either direction. We shall reduce this wide range of possibilities to four, briefly describe the features of each, and try to specify what determines the direction they may take. In what seems to us their order of probability in the United States today, we shall discuss (1) erratic marginal change —perpetuation of the *status quo* with slight changes vacillating left and right but tending ultimately to an integrated and corporate-dominated econopolitical system; (2) reactionary marginal change culminating relatively promptly (in, say, 10 to 15 years) in near-fundamental change to a system best termed totalitarian electoral fascism; (3) sustained marginal change with a reformist emphasis, resulting after a longer time span in something like welfare-state capitalism; and (4) revolution, generated by a left-oriented movement, which would result in a more rapid arrival of *either* fascism *or* socialism, depending on unforseeable circumstances developing as the revolution took place. In each case, we shall highlight those conditions and processes that our previous analysis suggests are of key importance.

1. *Erratic marginal change, culminating in a corporate-dominated system.* This scenario assumes that no major depression develops. Race conflict remains salient but more or less effectively suppressed through

the isolation and containment of black/brown/red peoples. Class consciousness remains low and radicalism-populism proves to be a minor and transitory phenomenon, genuinely rejected by workers and middle class alike and ultimately dissipated or suppressed. Threats of nuclear war continue but no major land war is fought outside the Western Hemisphere. In short, basic conditions create no major new dislocations and leave established elites entrenched and with full capacity to orchestrate popular support for their decisions.

Under these conditions, the level of perceived deprivation remains not much higher than it is at present, the government retains its legitimacy and authority, and established values are not seriously challenged. Racial tensions continue to be the chief source of social conflict, and the mass of relatively powerless people is thus divided and distracted. Established elites are relatively unthreatened, and thus able to respond to what seem to them the most important needs of the nation. Their concerns center on the continued stability and growth of the economy. More and more, the continued success of the dominant large corporations (and thus full employment and continued prosperity for most) depends on the use of government power. Hence, government undertakes management of the basic conditions of social life, financing of research and development, underwriting of major risks through subsidies and guarantees, and military protection of overseas activities. And it repels all efforts to change such priorities.

Thus, elites perceive no acceptable alternatives to the growing (and, in the eyes of most, welcome) domination of both the society and the polity by the major corporations. Greater and greater integration between business and government occurs, until the two are nearly indistinguishable. Because established values remain unchanged, economic attainments are the principal measure of progress, and in any event a steadily rising standard of living remains an unchallenged necessity. Existing social problems will also be dealt with, but only when serious incidents occur; even then, they will be second-priority and remedies will be applied to their symptoms rather than their causes. Occasionally, special efforts will be made to elicit popular support for space exploits, threats of nuclear war, or domestic "crusades" against the surface manifestations of problems that annoy many people. But the basic line of development will be an extension of the *status quo,* to the point that a corporate-managed society evolves. Conditions of life will not appear unfree or distasteful to most people, though to a small and permanent minority life will appear intolerably structured by the technological monsters of our own creation.

2. *Marginal reactionary change, culminating in fascism.* In this scenario, a stagnating economy causes unemployment to remain high and forces governments to cut back on services. The lowest levels of the white working class and all minorities feel the pinch quite seriously,

cesses are symbolic in character, for they create meanings and influence states of mind. If they also allocate values, they are both symbolic and instrumental.

The symbols that most powerfully inculcate support for the political system are those institutions we are taught to think of as the core of the democratic state—those that give the people control over the government. Probably the most reassuring are elections. Americans learn early in life to doubt that any state can be democratic without free elections, and they are inclined to assume that a country that holds elections must be democratic. Whatever else they accomplish, elections help create a belief in the reality of popular participation in government and popular control over policy. For the individual voter, elections also create a sense of personal participation and influence in government.

The belief is crucial whether or not it is accurate. Research discussed in Chapter 19 raises doubts that belief in popular control through elections is fully warranted. There is evidence that much of the electorate is neither especially interested in issues nor well-informed about them, and that votes are often cast on the basis of other considerations.[6] On the other hand, issues apparently do sometimes make a difference.[7] But if elections powerfully legitimate the political system and the regime, whether or not they are responsive to people's wants and demands, the realistic political analyst must recognize legitimation as one of their functions, and sometimes the major one.

Similarly, other institutions we are socialized to consider fundamental to democracy help inculcate broad support for the system and acquiescence in policies, even from those who do not like them. The publicized functioning of legislatures and courts promotes widespread confidence that majority will is reflected in the law, which is applied expertly and impartially to people who may have violated it. Here again, there is evidence that such belief is often not warranted. Legislative bodies chiefly reflect the needs of organized interests and strong pressure groups, and courts are more sensitive to the interests of some groups than others—regardless of the "mandate" of the voters in the last election.[8]

Besides legitimizing the political system, governmental actions also create support for, or acquiescence in, particular policies. A wide range of devices are used to evoke such acceptable responses to controversial

---

[6] See especially Angus Campbell, Philip Converse, Warren Miller, and Donald Stokes, *The American Voter* (New York: Wiley, 1960); Philip Converse, "The Nature of Belief Systems in Mass Publics," in *Ideology and Discontent*, ed. David Apter (New York: Free Press, 1964); Angus Campbell et al., *Elections and the Political Order* (New York: Wiley, 1966).

[7] For a study that tries to specify the conditions under which issues matter, and a review of the previous literature, see Gerald M. Pomper, "From Confusion to Clarity: Issues and American Voters, 1956–1968," *American Political Science Review* 66 (June 1972), pp. 415–428.

[8] For an exposition of the pertinent evidence and theory, see David B. Truman, *The Governmental Process* (New York: Knopf, 1951), chs. 11–15.

government acts. It is a challenging exercise to identify them and learn to recognize new ones, for the analyst usually has to overcome his or her own identification with their popular or conventional meanings in order to recognize their symbolic functions.

Reassurance: Protection Against Threats

Some types of governmental action create the belief that government is providing effective protection against widely feared threats or undesirable developments. One policy area in which this effect is especially dramatic is government regulation of business to protect the consumer against high prices. We have antitrust laws to insure that businesses compete, rather than conspiring to concentrate economic power and charge what the traffic will bear. We have many laws to prevent corporations that enjoy monopolies or special licenses in such fields as telephone, gas, electricity, and radio broadcasting from using their economic power to gouge the consumer with high prices or shoddy service. Antitrust actions are frequently in the news, as are the actions of public utility commissions, and politicians often declare their zeal to increase the effectiveness of protective legislation of this sort. Yet for many decades studies by economists and political scientists have shown that these laws and the agencies that administer them typically offer very little protection. They are usually highly sensitive to the economic interests of the businesses they "regulate," and far less so to the interests of consumers. The studies conclude that they become captives of these businesses, rationalizing rate increases while ostensibly protecting the consumer.[9]

If the regulatory laws and commissions come close to reversing the economic function they are established to perform, why are they not abolished? They clearly serve political and psychological functions, both for politicians and for the mass public; politicians find that support for them or for strengthening them still brings in votes. Those who fear the concentration of economic power are reassured when the government responds to their anxiety by setting up an agency to keep prices fair or regulate product quality. It is rarely clear to consumers just which price ceilings and product standards protect them and which exploit them. In short, the issues are ambiguous and complex. This combination of ambiguity and widespread public anxiety is precisely the climate in which people are eager for reassurance that they are being protected, and therefore eager to believe that publicized governmental actions have the effects they are supposed to have.

In many other fields of governmental action the same conditions prevail; public policies are partly, perhaps often chiefly, symbolic in char-

---

[9] See Chapter 13 for references to these studies and an analysis of the impact of regulatory agencies on power centers.

acter. New civil rights laws reassure liberals that progress is being made. But policemen and courts can still ignore the laws or interpret them to permit the very denials of civil liberties they were intended to prevent. And many among the poor and minorities lack the knowledge and legal counsel to assert their rights. The civil rights laws serve as reassuring symbols for affluent liberals, whose own civil rights are fairly well protected. But for the black or radical who is beaten up after being arrested on false charges, there is no ambiguity and no symbolic reassurance. For those who are worried about ecological catastrophe, the passage of laws against water and air pollution brings reassurance and a sense of victory. But again, it is usually far from clear that such laws provide the money or the capacity to act against influential industrial and governmental polluters. Nonetheless, such statutes and clean-up, paint-up, and anti-litter campaigns reassure many who would otherwise be aroused. Tokenism is a classic device for taking advantage of ambiguity and conveying a false sense of reassurance.

Reassurance: The Deprived Deserve It

Governmental or elitist actions also reassure people about worrisome conditions by instilling a conviction that the deprived deserve their fate and are personally benefiting from it. It is comforting to believe that those who are denied the good things of life suffer from personal pathology, deviance, or delinquency, and that they must be controlled, guided, or incarcerated as a form of "correction" or "rehabilitation." Such a rehabilitative and psychiatric ideology has increasingly dominated the laws, rhetoric, and bureaucracies of all the public institutions that have the power to impose severe penalties on the wayward and the dependent: prisons, mental hospitals, schools, and welfare departments. This is a "liberal" view, but its effects have been severely repressive, especially for the poor.[10] In this view, the person who steals is reacting not to poverty or alienating institutions but to psychopathic tendencies. The child who resists the school bureaucracy and its rules is "hostile" and must acquire "insight" by learning how inadequate he or she is. The person who is depressed or will not play conventional roles in life is a psychopath or schizophrenic who must be controlled, and possibly locked up, until he or she learns to behave in conventional ways. The welfare recipient is suffering less from lack of money than from personal inadequacies, for which he or she needs counseling and control. Because the staffs of these

---

[10] Cf. *Struggle for Justice: A Report on Crime and Punishment in America,* prepared for the American Friends Service Committee (New York: Hill and Wang, 1971); August Hollingshead and Frederick C. Redlich, *Social Class and Mental Illness* (New York: Wiley, 1958); Gideon Sjoberg, Richard A. Brymer, and Buford Farris, "Bureaucracy and the Lower Class," in *The National Administrative System,* ed. Dean A. Yarwood (New York: Wiley, 1971), pp. 369–377; Aaron Cicourel and John I. Kitsuse, *The Educational Decision-Makers* (Indianapolis: Bobbs-Merrill, 1963).

institutions enjoy wide latitude in defining deviance, the tendency is strong to perceive any behavior they dislike or that is uncommon in their own social circles as pathological and in need of "correction." Many people are unhappy or maladjusted; the problem lies in assuming that they themselves, rather than social institutions, are at fault.

For elites this way of defining the behavior of the poor and the unconventional has many advantages. It diverts attention from social and economic problems. It justifies repression of those who deviate from middle-class standards of behavior. It defines such repression as "rehabilitation," thereby enhancing the self-concepts of conservatives, liberals, professionals, and the administrative staff, who see themselves as altruistic. Finally, this ideology is accepted by many of the deprived themselves, making them docile and submissive. Docility and submission to authority are generously rewarded in schools, prisons, mental hospitals, and welfare agencies, while independence, insistence on personal dignity, and imagination are usually penalized, often severely.

Dissemination of the belief that the deprived are less deserving than others and must be controlled for their own good is a common and potent form of symbolic political action. Such labeling becomes a self-fulfilling prophecy, subtly or coercively requiring people to act as they are defined [11] and making it more likely that they will become recidivists—that they will revert to the behavior that got them into trouble in the first place. In a society in which economic and social rewards are very unevenly distributed, such social-psychological control supplements the use of coercive police powers and is more effective than naked coercion in maintaining quiescence. It minimizes resistance, maximizes support from the general public, and soothes people's consciences.

The confusion between psychological help and political repression that is characteristic of the definition and treatment of "deviance" takes still another form, with even more far-reaching political consequences. The sociologists who study deviance have come to recognize that the person who is labeled an offender against morality or normality is sometimes more useful to society as a deviant (sick, delinquent, psychopathic) than as a nondeviant. He or she serves as a reference-point, defining what behavior is acceptable and what is unacceptable and also making it clear that deviants are segregated and penalized. Consequently, institutions that keep people deviant by labeling them and then forcing them to maintain a pathological role are doing what many demand that they do to preserve the common conventions.[12] Repression of a conspicuous group of people in the name of "help," "rehabilitation," or "correction"

[11] In addition to the studies cited in footnote 7, see Erving Goffman, *Asylums* (Garden City, N.Y.: Doubleday, 1961).

[12] Lewis A. Coser, "Some Functions of Deviant Behavior and Normative Flexibility," *American Journal of Sociology* 68 (September 1962), pp. 172–174; Robert A. Dentler and Kai T. Erikson, "The Functions of Deviance in Groups," *Social Problems* 7 (1959), pp. 98–107.

powerfully shapes the beliefs and behavior of mass publics. Here we have one of the most striking, significant, and least obvious uses of political symbolism.

The Dynamics of Political Arousal

The Interpretation of Deprivation, Sacrifices, or Threats

For the student of mass political behavior, public quiescence and arousal are matters of central interest. We have just examined some of the ways large numbers of people are induced through governmental activity to remain quiescent, even though they may be deprived of much of the freedom, wealth, status, and dignity that others enjoy. Beliefs that arouse large numbers of people to militant action are also instilled by the use of symbols in ambiguous situations. We shall next examine the dynamics of the *escalation* of political conflict.

The symbols that promote quiescence create the widespread conviction that people are being protected from the threats they fear or that those who behave unconventionally need to be restrained or punished for their own good and that of society. Protection of the public is the key symbolic theme in either case. The symbols that arouse mass publics to protest or violence evoke the opposite expectation—that a widely feared threat to their interests is growing more ominous, that those who pose that threat are malevolent, and that these enemies must be resisted or, sometimes, exterminated. In the face of such a threat, people are led to set aside the lesser conflicts that ordinarily divide them and fight together against what they perceive as a more serious hazard to their common interests.

There might seem an easier explanation for political protest or militance—that those who are poor, oppressed, or trapped are driven to violence to try to better their conditions. There is certainly a large element of truth in this view. It is often the poor and the manifestly oppressed who protest and engage in violence. But this is far from a complete explanation.

First, those who are most deprived are often quiescent. The occasional slave rebellions in the pre-Civil War South were atypical; the great majority of slaves lived out their lives without participating in any such movement. Very few of the poor ever engage in mass riots or join revolutionary movements. The "untouchables," the lowest Hindu caste in India, long accepted their miserable condition as a manifestation of the divine order. Clearly, deprivation alone does not produce or escalate political conflict.

Second, people who are relatively well off sometimes engage in a politics of protest and violence. Affluent middle-class college students did so in massive numbers in the late 1960s. Revolutions typically occur after there has been substantial improvement in the condition of the deprived classes, not when they are most destitute.

Denial of the things people value is beyond question a major reason for political conflict; but the *meaning* of such deprivation is also critical. Is it seen as natural or divinely ordained or as unnecessary and unfairly imposed by the privileged? Is it seen as temporary, stable, or increasing? These *interpretations* of deprivation are influenced by symbols, and they are critical in influencing behavior.

How do people come to believe it necessary to resort to protest or violence outside the channels of conventional politics? How do large groups come to believe that those they fear are unrestrained by established governmental routines and represent an escalating threat that must be met by escalating counteraction?

The key condition is evidence that a group believed to be hostile is winning wider public support and preparing to attack, or to intensify attacks already in progress. Nothing helps American "hawks" win support for larger military budgets and incursions into foreign countries as much as allegations that hawkish sentiment and action is growing in foreign countries commonly believed to be hostile. It is therefore hardly surprising that hawks in rival countries are careful to observe, publicize, and exaggerate the militaristic actions and rhetoric of their adversaries. As they observe and exaggerate their enemies' alleged escalations, rival hawks serve each others' interests; they win added public support for their opponents as well as for themselves. Nothing so powerfully contributes to antipolice sentiment and behavior in American cities or on college campuses as allegations or evidence that police are arbitrarily harassing, beating, or arresting the poor, black, or ideologically unconventional. Political conflicts of these kinds engage more people and greater passions on both sides as each adversary group comes to see the other as its enemy, bent on its repression or extermination. A new and sudden step-up in harassment typically arouses widespread fear and support for escalation on the other side. This is the general pattern of escalating political conflict on any issue.

The Role of Myths in Escalating Conflicts

Another way to see this process is to recognize that people caught up in an escalating political conflict are likely to fit what they hear and see about it into a mythic form. A myth is a widely held belief based on social cues rather than observation of the world. Myth subtly but powerfully shapes the meaning of events. Myths about political conflict fall into a small number of archetypical patterns. One is the myth of an enemy plotting against one's own group or nation and who therefore must be suppressed or exterminated. Another is the myth of a leader-hero-savior who represents a social order ordained by God or sanctioned by the people; he must be followed and obeyed, and sacrifice or suffering on his behalf are seen as ennobling.

In the modern world, people hardly need to be reminded that political conflicts often escalate to the point that the costs and suffering become extremely high. Political history is largely a chronicle of mass violence in the form of wars, massacres, revolutions, and genocides. To understand how men and women become willing, even anxious, to kill and die for political causes, we must examine some perceptions of the enemy and the self that recur whenever political conflict is escalating.

A central feature of this process is the personification of adversaries. Hostile or potentially hostile groups or nations are not seen as internally divided, though this is bound to be true of every formal organization or nation. Instead, the enemy is seen as monolithic and resolute: as loyal followers of the alien leader or oligarchy, who symbolizes evil. This view simplifies the situation, substituting a vision of malevolence for the more realistic recognition that there is a large measure of drift in policymaking, that people change their positions from time to time, and that political leaders must respond to contending groups within their own countries in order to retain their positions. Simplification promotes solidarity against the enemy and eagerness to escalate attacks on him.

Those who participate in an escalating political conflict develop characteristic views of themselves and of their adversaries. Believing that they must defend their lives, their honor, their most vital interests, or their country against hostile outsiders, they take on a well-defined political role: fighter in a noble cause. Such a role gives their lives meaning; it is cherished and not easily abandoned, even in the face of evidence casting doubt on its validity. The cause, and belief in its righteousness or necessity, come to be part of the person's self-concept, reinforcing his or her zeal and willingness to sacrifice, hurt, or kill. Political beliefs, social movements, and self-concepts are not as distinct in real life as they are in textbooks. When a person becomes emotionally involved in a political cause, he or she takes on a particular all-encompassing view of his or her own identity and political role.

In several important ways, then, people involved in escalating political conflict develop particular beliefs and perceptions of the world and of themselves that may distort reality; they hold such beliefs tenaciously and emotionally, and interpret new developments so as to be consistent with and reinforce them.

Symbols, Organization, and Ritualization

The Meaning of Events

The central theme of symbolic analysis of politics is the gap between perceptions or beliefs, on the one hand, and actual gains or losses in money, power, status, or tangible goods on the other. As political conflict escalates, this gap becomes wider.

The winner of symbolic victories may not be the winner of tangible victories. As an international war or "police action" escalates, the low- and middle-income citizens of the country that is victorious on the battle- field may find their taxes far more burdensome, their lives more regi- mented, their sons and relatives killed or wounded. But they are "the winners." Defenders of civil rights who win a court decision guaranteeing that accused persons be provided with lawyers and information about their procedural rights may later learn that actual practices in the station- house have changed little or not at all. Citizens whose outcries against arbitrary rate increases and poor service by a public utility bring about legislation to protect consumer interests have won a symbolic victory. But this form of political triumph rarely brings about lower rates or better service for long. The regulatory agency often makes it easier to raise rates.

Other disparities between perceived and real changes in policy con- sequences become evident as political conflict widens and intensifies. Benefits often come to be perceived as deprivations, and vice versa. As international conflict grows hotter, the armed forces gain larger appro- priations for weapons, new powers to draft soldiers, higher status, and more influence on governmental decisions. It is the poor and the lower middle class whose sons are chiefly drafted to fight, whose incomes are disproportionately taxed, and whose influence on governmental decisions is least. Rather than appearing as real benefits and losses for a specific group of people, however, these changes are perceived and publicized as "costs" of defense, sacrifices the nation as a whole must valiantly as- sume to combat its enemies.

Even the identification of enemies and allies becomes confused and uncertain and may fail to correspond to observable reality as conflict escalates. Such confusion is not accidental, but a consistent and system- atic aspect of political conflict. It is important to create perceptions that induce people to fight, and to sacrifice if necessary, to serve a noble cause and defeat an evil one. In international conflict, the belief is fos- tered that the country is uniting to defeat a common enemy. In fact, there are always internal divisions about whether and how seriously the fight should be waged and whether the enemy is really harmful or malevolent. These internal divisions partly reflect the differences in interest noted above. Escalation means that the more hawkish or militant groups are winning more support than their dovish rivals. As already noted, hawkish groups win support for their foreign counterparts as they win it for themselves, though this tacit cooperation is systematically masked by belief in the implacable hostility of the two countries.

As civil rights conflict escalates, the same ambiguities appear. Here the symbolic conflict is between believers in "the rights of minorities" and believers in "law and order." These symbols unite people on both

community, human rights, and esthetic concerns would replace competition, property rights, and materialism. Structural manifestations would include effective political control and direction of the corporate economy, decentralized management of most governmental and productive functions, and widespread participation by ordinary citizens in various stages of policymaking and its implementation. Technological developments would be subordinated to questions about the desirability of their impact. Economic "progress" would be viewed in terms of worldwide, rather than domestic, circumstances. Redistribution of wealth within the United States would be steadily extended, until resources and productivity were shared with other nations generally.

4. *Immediate fundamental change by revolution leading to fascism or socialism.* Revolution, though hard to contemplate in a heretofore highly stable, advanced industrial nation where the means of large-scale violence are thoroughly monopolized by government, is nevertheless a possibility that must be considered. Revolution requires substantial economic crisis, such as a severe depression, which would create wide unrest. Change in consciousness is thus not limited to the young. But there must be a united cadre group to serve as the principal moving force. Social tensions that place militants, black and white, in a position to join together, accompanied by at least some organized workers, are essential. The crucial factor is a continuing source of provocation that overrides racial suspicions and class differences and brings youth and workers together to serve as the nucleus of the instrument of change.

For such people, and for those similarly affected by economic, social, or world conditions, value shifts are drastic. The government soon loses all legitimacy, and with it the power to restrain behavior. In response to militant behavior, polarization becomes sharp. Conditions nevertheless make a substantial segment of the population responsive to well-framed appeals by organizations of militants. Major strikes in key industries and occasional victories in local conflicts mark their growing power and capability. Elite repression adds to the organizations' constituencies. At this point the situation is ripe for the final spark that can—if the organizations' leaders are perceptive and determined enough—eventuate in revolution. The spark would have to be so dramatic, and the response of major leaders and groups so indecisive or mutually conflicting, that an impasse would be apparent and police and military forces divided or immobilized. A hopelessly deadlocked presidential election, or savage repression of a major strike, or the imminent prospect of nuclear war, might be capable of providing such a spark.

If a total effort to seize power in the national government is made, with no limitations on the means or sacrifice involved, it might succeed. Actions limited to what is perceived as possible rarely exceed such bounds; those based on "impractical" aspirations sometimes achieve most of them, much to everyone's surprise. Once the attempt at revolution begins, of course, uncontrollable forces are set in motion. An effort undertaken in the absence of the conditions necessary to success can be totally self-destructive. Whoever mobilizes the means of violence most effectively emerges the winner. Their goals could be the faintly concealed fascism that appeals to many of the powers on the American right, or the democratic socialism that motivates the left. But revolutionary processes assure only that the old order will not survive, and there is no guarantee that what results will be an improvement on it. The result *might* be either fascism or democratic socialism. But there is no way to foresee the outcome until after the revolution has run its course.

Prospects for Change in the American Political System

These four scenarios suggest the range of possibility that lies before us. Difficult as it is to see ahead, this is exactly what we must try to do if we are to play any significant part in helping to shape events. Let us speculate a bit about the American future.

We are confident of our basic premise: the United States and the world are experiencing an unprecedented era of transformation from which shall emerge a different economic and social order. One thing of which we can be sure is that the society we have known is in the process of being replaced by something different. Obvious preconditions of that change are visible in the economic pressures of the late 1970s and the ongoing social disintegration and underlying value change that have marked the last decade.

But the nature of the change we are experiencing is far less clear than is its existence. Multiple possibilities are open, each of them prefigured in part by our present circumstances. This brings us to our second major point: the eventual outcome will depend on what *people* do and think and seek in the next years. History often seems inexorable and predetermined. But there also occur times of change and multiple possibility when the actions of knowledgeable and determined people shape the future, and this is surely one of those times.

The four scenarios just described are listed in what we consider the order of their likelihood. The first two are almost interchangeable, and the events of the late 1970s may make the second the more probable. But these are only probabilities, not inevitabilities. Many people consider themselves helpless to affect the outcome of such momentous issues, of course. As we have seen, there is good reason for them to feel thus—at least as far as acting within the established ideological and political channels is concerned. That very helplessness, however, should be recognized as an outcome of the teachings of the American ideology: we are taught first that we must use only the established channels to seek political goals, and then that we are powerless anyhow.

Both of these self-imposed limits must be challenged, if people seek to avoid the worst of the prospective futures and to make something better. To withdraw into individual isolation, or to go along because everyone else seems to be accepting whatever happens, is to contribute personally to the likelihood that the worst possible future will come about. What is required instead is a re-examination of who we are as people and what kinds of people we want to be—and then of the kind of social relations and institutions that would be necessary to enable us to become such people. Just as our present circumstances are forcing change, some of which may well be very dangerous and undesirable, so do they bring opportunities to create a far more satisfying society and life. Free of the limitations of our present ideology and the narrow forms of political activity it prescribes for us, and possessing images of the social orders we *do not* and *do* want, Americans might well reconstruct their society. The first steps are the crucial ones, however, and those to which this book has been addressed: we must free ourselves from the grip of unexamined orthodoxy, see our present conditions and practices clearly, and recognize the pressing need to reshape them to serve our needs.

Appendix I

Tools of
Political Analysis

This Appendix takes up in detail certain tools of analysis that are referred to in Chapter 1 and applied in subsequent chapters. We explore three central questions of political analysis, criteria of evaluation, and some problems that often hamper sound analysis and evaluation.

Political Analysis: The Central Questions

How should analysts approach the problem of understanding the political process? We believe that three central questions lead most directly and efficiently to understanding.

1. What does government do with respect to various subjects, and what difference do its actions make for people and problems? In order to answer this question, we shall carefully assess the consequences of recent governmental activity in four subject areas. Our principal tool will be bodies of data about changes in peoples' lives—changes, for example, in their wealth, status, or power—as a result of specific government actions. We shall treat each subject area separately, and then ask whether the patterns of benefits and burdens from governmental action that are visible in one area are similar to those in others.

2. What interests, forces, or people cause government to act in such ways? Or, more briefly, **who rules?** In order to answer this question, we shall do three different but related things. First, we shall look at the explanations offered by the dominant American values and ideology, and contrast them with the charges made by radicalism-populism. This will tell us what some people consider the right answers to this question, and alert us to some things we must be sure to look at. Second, we shall start with the knowledge of who wins and who loses as a result of government action, and ask whether those people who win regularly are, in practical terms, the real rulers of the society. Third, we shall undertake to identify the people, groups, corporations, or other political participants that have large supplies of the resources of power, and try to see how their resources affect the actions of government.

These three approaches complement each other usefully. The contrasting ideologies suggest who and what to look at, as do the patterns of winners and losers from governmental actions; and our fresh analysis of where the resources of power lie serves as another independent focus. The final answer to the question, of course, can only emerge from the evidence and from the reader's interpretation of that evidence.

3. How does, and how might, change come about? Note that this question is partly factual (how has change happened in the past?) and partly speculative (what can be concluded from an analysis of power distribution and usage today about what might happen in the future?). There is a further component, one readers must resolve for themselves, that necessarily intrudes on any speculation about change. This is the question of whether change is desirable, and, if so, what sort of change —a value-preference issue properly considered in our section to come on evaluation.

In order to answer this third central question, we shall draw on theory and experience to construct categories for investigation. We first note that most political change is *marginal* change—that is, change that takes place without altering the basic outlines of established social and economic systems, or the distribution of wealth, status, and power within the society. *Fundamental* change—change in structures, basic distribution patterns, or the underlying values of the society—is much less frequent. Presumably, the latter is what we seek to understand, for marginal change may occur at any time as a result of a wide variety of frequently unpatterned causes.

Let us suggest, quite crudely at this early stage, that fundamental change is dependent on (1) certain preconditions, like an unsatisfactory level of economic well-being, social tensions such as race conflict, or international tensions; and (2) the political impact of those preconditions on the attitudes of people toward their government, the behavior of elites, and the power potential of change-seeking groups. We shall look closely throughout our analysis at developments relating to each of these preconditions, and at the political impact of such developments. By the close of our analysis of power and decision-making, we should be ready to expand greatly our understanding of how and when fundamental change occurs.

Evaluation in Politics: Standards of Judgment

Explaining how and why governmental policies take the form they do, and what difference that makes to people and problems in the society, is an interesting and important task. But it is only a preliminary for the person who wants to be more than a passive consumer of the products generated by the power and activity of others. One must decide whether a particular policy is good or bad, whether the political system is working well or not, and whether and how to seek improvements. To do this on a sound basis may seem to require more knowledge and greater wisdom than any person can really expect to develop. But this problem can be rendered manageable.

Several simplifying approaches can make it possible for a person to judge and act in politics in a responsible and still timely manner. One does not need to be intimidated by the fact that some scholars spend a lifetime studying particular governmental procedures or narrow subject areas. It is often enough that there be some solid evidence, especially if it pertains to the performance of government with respect to problems with which one is familiar. People can specialize in certain areas of the greatest interest to them. And they can avoid being diverted by rhetoric, ideology, or elaborate explanations about how the procedures of government operated to prevent accomplishment of their goals.

But perhaps the most important act in preparing oneself for sound evaluation in politics is clarification of the standards to be used in making judgments. Often, the standard applied contains the judgment within itself. For example, a standard that emphasizes maintaining established procedures or traditions is likely to lead to a status-quo-supporting judgment. So is a standard that emphasizes what is "practical" or "pragmatic" under the circumstances of today's power distribution. Today's procedures, of course, promote the interests and preferences of those who hold the balance of power now. What is "realistic" is what they can permit to take place without serious danger to their own predominance. In both cases, therefore, the use of such standards inevitably directs judgments toward minimal changes, which have the effect of supporting the basic outlines of today's power distribution.

On the other hand, standards that emphasize efficiency or economy in the solution of problems are likely to lead to severe judgments of the need for drastic change, often at the cost of important human values. Useful standards require explicit specification of the relative priorities to be assigned to each of several desired results. In the case of "equality," for example, it must be clear whether one means equality in the formal, legalistic sense or in the actual social and economic conditions of individuals. In the case of "democracy," it must be clear whether one means merely full participation in civil rights, or also consistency between popular needs and desires and the products of governmental action.

The key to all evaluation, however, is one's personal political philosophy, which each of us must construct and apply. This is easier said than done, of course. Developing one's own view of *what should be* is even more difficult and frustrating than understanding *what is* in politics. Most people can acquire facts about their political system, although they sometimes do so in the fashion of spectators at a game or passive memorizers in the classroom rather than as analytical, purposeful, and independent persons. Relatively few people make the effort to survey, self-consciously and comprehensively, alternative ends and means in politics and to arrive at their own set of standards and goals for political action. But not to do so is to commit oneself in advance to a passive role in the processes that determine the shape of the future. In effect, it means acquiescence in the decisions of those now in power about what is best for themselves, and perhaps for others. The person without an independent basis for analysis and evaluation in politics must be somebody's pawn, and the only remaining question is *whose.*

Centuries of reflection and writing by the great political theorists have not produced agreement among them, or among their respective followers, for reasons that are by now obvious to readers. But analysis of their work reveals remarkable consistency in the kinds of problems they found it essential to face. Because these problems also accord with our view of the intellectual issues involved, we shall use some classic categories to indicate the central questions that must be faced by a student of politics seeking to establish his or her own independent judgmental framework. Each individual must answer three basic questions, however temporary those answers may be, in order to evolve an independent political stance.

1. What is the nature of people and of their relationship to their society and environment?

To some extent these are factual questions, but for the most part we must simply assume or speculate—which means that our answers are more or less frank expressions of our value preferences. Some assume that human nature is fundamentally good—that a human being is essentially a cooperative, rational creature. If so, governing processes should be designed to maximize openness and participation, in confidence that the right decisions will be made. Others assume that people in general are selfish, emotional, likely to pursue short-range interests, and subject to demagogues, but that some people possess superior talents. According to these assumptions, a strong government run by the talented few is necessary to civilize people and maintain order and justice in the society. In other words, a whole series of conclusions and preferences is built on one's assumptions about human nature.

Assumptions must also be made about the character of society and the extent to which both people and their society are incapable of, or resistant to, change. For some, "society" is a term with real meaning—an independent entity with a life of its own, distinct from the people who happen to make it up at any given time. Such people are likely to value the "needs of the society" above any particular member's preferences. But some device for ascertaining those needs must be found. The net result is likely to be a form of government dominated by a relative few of the better-qualified persons in the society. A less mystical use of the term "society" is as a synonym for all, or a majority, of the individuals who happen to be present at any moment within the nation's geographical confines. According to such usage, the needs of the society and majority preference are one and the same, and an entirely different decision-making process is suggested.

Another set of assumptions concerns the extent to which people are irretrievably the product of something innate within their nature, or, alternatively, the product of their environment. If the latter is true, they can be improved (at least to some extent, but with accompanying risks) through manipulation of the environment. If the former is true, of course, such efforts are both hopeless and potentially very dangerous.

Which of these sets of alternative assumptions is better or more soundly based? At the moment, there seems to be no way in which a case for one or the other can be conclusively established or "proved." There are scraps of evidence regarding aspects of these issues, but they often can be used to support contrasting and equally plausible interpretations. People are therefore forced to adopt what seems to them the most reasonable set of assumptions. Because this is just another way of expressing one's preferences, such position-taking tells the listener or reader little about human nature but a great deal about the speaker's or author's political values.

2. What are the proper goals of social and political life, and in what order of priorities and at what cost should they be sought?

This is the area in which evidence is of least assistance. People must answer these questions in response to their own preferences and with only their personal values for guidance. Such questions are rarely put so bluntly, of course: they arise in the context of familiar concepts for the establishment of priorities among familiar and generally shared goals. For example, the concept of "freedom" carries several alternative meanings. To some it may mean freedom from governmental interference, leading them to seek severe limitations on the activities of government. To others, it may mean freedom to do what one could if only the handicaps of poverty and ignorance were removed. This stance would lead them to seek broad expansion of the social welfare activities of government.

The concept of "equality" is equally pliable according to one's preferences. It may mean the right to use one's talents, whatever they may be, in the pursuit of one's goals. Or it can be expanded slightly to include the right to at least a minimal education and standard of living. Or it can be broadened still further to signify that all persons are entitled to full social and economic parity with one another.

Economic equality is a much more ambitious goal than mere political equality, but even within the latter concept there is room for considerable difference of viewpoint. In the eighteenth century, some defined political equality in terms of suffrage—the right to vote—which was granted only to males who owned a certain amount of property. More recently, sharp controversy has developed about whether this generally agreed-upon goal requires the observance of "one man, one vote" at all levels of government. The fact that people who strongly subscribe to the goal of political equality can sincerely argue that some people should have more votes than others indicates that there is wide room for disagreement even when the basic goal is shared "in principle." Thus, it is determining the specific content of familiar terms that is critical in building one's own independent framework. No definition is necessarily preferable or "correct," for no person is the ultimate arbiter of the meanings of words. They mean for each citizen what he or she says they mean, and that is why there is bound to be disagreement in politics.

These differences in meaning may become apparent only when an issue arises that requires the concept to be put into practice (or "operationalized"). At other times, generalized agreement on the undefined concept of "freedom" or "equality" or "justice" may create the illusion of consensus. A similar illusion may be fostered by the widespread acknowledgment of these goals, despite sharply differing views as to which should be given first priority. Once again, the illusion is dispelled only when it is sought to actually *do* one or the other.

Consider the dilemma of the person who subscribes strongly to both "liberty" and "equality": at some point, he or she will have to decide which is paramount, because they frequently conflict. In order to provide equality for some, it may be necessary to limit the liberty of others to do as they wish with their property or their talents. If equality is defined as rough parity of opportunity to compete for the goals of life, and if it is a paramount goal, one must reluctantly conclude that in this instance liberty must be limited. But if one holds to a more restrictive view of equality, or considers liberty to be deserving of first priority, this would be an utterly wrong way for government to act. The same type of problem is involved in recent controversies over the proper priority rankings of "justice" and "order," two goals readily acknowledged as vital by all. To some, nothing is more important than order and tranquility, while to others the rights and privileges that are components of justice deserve precedence.

When neither specific meanings nor priority rankings have been established for these concepts, they are not much more than glittering generalities in citizens' minds. As such, they are aspects of ideology; we tend to believe that since all right-thinking people share the same views, all that needs to be done to resolve conflicts is to sit down and "reason together." Or we may believe that our leaders' views are the same as ours because they use these words in their explanations or exhortations. Clearly, these concepts offer us nothing but symbolic satisfactions and complacency until we undertake to define their specific content and relative valuations.

3. **What means—institutions and processes—offer the best prospects of reaching the goals we establish, given our assumptions about human nature?**

In other words, how can we get from specific assumptions about the nature of man to the characteristics of the good life? What logically consistent and empirically practicable means are there for reaching the goals desired? This is the area where we should be able to get the most assistance from factual knowledge about the workings of political institutions and processes. In seeking to establish some coherent connection between the nature of human beings and the realization of their goals in life, we have for guidance considerable evidence about how particular institutions work and why. We know, for example, that all members of the House of Representatives are not equally influential in determining the provisions of new statutes, and we would not rest our hopes for goal attainment on the illusion that they are. Thus, one of the first necessities in this area is to become familiar with the basic facts and processes that determine how the political system presently works, and to use this understanding to establish certain landmarks around which value preferences are to be exercised.

A second requirement in this area, as we suggested above, is logical consistency. If man is irrational and selfish, for example, one can hardly expect to achieve equality for all through political mechanisms that are highly responsive to individual preferences. The nature of each set of institutions and processes depends on the characteristics of the people who design and operate them, and in turn shapes the kinds of goals that can be attained through them. This is a crucial point: the nature of people, the character of institutions and processes, and the goals that can be realized, are interdependent in politics. When we study institutions and processes, we do so realizing that they have been structured by the values and natures of the people who created and animate them, and also knowing that their character determines in major ways the nature of the goals that can be achieved through them. Because this is so, we must organize our personal political positions to take this interdependence into account.

This is not to say that we must proceed consecutively from a definition of human nature to a vision of an ideal world, and finally to institutional tinkering necessary to link the two together. Most political thinkers probably start with certain highly valued goals and some convictions about what does and does not work in the real world, and then seek to fill in the gaps more or less consistently and adequately. Nor do all the possible questions and problems in these three areas have to be resolved before a personal framework becomes functional. It is enough to be aware of the interdependencies between them and, therefore, to perceive what is at stake when considering one area in apparent isolation, and to see the implications that findings or assumptions in one carry for the others. What *is* important is to begin to build a map in one's mind of what is, can be, and ought to be in politics. This, in turn, will make it possible to respond rationally and selectively to the urgings and pleadings of others and to shape one's own independent course in politics.

Problems in Analysis and Evaluation

It is time to become more rigorous about how one seeks to achieve understanding of a subject like politics, so embedded in emotions, patriotic loyalties, threats, and symbolic diversions. How can we assure ourselves that the understanding we acquire consists of valid interpretations, and not merely uncritical projections of our assumptions, hopes, or fears about American politics? We shall consider some of the technical problems of data collection and interpretation as they arise in later chapters. The more serious problems of nonobjectivity and misinterpretation, however, are conceptual in character. Let us try to identify some of them.

Culture-Bound or Ideological Premises and Assumptions

We are all more or less captives of our culture and products of years of indoctrination in its values and assumptions about what is right and good: what is, is right. And what exists in the United States is necessary, desirable, or at least the best that is practical given all the circumstances. These initial (and often subconscious) premises, to say nothing of social or official pressures to adhere to them, or the economic self-interest we may have in endorsing the *status quo,* cause even sophisticated observers to introduce approving evaluations into their supposedly objective "descriptions."

Every person who would be an objective analyst must go through a process of wrenching loose from such premises, assumptions, and conceptual blinders. The process is a lengthy and difficult one, for ideology reaches deep into the culture—into stereotypes (or "pictures in the mind"), symbols, even the language we use. Positive images are conjured up in most of us by such phrases as "Constitution," "free enterprise," "the rule of law," "free speech," and the use of such terms to describe what exists may lead us to believe that reality fits into such "good" patterns. Sometimes reality may indeed be what the words implicitly suggest, but reality is not determined by the words or assumptions used to describe it. Reality has its own independent set of characteristics and causes, and it may bear little resemblance to what the familiar words urge us to believe. If we are diverted from objective perception by symbols, stereotypes, and loaded words, we may never come to know reality as it is.

The Nature of Evidence

What do we need to know in order to say that a political institution or process works in a particular way? We cannot accept assumptions or speculations, exhortations about how they *should* work, or the self-serving assurances of their sponsors. No matter how hallowed and revered the authority that prescribes or declares how things work, we cannot accept such characterizations as truth. Instead, we must demand precise specification of who actually did what, when, and with what effects. We must be able to say with confidence that thus-and-so is the way the Congress works, or that voters respond to factors X, Y, and Z in deciding which candidates to support. To be able to do so, we must have enough data on hand for a comprehensive characterization—one that leaves no gaps to be filled by ideology-affected assumptions.

When we have achieved exhaustive and accurate description, we are ready to attempt explanation: *why* do people do what they do in politics? Again, we rest primarily on factual evidence—on cause-and-effect relationships that are demonstrable to us or at least inferable from the evidence—rather than on other people's explanations or wishful thinking. It is tempting, once one adapts to exclusively data-based analysis, to assume that the collection of empirical data is all-important and that we can accurately come to know and understand politics and the political process simply by building up larger amounts of more concrete and rigorous data. In seeking explanation for empirically identified patterns of behavior, however, analysis must be aided by theory. In this sense, theory means hypotheses (informed guesses about causes, which can be tested against available evidence) reflecting experience and sophistication about politics. In order to arrive at hypotheses, we must employ our knowledge of the wide range of possible causes, the many forces at work within a context, and the structure of relevant power relationships.

The Focus of Analysis

We must look comprehensively at the acts of all (or at least most) of the powerholders who are active in any given area, and not direct our analyses exclusively at the acts or words of leaders or the official decisions, laws, and regulations of organs of government. The easiest way to observe and analyze politics is to look at the public acts and words of political leaders, on the assumption that they make the key decisions and set the goals their followers accept. The political leader acts in public. One of his chief functions is to make a strong and widespread impression. Because he has a stake in being dramatic, he makes good copy for journalists. Journalistic accounts of politics consist very largely of descriptions of the statements, actions, and interactions of political leaders.

But the political analyst who confines his or her attention to leaders is likely to be led astray at every turn. If there is a riot, such a person assumes that ringleaders or outside agitators must have "caused" it. The social scientist looks deeper: at the social, economic, and political conditions that explain the willingness of rioters to engage in violence, to follow leaders who advocate it, and to ignore potential leaders who counsel patience or peaceful courses of action.

Another pitfall is the assumption that everything important in politics and policy formation takes place in the formal institutions and organs of government. A high proportion of decisions are made outside the corridors of government buildings, though their outcomes are closely tied to people's assumptions about how great the political power of the participants is. Even the actions that can be observed taking place within governmental institutions often convey a very superficial or misleading notion of what is going on. One reason formal government acts can be misleading is that they are frequently not put into practice. Almost twenty years after the Supreme Court had declared racial segregation in public schools unconstitutional, it still existed in a very high proportion of American classrooms. What goes on in courts, legislatures, bureaus, and United Nations meetings certainly has to be observed. But merely observing it usually reveals little about its meaning. To understand the significance of formal governmental actions, the political analyst has to observe many other activities as well. And he or she must have in mind a theoretical framework that describes how the observed activities are related to each other.

The Analytical Frame of Reference

A final barrier to accurate analysis is a narrow frame of reference within which, or the level at which, the analysis is conducted. Every effort at research and analysis must begin with some premises, or givens, about the world. But the act of making such beginning assumptions (an act that is frequently unconscious) may sharply confine the kinds of conclusions that can be reached. For example, if we assume the validity (or perpetuity) of existing American values, and if we assume that the present structure of power in government is fixed, then the only object on which to focus analysis or evaluation is the details of policies and the way in which they relate to the problems involved. This could be a relatively superficial analysis, because it might not penetrate to the real causes of a policy, or to the roots of the problem. Applied to the Vietnam War, for example, such an approach might conclude that its failure was due merely to tactical mistakes or errors of judgment on the part of particular policymakers, and that the whole matter could be rectified by replacing those people with better-informed individuals.

A more probing analysis would suggest that more fundamental causes were involved. Analysis might go one step beyond policies to look at the political system itself: perhaps the relative freedom of the President to commit the country, or overreliance on military assurances of capability, or the impotence of Congress in the area of foreign policy, or the influence of economic interests with investments in the Third World nations, are more significant causes of the Vietnam War. None of these potential explanations, of course, would have been suggested by an analysis limited in scope to policy alone. Or analysis could go further still and look at the underlying values that give rise to both the political system and the policy.

Using the same example, the causal origins of the Vietnam War may lie in fears of communism, cultural or racial arrogance, or the needs of the American economic system. The point is that exploration of such possibilities would have been unlikely unless the analyst's frame of reference extended beneath the policies to the political system itself and finally to the underlying values that sustain both. Only then, with such a deliberately broadened and deepened approach, could he or she be sure of including all possible sources of explanation and avoid building-in an ideological endorsement for the existing state of affairs. In some cases, clearly, the causes of problems lie at very fundamental levels, and failure to realize this may result in omitting from analysis the very characteristics or values that gave rise to the problem in the first place. A wide frame of reference that probes all three levels of analysis must be part of our approach.

Appendix II

The Declaration
of Independence

**The Unanimous Declaration
of the Thirteen United States of America**

When in the Course of human events, it becomes necessary for one
people to dissolve the political bands, which have connected them with
another, and to assume among the powers of the earth, the separate and
equal station to which the Laws of Nature and of Nature's God entitle
them, a decent respect to the opinions of mankind requires that they
should declare the causes which impel them to the separation.—We hold
these truths to be self-evident, that all men are created equal, that they
are endowed by their Creator with certain unalienable Rights, that
among these are Life, Liberty and the pursuit of Happiness.—That to
secure these rights, Governments are instituted among Men, deriving their
just powers from the consent of the governed,—That whenever any Form
of Government becomes destructive of these ends, it is the Right of the
People to alter or to abolish it, and to institute new Government, laying
its foundation on such principles and organizing its powers in such form,
as to them shall seem most likely to effect their Safety and Happiness.
Prudence, indeed, will dictate that Governments long established should
not be changed for light and transient causes; and accordingly all experience hath shewn, that mankind are more disposed to suffer, while evils
are sufferable, than to right themselves by abolishing the forms to which

they are accustomed. But when a long train of abuses and usurpations, pursuing invariably the same Object evinces a design to reduce them under absolute Despotism, it is their right, it is their duty, to throw off such Government, and to provide new Guards for their future security.— Such has been the patient sufferance of these Colonies; and such now the necessity which constrains them to alter their former Systems of Government. The history of the present King of Great Britain is a history of repeated injuries and usurpations, all having in direct object the establishment of an absolute Tyranny over these States. To prove this, let Facts be submitted to a candid world.—He has refused his Assent to Laws, the most wholesome and necessary for the public good.—He has forbidden his Governors to pass Laws of immediate and pressing importance, unless suspended in their operation till his Assent should be obtained, and when so suspended, he has utterly neglected to attend to them.—He has refused to pass other Laws for the accommodation of large districts of people, unless those people would relinquish the right of Representation in the Legislature, a right inestimable to them and formidable to tyrants only.—He has called together legislative bodies at places unusual, uncomfortable, and distant from the depository of their public Records, for the sole purpose of fatiguing them into compliance with his measures.—He has dissolved Representative Houses repeatedly for opposing with manly firmness his invasions on the rights of the people.—He has refused for a long time, after such dissolution, to cause others to be elected whereby the Legislative powers, incapable of Annihilation, have returned to the People at large for their exercise; the States remaining in the meantime exposed to all the dangers of invasion from without, and convulsions within.—He has endeavoured to prevent the population of these States; for that purpose obstructing the Laws for Naturalization of Foreigners; refusing to pass others to encourage their migrations hither, and raising the conditions of new Appropriations of Lands.—He has obstructed the Administration of Justice, by refusing his Assent to Laws for establishing Judiciary powers.—He has made Judges dependent on his Will alone, for the tenure of their offices, and the amount and payment of their salaries.—He has erected a multitude of New Offices, and sent hither swarms of Officers to harass our people, and eat out their substance.—He has kept among us, in times of peace, Standing Armies without the Consent of our legislatures.—He has affected to render the Military independent of and superior to the Civil power.— He has combined with others to subject us to a jurisdiction foreign to our constitution, and unacknowledged by our laws; giving his Assent to their Acts of pretended Legislation.—For quartering large bodies of armed troops among us:—For protecting them, by a mock Trial, from punishment for any Murders which they should commit on the Inhabitants of these States:—For cutting off our Trade with all parts of the world:—For imposing Taxes on us without our Consent:—For depriving us in many cases, of the benefits of Trial by Jury:—For transporting us beyond Seas to be tried for pretended offenses:—For abolishing the free System of English Laws in a neighboring Province, establishing therein an Arbitrary government, and enlarging its Boundaries so as to render it at once an example and fit instrument for introducing the same absolute rule into these Colonies:—For taking away our Charters, abolishing our most valuable Laws, and altering fundamentally the Forms of our Governments:—For suspending our own Legislatures, and declaring themselves invested with power to legislate for us in all cases whatsoever.—He has abdicated Government here, by declaring us out of his Protection and waging War against us.—He has plundered our seas, ravaged our Coasts, burnt our towns, and destroyed the lives of our people.—He is at this time transporting large Armies of Foreign Mercenaries to compleat the works of death, desolation and tyranny, already begun with circumstances of Cruelty & perfidy, scarcely paralleled in the most barbarous ages, and totally unworthy the Head of a civilized nation.—He has constrained our fellow Citizens taken Captive on the high Seas to bear Arms against their Country, to become the executioners of their friends and Brethren, or to fall themselves by their hands.—He has excited domestic insurrections amongst us, and has endeavoured to bring on the inhabitants of our frontiers, the Merciless Indian Savages, whose known rule of warfare, is an undistinguished destruction of all ages, sexes and conditions. In every stage of these Oppressions We have Petitioned for Redress in the most humble terms: Our repeated Petitions have been answered only by repeated injury. A Prince whose character is thus marked by every act which may define a Tyrant, is unfit to be the ruler of a free people. Nor have We been wanting in attentions to our British brethren. We have warned them from time to time of attempts by their legislature to extend an unwarrantable jurisdiction over us. We have reminded them of the circumstances of our emigration and settlement here. We have appealed to their native justice and magnanimity, and we have conjured them by the ties of our common kindred to disavow these usurpations, which would inevitably interrupt our connections and correspondence. They too have been deaf to the voice of justice and of consanguinity. We must, therefore, acquiesce in the necessity, which denounces our Separation, and hold them, as we hold the rest of mankind, Enemies in War, in Peace Friends.—

We, therefore, the Representatives of the United States of America, in General Congress, Assembled, appealing to the Supreme Judge of the world for the rectitude of our intentions do, in the Name, and by the Authority of the good People of these Colonies, solemnly publish and declare, That these United Colonies, are, and of Right ought to be Free and Independent States; that they are Absolved from all Allegiance to the British Crown, and that all political connection between them and the State of Great Britain, is and ought to be totally dissolved; and that as Free and Independent States, they have full Power to levy War, conclude Peace, contract Alliances, establish Commerce, and to do all other Acts and Things which Independent States may of right do.—And for the support of this Declaration, with a firm reliance on the protection of divine Providence, we mutually pledge to each other our Lives, our Fortunes and our sacred Honor.

The Constitution of the United States of America

We the People of the United States, in Order to form a more perfect Union, establish Justice, insure domestic Tranquility, provide for the common defence, promote the general Welfare, and secure the Blessings of Liberty to ourselves and our Posterity, do ordain and establish this Constitution for the United States of America.

Article I

Section 1. All legislative Powers herein granted shall be vested in a Congress of the United States, which shall consist of a Senate and House of Representatives.

Section 2. The House of Representatives shall be composed of Members chosen every second Year by the People of the several States, and the Electors in each State shall have the Qualifications requisite for Electors of the most numerous Branch of the State Legislature.

No Person shall be a Representative who shall not have attained to the age of twenty five Years, and been seven Years a Citizen of the United States, and who shall not, when elected, be an Inhabitant of that State in which he shall be chosen.

Representatives and direct Taxes shall be apportioned among the several States which may be included within this Union, according to their respective Numbers, *which shall be determined by adding to the whole Number of free Persons, including those bound to Service for a Term of Years,* and excluding Indians not taxed, *three fifths of all other persons.*[1] The actual Enumeration shall be made within three Years after the first Meeting of the Congress of the United States, and within every subsequent Term of ten Years, in such Manner as they shall by Law direct. The Number of Representatives shall not exceed one for every thirty Thousand, but each State shall have at Least one Representative; and until such enumeration shall be made, the State of New Hampshire shall be entitled to chuse three, Massachusetts eight, Rhode-Island and Providence Plantations one, Connecticut five, New-York six, New Jersey four, Pennsylvania eight, Delaware one, Maryland six, Virginia ten, North Carolina five, South Carolina five, and Georgia three.

When vacancies happen in the Representation from any State, the Executive Authority thereof shall issue Writs of Election to fill such Vacancies.

The House of Representatives shall chuse their Speaker and other Officers; and shall have the sole Power of Impeachment.

Section 3. The Senate of the United States shall be composed of two Senators from each State, *chosen by the Legislature thereof,*[2] for six Years; and each Senator shall have one Vote.

Immediately after they shall be assembled in Consequence of the first Election, they shall be divided as equally as may be into three Classes. The Seats of the Senators of the first Class shall be vacated at the Expiration of the second Year, of the second Class at the Expiration of the fourth Year, and of the third Class at the Expiration of the sixth Year, so that one third may be chosen every second Year; *and if Vacancies happen by Resignation, or otherwise, during the Recess of the Legislature of any State, the Executive thereof may make temporary Appointments until the next Meeting of the Legislature, which shall then fill such Vacancies.*[3]

No Person shall be a Senator who shall not have attained to the Age of thirty Years, and been nine Years a Citizen of the United States, and who shall not, when elected, be an Inhabitant of that State for which he shall be chosen.

The Vice President of the United States shall be President of the Senate, but shall have no Vote, unless they be equally divided.

The Senate shall chuse their other Officers, and also a President pro tempore, in the Absence of the Vice President, or when he shall exercise the Office of President of the United States.

---

[1] Italics are used throughout to indicate passages that have been altered by subsequent amendments. In this case, see Amendment XIV.

[2] See Amendment XVII.

[3] *Ibid.*

The Senate shall have the sole Power to try all Impeachments. When sitting for that Purpose, they shall be on Oath or Affirmation. When the President of the United States is tried, the Chief Justice shall preside: And no Person shall be convicted without the Concurrence of two thirds of the Members present.

Judgment in Cases of Impeachment shall not extend further than to removal from Office, and disqualification to hold and enjoy any Office of honor, Trust or Profit under the United States: but the Party convicted shall nevertheless be liable and subject to Indictment, Trial, Judgment and Punishment, according to Law.

Section 4. The Times, Places and Manner of holding Elections for Senators and Representatives, shall be prescribed in each State by the Legislature thereof; but the Congress may at any time by Law make or alter such Regulations, except as to the Places of chusing Senators.

The Congress shall assemble at least once in every Year, and such Meeting shall be on the first Monday in December, unless they shall by Law appoint a different Day.[4]

Section 5. Each House shall be the Judge of the Elections, Returns and Qualifications of its own Members, and a Majority of each shall constitute a Quorum to do Business; but a smaller Number may adjourn from day to day, and may be authorized to compel the Attendance of absent Members, in such Manner, and under such Penalties as each House may provide.

Each House may determine the Rules of its Proceedings, punish its Members for disorderly Behavior, and, with the Concurrence of two thirds, expel a Member.

Each House shall keep a journal of its Proceedings, and from time to time publish the same, excepting such Parts as may in their Judgment require Secrecy; and the Yeas and Nays of the Members of either House on any question shall, at the Desire of one fifth of those Present, be entered on the Journal.

Neither House, during the Session of Congress, shall, without the Consent of the other, adjourn for more than three days, nor to any other Place than that in which the two Houses shall be sitting.

Section 6. The Senators and Representatives shall receive a Compensation for their Services, to be ascertained by Law, and paid out of the Treasury of the United States. They shall in all Cases, except Treason, Felony and Breach of the Peace, be privileged from Arrest during their Attendance at the Session of their respective Houses, and in going to and returning from the same; and for any Speech or Debate in either House, they shall not be questioned in any other Place.

No Senator or Representative shall, during the Time for which he was elected, be appointed to any civil Office under the Authority of

[4] See Amendment XX.

the United States, which shall have been created, or the Emoluments whereof shall have been encreased during such time; and no Person holding any Office under the United States, shall be a Member of either House during his Continuance in Office.

Section 7. All Bills for raising Revenue shall originate in the House of Representatives; but the Senate may propose or concur with Amendments as on other Bills.

Every Bill which shall have passed the House of Representatives and the Senate, shall, before it become a Law, be presented to the President of the United States; if he approve he shall sign it, but if not he shall return it, with his Objections to that House in which it shall have originated, who shall enter the Objections at large on their Journal, and proceed to reconsider it. If after such Reconsideration two thirds of that House shall agree to pass the Bill, it shall be sent, together with the Objections, to the other House, by which it shall likewise be reconsidered, and if approved by two thirds of that House, it shall become a Law. But in all such Cases the Votes of both Houses shall be determined by Yeas and Nays, and the Names of the Persons voting for and against the Bill shall be entered on the Journal of each House respectively. If any Bill shall not be returned by the President within ten Days (Sundays excepted) after it shall have been presented to him, the Same shall be a Law, in like Manner as if he had signed it, unless Congress by their Adjournment prevent its Return, in which Case it shall not be a Law.

Every Order, Resolution, or Vote to which the Concurrence of the Senate and House of Representatives may be necessary (except on a question of Adjournment) shall be presented to the President of the United States; and before the Same shall take Effect, shall be approved by him, or being disapproved by him, shall be repassed by two thirds of the Senate and House of Representatives, according to the Rules and Limitations prescribed in the Case of a Bill.

Section 8. The Congress shall have Power To lay and collect Taxes, Duties, Imposts and Excises, to pay the Debts and provide for the common Defence and general Welfare of the United States; but all Duties, Imposts and Excises shall be uniform throughout the United States;

To borrow Money on the credit of the United States;

To regulate Commerce with foreign Nations, and among the several States, and with the Indian Tribes;

To establish an uniform Rule of Naturalization, and uniform Laws on the subject of Bankruptcies throughout the United States;

To coin Money, regulate the Value thereof, and of foreign Coin, and fix the Standard of Weights and Measures;

To provide for the Punishment of counterfeiting the Securities and Current Coin of the United States;

To establish Post Offices and post Roads;

To promote the Progress of Science and useful Arts, by securing for limited Times to Authors and Inventors the exclusive Right to their respective Writings and Discoveries;

To constitute Tribunals inferior to the Supreme Court;

To define and punish Piracies and Felonies committed on the high Seas, and Offences against the Law of Nations;

To declare War, grant Letters of Marque and Reprisal, and make Rules concerning Captures on Land and Water;

To raise and support Armies, but no Appropriation of Money to that Use shall be for a longer Term than two Years;

To provide and maintain a Navy;

To make Rules for the Government and Regulation of the land and naval Forces;

To provide for calling forth the Militia to execute the Laws of the Union, suppress Insurrections and repel Invasions;

To provide for organizing, arming, and disciplining, the Militia, and for governing such Part of them as may be employed in the Service of the United States, reserving to the States respectively, the Appointment of the Officers, and the Authority of training the Militia according to the discipline prescribed by Congress;

To exercise exclusive Legislation in all Cases whatsoever, over such District (not exceeding ten Miles square) as may, by Cession of particular States, and the Acceptance of Congress, become the Seat of the Government of the United States, and to exercise like Authority over all Places purchased by the Consent of the Legislature of the State in which the Same shall be, for the Erection of Forts, Magazines, Arsenals, dock-Yards, and other needful Buildings;—And

To make all Laws which shall be necessary and proper for carrying into Execution the foregoing Powers, and all other Powers vested by this Constitution in the Government of the United States, or in any Department or Officer thereof.

Section 9. The Migration or Importation of such Persons as any of the States now existing shall think proper to admit, shall not be prohibited by the Congress prior to the Year one thousand eight hundred and eight, but a Tax or duty may be imposed on such Importation, not exceeding ten dollars for each Person.

The Privilege of the Writ of Habeas Corpus shall not be suspended, unless when in Cases of Rebellion or Invasion the public Safety may require it.

No Bill of Attainder or ex post facto Law shall be passed.

No Capitation, or other direct, Tax shall be laid, unless in Proportion to the Census or Enumeration herein before directed to be taken.

No Tax or Duty shall be laid on Articles exported from any State.

No Preference shall be given by any Regulation of Commerce or Revenue to the Ports of one State over those of another: nor shall Vessels bound to, or from, one State, be obliged to enter, clear, or pay Duties in another.

No Money shall be drawn from the Treasury, but in Consequence of Appropriations made by Law; and a regular Statement and Account of the Receipts and Expenditures of all public Money shall be published from time to time.

No title of Nobility shall be granted by the United States: And no Person holding any Office of Profit or Trust under them, shall, without the Consent of the Congress, accept of any present, Emolument, Office, or Title, of any kind whatever, from any King, Prince, or foreign State.

Section 10. No State shall enter into any Treaty, Alliance, or Confederation; grant Letters of Marque and Reprisal; coin Money; emit Bills of Credit; make any Thing but gold and silver Coin a Tender in Payment of Debts; pass any Bill of Attainder, ex post facto Law, or Law impairing the Obligation of Contracts, or Grant any Title of Nobility.

No State shall, without the Consent of the Congress, lay any Imposts or Duties on Imports or Exports, except what may be absolutely necessary for executing its inspection Laws: and the net Produce of all Duties and Imposts, laid by any State on Imports or Exports, shall be for the Use of the Treasury of the United States; and all such Laws be subject to the Revision and Control of the Congress.

No State shall, without the Consent of Congress, lay any Duty of Tonnage, keep Troops, or Ships of War in time of Peace, enter into any Agreement or Compact with another State, or with a foreign Power, or engage in War, unless actually invaded, or in such imminent Danger as will not admit of delay.

Article II

Section 1. The executive Power shall be vested in a President of the United States of America. He shall hold his Office during the Term of four Years, and, together with the Vice President, chosen for the same Term be elected as follows:

Each State shall appoint, in such Manner as the Legislature thereof may direct, a Number of Electors, equal to the whole Number of Senators and Representatives to which the State may be entitled in the Congress: but no Senator or Representative, or Person holding an Office of Trust or Profit under the United States, shall be appointed an Elector.

The Electors shall meet in their respective States, and vote by Ballot for two Persons, of whom one at least shall not be an Inhabitant of the same State with themselves. And they shall make a List of all the Persons voted for, and of the Number of Votes for each; which List they shall sign and certify, and transmit sealed to the Seat of the Government of the United States, directed to the President of the Senate. The President of the Senate shall, in the Presence of the Senate and

House of Representatives, open all the Certificates, and the Votes shall then be counted. The Person having the greatest Number of Votes shall be the President, if such Number be a Majority of the whole Number of Electors appointed; and if there be more than one who have such Majority, and have an equal Number of Votes, then the House of Representatives shall immediately chuse by Ballot one of them for President; and if no Person have a Majority, then from the five highest on the List the said House shall in like Manner chuse the President. But in chusing the President, the votes shall be taken by States, the Representation from each State having one Vote; A quorum for this purpose shall consist of a Member or Members from two thirds of the States, and a Majority of all the States shall be necessary to a Choice. In every Case, after the Choice of the President, the Person having the Greatest Number of Votes of the Electors shall be the Vice President. But if there should remain two or more who have equal Votes, the Senate shall chuse from them by Ballot the Vice President.[5]

The Congress may determine the Time of chusing the Electors, and the Day on which they shall give their Votes; which Day shall be the same throughout the United States.

No Person except a natural born Citizen, or a Citizen of the United States, at the time of the Adoption of this Constitution, shall be eligible to the Office of President; neither shall any Person be eligible to that Office who shall not have attained to the Age of thirty five Years, and been fourteen Years a Resident within the United States.

The Case of the Removal of the President from Office, or of his Death, Resignation, or Inability to discharge the Powers and Duties of the said Office, the Same shall devolve on the Vice President, and the Congress may by Law provide for the Case of Removal, Death, Resignation or Inability, both of the President and Vice President, declaring what Officer shall then act as President, and such Officer shall act accordingly, until the Disability be removed, or a President shall be elected.

The President shall, at stated Times, receive for his Services, a Compensation which shall neither be encreased nor diminished during the Period for which he shall have been elected, and he shall not receive within that Period any other Emolument from the United States, or any of them.

Before he enter on the Execution of his Office, he shall take the following Oath or Affirmation:—"I do solemnly swear (or affirm) that I will faithfully execute the Office of President of the United States, and will to the best of my Ability, preserve, protect, and defend the Constitution of the United States."

Section 2. The President shall be Commander in Chief of the Army and Navy of the United States, and of the Militia of the several States,

[5] See Amendment XII.

when called into the actual service of the United States; he may require the Opinion, in writing, of the prinicpal Officer in each of the executive Departments, upon any Subject relating to the Duties of their respective Offices, and he shall have Power to grant Reprieves and Pardons for Offences against the United States, except in Case of Impeachment.

He shall have Power, by and with the Advice and Consent of the Senate, to make Treaties, provided two thirds of the Senators present concur; and he shall nominate, and by and with the Advice and Consent of the Senate, shall appoint Ambassadors, and other public Ministers and Consuls, Judges of the supreme Court, and all other Officers of the United States, whose Appointments are not herein otherwise provided for, and which shall be established by Law; but the Congress may by Law vest the Appointment of such inferior Officers, as they think proper, in the President alone, in the Courts of Law, or in the Heads of Departments.

The President shall have Power to fill up all Vacancies that may happen during the Recess of the Senate, by granting Commissions which shall expire at the End of their next Session.

Section 3. He shall from time to time give to the Congress Information of the State of the Union, and recommend to their Consideration such Measures as he shall judge necessary and expedient; he may, on extraordinary Occasions, convene both Houses, or either of them, and in Case of Disagreement between them, with Respect to the Time of Adjournment, he may adjourn them to such Time as he shall think proper; he shall receive Ambassadors and other public Ministers, he shall take Care that the Laws be faithfully executed, and shall Commission all the Officers of the United States.

Section 4. The President, Vice President, and all civil Officers of the United States, shall be removed from Office on Impeachment for, and Conviction of, Treason, Bribery, or other high Crimes and Misdemeanors.

Article III

Section 1. The judicial Power of the United States, shall be vested in one supreme Court and in such inferior Courts as the Congress may from time to time ordain and establish. The Judges, both of the supreme and inferior Courts, shall hold their Offices during good Behavior, and shall, at stated Times, receive for their Services, a Compensation, which shall not be diminished during their Continuance in Office.

Section 2. The Judicial Power shall extend to all Cases, in Law and Equity, arising under this Constitution, the Laws of the United States, and Treaties made, or which shall be made, under their Authority;—to all Cases affecting Ambassadors, other public Ministers and Consuls;—to all Cases of admiralty and maritime Jurisdiction;—to Controversies to which the United States shall be a Party;—to Controversies between two or more States;—*between a State and Citizens of another State;* [6]—between Citizens of different States;—between Citizens of the same State claiming Lands under Grants of different states, *and between a State, or the Citizens thereof, and foreign States, Citizens, or Subjects.* [7]

In all cases affecting Ambassadors, other public Ministers and Consuls, and those in which a State shall be Party, the supreme Court shall have original Jurisdiction. In all the other Cases before mentioned, the supreme Court shall have appellate Jurisdiction, both as to Law and Fact, with such Exceptions, and under such Regulations as the Congress shall make.

The Trial of all Crimes, except in Cases of Impeachment, shall be by Jury; and such Trial shall be held in the State where the said Crimes shall have been committed; but when not committed within any State, the Trial shall be at such Place or Places as the Congress may by Law have directed.

Section 3. Treason against the United States, shall consist only in levying War against them, or in adhering to their Enemies, giving them Aid and Comfort. No person shall be convicted of Treason unless on the Testimony of two Witnesses to the same overt Act, or on Confession in open Court.

The Congress shall have Power to declare the Punishment of Treason, but no Attainder of Treason shall work Corruption of Blood, or Forfeiture except during the Life of the Person attainted.

Section 1. Full Faith and Credit shall be given in each State to the public Acts, Records, and judicial Proceedings of every other State. And the Congress may by general Laws prescribe the Manner in which such Acts, Records, and Proceedings shall be proved, and the Effect thereof.

Section 2. The Citizens of each State shall be entitled to all Privileges and Immunities of Citizens in the several States.

A Person charged in any State with Treason, Felony, or other Crime, who shall flee from Justice, and be found in another State, shall on Demand of the executive Authority of the State from which he fled, be delivered up, to be removed to the State having jurisdiction of the Crime.

No Person held to Service or Labour in one State, under the Laws thereof, escaping into another, shall, in Consequence of any Law or Regulation therein, be discharged from such Service or Labour, but shall be delivered up on Claim of the Party to whom such Service or Labour may be due. [8]

[6] See Amendment XI.
[7] *Ibid.*
[8] See Amendment XIII.

Section 3. New States may be admitted by the Congress into this Union; but no new State shall be formed or erected within the Jurisdiction of any other State; nor any State be formed by the Junction of two or more States, or Parts of States, without the Consent of the Legislatures of the States concerned as well as of the Congress.

The Congress shall have Power to dispose of and make all needful Rules and Regulations respecting the Territory or other Property belonging to the United States; and nothing in this Constitution shall be so construed as to Prejudice any claims of the United States, or of any particular State.

Section 4. The United States shall guarantee to every State in this Union a Republican Form of Government, and shall protect each of them against Invasion; and on Application of the Legislature, or of the Executive (when the Legislature cannot be convened) against domestic Violence.

Article V

The Congress, whenever two thirds of both Houses shall deem it necessary, shall propose Amendments to this Constitution, or, on the Application of the Legislatures of two thirds of the several States, shall call a Convention for proposing Amendments, which, in either Case, shall be valid to all Intents and Purposes, as Part of this Constitution, when ratified by the Legislatures of three fourths of the several States, or by Conventions in three fourths thereof, as the one or the other Mode of Ratification may be proposed by the Congress; Provided that no Amendment which may be made prior to the Year One thousand eight hundred and eight shall in any Manner affect the first and fourth Clauses in the Ninth Section of the first Article; and that no State, without its Consent, shall be deprived of its equal Suffrage in the Senate.

Article VI

All Debts contracted and Engagements entered into, before the Adoption of this Constitution shall be as valid against the United States under this Constitution, as under the Confederation.

This Constitution, and the Laws of the United States which shall be made in Pursuance thereof; and all Treaties made, or which shall be made, under the Authority of the United States, shall be the supreme Law of the Land; and the Judges in every State shall be bound thereby, any Thing in the Constitution or Laws of any State to the Contrary notwithstanding.

The Senators and Representatives before mentioned, and the Members of the several State Legislatures, and all executive and judicial Officers, both of the United States and of the several States, shall be bound by Oath or Affirmation, to support this Constitution; but no religious Test shall ever be required as a Qualification to any Office or public Trust under the United States.

Article VII

The Ratification of the Conventions of nine States, shall be sufficient for the Establishment of this Constitution between the States so ratifying the Same.

Done in Convention by the Unanimous Consent of the States present the Seventeenth Day of September in the Year of our Lord one thousand seven hundred and eighty seven and of the Independence of the United States of America the twelfth. In witness whereof We have hereunto subscribed our Names.

* * *

Articles in addition to, and amendment of, the Constitution of the United States of America, proposed by Congress, and ratified by the several States, pursuant to the Fifth Article of the original Constitution.

Amendment I

[Ratification of the first ten amendments was completed December 15, 1791]

Congress shall make no law respecting an establishment of religion, or prohibiting the free exercise thereof; or abridging the freedom of speech, or of the press; or the right of the people peaceably to assemble, and to petition the Government for a redress of grievances.

Amendment II

A well regulated Militia, being necessary to the security of a free State, the right of the people to keep and bear Arms, shall not be infringed.

Amendment III

No Soldier shall, in time of peace be quartered in any house, without the consent of the Owner, nor in time of war, but in a manner to be prescribed by law.

Amendment IV

The right of the people to be secure in their persons, houses, papers, and effects, against unreasonable searches and seizures, shall not be violated, and no Warrants shall issue, but upon probable cause, supported by Oath or affirmation, and particularly describing the place to be searched, and the persons or things to be seized.

Amendment V

No person shall be held to answer for a capital, or otherwise infamous crime, unless on a presentment or indictment of a Grand Jury, except in cases arising in the land or naval forces, or in the Militia, when an actual service in time of War or public danger; nor shall any person be subject for the same offence to be twice put in jeopardy of life or limb; nor shall be compelled in any criminal case to be a witness against himself, nor be deprived of life, liberty, or property, without due process of law; nor shall private property be taken for public use, without just compensation.

Amendment VI

In all criminal prosecutions, the accused shall enjoy the right to a speedy and public trial, by an impartial jury of the State and district wherein the crime shall have been committed, which district shall have been previously ascertained by law, and to be informed of the nature and cause of the accusation; to be confronted with the witness against him; to have compulsory process for obtaining witness in his favor, and to have the Assistance of Counsel for his defence.

Amendment VII

In Suits at common law, where the value in controversy shall exceed twenty dollars, the right of trial by jury shall be preserved, and no fact tried by a jury, shall be otherwise re-examined in any Court of the United States, than according to the rules of the common law.

Amendment VIII

Excessive bail shall not be required, nor excessive fines imposed, nor cruel and unusual punishments inflicted.

Amendment IX

The enumeration in the Constitution, of certain rights, shall not be construed to deny or disparage others retained by the people.

The powers not delegated to the United States by the Constitution, nor prohibited by it to the States, are reserved to the States respectively, or to the people.

Amendment XI

[January 8, 1798]

The Judicial power of the United States shall not be construed to extend to any suit in law or equity, commenced or prosecuted against one of the United States by Citizens of another State, or by Citizens or Subjects of any Foreign State.

Amendment XII

[September 25, 1804]

The Electors shall meet in their respective states and vote by ballot for President and Vice President, one of whom, at least, shall not be an inhabitant of the same state with themselves; they shall name in their ballots the person voted for as President, and in distinct ballots the person voted for as Vice President, and they shall make distinct lists of all persons voted for as President, and of all persons voted for as Vice President, and of the number of votes for each, which lists they shall sign and certify, and transmit sealed to the seat of the government of the United States, directed to the President of the Senate;—The President of the Senate shall, in the presence of the Senate and House of Representatives, open all the certificates and the votes shall then be counted;—The person having the greatest number of votes for President, shall be the President, if such number be a majority of the whole number of Electors appointed; and if no person have such majority, then from the persons having the highest numbers not exceeding three on the list of those voted for as President, the House of Representatives shall choose immediately, by ballot, the President. But in choosing the President, the votes shall be taken by states, the representation from each state having one vote; a quorum for this purpose shall consist of a member or members from two thirds of the states, and a majority of all the states shall be necessary to a choice. And if the House of Representatives shall not choose a President whenever the right of choice shall devolve upon them, *before the fourth day of March next following,*[9] then the Vice President shall act as President as in the case of the death or other constitutional disability of the President.—The person having the greatest number of votes as Vice President, shall be the Vice President, if such number be a majority of the whole number of Electors appointed, and if no person have a majority, then from the two highest numbers on the list, the Senate shall choose the Vice President; a quorum for the purpose shall consist of two-thirds of the whole number of Senators, and a majority of the whole number shall be necessary to a choice. But no person constitutionally ineligible to the office of President shall be eligible to that of Vice President of the United States.

Amendment XIII

[December 18, 1865]

Section 1. Neither slavery nor involuntary servitude, except as a punish-

[9] See Amendment XX.

ment for crime whereof the party shall have been duly convicted, shall exist within the United States, or any place subject to their jurisdiction.

Section 2. Congress shall have power to enforce this article by appropriate legislation.

Amendment XIV

[July 28, 1868]

Section 1. All persons born or naturalized in the United States, and subject to the jurisdiction thereof, are citizens of the United States and of the State wherein they reside. No State shall make or enforce any law which shall abridge the privileges or immunities of citizens of the United States; nor shall any state deprive any person of life, liberty, or property, without due process of law; nor deny to any person, within its jurisdiction the equal protection of the laws.

Section 2. Representatives shall be apportioned among the several States according to their respective numbers, counting the whole number of persons in each State, excluding Indians not taxed. But when the right to vote at any election for the choice of electors for President and Vice President of the United States, Representatives in Congress, the Executive and Judicial officers of a State, or the members of the Legislature thereof, is denied to any of the male inhabitants of such State, being twenty one years of age, and citizens of the United States, or in any way abridged, except for participation in rebellion, or other crime, the basis of representation therein shall be reduced in the proportion which the number of such male citizens shall bear to the whole number of male citizens twenty one years of age in such State.

Section 3. No person shall be a Senator or Representative in Congress, or elector of President and Vice President, or hold any office, civil or military, under the United States, or under any State, who, having previously taken an oath, as a member of Congress, or as an officer of the United States, or as a member of any State legislature, or as an executive or judicial officer of any State, to support the Constitution of the United States, shall have engaged in insurrection or rebellion against the same, or given aid or comfort to the enemies thereof. But Congress may by a vote of two thirds of each House, remove such disability.

Section 4. The validity of the public debt of the United States, authorized by law, including debts incurred for payment of pensions and bounties for services in suppressing insurrection or rebellion, shall not be questioned. But neither the United States nor any State shall assume or pay any debt or obligation incurred in aid of insurrection or rebellion against the United States, or any claim for the loss or emancipation of any slave; but all such debts, obligations, and claims shall be held illegal and void.

Section 5. The Congress shall have power to enforce, by appropriate legislation, the provisions of this article.

Amendment XV

[March 30, 1870]

Section 1. The right of citizens of the United States to vote shall not be denied or abridged by the United States or by any State on account of race, color, or previous condition of servitude.

Section 2. The Congress shall have power to enforce this article by appropriate legislation.

Amendment XVI

[February 25, 1913]

The Congress shall have power to lay and collect taxes on incomes, from whatever source derived, without apportionment among the several States, and without regard to any census or enumeration.

Amendment XVII

[May 31, 1913]

The Senate of the United States shall be composed of two Senators from each State, elected by the people thereof, for six years; and each Senator shall have one vote. The electors in each State shall have the qualifications requisite for electors of the most numerous branch of the State legislatures.

When vacancies happen in the representation of any State in the Senate, the executive authority of such State shall issue writs of election to fill such vacancies: *Provided,* That the legislature of any State may empower the executive thereof to make temporary appointments until the people fill the vacancies by election as the legislature may direct.

This amendment shall not be so construed as to affect the election or term of any Senator chosen before it becomes valid as part of the Constitution.

Amendment XVIII

[January 29, 1919]

Section 1. *After one year from the ratification of this article the manufacture, sale, or transportation of intoxicating liquors within, the importa-*

tion thereof into, or the exportation thereof from the United States and all territory subject to the jurisdiction thereof for beverage purposes is hereby prohibited.

Section 2. The Congress and the several States shall have concurrent power to enforce this article by appropriate legislation.

Section 3. This article shall be inoperative unless it shall have been ratified as an amendment to the Constitution by the legislatures of the several States, as provided in the Constitution, within seven years from the date of submission hereof to the States by the Congress.[10]

Amendment XIX

[August 26, 1920]

The right of citizens of the United States to vote shall not be denied or abridged by the United States or by any State on account of sex.

Congress shall have power to enforce this article by appropriate legislation.

Amendment XX

[February 6, 1933]

Section 1. The terms of the President and Vice President shall end at noon on the 20th day of January, and the terms of Senators and Representatives at noon on the 3rd day of January, of the years in which such terms would have ended if this article had not been ratified; and the terms of their successors shall then begin.

Section 2. The Congress shall assemble at least once in every year, and such meeting shall begin at noon on the 3rd day of January, unless they shall by law appoint a different day.

Section 3. If, at the time fixed for the beginning of the term of the President, the President elect shall have died, the Vice President elect shall become President. If a President shall not have been chosen before the time fixed for the beginning of his term, or if the President elect shall have failed to qualify, then the Vice President elect shall act as President until a President shall have qualified; and the Congress may by law provide for the case wherein neither a President elect nor a Vice President elect shall have qualified, declaring who shall then act as President, or the manner in which one who is to act shall be selected, and such person shall act accordingly until a President or Vice President shall have qualified.

---

[10] Repealed by Amendment XXI.

Section 4. The Congress may by law provide for the case of the death of any of the persons from whom the House of Representatives may choose a President whenever the right of choice shall have devolved upon them, and for the case of the death of any of the persons from whom the Senate may choose a Vice President whenever the right of choice shall have devolved upon them.

Section 5. Sections 1 and 2 shall take effect on the 15th day of October following the ratification of this article.

Section 6. This article shall be inoperative unless it shall have been ratified as an amendment to the Constitution by the legislatures of three. fourths of the several States within seven years from the date of its submission.

Amendment XXI

[December 5, 1933]

Section 1. The eighteenth article of amendment to the Constitution of the United States is hereby repealed.

Section 2. The transportation or importation into any State, Territory, or possession of the United States for delivery or use therein of intoxicating liquors, in violation of the laws thereof, is hereby prohibited.

Section 3. This article shall be inoperative unless it shall have been ratified as an amendment to the Constitution by conventions in the several States, as provided in the Constitution, within seven years from the date of the submission hereof to the States by the Congress.

Amendment XXII

[February 26, 1951]

Section 1. No person shall be elected to the office of the President more than twice, and no person who has held the office of President, or acted as President, for more than two years of a term to which some other person was elected President shall be elected to the office of President more than once. But this Article shall not apply to any person holding the office of President when this Article was proposed by the Congress, and shall not prevent any person who may be holding the office of President, or acting as President, during the term within which this Article becomes operative from holding the office of President or acting as President during the remainder of such term.

Section 2. This article shall be inoperative unless it shall have been ratified as an amendment to the Constitution by the legislatures of three fourths of the several States within seven years from the date of its submission to the States by the Congress.

Amendment XXIII

[March 29, 1961]

Section 1. The District constituting the seat of Government of the United States shall appoint in such manner as the Congress may direct:

A number of electors of President and Vice President equal to the whole number of Senators and Representatives in Congress to which the district would be entitled if it were a State, but in no event more than the least populous State; they shall be in addition to those appointed by the States, but they shall be considered, for the purposes of the election of President and Vice President, to be electors appointed by a State; and they shall meet in the District and perform such duties as provided by the twelfth article of amendment.

Section 2. The Congress shall have power to enforce this article by appropriate legislation.

Amendment XXIV

[January 23, 1964]

Section 1. The right of citizens of the United States to vote in any primary or other election for President or Vice President, for electors for President or Vice President, or for Senator or Representative in Congress, shall not be denied or abridged by the United States or any state by reason of failure to pay any poll tax or other tax.

Section 2. The Congress shall have power to enforce this article by appropriate legislation.

Amendment XXV

[February 10, 1967]

Section 1. In case of the removal of the President from office or of his death or resignation, the Vice President shall become President.

Section 2. Whenever there is a vacancy in the office of the Vice President, the President shall nominate a Vice President who shall take office upon confirmation by a majority vote of both Houses of Congress.

Section 3. Whenever the President transmits to the President pro tempore of the Senate and the Speaker of the House of Representatives his written declaration that he is unable to discharge the powers and duties of his office, and until he transmits to them a written declaration to the contrary, such powers and duties shall be discharged by the Vice President as Acting President.

Section 4. Whenever the Vice President and a majority of either the principal officers of the executive departments or of such other body as Congress may by law provide, transmit to the President pro tempore of the Senate and the Speaker of the House of Representatives their written declaration that the President is unable to discharge the powers and duties of his office, the Vice President shall immediately assume the powers and duties of the office as Acting President.

Thereafter, when the President transmits to the President pro tempore of the Senate and the Speaker of the House of Representatives his written declaration that no inability exists, he shall resume the powers and duties of his office unless the Vice President and a majority of either the principal officers of the executive department[s] or of such other body as Congress may by law provide, transmit within four days to the President pro tempore of the Senate and the Speaker of the House of Representatives their written declaration that the President is unable to discharge the powers and duties of his office. Thereupon Congress shall decide the issue, assembling within forty-eight hours for that purpose if not in session. If the Congress, within twenty-one days after receipt of the latter written declaration, or, if Congress is not in session, within twenty-one days after Congress is required to assemble, determines by two-thirds vote of both Houses that the President is unable to discharge the powers and duties of his office, the Vice President shall continue to discharge the same as Acting President; otherwise, the President shall resume the powers and duties of his office.

Amendment XXVI

[*June 30, 1971*]

Section 1. The right of citizens of the United States, who are 18 years of age or older, to vote shall not be denied or abridged by the United States or by any state on account of age.

Section 2. The Congress shall have power to enforce this article by appropriate legislation.

Amendment XXVII

Which prohibits discrimination based on sex by any law or action of any government—federal, state or local—went to the states for ratification in March 1972.

Glossary

agribusiness. the term used to denote large-scale food and/or crop production as opposed to "farming" or "agriculture" as small-scale enterprise. It may be either a vertical industry—production through manufacture and marketing—or the overall controller of a series of small farms that contract their individual production to a single entity.

ambiguity. uncertainty; having several possible meanings.

ambivalence. contradictory feelings or thoughts about an issue or person.

anarchism. usually refers to the doctrine that government in any form is oppressive and should be abolished. It comes from a longstanding philosophical tradition, the core of which is an aversion to any kind of institutional management of people's lives. There are two main strands: communal and individual. The most common American version tends toward individualistic, or libertarian, anarchism; the main emphasis being the removal of all external restraints of any kind on the individual. For more discussion of libertarian anarchism, see Ch. 9.

Annapolis Convention. the precursor to the Constitutional Convention, it was called together in 1786 by Alexander Hamilton. Its purported purpose was to discuss the economic problems which merchants were encountering due to state and local particularism in credit laws, tariff policies, etc. These conditions were perceived to be "chaotic" by middle and upper classes.

Articles of Confederation. the document on which the government of matters of general concern to the newly independent colonies was based prior to the framing of the Constitution. In it, each state had an equal vote.

attitude. 1. a state of mind regarding some issue; 2. a predisposition to act in a particular way.

authority. that which is generally accepted as having the deciding voice, i.e., governmental authority would be that person and/or institution which is accepted as the controlling voice of the government.

authoritarian. a term, usually pejorative, used to imply that an entity is *too* controlling. When used in connection with a government, it implies there is too much ordering of citizens' lives.

bankruptcy. the financial condition in which an entity's liabilities so outnumber its assets that it is incapable of functioning.

business cycle. an assumption that the economy will expand and contract in a regular, predictable fashion. It is a *normal* aspect of capitalist society and assumed to be healthy as long as one or the other aspect of the cycle does not swing too widely.

capital. money or property available for use to produce more wealth.

capital gain. profit from the sale of capital.

capitalism. an economic system wherein production of goods and services is for *private* profit.

    world capitalism. the capitalist economic system that covers and crosses several national boundaries.

    capitalism/liberalism. the American combination of economic/government ideology and practice. See Ch. 9.

    capitalist countries. those countries whose economic system is devoted to *private* profit and production or at least whose main emphasis is private profit.

caucus. an informal group of like-minded and/or like-labelled persons who meet to devise common strategies and/or policies so as to present as united a front as possible.

change. see Ch. 22 and Appendix.

    fundamental. Ch. 22, "those instances of substantial alteration in the economic or political power structures or in key governmental policies bearing upon distribution of wealth and status."

    incremental. Ch. 22, alterations in minor policies, well within established power systems.

    marginal. Ch. 22, "alterations whose essential effect is to defend and promote established economic and political structures and existing patterns of distribution of wealth and status within the society."

political. alterations in the economic or governmental structures and/or policies.

process of. *how* alterations occur.

theory of. beliefs regarding how and types of alterations possible and/or probable.

class. a concept covering socioeconomic status; see Ch. 11.

class consciousness. *awareness* of the arbitrary nature of socioeconomic status and of one's place within it. As opposed to most definitions which rely on the objective indicators, this includes the subjective parameters included in distinctions of wealth, status, etc.

class system. existing patterns of distribution of socioeconomic status so that differences are apparent.

middle class. those whose socioeconomic indicators place them above poverty and below wealth.

ruling class. major owners of key banks and corporations; see Ch. 10.

working class. those who sell their labor power.

communism. a belief system whose end goal is the elimination of class distinctions and private profit enterprise so that *all* persons share in basic necessities and no one is in need; also a pejorative term used in the Western world to denigrate beliefs and/or nations which disagree with and/or challenge Western ideas, making "communism" something to be feared and destroyed by "anticommunists."

community control. the belief in the process of decentralization whereby local groups (from neighborhoods to cities) direct those policies and programs which affect them—i.e., local participation in school boards, zoning, police practice, etc.

competitive sector. that portion of the American economy composed of "small businesses, mostly retail or services-providing, in which real competition still exists and market principles apply." See Ch. 2.

concept. 1. a general idea based upon specific instances; 2. an idea that helps in ordering or interpreting data.

conceptual framework. that set of basic, underlying premises and assumptions that provide the ordering for data, argument, research, etc.

conservative. a term used in a variety of ways in the American polity; originally a distinctive ideology based on tradition and a notion of an organic society moving through time with societal interests paramount. In the United States (so strongly liberal in the classic mold), conservatives can be either those who draw on the original tradition or those who draw on classical, laissez faire liberalism. See Ch. 3.

fiscal conservative. one who prefers that the government refrain from spending ("excessive spending") and manipulation of the economy thereby.

constituency. a group of persons to which a representative is responsible, comprising the geographical area from which (s)he is elected.

contractualism.   the belief in ordering all relationships—person to person, person to business, person to government, entity to entity, etc.—by means of written, delineated benefits and obligations, rights and responsibilities.

co-optation.   the process whereby a dissenter or protester becomes a supporter by being given a share of the pie and/or a position of status so that his criticisms are eroded (almost subconsciously).

corporate-banking sector.   that portion of the American economy composed of the largest, often multinational, productive and financial institutions. See Ch. 2.

correlation.   1. a relationship between two comparable things; 2. the increase or decrease in the value of one variable as another one increases or decreases.

cost of living.   a statistical measure of the amount required to sustain human life, i.e., the cost of the basic necessities such as food, shelter, clothing, transportation, etc.

counterculture.   see "culture."

crisis.   a point at which a problem becomes critical; it can be "real," "imagined," and/or "manufactured."

> **energy crisis.**   an example of a "manufactured" crisis. When the oil companies discovered that their profits were dropping, it was declared that natural resources were finite, the Arabs were in control of the oil, demand outran supply, etc., so that prices had to rise and supply be carefully controlled.

> **fiscal crisis.**   the financial condition in which tax revenues and other state or governmentally collected monies cannot meet the loan and bond obligations (and similar forms of long-term debt obligations) with the result that the mutually supportive transfer of money between banks and governmental entities is in danger of collapsing.

> **population crisis.**   the world condition believed and advertised by some that the number of people on earth is outstripping the capacity of the earth to support human life in terms of basics such as food, space, etc. Those who argue that it is the *way* in which the earth's resources are distributed that causes the problem say that this crisis is ideologically based and thus "imagined."

culture.   the pattern of beliefs and institutions characteristic of a community or a population.

> **counterculture.**   the term covering a wide variety of "isms," emphasizing values new and/or opposite to the standard pattern.

currency.   paper money issued by national governments and supposedly backed by them.

> **devaluation.**   a national policy whereby the currency value relative to other nations' is deliberately lowered.

> **exchange rate.**   the value of the basic unit of currency of one nation relative to another's.

fixed exchange rate. a ratio established and agreed to by nations for currency exchange purposes.

floating exchange rate. the ratio that fluctuates according to the buying and selling of currency by those speculating in national currency value.

deflation. the economic condition in which money buys more. See "inflation."

democratic. in popular terms, pertaining to "the people's rule"; when examined more closely it covers many different ideas and is used when someone wishes to name a certain practice, institution, policy, etc. as a "good" one. For fuller discussion, see Ch. 8.

democratic pluralism. "the generally accepted view of the American political process . . . of negotiation and compromise among many factions and groups" so "that the product is a reasonable approximation of both democracy and the public interest." See Ch. 8.

demographic. pertaining to such characteristics of human populations as geographic distribution, size, growth, age distribution, birth rates, and death rates.

depreciation. a decrease in the value of something because of age or wear.

depression. "an extended period of decline in gross national product, industrial production, and employment." See Ch. 3.

détente. an uneasy truce between the United States and the Soviet Union, including the attempt to warm their relationship.

developed countries. those nations whose economic base is industrial and technologically advanced. It carries an ideological bias so that economic imperialism can be promoted as aiding the "development" of "*un*developed countries" in order that they will be enabled to grow up in the image of "developed" countries.

deviance. differing from what is accepted as normal; a term often applied to behavior perceived as criminal or mentally or morally abnormal.

discrimination. activities and/or policies, usually harmful, based upon personal characteristics such as race, sex, religion, etc., rather than merit or ability.

distribution. the manner in which resources (national, world, etc.) are shared and/or utilized.

maldistribution. when some have more or less than their fair share.

redistribution. to alter present patterns of resource usage and consumption.

dividend. a share of the profits received by owners of stock.

dollar glut. overabundance of dollars held by the major banks of foreign countries, primarily Western Europe.

Dred Scott v. Sanford. the case whereby the Missouri Compromise was declared unconstitutional as interfering with property rights without due process of law. A slave, Scott, had escaped from territory where slavery was permitted and gone to territory declared "free" by the Compromise; therefore, he argued, he was now a free man. The Court declared him "property" which had to be returned and that the Missouri Compromise declaring such territory "free" was unconstitutional since it interfered with property rights.

due process. the term covering the notion that governmental practices and implementation must be carried on by established procedures in a fair, reasonable, depersonalized, impartial, and neutral manner. See Amendment V to the U.S. Constitution in the Appendix.

ecological. pertaining to the balance of natural forces.

economic security. "steadily expanding opportunities for profitable investment and trade throughout the world so that constant growth is assured." See Ch. 4.

economists. those who study and attempt to make policy for the "economy." See Ch. 3.

> conservative economists. those who favor a return to a position of governmental hands off the economy.

> liberal economists. those who accept Keynesian notions of government/economy partnership in order to control and ameliorate the effects of business cycles, assuming that government can and is in control.

> radical economists. usually Marxian, those who perceive government as the servant of the major units of the economy, maintaining capitalism to the detriment of the people.

elite. those who hold more of the resources of power than others.

> governing elite. those members in the upper class in public positions.

> non-elites. the masses, those not in power and status positions.

> power elite. those members who have influence and power and can shape governmental events and policies for their benefit.

embargo. a refusal to ship.

empiricism. the way of thinking that bases truth only in tangible evidence, that which can be discovered through the use of the senses. The belief that there is a tangible world "out there" which can be discovered and defined.

energy crisis. see "crisis."

environmental. pertaining to the surrounding physical world.

equality. a notion covering many forms of belief in parity among *all* people, i.e., the right to compete (equal opportunity) economically, politically, etc. See Appendix.

egalitarianism. the belief system which emphasizes equality of all forms above all.

Establishment. "that large proportion of individuals holding positions of power (in government *and* private affairs) who have come to share roughly the same values, interests, political ideology, and sense of priorities about what government should be doing and a shared proprietary concern for the continued success of the American system in its familiar social, economic, and political dimensions." See Ch. 10.

executive agreement. an agreement with the head of a foreign state made by the President without senatorial ratification.

exploitation. extracting labor power or some other resource without a fair return and/or payment for the same.

expropriation. the take over of a private economic enterprise by a governmental entity. Usually used when a new government comes to power and nationalizes all industry, which includes that of foreign nationals, and is then used as a term of approbation. See also "nationalization."

fascism. a governmental system wherein economic and governmental spheres are merged and social control of all aspects of an individual's life is achieved, usually accompanied by police state apparatus to ensure compliance at all levels and to repress any and all dissent. For a fuller discussion, see Ch. 22.

    economic fascism. that system wherein government and economy are merged for the benefit of private profits and the population, as workers, is controlled. But this system is not necessarily accompanied by the entire police state apparatus, compliance being more voluntary on the part of the citizenry.

Federal Reserve System. the institutions and practices of the federal banks and management personnel (the Federal Reserve Board) which make and enforce national fiscal and monetary policy.

federalism. "the division of powers between constituent units (the states) and a single central unit (the national government) such that each has defined powers and is supreme in its own allotted sphere." See Ch. 12.

Federalist Party. the label for the group who, at the time of the drafting, ratification, and initial implementation of the U.S. Constitution, supported ratification and a subsequent policy of increasing utilization of national powers and centralization. It included men such as James Madison, Alexander Hamilton, George Washington, John Adams—but not Thomas Jefferson, a bitter enemy.

fiscal crisis. see "crisis."

fiscal year. a twelve-month period for which a government or organization plans its revenues and expenditures.

Framers. those men who drafted the body of the U.S. Constitution, in convention, in Philadelphia in 1787. Most of them remain unknown, but men such as Madison, Hamilton, Adams, Franklin, etc., generally evoke the image of "Framers."

freedom. in American ideology, the absence of restraint on an individual. Since total absence of restraint would lead to chaos, it also usually implies only those restraints necessary and includes a procedure whereby those restraints can be tested, with full coverage afforded by the Bill of Rights.

full employment. originally, "when the proportion of unemployed represented only those workers normally changing jobs or temporarily displaced by the advent of new technologies." It has shifted to mean "the level of unemployment that would maintain price stability and hold inflation down." See Ch. 3.

futurists. that group whose belief system emphasizes planning and preparing for the long term. Most, however, assume continuation of present policies, power structures, etc., and simply project them into the future, planning in order to maintain them.

government. the ongoing structure, institutions, and practices generally perceived to be public, carrying authority and granted legitimacy by its citizens.

gross national product. the total value of the goods and services a nation produces during a specified period of time.

growth rate. the proportion of increase or decrease in the gross national product from one year to the next. See Ch. 4.

hegemony. conformity. Usually refers to ideological conformity so that all agree, or at least publicly state that they agree, on goals, policies, etc. The "party line."

hierarchy. 1. a group of people ranked according to authority; 2. any ranked group of items.

Horatio Alger. an author who wrote a series of books about poor boys who, through luck and hard work, became rich men—who went from "rags to riches." The name came to be synonymous with the American myth of the self-made man, the idea that anyone can make it if they try hard enough (the "luck" part of the original stories being forgotten).

hortatory language. language intended to persuade.

humanism. the values based in the desire to improve the welfare and well-being of human beings as the end goal of any activity.

hypothesis. 1. a statement to be verified or falsified; 2. a guess that can be used as a basis for investigation or action.

ideology. "that collection of beliefs that people in a society hold about how their government works, or should work, and why." See Ch. 8.

imperialism. one nation's interference in the affairs of another. It can be through military dominance, economic capability, cultural arrogance, etc. and/or any combination so that the end result is that the dominant nation receives compliance from the subordinate.

incumbent. current office holder.

industrialized countries. those whose economy is based on industry, as opposed to those based primarily on agricultural or raw materials.

    industrial capitalist countries. those who are industrialized *and* capitalist; usually means the "Free World," such as the United States, Canada, Western Europe, etc.

inflation. "a general rise in the prices of goods and services such that the *real* or purchasing power value of money is reduced." See Ch. 3.

infrastructure. "underlying but necessary building blocks." See Ch. 2.

institutions. identifiable, longstanding structures and/or associations.

  economic institutions. those structures involved with the production of goods and services, such as corporations and trade unions.

  political (public) institutions. those structures such as Congress, the President, political parties, etc. that have open accountability and responsibility. See Ch. 2.

  private institutions. those structures such as churches, the family, corporations, with no governmental character.

interest. a concern and/or need.

  public interest. that which is of concern to *all* members of the polity.

  special interest. that which concerns a certain segment and/or group and/or institution, often assumed to be in contrast to the public interest, though it is advertised to be congruent with it by the special interest.

investment guaranty contract. insurance underwritten by the U.S. government for private enterprise involved in ventures in foreign nations so that the risks of such economic involvement is lessened.

judicial review. the power of the Supreme Court to declare acts of Congress unconstitutional and thus void; in other words, overseeing of "political" branches by "legal" branches.

just and justice. in the American context, denoting fair and neutral decisions and decisionmaking, almost exclusively procedural. See Ch. 13.

laissez faire. denotes the proponents and policies associated with the belief in "hands off" the economy by government. The belief that the government is best which governs least, especially with regard to property and economics.

law and order. a catch phrase denoting the American ideological belief in the need for prescribed rules to which everyone must adhere so that anarchy or chaos will not prevail. It became a political slogan covering repression of dissent and protest by terming dissenters lawless (thus criminal) and thus capable of bringing on anarchy.

left. those who lean toward support of a "wider distribution of power, wealth, and status within the society." See Ch. 22.

legalism. belief in procedural regularity and written rules for conduct and procedure as the best method of dispute settlement of *any* kind.

legitimacy. 1. the quality of a government by virtue of which it is regarded as lawful or as entitled to compliance with its orders; 2. "a status conferred by people generally upon the institutions, acts, and officials of their government . . . by believing that their government is the right one, that it works properly and for desirable ends, so that they place their trust in it and grant it their obedience." See Ch. 1.

liberal. another word for the American ideology, but used popularly only for those on the left side of the American ideology. See Ch. 8.

    liberal/capitalist. the peculiar interlocking combination of political and economic ideologies extant in the United States. See Ch. 8.

    liberal economist. see "economists."

liberation. freedom from oppression and/or domination. Often used by minority and/or revolutionary groups to denote their struggle against more powerful and exploitive forces.

libertarian anarchism. see "anarchism."

logrolling. the exchanging of votes by legislators. "You vote for my locally oriented bill, I'll vote for yours."

marginal. pertaining to a small difference or change. See also "wages" and "workers."

masses. those who hold little power, non-elites. See "elites" and Ch. 11.

median (in statistics). the middle value in a distribution, with an equal number of values above and below it.

military-industrial complex. the popular term for the interlocking and interchanging people and interests between the armed forces and the large private contractors and industries who benefit from arms and related production and require military protection for foreign investments.

multinationals. economic entities which exist in several nations and move easily through national boundaries, faithful only to themselves.

    multinational corporations. multinational industries and productive enterprises, e.g. the oil companies.

    multinational banks. the financial institutions servicing and dealing with the multinational corporations.

myth. a belief, based on suggestion from others, that may or may not be true.

national economic planning. the newest move to institute extensive government planning and controls to keep the economy running smoothly. See Ch. 3.

national income. the sum of the income residents of a nation receive in profits, interest, pensions, and wages.

national security. originally "military supremacy over the Soviet Union and other communist countries" and now becoming expanded and controversial as interference in other countries takes on multiple dimensions. See Ch. 4.

National Security Managers. American policymakers dealing with foreign affairs. See Ch. 4.

nationalization. the taking over by the government or other public bodies of the management and interest in a previously privately owned and managed enterprise. A "good" term when it is either accepted or at least not opposed by the business community. See also "expropriation."

net income. income after deductions for expenses, taxes, etc.

normative. based upon or prescribing a standard of acceptability, desirability, or typicality.

objective. 1. based upon observation; real; having material existence; 2. not influenced by emotions, values, or guesses.

OPEC. Organization of Petroleum Exporting Countries, the Third World organization of heads of state of those nations with oil resources and holding shares in multinational oil corporations, whose purpose is to unify and increase their bargaining power relative to the multinational American-dominated oil companies.

pluralist. see "democratic pluralist," also Ch. 12.

policy. an established set of rules, written or unwritten, and procedures, either formal or informal.

> **fiscal policy.** rules regarding government management of its own finances. See Ch. 3.

> **foreign policy.** rules regarding relations with other nations.

> **incomes policy.** rules regarding wages and prices. See Ch. 3.

> **monetary policy.** rules regarding the money supply. See Ch. 3.

> **public policy.** usually official, governmental rules and procedures (though it can be informal) regarding a certain subject area or areas.

political consciousness. awareness of and critical involvement and/or challenge of present ideological constraints and circumstances.

political economy. the conceptual approach that sees economic and political life as an integrated whole, interpenetrating and mutually supportive. See Ch. 2.

political science. that branch of study devoted to public institutions and relationships.

political socialization. the process by which children become imbued with the values and assumptions supportive of the present governmental arrangements—i.e. schools, family, television, etc.—and of nationalism and patriotism.

politics. "the process by which power is employed to affect whether and how government will be used in any given area." See Ch. 1.

pollution. the fouling of a previously clean and/or pure substance, i.e., water, air, etc.

population crisis. see "crisis."

populist. one critical of big government and big business and supportive of the "little people." See Ch. 9.

> **radical populist.** one who challenges the status quo on behalf of the "common man," emphasizing equality, democracy, community, etc. See Ch. 9.

pork barrel. a piece of legislation which enriches a certain district and/or area, such as a defense contract, a highway project, a new building, etc.

power. "the possession of those resources, ranging from money and prestige to official authority, that cause others to modify their behavior and conform to what they perceive the possessor of the resources prefers." See Ch. 1.

power structure. see Ch. 20.

pragmatic. a philosophy associated with William James, basing itself on the "possible." The current American variant reduces it to the "possible" that is totally within present terms, usually meaning a continuation of what presently exists and acceptance of all those boundaries and constraints.

private enterprise. the American ideological term for ownership and management and profits of production and other property uses adhering in individuals for individual benefit.

protectionism. belief in the use of governmental policy to shelter internal product prices from competitive pressure from the same or similar products from other localities.

psychopath. a person who engages in antisocial behavior because of a personality disorder.

public interest. see "interest."

radicalism. the belief in the need for drastic change at the roots of the social order. See Ch. 9.

radical populist. see "populist."

radical economist. see "economist."

rational. pertaining to a way of thinking that sees cause and effect as direct, so that if enough "facts" are obtained, the solution to a problem can be found and applied. A belief in the ability of man's reason and objectivity (as opposed to emotionalism and subjectivity).

rationalize. to make up reassuring but often inaccurate reasons for one's behavior.

rationing. a public policy of controlling production and consumption and enforcing it through control of amounts available to individuals and other entities by issuing certificates for the purchase of such commodities in limited quantities, requiring such certificates be presented before purchase is allowed.

real income. the amount of money received, adjusted to take account of increases or decreases in prices: income adjusted to reflect change in purchasing power.

real wages. see "wages."

reality. the "facts" and "laws" of the universe. Different ways of thinking pose different versions of what is "real" or "reality." American liberal empiricism's reality is that tangible world outside ourselves which can be discovered and measured and defined through the use of the scientific method.

reality testing. examining for truth or actual existence.

recession. a decline in economic activity, less severe and shorter than a depression; a temporary period of increase in unemployment and decline in investment and production.

repression. formal and informal methods and/or policies designed to prevent, discourage, and stop challenges and criticisms of the status quo.

republic. that form of government in which the public has a voice but does not absolutely rule; not strict majority rule, but tempered, checked, and balanced in a variety of ways.

revolution. a destruction of the old order and replacement with a new. Debate continues on what deserves the name, ranging from seizure of governmental power to total transformation of values, institutions, culture, etc. See Ch. 22.

right. those who lean toward insistence upon the status quo and/or even narrower and more restrictive distribution. See Ch. 22.

ritual. a procedure that is followed faithfully and regularly to express a belief.

robber barons. the name applied to the men who built vast economic empires by various and sundry not so legal or moral means during the turn of the century and into the 1920s.

role. the kind of behavior expected of a person as a result of his or her social position, job, or office.

separation of powers. the division of specific national governmental powers among the institutions of the national government. See Ch. 12.

social legislation. those statutes enacted to further policies designed to promote the health and well-being of the populace.

social mobility. 1. movement to a higher or lower social or economic position; 2. the ability to move to a higher or lower social position.

social structure. the pattern of personal relationships and institutions within a society.

socialism. a philosophy, with many variants, centering on human beings as social beings (as opposed to self-sufficient individuals) whose minimal material needs can and should be met through cooperative and communal efforts, thus allowing social relationships to grow and develop.

    socialist countries. those nations in opposition to the capitalism of the U.S. and its allies and/or who claim to be so. It is used in a variety of ways and for various countries by different people at different times depending upon the immediate issue at hand.

spoils system. the filling of governmental posts and bureaucratic positions by an incumbent (usually newly elected) as rewards for service rendered to the officeholder; supposedly replaced by the Civil Service system.

standard of living. the basic amenities required in order for individuals to maintain a decent existence and life.

state. the combined governmental units and practices of a nation.

status. personal rank and deference afforded one by others.

status quo. the present structure and distribution of power and resources.

SALT. Strategic Arms Limitation Talks, continuous negotiations between the U.S. and the U.S.S.R. regarding halting and/or limiting production and stockpiling of weapons of war.

structural. based upon economic or organizational positions or arrangements, as distinct from attitudes or beliefs alone.

structure of power. see "power structure," Ch. 20.

subjective. reflecting what is within an individual's mind; not verified by reality testing.

system. related and connected series of institutions, practices, and/or policies mutually beneficial and reinforcing.

> **class system.** a society wherein people occupy and possess differentiated material and status positions.
>
> **economic system.** the private enterprise connections.
>
> **econopolitical system.** the combined governmental and economic enterprises.
>
> **international monetary system.** the connections between world currencies so that international trade is possible.
>
> **political system.** the public enterprise connections.
>
> **"the" system.** a general term covering the institutionalized status quo.

systemic. based upon interdependent elements that form a persisting pattern; flowing from an economic, social, or political system.

tangible/intangible. comparable to the objective/subjective distinctions; another portion of the empirical thought process: tangible being that which can be touched, seen, heard, etc., something "hard" and definable; intangible being that which cannot be measured.

tariff. the taxes one has to pay in order to import articles.

theory. coherent and comprehensive understanding and analysis.

Third World. the term usually encompassing the "undeveloped" countries, those not firmly within the Western or the Soviet bloc, such as Africa, the Middle East, South America, etc.

trade war. the condition in which governmental policies are used to increase the advantage of home industries and the competing governmental entity retaliates with its own import/export restrictions.

Trilateral Commission. an international group of leading financiers and corporate executives, initiated by David Rockefeller of the Chase Manhattan Bank, which makes studies and proposals for economic coordination among capitalist countries.

tunnel vision. the acceptance of an ideology so that one can see only within its confines and interprets everything within its terms.

vacuum of authority. see "authority."

wages. payment for services rendered.

> **marginal wages.** just enough payment to maintain life, sometimes a little more but only so that the worker is in constant fear of any major or unforeseen expense.
>
> **real wages.** the purchasing power of the payment.

Warren Court. the term denoting the Supreme Court while Earl Warren was Chief Justice, actually came into widespread usage only as the Court's civil liberties decisions became more liberal and more controversial.

wealth. the combined total of income and other assets.

welfare capitalism. see Ch. 22.

welfare state. a term, often used pejoratively, to describe a government which aids its citizens through various programs supplementing income, such as unemployment compensation, Medicare, etc.

workers. those who must sell their labor power in order to survive.

    blue collar workers. menial laborers, assembly-line folks, derived from the dominant color of working clothes.

    marginal workers. those who do not make enough to be secure and/or are part-time or temporary laborers, seasonal workers, etc., so that survival is a constant problem.

World Bank. the financial institution created by the United Nations and dominated by the United States, which provides loans to developing nations, more affluent countries allowing their money to be loaned and used by less affluent ones.

world view. the comprehensive and consistent manner of perceiving humans and the natural world and their interrelationship, underlying and leading to more specific values, beliefs, ideologies, etc.

Zero Growth. the concept of limiting population and industrial and other kinds of expansion or increase to as close to a 0.0% growth rate for the world as possible.

Bibliography

The selections that follow have been drawn from the vast and rapidly growing literature on American politics. We have sought to identify additional reading, usually available in paperback, that will fill out each chapter in some important way. Sometimes these selections contrast sharply with our interpretation; at other times they extend it beyond the point that we consider supported by available evidence; or they represent reflections on approaches or methods worth examining. In no case, of course, can our selections be taken as a comprehensive bibliography. They are a beginning, and a highly diversified one.

CHAPTER 1 Politics: Some Tools of Analysis

Politics as an attempt to describe and explain:
Dahl, Robert A. *Modern Political Analysis.* Englewood Cliffs, N.J.: Prentice-Hall, 1963.
Eulau, Heinz. *The Behavioral Persuasion in Politics.* New York: Random House, 1963.
Sorauf, Frank J. *Political Science: An Informal Overview.* Columbus, Ohio: Charles E. Merrill, 1963.

Politics as an extension of ethical concerns:
Kaplan, Abraham. *American Ethics and Public Policy.* New York: Oxford University Press, 1963.

Kariel, Henry S. *The Promise of Politics*. Englewood Cliffs, N.J.: Prentice-Hall, 1966.

Pranger, Robert J. *The Eclipse of Citizenship*. New York: Holt, Rinehart, & Winston, 1968.

Approaches that mix the two in varying proportions:

Alinsky, Saul. *Reveille for Radicals*. New York: Vintage Books, 1969 (originally published in 1946).

Barber, James David. *Citizen Politics: An Introduction to Political Behavior*. Chicago: Markham, 1968.

Dalfiume, Richard M., ed. *American Politics Since 1945: A New York Times Book*. Chicago: Quadrangle Books, 1969.

Freedman, Leonard, ed. *Issues of the Seventies*. Belmont, Cal.: Wadsworth, 1970.

Laing, R. D. *The Politics of Experience*. New York: Ballantine, 1967.

Lipset, Seymour Martin, ed. *Politics and the Social Sciences*. New York: Oxford University Press, 1969.

Myrdal, Gunnar. *Objectivity in the Social Sciences*. New York: Random House, 1969.

Schuman, David. *Preface to Politics*. Lexington, Mass.: D. C. Heath, 1973.

Sherrill, Robert. *Why They Call It Politics*, 2nd ed. New York: Harcourt Brace Jovanovich, Inc., 1974.

CHAPTER 2   The American Political Economy

Baran, Paul A., and Sweezey, Paul M. *Monopoly Capital*. New York: Monthly Review Press, 1966.

Best, Michael, and Connolly, William E. *The Politicized Economy*. Lexington, Mass.: D. C. Heath, 1976.

Friedman, Milton. *Capitalism and Freedom*. Chicago: University of Chicago Press, 1962.

Galbraith, John K. *American Capitalism—The Concept of Countervailing Power*. Boston: Houghton Mifflin, 1952.

Galbraith, John K. *The Affluent Society*. New York: New American Library, 1958.

Galbraith, John K. *The New Industrial State*. New York: New American Library, 1968.

Greenberg, Edward S. *Serving the Few: Corporate Capitalism and the Bias of Government Policy*. New York: John Wiley & Sons, Inc., 1974.

Miliband, Ralph. *The State in Capitalist Society*. New York: Basic Books, 1969.

Musolf, Lloyd D. *Government and Economy*. Chicago: Scott, Foresman, 1965.

Potter, David M. *People of Plenty*. Chicago: Phoenix Books, 1954.

Reagan, Michael. *The Managed Economy*. New York: Oxford University Press, 1963.

Rostow, Walter W. *The Stages of Economic Growth*. Cambridge: Cambridge University Press, 1960.

CHAPTER 3   The 1970s: From Confidence to Crisis

Engler, Robert. *The Politics of Oil*. Chicago: The University of Chicago Press, 1969.

Galbraith, John Kenneth. *Economics and the Public Purpose*. Boston: Houghton Mifflin, 1973.

Kolko, Joyce. *America and the Crisis of World Capitalism*. Boston: Little, Brown & Co., 1975.

Mermelstein, David, ed. *The Economic Crisis Reader*. New York: Vintage Books, 1975.

Pirages, Dennis, and Ehrlich, Paul. *Ark II: Social Response to Environmental Imperatives*. San Francisco: W. H. Freeman and Company, 1974.

Samuelson, Paul A. *Economics*, 9th ed. New York: McGraw-Hill, 1973.

Tanzer, Michael. *The Sick Society: An Economic Examination*. New York: Holt, Rinehart, & Winston, 1971.

Watson, Donald, ed. *Price Theory in Action*. Boston: Houghton Mifflin, 1965.

Zeitlin, Maurice, ed. *American Society, Inc*. Chicago: Markham, 1970.

CHAPTER 4   Economic Security and Foreign Policy

Agee, Philip. *Inside the Company: CIA Diary*. New York: Stonehill Press, 1975.

Graubard, Stephen. *Kissinger: Portrait of a Mind*. New York: W. W. Norton and Co., 1974.

Horowitz, David, ed. *Corporations and the Cold War*. New York: Monthly Review Press, 1969.

Jenkins, Robin. *Exploitation: The World Power Structure and the Inequality of Nations*. London: MacGibbon & Kee, Ltd., 1970.

Magdoff, Harry. *The Age of Imperialism: The Economics of U.S. Foreign Policy*. New York: Monthly Review Press, 1969.

Parenti, Michael, ed. *Trends and Tragedies in American Foreign Policy*. Boston: Little, Brown & Co., 1971.

Tanzer, Michael. *The Political Economy of International Oil and the Underdeveloped Countries*. Boston: Beacon Press, 1970.

Williams, William A. *The Tragedy of American Diplomacy*. New York: Delta, 1959.

CHAPTER 5   National Security: The Military Aspects

Barnet, Richard J. *The Roots of War*. New York: Atheneum, 1972.

Barnet, Richard J. *The Economy of Death*. New York: Atheneum, 1969.

Bloomfield, Lincoln P., *et al. Khrushchev and the Arms Race.* Cambridge, Mass.: M.I.T. Press, 1966.

Boulding, Kenneth. *Conflict and Defense: A General Theory.* New York: Harper & Row, 1963.

Clayton, James L. *The Economic Impact of the Cold War.* New York: Harcourt Brace Jovanovich, 1970.

Donovan, John C. *The Cold Warriors: A Policy-Making Elite.* Lexington, Mass.: D. C. Heath & Co., 1974.

Huntington, Samuel. *The Common Defense.* New York: Columbia University Press, 1961.

Kaufmann, William E. *The McNamara Strategy.* New York: Harper & Row, 1964.

Lapp, Ralph E. *The Weapons Culture.* New York: W. W. Norton, 1968.

Marchetti, Victor, and Marks, John D. *The CIA and the Cult of Intelligence.* New York: Knopf, 1974.

Melman, Seymour. *Pentagon Capitalism.* New York: McGraw-Hill, 1970.

Melman, Seymour, ed. *The War Economy of the United States.* New York: St. Martin's Press, 1971.

Neiburg, H. L. *In the Name of Science.* Chicago: Quadrangle Books, 1966.

Prouty, L. Fletcher. *The Secret Team: The CIA and Its Allies in Control of the United States and the World.* Englewood Cliffs, N.J.: Prentice-Hall, 1973.

Thayer, George. *The War Business.* New York: Simon & Schuster, 1969.

CHAPTER 6   Income Distribution: Inequality, Poverty, and Welfare

Bachrach, Peter, and Baratz, Morton. *Power and Poverty.* New York: Oxford University Press, 1970.

Baltzell, E. Digby. *Philadelphia Gentlemen: The Making of a National Upper Class.* Glencoe, Ill.: The Free Press, 1958.

Bottomore, T. B. *Classes in Modern Society.* New York: Vintage Books, 1966.

Clark, Kenneth, and Hopkins, Jeanette. *A Relevant War on Poverty.* New York: Harper & Row, 1969.

Cloward, Richard A., and Piven, Frances Fox. *The Politics of Turmoil: Essays on Poverty, Race, and the Urban Crisis.* New York: Pantheon Books, 1974.

Dahrendorf, Ralf. *Class and Class Conflict in Industrial Societies.* Stanford, Cal.: Stanford University Press, 1959.

Donovan, John. *The Politics of Poverty.* New York: Pegasus, 1967.

Free, Lloyd A., and Cantril, Hadley. *The Political Beliefs of Americans.* New York: Simon & Schuster, 1968.

Ferman, Louis *et al. Poverty in America.* Ann Arbor: University of Michigan Press, 1965.

Harrington, Michael. *The Other America.* Baltimore: Penguin, 1967.

Kolko, Gabriel. *Wealth and Power in America.* New York: Praeger, 1962.

Lampman, Robert J. *Ends and Means of Reducing Income Poverty.* New York: Academic Press, 1971.

Lampman, Robert J. *The Share of Top Wealth-Holders in National Wealth.* Princeton: Princeton University Press, 1962.

Lenski, Gerhard. *Power and Privilege.* New York: McGraw-Hill, 1966.

Lundberg, Ferdinand. *The Rich and the Super-Rich.* New York: Bantam Books, 1968.

Matthews, Donald. *The Social Background of Political Decision-Makers.* New York: Random House, 1955.

Miller, S. M., and Roby, Pamela. *The Future of Inequality.* New York: Basic Books, 1970.

Mills, C. Wright. *The Power Elite.* New York: Oxford University Press, 1956.

Plotnick, Robert D. and Skidmore, Felicity. *Progress Against Poverty: A Review of the 1964–1974 Decade.* New York: Academic Press, 1975.

Rainwater, Lee, ed. *Inequality and Justice.* Chicago: Aldine Publishing Co., 1974.

CHAPTER 7 The Status of Racial Minorities

Allen, Robert. *Black Awakening in Capitalist America.* New York: Doubleday, 1969.

Brown, Dee. *Bury My Heart at Wounded Knee.* New York: Holt, Rinehart, & Winston, 1970.

Carmichael, Stokely, and Hamilton, Charles V. *Black Power: The Politics of Liberation in America.* New York: Vintage Books, 1967.

Clark, Kenneth B. *Dark Ghetto: Dilemmas of Social Power.* New York: Harper & Row, 1965.

Cleaver, Eldridge. *Soul on Ice.* New York: McGraw-Hill, 1968.

Coleman, James S., *et al. Equality of Educational Opportunity.* Washington: Government Printing Office, 1966.

Coles, Robert. *Children of Crisis.* New York: Dell, 1964.

Elkins, Stanley. *Slavery,* 2nd ed. Chicago: University of Chicago Press, 1968.

Friedman, Lawrence M. *Government and Slum Housing.* Chicago: Rand McNally, 1968.

Greenberg, Edward S., Milner, Neal, and Olson, David J., eds. *Black Politics.* New York: Holt, Rinehart, & Winston, Inc., 1971.

Herzog, Stephen J., ed. *Minority Group Politics.* New York: Holt, Rinehart, & Winston, Inc., 1971.

Jencks, Christopher, *et al. Inequality.* New York: Basic Books, 1972.

Knowles, Louis L., and Prewitt, Kenneth, eds. *Institutional Racism in America.* Englewood Cliffs, N.J.: Prentice-Hall, 1969.

Lewis, Oscar. *La Vida.* New York: Random House, 1966.

Lewis, Oscar. *The Children of Sanchez.* New York: Random House, 1961.

Liebow, Elliot. *Talley's Corner.* Boston: Little, Brown & Co., 1967.

Malcolm X. *Autobiography*. New York: Grove Press, 1964.

Matthews, Donald R., and Prothro, James W. *Negroes and the New Southern Politics*. New York: Harcourt Brace Jovanovich, 1966.

Moynihan, Daniel. *Maximum Feasible Misunderstanding*. New York: The Free Press, 1969.

Parsons, Talcott, and Clark, Kenneth B., eds. *The Negro American*. Boston: Houghton Mifflin, 1966.

Rendon, Armando. *Chicano Manifesto*. New York: Macmillan, 1971.

Report of the Advisory Commission on Civil Disorders. New York: Bantam Books, 1968.

Shockley, John S. *Chicano Revolt in a Texas Town*. Notre Dame: University of Notre Dame Press, 1974.

Van Den Berghe, Pierre L. *Race and Racism*. New York: John Wiley, 1967.

Walker, Jack L., and Aberbach, Joel D. "The Meanings of Black Power: A Comparison of White and Black Interpretations of a Political Slogan," *American Political Science Review* 64 (June 1970): 367–388.

Zinn, Howard. *SNCC: The New Abolitionists*. Boston: Beacon Press, 1964.

CHAPTER 8   Ideology: American Orthodoxy

Banfield, Edward. *The Unheavenly City Revisited*. Boston: Little, Brown & Co., 1974.

Becker, Carl. *Freedom and Responsibility in the American Way of Life*. New York: Vintage Books, 1960.

Boorstin, Daniel. *The Genius of American Politics*. Chicago: University of Chicago Press, 1960.

Cohane, John P. *White Papers of an Outraged Conservative*. Indianapolis: Bobbs-Merrill, 1971.

Devine, Donald. *The Political Culture of the United States*. Boston: Little, Brown & Co., 1972.

Girvetz, Harry. *The Evolution of Liberalism*. New York: Collier Books, 1963.

Grimes, Alan P. *American Political Thought*. New York: Holt, Rinehart, & Winston, 1966.

Hartz, Louis M. *The Liberal Tradition in America*. New York: Harcourt Brace Jovanovich, 1955.

Kristol, Irving. *On the Democratic Idea in America*. New York: Harper & Row, 1972.

Lane, Robert. *Political Ideology: Why the American Common Man Believes What He Does*. New York: Free Press, 1962.

Lerner, Max. *America as a Civilization*. New York: Simon & Schuster, 1957.

McGiffert, Michael, ed. *The Character of Americans*. Homewood, Ill.: Dorsey Press, 1964.

Rossiter, Clinton. *Conservatism in America: The Thankless Persuasion*. New York: Vintage Books, 1955.

CHAPTER 9   Ideology: The Radical Challenge

Albert, Michael. *What Is to Be Undone.* Boston: Porter Sargent Publisher, 1974.

Allen, Robert L. *Black Awakening in Capitalist America.* New York: Doubleday, 1969.

Boggs, James and Boggs, Grace Lee. *Revolution and Evolution in the Twentieth Century.* New York: Monthly Review Press, 1974.

Bond, Julian. *A Time to Speak, A Time to Act.* New York: Simon & Schuster, 1972.

Brown, Bruce. *Marx, Freud, and the Critique of Everyday Life: Toward a Permanent Cultural Revolution.* New York: Monthly Review Press, 1973.

Carmichael, Stokely, and Hamilton, Charles V. *Black Power: The Politics of Liberation in America.* New York: Vintage Books, 1967.

Cowan, Paul. *The Making of an Unamerican.* New York: Viking, 1969.

Dolbeare, Kenneth M., and Dolbeare, Patricia. *American Ideologies: The Competing Political Beliefs of the 1970's.* Chicago: Markham, 1971.

Harris, Fred. *Now Is the Time: A Populist Call to Action.* New York: Praeger, 1970.

Jacobs, Paul, and Landau, Saul, eds. *The New Radicals.* New York: Vintage Books, 1966.

Lowi, Theodore. *The End of Liberalism: Ideology, Policy and the Crisis of Authority.* New York: W. W. Norton, 1969.

Moore, Barrington. "Revolution in America." *The New York Review of Books,* 12 (30 January 1969): 6–12.

Newfield, Jack. *A Prophetic Minority.* New York: Signet Books, 1966.

Newfield, Jack, and Greenfield, Jeff. *A Populist Manifesto: The Making of a New Majority.* New York: Warner, 1972.

Seale, Bobby G. *Seize the Time: The Story of the Black Panther Party and Huey P. Newton.* New York: Random House, 1970.

Sherman, Howard. *Radical Political Economy.* New York: Basic Books, 1972.

Theodori, Massimo, ed. *The New Left: A Documentary History.* Indianapolis: Bobbs-Merrill, 1969.

CHAPTER 10   Managing the Political Economy

Bell, Daniel, and Kristol, Irving, eds. *Capitalism Today.* New York: Mentor Books, 1971.

Cook, Fred J. *The Welfare State.* New York: Collier Books, 1962.

Domhoff, G. William. *Who Rules America?* Englewood Cliffs, N.J.: Prentice-Hall, 1967.

Duverger, Maurice. *Political Parties.* New York: John Wiley, 1963.

Edelman, Murray. *The Symbolic Uses of Politics.* Champaign-Urbana: University of Illinois Press, 1964.

Hansen, Lee W., and Weisbrod, Burton A. *Benefits, Costs and Finance of Public Higher Education.* Chicago: Markham, 1969.

Hartnett, Rodney T. *College and University Trustees: Their Backgrounds, Roles, and Educational Attitudes.* Princeton, N.J.: Educational Testing Service, 1969.

Katz, Elihu, and Lazarsfeld, Paul F. *Personal Influence.* Glencoe, Ill.: Free Press, 1955.

Kelley, Stanley. *Professional Public Relations and Political Power.* Baltimore: Johns Hopkins, 1956.

Key, V. O. *Public Opinion and American Democracy.* New York: Knopf, 1961.

Klapp, Orrin. *Symbolic Leaders.* New York: Minerva Press, 1968.

Kolko, Gabriel. *Wealth and Power in the United States.* New York: Praeger, 1962.

Lang, Kurt, and Lang, Gladys. *Politics and Television.* Chicago: Quadrangle Books, 1968.

Lasswell, Harold. *Politics: Who Gets What, When, How.* Cleveland: Meridian Books, 1958.

Lowi, Theodore. "American Business, Public Policy, Case-Studies, and Political Theory," *World Politics,* 16 (July 1954): 677–715.

Lundberg, Ferdinand. *The Rich and the Super-Rich.* New York: Bantam Books, 1968.

Miliband, Ralph. *The State in Capitalist Society.* New York: Basic Books, 1969.

Mintz, Morton, and Cohen, Jerry. *America Inc.: Who Owns and Operates the United States?* New York: Dell, 1971.

Riker, William H. *Federalism: Origin, Operation, Significance.* Boston: Little, Brown & Co., 1964.

Schattschneider, E. E. *The Semi-Sovereign People.* New York: Holt, Rinehart & Winston, 1960.

CHAPTER 11 Managing the Government

Bauer, Raymond; de Sola Pool, Ithiel; and Dexter, Louis Anthony. *American Business and Public Policy.* New York: Atheneum Press, 1963.

Dahl, Robert A. *Who Governs?* New Haven, Conn.: Yale University Press, 1961

Harris, Richard. *A Sacred Trust.* New York: New American Library, 1966.

Kariel, Henry S. *The Decline of American Pluralism.* Stanford, Cal.: Stanford University Press, 1961.

Key, V. O. *Southern Politics.* New York: Vintage Books, 1949.

Lens, Sidney. *The Military-Industrial Complex.* Philadelphia: Pilgrim Press, 1970.

Matthews, Donald R. *Social Background of Political Decision Makers.* New York: Random House, 1954.

McConnell, Grant. *Private Power and American Democracy.* New York: Knopf, 1966.

Milbrath, Lester W. *The Washington Lobbyists*. Chicago: Rand McNally, 1963.

Mills, C. Wright. *The Power Elite*. New York: Oxford University Press, 1959.

Polsby, Nelson W. *Community Power and Political Theory*. New Haven, Conn.: Yale University Press, 1963.

Prewitt, Kenneth. *The Recruitment of Political Leaders*. Indianapolis: Bobbs-Merrill, 1970.

Rose, Arnold. *The Power Structure*. New York: Oxford University Press, 1967.

Truman, David. *The Governmental Process*. New York: Knopf, 1951.

Zeigler, Harmon. *Interest Groups in American Society*. Englewood Cliffs, N.J.: Prentice-Hall, 1964.

CHAPTER 12 The Constitution: Structure, Symbol, and Political Style

Andrews, William G. *Coordinate Magistrates: Constitutional Law by Congress and President*. New York: Van Nostrand, Reinhold, 1969.

Beard, Charles A. *An Economic Interpretation of the Constitution of the United States with New Introduction*. New York: Macmillan, 1954 (originally published in 1913).

Bickel, Alexander M. *The Least Dangerous Branch*. Indianapolis: Bobbs-Merrill, 1962.

Danelski, David J. *A Supreme Court Justice Is Appointed*. New York: Random House, 1964.

Krislov, Samuel. *The Supreme Court in the Political Process*. New York: Macmillan, 1965.

McCloskey, Robert G. *The American Supreme Court*. Chicago: University of Chicago Press, 1960.

Miller, Arthur S. *The Supreme Court and American Capitalism*. New York: The Free Press, 1968.

Mitau, G. Theodore. *Decade of Decision: The Supreme Court and the Constitutional Revolution, 1954–1964*. New York: Scribner's, 1967.

Pritchett, C. Herman. *The American Constitutional System*, 2nd ed. New York: McGraw-Hill, 1967.

Shapiro, Martin. *The Supreme Court and the Administrative Agencies*. New York: The Free Press, 1968.

Sutherland, Arthur E. *Constitution in America*. New York: Blaisdell, 1965.

CHAPTER 13 Law and the Courts

Abraham, Henry J. *The Judicial Process*, 2nd ed. New York: Oxford University Press, 1968.

Becker, Theodore L., ed. *The Impact of Supreme Court Decisions*. New York: Oxford University Press, 1969.

Cardozo, Benjamin. *The Nature of the Judicial Process.* New Haven, Conn.: Yale University Press, 1921.

Casper, Jonathan D. *American Criminal Justice: The Defendant's Perspective.* Englewood Cliffs, N.J.: Prentice-Hall, 1972.

Cole, George F., ed. *Criminal Justice: Law and Politics.* Belmont, Cal.: Wadsworth, 1972.

Frank, Jerome. *Law and the Modern Mind.* New York: Doubleday, 1930.

Goldman, Sheldon, and Jahnige, Thomas P. *The Federal Courts as a Political System.* New York: Harper & Row, 1971.

Jacob, Herbert. *Justice in America,* 2nd ed. Boston: Little, Brown & Co., 1972.

Klonoski, James R., and Mendelsohn, Robert I., eds. *The Politics of Local Justice.* Boston: Little, Brown & Co., 1970.

Lewis, Anthony. *Gideon's Trumpet.* New York: Vintage, 1964.

Murphy, Walter F., and Tanenhaus, Joseph. *The Study of Public Law.* New York: Random House, 1972.

Rodgers, Harrell R., and Bullock, Charles S., III. *Law and Social Change: Civil Rights Laws and Their Consequences.* New York: McGraw-Hill, 1972.

Scheingold, Stuart A. *The Politics of Rights: Lawyers, Public Policy, and Political Change.* New Haven: Yale University Press, 1974.

Schmidhauser, John R. *The Supreme Court: Its Politics, Personalities, and Procedures.* New York: Holt, Rinehart & Winston, 1960.

Wolff, Robert Paul, ed. *The Rule of Law.* New York: Simon & Schuster, 1971.

CHAPTER 14 Congress

Bailey, Stephen K. *The New Congress.* New York: St. Martin's Press, 1966.

Berman, Daniel M. *A Bill Becomes a Law: Congress Enacts Civil Rights Legislation,* 2nd ed. New York: Macmillan, 1966.

Bibby, John, and Davidson, Roger. *On Capitol Hill: Studies in the Legislative Process.* New York: Holt, Rinehart, & Winston, 1967.

Burns, James MacGregor. *The Deadlock of Democracy.* Englewood Cliffs, N.J.: Prentice-Hall, 1963.

Fenno, Richard F., Jr. *The Power of the Purse: Appropriations Politics in Congress.* Boston: Little, Brown & Co., 1966.

Froman, Lewis A., Jr. *Congressmen and the Constituencies.* Chicago: Rand McNally, 1963.

Green, Mark, *et al.* (Ralph Nader Congress Project). *Who Runs Congress?* New York: Grossman, 1972.

Herring, Pendleton. *Presidential Leadership.* New York: W. W. Norton, 1965.

Koenig, Louis W. *Congress and the President.* Chicago: Scott, Foresman, 1965.

March, James G., and Simon, Herbert A. *Organizations.* New York: John Wiley, 1958.

Mason, Alpheus T. *Harlan Fiske Stone: Pillar of the Law.* New York: Viking Press, 1956.

Matthews, Donald R. *U.S. Senators and Their World.* Chapel Hill, N.C.: University of North Carolina Press, 1960.

Murphy, Walter F. *Elements of Judicial Strategy.* Chicago: University of Chicago Press, 1964.

Polsby, Nelson W. *Congress and the Presidency.* Englewood Cliffs, N.J.: Prentice-Hall, 1964.

CHAPTER 15   The Presidency

Barber, James David, ed. *Choosing the President.* Englewood Cliffs, N.J.: Prentice-Hall, Inc., 1974.

Bernstein, Carl and Woodward, Bob. *All the President's Men.* New York: Warner Books, 1975.

Cornwell, Elmer. *Presidential Leadership of Public Opinion.* Bloomington: Indiana University Press, 1965.

Corwin, Edward. *The President: Office and Powers,* 4th ed. New York: New York University Press, 1957.

Cronin, Thomas E. *The State of the Presidency.* Boston: Little, Brown & Co., 1975.

Dunn, Delmer. *Financing Presidential Campaigns.* Washington: The Brookings Institution, 1972.

Fenno, Richard F. *The President's Cabinet.* Cambridge, Mass.: Harvard University Press, 1959.

Fisher, Louis. *President and Congress: Power and Policy.* New York: Free Press, 1972.

Hargrove, Edwin C. *The Power of the Modern Presidency.* New York: Knopf, 1974.

McConnell, Grant. *The Modern Presidency.* New York: St. Martin's Press, 1976.

Mueller, John E. *War, Presidents and Public Opinion.* New York: Wiley, 1973.

Neustadt, Richard. *Presidential Power.* New York: Wiley, 1960.

Osbourne, John. *The Third Year of the Nixon Watch.* New York: Liveright, 1972.

Polsby, Nelson, and Wildavsky, Aaron. *Presidential Elections,* 3rd ed. New York: Scribner's, 1972.

Schlesinger, Arthur M., Jr. *The Imperial Presidency.* Boston: Houghton Mifflin, 1973.

Sorenson, Theodore C. *Decision-Making in the White House.* New York: Columbia University Press, 1963.

CHAPTER 16 The Bureaucracy

Agee, Philip. *Inside the Company: CIA Diary.* Penguin Books, 1975.

Allison, Graham T. *Essence of Decision: Explaining the Cuban Missile Crisis.* Boston: Little, Brown & Co., 1971.

Barnet, Richard J. *Roots of War.* New York: Atheneum, 1972.

Downs, Anthony. *Inside Bureaucracy.* Boston: Little, Brown & Co., 1967.

Halperin, Morton H. *Bureaucratic Politics and Foreign Policy.* Washington: The Brookings Institution, 1974.

Janis, Irving L. *Victims of Groupthink.* Boston: Houghton Mifflin, 1972.

Melman, Seymour. *The Permanent War Economy.* New York: Simon & Schuster, 1974.

Perrow, Charles. *Complex Organizations.* Glenview: Scott, Foresman, 1972.

Pressman, Jeffrey and Wildavsky, Aaron. *Implementation.* Berkeley: University of California Press, 1973.

Rourke, Frances E., ed. *Bureaucracy, Politics, and Public Policy,* 2nd ed. Boston: Little, Brown & Co., 1976.

Simon, Herbert A. *Administrative Behavior,* 3rd ed. New York: Free Press, 1976.

Wildavsky, Aaron. *The Politics of the Budgetary Process.* Boston: Little, Brown & Co., 1964.

Wise, David. *The Politics of Lying.* New York: Random House, 1973.

CHAPTER 17 The Political Context of Non-Elites

Aronowitz, Stanley. *False Promises.* New York: McGraw-Hill, 1973.

Berelson, Bernard; Lazarsfeld, Paul F.; and McPhee, William N. *Voting.* Chicago: University of Chicago Press, 1954.

Blauner, Robert. *Racial Oppression in America.* New York: Harper & Row, 1972.

Braverman, Harry. *Labor and Monopoly Capital.* New York: Monthly Review Press, 1974.

Campbell, Angus, *et al. Elections and the Political Order.* New York: John Wiley, 1966.

Converse, Philip. "The Nature of Belief Systems in Mass Publics." In *Ideology and Discontent,* ed. David Apter. London: Free Press of Glencoe, 1964.

Converse, Philip, and Dupeux, Georges. "The Politicization of the Electorate in France and the United States," *Public Opinion Quarterly* 26 (Spring 1962): 1–24.

Converse, Philip, *et al.* "Continuity and Change in American Politics: Parties and Issues in the 1968 Election," *American Political Science Review* 63 (December 1969): 1083–1105.

Downs, Anthony. *An Economic Theory of Democracy.* New York: Harper & Row, 1957.

Easton, David, and Dennis, Jack. *Children in the Political System.* New York: McGraw-Hill, 1969.

Flanigan, William H. *Political Behavior of the American Electorate.* Boston: Allyn & Bacon, 1968.

Greenstein, Fred I. *Children and Politics,* rev. ed. New Haven, Conn.: Yale University Press, 1968.

Hartz, Louis. *The Liberal Tradition in America.* New York: Harcourt Brace Jovanovich, 1955.

Hess, Robert D., and Torney, Judith V. *The Development of Political Attitudes in Children.* Chicago: Aldine, 1967.

Huber, Joan, and Form, William. *Income and Ideology: An Analysis of the American Political Formula.* New York: Free Press, 1974.

Key, V. O. *The Responsible Electorate.* Cambridge, Mass.: Harvard University Press, 1966.

Langton, Kenneth. *Political Socialization.* New York: Oxford University Press, 1969.

Marvick, Dwayne. "The Political Socialization of American Negroes," *Annals* 361 (September 1965): 112–127.

Raskin, Marcus G. *Being and Doing.* New York: Random House, 1971.

Skolnick, Jerome H. *The Politics of Protest.* New York: Ballantine Books, 1969.

U.S. Department of Health, Education, and Welfare. *Toward a Social Report.* Washington: Government Printing Office, 1969.

Wolfenstein, Martha, and Kliman, Gilbert, eds. *Children and the Death of the President.* Garden City, N.Y.: Doubleday, 1965.

CHAPTER 18   The Political Attitudes of Non-Elites

Aronowitz, Stanley. *False Promises: The Shaping of American Working-Class Consciousness.* New York: McGraw-Hill, 1973.

Cantril, Albert, and Roll, Charles. *The Hopes and Fears of the American People.* New York: Universe Books, 1972.

Clausen, John A., ed. *Socialization and Society.* Boston: Little, Brown & Co., 1968.

Dawson, Richard, and Prewitt, Kenneth. *Political Socialization.* Boston: Little, Brown & Co., 1969.

Devine, Donald. *The Political Culture of the United States.* Boston: Little, Brown & Co., 1972.

Hamilton, Richard F. *Class and Politics in the United States.* New York: John Wiley, 1972.

Lane, Robert E. *Political Ideology: Why the American Common Man Believes What He Does.* New York: Free Press, 1962.

Lane, Robert E. *Political Thinking and Consciousness.* Chicago: Markham, 1962.

Lane, Robert E., and Sears, David O. *Public Opinion.* Englewood Cliffs, N.J.: Prentice-Hall, 1964.

Larson, Calvin, and Washburn, Philo. *Power, Participation, and Ideology.* New York: David McKay, 1969.

Marcuse, Herbert. *One-Dimensional Man.* Boston: Beacon Press, 1964.

Schoenberger, Robert A. *The American Right Wing: Readings in Political Behavior.* New York: Holt, Rinehart & Winston, 1969.

Stouffer, Samuel. *Communism, Conformity and Civil Liberties.* New York: John Wiley, 1966 (originally published in 1956).

CHAPTER 19   Participation: Voting and Alternatives

Almond, Gabriel, and Verba, Sidney. *The Civic Culture.* Princeton, N.J.: Princeton University Press, 1963.

Altshuler, Alan A. *Community Control: The Black Demand for Participation in Large American Cities.* New York: Pegasus, 1970.

Boyd, Richard W. "Electoral Trends in Postwar Politics," in Barber, David J., ed. *Choosing the President.* Englewood Cliffs, N.J.: Prentice-Hall, 1974.

Burnham, Walter Dean. *Critical Elections and the Mainsprings of American Politics.* New York: W. W. Norton, 1970.

Campbell, Angus, *et al. The American Voter.* New York: John Wiley, 1960.

Campbell, Angus, *et al. Elections and the Political Order.* New York: John Wiley, 1966.

Clark, Kenneth, and Hopkins, Jeanette. *A Relevant War Against Poverty.* New York: Harper & Row, 1970.

Cloward, Richard A. and Piven, Frances Fox. *The Politics of Turmoil.* New York: Pantheon Books, 1974.

Flanigan, William H. *Political Behavior of the American Electorate.* Boston: Allyn & Bacon, 1968.

Graham, Hugh Davis, and Gurr, Ted Robert (Task Force to the President's Commission on Violence). *Violence in America.* New York: Signet Books, 1969.

Greenstein, Fred I. *The American Party System and the American People.* Englewood Cliffs, N.J.: Prentice-Hall, 1963.

Gurr, Ted Robert. *Why Men Rebel.* Princeton, N.J.: Princeton University Press, 1970.

Jennings, M. Kent, and Zeigler, Harmon, eds. *The Electoral Process.* Englewood Cliffs, N.J.: Prentice-Hall, 1966.

Key, V. O. Jr. *The Responsible Electorate.* Cambridge, Mass.: Harvard University Press, 1966.

Kramer, Ralph M. *Participation of the Poor: Comparative Case Studies in the War on Poverty.* Englewood Cliffs, N.J.: Prentice-Hall, 1969.

Lipsky, Michael. *Protest in City Politics.* Chicago: Rand McNally, 1970.

Moynihan, Daniel P. *Maximum Feasible Misunderstanding.* New York: The Free Press, 1969.

Piven, Frances Fox and Cloward, Richard A. *Regulating the Poor.* New York: Vintage, 1971.

National Advisory Commission on Civil Disorders. *Report.* New York: Bantam Books, 1968.

Roszak, Theodore. *The Making of a Counter Culture.* Garden City, N.Y.: Doubleday, 1969.

Rubinstein, Richard E. *Rebels in Eden: Mass Political Violence in the United States.* Boston: Little, Brown & Co., 1970.

Sorauf, Frank J. *Party Politics in America.* Boston: Little, Brown & Co., 1968.

Spiegel, Hans B. C., ed. *Citizen Participation in Urban Development.* Washington: NTL Institute for Applied Behavioral Science, 1968.

Sundquist, James. *Dynamics of the Party System: Alignment and Realignment of Political Parties in the United States.* Washington, D.C.: The Brookings Institution, 1973.

Zeigler, L. Harmon and Peak, Wayne G. *Interest Groups in American Society,* 2nd ed. Englewood Cliffs, N.J.: Prentice-Hall, 1972.

CHAPTER 20   Power Structure: Alternative Interpretations

Barber, Richard J. *The American Corporation: Its Power, Its Money, Its Politics.* New York: E. P. Dutton, 1970.

Dahl, Robert A. *A Preface to Democratic Theory.* Chicago: University of Chicago Press, 1956.

Dahl, Robert A. *Who Governs? Democracy and Power in an American City.* New Haven, Conn.: Yale University Press, 1961.

Domhoff, G. William. *Bohemian Grove.* New York: Harper Colophon Books, 1975.

Domhoff, G. William. *Who Rules America?* Englewood Cliffs, N.J.: Prentice-Hall, 1967.

Domhoff, G. William, and Ballard, Hoyt B. C. *Wright Mills and the Power Elite.* Boston: Beacon Press, 1968.

Kariel, Henry S. *The Decline of American Pluralism.* Stanford, Cal.: Stanford University Press, 1961.

Kaufman, Arnold S. *The Radical Liberal: New Man in American Politics.* New York: Atherton Press, 1968.

Polsby, Nelson W. *Community Power and Political Theory.* New Haven, Conn.: Yale University Press, 1963.

Rose, Arnold M. *The Power Structure: Political Process in American Society.* New York: Oxford University Press, 1967.

Rowen, Hobart. *The Free Enterprisers: Kennedy, Johnson and the Business Establishment.* New York: G. P. Putnam, 1964.

Weinstein, James. *The Corporate Ideal in the Liberal State.* Boston: Beacon Press, 1968.

Zeitlin, Maurice, ed. *American Society, Inc.* Chicago: Markham, 1970.

CHAPTER 21   Symbolic Politics and Political Change

Cassirer, Ernst. *The Myth of the State*. New Haven: Yale University Press, 1946.

Cobb, Roger W. and Elder, Charles D. *Participation in American Politics*. Baltimore: The Johns Hopkins Press, 1972.

Edelman, Murray. *Politics As Symbolic Action*. New York: Academic Press, 1971.

Edelman, Murray. *The Symbolic Uses of Politics*. Urbana: University of Illinois Press, 1964.

Gusfield, Joseph R. *Symbolic Crusade*. Urbana: University of Illinois Press, 1964.

Lasswell, Harold D. *Psychopathology and Politics*. New York: Viking Press, 1930.

Mead, George Herbert. *Mind, Self, and Society*. Chicago: University of Chicago Press, 1934.

Moore, Barrington. *Reflections on the Causes of Human Misery and Upon Certain Proposals to Eliminate Them*. Boston: Beacon Press, 1972.

Mueller, Claus. *The Politics of Communication*. New York: Oxford University Press, 1974.

CHAPTER 22   Political Change

Dolbeare, Kenneth M. *Political Change in the United States: A Framework for Analysis*. New York: McGraw-Hill, 1974.

Dowd, Douglas. *The Twisted Dream: Capitalist Development in the United States Since 1776*. Cambridge, Mass.: Winthrop Publishers, Inc., 1974.

Georgakas, Dan, and Surkin, Marvin. *Detroit: I Do Mind Dying*. New York: St. Martin's Press, 1975.

Harrington, Michael. *The Twilight of Capitalism*. New York: Simon & Schuster, 1976.

Heilbroner, Robert. *An Inquiry Into the Human Prospect*. New York: W. W. Norton & Co., 1975.

Marcuse, Herbert. *Essay on Liberation*. Boston: Beacon Press, 1969.

Schroyer, Trent. *The Critique of Domination*. New York: George Braziller, 1973.

Index

1 2 3 4 5 6 7 8 9 10